A GENERAL HISTORY OF EUROPE

GENERAL EDITOR: DENYS HAY

STANDARD [   ]

UNLESS [   ]

A GENERAL HISTORY OF EUROPE

General Editor: Denys Hay

For many years the volumes of Denys Hay's distinguished *General History of Europe* have been standard recommendations for university students, sixth formers and general readers. They offer broad surveys of European history, in which the detailed discussion (on a regional or continent-wide basis) of social, economic, administrative and intellectual themes is woven into a clear framework of political events. They set out to combine scholarship with accessibility in texts which are both attractively written and intellectually vigorous. Now the entire sequence is under revision by its original authors – most of the volumes for the first time since they were published – and the books are being redesigned and reset. The revised *General History of Europe*, when complete, will contain twelve volumes, three of them wholly new.

★   *Available in the original edition*

◇   *New edition published in the revised format*

☐   *New title in preparation*

EUROPE IN THE
SEVENTEENTH CENTURY

SECOND EDITION

D. H. PENNINGTON

LONGMAN
LONDON AND NEW YORK

Longman Group UK Limited,
Longman House, Burnt Mill, Harlow,
Essex CM20 2JE, England
and Associated Companies throughout the world.

*Published in the United States of America
by Longman Inc., New York*

© Longman Group Limited 1970
Second edition © Longman Group UK Ltd 1989

First published as Seventeenth-Century Europe 1970
This edition 1989
Second impression 1990

British Library Cataloguing in Publication Data
Pennington, Donald
  Europe in the seventeenth century. – 2nd ed.
  1. Europe, 1600–1700
  I. Title II. Pennington, Donald.
  Seventeenth-century Europe
  940.2'52
  ISBN 0-582-03449-3 CSD
  ISBN 0-582-49388-9 PPR

Library of Congress Cataloging-in-Publication Data
Pennington, D. H. (Donald H.)
    Europe in the seventeenth century/D. H. Pennington. – 2nd ed.
      p. cm. – (A General history of Europe)
    'First published as Seventeenth century Europe, 1970' – T.p.
    verso.
    Bibliography: p.
    Includes index.
    ISBN 0-582-03449-3 ISBN 0-582-49388-9 (pbk.)
    1. Europe – History – 17th century. I. Pennington, D. H.
    (Donald H.). Seventeenth century Europe. II. Title. III. Title:
    Europe in the 17th century. IV. Series.
    D246.P446 1989   88-21873
    940.2'4 – dc19   CIP

Set in Linotron 202 10/12pt Bemboo

Produced by Longman Singapore Publishers (Pte) Ltd.
Printed in Singapore

CONTENTS

LISTS OF RULERS AND ROYAL FAMILIES

LIST OF MAPS

PREFACE AND ACKNOWLEDGEMENTS

PREFACE TO THE FIRST EDITION

In the inexcusably long period this volume has taken to produce, many people have helped, encouraged, and advised. The editor of the series, Professor Denys Hay, has given me most valuable guidance, and applied only the gentlest of pressure to get the book finished. Others who have read and commented on the drafts at various stages are Professor Gerald Aylmer, Professor Ivan Roots, and Dr Dennis Witcombe. I am grateful also to Mrs Mary Stableford for her expert work on the maps and genealogies; to Miss Pat Lloyd who did most of the typing; to Mr Michael Katz who corrected many blunders in east European names and transliterations without having the chance to scrutinize them all; and to Mr Christopher Grayson who read the proofs and took on a large part of the burden of indexing. My son and daughter have contributed in innumerable ways; and the deepest thanks of all must go to my wife, who has helped immensely both with the substance of the book and with the mechanical tasks of producing it, and has borne with endless patience the spells of depression and fury associated with Seventeenth-Century Europe. The errors, omissions, and confusions are all my own work.

D.H.P.

OXFORD, JANUARY 1970

We are grateful to the copyright owners, B. Arthaud, Grenoble, for permission to base maps 1, 2 and 4 on maps appearing in *La Civilisation de l'Europe Classique* by P. Chaunu.

PREFACE TO THE SECOND EDITION

Expansion and re-writing have added in all about 100 pages to this new edition, mainly in the descriptive and interpretative sections. I have tried to incorporate a manageable proportion of the huge output of recent work on the period and to give fairly cautious impressions of a few of the controversies that have occupied historians in the last twenty years. The belief that narrative and political history should be relegated to a status decisively lower than that of quantitative sociology is less well established than at one time seemed likely: rightly or wrongly the misdeeds of statesmen, diplomats and even generals are still given a good deal of space in the second half of the book. A major problem was to select material for the greatly enlarged bibliography: frequent excursions from rural Herefordshire to the Bodleian Library and the British Museum have not altogether prevented unjustifiable admissions and rejections.

Some topics, such as Islam, crime, and publishing that were neglected before have been given a little more space. The family, a subject hardly noticed by historians before 1970, has been inserted briefly. One of my many regrets is that linguistic ignorance and lack of enterprise have prevented much use of the mass of work on local history, which in its modern form shows that scholarship can still spread from France to the rest of Europe.

I am grateful to the editorial staff of Longman for all their help and forbearance in the face of the now familiar delays. The maps have been redrawn by Longman's patient artists, but only my interference is responsible for errors in them. Mrs Kathleen Betterton has given generous assistance with the new index; and as before my deepest thanks are due to my wife for her endless help, encouragement and tolerance.

LINTON HILL, HEREFORDSHIRE D.H.P.

NOTE ON DATES

Dates of birth and death, and of the reigns of monarchs, are generally given in the index and not in the text. Years are reckoned in the 'new style' which most countries except Britain, Russia, and the Ottoman Empire had adopted in the sixteenth century, with the year beginning on 1 January.

INTRODUCTION

The year 1600 in Europe was quite an ordinary one. There was a shortage of grain, but not a major famine; there were moderate local outbreaks of plague; in the west there were isolated rebellions while in Russia the new tsar was in danger of losing his throne. In Rome Giordano Bruno was burnt at the stake. He was described as an impenitent heretic, an upholder of Arian opinions on the Trinity, a magician. He was also – though the Inquisition was less interested in this – well disposed towards the ideas of Copernicus. Behind the elaborate accusations his unpardonable offence was to show too publicly his disbelief in the Church's ability to satisfy his quest for an understanding of mankind and the universe. Most of the other people who met the same fate as Bruno were guilty merely of witchcraft.

In Sweden four members of the royal council were executed for supporting King Sigismund III, the Catholic monarch who had just been deposed in favour of the Protestant Charles IX. In Madrid Philip III was, optimistically, organizing a new army to restore the rebellious Protestants of the northern Netherlands to their allegiance, though they were winning new victories in Flanders. Negotiations had begun for ending the state of war between Spain and England. Henri IV of France, now almost safe on his throne after the decades of religious civil war, settled a minor territorial argument with the Duke of Savoy by invading his country. At home Henri was proving that it was possible for Catholics and Protestants to live in the same state with much the same civil rights and protection. But this was achieved by separation, not by mutual acceptance. Nearly everywhere it was

1

assumed that religious minorities were a threat to internal security, and religion a major reason for international alliances, rivalries, and wars. The Emperor Rudolf II was facing irreconcilable conflict between the Catholic and Protestant states under his ineffective suzerainty. Meanwhile El Greco was completing some of his last paintings; Shakespeare was writing *Twelfth Night* and *Julius Caesar*; the building of St Peter's in Rome continued.

A hundred years later, in 1700, King Charles II of Spain died. Over the succession to his enfeebled empire the great powers were ready to fight another of the now familiar national wars in whose origins diplomatic, dynastic and strategic manoeuvres left little room for religious alignments, still less for any material interests of their people. Louis XIV in France and William III in the Netherlands and England were securely at the head of states in which their authority looked irresistible. Peter the Great, back from his journey through western Europe, had overcome the latest revolt of the *Streltsi*, the guards of Moscow, and was badly beaten by the Swedes in the war for supremacy among Baltic countries. It proved to be one of Sweden's last military triumphs. It was in 1700 too that the Emperor Leopold II signed the compact by which Prussia became a kingdom. In the same year the new king had founded the Berlin Academy of Sciences, with Leibnitz as its president. In England Isaac Newton was at the height of his career. Everywhere men of leisure and culture were avid for news of scientific curiosities, of travel in remote countries, of economic progress. The churches had lost some of their zeal for persecution and most of their hopes of new conquests in Europe. Nobles and princes demanded the best imitations of Versailles that were within their means. Opera was the fashionable entertainment. Swift and Defoe were perfecting their satirical techniques.

To most Europeans famine was as great a danger in 1700 as in 1600. Some landlords, the old-established as well as the newly risen, were making more productive use of their estates. The scale of industry and trade had grown; the accumulation of capital was easier and more secure. But increases in the amount of food and goods available had rarely been spectacular. In many places, such as Spain, Italy and the worst-damaged parts of central Europe, the general level of prosperity was probably lower in 1700 than in 1600. Even in France the improvements, never reliable, were confined to a few areas. The idea that this was a century of marked – even of 'revolutionary' – progress in economic affairs has given way to the well-measured evidence that there was greater and steadier production of food and goods in some places, stagnation and depression in others. Power and wealth remained in the hands of a minority hardly less small, even if it was different in some of its characteristics. Great territorial lords had become both less eager and less able to challenge or ignore the control of the state. Though their authority often seemed as extensive as ever, it was usually exercised through and not against that of the monarch. Their private armies of tenants and dependants had largely disappeared. Many had lost their exemption from taxes. Nearly everywhere large estates were still a main feature of the countryside; but they were less likely to be a source of secure wealth for their owners. Cities, some greatly enlarged, offered better and more varied prospects of enrichment than before. Successful town-dwellers still tended to see the acquisition of land as a necessary mark of social superiority. Nevertheless there had been, in the west at least, some movement towards the separation of landed property from power in the community. This had been the great age of the buying of 'office', and the age when kings had some success in imposing the principle that status should be linked with service to the Crown. For those not born into the highest circles, the quickest way to get there might well be to acquire a position in government, local or central. It was often a better means than land ownership of extracting wealth for oneself from one's fellow men. The rewards of enterprise, the penalties for inaction and miscalculation, and the hazards in the path of the propertied family were great enough to make society comparatively 'mobile'. Even so, the governing class had changed far less than seemed likely during the great conflicts of the century. Inherited wealth, family connection and patronage were still the essential means to success.

As at other times, many tremendous events failed to occur. The forces of the Counter-Reformation did not reconquer Europe; but the Holy Roman Empire was not destroyed by its Protestant enemies. The Turks did not overrun central Europe; but their empire too survived. The English monarchy was not permanently overthrown: despite the victory of men outside the normal ruling circle, the civil war had not established a decisive and permanent change in the distribution of political or of economic power. James II did not take England back to Catholicism. Of the many other rebellions only the one that made Portugal a kingdom independent of Spain had any lasting success. Sweden did not extend her territory round the whole Baltic coastline; France gained only minor improvements in her eastern frontier. Russia, in face of repeated massive threats from inside and out, did not disintegrate.

Is there, in this span of time defined by the accident of the calendar, any shape or coherence that is not artificially imposed? It is often suggested that it is divided into sharply contrasted halves by a mid-century crisis that marked the boundary between one historical era and another. For some historians the 1640s and 1650s have seemed to be a decisive moment in the transition from a feudal to a capitalist economy; for others they are a convenient dividing-line between the Renaissance and the Enlightenment; still others see them as ushering in the age of absolutism. There is no doubt that in much of Europe those decades were a time of even greater turmoil and instability than was normal. But 'crisis' has become the most overworked term in historical writing. When we find it applied equally to the economic, social, political, diplomatic, cultural, moral and scientific aspects of more or less the whole century,[1] it is hard to see what meaning it can have. There was a crisis of 'European, even worldwide proportions, centring on the year 1620'.[2] The 1640s, with a cluster of rebellions very different in size and character, provided the first evidence for the 'general crisis', or a crisis 'of the relation of the state to society'. More recently it has been suggested that there was a general European crisis in the 1680s,[3] something more material than the '*crise de la conscience européenne*' that was said to have lasted from 1680 to 1715.[4] It may not be entirely unfair to suspect historians of looking for a crisis in whatever they are studying, and being easily satisfied that they have found it. At least 'crisis' is a less provocative term than the earlier favourite, 'revolution'. Debates on that, in its Marxist and other connotations, tended too often to reduce themselves to arguments about the permissible uses of a word. But if we reject all the general terms that make it possible to compare and interpret, we cannot see much sense in anything. There is an element of deception in any picture worth painting; and the historian is bound sometimes to select and emphasize those parts of reality that make a perceptible pattern. The chapters that follow treat with a moderate dose of scepticism accounts of the seventeenth-century upheavals that push everything else into symmetrical subordination. It does not mean that nothing exciting happened – only that changes were less unified and decisive than it is satisfying to believe.

To impose a pattern of dramatic change on the century is one temptation. Another is to give it an undeserved identity of character. The notion that every period is 'the age of' something or other is not always merely a harmless response to the need for books to have a title. In one field of human activity, the visual arts, a distinctive style came into prominence in many western and central regions during the century. By 1700, at least where French culture predominated, it was outmoded. The name 'baroque' was only bestowed on it much later. With the gradual extension of the meaning of the term, the idea has developed that 'the baroque' was a whole *Weltanschauung*, an outlook on the world, in terms of which all behaviour in the period can be explained. It is a claim that can easily take us out of the realm of evidence into that of rhetoric. To some extent it has drawn attention away from the much more obvious fact that though in the first part of the century the influence of Italy was still predominant in many cultural matters, by the end France had become the unchallenged leader. And here there is a danger that has been revived in a new form – the danger of seeing the history of Europe as the history of France and its neighbours. The rise of France to its pre-eminence in art, letters and fashion coincided – by no means necessarily, as the role of Italy in the Renaissance shows – with the period when diplomacy and warfare were centred on the activities of Louis XIV and when a good many rulers regarded French methods of government as the ideal. Now that diplomatic and constitutional affairs tend to be less dominant in history than social and economic ones there is a different reason for the prominence of France: it is there that the most intensive and methodical study of the newer types of historical problems has been undertaken. In this the seventeenth century has had a large share of attention. At the moment therefore the supply of information encourages an unspoken assumption that what was French was either typical or especially important.

There is one corrective that can be applied to many of the distortions that enter into our impression of the century. Material is becoming increasingly available in western languages for the study of countries that were once of interest only through their wars in the west. The internal affairs of Sweden, and even – though still inadequately – of Turkey can now provide some instructive comparisons. But it is Russia above all that puts the trivial frontier wars and internal disorders of the west into proportion. There are no rational standards by which the huge territorial changes, the disastrous famines, rebellions, invasions, the brutalities of rulers and collapses of government in the east can be regarded as minor episodes in the history of the continent as a whole. It is equally absurd to leave England out of Europe. But a price has to be paid for attempts to give weight to a larger number of countries. Words, whether written or spoken, have a single dimension. History requires at least three – those of time and place and subject-matter. Chroniclers who narrated the deeds of kings had an easy life. To attempt to survey the manifold affairs of the government and peoples of even a dozen states and empires over a period of a hundred years involves a constant fight against confusion, repetition, and illogical selection. It is a fight that ends in compromise rather than victory.

The first half of this book is devoted to some of what seem the most important historical themes of the period, the second half to a mainly chronological account of separate areas or groups of states. France, despite the strictures above on its undue promi- nence in seventeenth-century history, has been given most space. (It cannot be denied that this is partly due to the accessibility of modern work about it.) Other topics could well have been chosen for special treatment – diplomacy, for instance, or colonization, or the life and structure of towns. Inevitably some events have been used as material for the topical chapters while others of a similar kind have found their way into the chronological ones. Cross-references in notes try to mitigate this. Revision of the book has on the whole produced a simpler subdivision of the narrative chapters into their separate countries. All the chapters have been amended – those in the first half of the volume more than most of the others. Some of the blunders in the first edition have been eliminated, to be replaced no doubt by others. The bibliography has been extended and moved to the end, where the maps have also been brought together. Notes have generally been more firmly restricted to cross-references and sources of quotations.

No-one can get far in understanding the history of any period without some knowledge of the sources from which that history is written. The first chapter will try to show a little of their character, their opportunities, and their dangers, and to indicate where original materials can be found. Those who find its details oppressive may well prefer to begin with Chapter 2 and turn back to consider the significance of the sources later.

NOTES AND REFERENCES

1　See the contents list in *Histoire générale des civilisations*, vol. 4 (Paris, 1956).

2　H. Kamen in *Past and Present*, no. 39 (1968), p. 45.

3　A. Lossky in *European Studies Review*, vol. 10 (1980), p. 177.

4　The book by P. Hazard with this title appears in English as *The European Mind* (London, 1953).

1

SOURCES

Historians like to think that their work is shaped by some consistent idea of what is important. In practice it has to be admitted that their choice of topics and the methods of dealing with them depend heavily on what sources are available The nature of the evidence that existed and has survived is itself part of the history of a period. But survival is not the only thing that matters. Even the most assiduous writer of scholarly monographs is unlikely to be able to make use of everything that would help. For all but the narrowest topics what is 'available' is mainly that part of the relevant material that has been assembled, classified, and indexed. There are taking place at the moment changes – greater than any since the invention of printing – in methods by which we can make use of historical sources. Microphotography and electronic devices for recording, sorting and extracting information may some day make the researcher who ploughs through inadequate indexes and travels with pencil and notebook round collections of archives look as inefficient as the monk copying out a chronicle. But so far we still rely mainly on what the individual worker can find and read. Sources that are printed, in full or in summarized 'calendars', are bound to have more influence than others of their kind that are not. Countries and towns where a large proportion of manuscripts can be seen in libraries and record offices get better historical treatment than those with fewer facilities.

For the seventeenth century, a period in which the vernacular was used more and more, another major problem is whether material is accessible, directly or indirectly, in a language the individual historian can understand. Despite what has been done in translating documents and secondary works there is no escaping the fact that, even within Europe, language barriers remain one of the greatest obstacles to a rationally balanced and comparative account of political and still more of economic and social history. The knowledge of Turkey, Poland, and even of Russia which westerners ignorant of East European languages can acquire is still deplorably small in comparison with what they know of France, England, or Spain. Historical scholarship is far slower than the sciences in becoming international.

Our period is richer in records than any earlier one. More documents were left behind by the processes of government, by economic activity, and by the conflict of ideas. Contemporaries wrote more narratives, memoirs and diaries. In the sixteenth century the amount of administration, and hence of its paper, had grown more rapidly in western than in eastern countries. The growth continued at every level; and by 1700 Russia, Sweden, and Brandenburg were – in central government at least – as bureaucratized as western monarchies. Archives were copied, sorted, and preserved not only for their immediate usefulness: men educated in the western Renaissance tradition were strongly aware of history, both as something they looked back to and as something they were themselves creating for the future. It was no longer the concern mainly of the churches and their chroniclers. 'That posterity may not be deceived . . .' – with these words the Earl of Clarendon opened his massive history of the English Civil War in which he had been the king's chief adviser. Among his enemies Sir Simonds D'Ewes was as zealous in writing his own account of the Long Parliament he sat in, as he was in compiling the records of Elizabethan ones, and its clerk John Rushworth used the opportunities his position gave him to amass his *Historical Collections* of state papers. His selection and comments discreetly favoured the Parliamentary cause. On the other side his rival John Nalson began, but never completed, a much larger *Impartial Collection*. Though no other country produced a statesman–historian of Clarendon's calibre, kings and ministers everywhere were concerned to write the memoirs and commentaries which were designed partly for the benefit of their immediate successors in office, partly for posterity in general. Often they reach us uncertainly through the work of secretaries or the amendments, additions, and forgeries of editors. But they give us closer contact with large numbers of the rulers of nations than is possible for any previous age.

THE RECORDS OF GOVERNMENT

The decisions and public enactments of most seventeenth-century governments are readily accessible. How much of the process by which they were produced and of the organization that enabled them to be put into effect can be reconstructed is more variable. The sphere of government that preserved its formal records most assiduously was probably diplomacy.[1] Increasingly collections of treaties became a popular addition to gentlemanly bookshelves. Such works as the *Acta Publica* of the Holy Roman Empire by Michael Caspar Lundorp (or Londorpius), which first appeared at Frankfurt in 1640, gave texts and commentaries starting with remoter periods but concentrating on what was still topical: Lundorp devoted a heavy volume to the years from 1608 to 1620. *Theatrum Europaeum*, a work begun by J. P. Abelin in the 1630s, gave the public version of international relations in narrative form. Continued by several other writers, it had reached 21 volumes by 1738. William III appointed his own historiographer, Thomas Rymer, to edit a complete collection of the treaties made by English monarchs, with their related documents. His *Foedera* took nine volumes to reach the 1650s. Two and a half were devoted to the seventeenth century. In the next century such publications were able to draw on documents previously kept secret: the negotiations that led to the Treaties of Westphalia appeared at Leipzig in the 1730s. A popular compilation published in French at Amsterdam, the *Corps universel diplomatique du droit des gens* (ed. J. Dumont, 1726–31) began with Charlemagne but devoted four of its eight volumes to the period since 1559. The market for such compilations continued to flourish. But it was only after the French Revolution that the archives of the great powers were generally thrown open and editing and printing became more exact. Then there came the great nineteenth-century boom in the official publication of state papers, whose products now provide the basic raw material of political histories. The most lavish undertakings were those of Britain and France, where the Public Records and the *Archives Nationales* have accumulated large if sometimes frustrating indexes. The series of *Documents inédits sur l'histoire de France* includes among its diplomatic material the *Negotiations relatives à la succession d'Espagne* (ed. F. A. M. Mignet, 4 vols, 1835–42). The collection of *Instructions données aux ambassadeurs et ministres de France depuis les traités de Westphalie* began in 1884 and still continues. The fate of the English *Calendar of State Papers Foreign* has shown how even before 1600 the sheer quantity of the surviving documents is a major problem: though publication began in 1863 with the papers for 1547, the Calendar had only reached 1589 in 1950, when it was abandoned in favour of a more abridged form. The material for the seventeenth century remains in manuscript. A collection that has been calendared down to 1673 is the *Venetian State Papers* – the letters of the Venetian ambassadors to London. Like their colleagues in other capitals they have provided one of the sources most quoted – and sometimes too readily believed – for internal as well as foreign affairs. The papers of the Venetian ambassadors to the Emperor were printed in another great series of state archives, the *Fontes Rerum Austriacarum* (vols 26 and 27). Formal reports to the Senate from ambassadors in Spain, France, Turkey and other states (*Relazioni . . . degli ambasciatori veneti nel secolo XVII*) were published in Italy between 1856 and 1871. Papal nuncios were expected to send back reports, often every week, of events in church and state: many of these have been printed in the countries concerned.

Massive though they are, the printed copies or summaries of government papers cover a small fraction of the material that survives in central and local archives. (For his volume on France under Richelieu and Mazarin Richard Bonney notes that he consulted 800 of the volumes of papers from the *conseil d'état* alone.) Historians are more dependent than they readily admit on how well, if at all, collections of manuscripts have been indexed or listed. The pleasure of finding a significant piece of information by good luck in a box of unclassified documents does not outweigh the frustrations of deciding that life is too short to search any longer for a document that must have existed. Nor is it easy to admit that a manuscript that has been found is illegible. In the west at least, standards of handwriting are often lower in the seventeenth century than in the Middle Ages – though this impression may be partly produced by the survival of more of the less formal documents. The thousands of letters that the

Emperor Leopold I wrote to his counsellors and emissaries may well contain evidence not found anywhere else; but they are said to be 'a well-nigh impenetrable graphological jungle'.[2]

Leopold was probably the most prolific of royal letter-writers, though the nine volumes of the letters of Henri IV in the *Documents inédits* (ed. B. de Xivrey and others, 1843–76) are a major source. The letters and papers of Peter the Great have been published in Russia at intervals over the last hundred years. Statesmen everywhere maintained a steady output of letters and memoranda, and most of them by now employed secretaries who copied outgoing mail and preserved it methodically. The *Lettres du Cardinal de Mazarin* occupy ten printed volumes (ed. M. A. Cheruel, 1872–1906) and the *Lettres, instructions et mémoires de Colbert*, eight volumes (ed. P. Clément, 1861–82). Richelieu's papers have been published in various incomplete collections: *Lettres, instructions diplomatiques et papiers d'État du Cardinal de Richelieu* edited in eight volumes by D. L. M. Avenel appeared between 1853 and 1877 and was followed in 1880 by his *Maximes d'État et fragments politiques* edited by G. Hanotaux. The *Société de l'histoire de France* produced a ten-volume edition of the 'memoirs' between 1907 and 1931. There are several collections of the letters of De Witt, beginning with six volumes of diplomatic correspondence that appeared in the 1720s. The Dutch archives series *Rijks Geschiedkundige Publicatien* includes among its great variety of correspondence three volumes of Oldenbarnevelt's letters.

It was a natural assumption of those who held office that their documents, like their job, were private property. Most of Richelieu's papers went, after his death, to his niece the Duchesse d'Aiguillon. Mazarin bequeathed his to Colbert who set in motion the formidable task of classifying them. (They were eventually bound into more than 400 volumes.) By this time the French central government was beginning to accept the idea that official papers should remain in its care. When Lionne died in 1671, Louis XIV ordered that the government should retain possession of all state documents. By the end of his reign an official repository for papers thought to be worth preserving for their historic interest had been established.[3] In England archives were still scattered among a number of collections. The Chancery records were in the Tower and at the 'Rolls' in Chancery Lane; the Exchequer had four separate repositories in Westminster; various private houses and cellars were used, with grievous effects on the documents.

State papers have constantly to be supplemented from the collections, great and small, of archives that either remained with the families of those originally in charge of them or passed into the hands of private collectors and often from them to the big libraries. Students of English history are more fortunate than any others in the quantity of private collections that have been calendared by the Historical Manuscripts Commission, though the quality of its work in its earlier years varied greatly. Even with central political questions, the loss of documents can have a decisive effect on the scope of historical writing. Evidence about Spanish government policies in this period is poor, partly because Olivares, having put the main decisions into the hands of his special juntas, kept their papers himself. Most of them were destroyed in the eighteenth century.[4] The collection of state papers in the *Archivo General de Simanacas* was seized by Napoleon, and many concerned with French affairs remain in Paris.

When we move from the level of monarchs and great ministers to that of detailed and local administration, the proportion of material that has survived and has been sorted – let alone printed – is naturally less representative; but there is still a vast amount of it. Among the various series in the *Documents inédits* are the *Mémoires militaires relatives à la succession d'Espagne* (11 vols, 1835–62), and the *Comtes des bâtiments du roi* (5 vols, 1881–91) for the period of Louis XIV. A well-known recent example of how historical study is influenced by the fate of documents is provided by the controversies on the local rebellions in France in the period before the Fronde. The Chancellor Séguier demanded from intendants and other local officials the most detailed reports of every episode. These remained in France until the Revolution, when an enthusiastic collector of archives attached to the Russian embassy, Peter Dubrovsky, acquired many, but not all, of Séguier's papers and took them home. It was consequently to Russian historians that they first became available, in the Saltykov Shchedrin library at Leningrad, and they formed the main source for the large-scale study of the rebellions by Boris Porchnev, who printed a small number of the reports. A larger, but still incomplete, selection has since been edited by Mme A. D. Lublinskaya. In the meantime Roland Mousnier in France had attacked Porchnev's interpretation of the revolts and edited a selection of the Séguier papers that were still in Paris (see p. 556).

One of the main modern developments in historical writing on the seventeenth century has been the recognition that to understand its conflicts and political changes we have to look at local and regional no less than at central affairs. Such work has been helped a great deal by the earlier activities of local historical societies in preserving and publishing records. Many French provinces and English counties have their record societies, though their output is often a good deal smaller now than it was at the end of the nineteenth century. As interest has shifted to more complex economic and demographic problems, the work of assiduous local antiquaries is proving immensely useful in methods of research that were quite unknown to them. Urban records are among those most often lost or destroyed; but they can provide a corrective to the impression of the effectiveness of central authority that comes only from its own reports. For the Thirty Years War the many collections of the archives of German towns are an essential source. Nevertheless, centralization itself created records of local affairs that would not otherwise have existed. The dossiers of the French Intendants, in the well-used 'series C' of the *Archives nationales*, provide a magnificent range of evidence on every aspect of urban and rural life.

Among the political records most thoroughly explored today are the proceedings of representative assemblies. In their struggle for survival most of them were strongly aware of the importance of precedent and of constitutional formality, and at the same time of protecting their members against criminal charges arising from their speeches. They were anxious therefore to keep full accounts of their decisions and formal actions, but not of the arguments that led to them. The *Journals* of the House of Commons and the House of Lords, in slightly different forms, are fuller than for any earlier period but rigorously exclude reports of debates. Many of the Commons records we should most like to have – such as those of its committees – have largely disappeared. The proceedings of the States-General of the Netherlands, which on foreign and military affairs held more detailed discussion than other national assemblies, also show how limited was its range of effective authority. Summarized versions of the *Resolutien der Staten-General* have been published at intervals in the series *Rijks Geschiedkundige Publicatien*. Another piece of modern editing has made the *Svenska Riksdagakter* available for the whole of the century.

Proceedings of the various German assemblies have not been brought together in any comprehensive form; but volumes such as the *Würtembergische Landtagsakten*, 1608–20 (1919) and the *Land-tagsakten von Jülich und Berg* (1925) are to be found for a good many states. Unofficial records of proceedings are often much more informative. None of the continental assemblies can produce accounts of debates as copious as those of the English parliamentary diarists. The task of piecing together the many fragmentary accounts is now occupying scholars in England and America, and is showing how much can still be added to knowledge even of so familiar a subject. After the Restoration the development of party in English politics was accompanied by more zealous circulation of parliamentary news and gossip. Unofficial lists of voting and allegiances, letters giving details of political alliances, and – despite the laws against them – accounts of debates became abundant.

REPORTING AND COMMENT

Mention of parliamentary diarists takes us outside the field of documents left behind from the process of political and administrative action into that of the reporting by individuals of events they had seen or taken part in. There were many occasions besides national assemblies of Estates where speeches were made that seemed worth writing down. The debates in the New Model Army in 1647 provided one of the first occasions when shorthand was used to make possible something like a verbatim record of impromptu speeches. Various accounts of the debates in the Paris *Parlement* in the period of the Fronde were produced for immediate publication. The makers of speeches, the preachers of sermons, even the victims of trials were beginning to realise the value of having their words preserved in print. Much more than before, printed material that was designed to inform and influence the contemporary public can – with suitable caution – be used by the historian.

It was in the seventeenth century that newspapers began. The earliest of them are naturally not of much value as sources of information on the events they report, though they are themselves a significant part of the history of the time. Augsburg had its *Relation oder Zeitung* in 1609, and other German printing centres brought out occasional publications of the same kind. In the

Netherlands the 'coranto' was familiar in the 1620s – usually no more than a single sheet containing news or rumour of foreign affairs and war. Richelieu's *Gazette de France* in the 1630s, which may well have been the first weekly, was an instrument of government propaganda, significant because the Cardinal himself supplied or controlled its diplomatic news. But it was the Civil War in England, the Fronde in France, and the Thirty Years War in Germany that made the printing of news, exhortation, and scurrility a thriving industry. The brilliantly vituperative royalist paper *Mercurius Aulicus* and its many parliamentarian rivals are sometimes, despite their capacity for invention, a help in piecing together details of the fighting. They are far more valuable in showing how the war and the political manoeuvres appeared to their readers.

There was no clear difference of purpose between the newspaper and the pamphlet. The *Mazarinades* – the broadsheets, pamphlets and verses that poured from Paris presses during the Fronde – offer some vivid examples of popular wit and malice and of more serious political thought. In the Netherlands the writing of political verses became a well-developed skill – used among other things for spreading Dutch ideas in the south.

From Germany in the early years of the Thirty Years War there came some of the best seventeenth-century specimens of another form of popular satire, the cartoon and caricature. Usually printed on a single sheet, with verses or dialogue to expound their point further, they offer crude but detailed pictures of the life of soldiers and civilians as well as indications of the black-and-white versions of the conflict that were thought to make good propaganda.

By 1660 the distribution of solid news was a well-established business, which governments had usually brought under fairly successful control. For the educated and leisured Parisians the *Mercure Galant* and the *Journal des Scavants* gave news not only of politics but of all the fashionable forms of cultural activity. Those who aspired to inside knowledge preferred the 'letters of intelligence', copied by hand and circulated at a high price. But no public source was yet felt to supply anything like the range of comment, gossip, and information of which the cultured gentleman felt in need. He – and his wife – continued to rely heavily on correspondents of their own, preferably in the capital or at court. Not every country or social circle could find the equivalent of Mme de Sévigné, whose witty and perceptive letters are the most quoted of all sources for the life of the court and of the provincial *noblesse*. But letter-writing was everywhere a form of art well developed among educated men and women. Collections of family correspondence like that of the Verneys in England, which covers the whole century; the strange correspondence between Philip IV of Spain and the nun Sor Maria de Agreda; the sorrowful outpourings of Elizabeth of Bohemia; the exhortations of St Francois de Sales and St Vincent de Paul; the voluminous comments on politics and literature from Jean Louis de Balzac – examples could be multiplied indefinitely.

Most important of all the correspondence is that between scholars. In the early part of the century, more perhaps than at any other time, it was through the interchange of letters that scientists, philosophers, and mathematicians made known their ideas and fought their intellectual battles. Marin Mersenne in Paris acted as something of a clearing-house for scientific discussion, handing on in particular the ideas of his most assiduous correspondent Descartes. Nor was it only to other scholars that letters containing major ideas and news of experiments were written. Governor John Winthrop of Connecticut was one of the more unexpected recipients of letters from Boyle, Hooke, Hartlib, and other leading scientists. Galileo sent his account of sunspots and their astronomical implications to an Augsburg merchant, Mark Welser – though these, like his celebrated Letter to the Grand Duchess Christina, were clearly meant for publication. The growth of bodies like the *Académie des Sciences* and the Royal Society, whose Proceedings are major sources for the impact of scientific developments on the wider intellectual community, did not make correspondence unnecessary. *The Correspondence of Isaac Newton* (ed. H. W. Turnbull, 1959–77) and the various collections of the letters of Leibnitz contain many of their ideas not found anywhere else.

MEMOIRS AND TRAVEL

The writing of memoirs was an occupation almost as widespread among cultured men and women, in the later part of the century at least, as correspondence. The French seemed especially addicted to it. *Les Sources de l'histoire de France*, 1610–1715 describes more

than 250 such works, many of them printed in the great collections – *Nouvelle Collection des mémoires pour servir à l'histoire de
France* (ed. F. Michaud and J.-J. F. Poujoulat, Paris, 1836–39) and
Collection des Mémoires relatifs à l'histoire de France (ed. M. Petitot
and others, Paris, 1815–29). Not all the writers are statesmen,
generals, or cultured ladies. Oudard Coquault was an ordinary
merchant in Rheims who described vividly the effects of warfare
on life in his town; Louis de Pontis was a minor army officer who
in old age retired to Port Royal and wrote his imaginative recollections. Memoirs can be more of a temptation than a help to the
historian. The much-quoted St Simon wrote up his account of
Louis XIV's later years from his own unreliable notes and recollections and from the journal of Philippe de Dangeau which he
mercilessly attacked. He has certainly been taken too seriously.
The literary ladies round the court, such as Anne of Austria's
devoted admirer Mme de Motteville, or Mlle de Montpensier,
daughter of Gaston of Orleans, have usually a narrow range of
observation even when they were closely involved in great events.
But men like de Retz, Omer Talon, and Molé give an insight into
the Fronde that can be matched in the same way for later periods.
The 'memoirs' of Louis XIV himself, even though they are a
compilation from his writings and dictated notes, are among the
most valuable of all.

If France was the most productive source of polished memoirs,
it had no equal of the two great English diarists. Pepys and
Evelyn were both well placed to give in their sustained daily
recollections a picture of English society a little below the court
and ministerial level. The only misfortune is that they were so
close together in time and in activities. But while Pepys was a
busy civil servant, Evelyn had leisure for the occupation that in
every country encouraged men to write of their experiences –
travel. The numerous editions and translations of the 'itineraries'
that appeared all over Europe show that there was a good market
for such works. Martin Zeiller, whose accounts of most of the
western countries appeared originally in Latin and later in several
other languages, was one of many popular writers. The quaint
story and the glib generalization were as much a part of travel
literature then as now. Endless curiosity about remote parts of the
world was rewarded by a spate of lurid accounts more relevant
for the insight they give into the minds of the writer and his audience than for factual information. But scholars, merchants, and

statesmen tried hard to collect more reliable evidence. Charles X of Sweden commissioned the *Account of Muscovy* by Grigory Kotoshikin which proved to be one of the most exact factual surveys. Sir William Petty's survey of Ireland brought a new standard of accuracy to topographical measuring and counting.

SOCIAL AND ECONOMIC HISTORY

Even for historians not primarily interested in politics or administration, the expansion of government activity in the seventeenth century provides a large part of the raw material. What has come to be called 'quantitative history' – the study of large-scale changes in economic activity and in the social structure by statistical rather than impressionistic methods – is for this period less hampered than might be imagined by lack of information. The demographer is not short of sources, even though much of his work consists of detecting and correcting their deficiencies. Most of his material comes either from the churches or from the tax-collectors. The Council of Trent had already made the recording of baptisms and marriages a well-defined part of the duty of parish clergy. In 1614 Pope Paul V announced that they must also record deaths and confirmations – the latter a valuable indication of the numbers surviving through childhood. Later in the century some registers – in France at least – become much more detailed. Parish registers are never infallible; but they survive in sufficient numbers to form the essential starting-point for demographic studies. Taxation, with its obvious incentives for inaccurate recording, nevertheless provides a mass of usable material, much of it still only roughly sorted. (It was mainly for this purpose that countries as unlike as Russia and the Netherlands held occasional and incomplete censuses.) Tax-collectors were also responsible for many of the figures that make it possible to build up more exact and detailed estimates on commerce than can be achieved for earlier centuries. Most ports and many inland towns kept records of taxable trade which often survive in a form that makes comparison between different periods feasible. The long series of statistics set out and analysed by H. and P. Chaunu in the eleven volumes of *Séville et l'Atlantique* (Paris, 1955–59) show what can be made of them.

The history of prices and wages has long been recognized as the starting-point for many lines of economic enquiry. With the spread of arabic numerals, account-keeping was a less laborious process used further down the social scale than was usual earlier. Compilations like those of Lord Beveridge for England, N. W. Posthumus for the Netherlands, and M. J. Elsas for Germany as well as innumerable local and specialized studies of prices show both the opportunities and the difficulties.[5] From every part of western and central Europe detailed series of price-movements have now been collected. The analysis of prices is naturally inseparable from that of wages, and here too the problem is to use the great abundance of sources with adequate technical skill. If historians in the past have sometimes been too ready to accept contemporary impressions because of their literary merit, the modern danger may well be the spurious authority of a column of figures. There is still a large gap between the general deductions that have to be relied on for most purposes and the elaborate methods of analysis used by French historians especially. Despite their difficulties, demographic and monetary statistics are more easily collected and used than those for agricultural or for industrial production. Long-term changes as well as sudden catastrophes in the yield of corn are one of the fundamental pieces of quantitative information. An obvious snag is that it is the exceptionally enterprising rather than the normal cultivator who is most likely to keep detailed records. In Protestant countries the lack of those meticulous monastic accounts of agriculture and housekeeping that are the basis of so much medieval economic history is a serious handicap. On the other hand landowners and tenants at every level were now acquiring, as a necessary part of property agreements, much more detailed and accurate surveys.

No-one was more assiduous than lawyers in making and keeping documents – even if their object was not always to convey the whole truth. The seventeenth century was notoriously an age of expansion for the legal profession. What in France are called *minutes notoriales* record in such forms as wills, inventories, contracts of service, agreements on tenures and loans a great variety of information about ordinary life and small-scale economic activity much of which has yet to be effectively used. The abundant records of the French *parlements* have yielded material for many different lines of enquiry. The depositions in innumerable tedious disputes that found their way into the Chancery records in London can give far better insight into the outlook of the members of a village community than most descriptions of it by detached observers. The rolls and order-books of Quarter Sessions that survive in nearly every English county for some if not all the century, monotonous though they may appear, are among the foundations for the study of local and regional conflicts that is proving one of the most rewarding fields of research. Types of crime, and the relative severity of punishments, can reveal a great deal about the underlying assumptions of any society; and here at least there is no lack of information. The processes by which authority harassed the poor but also kept them alive left a mass of documentation in the orders on settlement, bastardy, and recruiting. Lawyers were also involved in another essential part of social activity, the giving and receiving of charity. The extent and nature of bequests, and their unpredictable fate, can give insight into a wide assortment of social and economic changes.

Charity is one of the fields in which the records of the church are used alongside those of the state. Besides their demographic value, ecclesiastical records ranging from those in the parish chest to the massive archives of the Vatican can contribute to nearly every broad study of social and economic topics. The various kinds of 'visitation' by which church authorities gathered information were often more searching than any organised by the state. Religious sects, even the persecuted ones, often kept extensive records which their successors have been zealous in publishing. The registers of schools and universities are a major source for any social investigation that involves analysis of biographical information. Nor was it only institutions whose record-keeping improved. The chances are a good deal better for this than for earlier centuries of finding, from families down to the yeoman and artisan level, the collections of legal and financial papers that must be the basis of answers to many of the most formidable general questions.

NOTES AND REFERENCES

1   See the *Guide to the Diplomatic Archives of Western Europe*, ed. D. H. Thomas and C. M. Case (Philadelphia, 1959).

2   Robert Evans, *The Habsburg Monarchy*, p. 143

3   L. Delisle, 'L'origine des archives du ministère des affaires étrangères' in *École des Chartes*, vol. 35 (1874).

4   J. H. Elliott, *The Revolt of the Catalans* (Cambridge, 1963), p. 579.

5   The bibliography to chapter 7 of the *Cambridge Economic History of Europe*, vol. 4, lists a large number of these. See also the map on p. 486 of the same volume.

2

PEOPLE AND STATES

'Europe' is an awkward word. No-one looking at the earth from outside it would see this messily shaped western part of the greatest land-area as a separate unit; and it has never had a natural or political eastern boundary of any significance. The convention that its limit runs across the Black Sea, the Caucasus, and the Steppes to the rough south-to-north line of the Urals was not established until the nineteenth century. In the seventeenth the Volga or the Ob seemed more relevant. 'Christendom' was still a commoner term than 'Europe.' During the century several slow developments made Europe a better-defined unit, politically and even emotionally. Russia, which had seemed almost as remote as China from the diplomatic and economic affairs of the west, was by the time of Peter the Great's death in 1725 committed to the conflicts and many of the ways of life of the continent as a whole. (Siberia as a colonial area gave it few close links with Asia.) While Russia was drawn further into the European system, the Ottoman Empire made what proved to be its last serious attempt at westward expansion. It still held in some form of subjection much the same European territory at the end of the century as at the beginning; but the sultan was now of less concern to any but the masses he exploited. In place of the occasional calls for Christendom to unite against the Turk, the enemies of Louis XIV were speaking of the interest of Europe in curtailing the excessive power of one of its own states. It was already apparent that the virtues of a balanced and stable system were most readily upheld by those governments that felt threatened by any move to change it.

GROUPS AND LANGUAGES

In many ways the peoples of Europe now had less in common than in the centuries when Roman law, Roman Christianity, and the Latin language produced some cultural unity. Racially the differences between them did not mean much. There was a little more separation than there is today between the tall, Teutonic peoples of the north, the shorter, round-headed Celtic or Alpine peoples of the west, and the dark, longheaded Mediterranean peoples. The most distinctive major group was the Slavs – a word of disputed meaning with a mythology of its own. Originally they were the westward-moving tribes that Charlemagne had checked on a fairly well-defined boundary. The people regarded as their descendants were those who spoke Slavonic languages. The 'western' Slavs were becoming less identifiable as German speech spread into the Slav regions of the Holy Roman Empire; but Slavonic dialects were still the popular tongue well to the west of the Polish frontier. In Russia, the 'eastern' Slavs were absorbing their invaders of more recent Asiatic origin, whose countless languages were dying out. The 'southern' Slavs of the Balkans and parts of the Danube plain were largely cut off from the rest by the Germans and Magyars, but were by no means losing their identity under Ottoman or Austrian rule. One of the demonstrations that the Turks remained an alien power was that even after so many generations their language made little progress in the Balkans outside the bureaucracy.

The establishment of national languages was one of the achievements of the period by which Europeans were becoming more separate from each other (see also pp. 190–1). Luther's German, though the Catholic states long resisted it, came to be accepted as the language of literature and government over most of the Habsburg Empire. Parisian French was understood by the whole country, and then, in the wake of Louis XIV's diplomatic prestige, became a substitute for Latin as an international language of government and fashionable culture. Spain was ruled in Spanish; Galileo wrote not only in Latin but also in an Italian that would be familiar in most of the peninsula. The languages used by central governments were driving out Latin on one hand and popular local speech on the other. Since the latter often survived as the tongue of the uneducated, there was growing linguistic distinction between classes and sometimes between dominant and subject peoples. The Habsburg government had the greatest problem, and fear, of national languages. It organized, after the Bohemian revolt, a determined attack on Czech speech and literature; it banned the dictionary and grammars of the Slovene language that had appeared at the end of the previous century; later it tried to replace Magyar by German. In Poland, with a feebler government, minority languages survived, and Latin was still used for legal and cultural purposes. In Britain English became the only language of townsmen and landlords in regions where the poor of the countryside spoke Welsh or Gaelic. Cornish died out almost completely. Henri IV of France was reported to have asserted the principle that those who spoke the same language ought to belong to the same state. He was one of the few rulers whose territories would not have been divided by this: the others could only hope to force their language on those subjects who did not use it.

There were a few groups that constituted minorities in more than a linguistic sense. In southern Spain the Moriscoes, Christians of Moorish origin, formed, until they were ruthlessly expelled under Philip III, a prosperous and immensely valuable part of the community (see p. 381). At the other extreme, culturally as well as geographically, the Lapps of northern Scandinavia, a people of Mongolian origin who had mixed comparatively little with others, remained all but independent of the Danish or Swedish kings, and were only just being converted to Christianity. Almost everywhere there were the gypsies. As true nomads, avoiding as far as possible all contact with the state and its systems of law and property, they left little record of their existence. Inevitably they tended to become less identifiable as a racial group and to merge with the growing throng of vagabonds. Governments and propertied individuals were generally agreed that the number of vagrants was increasing. Victims of one form or another of economic misfortune, of war, and of persecution, they were a constant reminder that the state was not yet an all-inclusive institution.

The most firmly excluded minority was of course the Jews. Even they were not a 'race' in any scientific sense. Their own tradition emphasized the difference between the southern 'Sephardim', many of whom had fled from Spain to other parts of Europe, and the more numerous and generally less prosperous 'Ashkenazim' of the north and east. Nevertheless they were a group readily identifiable and seemingly made for persecution. Papists, witches, or Turks might be blamed in different places and periods for almost every evil; but the Jew was denounced unanimously. He was an enemy of Christianity, guilty, by some irrational hereditary principle, of the crucifixion and responsible for all kinds of desecration. For many believers in the millennium, the unconverted Jews were an obstacle to its arrival; and extermination was claimed, oddly, as a way of fulfilling the prophecies of their conversion and propitiating an angry god. If morality depended on religion, it followed that the Jews were totally immoral. As their exclusion from most other forms of economic activity led some of them to commerce and money-lending, the picture of Shylock was firmly established. In some towns, such as Rome, Metz, and Hamburg they were unofficially tolerated, especially if they underwent a nominal conversion. In Poland, where they formed perhaps 4 or 5 per cent of the population, many cities had a Yiddish-speaking ghetto, accepted as an almost independent community. But after the invasions in the middle decades of the century, attacks on the Jews became common and their prosperity ended. Elsewhere there was some improvement. The Great Elector admitted them, with restrictions and additional taxes. Cromwell, against widespread objections, declared that some should be admitted to England. Olivares tried in vain to relax their exclusion from Spain. Enforced migration sometimes made them more successful in international commerce: governments were ready simultaneously to exploit them and to pretend they were not there.

POPULATION

We do not know how many people there were in seventeenth-century Europe. Ninety million is a very rough approximation – about one-seventh of the present number. Even a more accurate total for the continent or for its various political units would not tell us much. To understand the effects of population changes on people and government it is necessary to see the changes in different age groups, different localities, and different social strata, and to distinguish long-term trends from the sudden ups and downs that were characteristic of the period. We need to know about the age of marriage, the size of families, changes in fertility and length of life, normal and abnormal movements of people. Such questions are now being investigated with possibly more thoroughness and refinement of technique than any other branch of historical study; and firm answers are slowly emerging. It was in the seventeenth century itself that the study of demography developed. The genealogist Gregory King in England, the Italian Jesuit Riccioli, and Marshal Vauban in France were three very different characters whose interests went beyond the crude counting of heads. Organizers of taxation and recruiting needed detailed information about the population of whole countries. Even in Russia, where the difficulties seemed more formidable than anywhere else, there was a large-scale census in 1678 and Peter the Great's 'registration of souls' produced a surprisingly comprehensive account. But all such sources have to be seen in the light of the motives and shortcomings of the compilers. Contemporary writers were often badly wrong in their impressions: Spaniards continued to deplore the disastrous decline in their population long after it had in fact begun to rise. No-one who saw the effects of sudden plague or war could have any idea how or for how long the various categories of the population had been affected.

At the beginning of the century the main regions of comparatively dense rural population appeared to run in a broad belt from north to south (see the map on pp. 584–5). There were forty to fifty people per square kilometre (about 100 to 130 per square mile) in south-east Ireland and south-east England, in the Netherlands and most of lowland France, in the regions of the Rhine and upper Danube, in northern Italy, and in much of Sicily and the Kingdom of Naples. Few regions showed any marked long-term increase during the century. England and Wales may have had about four and a half million people in 1600 and about five million in 1700, with slightly more in mid-century; both the northern and southern Netherlands had become more populous, and now had the highest density anywhere in Europe; at a much lower level parts of Scandinavia had also gained. In Spain, especially in Castile, the population fell drastically in the first half of the century – perhaps by a quarter. A slow recovery began after 1660. In Italy too there was a sharp fall between 1600 and 1660 and a revival thereafter. In Poland and much of Germany the decline in the first half of the century was made good more erratically.

France in 1600 was the most densely populated of the large states, with a fluctuating total of something like eighteen million. For Russia, where political frontiers and areas of cultivation varied rapidly, comparative figures mean little. Certainly there was lasting depopulation in many parts of it. The totals are still unreliable for rural populations; and for towns the difficulties in producing figures that can be compared are not much less. The sixteenth century had seen some great increases in the population of cities, through influx from the country rather than through an excess of births over deaths: the prospects of survival and reproduction were on the whole worse in the city than in the village. The biggest cities in 1600 were not those seen in the west as most important. Constantinople, with perhaps half a million people, was bigger than any in Christendom; Naples had about 300,000. London, if the whole urban area is included, had 250,000 and Paris, for which estimates vary widely, about the same. Venice, Rome, and Genoa were among the dozen or so over 100,000. A century later London and Paris had almost doubled their numbers. Amsterdam had increased from about 50,000 to 200,000. The Italian cities had, if anything, diminished. But comparison between two arbitrary dates hides the sudden disasters to which towns even more than the countryside were subject.

The two natural calamities most important in determining population were a sudden increase in hunger and an epidemic disease. Most parts of Europe were constantly on the edge of a 'crisis of subsistence'. If the normal food supply was curtailed for more than a single season, mortality could soon be doubled or trebled. Some of the very poor might literally starve to death; many more would suffer the hunger and malnutrition that increased the risk and severity of the ever-present diseases. In bleak statistical terms, a rise in food prices was regularly followed by an equivalent rise in the death-rate. Since in times of hunger marriages were delayed and infant mortality rose most of all, it could take many decades for the population to be restored. A *classe cruse* with a shortage of child-bearing women could carry the decline into the next generation. Hunger, like most other widespread calamities, was regularly followed by epidemics. Bubonic plague had existed, sometimes in comparatively mild and localized forms, ever since the fourteenth century. Why it became more severe and widespread around the end of the sixteenth century is still disputed. Crowded cities and armies were certainly places where it developed easily; ships sometimes carried it. But though these sources of infection had grown they had not done so as much as did the plague. There is argument, too, about whether it was carried only by the fleas of the black rat that migrated to human hosts or whether a wider flea community took part. An attractive theory that has now become unpopular is that the incidence of plague depended on a different war – that in which the brown rat, an Asiatic invader, fought and conquered the black rat. *Xenopsylla cheopia*, the plague parasite, apparently preferred the black rat. But in fact black rats were still common until the eighteenth century: it may be that variations in the potency of the bacillus were more important. Whatever the reasons, there were major epidemics in Spain in 1599, Switzerland in 1610 and 1615, Germany and the Netherlands in 1623–64 and 1634–65. Two of the most lethal were those of 1630 and 1656–57 in northern Italy. In 1661 there was a devastating outbreak in Turkey which, during the next ten years, spread over nearly all Europe. It hit the Netherlands in 1663, London in 1665, Austria in 1668. After that it disappeared, or at least diminished in severity, first in western countries and more slowly in the east. At its worst it could infect half of a local population, and most of its victims would die. No-one found a cure or mitigation, and the diminution is as hard to explain as the occurrence. Strict imposition of *cordons sanitaires* round infected places helped. It is all complicated by the fact that bubonic plague was not the only great epidemic. Pneumonic plague, even more deadly to those infected, was probably the main disease in the Black Death of the fourteenth century and though it was now – again for no clear reason – less prevalent it still existed. Typhus, spread by rat-fleas and human lice, was a threat wherever armies marched and more lethal than any of their weapons. The Thirty Years War took it everywhere in central Europe; Spain probably had a widespread epidemic in 1683–85. But unlike the unmistakable bubonic plague, typhus was not readily identified. There were many less terrible threats: influenza and smallpox were beginning to be recognized by the end of the century, and syphilis, less deadly than when it first appeared in the 1490s, was one of the few diseases with known or suspected hereditary consequences.

Statistically the effects of the 'demographic crises' caused by sudden disaster are hard to define. The normal death-rate in a region could be doubled or trebled for a year or two; but it was people whose expectation of life was already low who suffered most. A single town or city hit by plague might lose far more, through migration as well as death. In human terms the descriptions that come in abundance from every country leave the same impression of bewildered fear. Plague might be explained as a visitation from God (who was seen to behave in that way in the Old Testament) or as an infection brought by a foreigner, the wandering poor, the soldiers, or animals. It could produce irrational hatred, or acts of heroism. The very rich could often get away in time; the rest confronted it as part of a hostile and mysterious universe. A third source of suddenly increased mortality, more manifestly human in its origins, was almost as unpredictable. War, the greatest destroyer and waster of resources, could bring death in many more ways than on the battlefield. Spectacular disasters like the burning of Magdeburg in 1631 or the devastation of the Palatinate in 1688 were in the long run less important than the steady misuse of labour, the break-up of families, the seizure of money and materials. The worst damage was done by armies living on the countryside, ruining or consuming someone else's harvest while they left their own ungathered. But the ultimate effects of wars are the hardest of all to assess statistically. We can only be certain that every loss of production upset a cycle of output and consumption that seldom left anything to spare. It had been, and still was, possible for large increases in population to occur in some areas where living-space was available. In the long run the complex influences on birth and death achieved the inescapable result – that there were as many people as could, in the economic conditions of the time and place, get enough to eat.

FRONTIERS AND RULERS

An elementary source of error in early estimates of population change is that the area covered by one calculation was different from that of the next. Every unit, from a city to an empire, had limits that varied and could be defined in different ways. The modern map of Europe can nearly everywhere have firm black boundary-lines separating self-contained political units. All the territory of Switzerland is within its clear frontier, and all territory within it is Swiss. Within the black lines are others of varying thickness that separate smaller units of government, whose power is well defined. It all fulfils the ideal that seventeenth-century political theorists sought when they wrote of 'sovereignty'; and it is only just becoming accepted that a thinning of some black lines may be desirable and even possible. Most seventeenth-century boundaries, though rulers increasingly deplored the fact, had to be seen not in confident and continuous black, but as varying shades of grey, often broken and uncertain. Parts of the Russian frontier were until Peter the Great's reign a barrier that could be moved a hundred miles backwards or forwards in a minor campaign. Other parts were not demarcated at all. Even in the west, the Peace of Westphalia settled some local boundaries that had not been established before. Almost every ruler of any importance had islands of territory outside his borders and islands of someone else's within them. A monarch was unlikely to have the same relationship, in theory or in practice, with every piece of land over which he reigned. Though this was still true at the end of the century, there had been an unmistakable trend towards the nation-state and the sovereign ruler.

Sully, in his speculations about a logical rearrangement of European states, started from the common supposition that monarchies could be divided into the elective and the hereditary. 'Election' had often become a formality behind which the power of a single ruling family was built up; but electing the ruler involved the recognition of a firm distinction between political rule and proprietorship. It was still normal for the two to be intermingled. A monarch was for many purposes the first – or even the second – in a hierarchy that extended downward to the manorial lord. The same ruler could in one part of his territory be primarily a sovereign, while in another part he was primarily a great landowner. It was sometimes convenient to assume that the accepted laws concerning landed property applied to sovereignty – the notion which Louis XIV elaborated with more than usual chicanery in his claims to territory by 'devolution'. It was not easy to reconcile the fact that states were transferred from one monarch to another – by marriage, sale, barter, and bequest – with the supposed duty of subjects to give emotional and almost religious allegiance to their rulers. In a great many parts of the continent there were two monarchs, one of them the over-lord

31

in a real or nominal sense of the other. Sometimes the sovereign was too remote for his authority to be effective except through delegation. By the end of the century it seemed clear that the consolidated, centralised states were thriving and the huge empires declining. Pufendorf, writing in 1684, contrasted the weakness of Spain, whose provinces were 'mightily disjoined' and controlled by 'governors remote from the sight of the prince' with the strength of the unified French kingdom, 'swarming with people and sowed thick with cities and towns'. Germany had the disadvantage of being 'neither an entire kingdom nor properly a confederacy, but participating of both kinds'. On the other hand, some unified and prosperous states, such as England and Holland, were suffering from the decline of their zeal for war and the presumptuousness of the 'rabble'.[1]

THE OTTOMAN EMPIRE

Most of Europe belonged to one or other of three huge territorial units, each of which extended far beyond the continent. Russia and the Habsburg Empire were based firmly in Europe; the Ottoman Empire, though it occupied all the south-eastern lands and controlled the Aegean and the eastern end of the Mediterranean, was seen as an anti-European and anti-Christian threat. In 1600 it extended some 2000 miles both from east to west and from north to south. Its Asian possessions included all the southern shore of the Black Sea and the west of the Persian Gulf; in Africa it controlled nearly all the northern coast, Egypt, and the Red Sea. Thirty kingdoms, it was claimed, acknowledged the sultan as their overlord – though 'kingdom' had many different meanings. It was the sacred duty of the sultan to conquer the world; and his possessions in Europe especially were regarded as a source of men and money for his plans of further expansion. As part of the 'Domain of War' the lands peopled by Christians could, for the time being, retain their religion and pay their tribute. They were to be ruled by military commanders for military purposes. But the theory was by now, except on the rare occasions of a military campaign, remote from the facts. The great estates with which provincial warriors were rewarded did not encourage them to maintain their zeal as fighters. Unintentionally, the Turkish system was changing from one based on permanent warfare to one in which stable frontiers and landed property were more acceptable. It was a change which, even after the Turks were driven back from Vienna in 1683, was far from complete. The Tartar Khans of the Crimea, themselves members of the Moslem ruling house, repaid the sultan for accepting their virtual independence by giving, in their devastating raids, slightly better treatment to his lands than to those of his enemies. The three Barbary States of north Africa were governed, in theory, by pashas whom the sultan appointed and dismissed at will; in practice their pirate corporations could give or withhold their co-operation with impunity. The Grand Admiral in Constantinople who was supposed to control all the Mediterranean coastal lands of the Empire could never be sure of the obedience of their local rulers, and they in turn could not determine what the corsairs would do. By European standards of government the Ottoman Empire ought to have been too insecure to threaten anyone. Its multiplicity of peoples, languages, and ways of life, its overmighty subjects, and its thousands of miles of insecure frontiers seemed an exaggeration of everything that European rulers sought to avoid. Yet the sultans, the strong and the weak, kept their throne, and despite primitive means of cultivation there were usually some areas that produced a surplus of food. Caravans carrying high-value merchandise both eastward and westward contributed to an economy that enabled the sultans to equip armies and navies as strong as any that a single European power could raise. Even after Lepanto and the containment of Turkish expansion on land, the presence of the Ottoman Empire, and the diplomatic uses that could be made of it, were a background to almost every European conflict.

Three regions of conflict between the Turks and the Christian powers seemed to have become permanent. In the Mediterranean every maritime nation suffered from the activities of the corsairs. Algiers, Tunis, and Tripoli had become in the 1570s firmly defended Muslim states, and the Spanish attempts to reconquer them were never successful for long. Venice, whose wealth depended heavily on trade with or through the Ottoman Empire, was not prepared to act indefinitely as the sole upholder of western sea power. On land the Ukraine was still an area of undefined frontiers where Turkish power was being held back by the slow consolidation of both Russian and Polish defences. In the

Danube plain and the Balkans there had been constant local warfare between forces of the Christian magnates, more or less supported by the Habsburg emperors, and irregular Muslim fighters. It was easy for these to claim to be *ghazis*, warriors of the faith, even when their immediate concern was obviously land or just plunder. In 1593 the sultan had come to the rescue of the Bosnian *ghazis* and embarked on a full-scale war against the Habsburgs and their allies. Throughout the seventeenth century the possibility remained of a sudden Turkish campaign that could take them deep into central Europe and shatter the politics and the economy of the whole continent.

THE RUSSIAN EMPIRE

The empire of the tsar had only one defined frontier – in the west; and much of this was, at the beginning of the century, a negligible line in the path of successive invaders. Away from the central regions of Muscovy, land was there for the taking. 'A great many parts', Pufendorf still believed at the end of the century, 'are mere wildernesses scarce inhabited at all'. Political control was a matter more of lines of communication from which taxing and recruiting authority could spread out than of permanently defended boundaries. The tsar held power over peoples rather than over territories. Little Russians east of the Dnieper sometimes fled from Turkish or Polish lands into those of the tsar; in the west many White Russians were under Polish rule. But though there were plenty of opportunities for future claims to territory, Muscovy had achieved greater expansion than any other European state. By the end of the fifteenth century it had absorbed most of the rival Russian kingdoms. Ivan the Terrible had conquered Kazan and Astrakhan on the Volga. Beyond the Urals he had extracted from the more or less nomadic tribes an uncertain recognition of the tsar's supremacy. In collecting up the shattered fragments of the Golden Horde, Russia became a colonial power, developing like the others as much by the private enterprise of traders and invaders as by the efforts of the monarchy, but with no oceans to define the difference between colony and homeland. To a Crown peasant in Muscovy the tsar was a monarch, a master, something approaching both a god and a devil; to a Siberian tribesman he was an incomprehensible and not very significant figure thousands of miles away. Between them were endless degrees of allegiance to Moscow.

The assorted peoples under the tsar's regime had one thing in common: there was abundant living-space. Russians were less remote than most Europeans from the centuries when great movements of population were an essential part of human life. Escape to the edges of cultivation, or just to a less unfavourable piece of land, was possible; and the measures to prevent it dominated Russian history in the century. In the south of the tsar's empire were the people furthest of all in Europe from the life of the frontier-enclosed community. The Cossacks were not a race, or nation, or tribe – they were a gang, or association of gangs; a defiance on a magnificent scale of the ordered society of the territorial sovereign. *Kazak*, said to mean a 'free warrior', was a word borrowed from the Tartars of the Golden Horde. It was applied first to the men who fought against them or alongside them in the steppe, and eventually to almost any landless inhabitant. As the Tartar organization broke up, the whole region north of the Caspian and Black Seas was shared between its settled inhabitants and these men who lived as warriors, hunters, herdsmen, and traders. The Cossacks were free – of land, property, taxes, and all the growing apparatus of the state. Men of all classes were reported to have abandoned their families and possessions to join the Cossacks, as others did to enter monasteries. Cossack organization was often a democratic one, but liable to be seized upon by a successful leader.

By the seventeenth century there were various groups of the Cossacks. Those of the lower Dnieper, the Zaporozhian Cossacks, were nominally in Polish territory. A few thousand were 'registered Cossacks', supposedly full subjects of the Polish state, but this did not effectively separate them from the mass of those with no such allegiance. It was common to lead a Cossack existence in the summer and return to a Polish town for the winter. Nevertheless, there were signs of a trend towards stability. Round the fortified camps, agrarian villages were appearing. The Cossack arsenal of Tretchnikov, a necessary base for military campaigns, was not far from being the capital city of a republic.

The Don Cossacks were less corrupted by civilization. The unlimited land of the steppe and the intermixture with the Tartars helped them to keep the character of a 'host'. Yet both Russia and

Poland were able sometimes to get the Cossacks to do their fighting on behalf of the state instead of against it, and the armies they could muster were perhaps the biggest in Europe. Much of the expansion of Russian territory was their work. Although the state, for them, usually meant oppression more than security, they were seeing themselves more and more as part of something greater in popular hope and imagination than the state had ever been: they belonged to 'holy Russia'.

In the sixteenth century there had been two great cohesive forces in Russia, the tsar and the Orthodox Church. The rulers who had long been venerated as 'saintly princes', almost Christ-like manifestations of God on earth, had by the time of Ivan the Terrible added another role in the eyes of their subjects, or at least of those whose awareness extended beyond their immediate locality. The tsars were the successors of Caesar and Byzantium; and under them Russia was to be the eternal empire of the Third Rome. The Church was identified with this vision of Russia no less closely than was the Moslem Institution with the empire of the sultan. In the Troubles after Ivan's death, when the rival tsars were far from venerable figures, the vision was focused more clearly on the cult of the nation, a nation that existed irrespective of frontiers, conquests, revolutions, or indeed of any historical reality. It was not an outlook that had much immediate impact on the tsars and their governments; but it helped them to survive attacks from inside and outside their country, and to make territorial gains on a scale that made the changes in western Europe look comparatively trivial.

THE HABSBURG EMPIRES

The myth of the Third Rome was not the exclusive property of Russia: Vienna had a rather less irrational claim than Moscow to be the capital of a coming universal empire. By the middle of the sixteenth century the Emperor Charles V had brought so much of Europe and the world under his supremacy that he could contemplate the union of Christendom as the destiny of the Habsburgs. The title 'Holy Roman Emperor' had a mystique that linked Charles, through his namesake Charlemagne, with Byzantium and with the universal *imperium* of Rome; and it added the vague notion of a defender of the Christian faith against the ˙ infidel. But it was held by the Habsburgs as a gift not from God but from the seven Electors, princes whose support had to be manoeuvred for whenever an emperor died or departed. Charles V's other dominions – Spain, the Netherlands, much of Italy, and a vast area of south and central America – had been in reality but not in name a far more formidable empire that could hope to dominate the world economically and strategically. The vision of a Habsburg triumph over the lesser rulers of the earth had been shattered during Charles's lifetime. The Habsburgs had never accepted that a strict system of heredity applied to them in any of their capacities; and the rivalry between Charles's son Philip and his brother Ferdinand, with the tangles of power-seeking that surrounded it, had produced on his abdication two separate Habsburg monarchies, seen only by their enemies as parts of a firm dynastic conspiracy. The divisions and alignments in Germany associated with the Reformation had destroyed the remnants of his authority in the northern Protestant states. Even so, the imperial title carried great weight; and the Habsburgs never failed to hold on to it.

In many of the lands that constituted the Empire it did not matter much to the effective rulers, still less to their subjects, whether their state was inside it or not. When its nominal frontiers were drawn, several doubts arose for map-makers. It was tacitly assumed that the Swiss Confederation, after successfully fighting against the emperor, no longer belonged. In the Netherlands struggle it had scarcely mattered that the frontier of the Empire ran through the disputed territory. Some Habsburg possessions were inside it; some were not. Yet even in 1648 the Netherlands, with Franche-Comté and Luxemburg, were supposed to constitute the Burgundian Circle, one of ten such groupings created by Maximilian I and now remembered as a possibly useful weapon in the conflicts. The most ludicrous doubt was whether Bohemia was in the Empire or not, though its throne, held by the Habsburgs themselves, certainly carried a vote in the imperial election.

Relations between the Empire and its constituent parts were inevitably an illogical mixture of legal theory and political practice. The emperor was the overlord of his vassals. Among them the 'Imperial Free Knights', though they could not claim to rule even the smallest political units, still boasted independence of everyone except the emperor. He alone bestowed imperial titles. Until the Peace of Westphalia, no other ruler was supposed to make treaties with foreign powers. The 'Free-Cities', which could include considerable rural areas, guarded the independent status upheld by the emperor's charters. Bishops, whose appointments often depended more on princely families than on the Church, owed homage to the emperor for the lands they ruled. Principalities and duchies were divided between brothers and cousins as casually as the fields of a yeoman, and sometimes retained ties with each other that were perpetuated in the familiar hyphenated names. The possessions of most rulers had grown and crumbled over generations of marriage, inheritance, purchase, and robbery. Nevertheless the major states in the Empire, such as Bavaria, Brandenburg, and Saxony, were well able to hold their own in conflicts with the emperor. There was even the remote possibility that a German empire might come into being that had no connection with dynastic ambitions. In the Protestant north, the idea of a German nation with a German language had an emotional appeal. Luther himself had called on 'the German nation' to throw off the domination of the Roman Law as well as the Roman Church. But pressure against the Habsburgs remained 'particularist' – the resistance of the small unit to the large. One of the decisive changes in the map of Europe during the century was to be the almost total fading of the frontier of the Empire and the intensifying of those of the states, including Austria itself.

Partly inside and partly outside the Empire were the lands that were the hereditary possessions of the Habsburgs, and those that they aimed to make hereditary. They formed an agglomeration even more irrational than the Holy Roman Empire. Austria and the provinces of Styria, Carinthia and Carniola were well-established Habsburg territories, though not always under the same member of the permanently disunited family. The most bewildering changes anywhere in Europe in the last two centuries had been in Hungary and Bohemia, where Habsburg claims survived through a chaos of wars, intrigues, abdications, and usurpations. In 1526 the future Emperor Ferdinad I had become King of Bohemia, with its associated territories of Moravia, Lusatia, and Silesia. He then acquired the crown of Hungary too, which meant those parts of it not under the effective rule of the Turks. It was not merely a frontier area. From time to time it had seemed possible that an empire might be constructed there whose rulers could defy Turks, Germans, and Russians alike. Fifteenth-century Hungary had, briefly, extended from Belgrade almost to Berlin. In the sixteenth century Stephen Bathory, the Prince of Transylvania who became King of Poland in opposition to the Habsburgs, hoped to rule, some day, an empire including Hungary, Poland, and Russia. It would naturally involve the defeat of the sultan as well as of the tsar; and for such purposes Bathory was glad to make intermittent alliances with the Habsburg emperors. When the seventeenth century began, Hungarians were among the most wretched victims of prolonged warfare and bad government. Transylvania, together with the Danube principalities of Wallachia and Moldavia, had overthrown their Turkish rulers; and in the wide disputed borderland, Ottoman and Habsburg armies captured and recaptured the forts from which they controlled the surrounding areas. The Danube plains had been a region of expanding agriculture, able to export wheat, cattle, and wine to both Ottoman and western markets. The 'Great Hungarian War' – as it was called in Turkey – marked the beginning of their decline.

When the organized fighting ended in 1606 the Habsburgs had little to show for it. 'Royal Hungary' was still a narrow area that did not extend to Budapest; the 'kingdom' of Croatia linked it to the Adriatic. The Habsburg possessions were now a more or less unbroken area; but only the dynasty held them together. If the Habsburgs were to create from the hereditary lands any real empire, they would have to offer its peoples a cause worth supporting. The Catholic Church might conceivably provide it. The whole area was as diverse in religious allegiance as in everything else. Besides the Muslim and Orthodox churches, Protestantism in many forms flourished not only among lower orders of society but as a political force with its own sources of wealth and authority. In Austria itself many of the great landed families had become Lutherans. Bohemia and Moravia were centres of Protestant intellectual activity and places of refuge from Catholic persecution. The extirpation of heresy was a promising activity for an imperial government trying to establish its power. So at least it appeared to the militant Catholics at the courts of the Habsburg archdukes. In their eyes one of the greatest defects of the Emperor Rudolf II was his lack of enthusiasm for an anti-Protestant campaign. Protestant ideas were to his tortured mind as attractive as art and astrology; and in European politics he saw

the ancient conflicts between emperors and popes as one indication of the dangers of an inflexibly Catholic policy. When Rudolf
was deposed his successors could hope for an empire united by
its church if by nothing else.

SPAIN

The other Habsburg monarchs were kings of Spain and Portugal.
Lacking the title of 'emperor' was a minor annoyance, and Philip
II had once or twice thought of taking it. Their status in their
world-wide dominions was as complicated as that of their
Austrian cousins. Though the sea and the Pyrenees gave to the
Iberian peninsula the best natural frontiers in mainland Europe,
other frontiers within them were still significant. Castile, and its
deceptively affluent ruling élite, asserted a supremacy over the
other states; but Madrid had been a capital city only since 1560
and the efforts of central governments there to extend their
hegemony over the whole peninsula were a constant source of
conflict. Aragon, Valencia, and Catalonia – the lands of the
medieval 'Crown of Aragon' – were attached firmly to each other;
their financial, legal, and military organizations were largely
independent of Castile. Of the three, Catalonia had been much
the most prosperous, with a rich merchant class and a tradition
of political liberty. The American conquests and the shift of economic power away from the Mediterranean had been a loss for the
Catalans, but also a further incentive to resist 'Castilianization'
and even to form new links with France. Certainly none of the
Aragonese kingdoms would be reduced to a status like that of
Granada. This thriving Moorish kingdom had been conquered at
the end of the fifteenth century, in a war that was the first joint
activity by the forces of the newly linked kingdoms of Castile and
Aragon. It brought under the Crown half a million Moorish
subjects, with a non-Christian religion and a non-European
language. Catholic clergy had accepted with enthusiasm the task
of converting them. Most had become nominally Christian
'Moriscoes'; but they remained a racial minority persecuted by
Church and state, rebellious, and growing in numbers. In 1580
another 'union of the crowns' had brought Portugal into the
possession of Philip II, who had asserted his claim to the inherit-

ance at the head of a largely Castilian army. Spanish forces had established themselves in the country to suppress national resistance. The kingdom was promised full independence, with a wholly Portuguese government and army. Castilian power infiltrated quietly; resentment was, for the time being, equally quiet.

Beyond the peninsula lay what no other Crown possessed – remote dependencies in Europe itself. Charles V had for most of his life seen the Netherlands rather than Spain or Austria as his home. It was only under Philip II that the monarchy became entirely Spanish, with the Netherlands governed by some available member of the royal family. On Philip's death they were ceded, nominally, in full sovereignty to his nephew and son-in-law the Archduke Albert. By then the revolt of the northern provinces had irrevocably divided the area into two states. For the Spanish government it was a disaster of a kind other rulers occasionally dreaded. Rebels, with no royal leader and hardly any outside help, had successfully set up a new independent and prosperous state, defying one of Europe's strongest armies. The remaining Spanish Netherlands were not in any sense a rational unit. The frontiers were a military accident, sometimes following established provincial boundaries, sometimes wholly new. The language division did not coincide with any political or geographical one: Flanders had predominantly Dutch-speaking and predominantly French-speaking areas, but the first language of an individual could be determined by class or simply family habit. Religious divisions overlapped all the others. Detached from the Netherlands, but no less oppressed by military and dynastic happenings, was another Spanish possession in the north. The ironically named Franche-Comté was the 'Free County' of the Burgundian Circle of the Holy Roman Empire; its chief town, Besancon, was an Imperial Free City. But it had been included with the Netherlands in the part of Charles V's empire acquired by Philip of Spain. It was also claimed by the French. In the Netherlands wars it was a vital part of Spain's military communications – the Spanish Road – and in the seventeenth century was to change hands repeatedly as wars and treaties required. Its inhabitants somehow survived.

The Italian possessions of the Spanish Crown suffered a more thoroughly colonial form of government than had the Netherlands. The old possessions of the Aragonese Crown, Sicily, Sardinia, and the Balearic Islands, had been extended in 1504 by the final conquest of Naples, a kingdom that covered the whole of southern Italy. That had been a Castilian victory; and the Spanish lands of the western Mediterranean were a large factor in the tensions between Castile and Aragon. Milan had been one of the casual inheritances of Charles V, who gave it to his son Philip long before the division of his empire. By 1600 the prospect of a great Spanish domain in the Mediterranean, which might have been completed by further victories over the Turks, looked less and less convincing. Milan was notoriously a region of declining wealth and population. Sicily, once the most prolific exporter of grain in Europe, no longer had any reliable surplus. The Spanish viceroys in Italy were meeting with opposition both from Estates, resentful of the insertion of Spaniards into local positions of authority, and from sporadic popular rebellion. The Council of Italy in Madrid was now a less prestigious department of the elaborate court government. It had all become a minor and unremunerative part of the Spanish possessions compared with the splendid wealth of the new world.

The combined overseas empires of Spain and Portugal were at the turn of the century an astonishing phenomenon. In south and central America an area much larger than Europe was recognized by other governments as effectively belonging to Philip of Spain. Only some minor claims by England and Holland on the east coast and the islands scratched the monopoly. The native population had suffered in the conquest, and in the subsequent horrors of hunger and disease, possibly the worst destruction of a people ever recorded. In Mexico it is now estimated that the population fell from twenty million to two million. Cities of the native civilizations had been wiped out; many survivors had become something close to slave-labourers. Most of the interior of the continent was completely unexplored and inaccessible. But the Vice-Royalty of New Spain included the whole of central America, and the Vice-Royalty of Peru all the former Empire of the Incas extending for two thousand miles down the western side. From Buenos Aires westward an area of settled territory along the rivers gave a route between the mountains and the Atlantic. On the new maps of the world it made the empire of the Austrian Habsburgs look insignificant. To the Castilians especially it gave opportunities of new power and wealth for the office-holding and landed classes and of at least a less hopeless life for unpropertied emigrants. Mining was no longer the only large-scale activity of European settlers. Graziers from the Castilian hills could find in America unlimited space for a way of life that was dying in Spain. The *encomiendas*, originally native villages granted to Spaniards to rule and exploit, were becoming centres of a successful agricultural system that could produce a marketable surplus. Once the conquest was completed it was not obvious that the native population was treated much worse than labourers anywhere else. The Indians were subjects of the Spanish Crown; a few of them had even become merchants or small landowners. Spanish justice was supposed to be available to all on equal terms. The Council of the Indies in Madrid supervised a system in which administration was separate from justice and the viceroys were firmly prevented from becoming monarchs independent of Spain. (The sultan was much less successful in similar aims.) It also appeared to the Spanish rulers that the natives had benefited immensely from the presence of the Church. It was, in the sixteenth century, mainly the mendicant friars who had provided missionaries in America, and they had won a greater acceptance of at least the forms of Christian religion than the higher ranks of the Catholic Church would have been likely to achieve. Churches were the most prominent of the new buildings and the centres of new communities. To some extent the missionary priests did uphold the converts in the quest for food and safety. To the Spanish rulers and employers Christianity encouraged labourers and near-serfs to accept the life that had been imposed on them. Whether in the long run Spain and Europe benefited from the wealth of South America is still disputable. In 1600 all that seemed to matter was that the output of the mines was declining.

THE KINGDOMS: POLAND

A distinction between 'empires' and 'kingdoms' is a modern and artificial one. No ruler in 1600 could claim a single permanently unified territory, and kingdoms for the most part were hardly less complex in their constitutions and populations than empires. By far the largest kingdom was Poland. Since the formal merging in 1569 of the crowns of Poland and Lithuania, which had been personally united since 1386, their lands stretched for nearly a thousand miles from far beyond the Dnieper almost to the Oder, and from the Baltic almost to the Black Sea. They had come together partly because the Polish kings had seemed to offer to ordinary landowners some protection against foreign conquest and against the power of territorial magnates without imposing too much authority or taxation. In the 'royal republic' relations between the monarch and his subjects depended more on their revocable agreement than on national loyalties. The Jagiello dynasty which had brought about the union, had been a family of magnates like many others, with the same type of great estates carrying almost limitless power over the tenants. When it came to an end in 1572 there began the practice of electing as kings outsiders who might be expected to bring useful alliances as well as being dependent on the nobles who had supported them. Despite the scorn that has been poured on it, the practice did something to avoid the civil wars that few other monarchies escaped. It was a typical process of bargaining that had given the throne in 1587 to Sigismund, son and heir of the King and Sweden. Only his deposition in Stockholm prevented the formation of what would have been a fantastically large and disunited realm.

Even without Sweden, Sigismund's lands were assorted enough. He offered to hand over to the Polish state his personal possession of Estonia – for which the Polish nobility showed no enthusiasm, since the Swedes remained in military occupation. In eastern ('Ducal') Prussia, he was a nominal overlord. The western ('Royal') part was attached more firmly to the Polish state and contributed money and men. Danzig was a free city recognizing only the most shadowy allegiance to the crown. In the south was the border region that enabled Polish writers to claim for their country the role of a 'bulwark' of Christendom, or even of civilization. The Zaporozhian Cossacks, nominally within the state, and the Crim Tartars outside it were a constant threat, greater than that from the armies of the Sultan. But to Catholics especially the bulwark was also against the Orthodox Church. No other state suffered as much as Poland from religious rivalries. Though both Lutheran and Calvinist Protestantism had been highly successful in the sixteenth century, neither had built up anything like a national church. By many gentry and nobility they were regarded as German and urban religions. The most decisive territorial victory of the Counter-Reformation had been the re-establishment of Polish Catholicism. The Jesuits and other teaching orders increased their control of schools and colleges until Catholicism had almost a monopoly of education. The cult of the Virgin grew into a symbol of resistance to oppression. Yet in large areas of the east the Orthodox Church kept its hold on the peasants and townsmen. In 1595 the papacy had approved the 'uniate church' which was supposed to offer to the Orthodox a compromise, recognizing both the supremacy of the Pope and Orthodox ritual. In practice it was regarded by Catholics as an inferior substitute and by Orthodox Christians as heresy. Conflicts, persecutions, and even flight were the inevitable consequence of the multiplicity of beliefs. The Polish state was in a sense tolerant: Catholic monarchs and their magnate supporters had been upheld by the Habsburgs, and the tsars, when it suited them, could appear as protectors of their fellow-worshippers. In a kingdom whose enormous frontier was devoid of natural defences, none of the established religions could be threatened too severely without giving allies to a possible invader.

DENMARK AND SWEDEN

The Polish king, for all his troubles, came very near to ruling over a consolidated block of territory. In the Baltic region, which seemed to offer some magnificent natural frontiers, political divisions were erratic. The two Scandinavian kingdoms, solidly Lutheran and hitherto not much involved in the conflicts of the rest of Europe, were bitter rivals in expansion. The possessions of the kings of Denmark comprised the Jutland peninsula, extending southward to include, as a personal estate of the Oldenburg family, the German Duchy of Holstein which was also a part of the Holy Roman Empire. There were the islands of Funen and Zealand, and across the Sound the provinces of Halland and Scania. The remoter islands, Bornholm, Gotland, and Osel, gave the Danes a line leading to the eastern shore of the Baltic. Norway was theirs too, one of the poorest and least populous areas of the continent but developing a little its trade in timber. Its most easterly province, Jämtland, extended far to the Swedish side of the mountains. The Danish king and nobility had never recognized as permanent the rebellion by which in 1523 the first Gustav Vasa had made himself king of an independent Sweden. It was fortunate for the Danes that they had been able to keep their hold on Scania, which gave them complete control of the entrance to the Baltic – a sound too narrow for ships to escape the levy of the lucrative dues – and a base for any future reconquest of Sweden. On the other hand the Swedes had retained a precarious outlet to the North Sea at Älvsborg, where they were able to build the port of Göteborg. (There were even schemes for a canal to link it with the Baltic.) Swedish kings had already established a firm hold on the much-contested east shore. Finland was occupied; and in 1595 the tsar had accepted their conquest of Estonia and Narva, almost cutting off the Russians from the Baltic. In the far north frontiers were vague. Sweden, Denmark, and Russia had since the 1580s thought it worth while to contest territories there, and the Swedes held firmly to their access to the Arctic Ocean. Charles IX's claim to the poetic title of 'King of the Lapps of the Northland' meant that he hoped Swedish agents could occasionally collect taxes from them. Clearly conflict between the two kingdoms would continue, though it would have been hard to foresee that of the two Sweden would become the great European power and Denmark suffer repeated defeat.

BRITAIN

The most fortunate of early seventeenth-century monarchs was James VI of Scotland, who in 1603 acquired through the accidents of royal marriage and non-marriage the crown of England, Wales, and Ireland. With an absence of opposition that a decade earlier would have seemed too much to hope for, he inherited a kingdom more stable and more uniform in its machinery of government than any of comparable size in Europe. Yet taken as a whole his dominions presented many of the familiar anomalies. All moves towards a political and administrative union of the two kingdoms were rejected by the alarmingly powerful parliament in England. Though Scots born after 1603 were grudgingly accepted as subjects of the English Crown, they remained for many legal purposes foreigners – as they did in the popular opinion of Englishmen. It was not forgotten that Mary Queen of Scots had been the most dangerous conspirator against the stability of Elizabethan England. Indeed the Tudors, probably more respected by their subjects than any other monarchy, had been involved in some of the most frightening dynastic absurdities. They had fought off threats from their traditional enemies the French, the Spaniards, and the Scots, but then faced the dangers of foreign claimants to the succession. Heirs could be more important to monarchs than armies. In the 1550s Mary Tudor had brought England into alarmingly close association with Spain. The status of her husband Philip II had been an embarrassment to nearly everyone concerned. By the marriage treaty he was to be joint sovereign with Mary: children of the marriage were to inherit England and the Netherlands, but not Spain. At the end of Elizabeth I's life the Infanta, backed by English and foreign Catholics, was a possible successor. Even James VI was better than that. But England was now sharing its monarch with one of the poorest countries in Europe, dominated by the conflicts of nobility and of clergy. Poorer still, and much less effectively governed, was Ireland. There royal administration was a precarious business, extended with difficulty from the fortified 'Pale of Dublin' to the remoter areas. Like other frontier zones, it had been a region of land-grabbing for successive generations of lords, gentry, and soldiers. But it was not simply a colonial possession of the English. Settlers, however firmly separated from the 'mere Irish', had a common interest in resisting those who followed them. Throughout Elizabeth's reign there had been a succession of attempts to dispossess, under one excuse or another, existing landowners and tenants and replace them with new profit-seeking Englishmen. The 'plantations' had produced even deeper bitterness. Now that a religious division was added to those of nationality and class the fear and hope of rebellion were unending.

FRANCE

The Tudors had risen from the nobility to seize the throne in 1485. For Henri IV of France it had only happened in 1590. The long civil wars had shown how close France still was to being a federation of provinces, with frontiers highly insecure. Henri's accession had brought his own lands in the Pyrenees more firmly under the Crown; and in 1598 he had devoted all his military resources to the reconquest of Brittany. Its submission had been ratified by a formal treaty in which its military ruler, the Duc de Mercœur, had appeared more as a foreign sovereign than a French rebel. It was this expedition that made Nantes, where the king had been forced to negotiate with the local Estates, the place from which he issued the Edict conceding some of the demands of the Huguenots. Perhaps a tenth of all Frenchmen were Protestants, most numerous in the south and west but also in many towns throughout the country. When Henri, as a necessary step towards securing the crown, had renounced his own Protestant allegiance he was bound to be seen by his Huguenot supporters as a traitor to the cause. But Huguenotism was now more a political party led by a few noble families than a strong religious movement. Compromise would be possible. The state would have to abandon all idea of a united national church and accept a limiting of its central authority. Protestants were to have completely equal rights wherever their religion was already established, and access to public office throughout the country. The only major restriction was that they would not too openly try to extend the areas of Protestantism. No other religious minority in Europe had such privileged treatment. Even so, Huguenot leaders could compare the Edict not with the position of Protestants in Spain or Catholics in England but with the demands they had announced four years earlier at Sainte-Foy. In these the whole kingdom was to be divided into Protestant 'circles' and in effect two equally powerful states were to exist in the same territory. It seemed unlikely that the compromise would satisfy either side for long.

Nothing at the beginning of the century gave any hint that by the end of it France would be seen as the mainspring of European politics and culture. Central authority was so shaken by the civil wars, and the privileges of the nobility so firmly held, that the French Crown seemed at least as likely as any other to remain short of money. Much of what it had was being spent on those disputes about patches of territory along the eastern boundaries that were to continue throughout the century. The intricacies of legality, diplomacy, and conquest are among the most tedious topics of history. But warfare for apparently trivial scraps of land was part of the European power-game which monarchs and generals found constantly attractive. Henri in 1600 was involved in a long-standing quarrel over the Marquisate of Saluzzo, a region surrounded by the territories of Charles Emmanuel of

Savoy. By covering the main French route into Italy the Marquisate had some military importance, and had been, more or less, a part of France until Charles Emmanuel had invaded it. Savoy was a state that reproduced in miniature some of the worst characteristics of the great powers. It maintained its political independence almost entirely by war and diplomacy; Savoyard soldiers were some of the most valued in Europe; and the dukes by selling and withdrawing their support at the right moments could profit from the needs or misfortunes of other states – France most of all. This time the duke decided not to resist long, and the French army claimed a victory that did not cost much. But Henri IV had shown that wars great or small remained part of his way of kingship: his schemes to reform the government and the economy might have to take second place.

FEDERAL REPUBLICS: SWITZERLAND AND THE NETHERLANDS

Nearly all Europe was ruled by monarchs – a group almost, from their habitual intermarriage, a family – who were generally accepted by their subjects at every level as a necessity. But there were a few territorial units over which no individual was sovereign. Switzerland was hardly even a confederation of states. It was an alliance of thirteen cantons, with other associates that included the Bishopric of Basel in the north and the 'Grey Leagues' in the south-east. An assortment of subject or vaguely allied lands and towns had become attached to one or more of the cantons. Four of the cantons were Protestant; two tolerated both religions; the rest were Catholic. Six were large rural areas, seven were towns with their dependent countryside. Though the three 'forest cantons' of Schwyz, Uri, and Unterwalden that had originated the confederation successfully resisted any attack on their independence, it was the towns that now dominated such joint activities as there were. The only federal institution was a Diet called at irregular intervals on the initiative of the Canton of Zurich. Consequently it was almost impossible for Switzerland to be involved collectively in European politics. The advantages were great. The development of Swiss towns as international financial centres began during the century; and the occasional wars between cantons never brought in the allies that would have enabled them to be prolonged. But the Swiss from time to time tried to establish one of the first essentials of a unified state – an army. Since agreements to maintain it were abandoned when each successive danger was over, it was never a very formidable one. Swiss soldiers preferred to serve in foreign armies where pay and prospects of plunder were better, and had become the most valued of mercenaries. The lack of a royal family, a capital city, and a national foreign policy did not appear to be a great deprivation. Nevertheless the picture of Switzerland as a land of peace and freedom was unrealistic. The Catholic cantons had been sporadically at war with the Protestant ones, and had expected support from the Empire or Spain. In the west there had been attacks by Savoy, which led to some French protection. It had not caused any serious devastation or loss of territory.

While the Swiss remained precariously independent, the history of the 'free lands, provinces, and towns' of the Netherlands – as they described themselves in the truce with their former Spanish sovereign, showed that a federation more vulnerable to attack could become a rich and powerful state. It was also about to show how a republic could turn by harassed stages into a monarchy. In 1600 neither the statesmen of the United Provinces nor their enemies accepted that a permanent state had come into being. The notion of a Greater Netherlands, reuniting north and south, never ceased to be a political issue on both sides of the arbitrary frontier. The Union of Utrecht in 1579 had been a temporary expedient for getting the northern provinces to fight more effectively against Spain. Gradually the terms of the Union acquired almost the status of a written constitution – not because they created a unified state but because they were seen as a guarantee against centralization. The one effective institution created by the Union – the States General – was a meeting at The Hague of mandated delegates from the seven provincial assemblies. Only through the States General could the Union control its armies and navies, raise money, and establish relations with other powers. But it was far from being a representative body for the whole country. The part of Brabant that was held by the Union, and the province of Drente in the north-east had no voice in it at all. The states of the Union had not much in common. The inland provinces of Guelderland, Utrecht, and Overyssel, closer in speech and culture to the Empire than to France, were dominated by landholders, mostly small, against whom the towns tried to uphold their privileges. The fortified city of Groningen was in constant conflict with the impoverished countryside of its province. In Friesland the eleven towns, meeting in one section of the exceptionally democratic provincial Estates, shared power with the three country sections. Zeeland, where landholders had only as much representation in the Estates as each of six towns, reproduced on a small scale the extraordinary political conditions of its great neighbour and ally Holland. The English could scarcely be blamed for applying the name of this one province to the whole Union, not only because it was the naval and commercial power of Holland that chiefly concerned them, but because the ruling class of Holland itself regarded the other provinces, with some justification, as its dependencies. Holland provided more revenue than all the rest together. It provided the ships, the capital, and the enterprise that turned the provinces into a great power. All this was the achievement of the closed bourgeois oligarchy of the 'Regents'. While in every other state of any size effective authority was in one way or another bound up with the ownership of land, it was the great urban families in the towns of Holland who determined the policies of the province and for long periods dominated the whole Union. They controlled the delegations from the eighteen towns, each of which had as much power in the Estates as the single delegation of the nobility. The only effective challenge to them came not from the rural provinces as such but from the military leadership that gave to the House of Orange a unique position from which to build up opposition to the Regents. In the long internal struggle that followed the final defeat of the Spaniards, the dynasty was eventually victorious – but not to the extent of destroying urban power.

THE SMALLER STATES

The power of townsmen had not long been such a rare phenomenon. One of the least spectacular but most decisive changes in sixteenth-century Europe had been the decline of the medieval city-state. Maintaining complete separation from larger political units no longer paid. Novgorod had lost its independence before 1500; Lübeck in 1536 made the peace with Denmark that ended its days as the leading city of the Hanseatic League; Florence, after a gradual transfer of power from the city to the Medici family, became in 1569 the Grand Duchy of Tuscany. Even so, urban independence, in one form or another, was still in 1600 an essential characteristic of European life. Towns, however small, guarded jealously their control over their own tolls and regulations. Seville and Antwerp largely ran their own affairs within the Spanish monarchy. There were still in name about fifty Imperial Free Cities of which a few, such as Nüremberg and Frankfurt, remained as strong as ever. Two cities of northern Italy, Genoa and Venice, still controlled large rural and coastal dependencies; but the days of their greatest glory were over. Genoa had already lost its Mediterranean possessions, and become, despite occasional opposition, a subordinate ally of Spain. Venice, a century earlier, had been one of the most formidable of all European states, not only in commerce but in armed strength and diplomatic influence. By 1600 it was an anomaly, living on the prestige of the past. Despite the diminution of its trading activity, its agents and ambassadors were still leading figures in most of the courts and capitals of the continent. Though its government was not noticeably less oligarchic than those of other cities, there had developed a convention among writers on politics to praise the Venetian constitution as the ideal combination of liberty and order. The ordinary inhabitant of the city was not likely to appreciate this. It was less evident still in the mainland territories that had been expanding for two centuries until they now covered an area of north-eastern Italy almost as far as the city of Milan. No other European state was now so much under the domination of a single city. For the large Venetian nobility the liberties were more real. They were still, despite a growing tendency to move out into the countryside, a largely urban élite, serving the state institutions without the incentives of venal office-holding. Internal conflicts did not reach a scale that threatened the state itself; and by 1600 Venice was less able to get involved in costly European warfare. It had local rivalries to cope with. The smaller city-state of Ragusa (Dubrovnik) managed, by accepting the nominal overlordship of the sultan, to stay virtually independent and prevent Venice from controlling the Dalmatian coast. No less annoying were the Uskoks, the Adriatic corsairs whose successfully organized piracy made them almost a state without a country. But the fatal competition had come already from Antwerp, to which English, Portuguese, and German merchants had transferred most of their credit activities. Antwerp in turn was, in 1600, surrendering its position to Amsterdam.

The ruler of one small state could claim to be also the head of the most powerful organization in the world. The area of central Italy that had been drawn together by the wealth and military strength of the popes into the 'Papal States' was as corrupt and mismanaged as any European country. Popes and cardinals concerned with the peoples and governments of Christendom were content to leave the administration of their Italian possessions to an assortment of local aristocrats and clerics. But Rome itself, far from being ruined by the Reformation, had grown and flourished astonishingly. The tourist trade, lay and clerical, and the contributions extracted from Catholic churches everywhere, were an excellent substitute for more ordinary resources. It was by no means the only ecclesiastical state. Throughout Catholic Europe, bishoprics retained their temporal independence and their sometimes extensive lands. Something like a third of the western half of the Holy Roman Empire was church land of one sort or another. As Electors, the Archbishops of Mainz, Cologne, and Trier were powers the emperor could not afford to ignore. The Bishopric of Liège formed a major piece of territory dividing the Spanish Netherlands, and was subjected to repeated invasions by the great armies. Münster was another large bishopric within the Empire. The difference between these and non-episcopal states was that their rulers were not hereditary but were chosen by the elaborate politics of the Church: religious matters sometimes played a part. The ludicrous procedures by which Prince Ernst of Bavaria had acquired five bishoprics, including Liège, Münster, and Cologne, had been important to the Habsburgs who were already concerned about the rise of Bavaria as a threat to their control of the Empire. The absurdities were to continue in the seventeenth century, when for instance the See of Osnabrück was the subject of bitter contest and, according to the terms of the Peace of Westphalia, was to alternate between Catholic and Protestant bishops. Neither the faith nor the prosperity of the inhabitants mattered much.

In 1600 the notion of a Europe of sovereign states claiming the uniform allegiance of their subjects and affording them protection and justice was a myth further from reality in some places than others. By 1700 it had become, here and there, rather nearer to the truth. But the frontiers, the wars, and the bargains of the rulers remained for the great majority of Europeans more a meaningless burden and a threat of disaster than a source of emotional or material benefit. The situation has not entirely changed.

REFERENCE

1 S. Pufendorf, *Introduction to the History of Europe* (English transl., 1697) pp. 138, 229, 261, 304.

3

THE ECONOMY

Most people in seventeenth-century Europe were uncertain whether, in the following year, they would be short of food. It depended most obviously on the weather; and behind its erratic fluctuations the weather was on the whole getting worse. In the fifteenth and early sixteenth century the continent and the Atlantic Ocean had been warmer than in most earlier ages. Since then average temperatures had been falling to levels lower than any since the last Ice Age. Winters were colder; summers were wetter; devastating storms were more frequent. Evidence for this is necessarily indirect. It includes the dates of harvests, the growth of trees ('dendrochronology'), and the advance of alpine glaciers into the valleys. Reports of the freezing of the Thames and the Baltic Sound seem to confirm the unprecedented cold, though the state of rivers could be altered by other factors, such as the bridges that limit the inflow of salt tides. Exactly how the weather affected agriculture is a complex problem: grain harvests depend less on averages than on rain and sun at the right times. What is certain is that crop-failures hit large parts of the continent simultaneously. There was one around 1649, another in 1660 and 1661, and the worst of all in the 1690s. Local failures were frequent, such as those in Russia in 1601–03, France in 1629–30, and Spain in 1677. In most places two successive seasons of exceptionally bad weather were enough to make the difference between a small surplus and a frightening dearth. What caused climatic fluctuation is still a largely unanswered question. One suggestion is that the worst weather coincided with periods of minimum sunspot activity – which was observed well enough for detailed comparisons. (Historians have not yet been expected to explain what affected the sunspots.) Whatever the natural causes of scarcity, it was human failures that shaped their effects. European agriculture was feeding more people than ever before; but by the standards even of the next century it was wasting the resources of the land.

CROPS

The one essential economic activity was the growing of grain. Raising animals for food and clothing came next; and compared with these everything else, including the commerce and manufactures that occupy most of economic history, were secondary matters. The success of arable farming was determined both by the quality of the land and by the ways of coping with the great defect of nearly every kind of grain grown in temperate areas – its inability to thrive continuously on the same unaltered soil. Agriculture at its worst, in parts of central and northern Russia and of Sweden, meant raising a single crop on land from which forest had been cleared and then abandoning it. Normally some form of regular rotation enabled a piece of land to give a crop in alternate years, or in two out of three. The commonest grain, in 1600, was rye. Sown in either spring or autumn it provided a low but fairly reliable yield from which the bread eaten by the peasants who grew it was commonly made. Barley, the source of drink in the north and a food for animals, was sown in spring; so were oats, another cheap human food. Maize, the staple food of American civilizations, was becoming familiar in southern Europe. During the century wheat, the source of the bread demanded by nearly everyone in western Europe who could pay for it, became the chief crop for providing the peasant with the money he needed to pay rent and taxes and buy his few marketed goods. It was the most difficult of all to grow. Manure, and repeated ploughing, were usually needed; a three-year rotation with pasture and then some other grain suited it best; and even then the proportion of seed to harvest was lower than with most crops. Yields naturally varied from year to year and field to field; but a sixth of the crop in the west and a quarter in the east was a tolerable fraction to use for the next year's seed. The surplus that went through local or wider markets to feed such providers of money as townsmen, soldiers, and the households of the rich could disappear whenever output fell a little below normal. The high prices that hit the consumer when harvests were bad did not easily find their way back to the farmer – less still to the wage labourer. Amid the violent local fluctuations the normal price of wheat was fairly steady, in terms of gold or silver, until the middle of the century. Then in most countries, it began to fall. Though cheaper bread may have brought some benefit to townsmen, it did not mean that most Europeans were better fed or less afraid of a sudden dearth.

Exports of grain were a small fraction of the total amount consumed; but they could help to overcome shortages that would otherwise have been catastrophic. Only the Netherlands, with the highest proportion of town-dwellers, relied heavily on imported grain, though England, Spain, and occasionally France were other important markets. The great grain-exporting region of the sixteenth century, the Mediterranean, was no longer the main supplier. Some grain had come from countries under Ottoman rule, including Greece and Egypt, through Venetian traders. But it was in Italy especially that the arable farming that had flourished in every lowland area was declining by 1600 and did not recover. The Lombardy Plain, which had fed its cities by intensive cropping, was suffering from the inevitable exhaustion of the soil. In Naples farmers who had once grown rich on grain exports were running into debt as local prices went down. Surviving farms in Sicily were being reduced to more primitive forms of cultivation. In southern France perhaps half the cultivable land was now left unused, and much of the rest was tilled with hand-tools in a wasteful two-year cycle. Only in the few areas that supplied Paris and other cities was there a reliable market. Increased population in the countryside could lead not to increased production but to fragmentation of holdings and lower efficiency. In contrast eastern Europe was now the main source of grain imports. Most of it went by river to the Baltic – chiefly to Danzig – and thence through the Sound to western markets. Dutch ships soon captured nearly all the trade: in a peak year 5000 ships were estimated to carry 140,000 tons of grain – almost the whole consumption of the Netherlands. It was not due to any rich cornfields growing more than could be consumed: the exports came from land that was yielding less than was normal in the west. But the demand and the commercial organization brought prices up to western levels and gave an incentive to profit from them. In Poland, Bohemia, and eastern Germany large landowners tried to increase their output by imposing greater demands on an already wretched peasantry, for some of whom rye as well as wheat became a crop to sell rather than eat. By the middle of the century the supply of grain from Danzig was diminishing. Devastation by wars had reduced the output of some regions; and around 1650 drastic local shortages led to high market prices. After that, as productivity in the west slowly and erratically improved, there was less need for imports. In Poland especially, where trade along the Vistula diminished, there was less prospect of profitable agriculture. But the difference in exports does not seem enough to explain why the area of cultivation fell to two-thirds and the output of grain to a quarter of the levels early in the century. Poland seems to have followed Italy in paying the price of exploiting the land too hard in the wrong ways.

Southern Europe was fortunate in having a crop that was more reliable in both production and demand than grain. Throughout Mediterranean Christendom the whole population drank wine, apparently in huge quantities and without much concern about its quality. (Islamic rulers were usually happy to allow their Christian subjects to add the drinking of alcohol to their sins.) In the north wine was the drink of the rich; but during the sixteenth century more people above the peasant and artisan level had begun to buy it. In areas where the vine flourished, such as Champagne, the hinterland of Bordeaux, and the upper Rhine, it became the principal crop. The temptation to grow vines instead of cereals was even blamed for food shortages, and governments made sporadic efforts to have them destroyed. How profitable the sale of wine became depended partly on whether there was easy access to transport by river. Most of it was kept, like other alcoholic drinks, in barrels, where it deteriorated quickly. For peasants, to whom the grape harvest was one of the happy occasions in the year, local wine was an accessible luxury. But in both south and north there were alternatives. In areas within easy reach of cities, orchards – formerly more akin to natural woodland than to cultivation – were producing more selective varieties of pears and apples. Cider, a local oddity until the sixteenth century, became more widely accepted as a regular drink of agricultural workers, sometimes handed out as a part of their remuneration. Apple orchards could thrive on land difficult for cereals.

For the large-scale producer there was more benefit in the strongly alcoholic drinks made by distilling grapes, grain, or almost any tree-fruit. Brandy moved up the economic scale from being a potent medicament to a prestigious place at rich tables and then to its use as a stimulant for troops about to fight. But everywhere north of the wine-growing countries ale remained as universal as bread. Conveniently, barley or the other grains that were a necessary part of crop-rotation were the product best suited to brewing. Hops, the most successful ingredient for turning ale into a more durable and tasty beer, were slowly becoming popular. They rewarded growers who learned the techniques they need and helped commercial production to replace home-brewing. Beer-drinkers even more than wine-drinkers consumed amounts that by any modern standards look alarmingly high: two gallons a day appears to have been a common requirement. Whatever the drink, the crop that produced it was a vital part of rural economy both for marketing and for home consumption. There were other crops less prominent in economic statistics than they were in the diet of the peasant or the serf. The many varieties of beans, peas, and lentils that went under such collective names as 'pulse' or *légumes* could be grown with little labour on small plots as well as in fields, and eaten without the burdensome processing needed by grain. In a category of its own was the olive, the slow-growing shrub of the Mediterranean whose fruit was a necessity of life for the southerner and in the north one of many imported luxury foods. The division between the olive-oil consuming zone and the rest of Europe has remained surprisingly consistent.

ANIMALS

In animal-farming as in crop-growing, large-scale studies do not always say much about resources that in fact provided a large part of the food supply. As red meat became less accessible, poultry and their eggs remained important both to consume in the household and to sell in local markets. The basket of eggs that appears in so many pictures of rural life had cost little to produce. The one source of meat that could be raised by many of the poorest families was the pig: pork, salted for the winter, must have contributed a large but unrecorded amount of nourishment. It was not yet true that anyone who wanted could keep an enormous pig: though pulse, or acorns, or swill from rejected grain could make adequate pig-food, the comparative scarcity of root-crops made the diet of the pig less fattening than it soon became. There were other animals too that now seem to be on the fringe of economic activity but could be a major part of human life – the goats of southern Europe that lived on the poorest of land, the bees that were still the main source of sugar, the deer that were kept for food as well as for the amusement of the rich. An excuse for saying little about them is that they did not vitally affect agriculture as a whole.

In any farming system the relation between crops and animals was crucial. As a source of food, animals normally make less efficient use of the land than do cereals. But when manure from cattle and sheep was the main fertilizer they were indispensable. The bitter conflict between primarily arable farming and large-scale pasture had gone on for centuries and was still familiar in many areas. Which one predominated depended not only on the quality of the land but on a complex interplay of prices, power, and habit. There were large regions, and also small areas, where one type of agriculture was naturally more successful than another: England had its 'highland zone' where cattle and sheep occupied most of the land and its lowlands where cereals were combined with fewer animals; but within them districts of dairying, stock-fattening, sheep with corn, woodland and fen were intermingled. Wool still brought wealth; but the days of ever-expanding sheep-farming were over. In Spain the Mesta, though it still controlled something like two million sheep moving between north and south, was no longer making large profits. Spanish sheep-farming was as much in decline as the rest of its agriculture; but there, as in northern England and most other hill country, falling cereal prices later in the century made sheep comparatively profitable again.

The number of cattle must on the whole have been increasing; though all the evidence suggests that the amount of beef, as of other red meat, consumed by all but the rich was less than in earlier centuries. Winter feeding was becoming commoner, especially in England, the Netherlands, and Denmark, which was a great exporter of cattle. Most of them were now dairy cattle. It was more efficient to milk an animal than to kill it; and cheese was the great source of animal protein for workers in town and country alike. Armies lived on it, and it was an easily exported food. Swiss farmers could use mountain as well as lowland pastures to supply an export trade in dairy produce, importing their cereals in return. It was in Moldavia, Hungary, and more recently Brandenburg that large-scale rearing of cattle for slaughter was thriving. Where transport by water was difficult, a product that could walk was helpful, even if after being driven hundreds of miles oxen had to be fattened in pastures nearer the sea or the city. One function of cattle was slowly declining: on the richer arable lands the horse was replacing the ox for ploughing. Its more exacting demands for food were outweighed by the strength and speed that made it the source of mobile power for every purpose. In Spain and other southern areas the mule was the best the peasant could hope for; indeed the type and number of draught animals was a good indicator of the state of the economy. The life of a household could be ruined by their loss more than by almost any other calamity.

AGRICULTURAL CHANGES

Evidence about the progress or deterioration of agriculture, unless it relates to a very small area, is confusing and inconclusive. There are many different ways of measuring any change, and they are not easily translated into terms of human welfare. Certainly not much is left of the idea that agriculture was much the same from the Early Middle Ages until the eighteenth century. Yet many of the developments were local, uncertain, and marginal; the normal peasant ploughed and sowed as his ancestors had, and felt with good reason that he was worse off than they had been. It was not surprising that the Netherlands, with the largest proportion of town dwellers and a constant shortage of grain, was the leader in innovation. There were new systems of rotation that included such crops as parsnips and turnips. Peat and lime provided artificial fertilization of the soil. Industrial crops, including oil-seed, flax, and madder, helped to make use of every acre of land; so did the market gardens around towns. In the 1630s a boom in tulip-growing collapsed in one of the first speculative 'bubbles'. Netherlands engineers like Cornelius Vermuyden and Jan Leeghwater developed the methods of drainage that added six or seven square miles a year to the area available for cultivation – an important gain to the Netherlands but trivial in comparison with the amount neglected or devastated in the rest of Europe. In England too there was a gradual increase in the output of cereals, partly no doubt through better cultivation but also because more land was taken into cultivation. For most of Mediterranean Europe the one improvement in the productivity of the land came from the introduction of maize, first into Spain and then into Italy. While the yield of wheat was on the whole declining, maize proved astonishingly prolific and solved some of the problems of exhausted soil. It did not require much preparation of the land; and shortage of labour was, in later decades of the century, a widespread problem.

Whatever the barriers to practical improvements in farming, there was no lack of theoretical information about the ways in which land could be better used. 'Farming books' were among the best-selling literature of the day. The classic sixteenth-century writers like Tusser were superseded in England by Gervase Markham on horse- and cattle-breeding and Sir Richard Weston whose *Discourse of the husbandry used in Brabant and Flanders* was the best-known of many eulogies of Netherlands farming. It owed its success largely to its editor, Samuel Hartlib. Like John Dury and their master Comenius himself, Hartlib regarded reform of agriculture as one of the greatest practical forms of enlightenment, and the zeal of these writers was communicated to some of their puritan associates. In France the *Théâtre d'agriculture* of Olivier de Serres was reprinted throughout the century, and there were handbooks on similar lines in German. Some of their readers were landlords to whom new methods of agriculture were largely a gentlemanly hobby. There was an immense difference between the cattle and horses that were bred by landowners, ranging from English gentry to the Tsar Alexis, and the animals available to the ordinary tenant. But it was from the landlord that improvement was bound to originate. It was made possible partly by extending the demesne at the expense of peasant holdings, a process that had been common in the sixteenth century and was still spreading. To the ordinary countryman ideas that looked so salutary to readers of Hartlib were an added threat to his livelihood. 'Better' use of land could mean the loss of the extra food and fuel provided by woodland, waste, or common.

Men who lived a savage existence in English fens or Italian swamps did not easily see benefits in drainage. The Breton peasant, lacking barns, stables, and heavy ploughs, had no prospect of profiting from thoroughbred cattle. The French nobility were among the landlords most inclined to survive by extracting more labour, at little or no cost, from the tenant, his wife, and often his very young children.

Failure of the land to produce more food did not always mean failure to bring more wealth to its owners. It depended on the laws, the social conventions, and the whole ethos of landed society. If owners sought a more direct and profitable control over the farming of their estates, it was often because the real value of rents and dues was falling. It might be improved by such devices as enclosure in the English midlands or the tightening and legalizing of chaotic seigneurial rights in France. To enlarge and improve the demesne, land farmed for the direct benefit of the owner, required both labour and capital. In the east shortage of labour could be overcome by serfdom, or by increased obligations that came near to it (see pp. 97–102). The state, with its judicial powers firmly in the hands of landowners, offered little resistance to the tightening of bondage. In England and the Netherlands farm-labourers could usually be hired at a rate of wages that did not increase much; and it was there too that money could flow most easily into the land. Merchants could easily acquire the landed estates their social advancement required; landed families could be involved in commercial and industrial enterprises and subsidize their estates from the profits. In most other countries landed nobilities still preferred to preserve themselves from contamination by trade. In Germany and the Habsburg lands the rigid distinction between noble and non-noble estates made it hard for the ambitious outsider to reach the highest levels of landed society. But the success of the Prussian Junker showed how such obstacles could be overcome (see p. 366). *Gutswirtschaft* and *Gutsherrschaft*, the tenurial systems that gave the landlord the benefits of feudal authority with few of its obligations, helped to establish the prosperity of great estates at the cost of turning the tenants into labourers. The state tended to favour large-scale agriculture. In Poland the Crown was the greatest of the holders of huge areas of land that were managed for profit. The Danish monarchy, which was reckoned to hold, at the beginning of the century, about half the land in the country, granted it in abundance to loyal magnates and encouraged the outright confiscation of peasant holdings. But only in Russia were there estates on the scale of the Trinity-Sergius monastery with its population of 100,000 or owners like Basil Ostrogorsky who claimed an income higher than the tsar's. The great concern of the magnate was the same as that of the peasant – to keep his land in cultivation and in his possession. Changes in the way it was used were more likely to be an unhappy necessity than an enlightened enterprise.

WOODLAND AND SEA

Neither rich nor poor lived entirely on the produce of farming. Killing the abundant wild animals and birds was a major rural occupation; and in times of dearth it was often possible to turn from the barren fields to the woodlands, where chestnuts or acorns could make flour. In every country north of the Alps, trees occupied a large part of the landscape, and in the far north nearly all of it. How much food and fuel came directly from the woodland to the consumer we can never know: certainly for the peasant to be deprived of it was felt to be a disaster. But the forest that provided so much to the household was also a source of large-scale profits. The demand for timber was growing, with shipbuilding and the iron industry the biggest consumers. The one well-known instance of an awareness that the produce of the earth was being squandered was the widespread hostility to the destruction of woodlands. It was even suggested, in Cromwellian England, that the right to cut down a tree should carry an obligation to plant two or three more. The tenant or owner who ruined the timber on an estate for quick profit was depriving his successors; and the state was often among the most guilty. But it was easy to suppose that any extension of arable into former waste or woodland was beneficial, and that the great forests of Germany, Scandinavia, and Russia were virtually indestructible.

Another source exploited by both the poor man and the large organization was the sea. Here, at least, human intervention could seem insignificant; but the resources were not really unchanging or unlimited. Markets everywhere supplied fish. Much of it, of course, was caught locally as a spare-time occupation. But fishing in European seas and in the oceans had long been one of the biggest commercial enterprises. Dried and salted deep-sea fish was distributed far inland to form a major part of the diet at every social level. Perhaps the chief material benefit conferred by the Catholic Church was the compulsory eating of fish on fast-days that could amount to nearly half the year; though it would be hard to show whether Protestants consumed less than Catholics in the same economic circumstances. The Mediterranean was not a prolific source of the most attractive fish. Until the fifteenth century the southern Baltic, the great spawning-ground of herrings, was the biggest fishing area: one of the chief activities of the Hanse had been the transport of salt and herrings. Whether, as is often claimed, the trade declined because herrings began to prefer the North Sea (possibly through changes in salinity or temperature) is arguable. Exports through the Sound were still high in the mid-seventeenth century. By then much of the Baltic fishing and exporting had been captured by the Dutch, who found it even more profitable to exploit the seas nearer home. The *buiz* was a ship equipped to salt and pack the fish on board and to remain at sea for months at a time. A regular seasonal pattern was established in which fishing fleets moved between the Shetlands and the East Anglian coast. Selling their catch in ports that regarded them as trespassers in British waters was not always easy. But the disputes about rights over coastal waters and fishing grounds were based on even less well-defined claims than they are now. (Charles I's governments tried to make the Dutch buy licences to fish off the English coast.) The real danger was the privateers who found fishing boats easy victims. In more distant waters English fishing fleets prospered. Cod was caught off Iceland and North America: the Newfoundland coast, mainly under English control, was a convenient place for processing it. By the end of the century whale-hunting, the most difficult and profitable of all the ways to exploit the sea, was also dominated by the English. When the Dutch industry based in Spitzbergen declined through excessive catching which destroyed the whale population, the market for whale-oil was supplied by spectacular voyages to remote parts of the oceans. Meanwhile, to the scarcely changing village ports along every coast of Europe, the little boats of self-employed fishermen brought back catches that fed a population almost as close to hunger as inland labourers.

The distribution of fish, and indeed the whole dietary system of Europe, depended on the one commodity that was demanded everywhere always. Salt came from mines, from sea-water, and from the impregnated turf of estuaries. Its movement over long distances was essential because it was virtually the only way in which food could be preserved. Salt-mines, formerly exploited by pumping water in and out, were beginning to use direct extraction of the rock or the building of dams to create salt lakes. Either way required capital and expertise. The mines of Lüneburg Heath supplied not only German markets but the fisheries of Sweden and Denmark. Any coastal waters, but especially the Atlantic shores of France, Spain, and Portugal, gave opportunities for the extraction of salt by evaporation, as a small local industry or a bigger one. The trade, increasingly in the hands of the Dutch, was one of the economic activities too important to be affected by such matters as wars. Salt found its way to every market, farm, and household – usually through the hands of middlemen and tax-collectors who made its cost a common grievance.

INDUSTRY

At least nine-tenths of the people of Europe worked on the land. Manufacture was, in that sense, a minor activity. There was less difference between one part of Europe and another in industry than in agriculture. Industry – or pre-industry as Braudel and others call it – meant, nearly everywhere, the villager with his forge, water-mill, or hand-loom or the small urban master helped by his few journeymen and apprentices. They conducted it with their own capital, in the form of equipment unchanged for centuries, and sold their output directly to the consumer. The tanner, the blacksmith, and the miller are inconspicuous in economic histories only because their production made little impact on wider markets and their prosperity or poverty went largely unrecorded. But they were not insignificant. Such men, whose work was indispensable to their communities, had better opportunities to thrive than the ordinary villagers. The English midland blacksmith was a founder of the Black Country iron industry; the Russian miller was the villager most likely to become a money-lender and a 'rich' peasant. They had the chance to rise higher than the countrymen who got part of their living through specializing in the kind of work their neighbours could at a pinch do for themselves – the coopers, wheelwrights, and sawyers with neither the means nor the incentive to expand their activities.

The output of many kinds of goods rose during the century, though nowhere to a spectacular extent. Certainly in the west more metal goods, pottery, and glass were produced in 1700 than in 1600. But it would be wrong to suggest that there was a steady or universal expansion of industry and commerce. What looks like an increase in one area may often be a change of location or the substitution of one product for another. The most widespread development was the movement of industries away from towns into the countryside. The town, with its higher taxation, higher wages, greater hazards of fire, plague, and enemy action, was a place the enterprising organizer of industry might well prefer to avoid. Most of all it suffered through the guild system, which now seemed antiquated and restrictive. It was strongest in central Europe, but in one form or another it survived in large towns everywhere. For centuries the virtues of maintaining qualities and skills, protecting workers, and upholding the town's status had conflicted with the vices of obstructing change and enterprise. The brewing industry was typical. In the north, large-scale production of beer and spirits made possible the varied qualities that were more attractive to those who could pay for them than anything the household or estate could provide. Towns, with markets and ready access to transport, were the obvious places to manufacture a bulky product; but restrictions and costs could make it better to move out into the adjoining country. There were also the larger and slower movements, influenced by changes in demand – including increasingly, that from overseas – and by the interference of governments. Italy suffered first the shift of industries from the south to the north and then the disastrous decline of the northern centres that was part of a long and erratic fall in the economic activity of the Mediterranean as a whole. Most of the movement was of course in the one great industry that dominated European commerce – textiles.

TEXTILES

Making cloth involves so many processes and such varied equipment that it could be done only in the most primitive way without employers and markets. The early seventeenth-century was the climax of slow but drastic changes in both the products and their distribution. The use of water-power or wind-power to drive complex machinery for spinning, weaving, and 'fulling' shows how close the industry was to the revolution that began a century later. (Why it got as yet no further is one of the much-disputed problems of the period: the barriers seem to be effective demand and the availability of capital rather than techniques or materials.) In the last quarter of the sixteenth century the international market in 'woollens' – blanket-like material made from short-staple wool – had diminished as more varied fabrics were distributed widely. Germany and northern Europe continued to use the older types of cloth produced locally while in the west, the Mediterranean and the growing markets of the Near East the 'new draperies' formed the main stocks of successful merchants. They were 'worsteds', made from fine, long-staple wool that produced a lighter and more adaptable cloth. The popular varieties were cheaper to buy, though not as hard-wearing, as the older cloths. From their original source in the Netherlands they were by 1600 being adopted by both old and new centres of the industry. Each of the successive economic depressions, local or general, hit the older textiles harder than the more marketable ones. There was one essential condition for their development: everywhere spinning and weaving were able to expand by becoming an activity of the countryside.

This was the great age of the 'putting-out system', the *Verlagswesen*, in which an organizing merchant provided raw materials to workers in their homes, and bought back the finished product, paying less than any regular wage. It had existed since the Middle Ages in other manufactures too – metal-work, leather, even boat-building. But the making of every kind of textile now became a regular part of rural life. An industry seeking new markets for new products amid keen competition was less likely than more conservative ones to tolerate urban restrictions. At the same time countrymen who faced intermittent poverty were glad to undertake work which, not having its own seasonal fluctuation, could be increased when labour in the fields diminished. While actual manufacture was on the smallest scale, a merchant could be using the labour of several hundred homes and selling in worldwide markets.

The prominence of wool makes it easy to overlook the other

materials that were used in textiles both cheap and dear. Many were a mixture of animal with vegetable fibres known, in English and other languages, by a bewildering variety of names. Flax imported from Riga was an important item in Netherlands trade, and linen was the commonest fabric woven in the German countryside. English governments tried without much success to encourage the growing of flax and hemp. Cotton was already familiar as an import from the near east. But the bitterest rivalries concerned silk, no longer a rare and mysterious substance. In the sixteenth century silken clothing had become one of the greatest demonstrations of wealth and status, and its use spread slowly down the social scale. Dutch merchants had access to supplies of silk from Persia, Bengal, and China. But it was in Spain, and above all Italy, that successful production had begun. While other north Italian towns were losing both trade and industries, Genoese merchants built up something close to a monopoly in the supply of Mediterranean silk to the rest of Europe. The French, despite the insistence of Sully and Laffemas that silk ought to be produced at home, never managed to grow the right kind of mulberry in adequate amounts. Silk manufacture became the great industry of Lyons; but it depended on buying Italian silk from Genoa and on prolonged efforts to restrict the competition of other French towns such as Tours and Rouen.

Success in producing raw materials for textiles was not a substitute for profitable manufactures. The Italian towns and cities that until the end of the sixteenth century had shown their wealth in the magnificence of their buildings became in the next fifty years dependent largely on the inadequate agriculture of the surrounding countryside. The cloth produced in Venice was reduced during the seventeenth century to a tenth of its former amount. Milan and Florence suffered almost as badly as their luxury textiles were driven out by the lower costs of the French and the Dutch. The industry of Castile was in the same plight: the general economic troubles of Spain helped to make imported cloth, even when woven from Spanish wool, cheaper than their own. The captive market of South America was lost as industries grew up there. Spanish wool was still used in high-quality cloth, and was a normal ingredient of the 'new draperies'. But the wretched Spanish peasant, who had little chance to produce cloth for the market, saw the benefit from his few sheep disappear.

Further north there were many areas where a new rural textile industry flourished. In Switzerland at the beginning of the century the valleys round Zurich began to prosper through the weaving previously monopolized by the city. In Picardy, Normandy, and Brittany the production of cheap textiles for export became in some of the villages the main source of income, again to the distress of the towns. There was specialization both in the type of material and in the work done. Some villages devoted themselves entirely to the various finishing processes. Elsewhere in France the old *métiers* of the towns made little effort to adapt their high-quality products to the wider markets, and by the middle of the century the industry was at a low ebb. One of Colbert's successful acts of economic intervention was to call in Flemish and Dutch merchants to help its revival. Van Robais established at Abbeville one of the few large textile factories of its day, with two or three thousand workers bringing together all the processes from spinning to dyeing. In Germany, where the wars completed the collapse of many urban centres of industry, the impoverishment of the countryside was often mitigated a little by the extension of the already familiar putting-out of textile work; but foreign cloth was soon able to take over most of the market. The shift of the industry in the Netherlands took a different form. The medieval clothing towns of Flanders suffered badly from the revolt. Many of their weavers fled to the north and re-established the industry in Leiden and the surrounding area. Technically they were in advance of the rest of Europe: despite opposition by owners of old single looms, machines with twelve shuttles worked by one weaver were well established by the 1620s. But spinning and weaving were the least profitable part of the textile trade. With little sheep-farming of their own, Dutch clothiers had to rely on imported wool, mainly high-quality varieties from Spain. The business was dominated not by clothiers but by the merchants who dealt in finished cloth, and it was in the finishing processes – dressing, bleaching, and above all dyeing – that Netherlands superiority was most evident. Even this industry, much of it in large urban units, was a poor relation of commerce. The wealth of the trading community contrasted sharply with the poverty of the men, women, and children who were employed in the clothing industry but kept alive partly by charity. There were many complaints that cloth made abroad was dyed and re-exported as a Dutch product. England and Holland were rivals who nevertheless needed each other's activities; though as the disastrous project of Alderman Cockayne in 1614 demonstrated, the Dutch were not dependent on a single source for their imports of cloth (see p. 452). Only when Colbert's tariffs added to the slowly growing difficulties of the Leiden cloth industry did it suffer a depression as severe as those England had known half a century earlier. It was then the turn of the Dutch merchants to discover the virtues of scattered rural manufactures. In Brabant, as elsewhere, villagers worked for even lower wages than townsmen.

MINING AND METALS

The other field in which there were big changes in technique and organization was mining and metal-working. The loss of woodlands, for which the demands of iron-smelting were held partly responsible, led to more urgent need for coal. Armies and navies were using more iron and steel; copper coinage was becoming as important as silver. Some kinds of mining could still be local industries: in many places from the Cornish Stannaries to the Urals it was a co-operative business of independent artisans who held traditional rights to exploit shallow or open-cast workings. But it was deep mines, run by entrepreneurs who could provide the capital to create and maintain them and to ensure the transport and marketing of their products, that were giving new opportunities for profit. Drains and pumps, props and haulage equipment all developed in a manner that gave hints of the industrial changes of the next two centuries. In England and northern France coal was replacing wood both as the cheapest domestic fuel in towns and for many industrial purposes – though it was not yet used successfully in iron-smelting. Collieries employing a hundred or so workers were the largest units. Mining was seldom a secure occupation: problems of exhausted seams and uncertain demand were already familiar. The landowner with coal or iron on his estate had a tempting source of profit that was often exploited and then abandoned. It was one way in which landed families could discover the benefits and risks of commercial activity.

The problems of a rapidly growing mineral industry were shown very clearly in Sweden (see p. 407). The great copper mine of Falun was a source of wealth which, though not comparable with the silver of Peru, expanded rapidly enough in the first half of the century to transform the fortunes of the Swedish Crown. It would have been more important still if the economic aspects had been as well managed as the technical ones. The methods of extraction were designed by German experts. The actual working was run by a closed democratic body of some five hundred miners. The Crown controlled them partly by legislation, partly by organizing the processing and marketing of the ore either directly or through a monopoly company. The company repeatedly got into difficulties. The Crown demanded more for its war expenditure than the mine, properly worked, could afford; and though Sweden was practically the only source of copper in Europe the price tended to fall rapidly as supplies increased. In 1628 the Dutch financier Louis de Geer, already a shareholder in the company, was given what soon amounted to complete control. But efforts to rig the market and to consume large amounts of copper by minting it were constantly unsuccessful. Behind the immediate incompetence lay the inescapable fact that one piece of industrial progress could not get far unless demand for its product was kept up by others. Swedish iron-mining, much less spectacular in its expansion than copper, proved by 1700 a better source of wealth for the country as a whole. It had the advantages of widespread supplies of high-grade ore and of still abundant forests. At the beginning of the century the industry was at every stage on a small scale, dependent on French and German immigrant workers for such technical advance as there was. By the end the great ironmasters and exporters were controlling undertakings that supplied nearly half the iron used in England, and prospered on the demands of continental armies. The greatest single contribution to the change had again come from Louis de Geer. He was outstanding among the few financiers who were now, in close association with governments, putting capital into large-scale industry. His first big profits had come from the sale of guns and bullets to France, Venice, and the States General. Then, from his control of the copper industry, he came to dominate the economic life of Sweden. From the Netherlands he introduced new mining techniques and the men who applied them. More important to the government, his links with Amsterdam enabled him to raise loans of many kinds. He virtually financed Gustav Adolf's expedition to Germany, and most of its equipment came from one or other of his concerns.

But this was only one of the armies he supplied: Mansfeld was a customer, and debtor; Danish, French, and Dutch armies depended on supplies that he had controlled. One of his later achievements was to assemble and equip in Holland the Swedish navy that in 1645 defeated a Danish one supplied from the same sources. De Geer was in fact the first great international armament magnate. But he was by no means the only one of his kind: his nephews of the Trip family in Amsterdam and his partner De Besche in Sweden operated on almost the same scale. When he died, a member of the Swedish nobility and perhaps the richest subject Europe had yet seen, he had plenty of successors to benefit from the wars of Louis XIV.

CITIES

Trade and finance on a large scale depended on a few great cities. Beyond that it is hard to reach any general conclusions about the cities of Europe at this stage – or even about those of zones or countries. Each had its own history that was shaped by local, national, and world economies as well as by political and military events. We can see that the expansion of London and Paris were exceptional: most cities, despite their attractions for the dispossessed and the ambitious of the countryside, grew only slowly; some became less populous. The city-state inevitably lost some of its economic importance as its political functions were subordinated to the nation. Berlin and Madrid, on the other hand, achieved the status of major cities by becoming the capitals of national governments. But more often the rise and fall of a city reflected, sometimes belatedly, changes in the financial and commercial systems that centred on it. Sometimes there is an obvious immediate cause. The rapid decline of Antwerp had begun in the 1570s when the warfare against Spain and the blockade of the Scheldt ruined the industries and trade of the entire southern Netherlands. The contrast between the re-established Spanish government in the south and the merchant-led republic in the north was enough to ensure a permanent shift. In Germany the decline of the Hanseatic League and of many Imperial Free Cities had begun long before the Thirty Years War. Competition from England and the Netherlands in the north and the loss of the Italian trade in the south were irredeemable disasters. Munich, capital city of the Electors of Bavaria, suffered no less than Nüremberg and Augsburg. It is sometimes suggested that the failure to adapt to change sprang from the urban communities themselves. Later generations of the Fuggers and their kind became landed aristocrats and office-seekers rather than mercantile or financial entrepreneurs; old-established towns had evolved a mass of restrictions designed to preserve exclusive privileges rather than admit new enterprise and new capital. But it seems unlikely that any innovations would have avoided the worst urban collapse: that of northern Italy.

In the first decades of the century the great example of Italian prosperity was Genoa. Trade in such eastern commodities as coral and slaves, the penetration of European markets, and the provision of shipping to many western countries had helped it to become, briefly, the greatest centre of international finance. By linking their bills of exchange both to the silver of America and to the varied produce of Italy, the Genoese were able to finance both the armies of Spain and the transactions of Mediterranean and northern merchants. But with its restricted site and a hinterland of poor villages it had no alternative source of wealth and had never been as conspicuously rich as its chief rival, Venice. In 1600 the independence and diplomatic prestige of Venice might have been expected to bring it economic benefits from the wars that were depleting the resources of greater states. But there were already signs of the limitations that by 1700 made it comparatively poor. No other city was as dependent on shipping as this small urban island. Its ships still dominated the Mediterranean; but many were now being built elsewhere. Timber, despite the efforts of earlier Venetian governments to preserve the oak forests of the mainland, was inadequate for ocean-going ships. Venetian trade diminished as Mediterranean supplies of food and cloth were less wanted in the rest of Europe. Rich Venetians were already putting more of their wealth into acquiring estates on the mainland. With the introduction of maize and the reclaiming of uncultivated land, agriculture could be a more profitable use of capital than commerce. A sudden blow to the city's economy was the great plague of 1629–30, which reduced the population by something between a third and a quarter. Unlike earlier plagues it was not followed by a quick recovery. Labour was scarce. For the wars against the Turks that continued until the end of the century, soldiers and seamen now had to be recruited at growing expense from all over Europe. Despite all this, the city nobility were still rich and secure enough to keep the treasures of art and architecture that eventually turned Venice into a splendid museum. As the greatest example of commercial success it was replaced decisively by Amsterdam.

Amsterdam's dominant position in the merchant activity of the world has never been equalled. Once its pre-eminence had been established after the division of the Netherlands and the swift decline of Antwerp, no other northern city could come anywhere near to Amsterdam's progress. Like Venice, it was almost surrounded by water and divided by canals. But Amsterdam's equivalent of the Venetian terrafirma was a province whose many towns were easily drawn into its economic sphere. It was the most cosmopolitan of Europe's cities, welcoming refugees with little regard to religion or even race: Jews were among its leading financiers. Almost unassailable by armies, it could profit from war. It profited too from famine, switching its grain trade and – so it was generally believed – hoarding supplies in the huge warehouses that held a significant part of its capital in the form of food. Buying and selling commodities abroad was a better way to grow richer than becoming an owner of the limited available land; and an estate in the country was not, for the great men of Amsterdam, a necessary mark of social status.

The twelve-year truce with Spain provided the opportunity for Amsterdam to establish itself completely as the new centre round which the international economic life of Europe revolved. The exchange and deposit bank opened in 1609 was closely linked with the state. For the first time it became normal for bullion and coin to stay in the bank's vaults while payments were made by paper. More and more of Europe's silver came to Amsterdam, and it was largely through transactions there that rates of exchange among the chaotic currencies of Europe were settled. In the political upheavals of one country after another, merchants and politicians alike used it as a refuge for capital. Though the bank itself did not lend money except to the government, its facilities made borrowing easy and helped to preserve one of the city's great commercial assets: rates of interest, at 4 per cent or less, were the lowest in Europe. In 1611 came a second institution, the new Exchange. Originally a market for commodities, whose prices often determined those for much of the world, it became the scene of purely speculative dealing. By the middle of the century there developed the traffic in 'futures' and in options to buy or sell which meant that fortunes could be made and lost by speculation in goods that never existed at all. Efforts by the States General to prevent these aspects of capitalist activity had not much success.

Amsterdam's position in European finance was inseparable from its growing command of shipping. Beginning with the Baltic grain-trade and the export of manufactured goods to Spain in return for bullion, its shipping penetrated into nearly every European port, including those of the Mediterranean. When the supply of Baltic grain diminished, there was still timber. Firs from the vast Russian forests came through Memel. Much of the Scandinavian timber and timber products escaped the dues levied by the Danes by using Göteborg and the smaller Norwegian ports. By far the greatest part of it was carried in ships from Amsterdam, which took back textiles, including some from England and France, Mediterranean wine, and overseas luxuries. From the best of the timber, more ships were built in the Amsterdam yards. Dutch shipbuilding was probably the most technically advanced of all the industries of Europe. With cranes and wind-powered sawmills it could produce ships at half the cost of foreign rivals. The *fluit* was a merchant vessel easy to build and man. Unlike English and Spanish ships designed for the hazardous life of the Mediterranean, it was not armed; and it was readily adaptable to new types of cargo. Often its owners were a small co-operative group able to switch quickly from one enterprise to another. Even when, in the later part of the century, England and France made great efforts to increase their own merchant shipping, some of their ships were bought in Amsterdam. It could not last for ever: by 1700 the proportion of European shipping that used Amsterdam was shrinking; investment in financial institutions continued to grow while that in commerce and industry diminished. Unlike their fathers and grandfathers, leading Amsterdam citizens were buying country estates and becoming conspicuous spenders. The wars of the Orange monarchy were producing taxation that was not matched by profits. It is rash to talk too confidently of 'decline'. The city still had a large share in a booming overseas commerce; its population was still growing, without any large influx of the poor; governments of the union and the province might resent its power but were still dependent on it. But in the European economy it now had an evident successor – London.

London was very different from the earlier dominant cities. The port and financial centre were part of the larger city that was the capital of a diverse and prosperous state. It was the home of a monarch whose court drew to itself the leaders of a rich landed nobility. They set a pattern of life to which merchants naturally aspired. The best-known London merchant at the beginning of the century was Lionel Cranfield, future Earl of Middlesex. In 1600 he was a mercer, buying cloth from all the English producing regions and exporting it to markets all over Europe. He was buying other things too – a receivership of Crown revenues, and then a share in the Great Farm of the Customs. He was compiling details of the lands in various English counties that would bring profit as well as status. He was moving on from simple credit transactions to money-lending and international banking. No-one else in the city matched his achievement in acquiring the offices of Master of the Court of Wards and Liveries and finally that of Lord Treasurer, which led to his impeachment. But there were normally several city merchants who, like Cranfield, won seats in the Commons, and a few others in the Lords. The links of the city with government were made stronger by the Civil War, when it was able to provide not only loans but essential parts of the financial administration. After the Restoration it appeared to suffer – and survive – an assortment of misfortunes. Plague and fire, the Anglo-Dutch wars that brought an enemy fleet into the Thames, the constant disputes with royal governments, culminating in the forfeiture of London's charter in 1683, the panic produced by the 'Stop of the Exchequer' in 1672 which ruined many of the bankers, and the great crisis of the 1690s when confidence in both the financiers and the trading companies collapsed – none of these interfered with the underlying strength.

By 1700 London had expanded so much in building and population that no other city in Europe could match it. Three-quarters of English imports and exports went through the port of London. Coastal shipping, the Thames, and a road system that had always been focused on London enabled it to draw in every kind of marketable produce from the whole country, much of it for redistribution at home as well as for export. There were no internal trade barriers, no differing currencies, no powerful regional legislatures to resist London's domination. Though the poor were always there, it was not threatened by any mass star-vation. At every level the opportunities for improved standards of living were greater than elsewhere. This was the time when the shop, and the shop window, began to replace the open market stall in retail trade; and London, as its shops spread from the city to the west, was ahead of other European towns in developing them. A less evident help to its commerce was the stability of sterling. Despite occasional demands from exporters for a reduc-tion in its exchange rate, and despite the clipping of coins in circulation at home, the pound remained at exactly the same value abroad in terms of silver. The Dutch guilder was almost as steady; and until the 1690s London was only slowly catching up with Amsterdam in the facilities and security it could offer to finan-ciers. Then came the upheaval brought about by the unprece-dented cost of wars and the general economic depression. The city could no longer meet the needs of a government committed to unprecedented expenditure on war; and many Tory landowners were reluctant to help either of them. Government schemes that included a national lottery and a variety of devices for increasing taxation did not produce nearly enough. It was hoped to persuade people with a little capital to invest it directly in government funds by offering annuities for life as an alternative to straight interest, under the guarantee of an Act of Parliament. It still appeared that there was more confidence in city companies than in the national exchequer. In 1694 a partial solution was found in the creation of the Bank of England, an institution managed by a group of city financiers but with close government control as the price of its privileges. Though its first issue of banknotes was followed by financial panic and plots by older banking interests, London was soon as attractive as Amsterdam in the growing intricacies of international finance.

The leading figures in all this were a strange assortment. Edward Backwell, younger son of a Somerset squire, had been an outstanding member of the Goldsmiths' Company and de-veloped a private banking system, partly the goldsmiths' and partly his own. Cromwell and Charles II each relied on his help. With the collapse of his credit in the 1670s his 'goldsmiths' notes' and most of his own fortune disappeared. Josiah Child came from a London merchant family and made his fortune orig-inally from naval supplies. In the 1670s he gradually took control of the East India Company. Throughout the 1680s and the less

profitable 1690s he was a virtual dictator of the company, notorious for his bribery and nepotism but keeping most of the time
the favour of the royal court. He acquired great estates around
London; and though he was content with a baronetcy for himself,
his son became an earl and his grandson a duke. But the men who
had the most manifest and lasting influence on London were those
whose profits went into building. Most surprising of all in his
origin was Nicholas Barbon. He was believed, with some uncertainty, to be the son of 'Praisegod Barebones' of the Parliament.
He took a medical degree in Holland, became involved in London
financial circles, wrote on economic theory, but devoted most of
his life to organizing the rebuilding of the whole region between
the city and Westminster. It was development that had been
started a generation earlier by two of the great aristocrats who
became part-time Londoners, the Earls of Bedford and
Southampton, who were bringing capital from the counties into
the service of the city and drawing ample rents in return. The
multiplicity of resources represented by people like these made
London's prosperity almost indestructible. Paris was not comparable, even in the decades of France's greatest power: French
internal commerce was never concentrated in a single city but
shared with Nantes, Lyons, and other provincial towns. Nor were
any German cities. Leipzig, despite its losses in the Thirty Years
War, became the greatest market in central Europe, with permanent warehouses and auctions gradually replacing the celebrated
fairs; but its rival Frankfurt-am-Main remained a stronger financial centre. The trade between west and east within Europe was
still on a larger scale than the overseas commerce over which the
great conflicts were fought.

OVERSEAS TRADE AND COLONIES

The Netherlands and England were sending perhaps a tenth of
their exports across the Atlantic and a little more to the Far East.
France, by the end of the century, was developing its overseas
trade quickly. Between them they supplied Europe with the overseas products that became for the first time an essential part of
the consumption of families down to the artisan level. Sugar,
mainly West Indian, was in demand everywhere, though wars and
the exhaustion of the first plantations caused big fluctuations in

supply. Coffee, still a rarity in 1660, was by the end of the century a notorious feature of urban life and a major part of Asian trade. Tea was still an upper-class drink, but imports from China were beginning to grow. More alarming both to economic theorists and to the workers who thought themselves threatened was the sudden boom in Asiatic textiles. Printed calicoes, the merchants discovered to their surprise, could be imported cheaply enough to be sold in large quantities to the 'poor people'. The French government in 1686 tried, with only partial success, to impose a complete ban. In England the use of imported textiles was denounced year after year until in 1696 a bill to restrict them was supported by riots of weavers at Westminster. The East Indian interests in the House of Lords were strong enough to defeat it.

In 1600 Spain and Portugal were still the most active countries in overseas trade, and the only ones with colonial possessions of any size. In the east the Portuguese base at Goa was the centre of a trading system that extended from East Africa to China and Japan. The Cape route had formidable difficulties for the big ships that the Portuguese, short of timber and of sailors, found most economical: something like a fifth of the vessels that set out from Lisbon failed to return. There was little support at home in either supplies of exportable goods or new capital. Nevertheless for more than a century the Portuguese had no effective rivals. Their eventual decline was due partly to the misfortune of being involved first in Spain's war against the Dutch and then, after 1640, in war with Spain. Not that peace or war in Europe made much difference to such activities as the Dutch blockade of Goa that began in 1637. It was the superiority of Dutch and English organization and the support of their states that proved decisive. In the west too Portuguese commerce was slowly eroded by the pressure of Dutch and English rivals. The distinctions between peace and war, trade and robbery, hardly existed in the contest for American wealth. Spain's commercial position deteriorated more rapidly. The output of the silver mines began to decline; the dead hand of the Castilian aristocracy and the poverty of the Crown prevented the expansion of a merchant community; the constant wars in Europe made it impossible to protect the Atlantic traders or attack the pirates and smugglers. In the 1640s the annual sailing of the fleet from Seville and arrival of the silver supplies came to an end. Even so, in terms of territory controlled the South American empires of Spain and Portugal made them still the greatest colonial powers. Portuguese Brazil enjoyed a new boom in gold and diamond mining at the end of the century.

The Dutch, in contrast to their easy mastery of the sea-borne trade within Europe, had to fight a constant and in the end a losing battle in Asian and Near Eastern commerce. At the beginning of the century they seemed capable of driving out their rivals rapidly. The Dutch East India Company was founded in 1602 when the States General as part of the war against Spain demanded the merging of the separate enterprises that were attacking Portugal's trading empire. From its beginning it had the strikingly modern characteristic of being run by a few highly rewarded directors while most of its capital came from a much larger body of investors. Yet like the Netherlands state itself, the company was an awkward compromise between centralised power and federal equality. The Amsterdam members, who controlled most of the capital, increasingly imposed their schemes on the other five towns involved. The seventeen directors, mainly men of the Regent class who could ensure political support for almost anything the company did, were nominally elected but in fact a closed oligarchy. It was therefore not difficult for the company to become virtually the government of Dutch overseas territories. It could wage war and make treaties, establish military as well as trading bases, and set up Calvinist missions which – no doubt incidentally – helped to undermine the authority of the Catholic Portuguese. There was no clear intention that the company should become a territorial power; but in Ceylon and Java, the process of excluding the Portuguese and asserting enough power over local rulers to get the trading conditions they wanted led rapidly to political control. Dutch rule involved a good deal of brutality, which the respectable assemblies at home were happy to accept without being involved. The most determined 'colonist' in the early years of the company, Jan Pieterszoon Coen, told the directors that it was impossible 'to carry on trade without war or war without trade'. In 1619 he seized the port of Jakarta and established himself as virtual ruler of a new state. In South Africa it was mainly the incentive to supply ships rounding the Cape with stores produced on the spot that led to the slow growth of a Dutch colony. Van Riebeeck, who made the first territorial claim in 1652, tried in vain to use Chinese labourers or African slaves to make farming possible; but by the end of the century an assortment of immigrants began to occupy territory inland.

For the theorists who measured the wealth of a state entirely in terms of bullion, trade with Asia was highly undesirable: it drained bullion away from Europe, in contrast to the American trade which brought it in. This did not prevent East India companies from appearing at one time or another not only in the established commercial countries but in Sweden, Denmark, and Prussia. The English East India Company tried from its foundation in 1601 to justify its activities by sending goods rather than money and by showing that the bullion it did export was balanced by payments for the Indian produce it re-exported to European markets. A common complaint was that it attracted capital that had formerly gone into the older and less dangerous undertakings. Its leading members came mainly from the Levant Company and the Russia Company, and the purpose of their charter was largely to establish a monopoly excluding other Englishmen from the trade of the Far East. At first it collected a separate 'stock' for each voyage. The first two of these eventually yielded a profit of nearly 100 per cent; some of the others did even better, and some on which ships were lost produced nothing. On average it must have compared well with the 30 per cent paid by the Dutch company in its first ten years. In 1613 the first 'joint stock' for a longer period was raised, and thereafter there was frequent argument about the merits of the two forms of organization. It was only when Cromwell revised the charter in 1657 that the company finally established a big permanent capital, to which it added money borrowed at a fixed rate of interest. Despite the backing of the state in its early years, the loosely organized English company was not ideally fitted to compete with the Dutch. It was not until the post-Restoration period that the company abandoned its policy of reliance on agreements with local rulers rather than on military strength. By then its fortunes were deeply involved with political disputes at home. Puritan, and later Whig, groups among the merchants and politicians regarded the company as a creature of the Stuart court and resisted the continuation of its monopoly. For some years after 1698 the existence of two rival English companies made eastern trade unprofitable, at a time when it had almost overtaken that of the Dutch.

The French companies in the east were significant only as demonstrations of the weakness of commerce that sprang from political rather than economic initiative. Henri IV had set up an East India Company that hardly got as far as any serious trading activity at all. Richelieu's two companies for eastern trade also died at birth. Colbert's so-called East India Company, launched in 1664 with the glory of royal subscription to its shares and full monopolistic powers, was originally concerned mainly with Madagascar. It failed to get the capital it needed, and only by shedding its exclusive privileges and allowing independent merchants to use its ships and bases was it able to survive. In North America France had the prospect of much greater success. In spite of manifest lack of support from the merchant community for such ventures, the French conquest of a huge if ill-defined area of Canada was the biggest piece of true colonisation since the achievements of Spain a century earlier. In 1663 a grand scheme for French America was adopted. Canada became Crown property, administered like a French province. A new West India Company was to organize an economic system in which the northern colony and the tropical possessions in the Antilles would supply each other as well as conducting a balanced trade with the home country. All this was to make possible territorial conquests that would extend westward to the Pacific and southward to Mexico. But the ambitions of the 'expansionist' rulers such as Jean Talon and Frontenac did not coincide with those of the fur traders or of the Jesuits, neither of whom regarded political organization as much of a help to their activities. Canada could rely on neither men nor money from home. Though Colbert gave cautious promises of support, it was soon apparent that wars for scraps of territory in Europe were regarded as vastly more important than the acquisition of a continent. The limits to French expansion in Canada were set not by the successes and failures of the few thousand colonists but by the Treaty of Utrecht. In the West Indies the French buccaneers were able to fight their sporadic warfare against both English and Spanish rivals with less regard to Louis' diplomacy. The sugar plantations of Guadeloupe and the slave trade that supplied them made fortunes for the independent merchants of Nantes and the other Atlantic ports. But the problem of political control was unsolved. The companies that began the settlements in the 1620s sold them piecemeal to small groups of merchants, from whom Colbert recovered them for the benefit of his new West India Company. In the seventies the company, its bankruptcy completed by the wars with the Dutch, was replaced by the system of rule by colonial governors, varying in their power and their relations with the planters.

If America brought only a few successes to the French, for the Dutch it was the one disaster in their century of economic triumph. The Dutch West India Company, set up in 1621 on much the same lines as the eastern one, never produced comparable profits. It assumed from the outset that there would be easy profits from plundering but that the eventual aim was nothing less than capturing the trade and then the possessions of Spain and Portugal. There were a few encouraging episodes, such as the capture of the silver fleet in 1628; but the efforts to drive the Portuguese out of Brazil were slow and costly. The sugar industry remained in Portuguese hands: the Dutch company was more interested in exporting the sugar and in selling to the planters the slaves on whom they depended. The wars in the 1640s to preserve Dutch territory were run more by the company, and hence the financiers of Amsterdam, than by the government, though many of the ships of the Dutch navy were occupied in supporting them. In the end it was accepted that the costs were not going to be justified by reasonably assured profits. The Dutch garrisons were abandoned. In the West Indies it was possible to aim at economic predominance without holding much territory. From the small base at Curaçao the Dutch were able to sell to the Spaniards slaves from African ports they had seized from Portugal. Religious objections to slavery were overcome as profits rose: after all, the slaves might be taught the virtues of Christianity. The English were slower to claim a share in the wealth of the Caribbean. Peace with Spain, established in 1604, discouraged piracy and boosted legitimate trade with Spanish possessions. In the 1620s, when Charles I made the Earl of Carlisle 'Lord Proprietor of the Caribees', London merchants were beginning to stake out claims in the West Indies. But it was only after the Cromwellian conquest of Jamaica that there was large English investment in the region, with the Royal African Company supplying slaves to the sugar plantations. Its relations with the planters were always bad, the company complaining that their fellow-countrymen did not pay as well as the Spaniards and the planters denouncing it as an inefficient court-sponsored monopoly. In spite of the efforts, towards the end of the century, to establish the rule of law in the area, none of the companies seems to have done as well as the international pirates.

The North American colonies were still in 1700 of very minor economic interest to European powers. In 1674 the States General were happy, in return for acceptance of their claim to Surinam, to hand over New Amsterdam to English possession. (Charles II had granted the task of occupying the area to his brother James, Duke of York, whose later misfortunes made the name New York an unhappy choice.) English colonies on the Atlantic coast had come through their first difficulties. The failure of the Virginia Company had shown that the colonizing of northern lands was not a source of the quick profits that investors demanded. But the 'Pilgrim Fathers' found that the mixture of economic enterprise with flight from religious oppression was a good formula for survival in unpromising conditions. Two English ventures, the Providence Island Company and the Massachusetts Bay Company, had a strong connection with opponents of the Stuart regime. The Massachusetts charter was granted in 1629 at a moment when the incentive for puritan emigration was at its greatest. The colony claimed something like 4,000 settlers in its first five years and 40,000 by 1660. They were naturally not the most eager of men to agree on a political organization; but between them the small English companies had established their control over most of the eastern seaboard by the time the stream of assorted European refugees began to arrive in the eighties and nineties. They had also become involved in the first of the disputes that were to explode in the next century over the relations between colonial assemblies and the English Crown and parliament.

THE STATE AND THE ECONOMY

There was a world of difference between the attitude of western governments to their tropical colonies and traders, who were expected to be a source of wealth for the home country, and that towards the North American settlements most of which were at best a reluctant and impoverished market for home produce. Behind the quarrels that developed lay the whole question of the role of the state in economic activity. It was generally agreed that one of the functions of central government was to encourage trade and industry. How this should be done was another matter. The simplest process was collaboration between a government and a few of its favoured subjects to produce an industrial or commercial monopoly. It could be a means of using the power of the state to encourage investment and enterprise while taking its share of the profits; but it also became – as the English opposition insisted – a device of the courtiers and the office-holders to extract money for themselves and the Treasury (see p. 481). Everywhere monarchs and ministers included among the achievements for which they took credit a rather monotonous list of services to the cause of economic superiority. From Henri IV, and his theorist of state enterprise Barthelmy Laffemas, to Peter the Great, the process of using the power of the Crown to establish manufactures, improve transport and agriculture, capture markets, and bring bullion into the country has much the same character. Economic prosperity was sought for its own sake, and as a direct demonstration of national greatness; but it was sought also as a means of strengthening the state for war. With dismal regularity war became the main purpose, and its cost and destruction absorbed the material gains.

Two of the rulers whose sponsoring of economic expansion had the greatest difficulties to overcome and the most emphatic results were in the east. In Brandenburg after the worst of the Thirty Years War was over, the Great Elector became the first German ruler to use the power of the state on a large scale for economic development. He did not so much help his subjects to achieve prosperity as impose it on them. The agricultural and industrial reforms, the trading companies, the canals and roads, the immigration of skilled foreigners were schemes devised by the state with little positive support either from the aristocracy in general or from the towns. They were inseparable from his struggle for heavier and more widespread taxation, and from his interference, for the benefit of his military power, with the old order of landholding and privilege. There was no serious attempt to plan the use of land or find means of applying to it an economic system that would make the most of its potentialities. The mulberry trees flourished and the African trading company did not; but the state continued to assume – not unreasonably – that any economic development was better than stagnation. The main test of success was whether the land would eventually support more men (see pp. 251, 362).

Even the Great Elector's experiments were more realistic than much of the state-created economic progress that Peter the Great imposed on Russia. The tsar's celebrated imitation of western methods was largely a matter of technical detail: his real assumption was that the free capital and enterprise of Holland or England could be dispensed with in a state that could supply conscript labour, own materials and equipment, and coerce merchants into undertaking the tasks it required. The aim generally was to transfer state-established factories to private possession – and punish the owners if they were not successful. The endless regulations governing economic life were often made without much regard to what was feasible. When foreign cloth was believed to be preferred because it was wider, the state decreed that Russian weavers must make it wider too, without suggesting how they would acquire and house new looms. The foreign traders and technicians Peter attracted in his early years were to be replaced by Russians, competent or not. (The fact that many foreigners evaded such decrees at least indicated that Russian economy had something to offer them.) In making Russia more a part of the western commercial system and less an area for foreign exploitation, Peter's intervention was certainly effective. His internal measures proved on the whole a small and temporary part of the growth of the war-making service-state.

COLBERT

Jean-Baptiste Colbert perhaps appears outstanding in the history of state-sponsored economy more through the status his country achieved than through any unique success of his own. The notion that all Europe imitated a new French economic system known as 'Colbertism' has long been discredited, and with it the picture of Colbert as a benefactor whose good work was destroyed by a quest for 'glory' of which he disapproved. More money, he said 'would increase the power, the greatness, and the affluence of the state'. It was in that order that most statesmen would have put the aims of their governments in increasing the initiative and control they applied to economic affairs. How far the state's intervention succeeded is another matter. Colbert himself was distressed by the stagnation of France compared with the Netherlands. To combat it he was prepared to use every possible variety of state assistance to industry. The establishments formed of local groups of small craftsmen, like the hosiers of Troyes, were given the status of *manufactures royales* with protection from home and foreign competition. State capital was put into large-scale enterprises: van Robais at Abbeville got subsidies for his great textile factory in return for close state supervision. In some industries – especially those involved in army and naval supplies – outright nationalization was the favoured method. The successful entrepreneur was as much the state's servant as was the intendant or the captain of horse; and though it was seldom easy to persuade the nobility to involve themselves in industry, it was made clear that one way to royal favour was to invest in state enterprises. Ambitious industrialists were from time to time ennobled.

There were many forms of state intervention. One was simply to make the worker work harder. Colbert's ideal workshop was a place of quasimilitary discipline, where idleness and inefficiency were punished. It was not only Protestantism that could bring religion into the service of productivity: the workers of Paris and Lyons found their festival days reduced, and religious observances introduced into the workshop itself as an antidote to idleness. An occasional royal visit to great new industries was held to be a valuable encouragement. It was part of the state's concern to raise the quality of French produce – not simply by taking over the traditional guild regulation of standards in craftsmanship, but by emulating the most sought-after specialities of other countries. Every technician or craftsman won from abroad was a minor victory. The Academy was expected to apply scientific skill to the invention of new industrial processes. The improvement of inland communications – with the Languedoc Canal as the great show-piece – was a form of assistance for which provincial governments had to pay their share. Colbert managed it all like any other process of government. Lists of industries and their products were assembled, scrutinized, compared. Regulations and edicts poured steadily through the machinery of royal government. In 1670 two outstanding merchants, Savary and Bellinzani, were put at the head of a new campaign to bring every individual town and village under the care of a *commis* who would supervise existing organizations or impose new ones. To those involved it meant the constant presence of the malevolent but usually corruptible inspector. Every stage of manufacture and marketing was supposed to be controlled. Inferior articles would be destroyed, and those responsible could find themselves in the pillory. It seems to have surprised Colbert that his orders were evaded. Masters continued to make the goods that brought them the best profits rather than those they were told should be exported; workers monotonously earned one of his most damning terms of reproof – 'idle'.

There was no doubt that by his own practical tests Colbert's activities seemed to have some success. Output did increase; French products acquired a reputation for the highest quality and most fashionable style; real wages of the skilled worker were, by comparison with other western countries, high. Some of the success could be attributed to a decade of good harvests that kept food prices low; some to the fact he refused to recognize – that world demand was increasing. Colbert's theories of foreign trade, familiar enough in themselves but asserted with new dogmatic confidence, were, on the surface, nonsense. After a century and a half in which new overseas markets were being constantly developed, he could claim that the total amount of trade was fixed. After the immense changes produced by South American silver, he could say the same about the amount of bullion. But these were truths in a religious rather then a scientific sense: they showed the way to salvation. French commerce could expand only at the expense of the Dutch and to a lesser extent of the English. There was, in spite of the growth of devices like the Bill of Exchange, an apparent shortage of bullion in France and no means of acquiring it except by trade. Asia was absorbing more than before, Spain supplying less. Bullion was the only form of wealth the government could use for most of its purposes, and Colbert was well aware that everything depended on its circulation. Only money that found its way into the hands of tax-paying classes would return to the Treasury. That some of it was also invested in commercial and industrial enterprise was more important, even for his own purposes, than Colbert saw. His object was, more and more, to defeat the national enemies – which to him meant the Dutch above all. Tariffs directed against them, which began in 1664 as a comparatively small part of his industrial policy, quickly turned into commercial war. In 1667 duties on textiles were doubled, and on some other manufactures increased still more.

Colbert's tariffs did not in their extreme form last long: the Dutch after their success in the war made reduced tariffs one of the first conditions of peace. But they had brought France into the struggle for world trade which England had long been fighting. The damage inflicted on the Netherlands at this stage by French and English hostility was not decisive: European trade was still, in Colbert's day, overwhelmingly a Dutch affair. English attempts to restrict it had produced one outstanding specimen of the state's relations with economic activity, the Navigation Act of 1651. It was not a deeply thought-out policy: the Rump Parliament, unsure of its own survival, was manoeuvred by one group of the city merchants most hostile to Dutch overseas commerce into passing the law that prohibited imports in foreign ships or through a foreign country other than the one where they originated. It was too sudden and sweeping a measure to be fully enforceable in the conditions of the time; and it was only one of the sources of the quarrels that led to the outbreak of war between the two republics. In the successive renewals of the act after the Restoration there was better enforcement but more exceptions. Yet to England it marked a new attitude to trade. In place of the 'bullionist' idea that all export of precious metals, and therefore all avoidable imports, must be minimized – if necessary by state action – the emphasis shifted to the use of colonies as a cheap and unharmful source of raw materials and as a growing market. As the name of the acts suggested, their immediate object was to increase the number and activity of English merchant ships. In this they appeared to have great success. The quantity and prestige of shipping was one of the most visible ways in which state power and private wealth went hand in hand. It was one of the clearest applications of 'mercantilism'.

MERCANTILISM AND CAPITAL

Ever since the term was applied by Adam Smith to what he regarded as the evil seventeenth-century system, it has been commonly accepted that the economy of western states was 'mercantilist'. But the meaning of the word is elusive. The most celebrated contemporary account of such ideas came from the English merchant Thomas Mun, whose 'discourse' *England's Treasure by Foreign Trade* was written when he was a member of the commission set up by James I in 1622 to investigate the trade depression, but only published after the Restoration. It was already a commonplace that the loss of coin and bullion was the root of the state's economic troubles. Mun's objection was that remedies which concentrated on reducing the amount of coin paid out obscured the simple first necessity: 'we must ever observe this rule; to sell more to strangers yearly than we consume of theirs in value'. Bullion was only a means whereby the economic activity of the country could be increased. Though Mun did not stress the idea of a fixed amount of world trade that had to be fought for, he certainly assumed that 'strangers' were rivals and that to increase English wealth at their expense entailed the intervention of the state. One source of confusion is that mercantilism has sometimes been regarded as a system that put the profit of merchants before the good of the state, and sometimes as the reverse of this. The usual assumption was that the two were inseparable. The merchant needed state support – in the privileges granted and upheld by the sovereign, in the treaties, the threats, the convoys by which foreign interference was restricted, and from time to time in war itself. Mercantilists, though they expected monarchs to behave frugally and find their own sources of treasure, seldom condemned expenditure on war as such. It was the willingness of Colbert and the other statesmen who devoted themselves to economic expansion to see their schemes used and destroyed in war that led to the description of mercantilism as 'a system for forcing economic policy into the service of power as an end in itself'.[1] It could be claimed that a powerful state gave security to the rich and work to the poor. But mercantilists, like some of their modern successors in economic theory, approached their arguments from the points of view of the financier, the exporter and importer, the proprietor, and the government. The rest of the community, as consumers and wage-earners, would benefit eventually from the state's success, but must not endanger it by increasing the cost of exports through higher wages and greater consumption of goods at home. The balance of trade was reckoned on the assumption that bringing bullion in and sending goods out was necessarily beneficial. Among the calculations that were not made was the real cost of the wars that were fought for trade.

In the later part of the century the purely 'bullionist' element in mercantilist theory was giving way to what looked on the surface a more enlightened view of the economy as a whole. The Austrian manufacturer Johan Becher, whose *Politische Discurs* was

published in 1668, was one of the first writers to regard employment, and the maintenance of the level of the population, as more
significant tests of success than the accumulation of gold. Human-
itarian considerations did not interest him. He was among the
originators of the economic aspect of what became known as
'cameralism'. The power of the state would be best enhanced by
a prosperous people, thoroughly organized in their activities by
the skilled administrators of the government. One of his
immediate themes was the contrast between the backwardness of
the Habsburg territories and the success of the Netherlands. He
did not emphasize the fact that the Dutch, though they insisted
that the state must support economic activity, did not want the
central government to interfere with it. Dutch wars were fought
both for commercial gain and for territorial competition; but the
normal course of trade was expected to continue with as little
regard as possible to diplomatic or military hostilities. In the
Netherlands at least, the strong state was the means and prosperity the end.

DEPRESSION AND RECOVERY

Mercantilist ideas owed much of their success to the belief that
one country could only expand its trade, and hence its general
prosperity, at the expense of others. All the evidence seemed to
show that left to itself trade stagnated or declined. Complaints of
economic decay, often supported by memories of more land
under the plough, more looms, more ships a generation or two
earlier, came from almost every part of Europe. The impressions
of contemporaries can now be compared with quantitative studies
that are becoming ever more complex, both through the accumulation of raw statistical material and through new techniques and
apparatus for using it. The most favoured basis for investigating
economic change is still the history of prices: tables and graphs
summarizing these can perhaps be taken too confidently as indications of prosperity, and the quest for comprehensive patterns
behind local fluctuations becomes a mathematical challenge. There
is no doubt that when the sharp rises and falls in prices are
reduced to a broad average they confirm that the inflation of the
sixteenth century came to an end and was followed by compara-

tive stability or slow and erratic decline. Price-changes of course can only be measured in terms of some other variable – gold, silver, or the local 'monies of account' that were designed to be more stable than ordinary currency. When the price-changes are compared with measurements of the output of commodities such as grain, cloth, and metals and with commercial transactions, it can be claimed that 'trade and prices move in broad unison'. On the mass of short-term and long-term fluctuations can be based a seemingly endless variety of attempts to discern 'cycles' of rise and fall, expansion and contraction. One idea, cautiously expounded by Braudel, is of a vast 'secular' pattern extending from the thirteenth century to the twentieth. Its second cycle, with an upward phase from the early sixteenth century to the mid-seventeenth followed by a downward one lasting until about 1730, fits well enough the accepted picture. An earlier suggestion was the *Kondratieff* cycle of fifty years; but this was derived from later periods and is applied with difficulty to the seventeenth century. The process of discerning shorter and shorter cycles, with occasional 'intercycles' has produced some incredulity among unmathematical historians; and the doubts are not diminished when the significance of the cycles is extended from economic measurement to include a 'conjuncture' of every aspect of life.

Whether the cyclic theories have any validity or not, it is possible to arrive at some tentative conclusions on the sequence of economic changes. The various signs of depression appeared at different times and in different degree during the first quarter of the century. Spain, with plague in 1599 and 1600 followed by the expulsion of the Moriscoes and the decline in imports of silver, was one of the first places to suffer (see p. 380). In England the general rise in prices was halted by 1614. Then Cockayne's Project (see p. 452) proved a sudden blow to the textile trade, and the early twenties were still years of stagnation and uncertainty. But English trade thereafter recovered a good deal of its prosperity and the rise in prices was resumed. For France, where the early depression had been less sudden, the 1630s produced a mixture of further decline, such as that of the eastern trade, with some signs of recovery. Here, as in many other places, there was a great difference between the fate of the merchant and that of the peasant or the poor townsman. Shortage of good currency combined with fluctuating prices and high taxation to produce a feeling of growing poverty. In Germany debasement of currency in the early stages of the Thirty Years War – the *Kipper- und Wipperzeit* – helped to make the twenties a time of depression. Italy had its critical years between 1619 and 1622, in the north especially. For Poland it was not until well into the thirties that the collapse of agricultural prosperity became decisive.

It is in the middle decades of the century that the idea of regular cycles becomes most attractive. In many parts of the continent there were high prices around 1643, 1649, and 1653 – but they were the high prices of scarcity rather than of prosperity. The 1660s, in the west at least, were a period of recovery. But by 1670 there were again signs of a severe shortage of currency – a problem that continued to the end of the century. In the nineties most of the great commercial enterprises were finding their markets less reliable, though the industries like timber and iron that provided materials for war seemed to have brilliant prospects. For the mass of the population scarcity of food, uncertain employment, and high taxation were the main facts of economic life. Neither statistics nor contemporary impressions make it possible to generalize confidently about the human impact of the fluctuations. The questions that quantitative studies find it hardest to answer are those concerning real standards of living. For the sixteenth century it can be said confidently that wages almost everywhere rose more slowly than prices, and even when it is recognized that wages were often only one of a variety of sources of subsistence there is little doubt that the effective incomes of all but the prosperous minority fell. For the seventeenth there are more doubts and inconsistencies. Abundant lists have been compiled of the money wages paid over the whole century to particular categories of workers; and the standard methods of comparing these with the prices, in the same places and years, of the goods consumed by a household give a reasonably significant figure for 'real' wages. Averaged over periods such as five or ten years, there was commonly a slow rise, with sometimes a slight fall in the last decade or two. But a statistical average does not throw much light on sudden subsistence crises. The rate of daily wages only mattered if they were actually paid; and there were not many occupations in which a full wage could be expected every week in the year. (Two of the familiar interruptions that in many countries were becoming more frequent were wars and religious festivals.) One fact at least does seem to be well established: the rise and fall of economic activity as a whole did not correspond to the rise and fall in the wellbeing of ordinary people. If anything the periods of expansion for the rich were periods of decline for the poor. Neither made much difference to the great variety of hazards on which the material life of the majority depended.

The modern emphasis on uncertainty and recession in the seventeenth century is not totally incompatible with the claim that this was the time when feudal society gave way decisively to an expanding capitalism. But on this too fuller and more exact information makes any simple pattern unconvincing. For western Europe the whole period is still labelled, in Marx's phrase, as that of 'primary accumulation'. The accumulation of capital is a notion that puts together many processes – the acquisition of land by men who used it to produce a surplus of real wealth, the lending of money to governments and enterprises that were expected to repay it out of revenue, the development of banking and credit systems, and so on. It is here that the contrast between greater economic activity and falling real wages is seen not as an unexplained paradox but as an essential part of the events. Inflation, and the other factors that kept real wages low, helped to provide the surplus that was put into industry and trade. Behind all the waste and destruction, all the hunger, failure, and brutality, conditions were developing from which the new age of industrial expansion could emerge.

REFERENCE

1   E. F. Heckscher, *Mercantilism* (London, 1955), vol. 2, p. 17.

4

SOCIETY

At least four-fifths of European families lived by working on the land. Most were threatened sometimes by desperate poverty; a few had opportunities to become more prosperous; but in the west at least they lived in much the same way and with much the same variations in their fate as had their parents and grandparents. The economic developments of the seventeenth century, impressive as they seem in themselves, did not make much difference to this. Nor, despite all the expansion in some parts of industry and commerce, was there a spectacular alteration in the lives of most townsmen or of those villagers who were on the fringes of land-working. The great changes arose among the small minority who owned the land, or in some less permanent way controlled it. In this chapter we shall look at some aspects of the ordinary life of the main groups in society, beginning with the majority – the peasants, as they can be labelled in most places – and moving on to the minorities.

For even the lowest social groups information on material life is now abundant, though it remains more readily available for some countries – notably France – than others. The questions that are being answered successfully are inevitably those to which quantitative methods can be applied. We can arrive at detailed estimates, for any given area, of the numbers in whatever categories are invented. We can study arithmetically the changes in their resources, in the size and composition of their households, in their expectation of life, their food, their contacts with the law, the armies, the tax-gatherers, and the churches. We can examine, on a solid if incomplete numerical basis, the mobility of individuals and families between social groups, the migrations between town and country, the consequences of differing customs of marriage and inheritance. Progress is far less easy in understanding collective attitudes or behaviour. The terminology and methods of the sociologist are still distrusted by the historian, for whom sources must often be less exact and static conclusions less helpful. Firm classifications and countable evidence do not answer all the historical questions.

For the social historian one advantage of the seventeenth century is that the main categories into which the population was divided were still comparatively few and simple. It was often easier and more relevant to define a man's social group than to define his nationality. The English gentleman travelling in Italy or the French *seigneur* in western Germany might make the alleged national characteristics of his hosts the subject of a stock joke or a neat turn of phrase; but little in his way of life was essentially different from that of his equals abroad. Costume, retinue, and manner made apparent a man's 'degree' and assured him of the respect that was his due. At home they would indicate his relationship to the state and to the community. The individual was part of a triangle of service and protection. One side of this was the link between master and man, landlord and tenant; the other two sides were formed by the state's connection with each of these. The notion that all subjects should be equal in their relationship with the state seemed an odd philosophical concept remote from reality. Everyone had his duty to the state; everyone received benefits from it; but they were entirely different according to his place in the social order. Those most heavily dependent on their superiors could lose almost all direct connections with the state, since their duties and – such as they were – rights were exercised through the man they served. The common instance of this was the serf.

SERFDOM

The one great exception to the absence of major change in the lives of the peasants was the extension of serfdom. Even that can be made to appear more dramatic than it was. Sometimes it is suggested that a line can be drawn between an eastern part of

Europe where, by the second half of the century, the peasants were reduced to serfdom and abysmal poverty and a western part where they were free and comparatively prosperous. The differences were a good deal more complex than that. Serfdom meant the lack of freedom to move from a master's territory, but without the total subjection to him that constituted slavery. It was normally accompanied by a mass of other burdens, though these were of the kind that could exist without serfdom. Labour dues might be increased almost without limit; the lord might have more or less complete jurisdiction on his estate; and he could use every major event in the peasant's life – marriage, children, inheritance, death – as an opportunity for new exactions. But the serf who had a fair prospect of running away and eluding recapture was often in a less hopeless plight than the free peasant who in practice was bound to his lord by debt or by the sheer lack of any alternative short of vagabondage.

In Russia the oppression of the peasants had been growing worse throughout the sixteenth century as the demand for labour and the exactions of the state increased. Ivan the Terrible's fantastic institution of the *oprichnina*, the supposed personal domain of the tsar where peasants could be exploited with little restriction, did not survive after his death. The villages and districts where the privileged *oprichniki* had been ready at any time to hand over their tenants to the military service of the state reverted to more familiar conditions. But the *pomieshchiki*, holders of comparatively small estates, were also obliged to provide soldiers as well as serving when required themselves: their numbers grew in the first half of the century. The areas of 'black land' where peasants held, for tolerable payments, land they could pass on to their heirs were shrinking. Outside them were areas where *barshchina*, compulsory labour on the lord's demesne, was the common form of payment. As estates grew and labourers tended to escape in search of better conditions the *barshchina* was extended from one day a week to three, four, or even more. More and more peasants were becoming *bobyli*, landless labourers. (The normal word for a peasant, *krestyanin*, originally distinguishing him from non-Christian nomads, now meant usually one cultivating some land for himself.) The least free of all were the *kabala* slaves, bound irrevocably to their lords by debt. Repaying the money did not, since the end of the sixteenth century, end the servitude: landlords desperate for labour could not lawfully acquire slaves by transferring the debts. But the *kabala* made clear that whatever western theorists might say, 'freedom' is not always a blessing to the poor. Peasants could virtually sell themselves into slavery. Having no property the slave could not easily be taxed; nor could the army seize him without violating the rights of his owner. He might even thrive as a craftsman or small trader; and like the nominally freer peasants he had a good chance of being able to escape his troubles by running away.

The movement of peasants – to the north, to the newly colonized areas in the east, and most of all to the Ukraine (a word meaning 'borderland') – had grown in the sixteenth century. By 1600 the depopulation of the central area of Muscovy was disastrous. Taxation and conscription were shared among a smaller community. The lord's own standard of living was reduced when he had to use his household slaves in the fields or let land go out of cultivation altogether. From Ivan IV's time particular years were proclaimed as 'forbidden years' in which no-one was allowed to leave the land he worked on. After about 1610 hardly any years were not 'forbidden'. The peasants still disappeared. In the first three years of the century the harvest over most of European Russia was bad. Hoarding by landlords and speculators, and the spread of disease, completed the ruin. Village communities broke down completely. Men left their homes no longer always in the hope of finding new ones but to join the nomadic groups that plundered and killed to survive. Whether the disasters of this period or the slowly growing pressure on the peasants contributed more to the depopulation can be disputed. It can even be argued that 'nomadism' had always been common and that the losses of population were exaggerated to avoid taxation. What is certain is that even when economic prosperity and political stability returned in the 1620s to a level no worse than usual, and deserted lands began to be repopulated, the problem of labour shortage remained. The wealth of a landowner was reckoned by the number of 'souls' on his estates rather than by their money value. It was more important that control of men should be secure and hereditary than that all the land should remain in the family. With or without legal sanction, every effort was made to deprive the peasant of all his mobility and of all restriction on the burdens he had to bear. The chaotic legal code of 1649 (see p. 431), a convenient point from which to date the full imposition of serfdom, contained no new principle. But it brought together and extended the provisions for dealing with the runaway peasant. There was no longer to be any time limit after which it was illegal to recapture him. A lord who employed fugitives therefore took the risk of losing them if someone else could claim them back, and as a sort of interest on his capital the claimant could have them with their children and the families of their children. Serfs could be transferred without restriction from one estate to another, except that the state protected its own interests by forbidding their removal from land held on one type of tenure to land held on another. To these demonstrations of the serf's status as movable property were added several colourful touches, such as the rule that if he murdered the serf of another lord he was not to be hanged but, after the routine flogging, handed over to replace his victim – unless he was no longer in good condition. In that case a better substitute could be claimed.

There naturally remained a good many gaps between legislation and practice. But in the decades after 1649 serfdom as an almost universal system was gradually established, until under Peter the Great perhaps nine-tenths of the working population were serfs, or in one of the enormous variety of categories on the fringes of serfdom. So far as documents made any difference, the peasant might be affected less by the law than by the contract he or his forebears made with his lord. This no longer laid down any limit to the amount of work he was to do on the lord's land, or to the size of his own holding; but it might promise a plot of land of some sort. Often it would appear to bind the serf to the lord personally even if legally he was bound to the land. One consequence of the combination of servitude, insecurity, and new forms of tenure was the decline of the *mir*, the village community, and its organised form, the *volost*. To many peasants the village had been as much a part of their individual existence as the family. Their misfortunes, the land allotted for their own livelihood, their burdens of tax and service were shared with the rest of the village. Its customs were not to be broken; its leaders and its collective decisions were accepted readily. Now, slowly, the power of the *mir* receded. Even so, devotion to village traditions still offered a shred of protection. If no natural disaster or outside enemy upset completely the routine of the estate, the lord who tried to make sudden and drastic changes for the worse in the life of his peasants was quite likely to face the risk of local rebellion. He could not count on much effective help from the state in suppressing it.

It was not only Russia that produced the 'second serfdom': it was almost as widespread in many parts of the Habsburg Empire and of Poland. In northern and eastern Germany the tightening of the landlord's powers had been going on since the fifteenth century. What now looked like new developments were often the legal ratification of earlier piecemeal changes. The demand in the west for imported corn (see p. 57) made demesne farming profitable at a time when here too there were not enough peasants to supply all the labour that could be used. By turning some tenants off the land to increase the demesne and imposing new labour services on those who remained, landowners in the great corn-producing areas started the same process as in Russia of more migrations and greater measures to stop them. In Brandenburg there was legislation against the runaway peasant as early as 1518. A century later the Estates of Pomerania resolved that all peasants were bound to the land but liable to be evicted from it at the will of their lord. They could be made to do unlimited labour on his lands, and they had no rights of inheritance. It proved a matter of bitter political dispute.[1] Towns not involved in the export trade suffered from the impoverishment of peasants and the loss of rural markets. At least one great city – Königsberg – resisted serfdom and refused to allow runaway peasants within its jurisdiction to be recaptured. In Saxony peasant obligations remained for the most part limited by law. Generally a free and prosperous peasantry was in the interests of German rulers, who (since landowners were exempt from most forms of taxation) relied on the tenant for their revenue. During and after the Thirty Years War the movement of peasants increased. Many went into the devastated regions where the demand for labour was highest and land abundant. Others fled from persecution: Austrian and Bohemian Protestants were found in Saxony and even in East Prussia. But the Catholic south was on the whole an area more free from serfdom. With a smaller market for their produce, the landlords had little of the enthusiasm shown by the Junkers for profitable exploitation.

Even in the countries where serfdom was most rigidly and widely enforced, the 'free peasant' was a fairly familiar figure. The Russian 'Black Lands', though grants by tsars and robbery by magnates had reduced their size, still maintained peasants whose only allegiance was to the Crown or the state and who had few of the agrarian burdens of the landlords' serfs. Since they were drawn on heavily for military service they were often in practice no less restricted than those on seignorial lands. Peter the Great's efforts to increase the number of 'state' or 'treasury' peasants was certainly not a move towards the alleviation of misery. Nevertheless there were the few among them who found it possible to increase their holdings, to bring others into their subjection through keeping them in their debt, and to buy their way out of most of their obligations. Prussia had a far more flourishing class of free peasants, the *Cölmer*, who not only remained exempt from compulsory labour but often became large farmers not far removed in the size of their holdings and their way the life from the smallest of the nobility. Even in the most firmly ordered rural society, there was always some possibility of rising a little above the economic level of the majority; and once money began to accumulate it could usually be the means of an advance in social status.

THE WESTERN PEASANT

Though there was among the peasants of eastern Europe a great variety of burdens and opportunities, the vast majority were experiencing tighter obligations and greater poverty. In the west not even such hazy generalizations as these can be made. There was little in common between the thriving yeoman of the English midlands and the half-starved Neapolitan or Castilian struggling to live on what landlord and tax-collector left him from the produce of a patch of stony earth. Differences within the same country and the same region were often almost as great. The more intensively the French peasantry in particular have been examined, the more meaningless any broad categories, whether legal or economic, have proved. In times of famine or man-made disaster it was generally easier in western than in eastern Europe for some families to prosper at the expense of the rest: possibly the most important of all lines of division was between those with enough reserves to enable them to profit by general scarcity and the majority who faced the threat of hunger, debt, eviction, and vagabondage. In times of abundance a little capital and the accidents of temperament and family circumstance could be decisive in distinguishing those able to profit by their surplus from those

who found low market prices ruinous. Both upward and downward movements were on the whole greater in the more advanced
economies.

The French peasant was intensely aware of his social status. The
laboureur – a term dangerously easy to mistranslate into English
and originally meaning 'ploughman' – was as conscious of his
superiority as any inheritor or purchaser of title or office. His
status depended a good deal on local usage. In the Beauvais region
he was 'almost by definition a man who owned a plough and a
pair of horses'[2]; in Poitou he could be poorer; in Burgundy the
term covered a wide range of prosperity. In the course of the
century the number of *laboureurs* fell: their disappearance was one
of the signs of depression repeatedly noted by the officials of
Louis XIV. The fortunate few might build up their holdings at
the expense of the rest and join the exalted circle of the *fermiers*,
owning land or holding it on long leases, employing wage-
labourers (*journaliers*), lending out money, and sometimes terror-
ising the villagers more ruthlessly than did the *seigneur*. The usual
fate of the *laboureur* was to sink to the level of the *manœuvrier*. This
was the ordinary term for the majority who held by *métayage* –
the system in which the landlord owned land, stock, seed, and
farm implements and took a fixed share, usually half, of the
produce – or by one of the many other varieties of heavily
burdened tenure. Usually the holding was barely adequate to feed
their families, even in years of plenty and even on the poorest diet
of rye-bread and peas. The *seigneur*, besides his claim to a third
or a half of their corn-crop, commonly exercised an assortment
of rights such as his monopoly of mills or wine-presses. Taxes
and tithes seemed to remove nearly everything that was left. In
practice their standard of life varied greatly. The comparatively
fortunate were those living in a district of the *pays d'état* that
escaped the heaviest forms of taxation; or those in areas of
thriving rural industry whose families could pick up a fairly
regular money wage; or even those for whom a pig, a cow, or
the cultivation of vines provided a source of money income. It
was always the poorest who were hardest hit by unpredictable
calamities. Not only famine and the depredation of armies, but
a lordly hunting party, a sudden increase in the demands of the
landlord, or simply accumulated debt could bring the moment
when they were turned off the land and found such possessions

as they had seized by the bailiff. Able-bodied men might resort
to the army; for the rest there was nothing left but to drift on to
the roads, beg, steal, and die.

It is not obvious that the French peasant in general was more
free or prosperous than the eastern serf. The authority of the *seigneur*, to whom even the richest tenants still took solemn oaths of
subjection, was in most areas enormous. Manorial powers of
justice could be more limited in theory than in practice. The *corvée
seigneuriale* amounting to a few days' unpaid labour in the year
was not comparable to the weekly work of the serf; but the
difference between devoting half the time to growing the lord's
crop and surrendering to him half what was produced on the
tenant's holding was not much more than a technicality. In a land
that had reached the limit of the population it could support in
existing agrarian conditions, the French peasant might often be
tied to his soil more effectively than was the Russian who could
flee to the frontier areas. A great many were like the *censitaires* in
Burgundy, whose condition in 1672 was described simply as
'servitude'. The situation in western Germany was much the
same. The free peasant in the north, the *Meier*, sometimes had a
heritable tenancy with abundant opportunity to compete with his
neighbours for the extension of his lands; sometimes he held only
on a year-to-year basis. Since he provided most of the state's
revenue from taxation, it was in the interest of governments to
support him and to prevent any threat of large-scale evictions. In
Bavaria life-tenure was common, but conscription and the quar-
tering of troops were among the causes of a slow deterioration in
the peasants' prosperity. In Spain, and especially Castile, conditions had been getting worse ever since the mid-sixteenth century.
Deserted villages, a few rich peasants exploiting the indebtedness
of the majority, and an unceasing drift from the country into the
cities were accepted as normal.

Most European peasants had reason to envy the English
yeoman – a term that could now apply to a wide range of society
between gentry and husbandmen. The ordinary leaseholder,
secure for three lives or ninety-nine years, was often paying in
his entry fine and his rent a good deal less than the current value
of the land. He could easily aspire, with energy and luck, to
become a substantial freeholder with the not too closely guarded
status of 'gentleman'. The number of lords of manors whose
ancestors had been on the yeoman level a few generations back

was everywhere high. Not much was left of the rough equality between medieval holders of the yardland or virgate in the common fields. But even the copyholder, whose tenure was secured by manorial custom rather than contract, was unlikely to lose it unless a succession of misfortunes brought him to the point where rents went unpaid and debts accumulated. With a burden of taxation that would have seemed negligible to his continental equivalents, he had less cause for complaint than he believed. Nevertheless, for the younger son, for the family dependent on a decaying part of the textile industry, or for the victim of unrelenting increase in rent the outlook could still be grim. It was, surprisingly, in England that completely landless labourers were proportionately most numerous. In other western countries, though large numbers had no land to cultivate for their own benefit, many more had holdings, however small, without which they could not have survived. Failure of the harvest could be more disastrous for them than for those who earned a living wage.

FAMILIES AND MOBILITY

Even in discussing the peasantry, the huge stable mass on which the slender structure of the remainder of society rested, we have repeatedly encountered the question of 'mobility'. (The term has both a geographical sense and an economic one; but since hardly anyone moved from one place to another unless forced by poverty or attracted by prosperity; 'social mobility' is often a combination of both.) The problem of comparing mobility in different classes, countries, and periods has in recent decades produced abundant controversy and confusion. It involves both the movement of individuals and families from one group to another and the change in character of the groups themselves. The questions would be complex enough if they could be answered in measurable economic terms. But social groups are created by opinion as well as by possessions. Their members, except on the lowest level, have an interest in concealing the existence of mobility: the newcomer puts up a pretence of ancient lineage and the old-established reject the upstart. The theory in France was that three generations was the time needed to remove the stigma of manual labour and to enable the *noblesse de la robe* to acquire the status of *noblesse d'épée*, within which the gradations were increasingly complicated. When men insisted on the importance of degree and on a divinely ordered social hierarchy, they appeared to be denying the manifest changes in it. However illogically, both the newly risen and the established seem to have been gratified by the pretence that society was immutable.

It has only recently been generally recognized that a study of changing population should be less concerned with the unhelpful totals for states or cities and more with the smallest unit, the family. One of the greatest changes in early-modern times was that the small 'nuclear' family of husband, wife, and unmarried children was becoming more significant in ordinary life than the large patriarchal household or the village community. It happened more readily in comparatively prosperous agrarian regions, especially where the land was enclosed. The small family began to expect a house designed for privacy and seclusion, from which most offspring would sooner or later depart. If servants were included in it, many of them would eventually leave to set up households of their own. In the east, and in the woodland or mountain areas of the west and south, the larger household, sometimes with two or more married couples, was still common. Families were in either case not as large as has sometimes been supposed: three or four children surviving to maturity was a frequent number in a peasant home, with perhaps two or three dying in infancy or childhood. About one in five could expect to remain unmarried. The rest were likely to marry fairly late – sons in their late twenties and daughters a few years earlier. Often the father died before the eldest son felt able to marry and take over the home. But generalizations like this conceal enormous variety. Marriage was often earlier in the east, where a separate house was less necessary for it. A population disaster could be followed by a period of earlier marriages; and of course in rich households there was less incentive to delay marriage and a slightly better chance of survival. It is not clear why, in the seventeenth century, the number of children was not larger, especially where their labour was economically beneficial. Contraception was not unknown; and the Catholic church taught the virtues of abstinence, especially at times such as lent. But more decisive is probably the fact that fertility, and the avoidance of miscarriages, depend on nourishment.

Where property, however small, was involved it was the

normal task of parents to preserve or enhance the status of the family, and if possible extend its possessions by organizing marriage alliances. How far love as a reason for marriage was a literary myth is still a disputed question. The lowly maiden winning the heart and hence the wealth of a lord is not a plausible factor in social mobility. Elaborate marriage treaties, schemes for acquiring dowries, and for not paying them, entails and trusts were a crucial part of life for the peasant-proprietor as well as for the aristocrat. The greatest prize was naturally the heiress or co-heiress. Having to divide an estate among married daughters could be the final disaster for a landed family, though descendants in the female line might disguise the break by adopting the name, and even acquiring the titles, of their ancestor. In many ways the marriageable daughter had better prospects than the younger son. For him everything depended on the complex laws and customs of inheritance, which varied within as well as between countries. Most families of greater and lesser nobilities expected the eldest son to inherit the whole of their main estate. Only in that way could the status of the family be preserved; and on that there depended the structure of the rural society over which they presided. Among lesser holders of land it was only in England that primogeniture was the strict rule. In other northern regions a laxer custom of inheritance left the father with more choice, though however generous he was to younger members of the family he was likely to hold its essential lands together. France notoriously was plagued by the problems of divided inheritances that led to the multiplication of small estates. Even there the theory of equal inheritance was mitigated by a recognition that the crumbling away of estates was economically and politically dangerous. At the end of the century the tendency everywhere was for egalitarian inheritance to disappear. The deprived younger son, both of the gentleman and of the peasant proprietor, was therefore a common figure. The town was his natural refuge. Despite the occasional stories of men who made fortunes in commerce and returned to the country to buy greater estates than their elder brothers could hope for, mobility for the younger son and his family was likely to be rapidly downward. At the higher social levels, trade as a way of life rather than a profitable sideline still carried a stigma. The insistence by Spaniards that any partici-pation in commerce or manufacturing was a barrier to nobility was gradually seen to be economic folly: a royal edict in 1682 declared that such activities were compatible with noble status – provided of course that they did not involve manual labour. Less openly, some such exclusiveness existed in most countries. The merchant and the artisan, however successful in their sphere, were not a part of the hierarchy of land-tenure that brought stability and authority. For sons of the nobility respectable alternatives were the occupations on the fringe of landed society. The Church, at any rate in Orthodox and Catholic countries, still in a limited way offered the chance of education and admission into its ranks even to sons of the poor. Its richer posts were naturally the preserve of those whose high birth demonstrated their spiritual merits. The law had some of the same characteristics: the lower levels, more sparse than those of the Church, gave some opportunities to the literate but unprivileged, while its great offices carried impressive rewards. Between these it had what the Church lacked – a large middle section comparable in status to the minor gentry and giving access to a variety of positions that could be the way to riches and authority. The expansion of armies gave another opening. Military service, a ruinous burden for some, could offer an alternative for the man lacking a stable future in the conditions he knew as a child. Though the barriers between upper and lower ranks were even stronger than in most civilian societies, military communities had their own ways to success. When all the possibilities are put together there must have been many men, high and low, who lost both their home and their status. Younger sons, or at least their descendants, could fall far outside propertied society, as the number of obscure families who bore a distinguished name suggests.

Many circumstances were still restricting the tendency for households to consist of single nuclear families. Houses above the labourer grade were likely to include servants, unattached workers, or urban apprentices. Among the aristocracy the ostentatious retinue was still a frequent source of prestige, providing access to a highly competitive way of life in which the pageboy might someday become a duke of Buckingham. There were few better ways of advancement than to abandon the parental home for the household of a rising patron, or even for the royal court itself. It was accepted that great men would, in dispensing their patronage, remember the claims of relations far removed from the main family line. Huge noble households were a relic of what in most western countries was becoming an obsolete way of life. So too were the loyalties that lay somewhere between the family and the tribe; but there were regions, chiefly those in which the stable hierarchy of the manorial village or small estate were less common, where the wider family and the clan were still units that held the allegiance of their members. The Scots and Irish remained intensely loyal to clans that constituted the widest of 'families', and they were generally believed to show inadequate respect to their superiors within them. Wherever geographical mobility was at its lowest, in the villages remote from towns and trade-routes, loyalty to the local community was almost indistinguishable from loyalty to the extended family.

LAND AND TITLE

The character of landed families is a subject that lends itself to endless investigation and argument; and naturally the finer the detail the more significant the differences seem to be. It is easy to forget how much, despite all the geographical, economic, and institutional differences, the Russian *dvorianin* continued to have in common with the Austrian *Freiherr*, the Swedish *Knapar*, and the English squire. It was a status in which management of the estate and the household were combined with a natural authority over the local communities that in one form or another survived all the centralizing tendencies. Exercising judicial power was a regular interlude in life, in the west at a duly authorized court of law, in Russia sometimes with the personal wielding of the knout. Nearly everywhere landowners also devoted themselves to mimicking their ancient function of fighting wars. The one seemingly indispensable occupation of the nobility was the hunt. It was a game that offered the pleasures of victorious war with fewer dangers or discomforts. There was a mixture of discipline and freedom, an aggression in which the victim might not lose but could not win, a satisfaction of the primitive blood-lust. No assertion of superiority over the tenants was quite as pleasant as riding through his crops. Other war-games were nearer to reality. Against constant governmental disapproval, the French nobility guarded their privilege of killing each other in duels. Private armies had generally been reduced to the level of liveried retainers; but there were few countries in which fighting between noble houses was impossible, even though it was likely to be disguised as part of some worthier cause. Rivalry could take more productive forms: the passion for building great houses and furnishing them with costly works of art percolated downwards. Throughout the century, but especially towards its end, the 'great rebuilding' was a phenomenon recognizable in every reasonably prosperous area. It included the reconstruction, for enjoyment and display, of large areas of landscape.

The nobility had long since ceased to be primarily warriors in the service of the monarch. Nevertheless, armies provided the only clear line between two levels of mankind. Whatever the variations and complexities in defining a civilian noble class, there was no blurring of the distinction between a commander and his men. Though it was not impossible for the rich and titled to serve briefly in the ranks, it was not doubted that the qualities of an officer belonged naturally to people of wealth or ancient lineage. In both the artificial society of the army and the real one of ordinary life, the variety of subdivisions within each group or 'order' was growing. The one distinctive way to assert a funda-mental status equivalent to that of an officer was to possess a title, preferably a hereditary one. The significance of any seventeenth-century title needs careful assessment. There are many linguistic confusions, such as that between the English word 'nobility' and the French '*noblesse*'; and the value of titles was being diminished by the widespread practice of putting them up for sale. For governments it was an excellent way of raising money: they had a virtual monopoly of a product that cost nothing to make and was in constant demand. 'Inflation of honours' became a charac-teristic phenomenon of the century. One of the most ingenious devices was the new order, introduced by James I of England, of 'baronet'. Hereditary – and thus commanding a good price – but not conferring the political rights of peerages, it was intended to supply a market in which knighthood had become so common that Charles I later attempted to make it compulsory for those with the prescribed amount of property. In Spain Philip III increased the higher ranks of the peerage by about half, and sales of titles continued under his successors. The French *officier* normally expected at the appropriate stage in his career to pay a substantial extra sum for his letters of nobility – or, since he hated to admit that the title was a new one – of 'rehabilitation'. It was a nice illustration of the general problems of title-holding: the state wanted to make rank dependent on service and yet to sell it to whoever would buy; the seeker of a title wanted it to be easily acquired at reasonable price, but when he had it he demanded that others should be excluded. Both were prepared, to the disgust of the old landed classes, to separate title-holding from territorial possessions.

Considering the many ways in which titles were acquired, they coresponded surprisingly well to current gradations of wealth. Only occasionally did venality reduce them to complete absurdity: Venice at the beginning of the century had 25 princes, 41 dukes, 147 marquises and counts, and 600 barons. It was usually only at a level of nobility clearly marked off as inferior that 'inflation' got out of bounds. In Spain the barrier between commoners and *hidalgos*, the lowest grade of nobility, was of the utmost practical importance. In theory only the Crown could confer the status and privileges of *hidalguia*. In practice wild claims to forgotten hereditary nobility were made until in many places almost every head of a household who was not a manual worker proclaimed himself a *hidalgo*. In Poland there was a lower nobility so extensive that it included men on much the same level as the English yeoman or the French *fermier*. The *szlachta* was not the product of a recent sale of titles but of the efforts of medieval kings to buy military support. More successful than most lesser nobilities they had built up a strong constitutional position. Even the creation of new noblemen was now in their hands rather than the king's. But the gap between magnates and lesser nobility was as great in Poland as anywhere else. The increasingly powerful regional assemblies, and the main offices in central government, were dominated by members of the higher nobility.

There was in many countries one perfectly rational motive for buying a title. Though nobility had long since ceased to carry the obligation of military service, it was often in effect a certificate of exemption from direct taxes. But in England, where no such exemption in practice existed, there was little sign that titles sold any less well. As in so many other matters, power and prestige were driving forces at least as important as money. In the countryside even those who did not seek authority needed an adequate label of status to escape the presumption of those who did. At the centre there was usually a strong probability that the politically eminent would not for long lack a title appropriate to their authority. For many monarchs the age-old problem of the over-mighty subject was taking a new and complex form. Landed nobilities still claimed, when it suited them, a right to power in the state. New office-holders asserted their equality in rank, esteem, and way of life with the ancient aristocrats. Almost every system of representative Estates (see pp. 249–55), so long as they kept any effective function, gave to each member of the nobility, or at least of its higher orders, a chance to sit in the upper house of the legislature. Between the higher nobility and the monarch there was everywhere an unstable mixture of alliance and rivalry. The royal court was a natural centre for great nobles; and it was often the Crown's policy to keep them there as much as it could. But not even Louis XIV could overcome the attraction for many of the independent power exercised in a great provincial estate. Sometimes the only way to lasting success was to commute between the two.

THE NOBILITY AND THE STATE

One of the most carefully planned attacks on the problem of the state's relationship with the nobles was in Sweden. Gustav Adolf owed his throne to their support: his aim was to make them its active and almost its sole servants. Some of their privileges, including exemption from taxation, were curtailed, but the pride and solidarity of the caste were to be strengthened by excluding from it anyone whose conduct or economic position made him unworthy. At the same time it was made clear that the Crown would if it chose employ a complete outsider, ennoble him, and expect him to be received as an equal. The notion of a service-nobility with easy access to its ranks did not work smoothly. The ancient aristocracy grew more resentful of the intruders, built up their own provincial power, and became the political opponents of both Crown and commoners. Grants of new peerages went not only to Crown servants but to the professions and the townsmen. In the 1650s there began the long struggle between the monarchy and the old nobility that made possible the 'popular absolutism' of Charles XI and Charles XII (see pp. 416–18).

In Russia, inevitably, the role of the higher nobility in the state was settled not by political bargaining but in wars, mass executions, and vast confiscations of property. The only title recognized everywhere was that of prince – *kniaz* – and the 'sovereign princes' regarded themselves as indispensable allies of the tsar. The rest of the high nobility, the boyars, claimed to be hereditary counsellors on whose goodwill the power if not the life of the monarch depended. They behaved to each other with all the jealousy and unscrupulous anarchism of ˌrulers of nations. Precedence among them, in theory settled by the elaborate points system of the *mestnichestvo* according to their genealogy and the offices they held, was a matter for bloodthirsty disputes. Ivan IV's massive attack on the princes and the boyars in the 1560s had destroyed many of the greatest estates and some of their owners; but it had left the angry survivors who fought each other and the Crown in the Time of Troubles at the beginning of the new century. The Romanovs, boyars themselves, were able to create their own inner circle of twenty or thirty great families, some from the ancient nobility, others made rich by grants of Crown land. The Council of Boyars became a meeting of the chosen favourites and office-holders rather than an assembly of magnates as a class. By Peter the Great's time the notion of nobility as a reward for service was becoming accepted. Peter's 'Table of Ranks' expressed in precise terms what was happening in one way or another throughout Europe. Ancient families retained their dignities: indeed it was Peter who introduced for them a variety of titles in the western style. But only meritorious service could give their members a place in the complex arrangement of ranks. He had perhaps more success than any other ruler in making those who attained nobility through service the equals and even the superiors of the holders of ancient titles.

There was an increasing division, in the words of the sociologist Pareto, between a 'governing élite' and a 'non-governing élite'. This is what Louis XIV to some extent achieved. Certainly in the great days of Versailles the nobility were more sharply divided than before into those who were attached to the court and the *noblesse campagnarde* who remained on their estates and took little part in the affairs of the monarchy. It did not mean that a rigid line could be drawn separating courtiers who devoted themselves entirely to the splendour and ceremony surrounding the king from the men who got on with the job of running the state. The old landed nobility could no longer assume that political power and office were theirs for the taking. But few of those who had risen to high positions in central government were content to leave the titles and privileges of nobility to others. The status and security of the family was as important to them as it was at nearly every other level of French society. Louis was generally willing enough to ensure that the statesmen and administrators were respected and rewarded. The distinction that was still clearly recognized between the *noblesse d'épée* and the *noblesse de robe* did not mean that those involved in the running of the state were inferior. The *noblesse d'épée* had long since ceased to be the preserve of ancient families. Sales of honours, and evasion of the rules that were supposed to govern admission to its ranks, made it easier to enter this than the well-guarded select circle of the *'grande robe'*. Those who belonged, or pretended to belong, to the old-established nobility did not accept without protest either the infiltration of outsiders or the diminution of power. The commissions set up by Colbert to investigate titles to nobility and preserve some of the exclusiveness of their order was one attempt to mitigate a problem that had confronted every French government for a century or more: even in the worst moments of financial distress, not much could be done to encroach on their exemption from taxation.

THE TOWNSMEN

Despite all the instincts of the rural élites to exclude townsmen, the distinction between the property-owners of town and country was becoming less important. Not only was land being constantly acquired with money made in the cities, but – in the west at least – the landed nobility great and small was becoming more urbanized. Income from commerce was often an essential supplement to landed revenues that were barely enough to maintain an estate and the standards of life associated with it. For anyone with political ambitions, a house in the capital was increasingly necessary. The city might be evil-smelling, plague-ridden, and disorderly; but it was acquiring ornate buildings, new avenues and squares, even – by the end of the century – street-lighting. It was a centre of cultured life that only the very richest patrons of the arts could rival. Regular contacts with regional towns or with capitals were a part of the life of landed gentlemen as well as of their superiors. The law, at all but the lowest levels, functioned in towns. An office in government, even a local one, involved regular visits to the provincial or national capital. The city-dwelling landowner who spent part of the year on his estates was becoming more common. He was not always, in his way of life, as distinct as he liked to think from the successful bourgeois. The habits and accomplishments of the landowner remained the standard to which the social climber of the towns aspired. If Molière's *bourgeois gentilhomme* was a successful figure of fun, the Paris audiences that rejoiced in his blunders must have included many with a foot on each side of the barrier. There was little to distinguish the Parisian whose capital was invested mainly in the *rentes* – the loans to the government which were backed by the Paris municipality – from his neighbour who drew rents from a landed estate.

Both in the city and in the lesser town power was likely to be in the hands of a narrow ruling group no longer tightly controlled by the nominally democratic institutions. Its character varied a good deal. In many places it was composed of men who took no active part in commerce or industry. They were successful lawyers, financiers, or purchasers of office, sometimes closely connected by marriage or cousinhood with the court and the landed nobility. It was still possible for a merchant oligarchy to remain comparatively self-contained; but the temptations and opportunities for the townsman who had achieved power and wealth to break away from his commercial background were strong. Though some of the Amsterdam regents continued to divide their time between government and commerce, many became purely office-holders and investors. In French towns the *parlementaires* were often a group of families who fought hard to prevent outsiders from joining them. The leading *marchands-fabricants* of Paris, the men involved in an assortment of industrial and commercial enterprises who belonged to the exclusive *Six-Corps*, had many relations in the high offices of state. By looking at the careers of individuals prominent in the urban community it is easy to get the impression that they were firmly separated in their status and way of life from the landowners. It is only when they are seen as part of their families that the links become apparent.

For those lower down the scale, opportunities of advancement, and even of security, in the towns seemed to be diminishing. It was not only the ruling oligarchy that kept entry to its circle almost impossible for those outside the privileged families. The status of master, once the realistic aim of every member of a guild, was now more easily acquired by heredity than by excellence. Prospects for the urban journeyman were seldom brighter than for the rural tenant; and the discontent of men who felt themselves to be oppressed wage-labourers was a notorious source of unrest. Their complaints all over western Europe and the Empire seemed to be much the same: masters used guild regulations as a means of keeping down wages, extracting an assortment of dues and fines, and restricting the numbers employed. From time to time there arose the secret *compagnonnages* which very occasionally managed to organize something approaching a strike. Fears of their sinister activities were seldom well-founded, though the Dutch thought it worth while to legislate against them.

THE URBAN POOR

Towns, notoriously, were centres of instability in contrast to the supposedly unchanging countryside. A frequent complaint was that the old-style working population was being replaced both by the rich and by the very poor. In London and Paris authorities tried, without much success, to restrict the building of new houses. Londoners were already worried about the traffic problem in the streets, and this too was a subject of occasional legislation. In Russia the concern was more about a decline in urban population. It was not only peasants who were forbidden by the code of 1649 to move: townsmen too were ordered to remain where they were – though for the rest of the century the law had to be repeated and penalties strengthened. The Russian burgher aimed in moving to escape both taxation and restrictions on industry – a tendency familiar enough in the west. Another section of the code tried to restrict the *sloboda*, the settlements, often controlled by monasteries or landlords, that had grown up outside the walls. But the great threat to urban life everywhere was thought to be the growing numbers of men, women, and children with no means of subsistence. How many of them were refugees from the countryside who thought food and shelter easier to find in towns is impossible to say: to some extent the poor were more conspicuous rather than merely more numerous. But evidence of the extent of urban destitution was consistent everywhere. Inevitably the homeless poor were the least countable part of the population, and precise figures like that of 65,000 beggars in Paris in 1634 have to be taken cautiously. A common guess is that something between a third and a fifth of the people in big towns were paupers. They lived at the expense of the employed population – men and children as beggars, women often as prostitutes. Since the prospects of newborn children being cared for in the conditions of this underworld were poor, many were abandoned to become foundlings. The dead were often abandoned too, to receive a perfunctory unidentified burial.

The fate of the poor depended above all on the attitude of the rich to the human misery that surrounded them; and this as always was inconsistent. Charity was a virtue required of Christians and their churches. Both found it satisfying to distinguish between the deserving poor on whom good works could be bestowed and the idle or criminal who could be denounced for a wickedness that manifestly contrasted with the righteousness of the rich and was responsible for many economic and social evils. A worthy citizen whose charitable gifts were associated with the salvation of his soul was often greatly concerned to remove paupers and vagabonds from his neighbourhood. In some ways it was better to be poor in a Catholic than a Protestant town: relieving poverty was an essential duty of monastic orders, which did not regard failure to engage in productive work as a sin. In France a great variety of newly established orders like the Company of the Blessed Sacrament devoted themselves to rescuing the poor. Vincent de Paul, one of the very few men to achieve lasting fame through practical efforts to help the poor without discrimination, made both wealthy Parisians and churchmen aware of the realities of poverty and ready to take part in charitable activities that were combined with evangelism. But his organizations, the Lazarists and the Daughters of Charity, declined after his death in 1660. In France as much as in Protestant countries poor-relief was coming to depend on removing the destitute into secular institutions and insisting that the able-bodied ought to be at work. The French 'hospitals' for the old, the sick, and the foundlings grew steadily in numbers and were imitated in most Catholic countries. Usually the state or local governments were prepared to establish them and leave their running to private charities. English governments intervened more actively. Since the mid-sixteenth century legislation to deal with destitution and with conditions of labour had been produced in nearly every parliament. Its principles stayed essentially the same: the sturdy beggar must be flogged, but the employer of labour must be made to pay adequate wages. Local authorities must administer and pay for a process of 'setting the poor on work', and relieving the genuinely necessitous. Private charity was to be encouraged; but it was not a substitute for a properly organized system of compulsory payments. One of the most impressive achievements in administration was the construction begun in Charles I's Book of Orders of a scheme for management of the poor in which parish officers, JPs, sheriffs, and justices in assize had their precisely defined roles. Its cost, coming mainly from locally assessed and levied poor-rates, grew implacably. It was tolerated by most of those who paid, not from beneficence but from fear. The immediate cause for alarm was simply that the poor robbed the rich, violently or not. But behind it was the deeper fear – that propertied society would sooner or later be overturned by mass rebellion.

CRIME

There should perhaps be added to war, hunger, and pestilence a fourth ever-present danger in the ordinary life of the period. Crime has not on the whole been studied by historians as much as it deserves; and the processes of apprehending, trying, and punishing the criminal have been treated as a very minor aspect of government. It is not a subject easily defined. The condemnation of rebel leaders and overthrown statesmen has not much in common with that of a petty thief. The nobleman arrested for a brawl or duel, the merchant imprisoned at the behest of a creditor, and the printer who fell foul of a censorship law did not regard themselves as criminals, though such people occupied a large part of the time of the courts. The crimes that really concerned the community as a whole were committed usually by the people who had no place in the economic system. The decree of 1606 in Paris that beggars should be whipped, branded, shorn, and driven out was recognizing the assumption that idle poverty and crime were inseparable. Both were believed, with good reason, to be increasing.

Statistics about crime are among the most unreliable. They concern, inevitably, offences known to some authority, and often they are only for criminals caught and punished. As in later centuries, the numbers recorded depended as much on the activity of the judicial system as on that of the criminals. Even so, the evidence for a general increase in crime in the seventeenth century is impressive. It comes from a great variety of sources, local and central, in a great number of countries; and it follows patterns that are not due to detection and punishment, rising more sharply in times of dearth, greater in poor than in rich areas, divided evenly between regions with high and low rates of law enforcement. There is consistency too in the marked difference between urban and rural crime: it was in large towns that the professional thief, alone or in organized gangs, flourished. Tradesmen and artisans had no doubt about his origins. The poor of the countryside, when they found their way into a town, were seen by respectable citizens as a threat to order and prosperity. Any murder, rape, or robbery could be blamed on them. Constables and courts tended automatically to treat them more harshly than they would the known inhabitant; and the division of the population into the accepted and the rejected seemed to perpetuate itself. Though the incomers were not in the seventeenth century of a different race and colour, they could sometimes be of a different nationality. Vagabonds who had reason to flee could easily cross a frontier; and the disbanded soldier, who could well have been serving in a foreign army in the first place, was notoriously a bad character who had learnt to live by plunder and violence. The underground community was likely to be more cosmopolitan than the established one. Partly, no doubt, for that reason there had grown a language of the beggars, the 'jargon of the brotherhood', as it was called in Spain, that combined local phrases with international ones related to gipsy speech. It was the bond of the semi-secret beggar fraternity that existed in most cities. Often, if the colourful contemporary accounts are to be believed, it was divided into sections specializing in different devices for extracting money. There may even be some foundation for the stories of the beggar-kings, living in splendour, ruling over their subjects, and levying taxation in a parody of the national state. The true beggar-thief was not interested in charity.

In the countryside the impact of crime was lighter. Petty theft, drunken brawls, and the occasional murder were common enough in the routine of local justices; but much of the crime seems to have originated in personal or family quarrels rather than in any general defiance of the law. In times of dearth the hungry naturally stole from whoever had supplies of food. When life, however hard, was unchanging the village seems to have been a fairly secure and tranquil place. Outside the settled rural community there were the wandering poor. In areas of serfdom they were guilty of the crime of running away, which in one way or another was likely to be almost as reprehensible in the west. The attitude of the settled population to them was ambiguous. If the urban beggar was assumed to be a pick-pocket or worse, the homeless wanderer could be deemed a horse- or cattle-thief. Nevertheless there remained some of the tradition of sympathy with the people who had escaped the oppression of law-abiding and labouring society. They could be welcome entertainers, fortune-tellers, and pedlars; and sheltering the fugitive from justice was itself a common offence. Perhaps the picturesque vagabond was now a literary rather than a real figure. The Spanish novels about the *picaro*, the outlaw whose hidden qualities might include noble origins, were a recognized category of writing. Autolycus was a delightful character. But as the numbers of outcasts grew those who remained in the countryside were more likely to form communities as coherent as those of the urban beggars. 'Bandits', a word of Italian origin, became in many languages the term for the gangs that were inevitably more common in war-stricken areas. In them poverty and crime verged on rebellion: the *croquants* were bands of outlaws, and so in a different way were the pirate Uskoks. They could be the origin of irrational fears and rumours which though they did not reach the scale of the *grande peur* of the next century had the same features. Bohemia and the eastern Alps were two of the regions in which tales spread of the magical powers of the wandering bands. Storms, plagues, and crop failures were attributed to them; and their satanic orgies were described in detail. They could usually escape lawful punishment; and alternative rumours saw their magic as a beneficent force against the oppressions of the rich.

There was a lot of confusion, both in theory and in practice, about how crime should be dealt with. To the owner of property, great or small, it was not obvious why there was a difference between civil and criminal law: thieves who stole his cattle, debtors who refused to pay, cousins who laid claim to part of his inheritance were equally people from whom he wanted restitution. The principle that crime was a matter for the state or its local representatives had not entirely replaced the feeling that proceedings against an offender should be initiated by or on behalf of the victim of the crime. For the victim it was better to win restitution or recompense than merely to have the satisfaction of seeing the guilty person punished – though the popularity of public executions suggested that they supplied a need of some sort. Roman law, with its emphasis on obedience to authority, was the basis of most of the new or consolidated systems that were a regular part of the increased activity of governments. (The *Rules for Judges* published in Sweden in 1616 were exceptional in mentioning reform of the criminal as one of the aims.) The law as an impartial protector of individuals was becoming less prominent than its duty to punish severely anything that upset the political and social order. In practice the wronged individual might well turn criminal law to his advantage. A large number of reported crimes came to the courts as part of a complex dispute in which accusations and counter-accusations multiplied. It was felt at the time that a characteristic of sixteenth- and seventeenth-century society was the immense amount of energy devoted to litigation. Lawyers were a bitter joke for their profitable delays, pompous verbiage, and professional secrecy. But their services were in such demand that the law as a profession expanded incessantly. Every gentleman and lesser noble was assumed to have a working knowledge of the law as it affected his interests. The inventories of French village households have been found to contain more *coutumes* – books of customary law – than bibles. The English JP was a demonstration of how the informed amateur could play a crucial part in the administration of state-imposed justice, which included naturally upholding the superiority of his class. Machinery for trying and punishing the criminal was becoming more efficient; and though the use of some penalties such as burning alive diminished, the others were brutal enough. Torture was still, in most countries, a common part of the judicial process. The one comfort for the criminals was that the means of catching them were far less efficient than those of retribution. The thinly linked community of outcasts from society was growing larger.

REFERENCES

1 F. L. Carsten, *The Origins of Prussia* (Oxford, 1964), ch. 11.

2 P. Goubert in *Past and Present*, no. 10 (1956), p. 13.

5

RELIGION AND THE CHURCHES

Europeans in the seventeenth century believed in God. His activities were the obvious explanation of the ordinary events of the world. His wishes were the guide to approved human conduct. His purposes were, however mysteriously, fulfilled as much by wars, plagues, and famines as by prosperity. In the twentieth century it is hard to grasp that to all but an eccentric few God was a normal part of life. Harder still is to see how, amid all the religious turmoil and pressures, there began a separation of belief in God from the daily working of a mechanical universe. Imperceptibly it came to be assumed that natural events usually had natural causes; supernatural influences on them could be seen as a supplement – sometimes comforting, more often alarming. Today in every western culture there is a barrier, however shaky, between the normal and the religious. There are other barriers between these and the subdued magic that lingers on in, for instance, popular astrology, numerology, palmistry, and some parts of 'fringe' medicine. These separations too were developing slowly in the seventeenth century. Attempts of sociologists, philosophers, psychologists, and historians to elucidate the roles of religion and of the supernatural in human behaviour have not led to very satisfying conclusions. On this, even more than on most other topics, reconstructing the past involves disturbingly indirect use of evidence. All we can investigate confidently is the outward manifestations of religion that everywhere remained an essential part of life. Sunday, the annual Christian festivals, the ceremonies associated with birth, marriage, and death survived, however much the details of their observance were reformed. Parents saw the benefits of teaching their children that religion and virtue were identical and that disobedience would lead to divine punishment. Prayer was a household and personal routine, at least for the higher and middling ranks of society. The law assumed that an oath on the Bible was the best guarantee of truthfulness. In Protestant countries especially the language and anecdotes of the Bible were a necessary part of normal speech; biblical episodes were the commonest subject of artists. Above all there was in every community the Church. Seen from below, the distinction between the Church and other sources of authority was by no means clear. Every established church was in one way or another a law-giving authority. On the whole to the law-abiding peasants or artisans the Church rather than the state represented the organized community. It was the Church that educated them, the Church that laid down codes of moral and social behaviour, the Church that would relieve them in destitution. Maintaining it often added to their poverty. Men might quarrel about the kind of religious organization they wanted; hardly anyone could conceive of a society with no such organization at all. The minorities who broke away from an established church had to set up another, which was likely to have an even firmer hold on the lives of its adherents.

The collapse in the previous century of the Roman Catholic monopoly had such vast consequences that it is easily forgotten how little the beliefs and even the practices that made an impact on ordinary men had changed. For Catholic and Protestant alike the God who had created the universe still intervened habitually in its working, especially in the fate of human beings. There was a life after death, in which there would be rewards or punishments related in one way or another to the conduct and faith of the individual on earth. The Fall of Man and salvation through Jesus Christ must have been among the teachings that were recited rather than understood; but salvation through the Church, for those who fulfilled its minimum requirements, was the constant message of the clergy of every kind. (The apparent incompatibility of this with the doctrine of predestination was one of the mysteries argued by theologians but unlikely to worry the majority of Christians.) Leaders of all churches made use of a part of Christian belief that was readily comprehensible: besides God there was the Devil, who was responsible for countless personal and collective disasters. The malign force manifested itself not only in the future terrors of hell but on earth. Among other ways it was to be seen in the existence of bogus Christian churches – a view held most avidly by protestants in their confrontations with Rome. Belief in the utter evil of a different version of Christianity was not as permanent among ordinary laymen as it was among some of their superiors. It could arouse passions in war and occasional panics locally or nationally. But a conquering power or a new monarchy could impose a new religion with good prospects of eventually having it accepted. For most people churches provided neither terror nor zeal but security. Coming together in a ritual to which a whole community conformed; knowing a few accepted conventions about conduct and ceremony; feeling that something could be done, with guidance from the Church and clergy, to influence events that were otherwise uncertain – comforts like these were most important when the outside world was most hostile and inexplicable. For those excluded from the community of the majority there could be the greater consolation of belonging to a limited body of people who knew themselves to be the 'saved' or the 'elect'. To governments and men of property the churches had the immense attraction of instilling respect for authority and acceptance of existing hierarchies. The danger was that religion could so easily have the opposite effect. In literate societies it was not always possible to hide the awkward fact that, despite all the biblical texts demanding obedience to the powers that be, Christianity itself was based on resistance to them. So, originally, was every variety of Protestantism. But their history showed that the most rebellious religion tended in time to find itself on the side of the state. Even radical sects like those of mid-century England became the penalized but passive dissenters of later generations. The process of 'secularization' in government and in scholarly thought was still, in 1700, hardly perceptible to ordinary people. Panics about popish plots in England, the power of the priest in a Catholic parish and of the Jesuit confessor at a royal court, the passionate self-sacrifice of the Old Believers in Russia seemed to suggest that nothing had changed. But government, warfare, and the quest for understanding of the universe were all moving away from the domination of the churches. It was a very slow process.

CLERGY AND STATE

The period of large-scale religious strife that began with Luther was over by the middle of the seventeenth century. Shattering though it had been for those closely involved, it had not destroyed the outward structure of religion. In both Catholic and Protestant areas the parish survived, a natural unit in rural society though it was becoming less relevant in towns. Even Calvinism had found the need to take over both the buildings and often the clergy of the old Church and to fit itself into an existing pattern. As the baroque churches of southern Europe and Wren's rebuilding in London suggested, there was no general lack of money or energy to keep the parochial system going. Every village had its clergyman, whose standard of living was usually not much higher than that of his ordinary parishioners. In France he could be anywhere between the level of the poorest peasant and that of the prosperous small farmer: in any case he probably cultivated some land himself. In England the richer and pleasanter parishes were increasingly used by the gentry as an acceptable occupation for their younger sons, while in others vicars were almost as poor as dissenting ministers. The peasant-priests of Lutheran Germany were among the lowest of European clergy in social status and often in education. The poverty of local clergy could be blamed largely on the gradual and varied taking of the Church's resources by the state or its rich subjects. Tithe was now more a source of resentment to the payer than of adequate income to the clergy. In Sweden two-thirds of it went to the Crown or the landlord; and in one way or another the Reformation everywhere had benefited the rich at the expense of the clerical poor. But attempts by some Protestant churches and sects to abolish the clergy altogether had little success. However feeble his spiritual guidance, the local clergyman was an indispensable administrator and his diminished rituals an accepted routine. In most Catholic countries the priest, robed and celibate, was a dominant influence in the village community. Anticlericalism was a well-established sentiment, but usually expressed as hostility to priests rather than their office.

Resources paid to the Church went less to the parishes than to the dioceses and the monasteries. Spain and Muscovy had in common the fact that in 1600 much of their richest land belonged to the 'regular' clergy who contributed little apparent benefit to the outside world. Olivares and Alexis I were equally unsuccessful in trying to restrict them. The monastic orders were perhaps the greatest gap in the state's omnipotence, and were correspondingly unpopular with absolutist politicians. Here at least Protestant states were free from a material burden. But they had not lost a third section of the Church most involved in struggles for power – the clerical aristocracy. There are few countries in the first half of the century that did not see some high church dignitary playing a leading part in lay politics. For some their ecclesiastical position was a more or less nominal addition to other sources of wealth and power. It was royal connections that made Archduke Albert of the Spanish Netherlands an archbishop and a cardinal, and Filaret in Russia a patriarch. Richelieu's bishopric showed how the French aristocracy inserted themselves into the Church at the top. Both he and Mazarin became cardinals because they were politicians, not the other way round. Rich bishoprics were among the normal possessions of the aristocracy; cardinals' hats were a matter for political pressure. Laud, on the other hand, was a bishop first, a statesman and courtier second. In Sweden, one of the most priest-ridden of all countries, the Lutheran bishops were often large landholders with all the privileges and attitudes of the nobility. In every state and almost every locality the holders of political power recognized the importance of controlling, or sharing, ecclesiastical power. Appointments to Church office, high and low, were made more by the state and the owners of land than by the Church itself. It was not an unmixed evil: towards the end of the century it was increasingly recognized that the 'good priest' was an important asset to the state.

THE PAPACY

With the end of the religious wars in France it was evident that there was no prospect of Protestantism spreading over the whole of Europe: the Catholic Church would remain, at least in the southern half of the continent, an international power. The Papacy, run as much as other monarchies by venality, corruption and faction, was a unique institution in the world of diplomacy. Though papal nuncios were sent only to Catholic countries, the pope as head of an Italian state had his envoys and agents in Protestant capitals, and an intelligence service better than most. He could never be an ordinary member of the community of rulers. Popes, once elected, were virtually irremovable monarchs with the manifold powers and inducements they could use as vicars of Christ to back their diplomacy. On the other hand they were chosen by the College of Cardinals which was formed and influenced by a great diversity of pressures, among which those of Catholic sovereigns were prominent. Henri IV had found that military success convinced the College of Cardinals of the depth of his penitence, and that divorce from his first wife became possible when he chose a Habsburg as his second. He then spent, it was alleged, 300,000 ducats to secure – against the wishes of Philip III – a Medici as the next pope. It proved a poor investment, since Leo XI died after three weeks in office. Useful as the power of the Papacy was to rulers who could exploit it skilfully, it could never fit happily into the Europe of absolutist states. Though religion was a great unifying force in the Habsburg Empire, the pope could no longer dispute with the emperor as an equal, and was not prepared to be the Habsburg Minister of Propaganda.

In Italy at least, the Papacy seemed to have a chance to become a great political power. In the 1560s and 1570s it had been dominated by a nobility as anarchic and destructive as any in Europe. Sixtus V had improved its administration a little. In 1605 there appeared in Paul V the first modern absolutist among the popes, who by the familiar process of handing out titles and estates to his family, created something of a 'Tudor aristocracy'. It was his mission,. he proclaimed, to free the church from 'usurpation and violence'. In spite of a few gestures, such as his order that English Catholics should refuse the Oath of Allegiance, he did not seriously plan a campaign against Protestantism. Much more important to him were his visions of Rome becoming once more the capital of the peninsula. The result was to demonstrate that the pope's standing in power politics was a lowly one. Paul's conflict with Venice, where the state had just tightened its already strong control over the clergy, ended in failure. The Venetian clergy, led by the friar Paolo Sarpi, supported the Republic; and the assassins sent by the pope's nephew to deal with Sarpi bungled their job. In the Valtelline, papal troops who were supposed to be the guardians of the valley did not risk a clash with Spain or France (see pp. 128–9). But in 1626 Urban VIII was able to spite both France and Venice with the smart diplomacy that encouraged France in the Treaty of Monzon to desert her ally. As the European struggle developed, Urban faced the difficulty that his diplomatic interests were in supporting not the loyally Catholic Spaniards but the Gallican French, and worse still the heretical Swedes. The Papacy did not maintain an army worth having by the new standards; and at the Treaty of Westphalia its pronouncements were treated with contempt. Innocent X, refusing to recognize the religious division of Europe and the seizure of Church lands, pronounced the settlement null and void. No-one took much notice.

THE JESUITS

In spite of the political weakness of the Papacy, the settlement in 1648 was far from being a disaster for Catholicism. On the contrary it marked the end of Protestant progress in Europe and the acceptance of Catholic reconquests. Poland, Bohemia, and royal Hungary were now firmly Catholic. The Huguenots were no longer a threat to the French Church or state. Catholics had reason to hope for further progress in Germany, and even conceivably in Scandinavia. An eastward drive into the territory of the Orthodox Church was not impossible. The pope had to co-exist with both Protestantism and Gallicanism; but he could not altogether desert the 'lost sheep' of Europe or repudiate outright the efforts of those exponents of the true faith who tried to recapture them. The expansion of Catholicism was still the great task of the Society of Jesus. Indeed the Jesuits and their general seemed to have taken over from the pope a good many of his functions in the effective leadership of the church. In politics they found it expedient to remain on the side of Spain and the great armies. In religion they were their own masters; and they did not intend to allow dogmatic niceties to stand in the way of the growth of the Church's power. They demanded of their followers unquestioning and active allegiance rather than personal morality or doctrinal rigidity. Moral problems were solved by the system of 'casuistry' whereby the confessor could justify almost anything if its 'intent' was good – that is in the interests of the faith and in particular of the Order. According to the theory of 'probabilism' an opinion not manifestly absurd or explicitly condemned by the church could be accepted – especially if some clerical scholar could be found to have mentioned it – even in preference to one that was better supported. How far this could go was a matter of technical dispute between the Probabilists who required a reasonable degree of plausibility and the 'Laxists' who would accept anything not held to be positively disproved. No-one on the right side of the rigid barrier that excluded heresy and the few mortal sins needed to worry about his salvation provided he remained loyal to the Church and to his confessor. By bringing the consolations of this attitude to the rich and the powerful, Jesuit confessors were naturally welcomed into the most influential circles; and the confessional became one of the chief means of propaganda.

The Jesuit attitude was an extraordinary mixture. On the one hand they were using sinister methods of securing a hold on the minds and actions of their followers; on the other they were taking a tolerant and almost humanist standpoint. Man, they claimed, could work for the greater glory of God through art, literature, even science rather than merely through piety. The first step in saving one's neighbour was to educate him. By providing tutors and seminaries acceptable to the courts and aristocracies, Jesuits could see that the seats of power were occupied by men whose underlying assumptions were theirs. The general pattern instilled by the teacher could be filled in by the day-to-day advice of the confessor. Ferdinand II was the outstanding royal product of Jesuit control. Louis XIV's confessors, La Chaise and his succesor Le Tellier, were among the strongest influences, at least on his religious policies. In Spain Nithard, the Austrian confessor of the queen mother, became the greatest political power at the court of Charles II. Sigismund III, 'King of the Jesuits', had owed them much of the credit for his reconquest of Poland and enabled them to establish a complete control over the religion and education of the country (see p. 411).

Jesuits did not accept as permanent any division of the world into Catholic and Protestant territories. The English view of them as a sinister underground conspiracy against the state was exaggerated but not totally unfounded. Overseas they were both the allies and the rivals of the trading companies, eager to extend European power but often defending their converts against the unscrupulous behaviour of merchants and colonists. There too the

Jesuit technique was to start at the top and to adapt their teaching to the audience. Roberto de Nobili in southern India, ignoring the conversions made among the poor by the Portuguese, appealed entirely to the Brahmin caste, adopting their costume, learning their language, and preaching not the contrast between Christianity and evil paganism but how, with a little stretching, the two religions could be shown to have much in common. Indians enrolled into the Jesuit order gave up neither their caste nor much of their ritual. In China Jesuits suggested that the emperor might help to merge Christian and Confucian religions. In Japan they met with their one reverse when the Samurai became disillusioned with a religion that no longer seemed to hold the only key to trade with the west.

In South America the Jesuits achieved something like their ultimate ideal, the theocracy of Paraguay. Philip III conceded to them full control, subject only to his own sovereignty over the Guarani, in the River Plate region. By a mixture of force, propaganda, and material benefits they created the villages where the natives were 'reduced' to Catholic, monogamous, authoritarian life. Spanish colonists and slave-traders were kept out by well-equipped native forces; mines, foundries, and weaving sheds were added to the resources of collective agriculture. Clothes and tea replaced feathers and alcohol; the whip was used, but not the death penalty, since the vows of the Jesuits prevented them from carrying it out and no-one else could be trusted to do so. It was a society that paid for its sudden security and prosperity by submission to the minute and rigid control of the European priesthood. Here the divine summons to the religious life came only to white men. Services were conducted in local languages; but the Bible, apt to be misunderstood, remained – as it had formerly been for so many laymen in Europe – in the secrecy of a foreign tongue. The native was taught to be content with two days' work on his own land and four on the property of God, of which the Jesuits were custodians. The idealism was soon whittled away. New generations of missionaries became more closely connected with the ruling aristocrats of the Spanish colonies. A good deal of energy went into keeping out the rival Paulist missionaries. It all became a revealing parody of the Church's relations with state and society in seventeenth-century Europe.

The Jesuits could reasonably claim to be a progressive element in the Church, adapting it to the realities of political and economic change. Other orders too were involved in the mixture of temporal and spiritual activity and in the tendency towards a centralized and 'aristocratic' form of organization. The Capucins, founded in 1525 as a further Franciscan order, did not confine themselves to helping the victims of poverty, plague, and war. They came to specialize in diplomacy. Father Joseph was a Capucin; so was Father Hyacinth whom Maximilian of Bavaria employed as an agent to win Catholic support in Germany against the Habsburgs. Indeed the Capucins were generally identified with anti-Habsburg movements among Catholic powers and Jesuits with the pro-Habsburg ones. Overseas, Franciscans, Dominicans, and Augustinians quarrelled with each other and with the Jesuits over spoils that were not solely religious ones.

POPULAR CATHOLICISM UNDER THE HABSBURGS

Jesuits, however adaptable in theological niceties, had embraced by 1600 one doctrine that proved immensely popular both in the solidly Catholic areas of southern Europe and in those of central Europe retrieved from Protestantism. The theory that the Virgin Mary must herself have been conceived without the taint of sex had long been a matter on which the Church permitted more than one opinion. It now became part of the cult of the Virgin that flourished as never before. Why this happened in the seventeenth century especially is a problem that the study of mass psychology does not seem to have solved. Belief in one god, or in an incomprehensible trinity, had never satisfied the religious cravings of the majority. Saints with quasi-divine powers were in effect worshipped, however much it was stressed that they were mere agents. A female near-deity who represented motherhood and who was miraculously removed from the sins of the flesh was evidently a source of comfort that the all-male religious establishment failed to provide. In Spain the importance of Mary had been growing steadily. Under Philip III both the Crown and the Cortes of Castile tried to have the Immaculate Conception made into a central dogma of the faith. Academic doubts about the imposition of an oath upholding it were a cause of university riots. Representations of the Virgin, from the paintings of Velasquez and his followers to the crude statues carried in every village procession, were as powerful a visual image as the crucifixion. A theory that the body and blood of Mary appeared equally with that of Christ in the Sacrament was regarded as a punishable heresy; but there was no reason for the government of state or Church to repudiate the benefits of the cult. In Austrian and Bohemian towns the Marian 'sodalities' became popular associations, some for the rich and others for the lesser citizens. Pilgrimages to Marienzell and other miracle-working shrines were a popular activity. In Hungary the Virgin acquired a special function as protector against both the Turk and the Orthodox Church. Even St Stephen took second place in this. The reluctance of the Papacy to give its full support to the cult of Mary may have come partly from a feeling that all this depended too little on the priest and the local church. The multiplication of shrines, though it helped in the extirpation of Protestantism, carried a hint of primitive religion that had only an uncertain connection with the teachings of the Church: the worshipper there was not dependent on the intervention of the clergy. Even at the height of the Catholic revival anticlericalism was constantly reported. The clergy might be necessary to salvation, but not in quite such large numbers.

RELIGION IN FRANCE

In France opposition to the Jesuits came both from the rival orders and from the various movements of a mystical and individualist character that arose within the Church at the beginning of the century. Against the Jesuit concentration on free will was set the theocratic outlook of Pierre de Bérulle, a Jesuit pupil who was made a cardinal not long before his death. His ideal man was expected to merge himself into Christ and God by prayer and contemplation. Bérulle's followers were by no means cut off from political or social activity. His ideas were popular with the exclusive groups at court, and later in the literary salons. In 1611 he founded the Oratory, an association of Catholic clergy devoted to improving the status and morals of the parish priests and to ending the Jesuit domination of education. Bérulle himself and many of the leading figures in Paris were involved in the kind of mysticism that led them to the circle of visionary women like

Mme Acarie and Marie de Valence. Two of Bérulle's associates were in due course canonized. Francois de Sales, the Catholic Bishop of Geneva, claimed massive conversions among Swiss and French Protestants. Vincent de Paul had a genius for leadership and organization that produced the Lazarists, the *filles de la charité*, and the schemes for bringing help and the consolations of religion to galley-slaves and the starving poor of Paris. His devotion did something to make life tolerable for victims of war and hunger; but it did not lead him to question or break away from the high political and social circles of the capital.

From different theological starting-points, both the Jesuit and the Bérullien religions could comfort their followers with the assurance that the world and its customs were not altogether evil and that religious duty was compatible with a pleasant and privileged life. The price of it was to accept clerical domination in a wide range of activities. The *cabale des dévots* made great efforts to use state authority in stamping out heresy and indifference. They were alarmed to see the growth of tolerant cultural and literary groups in which Catholics and Huguenots met in each other's houses. But militant Catholics had always to face the problems that arose from France's relations with the Papacy. In the year of Henri's death, 1610, literate Frenchmen were excited by the reappearance of *De Regis et Rege Institutione*, a pamphlet by the Jesuit Mariana arguing that the subject might be absolved through his faith from obedience to the sovereign, and justifying the assassination of kings who failed to further the interests of the faith. An opposite view was put in Edmond Richer's *De Ecclesiastica et Politica Potestate* (1611) which claimed apostolic succession for all priests independently of the pope. Divine power would be exercised primarily by bishops, who could of course be good Frenchmen. This was a form of Gallicanism directed as much against the king as against the pope. To those who believed that the success of French Catholicism depended on a firm alliance with the Papacy it was a help that Louis XIII was legitimate only because the pope had allowed his father to remarry: the nobles hostile to the king had more reason to challenge papal supremacy. Under Louis XIV Gallican theories became, as they had been in the sixteenth century and earlier, involved with royal claims to revenue and authority, as well as with diplomatic alignments (see p. 512). Catholicism by then was safe; but its character remained uncertain. While some were seeking a religion in which they could feel intellectually satisfied, the devotion which Louis in his later years supported meant increasingly the cult of the Virgin Mary and the Sacred Heart, visions and miracles.

Henri IV's conversion and the Edict of Nantes did not mark an obvious end to the possibilty of new attempts by the Huguenots to conquer the country. It was not until the Peace of Alais in 1629 that their internal dispute on the merits of armed resistance was settled in favour of loyalty to the state. Politically and socially there seemed good reason for France to become a Protestant state. French Jesuits were making little headway against Huguenots. There was no apparent weakening of the discipline imposed by the national synods or of their conviction that Catholicism was the essence of evil. Yet once the revolts of the 1620s were defeated, the French Protestant Church became the first to accept the role of pacific dissent (see p. 317). The Huguenots had lost the factious nobility who led them into the sixteenth-century wars; the townsmen and men of the *robe* who now made their policy were not disposed to risk their lives and property in a losing battle against the state. (See pp. 513–15).

THE PROTESTANT CHURCHES

Whatever religious or material factors may have determined the original spread of the Reformation, the boundaries between Catholic and Protestant Europe were eventually drawn by political power. So, very largely, were those between the various Protestant Churches, which now had little in common beyond their rejection of the pope and their faith in the Bible as the ultimate spiritual authority. Lutheranism was by the mid-seventeenth century an orthodoxy at least as rigid in theory as Catholicism. Theologians devoted themselves to expounding the arid minutiae of such doctrines as the 'ubiquity' of Christ and attacking the errors of Calvinism. The Lutheran Church demanded the support of the state. Great ecclesiastical families, who held bishoprics and prebends almost as hereditary titles and Church lands as private estates, relied on orthodoxy to preserve what was now the established order. In Germany especially (see maps 3 and 4 on pp. 586–7). Lutheranism was conservative in outlook and ready to accept a good deal of secular authority in religious affairs in return for defence against its enemies. It did not draw much distinction between Calvinism and Catholicism as threats. The Lutheran Berliners stoned Calvinist troops from Saxony who came to their aid in the Thirty Years War. In Gustav Adolf's Sweden the Church imposed its moral code almost as fiercely as in Calvin's Geneva. It also became a local administrative machine of the state, assessing and collecting taxes, and even helping to organize conscription. In spite of this the Clerical Estate often acted, in Gustav's phrase, as 'Tribunes of the People', resisting more effectively than the fourth Estate could, the burdens imposed both by the state and by the landowners.

If Lutheranism now tended to be a religion of conformity and of collaboration with the state, Calvinism could not be regarded as simply the opposite: it could be adapted to submission as well as to challenge. Once they had succeeded in winning power, Calvinists could use the state as a means of imposing the most tyrannical orthodoxy. Their founder had shown what could be achieved in this; and Geneva was still an absolutism in which power was shared by clerical and civil authorities. Scottish Presbyterianism fought a fluctuating battle for power against the Stuart kings before the clumsy efforts of the English government to destroy it made it the centre of the national resistance that produced the Bishops' Wars. It had not always been a united movement: after Knox's death there had been incessant conflicts about its organization. Edinburgh militancy was still resisted by Aberdeen conservatism. But in the General Assembly and the mixed lay and clerical hierarchy the Kirk had a set of institutions well adapted to the exercise of political power and to winning support from a wide range of the community. The Covenant of 1638 was a magnificent example of how religious zeal could be organized for political ends: momentarily it achieved something approaching national unity in the most unlikely conditions. On the other hand, Calvinism had characteristics that were bound to lead to fragmentation. In religion as in politics, the more radical the beliefs the harder it was to hold them together. Predestination was above all the faith of sects, each believing itself to be the 'elect' minority. Its appeal was strongest to men striving to assert a status they had made for themselves; for whoever the elect were, they would not be known by inherited wealth or power.

ARMINIANISM

England and the Netherlands showed these conflicting traits well; though while in England it was the Puritan opposition to established doctrine that was more firmly Calvinist, in the Netherlands it was the official Church. In both the resistance to rigid Calvinism made use of the doctrines that had been expounded, with caution and ambiguity, by Jacob Harmensz – 'Arminius' – a Professor of Theology at Leiden (see p. 471). Out of the turgid 'supralapsarian' versus 'infralapsarian' controversy, he developed ideas that left little of predestination in any recognizable form. All who had faith retained a chance of salvation; only those who rejected 'grace' were damned. Moreover he was prepared to introduce a certain amount of decoration and ceremony into the austere Dutch churches. In 1610 his ideas were incorporated into the 'Remonstrance' presented to the Estates of Holland and Friesland, which asked merely that men should not be bound to doctrines they found incredible. To the Calvinist clergy and their followers all this seemed a move towards popery, and hence towards subjection to Spain. Anything stressing doubt rather than certainty was bad for clerical power. The orthodox faith was defended by Francis Gomar, a colleague of Arminius at Leiden and an unrelenting preacher of damnation. The Remonstrants, generally speaking, were the party of the prosperous merchants against the countryside, of Holland and the maritime provinces against the less advanced areas, of Republicanism against the House of Orange. The Synod of Dort, which met in 1618 at the height of the political crisis that absorbed the religious quarrel, was a 'Counter-Remonstrant' assembly that listened to Remonstrant ministers only to condemn them. It produced a set of canons defining doctrine on strict Gomarist lines; Remonstrant ministers were ejected; dissenters were in theory to be excluded from office and from many of the benefits of citizenship. In practice not many of the civil authorities were prepared, except against Catholics, to impose the full claims of the Church. In 1627 power in Amsterdam went to the 'libertine' party of Andries Bicker which had some success in maintaining religious tolerance. Protestant sectaries and even Catholics found that discretion, and perhaps money, could cause laws to be forgotten. Amsterdam, against the protests of the clergy, became the scene of flourishing intellectual and cultural activity.

What was now in Holland the heresy of a sect became in England the religion imposed by the monarchy and resisted by an opposition that found in its own version of Calvinism abundant support for its political and commercial interests. Arminianism, it is true, was a label more or less accidentally attached to the Laudian Church. In England it meant not a liberalizing of Calvinism but a form of worship that demonstrated in the repetitive ceremonies, the priestly vestments, and the railed-off altar the notion of salvation through obedience to those in power. English clergy, secure in the ambiguities of the thirty-nine articles, were not much concerned about supralapsarianism or irresistible grace. 'People', Charles I remarked, 'are more governed by the pulpit than the sword in peace'; and when Laud became Archbishop of Canterbury in 1633 the king expected him to maintain the Church as 'the chiefest support of royal authority'. The virtues of submission and passive acceptance of the existing order of society were instilled through careful central control of both the organization and the services of the Church. Doctrine and political purpose apart, it was certainly in need of reform. The 'visitations' reporting on every diocese revealed not only the opposition of Puritan clergy but in many areas a dismal state of poverty and incompetence. There were some signs of improvement, such as the marked increase since the sixteenth century in the number of graduate clergy. How far reform could have been extended by Laud's system can only be guessed: all it achieved in the end was to contribute to the revolution that brought the archbishop to his death.

PURITANISM

Against the Laudian Church was an alliance of religious beliefs known, mainly to their enemies, as Puritan. The term had such wide application that Puritanism is more easily defined by what it opposed than by what it upheld. Inevitably when it triumphed in the Civil War it broke into fragments, ranging from supporters of an established Presbyterian Church to the multitude of radical sects. But in the 1630s it was united in the conviction that Arminianism was half-way to popery and that the bishops and the whole Church organization were making religion the instrument of tyranny instead of the faith of individuals. Nearly all Puritans accepted in some form the Calvinist division of mankind into the elect and the damned. In theory the damned included the unfortunate passive majority. In practice the struggle was against all who participated, however unwittingly, in the great campaign of evil led by the Popish Antichrist. Among the elect all were equal in the eyes of the Lord, though not in earthly status and possessions. Their election might be made manifest in their godly life and the success with which their just endeavours to improve their lot on earth would in due course be blessed. Having undergone the great inner experience of conversion, they must constantly receive the word of God through the scriptures and through preaching.

The scriptures – though Puritans would have been horrified at such a suggestion – were not important mainly for what they said. It would have been difficult for the unguided reader to derive much moral or spiritual message from such a mass of apparent inconsistencies. The primary function of the Bible was to be for every individual a talisman that gave him the assurance of direct contact with God irrespective of the mediation of a superior clerical caste. Of course the Puritan convinced himself and others, with massive quotation and summary, that he derived directly from the Bible the whole of his faith and his habits of thought and behaviour. But to do this he needed other parts of the Puritan system. One was the 'godly preaching ministry' whose sermons were for most of the flock the principal means of contact with the great conflict in the rest of the world. But the minister was not the voice of priestly authority: he differed from the congregation only in his professional skill and knowledge. Puritans learned their creed as much from their fellow laymen as from the experts.

In the successes and failures of Puritanism under Elizabeth there had emerged a difference of emphasis between those who tried to meet these needs within the established Church and the sectarians who repudiated all existing organizations and claimed a monopoly of salvation for their own saintly minority. For most, the ideal was the 'gathered church' in which all believers joined to build from below whatever organization was needed. It could take many different forms. Individual congregations, like the celebrated Coleman Street church of the City Puritans, could achieve a spontaneous unity of their own within the old establishment. During the Interregnum the English Presbyterian

Church imposed its new system, with lay participation, uneasily on the old parish structure. It never seemed to have much popular zeal behind it. The more active Puritans tended to be 'Independents' who rejected Presbyterianism as a compromise with evil and envisaged a loose alliance of congregations with a minimum of imposed uniformity. The Parlimentary army, with its regimental preachers, provided a form of 'gathering' that was hardly spontaneous but could give to its captive audience the rare satisfaction that came from proof of the Lord's blessing on their cause: they had already, by their own efforts, destroyed the power of Antichrist in its Royalist guise. How easily leadership of the cause of individualism in religion could turn into a new authoritarianism was soon apparent.

The moment when the state seemed to have disintegrated was also the great opportunity for the sects. To the true sectary the smaller his group and the further removed from temporal power, the stronger his assurance. The 'Saints' were in his view a tiny minority, unrecognized except by each other, but about to come – in some not too closely defined way – into their own. Some of the sects had sixteenth-century orgins and widespread connections. Each of them in theory should, as the sole elect, have been intolerant of all its rivals; but their common struggle against persecution made them, pending their triumph, advocate toleration for other forms of Christianity. To the vast majority the term naturally excluded popery.

Anabaptism, with its convenient insistence that infant baptism could not compel anyone to belong to a church he had not freely chosen, survived incessant attacks, particularly in England and the Netherlands. In Holland it became the creed of the urban poor, whose interests neither Remonstrants nor Counter-Remonstrants represented. It was from an alliance between Dutch and English Anabaptists that the Pilgrim Fathers sprang. Several of the civil war sects originated in Anabaptism. One of the most effective sectarian beliefs was an emphasis on the prophecies of the millennium. To the most successful of the millenarian groups, the Fifth Monarchists, the reign of Christ on earth was an immediate practical prospect, for which they could work by rebellion against the existing political order. Most of the sects were less concerned with actual revolt than with survival as an unrecognized elect. Messianic characters like Lodowick Muggleton or James Naylor could collect for a time a passionate following. Groups like the Ranters and the Family of Love sometimes attracted support and horror by meetings that turned into orgies. But the crime of most was simply to take the moral and social teaching of the New Testament seriously.

The whole period of the Civil War and Interregnum was for the sects a struggle in which the moment of triumph seemed always at hand but always postponed as one authority after another rejected the light of sainthood and imposed the tyranny of the state. Determination to resist was part of their common creed. Often they refused to pay tithe to the church they had rejected; for tithe was part not only of the hated clerical system but of the distinction between property-owner and poor. When the Presbyterian Thomas Edwards denounced sectarian principles as 'destructive to human society, to all kinds of government, political, ecclesiastical, and economical'[1] he was only exaggerating what was at that stage certainly true. Religious radicalism was inseparable from political and social radicalism. It seemed possible at last for the levelling ideas of Christianity to take on a practical meaning. Extreme Puritanism flourished most in the towns and in the army. It drew support from the artisans, the apprentices, the ordinary soldiers who were also the mainstay of democratic political movements. Puritanism was a religion of revolt. But successful revolt, in this as in everything else, could only be achieved by accepting some form of authority. To many sectaries successive new authorities seemed as bad as the old.

Some sects seemed to thrive on defeat and contraction; but for many the Protectorate and the Restoration were disappointments difficult to explain away. They tended to move away from militancy towards faith in a more remote millennium or towards renunciation of worldly activity. Partial toleration, as was intended, removed some of their appeal. The most assertive group of English dissenters after the Restoration was the Quakers. In the days of George Fox they were anything but pacific; but their energy was directed more to denouncing the sins of the church than to advertising a positive creed of their own. Dogma was the great evil; non-conformity a virtue in itself. An organized sect or systematized worship would have been seen as barriers to the direct experience of the 'inner light' that was their great source of reassurance. Under the leadership of William Penn they made toleration a major principle rather than a matter of expediency. Conversion ceased to be an important aim. Within their society there was room for a range of beliefs from visionary mysticism to an emphasis on the moral aspect of Christianity that left little of the supernatural in it. It was the Quakers who made notorious the self-conscious idiosyncrasies of dress and speech often attributed to Puritans in general. Where the law was wrong, as it usually was, it had to be rejected at whatever cost. They thrived on martyrdom, which the Stuart government provided rather half-heartedly. But they did not seek revenge. The combination of Christ-like morality with the repudiation of the state led them eventually to denounce the most universally accepted of the state's activities, war. Other Christians continued to find it compatible with their devotion to New Testament texts.

MYSTICS, PIETISTS, AND QUIETISTS

In their asceticism, introspection, and determination to save religion from the clergy, the Quakers had a good deal in common with the various forms of mystical religion that were managing to survive in both Protestant and Catholic Europe. Popular movements that asserted the power of the 'inner light' against the wealth and wordly authority of the church had existed in every age. Early in the century one of the most successful preachers and writers in this tradition was Jakob Boehme, the shoe-maker who despite Lutheran persecution spread the news of his visions of the conflict between good and evil, and the 're-birth' that would bring salvation. Half a century later Philip Spener popularized a doctrine of individual piety attractive to those who resented Calvinist or Lutheran discipline but were not consciously affected by rational doubts. If knowledge increasingly eroded the old sources of religious certainty, it was still possible to claim others that were incommunicable in words. The 'Pietists' were repelled by scholastic argument, and by what they saw as the growing worldliness and indifference of the clergy. They wanted a religion neither frightening nor complex in its creed, but giving a sense of zeal and virtue. Some found it in meeting to sing emotional hymns like those of Paul Gerhardt. Others devoted themselves to religious teaching and organized charity. In Brandenburg at the end of the century, Halle became a great centre of Pietist activity, with its new university, a model orphanage, schools, and religious presses. Amorphous though Pietism was, a variety of later dissenting groups, including the Moravian Brethren and the Methodists, claimed it as one of their origins.

'Quietism' was a cult different from Pietism less in its mood than in the people to whom it appealed. This too was an anti-clerical, individualist form of religion with strongly mystical tendencies. It began in the followers of the Spanish priest Miguel Molinos who acquired a fashionable reputation in both Rome and Paris – though he was eventually imprisoned by the Inquisition. In the 1680s French high society was full of the reputation of Madame Guyon, whose claims to direct divine guidance closely resembled those of modern spiritualist mediums, and who won devotees in much the same way. The Quietists sought only the annihilation of all individual activity in the love of God. Nevertheless, Madame Guyon became a centre less of tranquillity than of intrigue and faction. Not only the dilettante philosophers of the court were involved, but also the two outstanding French theologians, François Fénelon and Jacques-Bénigne Bossuet. Fénelon, the passionate intellectual, the believer in educational reform and cautious critic of the monarchy, came completely under her spell. Bossuet, the bishop, historian, and rigid upholder of authority, was one of the principal destroyers of the cult.

JANSENISM

The most effective independent religious movement in Louis XIV's France, Jansenism, managed to combine an element of mysticism with an almost Calvinist view of redemption. Cornelius Jansen was an old-style theologian at Louvain, who in his *Augustinus* set out, like countless other writers, the views of St Augustine in a manner slanted for his own purpose – to attack the Jesuits. Obedience, and the power of the confessor, on which Jesuit influence was based, depended on free will. To extol the role in salvation of Grace at the expense of free will was therefore to diminish Jesuit authority. Jansen's two associates, Duvergier de Hauranne, Abbé de St Cyran, and Antoine Arnauld, were largely responsible for reforming the two Convents of Port Royal, one in Paris and one in the country, which became the headquarters of an aristocratic and intellectual clique devoted to propaganda and to educational work. Arnauld's daughter was made abbess at the age of seven. His son, the younger Antoine, who became its effective master, was the author of the tract, *De la Fréquente Communion*, which provided the popular source of Jansenist arguments. With its associated semi-monastic male group, Port Royal was a fashionable centre of hostility to the court. Its reputation was enhanced by the miraculous powers of its fragment of the Crown of Thorns. But Jansenism was not simply an affair of a rich intellectual clique. It managed to fulfil in a small way the role of an opposition creed which Puritanism played in England. De Retz and many of the Frondeurs held Jansenist views. Against it the Jesuits had the support of the Sorbonne, and of Pope Innocent X. His Bull of 1653 condemning five 'Propositions' which it said were in the *Augustinus* led to an intricate argument that involved the vital question of the relationship between faith defined authoritatively and observed fact. If the pope said the Propositions were heretical, the Jansenists would accept his ruling. But on the factual question of whether they were in Jansen's book, they insisted that he was wrong. The style of the law-courts was mixed with that of theologians in the quarrel, and in the intermittent attempts at compromise. In 1661 the nuns of Port Royal were expelled and their schools closed. In 1667, after approaches from the French diplomat Lionne, Clement IX produced a formula in which the crucial phrase 'purely and simply' was replaced by 'sincerely'. Since this, for reasons clear to theologians, made all the difference, Port Royal was restored, and was more readily tolerated in Rome because of its continued disagreements with Gallicanism. Only in Louis' fanatical last years was it eventually destroyed.

The greatest figure in the controversy was not regarded as a thorough-going Jansenist. Blaise Pascal, whose *Lettres Provinciales*, written at Port Royal des Champs between 1655 and 1657, are a masterpiece of ironical denunciation, did not find in Jansenism a complete answer to his quest for certainty. His attack on Jesuit casuistry was so merciless and enjoyable that he came to fear the popularity it achieved among people who might apply it more widely than he intended. Jansenism, in attacking the Jesuit version of Catholic dogma, sometimes seemed close to rejecting the Church, or even Churches in general. Its later leaders Pierre Nicole and his successor the fiery Pasquier Quesnel, were eager to provoke a further conflict with the Jesuits in the hope of getting them expelled from the country entirely. But the new Jansenist writings were condemned uncompromisingly in two Papal Bulls, *Vineam Domini* in 1705 and *Unigenitus* in 1713. By then the movement was more deeply involved in a struggle of quite different origins – for the 'liberties' of the Gallican Church. Jansenist bishops were the first to oppose the extension of the *régale* (see pp. 511–2), while Jesuits, on bad terms with Innocent X, found themselves supporting the Crown. Neither now appeared to find their theological views relevant to any serious criticism of the society or state they lived in.

THE ORTHODOX CHURCH

In 1600 there were something like 42 million Europeans in Catholic areas and 28 million under some form of Protestantism. It is easy to forget that perhaps another 28 million belonged to the Orthodox Churches. In the fifteenth century the Russian Church had broken with the Greek Church, and each now claimed to be the only guardian of the true Christian religion. Some two-thirds of Orthodox Christians were Russian, with about half a million more in Poland; the rest were subjects of the Ottoman Empire, in whose European territories Islam was in general the religion of the rulers, Greek Orthodox Christianity that of the ruled. The Christians were not greatly oppressed. The Greek patriarchs and bishops were encouraged to exercise some of the judicial authority that was an essential part of the functions of the Moslem Institution. The Greek Church was too disunited to be much of a threat to Moslem power. The Patriarch of Ipek, the Archbishop of Ohrid, and the Bishops of Cetinje were ecclesiastical magnates largely independent of the Patriarch of Constantinople. In Bosnia, formerly the centre of the Bogomil heresy, native landowners had accepted Islam and left Christianity an ill-organized religion of the poor. In Albania it had almost disappeared. Greek Orthodoxy had been as inflexible and authoritarian as any creed could be; but during the century it became a little more tolerant, at least of Catholicism. The retreat of the Turks after their attack on Vienna in 1683 enabled Catholics to penetrate into areas from which they had been firmly excluded. It even seemed possible that the Papacy might achieve a partial reunion with the Greek Church, as had been attempted in Poland. But when the Turkish frontiers became more stable, the Orthodox Church remained isolated and politically ineffective. The one source of concern about it to the Ottoman rulers was that despite the theological disputes it provided a link between the Christian minorities and Russia.

In religion, as in so much else, Russia provided a grim exaggeration of the troubles of the west. The claims of the Russian Orthodox Church to a monopoly of true belief were demonstrated largely by passionate adherence to its garbled and often nonsensical texts and to its ritual. There were a few matters still open to learned dispute: the question whether 'Alleluia' should be said three times or only twice had been debated for a hundred years or so. But the service as a whole remained in theory untouchable, even if its insufferable length had been mitigated sometimes by performing three different parts of it simultaneously. The sacred words moved gradually further from their Greek origins, through being learnt parrot-wise by generations of illiterate clergy who knew no Greek at all. It was a magical religion, in which neither moral teaching nor biblical history played much part. The redemption of the soul, the curing of disease, and the growth of crops were among the benefits to be secured through the exact repetition by the priest of formulae meaningless to his flock and usually to himself. Equally necessary was the worship of icons, which at due times provided miraculous demonstrations of their power. Village priests lived on much the same level of poverty and ignorance as the peasants; but they were the lowest stratum of a clerical society comparable in wealth and power with the state itself.

The wealth of the Church had increased enormously during the sixteenth century, partly through acquisitions in newly conquered areas, partly by growing pressure on landowners to save their souls by bequests to the church. Since Church property escaped taxation, the landowner often found it profitable to hand over his estate and retain the use of it during his life. In some central areas the Church now held a third of all the arable land. Over the inhabitants of its estates it exercised almost complete judicial power, as it did over clergy everywhere. Most of its land was monastic. Even more than in Spain monastic life offered the best prospect of escape from the brutalities of the state and the landlord The Trinity Sergius Monastery became, in the years of the 'Troubles', a capital of the religious and intellectual community more effective than was Moscow for the laity. Loyalty to the state was inseparable from loyalty to the Church. For a century or more Moscow had been seen by those of its subjects who were aware of such things as the 'Third Rome', the empire chosen to guard the true faith until the millennium. The tsar was the 'Holy Father', a figure who, whatever the failings of his real manifestation in the palaces, could be presented to village congregations as a god-like, even an immortal, being. Any serious attack on the ways of the Church could only be the work of an Antichrist who was equally an enemy of the tsar and was infallibly destined to be destroyed.

Nevertheless the seventeenth century saw such attacks develop. There was an enormous gulf between the unchanging church of the priests and lesser monasteries and that of the higher clergy at the centre, among whom doctrinal quarrels were familiar enough. Only they, at the beginning of the century, were aware of the pressure on the Orthodox Church, both from the Greek hierarchy which was reasserting its own theological superiority, and from the west. In 1595 the Polish Orthodox Church had announced its reunion with Rome – though many of its members refused to accept this and became a persecuted minority. Jesuits saw the new 'Uniate Church' as a means of extending their work into Russia. When Polish armies invaded an almost helpless Russia, bringing militant Catholicism with them, it seemed possible that Orthodoxy might begin to disintegrate at the centre. But Church and state survived the 'Troubles' together. The Church was rescued in the course of the century by the ruthless work of its two mighty Patriarchs. Filaret, appointed in 1619, was a Wolsey magnified to the Russian scale (see p. 426). His experiences in Poland had made him a ferocious opponent of everything tainted with Latinizing. After removing all potential rivals and enemies he used his authority to introduce a firmer clerical discipline and encouraged the monasteries to do something towards producing a rather more educated clergy. But he had no intention of giving the Church any institutional independence. The strengthening of the state in the 30s and 40s brought the Church more closely into the civil machine. The legal code of 1649 (see pp. 431–2) established a new department to control its temporal affairs and encroached a good deal on its judicial functions. At the moment when a real secularization of the state seemed possible there appeared the second of the great Patriarchs, Nikon. On the face of it, Nikon's position was the same as that of Filaret. But their aims had not much in common. Nikon was a peasant, who had risen in the Church by his own ambition and unscrupulous skill. He did not merely seek for the Church an equal partnership in the landlord-dominated, isolated Holy Russia: he dreamed of the Universal Church, with the Russian Patriarch as its greatest potentate. To achieve this it was necessary to restore first the unity of the Greek and Russian forms of Orthodoxy – which meant accepting reform of the debased Russian texts and rituals. The corrected text, and the Greek view on such passionately argued matters as how many fingers should be used in making the sign of the cross, were imposed by Nikon almost without warning. From churches and houses images that did not fit the new rules were thrown out by Nikon's inquisitorial teams; and there was never a shortage of disasters for which this could be blamed. It could only be done haphazardly: clergy who resisted never knew whether they would be left to continue the old prac- tices in peace or sent to Siberia. Many did their best to cope with the incomprehensible demands; but year by year resistance grew, by every means from martyrdom to armed revolt. Russia soon experienced a phenomenon that most western countries knew only too well, a militant religious minority.

Nikon was not at first much alarmed by the appearance of the *staroveri*, the Old Believers. (The other term for them, *raskolniki* – schismatics – was used mainly by their opponents.) They would, he supposed, prove to be a mass of helpless peasants led by a few nobles and court intriguers exploiting the disputes for their own benefit. In fact they became a movement so widespread and diverse that almost any opposition to established authority could be attached to it. Its core came to be the 'easteners' who resisted the centralized state in every way. In 1666 Nikon, having quarrelled with the tsar and misjudged the extent of his support, was tried by a Church Council, with the tsar as prosecutor, and banished; but the Church had firmly accepted his reforms. In the priest Avvakum – Habakkuk – the Old Believers found a hero- figure who was eventually burnt at the stake. Successive waves of mass suicides by burning swept across the north. Old Believers fled from the state to set up primitive free communities in the forest. Some, paradoxically, arrived at the very new belief that the clergy had betrayed the true Church, and must be dispensed with entirely. The Cossacks happily retained the Old Belief. In the far north the Solovetsky monastery withstood a siege of eight years before it surrendered. Only very slowly could mass persecution on one side and mass hysteria on the other turn into the stolid conservatism of the outcast group.

ISLAM

There was another religion in Europe, about which Christians of every kind were very ignorant. How many true believers in Allah there were in the Turkish-occupied lands, and in southern Spain, is impossible to say. It was not as difficult as outsiders supposed to move between the two faiths or to conform as circumstances required to one or the other. Islam, no less than Christianity, was derived from the Hebrew scriptures. Allah, the one god, was readily identifiable with Jehovah. Christ had been one of the messengers of Allah, and the crucifixion was a sin perpetrated by the Jews that put them a stage further than Christians from being acceptable. Both were People of the Book who should be treated politely and told that they shared with Islam the same god. This remarkable tolerance might appear incompatible with the doctrine of the Jihad, the Holy War, to participate in which was the surest way to salvation. Its aim now was territorial conquest rather than destruction of unbelievers. The Jihad was an incentive to war better than any that Christianity had provided since the crusades, and could excuse most of the usual war atrocities; but it was not an obstacle to forming alliances either with the west or with conquered nations. Christians especially could be taken, forcibly or otherwise, into the service of the sultan and his subjects.

Islam had in origin an advantage over western Christianity: the supposedly historical events on which it rested did not occur in some remote part of the world or in a society different in its life and environment from the one that read the holy writings, but in and around the central possessions of its empire. Wildernesses, camels, and plagues of locusts were familiar; Arabic language and culture had changed comparatively little. Mohammed had been a ruler as well as a prophet, and the Shari'a, the sacred law derived from his teaching, was to a great extent the civil and criminal law of the state. The Koran, chaotic though it was, laid down practical rules for living that were still applicable. When Mecca had replaced Jerusalem as the Holy City, it was already a place of pilgrimage and a centre of caravan routes accessible to the great majority of the faithful. Successive caliphs had a temporal power greater than any pope had achieved. But even more than the popes they had faced divisions within the faith that curtailed their authority. The disputes had arisen soon after the death of the Prophet, in a form that to the west looked more like a royal succession question than a religious schism. The Shi'a were those who insisted that Mohammed's successors were the descendants of his son-in-law Ali; the Sunni claimed that his authority had passed to his disciples or counsellors, the leader of whom, Abu-Bakr, became the first caliph. The Ottoman Empire in the seventeenth century was controlled by the established Sunni rulers; the Shi'a were a minority from whom an assortment of local sects, orders and communities had arisen. The long wars against Persia were in origin a conflict between the Sunni Ottoman sultans and a Shi'a sect that in the early sixteenth century had built up an army in the Caspian region and conquered a vast area of modern Iraq and Iran. The victories of European Protestantism were slow and tepid in comparison. But they had something in common. Allah, it was agreed, would on the last day divide all men between heaven and hell. It left open the possibility of predestination; and the minority sects were often convinced of their own exclusive guarantee of salvation. The Sunni rulers could afford to be more tolerant; Allah demanded generosity to the weak, the poor, and the oppressed. It could include unorthodox sects, holy men, dervishes and preachers – as long as they behaved themselves.

DOUBT

To look at the strength of churches almost everywhere, at the popular belief in miracle-working, divine retribution, and immortality, or at the learned disputes over the Gallican Articles in France and the complex theological feuds in Germany does not give the impression that religious belief was declining. Nevertheless, in the second half of the century many strands of thought and behaviour were leading away from the domination of life and thought by Christian doctrine. For ordinary people whose parents and grandparents had lived through a succession of religious changes imposed by armies or politicians it was not obvious that the clergy they happened to have now were endowed with the only true faith. For scholars the intellectual certainty even of the fundamental Christian beliefs had gone. New reasoning and new observation led to conclusions that might not disprove the existence of a god but were not compatible with the biblical accounts of the universe. In universities the most talked-of modern thinker was now Descartes (see pp. 166–7). Perhaps unjustly, he became the figurehead of the trend towards solving – or evading – the difficulties by treating the material and the spiritual as two separate spheres. Descartes' God, whose existence he proved by a version of the old 'ontological' argument, had created the material universe and now preserved it but did not interfere with its working. To Cartesians everything, from the stars to the newly found microscopic creatures, must be explained without reference to biblical texts or mystical principles. If some answers were wrong this did not matter as much as the recognition that better ones might be found. Descartes was in fact regarded by both disciples and enemies as the great advocate of the 'dualism' by which study of the material universe could continue unimpeded by faith in an immaterial one. However certain his conclusions appeared to him, he would not, he claimed, 'for anything in the world uphold them against the authority of the Church'.[2] The Church refrained from persecuting him; but his works remained on the index of forbidden books. The more popular Cartesianism became with educated Frenchmen, the greater the Church's hostility.

Most of the eminent philosophers in one way or another rejected ecclesiastical authority without coming near to atheism. Gottfried Liebnitz (see p. 178), despite his own complex ideas of the relation between God and the universe, was a Protestant willing to defend orthodox Christianity, miracles included, not as a certainty but as a possibility. He took up energetically the cause of union between all the Churches, with arguments that led him sometimes to a general questioning of scriptural authority. That, in the opinion of his antagonist Bossuet, showed the danger of specious attempts at harmony in religion. Benedict Spinoza (see p. 223) was, as a Jew, unencumbered by attachment to any Christian church. His God was the whole substance of the universe, timeless, self-creating, unconcerned with human affairs.

The Old Testament showed how religion was exploited by monarchs as a means of strengthening their own rule. Religious authorities had designed their doctrines to 'impress the minds of the masses with devotion'. The feeling that to question established religion was to encourage sedition and discontent was common everywhere. Hobbes (see pp. 219–22) had devoted a large part of *Leviathan* to investigation of scripture and miracles, making his own scepticism clear but insisting that whatever intelligent men might think in private they should uphold religion in public for the good of the state. Doctrine must be determined 'by them that under God have sovereign power'.

Hobbes was writing at a time when 'sovereign power' was changing hands with bewildering frequency. But through all the bitter religious conflicts in England there had survived a quiet humanism that deplored both Laudian authority and Puritan fanaticism. Before the Civil War the little circle of scholarly gentry at Great Tew discussed the virtues of tolerance and Christian unity. After the war the Cambridge Platonists, aware of the implications of scientific discovery, argued that if complex religious dogma could be escaped reason and revelation would somehow lead to the same conclusions. The Latitudinarian movement within the Church offered to scientists the assurance that all their discoveries were demonstrating the power and goodness of the Creator and thereby strengthening religious belief. But behind the effort of all these schools of thought there was anxiety: to say that reason and new knowledge were compatible with the existence of a God did not mean they supported faith in the biblical story of the creation, the fall, and the redemption or in the God who upset the course of nature in response to persuasion by prayer. A different solution to the contradictions was put forward by the Deists, who by stressing the perfection of God's works, including the rational faculty in man, were able to leave Christian revelation as either a supplement to reason or, for the more daring, a contradiction to be rejected. The most soothing version of it was that of John Toland who asserted that once the absurd accretions of theologians had been removed there was nothing mysterious or irrational in the essentials of Christianity. It was a view that left many obvious difficulties unanswered.

A few writers were able to face the conflict between faith and reason openly. France produced – and drove out – one figure who was always sure of an audience for the most unconventional religious views. Pierre Bayle has a good claim to be the first popular journalist of literary and intellectual criticism. In his monthly *Nouvelles de la République des Lettres*, published in the Netherlands, he poured forth, from 1684 to 1687, a spate of brilliant invective against Catholic tyranny and intolerance. He flatly denounced belief in miracles as an insult to a God who had no cause to break his own laws. Then, in the *Dictionnaire historique et critique*, he adopted a new technique. In the guise of factual information he was able to present to those prepared to search for it a massive demonstration of the inconsistencies, distortions, and pretentious nonsense that filled the work of the most respected writers. His own conviction that nothing was certain grew as the work went on. This was not the doubt of Descartes that had permitted a selective re-establishing of beliefs. It was doubt that remained universal. The scriptures were not exempt from the process of questioning. Between the religious and the rational outlooks, no compromise was defensible. This did not mean that reason could offer definitive answers to fundamental questions; but at least it could admit its inability to do so.

Bayle never claimed to have formulated a coherent system of thought. He did not admit to being an atheist, though he had come to attack the Protestantism in which he had once believed as bitterly as all other religions. Some of his pronouncements make him appear to be a Deist, accepting a God unrelated to revelation, salvation, or morality. But the term his innumerable enemies commonly applied to him was 'Socinian'. The sect that derived its name and original form from the ideas of the Italians Laelius Socinus and his nephew Faustus had a different character from most of its kind. Faustus, who had travelled through Europe on his heretical missions, had his first successes in Poland and Transylvania. After popular demonstrations were organized against them by the church, their followers migrated to Germany, France and Holland, from which the creed soon spread to England. Their shocking belief was in unitarianism. To deny the Trinity, and hence the divinity of Christ, was regarded as tantamount to atheism. In many western countries, Socinianism in a more questioning form became a creed of intellectuals who sought to reconcile rationalism with some kind of religious belief. From Grotius at the beginning of the century to Newton at the end, some outstanding minds found themselves nearer to Socinianism than to any other religion. Its emphasis now was less on a set of heretical opinions than on the application of rational tests to every element of religious dogma. The moral aspect of Christianity could, it was implied, be separated from the miraculous.

It was another Frenchman, Richard Simon, who made the critical study of the Bible a matter for public dispute. One demonstration of the power religion had held is that through so many centuries the text of the scriptures had been minutely studied and debated by men of high intelligence with hardly a thought being given to the obvious human explanations of the contradictions and improbabilities. Textual corruption had been considered as an explanation of minor difficulties; but it was not contemplated that biblical writers or their sources could be subject to human fallibility, let alone ulterior motives. The notion of biblical narratives as allegories had appeared from time to time as a daring aberration. Spinoza had set out principles on which scientific method could be applied to an investigation of the Bible. That could be brushed aside as the blaspheming of a Jew. But Simon was a Christian priest and a member of the Oratory until it expelled him. Despite the immense learning in his work, its conclusions were readily comprehensible. His *Histoire critique du Vieux Testament* of 1678 was followed by a series of studies of the New Testament on the same lines. All the powers of suppression that state and Church could muster were used to prevent him from becoming widely known. His enemies may well have seen more clearly than he did where his ideas would lead: for Simon himself claimed to remain a good Catholic.

WITCHCRAFT

In religion as in most things we know very little about the thinking of ordinary people. But in one form of belief in the supernatural there were spectacular changes that depended almost entirely on popular notions. For at least the first half of the century most of the people in most of Europe had no doubt that witchcraft was a constant and menacing reality; by 1700 the belief had retreated into the background of vague superstitions. The medieval Church had attacked witchcraft and sorcery, but on the whole had treated it as an unimportant aberration of the ignorant. Village communities commonly included eccentric men and women who claimed supernatural powers, especially of healing and prophecy. Some of their purported achievements had an awkward similarity to those of the clergy themselves: the uneducated might not distinguish clearly the Latin text and the holy relic from the magic incantation and the hare's foot. It was helpful to the Church to denounce witches as agents of Satan. At the end of the fifteenth century papal pronouncements made the pact with the Devil a central feature of witchcraft. The white witch and the cunning man became gradually less notorious than the sinister woman who brought about all the unexplained deaths, crop failures, storms, and murrains. Rural society was never short of disasters. Throughout the sixteenth century the fear had grown. Men and women of every religious allegiance and every social class seemed equally ready to believe that they were surrounded by wielders of diabolical power who must be sought out and extirpated. As the churches reiterated, there was authority in the Book of Exodus for slaying witches. All too clearly the trials and executions brought not only temporary relief from fear but the pleasures of mass revenge. Inevitably the evidence about witchcraft comes mainly from the records of the persecutors. Confessions that were built up from legal and popular tradition were easily put into the mouths of victims who knew just what was expected, and could often be reduced to believing or half-believing the stories. Torture or the threat of it was useful – though torture was not used in England where nevertheless much the same evidence was produced. It is disturbing for the historian who has to compare the value of his sources to realize that the habits of the Devil when he appeared in human or animal form are recorded more voluminously and with greater precision than many of the social and economic facts we rely on. The subject has been studied intensively in recent years; and the more is known the less likely it seems that there was any residue of fact in the idea that witchcraft was a survival from a pre-Christian religion or that members of an underground cult assembled on local hilltops on the High Days to indulge in frenzied sexual orgies. Magic was certainly a part of folk-lore everywhere; diabolical witchcraft was largely the creation of churches, writers, and lawyers.

There is no single explanation of the rise of witch beliefs. If the Reformation contributed to the panics, it was not because of any great difference between Catholic, Lutheran, and Calvinist atti-

tudes. The ending of a single unquestioned religion may sometimes have added to the zeal for persecuting unaccepted practices.
There was little witch-hunting in Spain or Portugal, where the
Inquisition upheld conformity and provided other victims for
popular hostility. There was little in Protestant Holland. Some
witches had been executed there in the sixteenth century; but the
last were in the 1590s, the time when in equally Protestant Scotland James VI himself was leading one of the most extensive
persecutions in Europe. A thousand executions in Scotland seems
to be a fair estimate, most of them in the more prosperous
regions. James developed a belief that witches were responsible
for all his troubles, and became an expert about them. His work
on demonology put him among the many pamphleteers whose
popularity showed how printing and literacy could spread darkness as well as light. Before he came to the English throne he had
grown cautiously sceptical and enjoyed exposing cases of
fraudulent or hysterical 'possession'. Local Scottish courts were
forbidden to try witches. In England the first wave of witch-
hunting had been in the middle Elizabethan decades: there is no
evidence that James was responsible for its revival in his reign.
The Civil War was another period of persecution. But it cannot
be explained simply by wartime distress. Matthew Hopkins, the
notorious 'witch-finder general' carried out most of his work in
Essex and East Anglia, prosperous and comparatively little
affected by the fighting. Nor was there any decisive link with
puritanism: a witch-panic could explode in almost any village
community. English witches probably had a better chance of
acquittal than most; and the sentence on them was hanging, not
burning. German states produced some of the worst horrors. In
the 1620s the Prince-Bishops of Bamberg and Würzburg between
them held well over a thousand burnings. The Rhineland bishoprics were almost as bad. Here too there was no great difference
between Catholic and Protestant areas; and though the distress
and disorder produced by the Thirty Years War provided conditions that favoured the panics, local disasters were less important
than the presence of a few enthusiastic and powerful witch-
hunters. The western side of the Rhine, Franche-Comté and
Lorraine, claimed as many witches as the eastern. German and
French victims were by no means always old women. The
isolated widow was always the obvious character to fit the standard definitions of a witch; but children, equally defenceless, were

also liable to behave in ways that indicated possession by the Devil. Even clergy could occasionally find that the line between their activities and those of witches was thin enough to put them among the accused instead of the accusers.

One witch trial and one public execution regularly led to others. Much of the evidence consisted of events that were in reality happening all the time; and the aim of the prosecutor was not only to convict one witch but to extract the names of others. It provided a way for the victim to have posthumous revenge on old enemies, and for one village or group to damage another. Possibly the danger of witch-panics was increased when religious conformity had been shaken and was being re-imposed. Calvinists and Jesuits alike were, it can be claimed, more zealous witch-hunters than their less ardent contemporaries. Both stressed the doctrines of sin and damnation. One of the last episodes of persecution was in Sweden, where the Lutheran Church after the defection of Queen Christina became more zealous and intolerant than before. Churches, governments, lawyers and landowners had obvious reasons for at least not discouraging popular hostility that was turned against an insignificant few. There remains the most alarming aspect of all – that intellectual leaders of every kind joined in the outcries or at best kept silent. Bacon, Descartes, and Kepler all accepted witchcraft as a reality. Bodin had been one of the most insistent persecutors. Those who opposed the fear and cruelty did not question the existence of witchcraft: they merely claimed that malicious denunciations or confessions extracted under torture were not adequate proof of guilt and that some professed witches were deluded or fraudulent. Only a few eccentrics like the Dutchman Balthasar Bekker in the 1690s went so far as to deny that the Devil interfered in human affairs at all. Bekker had little support.

The decline of witch-hunting could not be acclaimed as a triumph of reason over superstition. When the fears of great evil conspiracies receded, most people still believed in lesser forms of magic. To the peasant it remained as much a part of life as the laws of the landlord and the state. There were still many statesmen, generals, and scientists who thought astrology worth taking into account. Throughout literate society it was necessary for all but the most defiant to adopt a double, or rather a multiple, standard of belief. For most practical purposes the universe had become a mechanistic one. The supernatural could occupy a larger or a smaller segment of the mind according to circumstances; and this applied to Christian as well as to non-Christian beliefs. The connection was proclaimed, for his own ends, by Jopseh Glanvill, the most popular of the English defenders of witch-beliefs at the time when they were receding into the background:

Those that dare not bluntly say, 'There is no God' content themselves (for a fair step and introduction) to deny that there are spirits and witches.[3]

It was a smear with some logical sense behind it. Most of those who believed in sporadic divine interference with the workings of nature, and who accepted the Christian doctrine of a personal Devil as well as a personal God, now denounced the hysteria and injustice of witch persecution. They could not easily claim that the supposed supernatural happenings were either impossible or unimportant. Total rejection of the discredited notion of witchcraft could only come as part of a separation of religious ways of thought from those on which daily life was based. All who were aware of the general field of human knowledge and thought could see that within it the area of the scientific and the material was expanding at the expense of that of the divine and the magical. In the first, certainty was steadily increasing, in the second, doubt. If between the two there was a vast no-man's-land of ambiguity and hypocrisy, we are in no position to sneer today.

NOTES AND REFERENCES

1 *Gangraena* (1646), part III, p. 262, reprinted by *Rota* (Exeter, 1977) and quoted in C. Hill and E. Dell (eds), *The Good Old Cause* (London, 1949), p. 320.

2 Letter from Descartes to Mersenne, April 1634.

3 *Philosophical Considerations touching Witches and Witchcraft* (1667).

6

SCIENCE

In most kinds of human activity the seventeenth century was, in the end, a time of failure. Hopeful revolutions were crushed; political and social ideals faded; intolerance and oppression flourished; hardly anything was done to mitigate disease and famine; where material resources increased, they were squandered in war. No other century until the twentieth produced so much deliberate destruction. But in one achievement these years are outstanding: the great barriers in human thought that held back the understanding of the material universe were decisively breached. The 'Scientific[1] Revolution', a term that would have meant nothing to historians of the period a couple of generations ago, is now recognized as one of its most significant aspects. Those who reject the word 'revolution' in this context are usually concerned not to deny the achievements of the century but to stress that, for instance, Greece, medieval Europe, and the renaissance made impressive discoveries. None of them came anything like as close to an understanding of how factual information could be tested, quantified, and improved.

There are in practice two ways in which knowledge of the world and its inhabitants can be accepted: statements can be believed because they have 'always' been believed, because 'everyone' believes them, because they are asserted by unchallenged authorities; or they can be believed because observation and reasoning make them appear more likely than any alternatives, and because they are compatible with other beliefs established in the same way. Few individuals have exclusively one kind of outlook or the other; and it cannot be claimed that any seventeenth-century scientist crossed completely the barriers that were maintained by tradition and authority. Everyone knows the legend of Galileo recanting his errors before the Inquisition and murmuring 'All the same, it does move.' The story itself is as unscientific a piece of history as anyone could find: it seems to have been invented in the eighteenth century. But Galileo and most such men did behave in the way the remark suggests. They were neither martyrs nor rebels by nature: they insisted that new knowledge was compatible with old belief. From Kepler at the beginning of the century to Newton at the end, the most eminent scientists were fascinated by such pursuits as alchemy, astrology, or numerology that now seem wholly irrational.

Galileo made his explanation of the Bible's misstatements about the material universe perfectly clear: they were there because it was intended for the common people who would be confused by more unfamiliar versions. He did not claim any originality for such a view. St Augustine had insisted that the scriptures should not be taken as a literal explanation of physical phenomena: for 'why should the Bible be believed concerning the resurrection of the dead . . . when it is considered to be erroneously written as to points which admit of direct demonstration or unquestionable reasoning?'[2] Even the later enthusiasm for the study of geology and of fossils led men to ask not whether but how their evidence could be reconciled with the story of the creation and the flood. But religion was not the only kind of dogma. If the authority of the Bible could not be attacked, the authority of the 'ancients', and in particular of Aristotle, undoubtedly could. A century earlier the concern of Renaissance philosophy with Plato had deprived Aristotle of some of his pre-eminence. To denounce him – or at least his devotees – as the personification of an anti-scientific attitude now became a typical mark of the new scholarship.

BACON

One of the most forthright enemies of all authority that restricted the quest for knowledge was Francis Bacon. Whatever his merits as a lawyer and writer, he has never had unqualified admiration from scientists. He rejected Copernicus, saw no useful connection between science and mathematics, believed in indiscriminate rather than planned experiments, distrusted deduction from general principles. He also had a great capacity for proclaiming other people's ideas as his own. Nevertheless, even though he did not always stress the infinite amount that was yet to be discovered, he did more than anyone to destroy the idea of the Aristotelians that little of importance remained to be added to human knowledge. He had no patience with those who 'almost incorporated the contentious philosophy of Aristotle into the Christian religion', and who thought that 'the secrets of nature were secrets of God' into which men should not probe.[3] Baconian science, whatever its intellectual shortcomings, was full of optimism and of practical purpose. His scheme for the 'advancement of learning' blended – some would say confused – its utilitarian aspect with a vision of knowledge expanding for its own sake. In England at least, his prestige and the popularity of his writings did much to make scientific activity reputable.

ASTRONOMY

The most controversial of the early seventeenth-century scientific activities was clearly that of the astronomers. They could claim practical reasons for their studies: predictions about the moon and tides, charts of the stars for navigation, and even the calendar itself were notoriously inaccurate; and any mistakes in astrological prediction of human affairs were likewise attributed to mistakes in observation. By 1600 the work of Copernicus, written seventy years before, was fairly well known to scholars. It had been designed partly to remove the observational inconsistencies and unnecessary complexities in Ptolemy's system of spheres, partly perhaps to uphold a mystical belief in the sun as the source of life. The idea of the sun as the centre of the universe was not entirely novel, and though Protestants attacked it as contrary to biblical texts, the Catholic Church was not at first much worried. The strong religious objections only came when followers of Copernicus suggested that a universe that appears unchanged from different positions of a moving earth must be infinitely large and presumably contained other inhabited planets. One of the offences of Giordano Bruno was that he had supported this notion of the 'Plurality of worlds'. A multiplicity of redeeming Christs was an intolerable heresy. This was an objection of theologians. The greater danger to religion came when observation of the universe seemed to suggest that it could keep going without a divine power to drive it. When the churches found that astronomers, whatever they said, were making a personal God less necessary, they began to attack them with the familiar weapon of biblical texts. It was this attack that first showed the Catholic Church as more hostile than Protestantism to the 'new philosphy'.

GALILEO

In 1609 Galileo Galilei heard how 'a certain Fleming' had devised a glass by which distant objects were made to appear nearer. Here, he realized, was an invention that might help to settle through observation the conflict between the Ptolemaic and the Copernican systems. But Galileo was not primarily an observer or experimenter. He had become a distinguished Professor of Mathematics at Padua, already a centre of scientific ideas and of comparative freedom from authoritarian interference with scholarship. It was through mathematics rather than through the unreliable evidence of the senses that Galileo sought to discover laws of motion. But though his theories were those of Plato's idealism, he could never resist the pleasure of experiment – and not always the temptation to be too readily convinced that it had given the right result. Aristotle's view that the heavier a body the more rapidly it fell could be questioned simply by imagining what happens if two stones of unequal weight are tied together and dropped. Mathematics alone could show what the rate of acceleration must be. Galielo still spent enormous energy on the famous experiments with pendulums and with balls rolled down an inclined plane. In his first sophisticated formulae relating weight, acceleration, and motion, he accepted the idea that motion must arise either from 'impetus' or from the 'tendency' of bodies to return to their original place. Gradually his emphasis turned from the cause of motion to the calculation of its change. The idea of an 'inertia' of motion as well as of rest replaced the Aristotelian assumption that only continued force could maintain movement. No experiment on earth could show this directly. But the orbits of the planets could be an instance of motion without resistance; this mathematical aspect of astronomy was naturally not grasped by those who saw his teachings simply as an attack on established belief. Nor was it the only thing that mattered to Galileo himself.

Within a few months of his first experiment with lenses, he had a telescope that revealed the moons revolving round Jupiter and the innumerable stars of the Milky Way. A year later, in 1610, his pamphlet *Siderius Nuncius* (meaning, he said, news of the stars – not that he was claiming to be a messenger of heaven) set down some of the revelations of the telescope. Its success among scholars made the Jesuits and the Inquisition take up Copernican astronomy as a major topic of theological arguments – some highly abstruse, some on the level of 'How did Joshua stop the sun if it was not moving?' At this stage the new ideas were regarded not as damnable heresy but as matter for argument, sometimes bitter, sometimes good-humoured. 'Ye Galileans, why stand ye gazing up into heaven?'[4] Father Cacchini, who was reported to have taken this as the text of a sermon that became celebrated for its violence, was so sweeping and irresponsible in his denunciation of every intelligent idea that Galileo could make good use of him. The replies, written in Italian and full of gently ironical concessions, avoided outright heresy. But they established his success, unique among the leaders of the new thought, as a popular writer, and it was popularity that made him a menace to the authority of the Church. He could no longer be taken lightly. Hence in 1615 came Galileo's first trial by the Holy Office, in which he recanted his errors and was let off with the penalty of reciting seven psalms a week. If it was hoped that this would cure him, the optimism was mutual. For Galileo did not question that the Catholic Church was a desirable institution: so great was its wisdom that eventually it would see it was mistaken in per-secuting him. Meanwhile it was better to accept its mistakes than let it make a worse one in killing him.

In 1632 Galileo produced his *Dialogue on the two chief systems of the world*, ostensibly an impartial debate between Copernican ideas and those of the Ptolemaics and Aristotelians who 'make an oracle of a log'. It was enjoyed everywhere as a triumph for heliocentric theory over the church. The church returned to the attack and, despite further abjurations, he spent his last years in fairly lenient imprisonment. By then he had produced arguments that, imperfect and sometimes self-contradictory though they were, destroyed all rational belief in Aristotle's tightly knit system. He had no equally comprehensive or unified system to put in its place: his answers were not complete, and usually not quite right. He did not use the telescope for accurate observation. His own preconceptions in favour of simplicity – especially his belief that all orbits are circular – were almost as unscientific as those he scoffed at. He was by no means averse from constructing a theory first, making observations second, and if they disagreed concluding that the observations must be wrong. His mathematical knowledge was applied more in formulae than in measurement. His conclusions are qualitative rather than quantitative, and very many of them destructive rather than constructive. But ignorance has never, since his attack, been quite as easy to preserve.

KEPLER

The astronomer who went furthest towards our own notions of the universe, Johann Kepler, was completely different in outlook, achievement, and mistakes. Kepler was a German and a Protestant. His interest in mathematics was a more abstract one: his work on astronomy arose from a study of conic sections rather than weights and cannon-balls. Driven from the University of Graz by religious persecution, he joined and afterwards succeeded Tycho Brahe as 'court mathematician' to Rudolph II, an indiscriminate patron of scholars and pseudo-scholars. But like most of the emperor's financial affairs, this patronage of learning was heavily in arrears, and Kepler lived largely on the proceeds of freelance astrology, in which he appears to have had a convenient half belief. Indeed, no-one typified better the outlook of the new scientists: his idea that the divine harmony of the universe was expressed in some hidden magic of numbers led him to fantastic efforts to find a pattern in the stars that would fit the shapes of regular solids or the spacing of notes in musical scales. But his work was more fruitful than that of any contemporary astronomer. His indefatigable labour on charts and calculations, and his rejection of failure after failure in the belief that a true solution would turn up eventually, were sometimes in the spirit of the medieval alchemist rather than the modern researcher. Yet where Galileo wrote popular controversial works, Kepler wrote for mathematicians. His three 'laws' were arrived at largely by checking, with the help of the observation tower designed by Tycho and of some laborious and skilful mathematics, a whole series of imagined explanations of planetary motions. The first, that planets move round the sun in elliptical orbits, was apparently what Copernicus and others had accepted, but Kepler's ellipses were established by exact measurement. The second law showed that as a planet moves further from the sun, its speed decreases, so that a line from planet to sun always sweeps across the same area in any given time. It was actually discovered before the 'first' law, on the assumption that orbits were circular. Kepler's mathematics had produced, he admitted, an approximation to this simple solution. He established it by first trying a variety of theories that would give some mathematical law to fit the apparently irregular speed and then hitting on the calculations that led to the theory of equal areas. In the course of investigating the discrepancies that remained, the idea of elliptical orbits emerged. These two principles were announced in 1609. It was not until ten years later that the third law appeared as something of an afterthought. It stated that the square of the time taken by a planet to complete its orbit bears a constant ratio to the cube of its mean distance from the sun. Kepler was never anxious to proclaim his 'laws' as great new discoveries. He had fulfilled his ambitions not by overturning old misconceptions but by confirming ancient beliefs in the essential harmony of the universe; and by processes of thought that now look astonishingly inconsistent his years of sophisticated mathematical labour did not destroy his fascination with almost mystical concepts of shape and number. But he did not accept harmony as a sufficient explanation of the heavens. The problem of how and why the planets moved in these regular orbits always baffled him. They could not be depicted as the result of independent spirits moving each planet separately. If the word 'soul' (*anima*) is replaced by 'force' (*vis*), he said, we have the principle on which his physics rests.[5] It was a principle that remained unexplained, even by Newton.

DESCARTES

In 1637, when Galileo's work was almost at an end, there appeared from the freer printing presses of Leiden an anonymous book, in French, that attracted little attention – the *Discourse on Method*. René Descartes was the son of a minor office-holder in Brittany with aspirations towards the *noblesse*. He had suffered what he regarded as the misfortune of a Jesuit education, fought as a gentleman volunteer in the Thirty Years War, and – for reasons which he insisted had nothing to do with persecution – settled in Holland. Throughout his youth, as he explained in the *Discourse*, his scepticism about the contradictory and ill-founded teachings of scholastics had grown. He devoted himself not to reading but to thinking; and thinking had led to his three 'principles' – to accept as certain nothing of which the least doubt was possible, to divide the problems he studied into the smallest possible 'packets'; and to reason always from the simpler to the more complex questions. His aim was nothing less than to construct a new universal system of knowledge. Seeking the starting-point for the deductive process that would make this possible, he arrived at the statement – much less clear in its meaning than he imagined – 'I think, therefore I am.' From this he went on (by a process very like the familiar arguments of the schoolmen he purported to reject) to discover that 'God' also exists. So, for reasons that were moving rapidly away from the proclaimed principle of certainty, did a material universe entirely distinct from the human mind. To the study of this he was now ready to devote himself.

It is at first sight astonishing that a writer whose methods became the basis of a widely accepted system of scientific thought produced theories of the universe most of which were easily shown to be wrong. One of his professed purposes and achievements was to explain all material events and objects in terms of mathematics – the only kind of knowledge demonstrably true. The hundreds of 'principles' in which this enormous quantity of exposition was set out do not in fact contain much mathematics in any ordinary sense, and even less experimental proof. But their concise assertions covering all the questions about the material universe he could think of, including its divine origins, are a formidable intellectual construction. An object, he decided, had two essential qualities – extension (length, breadth, height and hence shape) and motion. Everything else was either a sensation of the observer or a hidden motion. All matter consisted of particles, of three degrees of coarseness that corresponded to the elements of fire, air, and earth. But the middle category formed the 'subtle matter' that filled all space: no vacuum was possible. The particles were not atoms: they were infinitely divisible. From their movement arose the 'vortices' that accounted for light and heat. It is all so complicated and so unreal that later Cartesian philosophers had to ignore or explain away its most untenable statements. But sometimes it came close to genuine perceptions. Descartes' 'first law' was that objects remain in the same state unless something changes it, and this includes a state of motion as well as of rest. The second law is that every piece of matter tends to move in a straight line, though it will often encounter other bodies that divert it into a circle. The explanation of this is typical of his ways of thinking. It is illustrated by the behaviour of a stone released from a sling; but the reason for this law, and for the first, is that God is immutable and so conserves the motion he has created. Not all Descartes' ways of reconciling a mechanical universe with religion are as crude as this. When he moves to the consideration of mankind he accepts the existence of something more than particles. In man, though not in animals, there is a soul and its attribute, thought. They can to some extent control the working of the body; they can produce emotions; and they can make mistakes, especially about what they perceive. How the mistakes are to be corrected is less clear: sometimes the only answer seems to be to read Descartes. There was a complete contrast between the arrogance of Descartes and the gentle questioning of his successor as the leading French philosopher, Pascal. Descartes decided that there was no such thing as a vacuum, because a vessel emptied of everything would still form an extension, and there could be no extension without matter. If God decided to empty the vessel completely, its sides would fall in. Pascal's approach to this was to climb to the top of the Puy de Dome with what was later known as a mercury barometer. The mercury in the tube fell, and no air could have replaced it. The small experiment produced passionate controversy, with Cartesians giving the easy answer that 'subtle matter' had passed through the glass wall of the tube. Experiments with the vacuum became a popular demonstration of scientific methods.

MEASUREMENT

Galileo, Kepler, Descartes, and Pascal all in different ways recognized that the basis of any new understanding of the universe must be a mathematical one. Already a fashionable part of the interest of educated gentlemen, mathematics in the seventeenth century made progress that took it far beyond the understanding of all who lack the special talents it demands. But many of the most necessary advances of the mathematicians concerned simply the equipment and terminology they used. Far from being the most abstruse part of the new science, it had immediate practical application. Arabic numerals, already familiar to scholars, came into general use around the middle of the century. Simon Stevin, the military engineer, introduced another necessity for exact calculation – the decimal point. The slide-rule, and the table of logarithms worked out by John Napier, became common aids to reckoning. A more fundamental change in the working of mathematics came with the application to classical geometry of the new algebra. From the work of mathematicians all over Europe there developed the whole new system of analytic geometry and the measurement of change. Kepler and many others saw the possibilities of measuring a curve by imagining it to consist of a very large number of very small straight lines. From this the stage was reached where Newton and Leibnitz produced at the same time and in slightly different forms the differential and the integral calculus. Without it astronomical measurements, however good, could not make complete sense.

Side by side with higher mathematics, the simple apparatus of measurements was improving all the time. The links between craftsman and scientist were closer in the seventeenth century than in the generations before and after; and it was in measurement that they were most apparent. Realisation of the need for agreed quantitative standards in everything came very slowly. For a few purposes anyone can devise his own ways of measuring. Galileo made a thermometer, as did several of his contemporaries, each using his own arbitrary scale, It was not until 1724 that Gabriel Fahrenheit calibrated his mercury thermometer with the system that is only now slowly going out of use. In the same way the principle of the barometer was known long before it was used to give precise measurements of atmospheric pressure. Even with weight, vital to trade and finance as well as manufactures and science, the balance was in the seventeenth century more accurate than the units it compared. The distance of the moon, or the focal length of a lens, were still worked out in units derived from the plough or the thumb. Only angular measurement, as fractions of the circle, could be indefinitely narrowed in accuracy just by more precisely made instruments.

One measuring device, whose production was an industry in itself, was everywhere the same and was steadily improved by practical skill and scientific knowledge. The accuracy of clocks could be tested fairly well by the sun; in them the astronomer and the navigator seeking to measure longitude at sea both demanded precision and reliability. The Dutch physicist Christian Huygens constructed in the 1650s clocks specifically for use in navigation. He had already seen that the simple pendulum is not quite 'isochronous'; to discover the curve that it needs to follow to be really accurate involved a major mathematical achievement that occupied him for twenty years and contributed directly to the work of Newton. The difficulties were not only in suspension: they came from the differences in the earth's gravity and axial motion, and from heat expansion. While Huygens was working on the problems, the *Académie des Sciences* organized the expedition to Cayenne in French Guiana which found that a one-second pendulum is one-tenth of an inch shorter near the equator than in Paris. It was comparatively easy to calculate, and demonstrate, that taking a pendulum clock up a mountain would make it lose time. Both Huygens and Hooke had examined the alternative to the pendulum, the balance wheel and hair spring; but these too demand temperature compensation. The clock is only the most obvious instance of the links between mathematics, experimental science, craftsmanship, and demand. The development of lens-making is a similar story. But it cannot be claimed that the scientist and the craftsman always worked in happy collaboration. If anything by the end of the century the social barriers between them seemed more rigid than before, and scientific interest shifted away from the topics of immediate practical value.

THE HUMAN BODY

Besides the universe, the thing most mysterious and important for men to observe was their own bodies. Here too new knowledge had to confront entrenched belief. Hippocrates and Galen were for the student of anatomy and medicine authorities no less exalted than was Aristotle for the physicist. To most people the body was as directly governed by its soul as the universe by its maker; but, like the universe, the body was also the site of an endless conflict between good and evil. There was no rigid distinction between a possessing 'spirit' and a material fluid. The four 'humours' of the body, vaguely linking visible substances with mental and physical states, were accepted with just the pseudo-scientific credulity doctors and patients always find helpful. Remedies were derived partly from the principles of magic, partly from more or less successful trial and error. As in other ages, there was not much connection between their popularity and their efficacy. In understanding the chemistry of the body the seventeenth century made little headway, and the understanding of it as a machine brought few practical benefits. Men suffered and died with about the same balance of benefit and harm from their physicians and surgeons in 1700 as in 1600. But ways to improvement previously closed were now wide open.

There was no obvious reason to dispute Galen's anatomical system: indeed, it seemed to show admirably the perfect wisdom of God. From the liver, the source of the vital spirit, or 'pneuma', the nourishing blood of the veins was sent outward through the body. Some of it was drawn in by the heart, where, as it passed from the right ventricle to the left, the life-giving spirit was infused into it. Then it went outward as the different blood of the arteries. The lungs were primarily a cooling system supplying the heart with air. Several anatomists, notably Vesalius and Cesalpino in the sixteenth century, had come near to recognising the circulation of the blood without achieving the rejection of Galen that would have led to the simplest explanation of what they saw. Hieronymus Fabricius, professor of anatomy at Padua, had described the valves that prevent blood in the veins from going outwards, without drawing the obvious conclusion. William Harvey was a pupil of Fabricius at Padua in Galileo's time, but his career was spent mainly at St Bartholomew's Hospital and at the court of James I and Charles I. (One of his jobs was the physical examination of witches.) He was at first a faithful follower of Aristotle and Galen, anxious to reconcile their statements with his own observation. But on the heart this was impossible: even the crudest measurement showed that it pumped out blood much faster than the body could conceivably manufacture and absorb it. Circulation was the only possible solution. How it was achieved Harvey did not know: the microscope involved more difficult problems of accurate lens grinding than the telescope, and the capillaries that link veins with arteries were not seen until half a century later. What is now regarded as Harvey's great discovery was not proclaimed, and probably not seen, by him as a challenging new revelation. His book *On the Motion of the Heart*, published (in Latin) in Frankfurt in 1628, flattered Charles I with the conventional analogies between the heart, the sun, and the king, and identified the blood with the 'spirit'. Later he seemed to regard the blood as the real source of life. Whether a social and political significance can be attached to his 'dethroning of the heart' has been hotly argued.[6] What in practice mattered more was his increasing escape from analogies and from 'spirits' into a purely material view of the body. Like Descartes, he reduced the soul almost to the status of a chemical component of the body. The danger in the enthusiasm for studying the body as a machine was that nearly all those who did so convinced themselves that a complete explanation of its working was within their grasp and when they were defeated resorted to specious theories and undefined terms which they confused with observed facts.

REPRODUCTION

Men, animals, and plants had one characteristic in common which contained disturbing scientific and religious implications. They reproduced themselves, and in doing so handed on recognizable characteristics to their descendants. With animals reproduction was not the only way. One of the most firmly held of the scientific teachings of Aristotle, expanded by many medieval writers, was spontaneous generation. To question this, Sir Thomas Browne had said, 'is to question reason, sense, and experience'. Johann van Helmont, the discoverer of carbon dioxide, produced a recipe for making mice out of cheese and dirty linen. Everyone knew that putrefied meat generated maggots; but some accounts of the spontaneous appearance of bees and frogs reached almost the same level of mythology as the phoenix. Harvey was uncertain about it. It was not until 1688 that Francesco Redi, after experiments and observations that included the not very difficult one of protecting the meat from flies, claimed that all life arises from reproduction.

Some of the most absurd theories arose from the most successful scientific studies. Marcello Malpighi in Italy and Jan Swammerdam in Holland made microscopic studies of the foetus in eggs and of minute insects that proved to have organs not unlike those of larger animals. It led to the popular theory of 'preformation' – that a tiny but complete animal existed in the ovum. The apparently logical extension of this was the doctrine of 'encapsulation': every female would contain all her descendants inside each other in ever-diminishing scale. Eve had therefore contained the entire human species which at some predetermined time would come to an end. The role of the male was merely to stimulate the development of the next generation. This seemed to threaten one of the fundamental assumptions of European society – that the noble qualities inherent in the upper classes descended, like property, in the male line. The greatest of the Dutch microscopists of his generation, Antoni van Leeuwenhoek, who in the 1670s discovered the existence of male spermatozoa, modified these distressingly feminist notions in favour of what came to be called animalculism. It was after all the male, as Aristotle had said, who mattered. He provided the tiny animal: the female was merely a convenient place for it to develop. Neither view of course was remotely compatible with the then familiar facts about heredity. Yet fantasy of this kind was combined with an insatiable zeal in observing forms of life as small as the single cell. Leeuwenhoek's microscope was not improved on for well over a century. The capacity to observe was at this point far ahead of the developments in chemistry that were necessary to make sense of what was seen.

CLASSIFICATION

Observation –·patient, unprejudiced, and on a large scale – was in many fields of science the greatest advance that could be made. Many writers, both classical and medieval, had named and classified plants and animals. Interest in this had received a new impetus from the unheard-of specimens brought back from

America and the tropics. Bestiaries and catalogues of herbs abounded. The fascination of mere lists of names was delightfully exploited by Shakespeare and Milton. But naturalists were seeking more meaningful nomenclature and grouping. A great variety of publications attempted this. The Swiss Konrad Gesner had produced in the sixteenth century encyclopaedic works on all the known plants and animals. New methods of classification appeared constantly in the next hundred years, and new plants were constantly being identified. Perhaps the greatest name in this field is that of the Englishman John Ray, who had the best kind of collector's mind – full of zeal for additions to his catalogues, meticulous in his knowledge and accuracy. Many of his methods of grouping and naming were taken over by Linnaeus and others in the next generation to form the basis of modern classification. But like the men in so many fields who achieved the break-through to the scientific method, Ray was original mainly in his rejection of irrational assumptions and his readiness to admit imperfection.

Biology was almost as deeply involved as astronomy in awkward religious questions. How were ovist and animalculist theories reconciled with the miraculous birth of Christ? Was the last judgment timed for the moment when the stock of human beings was exhausted? Could all the newly discovered species have fitted into the ark? Arguments of this kind, though a great deal of print was devoted to them, did not produce in England and Holland anything like the organized repression that had almost killed scientific studies in Italy after Galileo. English Puritanism and the more tolerant Dutch Calvinism not merely refrained from persecuting science: they were, within limits, favourable to it. The Puritan believed in utility and in knowledge, and he hated obscurantist theology. He was prepared both to applaud the practical application of studies of nature and to see them as a tribute to the glory of God. Whether this undoubted shift of the main centres of scientific activity from Catholic to Protestant countries can be extended to the claim that individuals who held strongly Protestant views were more likely than others to become scientists is another matter. The numbers involved are so small that arguments about it tend to turn into the inconclusive listing of names. What is certain is that there existed everywhere, in greater or less degree, conservative forces in the churches and in the universities that were hostile to every manifestation of the 'new philosophy'. Victory over these would come less through the persuasive powers of a few men of genuis, than through the acceptance of science that spread through a large part of politically and economically powerful society. Merchant communities were interested in the practical value of scientific discovery in such fields as navigation, and prepared to some extent to patronise them. But it was among men of leisure as well as education that there appeared the enthusiastic amateurs who formed the link between the scholars and the community at large.

SCIENTIFIC SOCIETIES

Organized assemblies for the exchange of scholarly information were by·no means new. The literary 'academy' had been fashionable in Renaissance Italy. One of Bacon's schemes had been for large-scale corporate activity in which he believed anyone with leisure could contribute to knowledge. Galileo belonged to the *Accademia dei Lincei*; but this was no more than an association of men who corresponded without attempting any collective enterprise. The first of the active societies – and for a long time the last notable Italian contribution to science – was the *Accademia del Cimento*, founded in 1657 by the Grand Duke of Tuscany. If the Medici could no longer afford splendid palaces, they could pay for the best laboratories and instruments available, and though they allowed the project to die after ten years, it had shown the attractions of co-operative work and publication of results. Societies of this character arose in Germany, but they lacked the opportunity to develop beyond a local scale; and despite the example of the *Académie française*, which Richelieu established as an official institution in 1635, the French societies before Louis XIV were small groups of friends and correspondents.

Elizabethan England had produced the unique institution of Gresham College, endowed by the great financier and supported by merchants of the city as a centre for a form of education more practical than any the universities provided. It was also a meeting-place of scientists; and from it derived the informal groups of mathematicians, astronomers, physicians, and others who began during the Civil War to hold weekly meetings. One of them was Cromwell's brother-in-law John Wilkins, who asked why his age had not the same means as the ancient Romans to attempt 'mechanical discoveries'. Another was the German refugee Theodore Haak, a correspondent of most of the chief European scholars. A second group with a more technological bias, that gathered round the versatile Polish refugee Samuel Hartlib, a merchant with a wide interest in science but no claim to academic learning, was associated with what Boyle occasionally called the 'Invisible College'. Under the Commonwealth members of these informal associations who moved to Oxford established the discussion group that was later regarded as a precursor of the Royal Society. (Arguments about the origin of the Society have often made the various groups appear more distinct and organized than the evidence justifies.) When Charles II gave it the sponsorship that justified its title many of its fellows were as amateur as the king himself, who was proudly reported to spend long hours in his laboratory. Lacking substantial resources and genuine state encouragement, it never approached the ideals of collective discovery expounded by Bacon and Comenius. Some members never got beyond the zeal for reporting curious natural phenomena; others were closely concerned with the collection of information that had immediate economic value; a few were among the great original experimenters. To all of them the Society gave a reliable means of communication. The *Philosophical Transactions*, to which scholars in many other countries subscribed and contributed, established the modern means of circulating news of scientific and academic activities through the 'learned journal' rather than prolific individual correspondence.

In France one of the most assiduous of correspondents, the friar Marin Mersenne, helped to create the group of Paris scientists which after his death developed into a circle perhaps too fashionable for high scholarly standards. But from it arose in 1666, with Colbert's backing, the *Académie royale des Sciences*. Unlike the Royal Society it had abundant state support. To its observatory – better than Greenwich – came Cassini from Italy, Roemer from Denmark, Huygens from Holland. Astronomy here was a matter not for half-theological theory but for accurate measurement. The shape of the solar system was already recognized: the *Académie* and its outstanding native member Jean Picard began the assessment of its size. The expedition to Cayenne made possible a fairly accurate measurement of the distances of Mars and of the sun. Louis' government was the first to invest generously in discoveries that combined the prestige of spectacular achievement with information of direct value to the state. Colbert, to whom the *Académie royale des Sciences* was only a part of the centralization of learning under the state, occasionally reminded it of the relationship of science to industry. It was this aspect of the learned society that appealed strongly to the German princes and municipal governments who encouraged small-scale learned societies of their own. The Scientific Academy created by the Elector of Brandenburg in 1700 was, as even Leibnitz wanted it to be, wholly devoted to the prestige and well-being of the state. By this time the days when the gentlemanly dilettante and the scientist could work happily together were coming to an end. As higher mathematics became an essential part of most of the arguments, the squires and rich townsmen were less and less able to understand what it was all about.

BOYLE

The most distinguished of the Royal Society's members was a man whose life and outlook were typical of many aspects of European science in the second half of the century. Robert Boyle, son of the Earl of Cork and educated in the normal manner of his class, combined his scientific work with the study of ancient languages, a directorship of the East India Company, and a zeal for the propagation of the gospel. To try to understand the phenomena of nature was a Christian duty. They should be studied both for the sake of knowledge itself and as a means to economic progress. He showed no contempt for the Baconian type of random experiment and observation. His work with air pumps was at first concerned only with the quality of 'elasticity'. It was in response to criticism of it that he began the quantitative measurements leading to the 'law' – 'that pressures and expansions be in reciprocal proportions' – which immortalized his name. The experiments were also intended to uphold a theory of the nature of matter.

None of the 'ancient' beliefs had shown more staying-power than the Aristotelian theory of the four elements and the rival doctrine of Paracelsus that matter consisted of the three 'principles' of salt, sulphur, and mercury. Descartes' explanation of matter, though claiming to reject all the magical and metaphysical trappings of earlier ideas, started from the assumption that three 'elements' had to be accounted for. It had something in common with another of classical origin now refurbished by the French mathematician Pierre Gassen – Gassendi – that matter consisted of atoms with nothing between them. Boyle in his *Sceptical Chymist* (1661) denounced the lack of proof for any of these, but at the same time put forward as a hypothesis a variant of the atomist theories stressing the idea that atoms form, according to their size and arrangement, elements of differing characteristics which can be blended into compounds. The notion of 'forms' and 'qualities' distinguishable from the material structure of substances was thrown out completely. It sounds like the basis of modern chemistry. But he never found how to identify specific substances as elements or compounds or how a chemical reaction could be explained. Even so, his chemical experiments were so well organized and so accurately recorded that it is hard to realize that while he was publishing these to the Royal Society he was also working secretly as an alchemist, seeking the Philosophers' Stone and the universal remedy for disease. To some extent his scientific activities were divided into compartments where different criteria applied. A similar separation provided his answer to the problem of divine revelation. It did not lead him to diminish his religious faith, nor to move from orthodox Anglican Christianity towards deism. He insisted that God continued to direct the machine he had created: things only worked in accordance with fixed laws because God saw to it that they did.

NEWTON

The seventeenth century never arrived at the terminology and method necessary for decisive progress in chemistry. Its greatest scientific achievement was the mathematical system that turned its idea of cosmology from coherent observation into measured and apparently irrefutable fact. Isaac Newton was not in his lifetime regarded, at any rate outside England, as a genius standing above all his contemporaries. His reputation was certainly not helped by the paranoiac tendencies that led to his disputes with Hooke and Leibnitz about who thought of what first. Coming from a family of minor gentry or higher yeomanry, he belonged first to a Cambridge purged of its Puritanism, later to the Royal Society and the highest London circles. His Socinian religious beliefs were hidden behind a nominal Anglicanism. Like Boyle, he accepted Holy Writ, and indeed was fascinated by its details. Gradually he seems to have come to regard some of it as allegory rather than fact.[7] Alchemy, and biblical chronology interpreted through astronomy were for long periods among his greatest enthusiasms. Science as a contribution to human welfare made no appeal to him at all: he did a good deal to destroy the links between the Royal Society and manufacturers. Much of his greatest work was done in short bursts of activity, and he was in no hurry to publish it. By the time he became a national figure in the 1690s he was no longer much of a working scientist. It was when Newton was a refugee from the plague in the mid sixties that he first worked on the binomial theorem and began to circulate among his friends the system of 'fluxions'. No full account of it had been published when in 1675 Gottfried Leibnitz, the philosopher to whom mathematics was also a sporadic interest, worked out the infinitesimal calculus which solved the same problems of the measurement of rates of change with a simpler notation. When Leibnitz published his account of the calculus in 1684 there developed the bitter controversy that almost broke off the connections of England with European mathematics. No substantial evidence for Newton's charges of plagiarism seems to have existed, and it was certainly Leibnitz whose reputation was enhanced.

Long before the quarrel with Leibnitz's supporters had developed its further implications, Newton was involved in another dispute arising from the optical experiments described in the *Philosophical Transactions*. The subject of light appeared to produce exceptional stubbornness among the scientists of the seventeenth century. For those who believed that everything consisted of matter, light was not easy to explain. There was a familiar dispute between the idea of 'corpuscles' and that of the movement of some kind of 'medium' through which light was transmitted. Descartes had compromised on corpuscles moving, and producing pressure, in his *matière subtile*. Robert Hooke, Newton's greatest English rival, and Christian Huygens independently developed 'wave' theories of transmission. A central problem in optics was that of the colours produced by a prism and – annoyingly – by a lens. If a beam of light fell obliquely on a transparent surface, Hooke argued that one 'edge' of it would hit the surface before the other, and if the new medium transmitted light less (or more) easily than the air, the beam would not only be bent, but 'confused', producing red lights at one 'edge' and blue at the other. Colours were therefore the confused version of pure white light. Working especially with thin layers of mica that produce 'Newton's rings', Hooke achieved some elaborate measurement and mathematical analysis: the rest was speculation with no solid experimental basis and as Newton pointed out was uncomfortably vague when it shifted from the 'waves' to the 'beam'.

Newton's experiments with prisms did not explain the fundamental nature of light: but he showed that colour was not an aberration but white light a 'heterogeneous mixture of rays'. Once separated by one prism, they were not changed further by a second, but could be recombined into white light. Hooke and Huygens bitterly attacked the idea without offering comparable evidence against it. On both sides the argument had something in it of the old philosophy as well as the new. Newton claimed that light must be a substance since only a substance could have the 'quality' of colour. His opponents resented the idea that the light of the sun was not the 'pure' form; coloured light *ought* to be the deviation from it. Nevertheless the controversy led both Hooke and Newton to modify their views; Newton adopted the idea of an 'ether' in which the corpuscles whose existence he still insisted on produced vibrations; Hooke considered the relation of colour to changes in the force of the vibrations. Ironically the man who came closest to the idea that light has a measurable wavelength, shortest for violet and longest for red, was Descartes' disciple Malebranche, who arrived at it from an analogy with sound and with comparatively little mathematical or experimental knowledge. He first put forward his theory in 1699, long after those of Newton and Hooke, but apparently without having heard of them.

When Newton at last brought together and published his work on light, in the *Optiks* of 1704, he referred to differences in the 'bigness' of the vibrations as a possible explanation of colour. This was in the 'Queries' which he appended to the book because as he said, in words that sound like a claim to divinity, 'I have not finished this part of my Design.' He was admittedly modifying his claim not to 'deal in conjectures' and he never answered the question, even though he had long ago performed an experiment that demonstrated the wavelength solution very clearly. (It showed that a ray of light of a single colour had regular short intervals – 'fits' as he called them – of easy penetration alternating with easy reflection.) Not only did Newton's reluctance to abandon corpuscles block his own acceptance of the best answer: when his towering reputation was established the wavelength idea came into thorough disrepute merely because he had not asserted it. A Newtonian orthodoxy became as rigid as once the Aristotelian one had been.

In the work that gave him this unique status, written in Latin and having the austere title *Mathematical Principles of Natural Philosophy*, Newton completed as certainties, calculated precisely and in vast detail, what Galileo, Kepler, Hooke, and many others had seen in part. The problem of gravitation seemed very like that of light: in each case something was transmitted that could not be accounted for in obvious mechanical terms. Borelli had suggested that the sun's rays could be acting like levers pushing the planets round. Even those who accepted the idea of an inertia of motion felt that there ought to be a material link between bodies that were attracted to each other – otherwise the mechanical universe was being spoilt by letting in occult qualities producing action at a distance. Descartes and his followers had talked of vortices in the subtle matter, diverting the moon and planets from the straight course they would otherwise have followed for ever. Newton showed that these did not make mathematical sense, and that universal gravitation did. There was nothing new in the idea that all heavenly bodies attracted each other. It could be found in Kepler's discussion of mutual attraction between earth and moon; Hooke had discussed it at the Royal Society, and in correspondence with Newton. The essential equation – that the force of gravity between two bodies varies in inverse proportion to the square of the distance between them – emerged in a way typical of Newton's mathematical mind. He had arrived at it, from work on Kepler's laws and his own measurements of centrifugal force, by 1666, and finding great mathematical difficulties in completing the proof had given it up. Only when Hooke put it to him in 1679 did he take up the idea again. With the help of Picard's accurate measurement of the size of the earth, and of some corrections from Hooke, Newton produced an exact explanation on this basis of the orbits of the planets. Five years later, when the manuscript of the *Principia* was presented to the Royal Society, Hooke and Newton began mutual accusations of plagiarism. In the final version of the *Principia*, Newton announced that Wren, Hooke, and Halley as well as himself had all independently deduced the inverse square law from Kepler's statement.

Newton had no particular yearning for immortality as the discoverer of the 'law of gravity', still less of 'nature's laws' as a whole. He was well aware that gravity was only one of the many phenomena of nature that might be understood in the same way. His real achievement was to establish a scientific outlook more fruitful and consistent than those of Bacon or Descartes. Neither observation nor deduction were enough in themselves: they must yield answers capable of exact measurement and mathematical verification. There should be no confusion between facts that had been proved in this way and theories that had not. The fact of universal gravitation was demonstrable. How it worked was still to be solved. It was this difficulty that the Cartesians seized on in their attack on Newton, who had dismissed their vortices and subtle matter with some contempt. Gravitation, they argued, was not a brilliant advance but a return to the idea of occult forces. Moreover Leibnitz was now their hero; and Newton's God who had to keep his universe going seemed inferior to Leibnitz's 'most perfect being'.

The differences between Newtonian and Cartesian universes were the subject of long and sterile argument. It was a difference altogether smaller than that between the agreed supremacy of observation and deduction and measurement over the ancient reliance on authority and magic. There was of course no total victory. The last years of the century in England saw the 'Battle of the Books' in which Sir William Temple and his friends came stoutly to the defence of ancient learning against the moderns. In France Bernard de Fontenelle, the most successful populariser of Cartesianism and of the new astronomy, was an early exponent of the idea of progress. Ancients and moderns would in the future, he asserted, be seen alike as contributors to the unlimited expansion of knowledge, which must now be made available to the masses as well as to the intelligentsia. Obstacles to such progress were still formidable. Catholic control over thought seemed stronger than ever over much of southern Europe; and Protestant

Churches were seldom ready to assimilate scientific ideas. But, usually without much inkling of the change, men whose grandfathers had lived in a world made of spirits as well as matter pushed these assumptions into a compartment of their thought where they did not interfere with a universe that worked in accordance with laws capable of mechanical explanation. The 'Scientific Revolution' had succeeded.

NOTES AND REFERENCES

1 The terms 'science' and 'scientific' are used here in their modern sense. In 1600 'science' usually meant something wider – almost 'knowledge' – and the study of the material universe was called 'natural philosophy.' By 1700 a more limited meaning of 'science' was common, though 'scientist' was not used until the nineteenth century.

2 Quoted by Galileo in his Letter to the Grand Duchess (S. Drake, *Discoveries and Opinions of Galileo* (New York, 1957), p. 208).

3 *Filum Labyrinthi*, Section 7.

4 Acts of the Apostles c. I v. 11 – but the pun may be one of the many apocryphal stories about Galileo.

5 E. J. Dijkserthuis, who quotes this (*The Mechanization of the World Picture* (Oxford, 1961, p. 310), gives Kepler more credit than do many writers for moving from an animistic to a mechanistic outlook.

6 See the article by Christopher Hill in *Past and Present*, no 27 (1964), pp. 54–72, and the discussion of it in nos. 30 and 31.

7 See his *General Scholium* in *Works* (2nd edn), p. 546.

7

EDUCATION AND THE ARTS

One of the hardest tasks in the study of human activities is to explain convincingly developments in art, music, and literature. Up to a point the influence of material conditions on cultural achievement is obvious enough. However brave and unselfish the creator of such work may be, the survival of his products depends on the demand for them, and therefore on the whole condition of the society in which he lives. Every class and country supports, to a greater or lesser degree, its own forms of art; and they can all be used for propaganda or just for prestige. Since writings must be printed and published, plays and music performed, painting displayed (to however restricted a number of people), someone is likely to intervene between the creator of any of these and the recipient. But when all interpretations of how patrons and audiences behaved have been exhausted, they seldom amount to a satisfying explanation of why, for instance, England did not produce a school of painting comparable to that of the Netherlands, or France a poet like Milton. The links between styles in the arts and the periods in which they flourished are no less elusive. Efforts to show the seventeenth century as the 'age of the baroque' in which the characteristics of politics, religion, and commerce were all related to the ornate and swirling shapes, the sense of movement and striving, that were fashionable in painting sometimes owe more to imagination than to evidence. Analysis and explanation of cultural history are a necessary part of the understanding of any period; but even more than most forms of history they need to be scrutinized with a wary eye for the pretentious unsupported assertion.

EDUCATION

The activities of schools and universities might be expected to have a major effect on the arts that would be a direct link with social conditions. In fact their positive influence on taste and creativity was lamentably small. The newness and vigour of seventeenth-century arts came from men whose education must have done more to crush initiative than to encourage it. The day-to-day work of most educational institutions in the period forms a dismal contrast with the ideas and energy of those who sought to reform and expand them. It contrasts too with the achievements in science and culture outside them. The sixteenth century had been in many countries a period of rapid expansion in the amount of schooling available, and in some the process still went on. It has been suggested that perhaps 'early seventeenth-century England was at all levels the most literate society the world had ever known' but that the level then declined sharply.[1] The Netherlands may well have maintained an equally high rate of elementary schooling. With Puritans and Jesuits having active, though very different, interests in education, and with the endowment of schools a widely accepted form of charitable virtue, the demand for literate workers and that for highly educated administrators was being met. But the distribution of schools was patchy and accidental: one village, town, or province could often be far better provided for than its neighbour. Against the instances of expansion must be set the grim decline of education in Germany during the Thirty Years War and in many similarly afflicted regions. Moreover, the character of teaching changed far less easily than the amount. Many enthusiasts for educating the lower orders still assumed that writing, simple religion, and useful trades were the limit of their ability. Prospects for the aspiring poor scholar were often worse than in earlier centuries. Even for those whose social position fitted them for more prolonged studies, Renaissance humanism had not left much mark on the process or content of teaching. The revival of classical learning could easily take the form of Latin grammar instilled with the help of the birch.

There was no lack of official concern with education. Kings, from Gustav Adolf to Peter the Great, took a personal interest in schemes to reform it; states and cities, as well as private benefactors, felt that they won prestige by financing it. But none of the activities of laymen did much to disturb the dominance of the churches over teaching at every level. There is not much doubt that in this part of the struggle Catholicism was on the whole doing better than any form of Protestanism. Lutherans, despite their theoretical belief that the scriptures should be available to everyone, did little to enable the poor to read. Their system of teaching for the minority who did receive a substantial education put the emphasis heavily on Latin grammar and verbal memorising. Calvin's educational ideas had survived rather better than Luther's, at least in extending the use of the vernacular in schools. But no-one brought to Protestant education anything like the zeal and systematic skill of the Jesuits. Their *Ratio Studiorum*, issued in its final form in 1599, established a system of primary and secondary schooling wider in its subject-matter and far more enlightened in its methods than any other in use. Though its ultimate purpose was the victory of Catholicism, religious conformity was instilled into pupils unobtrusively – or insidiously – rather than by the rigid discipline imposed within the Order itself. Aristotle and Aquinas remained the essential sources of knowledge and wisdom; some dangerous ideas were firmly banned; but within the rules there was room for a range of teaching wide enough to make the schools attractive to Protestants as well as to Catholics. Bacon remarked how much they had 'quickened and strengthened the state of learning',[2] and suggested that to 'consult the schools of the Jesuits' was the quickest way to see how education should be reformed. In France the number of great men in literature and scholarship who had been educated in Jesuit schools was very large, though Descartes was not alone in doubting the benefits of it. Their pupils were not drawn from any one social class. Investigation of their origins in various regions and years shows that sons of merchants and office-holders had the largest share of places; but those of artisans and *laboureurs* were something like a quarter or a third of the total.

Jesuit schools, open to literate pupils whatever their origin and aim, were not likely to appeal strongly to the nobility; and the demand for a type of education suited to the exclusive requirements of the court and the landed classes found its own response. In France Bérulle's Oratory began to offer to the sons of aristocrats as well as to future priests teaching rivalling that of the Jesuits; and from the middle of the century the schools of Port Royal became a centre of enlightened teaching for the courtly intelligentsia. In Germany after the Thirty Years War the 'knightly academies' (*Ritterakademien*), which soon came strongly under French influence, met the same need for an almost vocational training in the accomplishments of a gentleman. French became at least the equal of Latin as a language of the élite; useful subjects such as law, heraldry, and military science were included in the curriculum; and pupils were even encouraged to know enough about art and music for conversational purposes. Sweden's new *Gymnasia*, established mainly in the 1630s and 1640s, were controlled by the bishops and extended their scope only cautiously beyond the old religious and classical subjects; but they helped to produce a ruling class that was culturally equal to those of the other powers. Not that ambitious nobles and gentlemen necessarily regarded schools of any kind as suitable for their heirs. The best form of education was often felt – in England perhaps most of all – to be provided by the private tutor at home or during foreign travel. It was a job that offered a comfortable and reasonably leisured existence to scholars: Bossuet, Leibnitz, and Hobbes were among those who lived in this way.

The century was not a glorious one for universities. Between their functions as centres of ecclesiastical training and propaganda and as finishing-schools for gentlemen, up-to-date scholarship usually took a lesser place. There were exceptions. After the foundation of Leiden in 1574 several of the Netherlands cities and provinces created their own universities where new scientific and literary ideas held their own against traditional Aristotelian formulae. Strassburg, both under Imperial and under French control, had flourishing schools of mathematics and history. The opening of the University of Halle in 1694, intended by the Elector Frederick III as a mark of national prestige, came to be regarded as the beginning of a new era of enlightenment and freedom in German education. But few of the great intellectual achievements of the century owed much to the universities. In Galileo's day both Pisa and Padua still had a good deal of their Renaissance initiative and freedom. Their teaching of mathematics, medicine, and 'natural philosophy' brought them students from all over Europe. By the middle of the century their reputation had almost disappeared. Oxford under the Commonwealth enjoyed a brief period as a centre of the new science. There however, as at Cambridge, teaching was slow to respond to the demands of an enterprising minority for a less narrowly scholastic outlook. Geometry, Astronomy, and Natural Philosophy were added to the Oxford professorships; but they were handled on cautiously traditional lines. The establishment of the Royal Society was part of a general tendency for both leading scholars and intelligent amateurs to come together in societies and academies unconnected with the universities (see p. 174–6). The Inns of Court offered for lawyers a seven-year professional training and for the sons of gentlemen the opportunity in one year to pick up pleasantly a smattering of law.

Nearly everyone in a position to control education shared the same basic assumptions. Boys (and in a very limited way girls) must learn a definite and unquestioned body of factual information and acquire an appropriate degree of skill in written and spoken language. A few might move on from fact to understanding, but with the range of permissible investigation and dispute limited by authority. Throughout the century these assumptions were challenged by some of the most powerful writers, and revolutionary ideas on education were even, here and there, put into practice; but their achievement by 1700 did not amount to much. Richard Mulcaster, high master of St Paul's School until 1608, had advocated universal primary education and denounced the excessive importance attached to Latin with arguments some of which were renewed, and rejected, in twentieth-century Oxford. Bacon's *Advancement of Learning* was followed by a stream of English writings on educational reform, many of them from Puritans, among which Milton's *Treatise on Education* (1644) was the best-known but by no means the most radical.

The distinction between knowledge, understanding, and judgement was the basis of the elaborate schemes devised by the Czech Comenius – Jan Amos Komensky – who in Poland, Sweden, the Netherlands and briefly in England, campaigned for the reform of education on lines that owed a good deal to Bacon. 'The entire youth of both sexes, none being excepted' would be taught in a way that would make them 'learned in the sciences, pure in morals, trained in piety'[3] – a shocking order of priority. This was to be in local schools provided by lay authorities. For the few who could advance beyond mere knowledge there were to be gymnasia in every city and universities in every province. The aim of it all was not merely the improvement of the individual, but the achievement of a new civilization with universal peace. He was widely read, and ignored. The one philosopher who had a clear practical influence on education was Descartes. From him there came not theories on the method of teaching but the attitude to knowledge that firmly rejected the authoritarian scholastic tradition. If the way to achieve certainty was first to doubt everything that could be doubted, there was no room for the professor who thought it his main job to elucidate received texts. The test of truth was not whether a statement rested on ancient authority, but whether it was conceived clearly and demonstrably. Cartesian education aimed therefore not to impart ready-made beliefs, but to instil the habit of questioning and the method of distinguishing as far as may be truth from falsehood. There was usually a wide gap between the aim and the achievement.

PRINTING AND PUBLISHING

Despite all the obstacles and setbacks in education, the first half of the century was the period when the printing of books, pamphlets, and news, which had been spreading steadily beyond intellectual and clerical circles, became a major industry. It depended on the production of enough paper (one of the first products to get worse in quality as the demand for it grew) and on the complicated metallurgy involved in making founts of type that would not wear out too quickly. A printing-press could be a small machine operated by one man; but larger-scale output required workers with specialized skills, and means of distribution that would ensure quick sales. The industry became increasingly concentrated in a few university towns and in large cities such as London, Venice, and Paris which in the 1640s had 70 printers running 180 presses. In the Netherlands printing was rather more scattered. The towns of the southern as well as the northern Netherlands became notorious for the publication, more or less illegal, of religious and political material that was sold all over Europe. The mid-century conflicts created a sudden boom in popular pamphlets, newspapers, and broadsides – single large sheets. Printed sermons, and reports of speeches and debates, had an astonishingly large demand. Whatever the effect on opinion, material that now seems difficult reading was bought by people far outside the intellectual élite. There was a steady output also of practical manuals. Agriculture, travel, cooking, hunting, alchemy, architecture – every activity now had its printed information, and the ability to read it was necessary for success in urban trade or craftsmanship. But reading-matter was not inaccessible in the countryside. Fairs and markets, pedlars, and by the end of the century the chapmen or *colporteurs* who specialized in hawking small popular books were common sources. Books were not prohibitively dear even for the fairly prosperous peasant. An almanac could cost as much as a couple of large loaves and provide a miscellany of useful or mythical information. On the scholarly level there was no longer much difficulty in setting out material at whatever length was required. Though no writer could hope to make much money from books, the zeal for self-assertion in print seemed insatiable. Quick production and distribution meant that philosophical or scientific expositions could be enlivened by the controversies of great men who hated each other.

The limits to the growth of printing were set less by its producers or consumers than by the authorities who had reason to fear it. Rulers of church and state had always seen the spread of knowledge as a threat to the acceptance of their infallibility. In the seventeenth century censorship was sometimes a minor nuisance, often a major factor in the shaping of society. The warfare between writers and those who sought to restrict them varied in its ferocity and effect, but never completely stopped. Absolutist government and authoritarian religion saw the control of printing as a natural part of their functions; but on the whole both were fairly incompetent in enforcing it. In Catholic Europe the Index of prohibited books was not one document but a continuing series of orders, some unconditional, others to be rescinded when 'corrections' were made. The Spanish index was independent of the Roman one: the collected version of 1640 was no longer directed mainly at Protestant heresies but at anything non-Spanish or conceivably offensive to anyone. It was brutally enforced, but so inefficient that Galileo was among the writers too obscure to appear on it. In France the system was based partly on the prohibition of imported books and partly on the requirement that every book and pamphlet sold must be specifically licensed. Alarm at the newspapers and pamphlets that appeared so prolifically during the Fronde led to the suppression in the 1660s of every such production except the official *Gazette*. Protestant countries on the whole were not much more liberal. The English licensing system, often haphazard, had its periods of aggression. In 1637 attacks on the regime of Archbishop Laud led to a decree of Star Chamber limiting the number of printers in London to twenty and requiring stringent examination of everything they sold. The market for illegal literature benefited enormously. None of these centres could compete with the Netherlands, where every kind of forbidden writing could be printed and returned to its country of origin through the great commercial network. It was not only the banned religious and political works of writers in the Protestant north that made use of Amsterdam and Leyden presses. Jansenist as well as Huguenot pamphlets were among their vast output in French; Descartes, Galileo, Locke, and Comenius were a few of the authors published in the Netherlands when it suited them. The laxness of restrictions there, and in some German states, came more from political conditions than from high principles; and when during the mid-century conflicts effective censorship in England and France broke down it did not indicate any widespread pressure for complete freedom of expression. Milton and Cromwell saw a variety of benefits in relaxing censorship except for really intolerable views like catholicism; but the successive governments of the 1650s introduced restrictions on the press which they were able to enforce sporadically. After 1660 censorship was tightened again wherever it had been weakened. There were many ways of evading it besides underground circulation. Allegory, irony, bland assertion of accepted views in works that undermined them, and the allusive use of ancient history were easily recognized by the well-informed reader; but they could lead authorities to assume that anything they had not issued themselves probably had some sinister implications.

One reason both for the rise in the output of printing presses and for official distrust of them was the use of vernacular languages. 'Linguistic nationalism' was sometimes approved but more often feared by rulers. In 1569 Johanes Becanus (though he Latinized his own name of Jan van Hilvarenbeek) had announced his great discovery that Dutch, which was spoken by Adam, had been exempted from the unfortunate affair of the Tower of Babel. There was great enthusiasm during the Netherlands Revolt for making the greatest possible use of the language. In Sweden Skogekär Bergbo wrote in the 1630s a poem deploring the neglect of Swedish for literary and administrative purposes and its corruption by German and Latin infiltrations. Similar complaints were made about German itself by Martin Opitz, who thought that a rigid set of grammatical and stylistic rules was necessary to raise the level of native literature. Efforts to purify and define the French language had continued since the days of Ronsard and the *Pléiade*. In 1647 Claude Vaugelas published his *Remarques sur la langue française*, which laid down the rules for a pure and unambiguous literary French. The *Académie* had the same object. Its official dictionary, completed in the 1690s, was compiled on the principle that words and phrases had differences of status as clear and important as those between men. The language of the peasant and the bourgeois was not to be confused with that of the court and the *salon*; and it was only the purest literary French that was worthy to succeed Latin as the international language of diplomacy and culture.

VERNACULAR PROSE

Throughout the century most prose writings were meant to inform and convince rather than to entertain. But such works as the scientific arguments of Galileo, the political and religious pronouncements of Bossuet, the sermons of Donne or even such revolutionary pamphleteering as the best of the Mazarinades and Leveller tracts must be ranked as literature in their own right. With Pascal the '*pensée*', that might be a few words or a few sentences, was a form that lent itself to his aim of revealing unresolved conflicts. Less introspective writers like La Bruyère and La Rochefoucauld showed what the French language could make of the aphorism and the epigrammatic sketch. In England the miniature portrait of a type or an individual was a favourite amusement. John Earle's *Microcosmography* and John Aubrey's *Brief Lives* combined a gently satirical touch with satisfied observation of their society. More expansive writing could still too readily become ponderous and contrived. The scholarly belief that Latin, even though it was no longer exclusively Ciceronian Latin, was the perfect model for English died hard. But often sheer joy in the power of words and a readiness to experiment broke through the conventions. Sir Thomas Browne, even when he is manifestly striving for effect, gives the reader the feeling that he is being asked to take part in an exciting and not too strenuous diversion. On the whole the tendency as the century went on was for English prose to become less artificial, simpler, and more relaxed.

Vernacular prose was surprisingly slow to develop as a vehicle for purely imaginative writing. The *novella*, which had been a popular form of amusement in the sixteenth century, survived without growing into serious fiction. The one great work that has something in common with the modern novel is *Don Quixote*, the first part of which was finished in 1604. In using a tale in a familiar mould to attack the outdated assumptions of Spanish noble society, and in making out of the stereotyped figure of the *picaro* – the rootless, wandering rogue – a character so vivid and significant, Cervantes achieved a triumph that proved completely isolated. Perhaps its nearest successor was Grimmelhausen's *Simplicius Simplicissimus*, published anonymously in 1668; and this owes its modern reputation more to its realistic portrayal of Germany in the depths of wartime misfortune than to literary skill. Prolonged reading was still the activity of the scholar, the lawyer, and the seeker for religious truth rather than a pastime. In the later part of the century the popularity of Bunyan's *Pilgrim's Progress* suggested that at the lower levels of literate society the religious allegory that also made a good story was now more attractive than the printed sermon. The *Arabian Nights* appeared in French in twelve successive volumes during the Spanish Succession War. But it was only when Defoe produced his best works of fiction that this form of art took on anything like its modern importance.

Historians of literature seldom say much about the lower-level works that collectively had a larger circulation than all the immortal writings. It was the booklets, pamphlets, and broadsheets intended for the casual buyer that kept the printing industry thriving. News of battles, fires and floods, monstrous births, murders, and executions could be printed as separate items and illustrated with crude woodcuts. Traditional songs, often with verses that later rescuers of folklore were quick to suppress, gave the publisher the chance to add his own variations. What effect it all had on genuinely popular culture is hard to estimate. It may be that by destroying the memorized epic and the improvised ballad it debased creative activities that had given peasant society an artistic life of its own. But many songs and nursery rhymes and legends that are supposed to have survived through oral tradition must in fact have been established by printing even though they were handed on to the illiterate. Verse of every sort is easier to memorize than prose; and political denunciations in rhyme could find their way from the printed sheet to the alehouse singer and the travelling entertainer. There must have been many totally unknown versifiers who did more to shape popular attitudes than all the pamphleteers and preachers.

POETRY

Every kind of artistic creation was involved to some extent in a conflict between the quest for new freedom of thought and expression and the desire to conform to well-defined rules. Energy and movement had somehow to be reconciled with symmetry and harmony. In poetry such a conflict seems almost essential. Seventeenth-century verse was often rhymed and nearly always obeyed rigid metrical rules; yet it was generally felt to be the one form in which language could attain as high a level as painting. Poets were willing to accept the conventions and to rejoice in the astonishing variety of emotions, ideas, and sounds that could be created within them. At its best the combination of harmonious and predictable forms with adventurous imagery and vocabulary could make a more powerful impact than was possible in any other medium. But there was no doubt about the risks involved. The phrases, the allusions, and the themes could become as stereotyped as the arrangement of rhyme and rhythm. Artificiality and too self-conscious skill were seldom far away. The gap between the exalted and the ludicrous could be a very narrow one.

The ability to turn out a well-contrived sonnet was almost as much a part of the cultured western gentleman's accomplishments as fencing. Writers of indifferent verse were often patrons and avid readers of good: in England, France, and Italy poetry had a wide circulation in cultured society. But it was no less popular among the townsmen of the Netherlands. Though Dutch verse could not, for the obvious reason, achieve the international repute of Dutch painting, it was as important a part of the national culture. Constantin Huygens, the father of the scientist, was one highly popular poet, who despite his courtly and intellectual background took many of his themes from ordinary urban and rural life. Jacob Cats, Pensionary of Holland in the 1640s, 'whose works could be found alongside the Bible in every Dutch home for two centuries' had a reputation as a poet which Huizinga describes as 'somewhat of a blot on our national character'.[4] But the greatest of the Dutch poets, Joost van den Vondel, has been ranked with Milton as an outstanding writer of the century. He had, it is claimed, a majestic command of language which rose above the limitations of his scriptural subjects and his strict observance of classical rules.

In England religious themes in poetry had to compete more openly with courtly ones. The religious element was seldom specifically Puritan. Its typical products were the devotional poetry of George Herbert, who renounced the worldly pleasures that were open to him and brooded on his own unworthiness; of Henry Vaughan, who found his manifestations of God in nature as well as in immortality; and of Richard Crashaw, Laudian and eventually Catholic, whose imagery came as close as any English writing to the baroque atmosphere. The contrast between these and the 'Cavalier' poets is by no means complete. Thomas Carew, Robert Herrick, Richard Lovelace, and the rest were as ready to apply their deliberately far-fetched imagery to the fate of their souls as to the inconstancy of their mistresses. The incongruity between and within their poems was not accidental: behind it was the pervading suspicion that the universe as they had been taught to see it and the social conventions of their time did not altogether make sense. Both the devout and the courtly owed much to the most original of the early seventeenth-century poets, John Donne, who had more success than anyone else in combining intellectual argument and verbal ingenuity with lyrical beauty. The wit, the extravagant analogies, the sureness of touch with which he can switch from the colloquial to the classical seemed as apt in his early love-poems as in his later religious ones. Some of the same qualities appeared a generation later in Andrew Marvell, but with a more relaxed lyricism and a more light-hearted approach even to his most deeply felt arguments. He is the complete answer to the notion that a Cromwellian Puritan must be a mealy-mouthed prig.

Inevitably the dominant figure of the century in English poetry is Milton. Few poets have ever aroused so much angry controversy so long after their deaths: whether they are good poems or bad, it can scarcely be denied that some of the immense reputation of *Paradise Lost* and *Paradise Regained* has come less from their real qualities than from the firmly inculcated belief that they are mighty works of Christian faith. His decision to reject such topics as the legend of Arthur and to combine his ambition to write a great epic of conflict with the duty to teach Christian doctrine created, as he well knew, great literary difficulties. The unrelieved solemnity, the allusions that have now become formidably unfamiliar, and the ponderous evenness of the blank verse need not prevent us from recognizing the command of language and the vividly human qualities given to the superhuman characters. But they do make it difficult to enjoy them. The great works of the defeated post-Restoration Milton tend to obscure the Milton who was a passionate exponent of the Parliamentary cause, an enemy of censorship, and a poet with a wide range of style and subject-matter. By the end of the century the literary world of Donne and Milton seemed utterly remote. Doubt and incongruity had almost disappeared. English poetry was now the rational and usually restrained classicism of Dryden, ranging from political satire to the few emotional odes. The neatly rounded heroic couplet was more appropriate to self-satisfied wit than to lyrical beauty or tortured questioning. Dryden was a writer of prose no less than of poetry, and consciously minimized the difference between them. Analysis and criticism could be applied almost as much to religion as to politics. Pope and the 'Augustan age' were not far away.

THE THEATRE

Even in areas where education was most widespread, drama was at least as important as printed literature in enabling the products of creative imagination to reach large numbers of people. Everyone was familiar with it, often in forms that did not require a barrier between performer and spectator. The carnival that was a regular part of life in the whole of southern Europe and, in spite of the hostility of Protestant churches, to some extent in the north too, has been described as 'a huge play in which the main streets and squares became stages, the city became a theatre . . . and the inhabitants . . . actors and spectators.'[5] Villages had their lesser equivalents on the appropriate saint's day or festival. It all

involved the unfamiliar costumes, the stock characters, the songs
and slapstick comedy that were transferred to the formal theatre.
In sterner versions of popular drama, the mystery plays on biblical
themes had been an approved form of religious teaching; but by
the end of the sixteenth century they had been condemned along
with the idols, the bell-ringing, the maypoles, and the Christmas
and Easter festivities in which Protestant clergy saw elements not
only of Catholicism but of pagan ritual. Protestants were not
alone in their hostility. Jesuits took much the same view; and so
did the Russian reform movement which in 1648 secured an edict
against such superstitious practices. It was no doubt true that
popular dramatic festivals were partly derived from fertility rites
and portrayed sexual aspirations that would not be openly
accepted in real life. The formal theatre was naturally expected
to do the same.

It was only in the 1580s and 1590s that theatres as permanent
buildings and enterprises had become part of the life of cities.
There were two theatres in London when Shakespeare arrived
there in 1586, and five in 1600. By then a large number of Spanish
towns had theatres, and they were appearing in Italy and in some
German states. Paris was slow to follow. The *Théâtre du Marais*,
equipped for elaborate stage spectacles, was founded in 1624. Its
first rival was the *Hôtel de Bourgogne*, headquarters of the
Comédiens du Roi, where most of Corneille's plays were produced.
Molière first established himself in Paris in 1658 at the *Salle du
Petit-Bourbon*, which he had to share with an Italian company.
When this was demolished to make room for the extensions to
the Louvre, the king handed over the *Salle du Palais Royal*, which
later became the centre for the *Opéra*.

Nearly everywhere the company of players rather than the
building was the centre of organization. It was likely to depend
heavily on royal or noble patronage. Many French plays were
performed first at Versailles and afterwards in the city: court
approval was naturally an important step towards popular success.
It was Louis XIV's personal support that brought Molière to
prominence. Shakespeare began his career in a company maintained by the Earl of Leicester, and he had a succession of court
patrons before his players were taken under James's official
protection in 1603. Court fashion and taste were responsible for
the comedies of Restoration England as much as for the classical
tradition and stringent rules of French tragedy. But the theatre

was nowhere the exclusive preserve of the aristocratic or educated minority. The majority of early seventeenth-century plays, from *Hamlet* down to the hastily botched-up routine comedies, managed to include something for everybody. Noble theatregoers did not of course mingle excessively with the multitude: they occupied the *loges* of the Paris theatres, arranged in appropriate grades; they watched open-air performances in Spain from windows or balconies; everywhere they were liable to invade the stage and interfere with the performance. The approval of the 'groundlings', standing and – it was hoped – tightly packed together, was hardly less necessary for commercial success. Actors were often paid on the spot out of takings to which the cheaper parts of the theatre contributed substantially. It was a profession that could be close both to court luxury and to poverty. The view that players were much the same as other vagabonds was not confined to English Puritans.

The writer who provided the actors with their necessary material seldom had an easy or secure existence. Scripts were demanded in enormous quantities, and payment for them was usually very small. The manufacture of plays was an industry in which collaboration, open or anonymous, was common. Plots and characters were borrowed as freely as jokes. Alexandre Hardy, the first popular French playwright of the century, was said to have written six hundred plays, few of which were printed; Lope de Vega in Spain was credited with even more. Both for economic reasons and to acquire such status and protection as were possible, the writer of plays was more in need than the poet of patrons who were highly placed, or even merely rich. Corneille at the height of his success had to produce a ludicrously fulsome dedication to the tax-farmer who had subsidised his publication.[6] Calderon and Lope de Vega eventually found security in the church. Ben Jonson, despite his turbulent career, won both steady patronage and a wide circle of friends at the Jacobean court. But it was significant that Shakespeare achieved only the fringe of provincial gentility and that there was some difficulty in arranging a respectable Christian burial for Molière.

In this situation the choice of topics and attitudes was inevitably restricted in many ways. Fear of government or ecclesiastical censorship, powerful though these could be, was only one reason for the conservatism that was a common characteristic of drama everywhere. It was obviously believed that both the popular and the courtly audience preferred conformity to innovation. Spanish drama was perhaps the most heavily committed to patriotism, monarchy, and the old ideas of chivalry and virtue. Though in every country the lower orders could be treated sympathetically as well as humorously, rebellion was always evil. The sins and follies of the nobility could be denounced; but the hierarchical structure of society was as sacred as the institution of monarchy. The highest thoughts and deepest emotions were expected to be depicted in royal or at least in aristocratic personages. Marriage was sought almost exclusively on the appropriate social level. There was little indication that drama was widening its scope as the century went on. French classical tragedy, which became one of the dominant influences, was the most restricted of all forms. Its insistence on an unvarying verse form and on the 'dramatic unities' of time, place, and action was appropriate to an equally narrow range of themes.

Despite all the obstacles, seventeenth-century plays are among the greatest achievements of the age. Shakespeare is of course unmatched in the variety and power of his work. There is little point in arguing about the century, or the style, to which he should be attached. As it happens the patriotic histories and the lighter comedies are nearly all Elizabethan in date; all the great tragedies, *Cymbeline* and *Coriolanus, The Winter's Tale* and *The Tempest* belong to the seventeenth century. The emphasis has moved from success and ebullience to inward doubts and tensions and to struggles with a mysterious and generally malign fate. The Italian court, the London tavern, and the Warwickshire country-side become less prominent than the storm, the witch-haunted heath, the dark castle, and the magic island. He remained as much an entrepreneur of the theatrical industry in writing *Hamlet* as he was in the popular comedies and the serialized historical epic. But awareness of the demands of his various audiences did not bring him to introduce the political, social, or religious conflicts of the day directly into the plays. His kings, his mobs, his statesmen, and his soldiers are on the whole as timeless as his mental conflicts. Not all his contemporaries and immediate successors shared this attitude. Ben Jonson was a master of topical satire: projectors, monopolists, acquisitive and hypocritical Puritans were some of his victims. Philip Massinger's *New Way to Pay Old Debts* is a caricature of the troubles of landowners in their search for new sources of wealth in which Overreach is blatantly modelled on Sir Giles Mompesson who had just been impeached for his monopolistic abuses.

The Interregnum, despite the pressures of Puritanism and the removal of most sources of patronage, was not a total disaster for English drama. (One thing it ended was the exclusion of women from the stage.) But after it Restoration comedy, with its uninhibited commentary on the contrast between marriage for the sake of property or status and sexual competition outside it, was rarely more than highly skilled light entertainment. It was in France that Shakespeare found his real successors – sharply divided between the comic and the tragic and shunning variety of mood or scene. Molière – the merchant's son Jean-Baptiste Poquelin – was a magnificent counterpoise to court solemnity. The royal visit to *Les Précieuses Ridicules* in 1660 had no perceptible effect on the cultural pretensions of the court or the salons; but the play established Molière securely. Though the *Compagnie du Saint-Sacrament* succeeded in banning *Tartuffe*, the daring attack on religious hypocrisy and casuistry, *le Bourgeois Gentilhomme*, *le Medicin malgré lui*, *les Femmes Savantes*, and the other satires on familiar types and attitudes survived unscathed. The two great tragedians, Pierre Corneille and – more than thirty years younger – Jean Racine were less remote from contemporary conflicts than their classical subjects and their firm concentration on the inward struggles of the idealized hero or heroine would suggest. The glories of military conquest were a theme sure of official welcome. When Corneille repeatedly showed the power of the free will faced by a moral dilemma, he was not only using a dramatic device familiar to the Greeks but upholding one aspect of Jesuit theology. Racine the Jansenist was more concerned with the 'Hidden God' of Pascal, the mysterious fate that it was pointless to resist. Romantic love is, both for men and for the women to whom he devoted his greatest poetry and characterization, sufficient in itself. He was never sure of a favourable reception, and when *Phèdre* was attacked by his enemies at court he abandoned the theatre altogether, returning only to write the two biblical plays, *Esther* and *Athalie*, for schoolgirls patronised by Madame de Maintenon. It was no doubt a tremendous achievement to convey such passion through his monotonously balanced verse, his small stock of words and phrases, and his rigid exclusion of all irrelevance or ornamentation. Even the most enthusiastic devotees of the idea of an all-pervading baroque would find it hard to apply the term to Racine.

THE BAROQUE IN ITALY

It is generally agreed that the centre from which baroque art spread through Europe was the Italy of the Counter-Reformation. Here at least there was a clear connection between artistic style and ideas prevalent in other spheres. The demand by the church for the services of architects and painters was now more important than that of individuals or lay authorities; and the church insisted that art must be adapted to the glorifying of re-ligion in its Catholic form. Rome was the headquarters of the most expensive and spectacular advertising campaign ever devised. Everything was to be the opposite of the austerity and individ-ualism of the Protestants. Light and colour and aspiring move-ment beautified the churches. The heavens opening, hosts of angels glorifying God, biblical scenes with throngs of the faithful adoring Christ, splendour surrounding the Virgin and the Saints – all these were treated in a manner supposed to draw the spec-tator in rather than to overawe him. There was no separation between the functions of architect, sculptor, and painter. A side-line of the baroque was the 'Illusionism' that could disguise the boundary between three-dimensional structure and flat painting. It did not mean that artists were deliberately rejecting older habits: the painters most influential around 1600 such as Annibale Carracci and Polidoro da Caravaggio, had grown up in the Renaissance tradition much of which survived behind their strong individual traits. (Caravaggio was denounced by churchmen for the realistic poverty of some of his figures.) But it was the bold-ness and splendour of the new works that impressed visitors to the city. Sixtus V in 1585 had initiated a scheme for new streets in Rome; and a succession of seventeenth-century popes, Urban VIII, Innocent X, and Alexander VII, were anxious that the whole city as well as its churches should be a worthy attraction for the faithful.

Some of the most startling productions of mid-century Rome were the churches of Francesco Borromini with his insistence on using a curve rather than a straight line wherever it could be contrived. The greatest creator of Italian baroque, Gian Lorenzo Bernini, became a major European celebrity. Though it is for sculpture and architecture that he is remembered, he was at least as enthusiastic as a painter: the idea that the three could be different skills and their products unrelated would not have seemed tolerable to him. In 1629 he was appointed architect of the half-finished St Peter's, where he made the splendid colonnades of the piazza and the huge canopy, or *baldacchino*, on twisted pillars over the altar. (Bronze was torn from the roof of the Pantheon to provide material for it.) His sculpture and building, his fountains and altars, appeared everywhere in the city and in the other Italian towns. From the palaces of the cardinals downwards, baroque domestic architecture and decoration became the accepted mark of prestige. In gardens, squares, and the new broad avenues of planned city development, baroque ideas were proclaimed. The courts and towns of the rest of Europe adopted and modified the fashion with an enthusiasm that tended to diminish in proportion to their distance – physical and spiritual – from Rome. In Italy itself the stimulus given to art by the Church's patronage may well have been outweighed by the narrow range of subjects and manner it now approved.

RUBENS

At the turn of the century the Duke of Mantua appointed as court painter Peter-Paul Rubens, son of a prominent Antwerp magistrate. He visited Rome, Venice, and Genoa, and spent a year in Spain. In 1608 he returned to Antwerp, with a well-established reputation and style, and was received into the establishment of the Archduke Albert. The city that had lost its commercial pre-eminence became the centre of what turned into a minor industry of art. Though Rubens completed his greatest works and many of his courtly portraits himself, his output – like that of masters in other crafts – was expanded with the help of numerous apprentices and assistants, and he kept a careful eye on the market price. The styles of his great range of subjects were imitated in, and far beyond, the Spanish Netherlands. Much of his work seemed as passionately religious as anything in Rome. Before too much is made of the spiritual inspiration behind his scenes of apotheosis it is worth remembering that the figure borne heavenwards by cherubim is James I in one of them and Henri IV of France in another. Formal portraits, allegorical scenes of royal triumph like the series on the life of Marie de Medici, and episodes from pagan mythology were no less welcome as topics than the religious ones. It is undeniable that to most twentieth-century eyes the fat women with chinless insipid faces are not for their own sake attractive, and they have become – unjustly – the best-known characteristic feature of his work and even of baroque painting in general. He was capable of the most perceptive and sympathetic portraiture – as in the *Four Negro Heads* or the *Old Woman warming herself* – and of such realistic scenes as *The Prodigal Son* and *The Boar Hunt*. In his later years, when he claimed to have 'conceived a horror of Courts'[7] and had acquired a lavish country house, he produced more landscapes, peaceful and even subdued. But he never ceased to accept commissions for an immense variety of work. One of the orders for which he assembled a distinguished team of collaborators was the state entry of the Prince-Cardinal Ferdinand into Antwerp in 1635. The triumphal arches, the sculptures and paintings arranged in great open-air displays, the processions and ceremonies were co-ordinated into one huge theatrical display. The fact that it was temporary did not make it seem any less important.

There was nothing unheard-of in the 'entry of Ferdinand'. Seventeenth-century painters did not assume that their main task was to produce on an easel works that would hang in an art gallery or glorify the home of whatever rich purchaser could be found. They were part of a single continuing process of providing visual beauty. The chief beneficiaries were necessarily those who paid for it; but it was not only in churches or on the exteriors of buildings that the people as a whole saw the products of art. The festivals that provided popular drama were also, in their decorations, waxworks, costumes and fireworks a form of visual art, and as with the dramatic aspect it was one in which everyone could actively participate. When Louis XIV spent unlimited money on his water displays, cavalcades, ballets, dwarfs and monsters he was creating on the grand scale what the carnival and the travelling showman attempted amid the poverty of village life. Punch and Judy can claim baroque qualities as confidently as any sculptured ceiling or sculptured fountain; and it was in this period that their popularity became established.

THE BAROQUE IN CENTRAL EUROPE AND SPAIN

It was probably in the Catholic part of central Europe that the baroque was, by 1700, most prominently visible. The Thirty Years War did not altogether put a stop to lavish building: the palace that Wallenstein built for himself in Prague between 1625 and 1629, and filled with looted treasure, originated the popularity of the style in a city which in the next generation became full of it. After the Peace of Westphalia, both the landed nobility and the church were able to undertake an impressive amount of new building, much of it designed by Italians. In the 1680s and 1690s, when the greater sense of security after the defeat of the Turks may have been a further incentive to building, there appeared the first great German architects of the century. Johann Bernhardt Fischer von Erlach, 'Inspector of Royal Buildings' to the Emperor Joseph I, produced the original grandiose plans for the palace of Schönbrunn – which were drastically altered after his death – and a great variety of buildings in Vienna, Prague, and Salzburg. Lukas von Hildebrandt, once an engineer in the Imperial army, built in a rather less ponderous manner than Fischer's many of the huge palaces that were within the means not only of princes but of aristocrats who had reaped the benefits of successful war.

One difficulty about the claim that baroque art expressed the essence of Catholic civilization in the seventeenth century is that in Spain it was not a distinctively dominant style. The facade of Granada Cathedral, designed by Alonso Cano, was the first really impressive building of this kind, and it would have been completely unfamiliar in the north. Francisco de Herrera and Francisco de Zurbaran were far more restrained and realistic than their Italian contemporaries. Diego de Silva Velasquez, chosen by Philip IV as his principal court portrait-painter, produced naturalistic figures enlivened by a magnificent use of light and colour, but closer in manner to the later Renaissance than to the baroque. There was not much trace of religious passion in him. His *Coronation of the Virgin* treats the theme of heavenly glorification in a way that is comparatively rigid and angular. Indeed the Spanish church did remarkably little to make use of the attractions of great art: it was the court and the confident superiority of royalty and aristocracy that provided Velasquez with his subject-matter.

FRENCH ART

Harder still to fit into the idea of the all-pervading baroque is the Catholic country that by the end of the century dominated the whole culture of Europe. Though Bernini and Rubens had a prolonged influence in France, characteristics that in any other period would be unhesitatingly called 'classical' were prominent all the time and in the great days of Louis XIV's court clearly had the upper hand. Henri IV had ambitions for Paris comparable to those of the popes for Rome. He also led the way for the higher nobility in the building or expanding of chateaux. But it was not until Richelieu's time that successful state encouragement was given to French art. In 1627 Simon Vouet, who had spent most of his adult life in Rome, was invited to the French court. His painting in the Louvre and the other royal palaces, and his panels and altars in churches, established a style of decoration that was bright and luminous but a good deal more restrained than the Italian fashion. He did not achieve as much success with the Parisian aristocrats as did another French settler in Rome, Nicolas Poussin. Though Richelieu brought him to Paris in 1640, two years of the life of an approved court painter proved as much as he could stand. But when he returned to Italy he continued to work for French patrons. A landscape, a biblical scene, or a piece of ancient mythology by Poussin was a highly fashionable acquisition for any office-holder aspiring to social advancement. He became the recognized model for French artistic taste; and the qualities he imposed were predominantly classical ones. In his wide range of style and subject-matter his interest was always in carefully calculated geometric pattern and unity of theme rather than in excitement or splendour. His greatest source of guidance was antique sculpture. 'Cold' is one of the commonest terms applied to him; but through the various 'periods' into which his work has been analysed there runs a love of smooth, glowing light that may have been more apparent before the pictures became darker with age. More dramatic effects of light appear in many of the landscapes of Claude Lorrain, another Frenchman who lived almost entirely in Italy. He was much more responsive than Poussin to the beauty of country and sea – and less favoured by the best circles in Paris. In complete contrast to the followers of Poussin were the Le Nain brothers, Antoine, Louis, and Mathieu. They worked in the same studio, and often on the same picture, which they signed with the surname alone. Their one characteristic theme, realistic scenes of rural life and peasant faces, acquired something of a vogue of its own. They did not make fun of the peasant, or idealise him. They offered no comment on poverty or injustice. But they used the pictorial qualities of houses, dress, and furniture that had not been designed for ornament or ostentation, and of faces not apparently posed for the painter. They did not hide themselves away in the countryside that provided their material: they sought the same courtly patronage as others, and just before the deaths of Antoine and Louis they were admitted as original members of the *Académie de Peinture et de Sculpture*.

The foundation of the *Académie* in 1648 was a decisive step in the organization of French art for the glory of the state. But it was not until the energy of Colbert was applied to the integration of the nation's artistic resources that the great era of regulated art began. What remained of baroque freedom was firmly subordinated to an officially approved style for which classical sculpture and Raphael were highly recommended models. There was prolonged hesitation over the eastern façade of the Louvre. Though Bernini was brought from Rome and welcomed with adulation, in the end his plans were rejected in favour of classical severity. The first leaders of the new artistic hierarchy were the men who created Fouquet's great chateau at Vaux-le-Vicomte and were promptly conscripted by Colbert for Louis' own even more magnificent scheme. Louis le Vau had been employed by Fouquet not simply as an architect but as manager of a great company of painters, sculptors, and craftsmen of all kinds. Charles le Brun, the principal painter throughout Colbert's period in power, was himself an organizer and co-ordinator who would happily turn from his massive pictures such as *Louis XIV adoring the Risen Christ* to sketch out a tapestry, plan the complete decoration of a room, or settle contests for advancement among the artists as bitter as any among politicians. His own supremacy ended with the fall of Colbert. At least as important in the Versailles project and in the aggrandisement of Paris was the landscape-designer André le Nôtre, who brought buildings, lakes, woods, and gardens into designs of calculated symmetry and proportion. When le Vau was succeeded by Jules Hardouin Mansard no doubt remained about the classical emphasis in the immense exterior and even in the interior of Versailles.

THE DUTCH PAINTERS

An impressive piece of evidence for the effect on the arts of religious and social factors is the contrast between the painters of the United Provinces and those of the Spanish Netherlands. Before the revolt the mixture of Italian and native traditions had been much the same in Utrecht as it was in Antwerp. After it the artists of the north lived in a different world from that of Rubens. Though official and individual patronage was not unknown, the Dutch painter normally completed his canvas first and then offered it for sale in his studio or even in a fair. Much of the demand was for the realistic scenes of the household, the tavern, and the street, or for local landscapes, or for group portraits as well as individual ones. Dutch bourgeois art was firmly condemned by the French academies. But the modern assessment of Dutch painting can give a misleading impression. The Italian style was not driven out: men like Cornelis van Poelenburgh had great success with biblical and mythological subjects while some of what are now seen as the greatest pictures were unsold. Rembrandt was in his earlier years a successful portrait-painter in Amsterdam. He had many of the baroque techniques, even if they were applied to townsmen rather than angels. When he became introspective and tragic, painting Christ in tender humanity rather than glory, and landscapes that were more dreamlike than real, he went bankrupt. Jan Vermeer, disregarded and impoverished in his lifetime, achieved his powerful emotional effects by new techniques for the creation of luminosity and depth. Many of this generation of painters – Pieter de Hooch, Salomon and Jacob van Ruisdael, Jan Steen and others – died in the seventies or early eighties. After them Dutch art as we admire it was almost extinct: the influence of Antwerp and of Paris dominated the market.

It is hard to find in the art of other northern countries a style as distinctive or successful as that of the Dutch. The Stuarts drew their favoured painters from the Netherlands, Rubens' pupil Sir Anthony Van Dyck from Antwerp and Sir Peter Lely from Haarlem. Inigo Jones, whose ideas were formed in his visits to Italy, brought to the service of the Crown and the court nobility the 'Mannerist' style of Palladio, with its rules of symmetry and proportion, its columned façades and its restraint in exterior ornament. Sir Christopher Wren kept away from Italy: it was France that he recognized as a source of ideas, though not of rules.

In the work of this state architect who was originally a scientist and mathematician, and who could evade both conventional standards and the views of his patrons, it is easy to find traces of almost every European style. The connection of St Paul's with St Peter's was as recognizable but as restricted as that of Anglicanism with Catholicism. Sir John Vanbrugh produced at Blenheim and Castle Howard massive palaces that can certainly claim to be more baroque than Versailles. But it was not in great houses or in churches that a distinctive English architecture appeared. Perhaps the most successful buildings in combining function with appearance are the more modest gentry houses, often of brick, aping the aristocratic ones in some of their features – notably the long gallery – and adorned with the best portraits, furnishings, and plate the owner could afford to keep. A great deal of gentry wealth found its way to the craftsmen who produced what prestige and taste required.

MUSIC

The painter, the sculptor, and even for most purposes the architect had in 1600 materials that were as good as any available today. This was not true of the musician. There could not have been a musical equivalent of St Peter's because the instruments that existed were incapable of the range and richness of sound it would demand. The lute and viol, the virginals and clavichord, imposed severe limitations on the composer. It was in the course of the seventeenth century that the essentials of the modern orchestra appeared. The violin evolved slowly into the form produced by Nicolo Amati and his apprentice Antonio Stradivari. The oboe now gave more quantity than quality of sound; but the introduction from about 1690 of the clarinet made possible the successful combination of strings and woodwind. The mechanical developments were part of a change in the rôle of music in cultured life. Outside the church it had come mainly from the solo instruments the playing of which was an accomplishment familiar in the middle as well as upper ranks of society, from small professional groups, and of course in song. The innovation that did most to expand its scope was the opera.

Many other art-forms contributed to the conventions of opera.

The secular cantata and the oratorio made the telling of a story the framework for large-scale vocal music with alternating 'recitative' and 'aria'; the French *ballet-de-cour* demanded elaborate instrumental accompaniment; the English masque blended music and drama with spectacular costume and scenic effects. But it was in Italy that the popularity of opera was first established. The Church accepted without controlling it; the nobility patronized it. As Italian artistic energy seemed to move from painting and sculpture towards music opera provided the perfect combination of skills. *Orfeo*, the most popular work of Claudio Monteverdi, was performed in 1608. In 1637 Venice had its Opera House – an institution that soon became necessary to most self-respecting cities and monarchs. Though Monteverdi was himself a writer of madrigals, his operas made more use of simple melodic solos than of verbally incomprehensible choral polyphony. A large orchestra was as much a part of them as the singers. Despite the fame of Italian opera, it was only under Louis XIV that the French developed an enthusiasm for it. Jean-Baptiste Lully was a court musician ready to turn his hand to whatever form of entertainment the king demanded. The dramatic plot tended to be rather more coherent than in Italy and the music unemotional; but orchestra and chorus, as well as the indispensable ballet, got plenty of prominence.

Protestant Germany was as open as Vienna itself to the influence of Italian music. Hamburg in the 1680s became a centre of opera, despite some religious opposition; in Dresden the Italian-trained *Kappellmeister* to the Elector of Saxony, Heinrich Schütz, turned from his early operatic work to religious choral music, and made the oratorio an opportunity for vast and unrestrained compositions. But the greatest German initiative was in writing for the organ. This too underwent great technical development during the century. Girolamo Frescobaldi as organist of St Peter's expanded the musical possibilities of the instrument and initiated the demand for improvement. It culminated at the end of the century in the great organ at Lübeck on which Dietrich Buxtehude worked out the organ chorales and toccatas that are seen as leading directly to Bach. Much more than opera, or than the sonata and concerto that were taking shape in the instrumental music performed in great and not so great houses, church music was accessible to everyone. Indeed it was inescapable. Despite the suspicions of some Protestant sects, the churches on the whole helped to give music its importance in the leisure of poor as well as rich. Not that much help was needed: enough has survived of the folk-songs and traditional airs of the period to show that the cultured élite had no monopoly in the creation of melodic beauty.

NOTES AND REFERENCES

1 Lawrence Stone in *Past and Present*, no. 28 (1964), p. 68.

2 *Works*, eds Spedding and Ellis, vol. 3, p. 300; vol. 4, p. 494.

3 From the full title of *The Great Didactic* (1642).

4 J. H. Huizinga, *Dutch Civilisation in the Seventeenth Century* (London, 1968), pp. 65–6, 70.

5 Peter Burke, *Popular Culture in Early Modern Europe* (1978) p. 182.

6 It is quoted in J. Lough, *Introduction to Seventeenth-Century France* (London, 1954), p. 187.

7 P. Cabanne, *Rubens* (London, 1967), p. 233.

8

POLITICAL IDEAS

Ideas about the working of the organized community, and about the duties of rulers and ruled, had always been an important part of European philosophy. The *Politics* was one of the most familiar books of Aristotle. Augustine and Aquinas had both regarded questions of justice and government as part of their theology. To early seventeenth-century writers who ranged, more or less selectively, over the whole expanse of human understanding, it was natural to treat political questions in the traditional way. They asked how the state originated, and answered the question with little regard to historical evidence. They defined, as Aristotle had, the various possible forms of the state; and the descriptions of them were usually remote from reality. The men they envisaged as its subjects were remarkably free from poverty, greed, and stupidity. To some extent this was a conventional pose, concealing a strong concern with current conflicts; but it was one that tended to keep the influence of the theorists on events small. While men were dying and destroying through the blunders and follies of the state, those who studied it seemed to devote themselves largely to such notions as the fictitious contract that justified political power and the ill-defined Natural Law that might limit it.

Even so, this was a period in which theories about fundamental political problems were closer than before to what was happening. The conflict between authority and doubt in religion was accompanied by a questioning of the accepted reasons for obeying earthly powers. Most theorists, heavily influenced by Bodin, agreed that there must be a 'sovereign' whose ultimate power no-one could challenge; and sovereignty was justified by an uneasy mixture of divine command, metaphors about the family or tribe, and general conceptions of justice and morality. But, increasingly, sheer expediency was added to these. The gap between theoretical pronouncements and the minister coping with an empty treasury or the crowd cheering a rebel leader, wide though it remained, was not unbridgeable. Within the concept of sovereignty there was room for argument about the ways in which a ruler might normally limit and share his power. It was possible to consider as a practical problem the circumstances in which a subject might resist his sovereign. Political theories were becoming less a preserve of the clergy and the intellectuals and closer to the mere craft of statesmanship. Many of the most relevant ideas about the state came from men directly involved in its working. In France Sully, Richelieu, Colbert, even Louis XIV himself, left in one form or another their thoughts on monarchy. England produced a rare assortment of political thinkers who were also practitioners. There was James I, the king who claimed to be a philosopher; Bacon the philosopher who became a Lord Chancellor; Eliot the hero of opposition who wrote in prison his treatise accepting royal sovereignty; Coke and Selden the state lawyers; Lilburne and Rainsborough the leaders of popular rebellion; Milton the poet and official propagandist. Descriptions of the various forms of government in Europe became a necessary part of the culti-vated gentleman's library. In the study of states, as of planets, accurate observation was now the first essential – with sometimes a dangerous assumption that both moved in unchanging orbits. The aim of observation was, for many writers, to construct a science of politics, in which principles could be laid down with mathematical certainty. By the end of the century there were the beginnings of political statistics, and investigations of national economies. It was a great advance on Aristotelian theorizing; but its confident ambition was liable to produce new unrealities.

Aristotle's 'state' had been a single self-sufficient community of villages, to which every human being belonged; and political theorists now tended to assume that the state was the one auth-ority that commanded the complete obedience of its subjects. In 1576 there had appeared Bodin's *République*, which became almost as great an authority as Aristotle himself; and Bodin too had seen the sovereignty of the state as the fundamental question of politics. A difficulty was that in many parts of Europe it was not at all clear what territory constituted the state. It was not much help when Bodin remarked that the Holy Roman Empire was a state where sovereignty was held by the seven electors and three hundred or so princes. Ferdinand II found several theorists ready to insist that the emperor was sovereign and entitled to veto the legislation of the states within the Empire. Against them such writers as Philip Chemnitz ('Hippolytus a Lapide') argued not only that the princes held sovereign power but that they had a duty to resist an emperor who claimed it for himself. A more widespread problem was that no-one could openly deny the overriding duty of obedience to God, which could easily be turned into obedience to the Church. But the medieval conflicts between *regnum* and *sacerdotium* had by this time been reduced to marginal or occasional clashes of interest. The restriction on sovereignty that now mattered more was that of the law. Even the Spanish Jesuit Francisco Suarez, though he was bound to uphold the pope's supremacy over kings in spiritual matters, used theology as a basis for limitation of the power of the ruler by Natural Law. God, he argued, had ordained that men should freely unite in an organized community, and had shown the Natural Law by which it should be governed for the common good. This of course was only distantly related to the laws that were in practice obeyed. Much as the churches and clergy had claimed to be the interpreters of the will of God, judges and lawyers were more and more able to claim for themselves a status independent of monarchies. The ruler who sought to make his power absolute had to make sure that the obedience owed to God and the law became in effect obedience to the state.

THE KING AND GOD

It was not difficult to take over for the king some of the individual's duty to God. James I, 'supreme head' of a church more closely bound to the Crown than any other in Europe, expounded for his subjects and for his son the notion of Divine Right: kings were established by God, they sit on God's throne, they are responsible to God alone.[1] This was little more than trumpet-blowing that did not greatly affect James's realistic appraisal of his relations with Parliament. But many writers on various levels went further, threatening damnation for resistance to the Lord's Anointed. Roger Manwaring announced in his sermons in the 1620s that to achieve salvation the will of the sovereign must be obeyed unless 'flatly against the law of God' – a larger loophole than he admitted. In France homilies on the Christian duty of obedience to kings were common – some of them in atrocious verse.

> Par moi règnent les rois, dit la bouche suprême;
> Ils tiennent de moi seule, en foi, leur diadème.[2]

Expositions of the unlimited power of monarchs were a favourite type of literature throughout the century. Sir Robert Filmer in England showed absolutism to be in harmony with all the other works of God; Prokopovitch in Russia blended Divine Right with consent by proving that God had commanded the people to confer their power on the tsar; tracts and sermons almost everywhere made God and kings inseparable. One of the last comprehensive expositions of divine right came from the French theologian and court preacher Jacques Bossuet. With massive biblical quotation he set out in a logical series of 'Propositions' to show that the law of God ordained absolute hereditary monarchy as the best of all forms of government.[3] Some of the reasons for this were practical, not to say cynical: people naturally show envy towards those in power, but a royal family can arouse their affection instead. The monarch whose kingdom will be passed on to his sons will feel that his own interests are so closely identified with those of the state that he will act entirely for its good. Royal authority was sacred, paternal, and absolute; but it was also subject to reason and to the law. This was the point at which Bossuet startlingly turned Divine Right into Divine Obligation. True the king could never be liable to the penalties of the law, or to coercion by his subjects. But the law to which he must submit was not simply the law of God: it included the law of the land. The monarch should be greatest in virtue as well as in power, and his virtue included setting an example to his subjects of obedience to his own just laws. It was the sacred duty of the monarch to rule in accordance with reason – the implications of which were set out in what was then the familiar form of a series of rather trite pieces of moral advice. The relation between the ruler of the state and 'law' had long been a much more pressing field of dispute than his relations with God.

THE KING AND LAW: GROTIUS

The term 'law' – or its Latin equivalent '*ius*' – had so many meanings that it was in itself a source of abundant confusion. 'Positive' law included what was ordained by monarchs, legislative assemblies, and those who derived authority from them; but it also included in England the Common Law that had grown out of the decisions of lawyers through the ages and in France and much of southern Europe the Roman Law that was accepted as the basis of the system of justice. 'Natural' law, a much overworked term, was a less definable notion, with both classical and religious origins. As could be expected , seventeenth-century philosophy increasingly separated Natural Law from its religious, and especially its scriptural aspects and put the emphasis on those versions that made it a statement of how men and communities behave and how in their own interest they ought to behave. In this sense Natural Law seemed to be one means of bringing to the study of men in communities the processes both of observation and of deduction from what was certain. The writer who first made this attitude obvious was the Dutch lawyer and statesman Huig van Groot, who Latinised his name as Grotius. To Netherlands theorists after the Revolt, conventional explanations of the need to obey the state and the monarch were embarrassing. The Dutch were almost bound to stress the importance of law as a safeguard against tyranny. Grotius was anything but remote from political realities or from religious conflict. As a leading theologian of the Remonstrants he was sentenced to life imprisonment when his patron Oldenbarnevelt was executed. After his celebrated escape in a load of books and dirty linen, he lived in Paris with a pension from Louis XIII, and for a time was in the diplomatic service of Sweden. He described the Law of Nature as emanating from God; but he noted that if – which it would of course be sinful to believe – God did not exist, the arguments would still be valid.[4] For his aim was to construct its principles with the precision and certainty of geometrical theorems. God could no more change Natural Law than he could make two and two into something other than four. Grotius was in fact firmly separating the principles on which societies should be founded from the revealed religion in which he continued to believe.

When it came to actual definition there was nothing startling in Grotius' Natural Law. Men should fulfil their promises and contracts, specific or implied; they should respect property; they should obey those whose authority they had accepted, and in groups with no such authority they should conform to the will of the majority; they should punish transgressors according to their deserts. Some of his precepts might seem to owe as much to the needs and habits of the Dutch commercial class as to universal truth. But Grotius claimed to distinguish firmly between principles and the differing positive laws which states could make within them. Unlike most theorists, he was concerned at least as much with international as with national questions. It was in relations between states that the problems of society without a sovereign could be seen. If the principles of Natural Law could be applied there, its benefits would be immediately obvious. *Mare Liberum*, intended as an attack on the trading and colonial monopolies of the Spaniards, used the theories as part of a pamphleteering war. But *De Jure Belli ac Pacis*, written during the early part of the Thirty Years War, set out in massive and dogmatic detail the rules by which the justness of wars could be tested and their inhumanity and inconvenience mitigated. Though the work had little perceptible effect in his own day, it eventually provided a basis for the polite conventions within which eighteenth-century conflicts were conducted, and even for a sketchy 'international law'.

THE SUPREMACY OF LAW: COKE

Grotius was using an artificially devised legal code to solve the difficulties that arose from an absence of sovereign power. In England another great codifier, Edward Coke, saw in it the way of settling disagreements between those who shared power. It was a familiar argument for absolutism that a division of power produced anarchy. An institution with power to settle differences within the ruling authorities would itself be the sovereign. To take refuge in appeals to Natural Law, or God, was merely to express the pious hope that the quarrel could be settled by argument. But a solution might exist if there were a set of laws so apt and so well defined that, at least among those skilled in such mysteries, there could be no doubt about what they meant. To this status Coke was ready to exalt the English Common Law. 'The Common Law', he reiterated, 'is the absolute perfection of reason.'[5] It was superior to Parliament, and when (not even 'if') an Act of Parliament is unreasonable the Common Law will declare it void.[6] According to his own account he told James I bluntly that 'his Majesty was not learned in the laws of England' and that kings were under the law as well as under God. But statements as uncompromising as these were not developed into any clear explanation of how they were to be applied. Coke is as guilty of muddle and self-contradiction as any of the philosophers.

For some purposes law, and the Common Law especially, appeared as unchangeable, needing only to be declared and applied by the professional experts. For others, such as the reform of the legal system itself, Coke was ready enough to stress that 'a transcendent and absolute power of legislation' was vested in parliament – which he could, by a convenient piece of antiquarianism, call a court. His intention was to attack the arbitrary power he believed the Crown to be acquiring; but the lawyer-dominated state he seemed to envisage was not attractive to the parliamentarians who wanted power for themselves as representatives of a large section of propertied society. It was one thing to attack such specific evils as the encroachment of ecclesiastical and prerogative courts, but quite another to show how law, or law in the light of reason, would always prevail against tyranny. The best he could offer as an unchallengeable source of ultimate authority was Magna Carta, already something of a legend. Its celebrated but ambiguous clauses protecting the 'free' man and the right of property were hardly more specific than the principles laid down by Grotius; and the rest of its massive text had little relevance four centuries later. Even so, his insistence that a body of law, as systematic and comprehensive as possible, should be used to protect the citizen became part of a professional tradition. Like Grotius, he was among the theorists who had a direct influence on events.

THE DIVISION OF POWER: ALTHUSIUS

In one essential the lawyers tended to agree with the absolutists: the greatest evils were those that came from disorder and conflict. Stability and beneficence of institutions mattered more than the individual's part in them. One of the first writers in the century to concern himself with the relations between ruler and ruled was the German Calvinist Johann Althusen – Althusius. Though he has never been highly regarded by political philosophers, his *Politica Methodice Digesta* (Analysis of Political Method) was, in spite of its artificially rigid and elaborate classifications, a realistic investigation of contemporary government. It was, he believed, natural for human beings to associate with each other in groups of different size and purpose. The family was the smallest of these, an entirely natural community into which some of the individual's rights and activities were merged. Similarly small voluntary associations (*collegia*) could offer other benefits of living together and have appropriate powers conceded to them by their members. Above them the various political institutions, local and regional, contributed to the authority of the state itself. The power of the group, including the unique majesty of the state, was derived from smaller groups that had come together to form it, and ultimately from the people themselves. This notion of authority derived from the whole people through intermediaries had the great attraction of justifying the power of assemblies and of such bodies as the cities and principalities of the Empire, without admitting a right of popular rebellion. The tyrannical monarch could be resisted, but only by the officials or institutions to whom the people had delegated their right to do so. Or at least they must be deemed to have delegated it: one of the difficulties Althusius never quite solved was the gap between 'the people' and the institutions with which he identified them. Somehow the men at every level who had been 'entrusted' with the administration of authority could, like the monarch, have their powers removed if they abused them. It all fitted well enough the teaching of Calvin himself.

THE CONTRACT

There was another essential ingredient in the scheme of Althusius, which he shared with most other theorists of the century: the power of rulers originated in a 'contract'. Only the most naive or unscrupulous could offer a historical basis for such an idea. Others had either to brush aside as irrelevant the question of whether a contract ever existed or to admit frankly that it was a myth. But in the thought both of the theorists and of their readers history played a much smaller part than law. The notion that obligation must rest on a solemn agreement was a central part of the lawyers' way of thought; and they were too familiar with the idea of a fictitious or implied contract to be put off by quibbles about its unreality. Moreover the notion of a contractual relation between the sovereign and his subjects was linked, vaguely, with that of feudal obligations. It could make obedience a moral duty – and could do so without reference to religious precepts.

The contract theory did not help to settle arguments about the power of the state. It could be asserted with equal plausibility either that the contract imposed obligations on the ruler or that it freed him from them. Part of the confusion came from haziness about who the 'contracting parties' were imagined to be. Althusius demanded a number of contracts, of two distinct kinds: all his groups were brought into being by contracts between the individuals, or between the smaller groups, that formed them. The group then made a second contract with the man, or men, who saw to the working of its organization. Looked at in this way the state was different from other associations in the extent but not in the origin of its power; and the monarch was only the dominant part of a complex machinery of government. If he broke his side of the contract, power would revert to the bodies that had made it, and ultimately to the people as a whole. The contract in this form was therefore an argument on the side of the 'monarchomachs' – the term applied loosely to those who justified some kind of resistance to the monarch. It could be used at the same time to rule out mere rebellion, by stressing that the contract setting up the community implied a promise to abide by the decisions of the majority – which could be quietly assumed to mean the majority of those who were able to take part in politics. But there was no logical reason why the contract should be assumed to leave ultimate power in the hands of the majority: it could just as well bestow it, more or less irrevocably, on one or more rulers. All that was necessary in using it to support absolutism was to play down the idea of a contract between government and people and think solely of an agreement to set up the state by surrendering the natural rights of individuals into the hands of a sovereign – an agreement which would be binding so long as a sovereign existed.

HOBBES

This was the version of the contract used by the most outspoken and exciting of all philosophers of the time, Thomas Hobbes. Next to Marx, Hobbes may well be the modern political theorist about whom most has been written. Commentators on the whole agree in praising the logical and uncompromising clarity of his argument and go on to differ fundamentally about what he meant. His life was full of contradictions. He was a dependant of the Cavendishes, one of the greatest aristocratic families, and fled to Paris before the outbreak of the Civil War; but the leading royalist political writers, Clarendon and Filmer, went out of their way to denounce him. Three of his principal works, the English translation of *De Cive, Leviathan*, and what was later entitled *The Elements of Law*, were published in England during the Rump Parliament and were soon alleged to be justifications of the rule of Cromwell. At the Restoration Charles welcomed him at court, and the presence of so wicked an atheist was one of the popular explanations of God's wrath manifested in the Plague and the Fire – though he had produced long and not grievously unorthodox expositions of Christianity. Perhaps the habit of simultaneously admiring him and either attacking or 'reinterpreting' him springs from a feeling that his pessimistic view of human nature and its political consequences can neither be refuted nor accepted. Before Hobbes, both the classical and the Christian strands in political thought had been concerned with morality: starting from such abstract notions as justice, virtue, and wisdom the theorists asked not what did happen in the creation and working of the state but what ought to happen. The answer tended to be, as Leo Strauss put it, 'that the simply best régime is the rule of the wise and the best practicable régime is the rule of gentlemen'.[7] For Hobbes politics was part of an all-embracing study of the material world, to be treated in the same way as mathematics or astronomy. His starting-point was the nature of human beings – a nature very different from anything the moralists or theologians imagined. Men are so nearly equal, in mind and body, that whatever one man has another can hope to acquire. The weakest can, with a little ingenuity, kill the strongest; everyone thinks himself among the wisest; material possessions are always liable to be stolen. Consequently men constantly quarrel with each other.

In the nature of man we find three principal causes of quarrel. First, competition; secondly, diffidence; thirdly, glory. The first maketh men invade for gain; the second, for safety; and the third for reputation.[8]

If there is no power to keep them 'in awe', they will be 'in that condition which is called Warre'. In this state, where life is dominated by fear, there can be no material or cultural improvement. 'The notions of right and wrong, justice and injustice have there no place.' It is not so much a condition men *were* in before government existed as a condition they *would* be in if the power of government were removed. It is also the condition that actually exists not between men but between nations.

To escape from the horrors of the 'State of Warre' Hobbesian men were deemed to have made with each other the contract that set up a sovereign government. In practice, states were usually founded by conquest; but it is still expedient to accept the conqueror as sovereign. It is here that Hobbes throws out completely the pious smugness of traditional theories. He does not divide governments into good and bad: they are all bad. The men who rule will be men who seek power – more power than they need for their own protection. That is one reason why a single person is not quite as bad a ruler as an assembly: his wealth and glory will be largely the same as the wealth and glory of the state. The corrupt and ambitious officers of a democracy will often do best for themselves by 'perfidious advice, a treacherous action, or a civil war'.[9] Not that subjects are essentially different from rulers: if they think they can benefit by breaking the laws, they will do so. In this they are mistaken. When the sovereign is there, it is in the ultimate interests of subjects to obey him whatever he may command, since nothing short of death could be worse than the reversion to anarchy that would result from disobedience. There seem to be only two circumstances in which resistance to the sovereign is desirable. One is when he tries to put the subject to death; since (for some reason not made clear) death is the one evil worse than living in anarchy. The other is when the sovereign has ceased to be able to offer protection, and order can be better preserved by transferring allegiance to another. The Civil War, Hobbes suggests in a postscript to *Leviathan*, might have thrown some light on the tricky problem of when the citizen, and the soldier, can lawfully transfer his obligation from the old sovereign to the new.

At this point Hobbes is introducing into his argument words such as 'lawful' and 'obligation' which seem to belong not to his strictly amoral outlook but to the familiar ideas of politics that involve some absolute ethical standards laid down if not by God at least by a 'law of Nature'. Indeed he often talks in such terms. In accepting the state, a man grants away his natural rights, and is then '*obliged* or *bound*' not to hinder those who now hold them. He '*ought* and it is his *duty* to avoid the *injustice* and *injury*' that would arise from breaking his covenant. (The emphasis is Hobbes's own.[10]) Similarly he discusses at length the duties as well as the rights of the sovereign. Many twentieth-century commentators have insisted that all this amounts to an explanation of political behaviour that is based on morality rather than expediency and is independent of his dismal view of human psychology.[11] Certainly he wrote a great deal, especially in the earlier statements of his ideas, in the familiar language of moral philosophy. But when he faced the question of how obligations came to exist his answer was generally that they depended on the state. In the condition of 'warre'

. . . nothing can be unjust . . . Force and fraud are the two cardinal virtues. Justice and injustice . . . relate to men in Society, not in Solitude.[12]

Perhaps the greatest difficulty was to explain how totally selfish men would be so enlightened as to make and keep the imaginary covenant with each other to set up the state. There is a good deal of confusion in the argument that it is a law of Nature, that is to say a 'precept or general rule found out by reason . . . that a man be willing, when others are so too, . . . to lay down this right to all things'. One modern comment is that the descriptions he applied to mankind in general were really derived from the 'market society' of his own time where feudal obligations had disappeared and sovereignty was manifestly necessary for the preservation of property.[13] But property-owners did not usually consider collective rather than individual interests. Hobbes avoids all the errors that arise from assuming that men are virtuous: he cannot always reconcile his ideas with the fact that they are stupid.

Part of the task of the Hobbesian sovereign is to cope with popular ignorance. 'Common people are not of capacity enough to be made to understand' the principles of government. They must be constantly taught to conform. It would be a help if times could be set aside from labour when they could 'hear their duties told them', and 'put in mind of the authority that maketh laws'. To this end the Jews had a sabbath, 'in the solemnity whereof they were put in mind that their King was God'. Without specifically relegating the Church to the role of a propaganda instrument for the state, Hobbes insists that the interests of the two are identical. Religious teaching, like every other aspect of life, is subject to the orders of the sovereign. If the subject is ordered to believe what in fact he does not, then though the cleric may reasonably suffer martyrdom for his faith, the layman must outwardly conform – and trust that God will hold the sovereign responsible. Hobbes's discussions of Christianity cannot however be written off easily as those of an atheist practising the outward conformity he advised. He compared religion to pills 'which swallowed whole have the virtue to cure, but chewed are for the most part cast up again without effect'.[14] He chewed a great deal himself. Sometimes he devotes all his intellectual power to an effort at reconciling Christianity with a rational theism and incorporates both into his explanation of politics. But his reflections on religion repeatedly turn away from what he insists are unprovable assertions to investigation of its role in human society. Delusion and deception have played a very great part in this. For a man to say that God 'hath spoken to him in a dream is no more than to say he dreamed that God spake to him'. Being a man, he 'may err, and (which is more) may lie'. Clergy who pretended to political wisdom and authority were to Hobbes an intolerable menace. 'It is not the Roman clergy only that pretends the Kingdom of God to be of this world, and thereby to have a power therein distinct from that of the Civil State.'[15]

PUFENDORF AND SPINOZA

Two of the century's later philosophers were especially influenced by Hobbes in their efforts to construct a comprehensive system of politics as part of a general philosophy. Samuel Pufendorf was a German scholar in the tradition of encyclopaedic learning. Like Althusius, he was very well aware that the idea of single sovereign states made no sense in Germany. Few of the philosophers had faced so honestly the need to reconcile theories of the state with historical and contemporary facts. He was perhaps less honest in admitting how hard it was to do so. He accepted the Hobbesian view that the sovereign state was necessary for civilized existence; but it must be a sovereignty that provided for such a relationship as that between the German states and the Empire. Security was no longer the sole purpose of sovereignty: it was the duty of princes and emperor alike to provide for the well-being of their people – in a largely material sense. *De jure Naturae et Gentium* – a title suggesting acceptance of the scholarly conventions – set out in massive and arid detail how Natural Law could be elaborated into a code of conduct for both subject and ruler. Pufendorf was an orthodox, though tolerant, Lutheran. But he was nearly thrown out of Sweden for laying down too precisely the need to separate the sphere of reason from that of religion. Swedish clergy were not taken in by his bland assertions that there need be no conflict between the two.

If Pufendorf shared Hobbes's empiricism, it was a more profound philosopher who completed his removal of Christian religion and orthodox morality from politics. Benedict (or Baruch) Spinoza was a man detached from all allegiances. His family were Portuguese Jews who had moved to Amsterdam, where he so quickly became a known heretic that at the age of twenty-four he was expelled with solemn curses from the Jewish community. He lived, a consumptive recluse, by making lenses. Even in Holland his *Tractatus Theologico-Politicus* had to be published under a false name, and his main works did not appear at all until after his death. His theories of the state showed the same mixture of idealism and scepticism as his theories of God (see p. 151). He did not put as much weight as did Hobbes on a rational decision of the subject that government, with all its horrors, was better than anarchy: the state survived by simultaneously making its citizens fear it and persuading them to love it. There are limits to what can be done by sheer terror: consequently the state needs to avoid rousing too much 'indignation' in the majority of subjects. Even though its sole aim is security, it will be responsive to the will of the majority. In this it is unlikely that monarchy will prove the best form of government, since the monarch will be concerned mainly with preserving his individual power. The *Tractatus* breaks off in the middle of the discussion of the three Aristotelian forms of government without coming to any conclusion about the merits and defects of democracy. But it is evident that Spinoza saw a good deal of virtue in the Netherlands government of de Witt, with effective power in the hands of a narrow but comparatively enlightened section of the community. It was in the Netherlands more than anywhere else that those in power were prepared to concede, however hesitantly, some freedom of thought and speech to whoever accepted the authority of the state. 'The true purpose of the state', he said, 'is liberty' – and what now sounds a platitude was then a startling declaration. But Spinoza's view of the practicable functions of the state appeared to change as he became increasingly disillusioned about the behaviour of those involved in its work. The assassination of the de Witts and the French victories have been seen as a cause of his retreat into a less hopeful view. The state, he continued to insist, was as much a part of the divine creation as everything else in the universe. Its purpose was more than merely enabling the individual to remain alive and secure: it should also make his life worth living – which for Spinoza was a spiritual rather than a material achievement. The idea that the state could contribute positively to the collective quest for the good life seemed to give way to the admission that the most that could be expected from it was the freedom and peace necessary for a cultured existence.

Among the great political philosophers there were not many who, like Bacon, were in a position to have much influence on immediate events. But the century produced a great variety of writers whose theories were designed as direct appeals for action by governments or rebels. They were not confined to such comparatively free societies as those of England or Holland. One of the most surprising phenomena is the appearance of a group of ardent advocates of reform in the most rigidly intolerant country of western Europe. The *arbitristas* – projectors – who over a period of several decades deplored and analysed the condition of Spain were united mainly in their belief that there was a desperate need to save the country that they saw as a sinking ship or a body wasted by disease. Some of their writing managed to appear in print; but far more was circulated cautiously in manuscript or presented as petitions or memoranda to officials who were sometimes willing to receive them. Some indeed were themselves involved in government; a few were merchants; there were army officers, and even clergy. Those whose names became well known included Martin Gonzàles de Cellorgio, whose '*Memorial* of the policies necessary and useful for the restoration of Spain' appeared in 1600, and Sancho de Moncada, whose work on the 'Political Restoration of Spain' was based on strikingly advanced research into the demographic and economic situation in the 1620s. Nearly all the writers agreed that it was for the government to undertake the healing process. They largely agreed too in looking back to some golden age of prosperity. It was not usually the sixteenth century: the Habsburgs were blamed for imposing, on Castile especially, the cost of wars and colonizing. Deserted villages and fields that had gone out of cultivation were visible proofs of prolonged failure while other countries prospered. What the remedies should be was less certain. Some even approved of the expulsion of the Moriscoes; some wanted above all to attack conspicuous wealth and idleness; some would assuage God's wrath by legislating against brothels and unseemly literature. Above all productive activities and trade must be made to increase. Hope diminished slowly.

PARLIAMENT IN ENGLAND: WHITELOCK AND PARKER

Most of the conventions of philosophical theorising about the state made it convenient to assume that the ruler was an individual. The other possibilities sometimes seemed a rather awkward afterthought. The failure to ask who in fact exercised power in the state was one of the main reasons for the unreality of so much of the argument. It was only in England that the problems of 'mixed monarchy' formed a central part of political debate; and the events of the century did not encourage Europeans to regard it as a desirable topic.

The decades of growing tension between English monarchs and their subjects did not produce any outstanding prophet who could explain either how or why royal power should be restricted. The notion of 'consent' was of course familiar; and parliament was readily deemed to 'represent' the freely expressed will of all citizens. The difficulty was to show why the representative body should share the king's power in some topics and circumstances but not in others. A favourite device for having the best of both worlds was the sovereignty of the king 'in' parliament. James Whitelock told the Commons in 1610 that the king had a twofold power, and that what he did alone could be overruled by what he did in parliament. The most relevant explanation of this was derived from the sanctity of property: it was only with the consent of an assembly representing owners of property that taxes could be justly imposed. But Whitelock extended this argument to apply to any alteration in the law. The Commons were always ready to welcome the idea that they were not merely the temporary representatives of taxpayers but an embodiment of the whole community. MPs claimed such privileges as freedom from arrest on the grounds that they were 'not now private men but supplied the room of a multitude'. This was the notion that was developed by Henry Parker in pamphlets that were intended merely as part of the rather arid debate between Charles and the Commons in the months before and after the outbreak of civil war. It was possible by then to say bluntly that all political power remained in the hands of the people, which in practice meant the hands of parliament, 'the people artificially congregated'. The invention of representative assemblies had solved the problem of reconciling order with protection against tyranny. Whatever laws parliament judged necessary the king must pass; his ministers must be approved by parliament and his resources provided by them. What would have seemed in 1610 a fantastic exaggeration of the theory of representation was now only a restatement of claims that the majority in parliament had made. What Parker did not make clear was whether they were an emergency measure – the assertion of parliament's ultimate authority against a tyrant – or a normal procedure that left the king as a mere servant of parliament.

THE STATE AND PROPERTY: HARRINGTON AND THE LEVELLERS

The English Civil War turned many of the stock ideas of political theory into practical reality. Resistance to the sovereign had actually happened – not as the rebellion of a faction but as an act of policy debated *ad nauseam*. While it went on, and when it was over, there were repeated attempts to draw up a real contract

between king and subjects. Mixed monarchy was to be defined
by a document and upheld by an agreed form of control over the
armed forces. The attempts were monotonously unsuccessful.
When it came to the point statesmen, lawyers, and gentlemen
fully conversant with the works of political thinkers from Plato
to Coke, and desperately anxious to find a workable settlement,
could not do it. With the state on the edge of dissolution there
appeared the theories that took account of a fact normally evaded:
citizens were not alike, but were divided into rich and poor,
powerful and powerless. From the early days of the war, some
pamphleteers had seen the conflict as one between different
sections of propertied society from which lesser men had nothing
to gain. But it was only when the fighting had ended that there
occurred, mainly in the army and in the City of London, the
astonishing episode of the Levellers. Speeches, pamphlets, and
broadsides were filled with the debate about the connection
between political rights and ownership of property. In the greatest
moment of the controversy, at Putney in 1647 when officers and
men of the army met on equal terms, the spokesmen of the
soldiers put forward the 'Agreement of the People', a draft for
a real social contract. Colonel Rainsborough, in his simple and
moving speeches, set out some principles of democracy:

Truly sir, I think it's clear that every man that is to live under a
government ought first by his own consent to put himself under that
government: and I do think that the poorest man that is in England is
not at all bound in a strict sense to that government he hath not had a
voice to put himself under . . .[16]

Rainsborough's most lucid opponent was not a supporter of
absolutism, or even of the mixed constitution the Stuarts were
alleged to have violated, but the future regicide Henry Ireton,
advocate of parliamentary sovereignty and a wide franchise.
Ireton's alarm was that any appeal to the natural equality of men
led logically to the abolition of private property. Power must be
restricted to those with a 'permanent fixed interest' in the country.
Rainsborough, firmly denying the allegation that the supporters
of the Agreement sought to take away property, stuck to the principle of universal – or perhaps only universal male – suffrage. But
the leading trio of Leveller pamphleteers, John Lilburne, Richard
Overton, and William Walwyn, were less confident when it came
to expanding the first Agreement into detailed constitutional

proposals. 'Servants', a conveniently vague term which seemed to apply to the whole body of a wage-labourers, were excluded from the franchise on the implausible grounds that they were 'included' in their masters and by accepting dependence had forfeited their 'birthright'. Recipients of alms had lost it too by their subjection to the charity of others. The franchise was in any case not the main part of Leveller demands. Parker had been content to assume that parliament was the voice of the people. The Levellers had seen the triumph of a parliament that then revealed itself as the voice of successive minorities. 'Having by woeful experience found the prevalence of corrupt interests' among men entrusted with authority, they concluded that the power naturally inherent in the people in general could only be protected by an irrevocable written constitution. 'The people', Lilburne proclaimed 'are now dissolved into the original Law of Nature'; and in this unique moment when the state could be created afresh there was available an instrument capable of doing so – the New Model Army. But in the end the army, under Cromwell, was kept loyal to the new privileged minority.

To the Levellers the state should have a constitution that would ensure the separation of power from wealth. To the most original – but hardly the most practical – of the republican philosophers it should redistribute wealth in a way that would produce political stability. James Harrington, former courtier and friend of Charles I, and a passive neutral in the war, was one of the few who recognized immediately the merit of Hobbes. ('He will in future ages be accounted the best writer, at this day, in the world.'[17]) But he loathed Hobbes's opinions, and applied a method no less rational and materialist to the design of a commonwealth in which power would be widely shared. *Oceana*, published – with Cromwell's reluctant consent – in 1656, was both an interpretation of English history and a future constitution based on economic determinism. From a study of history Harrington believed he had discovered an all-important scientific principle – that power depended on the possession of land. English history from the dissolution of the monasteries to the Civil War was a splendid demonstration of this: the growth of a new class of landowners had brought about the collapse of the old rule of monarch and nobility. The victors must now construct a new state in which the accumulation of property in the hands of the few would be prevented by an Agrarian Law limiting landed estates to the annual value of £2,000. The practical details of the constitution of Oceana were hardly a logical triumph. On Harrington's own calculation there could still be a landed minority of 5,000 people. Only by assuming that everyone would work out his own interests with perfect and law-abiding rationality (and by some very odd arithmetic) could he show why the republic should not be overthrown. But he did succeed in breaking away from the fiction of monarchies, aristocracies and democracies to invent a system that recognized what he regarded as the powers of leadership 'peculiar to the Genius of a Gentleman'. Only the Senators, consisting of gentry and nobility, had enough wisdom to debate. The assembly, chosen largely by 'the meaner sort' in a secret ballot, was to vote without discussion. Administration was to be done by elected councils and paid officials. Every position in the state was to be relinquished after a fixed period – for only a system of rotation could prevent the formation of parties. Given this perfect constitution, Oceana would be exempt from all the consequences of human wickedness and folly. It would last for ever, and as an imperial power and leader of a great alliance would spread its blessings over the whole earth. Cromwell, cast for the role of its founder, was unconvinced.

None of the theories about the just distribution of political power produced a practical form of government to replace the Stuart monarchy. Among the various radical opinions those of Milton proved more fragile than most. In 1650 he showed how it was justifiable for the people, from whom all political authority is derived, to slay a tyrant. By 1654 he had discovered that 'nothing is more pleasing to God or more agreeable to reason than that the most worthy should possess supreme power'.[18] One writer who seemed to achieve consistency was Gerrard Winstanley, the passionate spokesman of the little Digger community, who believed that only the abolition of property would end the evils of power. Mankind would then put away its covetousness, pride and oppression, and act in accordance with the 'great Creator, Reason' which Winstanley identifies with God. But when he too indulged in the exercise of drafting a constitution, the fruits of the Common Treasury of the earth were to be distributed under the control of 'overseers' with formidable powers of punishment. In 1660, though radicalism in its religious forms struggled on, the revolutionaries seemed to be silenced as well as defeated. In place of the conflict and disintegration that produced Lilburne, Harrington, and the great ferment of ideas and ideals, there came the compromises that produced Locke.

THE ENGLISH COMPROMISE: LOCKE

Though most countries found philosophers able to demonstrate that their current régime was exactly the one required by God or the Law of Nature, few of them made quite such comfortable reading as John Locke. Where writers of the previous generation had inculcated either angry hope or resigned despair, Locke offered to all who accepted the settlement of 1688–89 the assurance that while foreigners might live in the darkness of absolutism, in England justice and freedom had at last been reconciled with security. Locke's men in the state of nature were not the bloodthirsty savages of Hobbes: they recognized that 'no-one ought to harm another in his Life, Health, Liberty or Possessions'.[19] They agreed to set up government 'for the regulating and preserving of Property'. The agreement is a conditional one. Men have not consented to a government that would enslave them, or rule by arbitrary decrees, or seize their property, or hand over its power to others. What happens if governments do misbehave is not so clear. Where there lies no appeal on earth, men 'have just cause to make their appeal to Heaven', and only if they are confident of their success before 'a Tribunal that cannot be deceived' will they resort to armed revolt. The difficulty is partly that, though he asserts the distinction between what men do and what they have a right or a duty to do, Locke easily assumes that the people, if not always the politicians, will be both moral and rational. Representative government is the best form because an elected legislature 'is not nor can possibly be absolutely arbitrary' but 'is bound' to rule justly. Even so, since human frailty is tempted to grasp at power, the legislative and executive functions must be separated. The executive is completely subject to the legislative; but it must have some discretion to act for the public good 'without the prescription of the Law, and sometimes even against it'. The implications of this do not seem to worry Locke at all.

To make the England of William and Mary the ideal state, it was necessary to show that it depended on the free consent of its citizens. Ignoring the debates and experiments on the franchise forty years before, Locke was happy to regard the Commons as an assembly of representatives chosen by the people. Similarly the all-important institution of property was made compatible with equality. Private property was originally whatever the individual could acquire and use through his own labour. Then the happy invention of money had made possible the virtuous process of storing property without wasting it. Yet behind what now sounds like smug self-deception, Locke was upsetting a good many conventional attitudes of his time. Of all the political philosophers of the century, he was probably the most influential; and his influence was, within its limits, humane and liberalizing.

THE STATE AND THE INDIVIDUAL

One thing that separated Locke from the vast majority of earlier theorists was his view that excessive state authority was immoral whoever wielded it; and he was sometimes inclined to count as excessive what most politicians considered necessary for the security of the state. There had long been voices on the outer fringe of the world of political ideas arguing that freedom of speech was one right with which the state ought not to interfere too much. In 1644 Roger Williams, after being expelled from Massachusetts for his dangerous views, had published the *Bloudy Tenent of Persecution for the Cause of Conscience* in which he suggested that it was outside the proper sphere of the state's activity to disturb the worship even of 'Papists, Jews, Turks, or Indians'. It was almost the only plea for toleration that did not vitiate its principles by making exceptions to them. Milton's *Areopagitica*, which appeared in the same year, reached the heights of poetic prose in defending the right of uncensored printing. From its arguments for free expression, which rested on practical as well as historical and moral grounds, there were exceptions too obvious to need more than the briefest mention: what is 'impious or evil . . . no law can possibly permit that intends not to unlaw itself'. Naturally this included popery. The attack on censorship was one instance of a more general change that had taken place in political thinking during the century. In 1600 people who sought to reduce the powers of the monarch were usually concerned to defend those of some other authority – or to advocate one of the various forms of decentralization of state functions.

By 1700 they were more likely to be concerned with the 'rights' of the individual which authority of every kind ought to uphold.

Even within the absolutist states, the order of society was felt to be less rigid; the individual, by his own efforts, skill, or unscrupulousness, could more easily achieve rank and power. Attacks on authoritarian religion were becoming more linked with insistence that the state should uphold some degree of liberty for individual judgement. It was likewise the duty of the ruler to make it easy for individuals to increase by personal enterprise the wealth of the state and community. The expelled French Huguenot, Pierre Jurieu, in the anonymous pamphlets *Les soupirs de la France esclave* and in his open *Lettres pastorales*, denounced the despotism of Louis XIV's later years in contrast to the legitimate absolutism that his subjects had implicitly accepted. It was now their right to follow the example of the English and overthrow the monarchy. Even in the comparatively liberal Netherlands the notion of the state failing in its duties to the individual was well known. *The Interest of Holland*, an anti-Orangist pamphlet of the 1670s, became a popular manifesto of the uncompromising wing of de Witt's party, and was sometimes ascribed to the Grand Pensionary himself. Its real author, Pieter de la Court, had already produced works on the problem of reconciling liberty with good government that had been admired by Spinoza. He had now concluded that to attain 'the highest perfection of a political society', in Holland especially, 'there is an absolute necessity that the commonalty be left in as great a natural liberty as possible for seeking the welfare of their souls and bodies, and for the improvement of their estates'. A republic was, in de la Court's view, the only 'free government', in which the liberty of the individual would not conflict with the interest of the state. It was not an assumption that the old theorists of absolute monarchy would accept. Ludwig von Seckendorf was a widely read German Lutheran, whose *Princely State* and *Christian State* added to the conventional applauding of absolutism exhortations to the ruler to make the welfare of his subjects, both moral and economic, a main concern. It was the view taken up in Vienna under Leopold I by the economic theorists later known as 'cameralists'. But the title of one of the most popular of their works left no doubts about the purpose: Philip von Hornigk in his *Oesterreich über alles, wann es nur will* – Austria at the top when it shows the will to be – was continuing the teaching of his father-in-law Johan

Becher (see pp. 91–2). His nationalism was essentially an economic one, based not on the accumulation of bullion but on increasing the sale and output of goods. To achieve this the state must do everything to advance internal prosperity, enterprise, and education. In the jargon usually applied to the next century, despotism must be, for its own good, benevolent and enlightened. The ruler was ceasing to be a god and becoming a manager.

NOTES AND REFERENCES

1   *The Political Works of James I*, ed. C. H. McIlwain (Cambridge, Mass., 1918).

2   By P. de Nancel, quoted in E. Thuau, *Raison d'État et pensée politique à l'époque de Richelieu*, p. 18.

3   *La politique tirée des propres paroles de l'Écriture Sainte* (1709.)

4   *Prologemena* to *De Jure Belli ac Pacis*, sect. 8.

5   *II Institutes*, p. 179, quoted in Christopher Hill, *Intellectual Origins of the English Revolution* (Oxford, 1965), where the contradictions are abundantly illustrated.

6   *III Institutes*, p. 111.

7   K. C. Brown (ed.), *Hobbes Studies* (Oxford, 1965), p. 16.

8   *Leviathan* c. 13 (Everyman edition, p. 64).

9   *Leviathan* c. 19 (Everyman, p. 98). See also *De Cive* c. 5.

10   *Leviathan* c. 14 (Everyman, p. 67).

11   H. Warrender, *The Political Philosophy of Hobbes* (Oxford, 1957), puts this view uncompromisingly.

12   *Leviathan* c. 13 (Everyman edition, p. 66).

13   C. B. Macpherson, *The Political Theory of Possessive Individualism* (Oxford, 1962), part II, sect. 3.

14   *Leviathan* c. 32 (Everyman edition, p. 199).

15   *Leviathan* c. 47 (Everyman edition, p. 383).

16   A. S. P. Woodhouse, *Puritanism and Liberty*, p. 53.

17   Quoted in P. Zagorin, *A History of Political Thought in the English Revolution* (London, 1954), p. 34.

18   *Defensio secunda*.

19   *Civil Government* II, c. 6.

9

GOVERNMENT

Like most historical accounts of government, this chapter presents a distorted picture; for it is written almost entirely from the standpoint of the rulers, not of the ruled. Inevitably it is the rulers who provide the sources, both in the mass of documents left over from the process of government and to a great extent in the descriptions of what happened. But it is worth remembering that though government often seems to be a world of its own, concerned with the people outside it mainly in order to make them support an existing regime, it mattered only because of its effects on its subjects. Another distortion is the concentration on central rather than local institutions. In this historians are beginning to mend their ways: more is being written about the government of provinces, cities, and villages – and at a higher level of scholarship – than ever before. The seventeenth century was an age of centralization; nevertheless in 1700 government meant, for the great majority of people, the local tax-collector, the local law-court, the local organizers of armed forces, sometimes the local priest. The distinction between central and local authority was never simple. The state could function only through men who exercised power in smaller units. How far they felt themselves to be agents of the state and how far they were or became independent of it was a complex social as well as political question. Where subjects collectively continued to play any formal part in government, through representative assemblies, it was often provincial rather than national bodies that survived. Only in preparing and making war did the state become during the century truly 'absolute'; and even there it had to face the danger that armies, or those who commanded them, could become more powerful than the monarch and his civilian counsellors.

MONARCHY

The one institution of central government of which subjects were always aware was the monarch. Nearly every country was deeply affected by the history of its royal family, and by the personal characteristics of monarchs, their spouses, mistresses, heirs, and guardians. The king or queen could be anything from an irresistible controller of the state to an infant or half-wit. The only function they had in common was the ability by their mere existence to make the fate of their nation irrational and accidental. Because succession to the throne usually depended on rules of inheritance that were rigid but not entirely beyond argument, the matrimonial and reproductive affairs of royalty were sometimes more important politically than all the country's economic and military efforts. Almost the worst misdeed a monarch could commit was to die without providing an unquestioned adult heir; and the chances that this would happen seemed higher among royal families than others. The shape of English politics for ten years depended on Charles II's lack of a legitimate Protestant successor. The Russians, who were most in need of an effective monarch, suffered more than their share of minorities and disputed inheritance. The French and the Spanish thrones passed in orderly fashion from father to son. But the stability of the French state was shaken by two long regencies that became in effect the rule of women and their factions; and the incapacity of Charles II of Spain led to the most destructive succession dispute Europe had ever seen.

Illogically, doubts about the king's accession had little effect on his eventual status. The wearer of the crown, however he acquired it, became a sacred ruler, with such vestigial miraculous powers as the curing of the King's Evil. His coronation ceremony preserved a hazy recollection of pagan and Christian myths. Most of these rituals also contained reminders of his role as a popular leader: he was presented to and acclaimed by 'the people' and took oaths which often committed him vaguely to uphold their 'rights'. In an extreme form, the notion of power delegated by the people was occasionally used to defend rebellion and tyrannicide. There were traces of the theory of 'popular' monarchy in the royal elections, real or nominal, that were still common in 1600. The Polish Crown was outstanding in this only because for a time the choice was a genuinely open one (see pp. 411–4). Denmark, Bohemia, Hungary, and Russia all held elections for their monarchs, and though at this stage they seldom went outside the reigning dynasties, they could help to make some sort of bargain possible. But it was not a bargain with the people: the king in another of his aspects was the greatest of the landowners, ruling with their consent and in their interest. The kingdom was still, in part, regarded as a piece of property to be bequeathed and sometimes shared out among the family. Philip II had no difficulty in handing over the Spanish Netherlands to his daughter and her husband the Archduke Albert with provision for their reversion to the King of Spain if the two died childless. The tangled claims to the Spanish Succession depended on the wills made by Philip IV and his son Charles, and on the renunciation and transfer of rights under them (see p. 402). But perhaps the most ludicrous application of the notion of the monarch as proprietor was the invention, by a French official, of the claim to an assortment of little territories in the Netherlands on the grounds that local laws of land-inheritance would bring them by 'devolution' to Louis XIV's wife Maria Theresa (see pp. 505–6).

On the whole foreign matches proved a less important foundation for alliances and territorial unions than diplomats assumed. The earlier marriage alliance between France and Spain, in 1612, made little difference to the long hostility between them. England's relations with these two powers were not decisively affected by the unhappy fiasco of Charles I's journey to Madrid in 1623 or by his subsequent marriage to Henrietta Maria of France. Nor did it prove to matter very much that Gustav Adolf, after a similar incognito expedition to Berlin in 1620, succeeded in marrying the Elector's daughter in face of the rivalry of the Poles. One permanent consequence of diplomatic control over royal marriages was that the monarchs who were figureheads of national sentiment often had little claim to any nationality of their own by birth. Louis XIV's grandparents came from France, Italy, Spain, and Germany, James II's from Scotland, Denmark, France, and Italy. (His marriage to an English subject, Ann Hyde, was much more remarkable in the west than it would have been in

Russia, where the Romanovs took their brides from rival court families.) It is open to argument how far the other obvious fact of royal ancestry – the prolonged in-breeding – was responsible for physical and mental defects: they were common enough at every level of society. Considering the horrors of their upbringing and environment, seventeenth-century monarchs were a fairly normal sample of humanity.

Most kings worked hard for their living. If none was quite the model of industry that Philip II had been, there were plenty – Maximilian of Bavaria, the Great Elector, and for many years the *roi soleil* himself – who devoted an immense amount of time to the detailed tasks of government. Not only did the monarch combine the work of presiding over councils with a good deal of bureaucratic routine and with his indispensable ceremonial functions, he was often still expected to lead his armies in war. If warfare had been a rational activity it would have been absurd for kings, on whose survival so much depended, to risk the fate of Gustav Adolf and Charles XII. The king on the battlefield was part of the feudal tradition of monarchy, still appropriate in so far as he was directing the state's principal activity, but a serious hindrance both to efficiency and to political stability at home.

THE COURT

However important the accidents of the sovereign's personal life, the real centre of absolute monarchy was not so much the individual ruler as the court. It was here that the monarch encountered the organized pressures, from his relations, the nobles, the office-holders, the political factions, the financiers, the priests, confessors, and astrologers – anyone who could gain access to the royal ear. The two main types of court influence can be called loosely the 'aristocratic' and the 'bureaucratic'. The character of royal absolutism depended a great deal on the monarch's relations with on the one hand the men whose greatness was derived primarily from their status at the top of the landowning pyramid, and on the other those who owed it to the holding of office. The court was in its ancient form the household of the greatest of landowners, to which the high nobility tended to assume that they could belong if they wished. The Russian court in the Time of

Troubles and the Polish court, such as it was, for most of the century were grim examples of how it could be the battleground of fights for control of the Crown, which prevented it from being anyone's established home. In many countries it had only just become permanently fixed in the capital: though kings continued to move frequently about their territories, they could leave many of the functions of their courts behind. Instead of demanding hospitality from the nobles, the king was now assumed to give it. To great men no longer able to live in the style they deemed appropriate on the resources of their estates, the court was a source of wealth. Spanish kings suffered as badly as any. When Philip II established his court firmly at Madrid he kept its size and splendour within bounds; only a minority of the grandees were courtiers. Philip III allowed large numbers of aristocrats great and small to come there and to bring with them their households, on the size of which their prestige was thought to depend. The palace and the capital were filled with men seeking favours, sinecures, or active positions at whatever level they could reach. It was a vast and largely unproductive community, living ultimately on the rents and taxes of those outside it, and on growing debts. Efforts to make the nobles go back to their estates had little success, and court expenditure continued to grow under Philip IV and Charles II until it was estimated at a quarter of the whole revenue of Castile.

Louis XIV's Versailles was not quite the ingenious new invention for taming the nobility and keeping them out of politics it is sometimes alleged to have been: only the long process of centralization and the economic problems of landed families had made it possible. Louis was merely doing more magnificently what almost every monarch accepted as part of his life. The gorgeous costumes, the festivities, the lavish buildings and furnishings, the throngs of servants in strict order of rank formed a world of mingled luxury and squalor proclaiming that every man had his position, and must rise and fall according to the rules (see pp. 496–7). But just as most monarchs were the active heads of government, most courts were the frames within which power was both fought for and exercised. Under Gustav Adolf the 'Chancery Wing' was added to the palace at Stockholm: the bureaucratic function was different from the ceremonial one but closely attached to it. A clear line between household service and political service was almost impossible. The English Secretaries of State dined at court, and the great household officials were members of the Privy Council, even though government offices were recognized as different from purely household ones. At Vienna the court had the advantage, for the emperor, of being attached neither to the Holy Roman Empire nor to the Habsburg hereditary lands. Its principal officer, the *Obersthofmeister*, was often the emperor's chief minister (see p. 369). The Great Elector of Brandenburg made his court almost entirely a working body. But he was no more able than the rulers of greater states to escape one major problem in government – the quest for office as a source of profit and prestige.

OFFICE

The passion for holding offices, nominally or really in the work of central administration, and for acquiring titles, was an outstanding characteristic of seventeenth-century Europe. It led, since governments were always short of money, to the twin devices of 'venality of office' and 'inflation of honours'. Office and title were alike in the profit their sale brought to the Crown. But while the sale of titles was the most harmless way of raising money, the sale of offices had a profound and generally evil effect on government. A post in the king's service became a piece of property to be acquired, exploited, and handed on to heirs in much the same way as a piece of land. The supply of offices, unlike that of land, had no fixed limits: the Crown could create as many as it chose for the joint profit of itself and the favoured subject. As central government became more active, some new officials were undoubtedly needed. Many worked hard; and usually they were rewarded to a small extent by a fixed payment from the Crown. But their principal sources of income from office were the fees which they were entitled to charge the victim or beneficiary of their work, the proportion they kept of the money collected for the Crown, and the gifts and bribes that in greater or less degree were assumed to be their due. If an office enabled its holder to make in this way profit that depended on his energy and enterprise, it was natural that he should be ready to pay a lump sum for the opportunity; and from this it was an easy step for the Crown to multiply offices not in order to get necessary work of government done but in order to make money. There were many ways in which the man who wanted to work his way up the office-holding ladder might begin. He might buy directly from the Crown a post, or the 'reversion' of a post after its existing holder died or moved up. He might buy from the holder a post that had been granted not just for life but with the right to sell or bequeath it. Or he might pay the man who had acquired not the office but the 'gift' of it. At every stage the process probably involved suitable rewards to those in a position to put in a good word. The first Duke of Buckingham was believed, perhaps with some exaggeration, to have made himself the centre of a huge office-market, and under James I the great majority of posts in central government were probably sold in one way or another. But in England the disease took a mild form: jobs were not created in outrageous numbers, and the court did not concern itself with many of those in local government. Charles I reduced the sale of at least the higher offices and made an effort to remove some of the worst abuses of fees. Even so, many English landed families found office-holding an important part of their economy. The cleavage between those who were involved and those who were excluded has sometimes been made to appear too rigid; but progress in the royal service depended as much on family connection and patronage as on cash. Men who already belonged to the court and office-holding establishment naturally wanted to prevent its benefits from being too widely diffused by the admission of outsiders.

In Spain there was far less restriction. Under Philip IV the Castilian Cortes largely abandoned its opposition to a system that seemed for the Crown one of the few sources of genuine extra revenue and for the subject a way of acquiring some sort of distinction. Under Charles II it was estimated that a fifth of the population of Castile held a government office of some sort. But Spanish 'empleomania' was more a low-level than a high-level affair; most of the offices sold were trivial local ones not producing any opportunities for large profits, though the title of nobility attached to some of them was valued not only for its status but for the exemptions from taxation it carried. The higher offices, and places at court, were obtained more by bribery of individuals than by open sale; their holders grew rich through corruption rather than through recognized fees or allowances.

It was in France that the sale of offices reached its height. Even in proportion to its large population, France probably had more offices than any other country. Creating and selling them brought money to the Crown and was thought to make the purchaser loyal to the state. Buying an office, like lending to the state through the *rentes*, was a form of investment that seemed to most Frenchmen with capital available more attractive than industry or commerce. No-one knows how many offices there were. One estimate is that 50,000 new posts were made under Louis XIII. In Normandy there were more than 4,500 holders in 1638, two and a half times the number in the 1570s. In Dijon it was calculated that almost half the citizens were of families with some place in the great mass of municipal officials, lawyers, and so on. Henry IV's principal contractor for offices, Charles Paulet, devised the edict whereby in return for an annual payment to the Crown of one-sixtieth of the recognized value of the office, the holder could ensure its transfer to his successors. The *paulette* or *droit annuel* together with the sales, eventually produced between a quarter and a half of the state's whole revenue. Richelieu in 1625 announced his determination to abolish the sale of offices completely. But later, in the *Testament politique*, it was admitted that though in a newly established state it would be a 'crime' to allow venality of office, 'prudence did not permit' the destruction of the institution once it was there. By the time of Louis XIV, even though the creation of new offices had fallen off under Mazarin, administration was a major national industry. From the high legal and governing families of the *grande robe* to the swarm of local collectors and clerks, the office-holders had a common interest in protecting their *charge* and its profitable rights. To improve the efficiency of government and its yield of money to the Crown it was often necessary to create posts outside the old venal system. Richelieu's intendants were meant to cut across the vested interests and corruptions of officials. Their posts were not *charges* but *commissions*, which the Crown could grant and revoke at any time. Many came from the families of the *maîtres de requêtes*, local administrators of comparatively lowly origin who did much to strengthen royal authority in the provinces. Under Colbert the intendants and various *commissaires* gradually extended their functions into jealously guarded areas of local government. When they began to appoint a growing number of *sub-délégués* to do work that became permanent instead of temporary, there was something very like a rival bureaucracy imposing itself on top of the old one. The *sub-délégués*, whose existence the Crown had refused to recognise, succeeded in making their own positions marketable in much the same way as the old ones.

THE MINISTER

Neither the most energetic of monarchs nor the most efficient system of departments could function without the two institutions on whose character and relative power the nature of the regime depended – the minister and the royal council. Despite the obvious exceptions, this was in the west more an age of the great minister than of the great king. They had rare opportunities to combine the enormous power derived from effective central institutions with the wealth and half-regal patronage monarchy made possible. Perhaps the ideal ministerial figure of the period is the Swede Axel Oxenstiern, Chancellor to Gustav Adolf in 1612 and still in office at the abdication of Christina in 1654. He was born into the court nobility; he built up a great family connection and was succeeded by his son; he lived in considerable splendour. In return he devoted a calm precise mind and an unflagging capacity for work entirely to the service of the state. Below him was the collegiate system of administration in which departmental officials could make and uphold their own policies (see pp. 407–8). Above him was a king with whom he developed a confident, harmonious relationship. Unlike many of his European equals, he did not need to fear dismissal or worse. Though he often disagreed with Gustav's ideas – including military aggression in Germany – he adopted the 'civil service' habit of working out alternative lines of action, urging the one he thought best, but when necessary applying another. On the king's death he quickly became a virtual monarch, so confident of the Regency Council, which was dominated by his brother and cousin, that he could spend much of his time in Germany.

Most of Oxenstiern's contemporaries in ministerial power lived with one foot in the world of administration and the other in that of court ceremony and intrigue. Richelieu after his success in the 'Day of Dupes' affair (see p. 319) eventually made of Louis XIII a fairly reliable ally. He kept his grip on the royal mind only at the cost of incessant letter-writing and interviews and of intense concern with the activities of his enemies at court. Mazarin owed his power and sometimes his life to the ability and willingness of Anne of Austria to uphold him not only against the normal hazards of ministerial life but against the rare threat of popular revolt. For Frenchmen whose political ambitions were more limited, survival could be easier. Pierre Séguier, whom Richelieu made Chancellor in 1635, held his office until 1672. But this was an almost unique achievement. In Spain Olivares found that neither his huge array of dependants nor his zeal as a reforming minister could save him once it seemed to his master expedient to sacrifice him. No continental minister was quite so tragic a victim of the failure of the royal regime he managed as was Strafford (see p. 461); but Count Griffenfeld, the chief architect of Danish absolutism, spent his last twenty-two years in prison. Under Frederick III, who broke the grip of the old nobility and in 1660 was proclaimed as the first hereditary monarch, Griffenfeld presided over a centralised absolutism that had all the institutional apparatus of strong ministerial rule. But by the time of Frederick's successor, Christian V, a new court aristocracy had arisen, as hostile to reforming efficiency as the old. Griffenfeld was accused of treason by a faction that preferred military glory to good government. It was one of Louis XIV's great successes that he could cause ministers to rise and fall without every change being a matter of triumph or disaster. The dynasties of Colbert and Louvois shared out many, but never all, of the highest offices for most of the reign; yet as Colbert's own fall from favour showed, they were men whose services the king could use or discard without upsetting the steady work of government. In part this was connected with his management of the other instrument of royal absolutism, the council.

THE COUNCIL

In every state the distribution of power depended a good deal on who attended the various meetings of high political and administrative servants. To be a counsellor of the king was a right traditionally claimed by the greatest nobles; but it had long been a common practice for monarchs to draw their chief advisers from the ranks of the working servants of the Crown. It was equally common for such great men to turn themselves into a new aristocracy with all the characteristics of the old. The Austrian Habsburgs, in their various capacities, had an assortment of councils, whose changing functions were deeply involved in the struggle for power between emperor and princes. The members of the Imperial Privy Council (see pp. 369–70) were mainly high nobility – often nobles of the first or second generation whose rank was won by service. In Sweden membership of the council (the Råd) was still a right of the great aristocrats. Most of them in 1600 rarely attended and left its work to the five principal officers of state. Gustav and Oxenstiern, far from driving them out, persuaded them to spend more time in Stockholm or with the king. In the successive minorities and absences of the monarch that Sweden suffered throughout the century the council became the centre of a noble oligarchy so firmly entrenched by the time Charles XI was of age that he had to establish his royal authority by getting the Estates to declare that he had the power to act independently of the council. But it was again Spain that provided the most dismal specimen of conciliar government in excess. Philip II's Council of State (the *Consejo de Estado*), though endless faction quarrels occupied its time, was an instrument of royal authority that effectively resisted challenge from the councils of the various kingdoms. Under his two successors, councils multiplied almost as rapidly as offices. The Council of War, the Council of Finances, the Council of Aragon, which still resisted Castilian domination – these and many others became highly institutionalized bodies, with strong vested interests in preserving their own hierarchical structure. Against them were set up the juntas, small secret, informal committees of ministers which were supposed to cut through the elaborate procedures of the conciliar system but which rapidly became weapons in petty struggles for power. New juntas and old councils alike were composed of nobility, and in the main of the higher nobility – 'unintelligent, inexperienced, devoted entirely to their own interests', as the French Ambassador Villars put it. To him as to others the conciliar system of Louis XIV seemed the standard by which others should be tested.

If accounts of the French councils at the height of their importance in the 1670s or 1680s tend to be confused and contradictory, this comes partly from one of their merits: they were not so firmly organized that rights and procedures mattered more than functions. The innermost council had three, four, or five members, who belonged to it if the king summoned them and had no redress if he did not. Its meeting, commonly three times a week, was the moment in the royal routine when reports on any part of the work of government could be received, policy made, power redistributed. It did not even have an official name: it was often called the '*conseil d'en haut*' (because it met upstairs) but also the '*conseil d'état*', a name that in older terminology applied to the whole body of royal councillors. The *conseil d'en haut*, though it occasionally claimed a right to veto the decisions of lesser bodies, was never all-powerful. Most of its time was spent on foreign affairs; and it had little to do with finance. That was the sphere of the *conseil d'état et des finances*, run by the Chancellor and the *surintendants des finances*. Louis XIV replaced it by a *conseil royal des finances*, where the king and the *controlleur-general des finances* (Colbert's post) began to impose order on the chaos of receipts and payments. The work of lower councils was even less well-defined. The *conseil des dépêches* handled a great many of the problems arising from the papers of the intendants and from petitions; the *conseil privé*, also known as the *conseil des parties*, was a large body meeting usually without the king, which could be involved in almost any dispute or plea. The titles bestowed on holders of administrative posts were as confusing as their functions. The most impressive, '*conseiller du roi en ses conseils d'état et privé*', did not give the holder membership of anything at all; *conseiller d'état* was used mainly for members of the *conseil privé*; members of the *conseil d'en haut* were simply '*ministres*'. A Frenchman whose problems found their way to the centre could well despair of its complexities. Though most of the work of the councils emerged as directions to intendants and lesser local administrators, their decisions were often in effect judicial. They inserted themselves into the spheres of the old courts of justice, sometimes to the benefit of the subject, often by applying separate 'administrative justice' for the protection and support of the state or its officers. As the English opposition to the Stuarts had seen, mixing judicial with administrative functions was one of the characteristics of absolutism.

OTTOMAN GOVERNMENT

Western statesmen would not consider the government of the sultan as relevant to the politics of Christendom, except as a demonstration of the evils of tyranny and misrule. Conditions that even in Russia occurred only in the worst periods of chaos seemed in Turkey to be a normal feature of government. But in fact most of them lay only a little below the surface of western absolutism. The essential principle was that men should hold power, wealth, and status solely through service to the sultan, military or civil, central or local. If the system worked as intended it was a triumph of monarchy beyond the dreams of any western ruler. The difficulty in comprehending it was, and is, that whatever the theory the practice varied so much in time and place. The most consistent feature was that the court was the central government: departments of state could not separate themselves from it. Highest of all institutions was the harem, and the eunuchs who protected it. Only the Grand Vizir, whose ministerial power had grown in the last century, was its recognized superior; and at least four grand vizirs in the seventeenth century had a violent death. The sultan's numerous concubines were at the centre of the endless faction struggles. Their sons, all equally legitimate, ensured that every succession was likely to be disputed: the custom had been that the victor killed off his brothers. Below the harem the Inner Service now had many characteristics of a departmental administration, with the treasury and the chamber of war the largest ministries. But the departments were the households of the vizirs or lesser officers in which no-one's place or life was secure. The heads of all the sections of the service formed the Divan, a council that could now fall easily under the management of the grand vizir.

Not all of this was far from western practice. But the splendour in which high officials lived hid the astonishing fact that they were slaves, brought from the infidel provinces and lacking all inheritance or prospect of landed wealth. The institution of the *devshirme* had begun as the recruitment of prisoners of war into the service of their Muslim captors. Then it became a regular levy of the children of Christian subjects, partly in lieu of taxes. Having been converted to Islam, they served in the bureaucracy or the forces: they could rise as soldiers to the elect infantry companies of the janissaries or as servants of the court to offices as high as vizir. It was not of course possible completely to exclude born Muslims from serving their master and being duly rewarded. The ten *byelerbeys* in charge of provinces and the many more *sanjakbeys* below them were often sons of the sultan or lesser members of his household. It was supposed to train them in government and in Islamic culture. But the recognized link between land and service was the *timar*, the small fief that conferred not ownership of an estate but the non-hereditary right to collect dues from it. Holders of these were the *sipahis*, who had ill-defined local powers but were mainly cavalry soldiers. At the end of the sixteenth century there were said to be 130,000 of them in the provinces. Another 15,000 formed the palace guard, still recruited from the children of Christians. Sipahis at their worst could be frontier plunderers and potential rebels; but those living in peaceful areas could build up households and retainers and turn themselves into something resembling the lesser gentry of the west. Those attached to the household could be either allies or powerful rivals of the janissaries.

One large area of government was reserved for the native faithful. At court the *Sheikh-ul-Islam*, the interpreter of the sacred law, could claim equality with the grand vizir; and in the Outer Service of the palace the *ulema*, guardians of the Koran and of the law, exercised in their successful periods virtually the right of veto on government actions. No distinction existed between the faith and the law: a body of men who through much of the Empire were the equivalent both of the western priest and of the lawyer had almost unlimited opportunities. The sultan was not always their enemy. When Suleiman the Magnificent had proclaimed himself to be Caliph as well as Sultan he was acquiring a sacred as well as a temporal power – or in more practical terms a whole body of supporters separate from the factions and treacheries of the court. But the *ulema* too could rebel: it was mainly through them that the Sultan Mustafa and his grand vizir were overthrown in 1623. One source of danger however sultans did not suffer: nothing approaching a representative assembly existed.

REPRESENTATIVE ASSEMBLIES

In nearly every western state there were in 1600 representative bodies, regional or central or both, on which the government depended for much of its revenue. By 1700 some had disappeared; some had seen their powers whittled away in a series of conflicts with the monarchy; and even those that in theory survived with unchanged or enhanced authority were in practice more easily controlled than before by a strong ministry or monarch. It did not mean that virtuous, democratic, liberty-loving institutions had been crushed by reactionary tyranny. The assemblies 'represented' not subjects as individuals but the 'Estates of the Realm' into which, in medieval theory, men were necessarily divided. Since the thirteenth century, Assemblies of Estates had been the means by which subjects could fulfil their duty of giving aid and counsel to the sovereign. It was an increasingly unrealistic concept. Assemblies did not reflect the true distribution of power within the community; and the Crown had good reason to regard them as a source of obstruction rather than of the support it needed. The most flourishing, the English Parliament, was the one in which the notion of 'Estates' meant least. Peers and MPs were a homogeneous body of landowners, with a minority of townsmen and lawyers. Ministers of the Crown belonged to it and held the initiative in its proceedings. In contrast the French Estates-General had been of little use either to the Crown, whose ministers took little part in it, or to the deeply divided propertied groups. Hardly anyone regretted its extinction much. The great majority of assemblies lay somewhere between these two extremes in their activity and in their ability to survive. The growing need of governments for money and the firm tradition that extraordinary levies were a matter for consent and bargaining meant that it was often easier for monarchs to make use of the assemblies than to abolish them. Internal divisions were as important as government hostility in producing their decline.

In practice the Estates that could usually claim a voice in politics were the clergy, the 'nobility' – usually in the broad sense of landowners – and the towns. The 'assembly of Estates' did not necessarily include all of them – for a variety of reasons. In some German states the nobles were glad to avoid the obligations involved in attending the diets by acquiring the status of Imperial Free Knights. Clergy could often claim to hold entirely independent assemblies of their own, which might or might not accord to the temporal ruler a voluntary gift of money. One of the many illogicalities of the English system was that bishops continued to sit in the House of Lords while lower clergy were excluded from the Commons. The 'Convocations' of the Church, completely detached from Parliament, were a substitute for a clerical House. In Brandenburg (see pp. 365–6) the clergy as such had ceased to belong to the Estates at the Reformation; Saxony, where the bishops – almost invariably of noble family – had an assembly of their own, retained a vestigial clerical Estate with representatives of universities and cathedral chapters. There was endless variety in the representation of lesser landholders, however defined. Sometimes, as in the Cortes of Aragon, they met separately from the higher nobility and formed one of four Estates. In Poland they almost monopolized the lower of the two Houses of the Diet (see p. 255), from which towns had been largely excluded. Though townsmen on the whole remained in control of the 'third Estate', there were many signs of the decline in their power. The English House of Commons had by 1600, seen most of its 'borough' seats taken over by the gentry, though townsmen were usually the most numerous voters in the elections. The French *Tiers-État* had become mainly a preserve of lawyers and office-holders. In the Netherlands (see p. 253), the one outstanding example of a state where government was more in urban than in rural hands, the delegations from towns were normally drawn from an oligarchy that was becoming less representative of the merchant community and seldom considered the artisans. But ordinary townsmen were usually in a better position than the peasants. The theory that tenants and labourers were 'represented' by their masters provided a thin excuse for the exclusion of the rural poor. There were places where peasants still had a voice. Sweden had a peasant Estate, and though only freeholders and tenants of Crown lands were involved, their number was large and elections reasonably free. The snag was that the Crown often omitted to summon it. In Switzerland the rural cantons had assemblies that were elected on a much wider franchise than was common in the towns; and there was peasant representation of one sort or another in some of the south German states. Their governments did not show much concern.

The structure and powers of assemblies were in most countries a mixture of tradition and improvisation. England was exceptional again in having by this time an exactly defined membership of the two Houses and a rigid procedure. The Scottish parliament was more typical. Though the lesser landholders and representatives of royal burghs had been brought back into it to approve the succesive religious changes of the sixteenth century, the Crown and the nobility could each use various devices for preventing any initiative from below. The 'Convention of Estates' was a body not easily distinguished from a parliament but containing only those whom the Crown chose to summon. Its decisions could be ratified by a more formal parliament when it was politically safe to hold one. The 'Lords of the Articles' were a small executive committee chosen from the bishops, nobles, lesser landowners, and townsmen by an elaborate system that made opposition to the Crown almost impossible. But Charles I found that if he could adapt the system of assemblies of Estates to his own ends, others could do the same. In 1637 the opponents of Laud's religious innovations provided a rare instance of representative bodies coming together without the initiative or consent of the Crown. Each of the four Estates chose, by one improvised process or another, 'Commissioners' who in turn elected the 'Tables', the small committees that formed the nucleus of a resistance movement.

The Swedish assembly, the Riksdag, had in 1600 no fixed place of meeting, no recognized electoral system, no regular forms of legislating or petitioning. Which of the Estates attended depended on the immediate circumstances. Groups normally outside them, such as army officers, sometimes successfully claimed representation; many of those named as members failed to attend; sessions often ended in disorder and the drifting away of members rather than in formal dissolution. In the constitutional reforms of 1617 and 1626 Gustav Adolf and Oxenstiern brought more definition to the proceedings. One of their objects was to establish the noble Estate as the essential part of the Riksdag. The status of nobility was for the first time made to depend entirely on royal patent; three classes within the Estate were arranged; and the function of the nobles in leading the other Estates in the direction the king wanted them to go was made abundantly clear. The 'Form of Government' of 1634 (see p. 408) made the alliance between Crown and nobility closer still; but it kept the Riksdag as a regular part of the governing machinery. It survived because the elements that might have resisted the Crown were too weak to be a serious threat. All the initiative in legislation and discussion came from the monarch: the Estates were merely invited to debate what was brought before them. Though their enactments were unquestionably valid, the Crown could if it chose legislate without them. During Christina's reign the Estates made some progress. Taxation was levied only with their consent; policy, though never controlled, was at least debated. In 1650 they put forward demands that were clearly influenced by events in England. But it was only in the minority of Charles XI that the Riksdag contrived to extend its independence by uniting against the nobles of the Council of Regency. When the king came of age he had little difficulty in using the Riksdag to punish the regency nobles, while at the same time curtailing its own political influence. By 1686 the Estates were content to accept the convention that they no longer offered any comment at all on official expositions of the government's decisions, on the few occasions when the king was graciously pleased to give them. This rare specimen of a 'parliamentary absolutism' showed how mistaken was the assumption that the mere existence of a parliament was a protection against despotic rule. Lacking substantial provincial towns and prosperous gentry, Sweden could not establish an assembly able to resist any royal government that had aristocratic support.

In many other countries the fate of Assemblies of Estates was determined by conflicts between Crown and nobility. In Denmark (see pp. 418–9) Frederick III's triumph over the nobility was made possible by the support of the clerical and urban Estates, who resented the efforts of the nobles to extend both their exemption from taxation and their claims to Crown land. The Estates then accepted with hardly a murmur the destruction of their own power. German princes were able to use their power as members of the Imperial Diet to force the emperor to uphold them against their own Estates. In Brandenburg the diet most often summoned was now a small body. The nobility, who nearly everywhere else assumed that they could all attend, chose representatives, and the urban Estate was drawn only from a few big towns. The Thirty Years War was as damaging to the diet as to all the institutions of government; but the Great Elector, in the early years after his accession in 1640, was on better terms with the Estates than his predecessor had been. It was only when wars and the army became his main concern that there developed the triangular struggle between Elector, nobility, and towns. In 1652 a large 'General Diet', with all the nobles and wide urban representation, was expected to show how popular the Elector's policies were. Instead it proved determined to drive a hard bargain. Some of the demands were for constitutional rights; but the ones most effectively pressed, far from showing a concern for liberty, were for extensions of the servitude of the peasants. For the moment the Estates got most of what they wanted. But no General Diet met again: the Elector's hope of gaining the regular support of the Estates for his wars and the taxation they involved was not fulfilled, and for him the inevitable answer was to collect money on his own authority. The nobles, largely exempt from taxation, did not greatly mind. Not that the urban representatives put up much resistance: most of them came to accept a system that put the heaviest burdens on the ordinary townsmen. By the time of the Great Elector's death the urban Estate in Brandenburg had been virtually eliminated and the nobility could be relied on as supporters of official policy.

The Brandenburg Diet was not Frederick William's only assembly. He had similar difficulties with the Estates of Prussia (which at one stage tried to appeal to the King of Poland as the Elector's overlord); and the Estates in his western possessions of Cleves and Mark were more resolute and successful in preserving their powers. There was nothing unusual in this situation. The unification and centralization of states did not mean that assemblies necessarily followed the same pattern. In Spain the Cortes of Castile remained distinct from the Cortes of the Crown of Aragon; and within the territories of the Crown of Aragon there were in addition the three separate Cortes of Catalonia, Aragon, and Valencia. In France those provincial Estates that had a well-established traditional authority proved better able to resist the Crown than did the Estates-General. No other French assembly was as healthy as the Estates of Brittany, which kept under their own supervision a system of taxation quite unlike that of the rest of the country. In Normandy, where in the sixteenth century the Estates had consented to an exceptionally heavy share of national taxation in return for some attention to their own grievances, royal promises became increasingly vague and pleas for reduction a formality. Their meetings came to an end in 1657. In Provence the Estates put up some resistance to royal demands until 1671. Resistance to the consolidation of monarchical power in France was in the long run hindered rather than helped by the existence of a quite different institution through which opposition could be expressed. The Paris *parlement* was one of the four 'sovereign courts' of law. Princes of the blood, great nobles, and a few clergy kept the right to sit in the *Grand'Chambre*, along with the principal lawyers. Its *premier président*, appointed directly by the king, had a ceremonial status higher than that of the princes themselves. But the hundred or so ordinary members, who had got there by buying or inheriting their offices, came mainly from the leading Parisian families and, increasingly, from the *noblesse* too. Like the *parlements* that sat in some provincial towns, it was closely linked to municipal government and membership was a jealously guarded mark of privilege that separated the *magistrats* of the *parlement* from the urban community. Unlike them it showed some sign of developing into a national body. Its judicial area had extended to cover nearly a third of the country. Its right to register royal decrees had grown into a claim to discuss and even to reject them. This process of inserting itself into the legislative process came to an end in 1641, when it registered without serious protest a decree forbidding it to discuss matters of state except by specific royal command. Richelieu preferred to see it as part of the royal administrative machine, and as the scene of the king's occasional solemn *lit de justice* where his pronouncements acquired unchallengeable authority. A body of which Richelieu could more safely make use was the *assemblée des notables*, which had a brief importance in 1626–27. Convoked entirely on royal authority, and ranging from the princes down to members of the sovereign courts, it accepted its function of granting the war subsidies demanded and approving measures to strengthen government power. Once the taming of the nobility was complete there was no further use for it.

The States General of the Netherlands was unlike any other central assembly. With no medieval tradition of its own and little trace of the normal forms of representation, it looked in many ways more like a conference of sovereign states than a national parliament. The seven provinces from which it was constituted could send what representatives they chose. Only about thirty assembled at a time, not, it was said, from any constitutional decision but because they met in a small room. All members were required to vote in accordance with the mandate of their provincial assemblies, and debating was frequently interrupted so that they could go back for consultations. In theory decisions were only binding if they were unanimous. Despite all this, the States General played a more effective part in government than almost any conventional parliament. It met every day, conducting business that often looked like that of a monarch or his council. Foreign ambassadors were surprised to find that they had to present themselves to this committee instead of to a royal court. Foreign affairs were supposed to be under its sole control; so were the organization of the armed forces and of the national taxation that payed for them. How much authority it exercised in practice depended for most of the century on its relations with the head of the House of Orange, usually its ally, and with the provincial Estates. Each of these seven assemblies had its own constitution, based in one way or another on the distinction between the representation of landowners and that of towns. The Estates of Holland had their own unanimity rule: the nobility had a collective delegation giving a single vote. So had each of the eighteen towns, Amsterdam being supposedly no more important than the decayed boroughs around it. Elsewhere representation of the land ranged from the astonishing system in Zeeland, by which the First Noble – the Prince of Orange – was the sole delegate of the countryside to that of Groningen where small landholders could choose their delegates. Everywhere it was the task of permanent officials, usually the Advocate or Pensionary, to manage the negotiations that made decisions possible.

Netherlands assemblies depended on no superior authority for their summoning and dismissal. Most other such bodies accepted the uneasy dual status of representative institutions and advisers to the monarch, and were happy to come and go as he chose. The newest of them all, the Russian Zemsky Sobor, had originated as an assembly convoked by the tsar with no pretence of election or intention of regular meetings. Yet for the first half of the seventeenth century it appeared to be among the most active of representative institutions in Europe. It never acquired a formal structure: its very name of 'Assembly of the Land' was bestowed on it only after it had ceased to function. Its surviving records are slight. What they seem to show is a body influenced to some extent by western ideas of 'Estates' in a society where such divisions were scarcely recognized. It owed its success largely to the collapse of tsarist government in the 'Troubles', when successive claimants to the throne needed spectacular approbation and when any political body that could unify resistance to the invaders was in a strong position. The assembly that elected Michael Romanov to the throne was exercising in reality a power that in the west had become at most an antiquarian formality. During his reign it met frequently, and debated matters of foreign policy and war which few monarchs allowed their Estates to meddle with. The great Zemsky Sobor of 1648–49 not merely ratified the new code of law but extracted some concessions such as a restriction on tax-exempt lands that was demanded by the townsmen. An element of petitioning against grievances of local communities seems to have crept into its proceedings. But it did not come anywhere near to risking a serious dispute with the tsar: in the 1650s when its occasional complaints became a nuisance its meetings were brief and infrequent.

The great eastern example of a secure representative assembly was the Polish Diet. English and Dutch advocates of such institutions did not find it expedient to cite this as an example of their ideal form of government. But the comparisons were by no means irrelevant. The *Seym*, like the English parliament, was a two-chamber assembly in which landowners were completely dominant over the few townsmen and lawyers. Power in it was not monopolized by the magnates: the lower house, including some quite small freeholders, kept on equal terms with the upper. Perhaps 10 per cent of the population were involved in its election. Under Sigismund III there were signs of an organized opposition party, determined to resist the central authority of a monarch devoted to dynastic wars. But the Seym proved to be a grim example of the weakness that came from particularism: the overriding aim of most of its members was to prevent national authority from trespassing on local. The interests Polish landowners had in common seemed entirely negative ones. In 1652 their disputes culminated in the acceptance of the *liberum veto* whereby meetings of the Seym could be, and were, broken by a single dissenting voice. During the next forty years the use of the *liberum veto* was extended with disastrous effects on the raising of revenue especially. It was easy for western constitutional theorists, then and later, to scoff. But the problem of combining representative powers with effective political authority was one that no assembly managed to solve. Poland was already familiar with one obstacle to the supposed democracy of parliaments – that their members could be committed to decisions taken elsewhere. The 'dietines', regional assemblies sometimes dominated by higher nobles, could virtually decide who would sit in the lower house of the Seym and give them rigid mandates. Much more bizarre was the ancient right of 'confederation', by which any individual or group could legally organize an alliance whose members would be bound by oath to act in support of its specific demands. The line between a confederation and an armed rebellion was not always clear.

TAXATION

Assemblies, it was wisely and reasonably believed, depended above all for their survival on the need of kings for money. Their decline nevertheless came in a period when governments were spending far more, and raising a growing proportion of what they spent by taxation. It was still felt that the Crown, as a large land-owner itself, had resources which ought to enable it, in the familiar English phrase, to 'live of its own' except in times of special expense. But such an assumption was no longer compatible with the realities of government finance. The Crown had either to extract regular and, by earlier standards, huge sums from its subjects or to exhaust its capital and accumulate debts. The days when a national debt was an indispensable part of the economic system were still far ahead. France seemed at the beginning of the century to be closest to them. The *rentes*, loans to the Crown backed by the city of Paris, had since their introduction early in the sixteenth century become a form of investment so profitable that it was a normal upward move in the social scale for a trader to turn himself increasingly into a *rentier*. Unhappily the *rentes*, like offices, came to be sold for the benefit of the subject more than of the Crown, and one of Colbert's main financial aims was to redeem them. Generally the ability of a government to borrow depended on the easily shaken confidence of merchants and bankers in its capacity to repay. The debts a minister bequeathed were regarded as a mark of mismanagement, and his successor often appealed successfully for new taxes to pay them off. Official royal bankruptcies were a risky and discreditable but not uncommon device. Another was to get money by minting it, as cheaply as possible. Debasement of the coinage had been a process familiar in the sixteenth century and was still used at times and places as far apart as Philip III's Spain and Peter the Great's Russia. But such methods could not postpone for long the need to extract more wealth from the vulnerable sections of the community.

The development of regular systems of taxation, imposed with tolerable efficiency, was a slow achievement of western governments that was well on the way by 1700. For most of the century public finance was a matter of improvisation by the ruler and struggles by the subject to escape. The heavier the demands, the greater the incentive for those who could to win exemption for themselves at the expense of the less fortunate. It was not only nobilities who held or acquired such privileges: towns and provinces could often find means of mitigation. Indeed it was seldom assumed, outside England, that a uniform system for a whole country was possible. The sufferings of Frenchmen varied enormously according to where they lived. The *taille* was in some areas a tax on land, in others on personal property, in a few nonexistent. The regions of the *grandes gabelles* paid anything up to five times as much tax on their salt as those of the *petites gabelles*. In German states there was intricate conflict between town and country and between one small area and another. The unit with which most governments were concerned in administering taxation was not an individual but a district. Its contribution was fixed by tradition, bargaining, or threats, and local authorities were left to apportion it as their circumstances permitted. The collector was less likely than in earlier centuries to be a direct servant of the Crown: tax-farming had become the normal way of ensuring a quick return from every imposition granted or decreed. Though it was often believed that half or more of the amount paid failed to reach the government, the system at least gave to those who managed the collection an incentive to do the job thoroughly. But it was often necessary to collect taxes by the threat of force. The armies that absorbed most of the money also gave to the Crown a means of extracting it that sometimes avoided the necessity for constitutional formalities.

The need for making subjects pay more led governments to invent new devices. We have seen the wide effects of the sale of office and title; but only in France and Spain, of the larger countries, was their contribution to the revenue of great and lasting importance. New taxes were the only general solution. The simplest was the crude poll-tax or tax on households, which could to some extent be graded according to the apparent wealth of the victim. It was tried, with no great success, in England in 1641; in Russia it provided a large source of revenue, and under Peter a fairly advanced administrative machinery was evolved to assess and collect it. But it was an almost universal experience of governments that indirect taxes were more easily brought under the complete control of the Crown than direct ones. Customs duties, almost the only money-raising method that had also, by discouraging or regulating imports, a wider economic purpose, were constantly being extended. In the second half of the century the excise – the taxation of selected commodities, or even of everything that was sold – came rapidly into favour. The Spanish *alcabala*, in theory a general sales tax, and the *millones*, a tax on essential foods and other commodities, were already well established before 1600, though to some extent their impact was changed by allowing towns to compound for them at a fixed sum. France was only one of many countries that taxed salt, which was so necessary that an increase in price had little effect on demand and in many areas was so restricted in its sources that the tax was hard to evade. The Dutch were the first to use the excise widely, and probably raised more money per head than any other country. In England it was the most hated of the Civil War innovations. The Great Elector fought his bitterest political struggle to extend the excise to all the towns (see p. 366). But he never succeeded in imposing it universally. In taxation as in everything else the range within which governments could increase their authority over the rich was very limited.

Despite all their difficulties monarchs in 1700 had, by the standards of their great-grandfathers, enormous financial resources and enough military power to make successful rebellion by their subjects highly unlikely. They had, with few exceptions, destroyed the threat of opposition from representative institutions; they had reduced their dependence on aristocracies, on venal office-holders and on clerical magnates. Government was now far more of a profession, in which monarchs needed to become expert. But it was government with little consistent purpose beyond its own survival. The welfare of the subject certainly mattered no more than it had a century earlier. The burden governments imposed on him was decidedly heavier.

10

REBELLION

A large part of the history of seventeenth-century Europe is made up of violent resistance to authority. Rebellion at every level of society was as much a part of life as were famine, plague, and war. The word can be applied to events ranging from a local riot to a civil war; and efforts to define rigid categories have, as with many such words, led to forceful arguments but not to accepted conclusions. The simplest classification of rebellions depends on the people originally or chiefly involved. There were those among the aristocracy, often headed by rival claimants to a throne. There were those led by men of substance below the aristocratic level, such as French lawyers, English gentry, or the townsmen of Prague. And there were those of the urban and of the rural poor. It is more difficult to divide rebellions according to their purpose – to overthrow a central government, to establish local privileges, to secure the rights of a minority, or to remedy one form or another of oppression and poverty. The proclaimed objectives of a rebellion could change quickly and unpredictably: many participants must often have had only a vague knowledge of what they were. A popular rising could often be absorbed into, or originate from, a larger political movement. Which of those should be called 'revolutions' is another topic of massive argument. What is widely accepted is that any explanation of the outbreak of rebellion has to be sought in a multiplicity of circumstances. With each such event two separate questions can be asked – what were the backgrounds and aspirations of those who rebelled, and why at that time and place rather than another did they lead to violent action? When rebellions are looked at collectively far more complex questions arise, leading into the depths of historical and sociological theory. Only the surface of them can be touched here.

REBELLION AND REVOLUTION

The 1640s and 1650s were an age of rebellions. Men said so at the time, and tried to interpret the warning of comets, explain the prophecies of the millennium, or calculate the average lifetime of empires on the assumption that some cataclysmic moment had arrived. It is tempting to point to the English Civil War (see pp. 460–9), the successful revolt in Portugal against the Spanish monarchy, and the less successful ones in Catalonia, Sicily and Naples (see pp. 388–97), to the peaceful overthrow of the Orange stadtholderate in the Netherlands (see pp. 469–75) and to the Fronde in France (see pp. 326–31), and to insist that the occurrence of all these in the space of ten years cannot be just coincidence. The great rebellion in the Ukraine in 1649 is less tempting to include; and if the revolts that in the same years overthrew the Ming dynasty in China are added the claim that they are all part of the same crisis becomes embarrassing. Even in western Europe, if the revolts formed a single event marking the watershed between the world of the Renaissance and that of the Enlightenment, or between a feudal and a capitalist society, it is remarkable how little they affected each other in their outbreak or course. It is a familiar fallacy to suppose that if revolutions occurred independently they ought to be evenly spaced throughout whatever period is discussed. If the Revolt of the Netherlands or the Bohemian rising, or the later troubles in Hungary had occurred in the forties, they too would naturally have been hailed as part of the great revolutionary upheaval. It has been pointed out that at least as many rebellions can be found in the 1560s.[1] Risings of the poor and violent local opposition to governments were common all through the century. Nevertheless, after 1660 there were few revolts on as large a scale as the earlier ones. Governments nearly everywhere seemed to have overcome the threats: they were now defended by armies bigger than any their subjects could possess and had established stable systems of administration. For another century the absolutist state would survive.

The rebellions most feared by monarchs were those that began among their immediate supporters. Landed magnates who revolted against the king had always been the greatest internal threat to order and stability. If royal courts were intended to strengthen the loyalty of the great men who benefited directly from the power and wealth of the monarch, they were also places where conspiracies thrived and challenges to the innermost circles of privilege developed. Palace conspiracy could still easily turn into wider conflict. The discontented noble could call out his dependants, and could usually find plenty of allies against the established authority. A danger-signal for the French monarchy was when great men began to leave the court for their provincial homes – where some were virtually monarchs in courts of their own. Throughout the reign of Louis XIII and the minority of his successor, the threat remained that noble insurrection would bring France back to the chaos of the sixteenth-century Wars of Religion. Russia before 1613 suffered similar disasters on a scale nowhere else could match. Among the manifold origins of the English Revolution, the Bishops' Wars were at least in part a Scottish baronial revolt; and in the leadership of both the Royalist and the Parliamentary sides there were clear vestiges of the old-style wars of the nobility.[2] But the difference between the Earl of Essex under Charles I and his father under Elizabeth was significant: seventeenth-century noble rebels, much more often and prominently than their predecessors, acted in the name of a larger cause than the power and independence of their own kind. Often their role was that of the military leaders in movements for which much of the initiative came from lower down the scale.

Religion was naturally one of the most effective stimulants for revolt; and round it everyone from the duke to the beggar could unite in impassioned resistance. French Huguenots, Russian Old Believers, Irish Catholics, English Puritans, and Bohemian Protestants showed the same capacity for linking the claims of the religious minority with a great variety of aspirations and grievances. Regional loyalties could be as deeply felt as religious ones. It was not only places under alien rule that could rise in assertion of local privileges or separatist aims. From Bordeaux to Novgorod almost every city had its memories of struggles for independence in trade, law-making, and administration, and often of disputes with lords of the surrounding territory. They were memories that any new incentive could revive. But above all it was economic burdens that brought normally peace-loving subjects gradually to the side of the advocates of forcible resistance. One simple fact about the rebellions is evident: of the rational grievances behind them the most widespread was taxation – and especially new taxation. Exemption of the rich aristocracy from paying any tax at all, irrational differences between those of the other citizens who paid and those who did not, even the dishonesty and brutality of tax-farmers were often borne passively until some new imposition touched off the suppressed resentment. The 'illegal' exactions of Charles I, the fiscal devices of Mazarin, the Neapolitan fruit-tax – all were as bitterly hated as had been the burdens the Spaniards had imposed on the Netherlands in the previous century. Nothing else could so effectively concentrate awareness of the injustice of the whole social and economic order into a moment of united anger.

Theories about the deeper causes of the great revolutionary upheavals still multiply on every level of scholarship. The most indestructible seem to be those based, sometimes in simplistic terms, sometimes in highly sophisticated ones, on the claim that it was all part of an inevitable conflict of classes: the revolutionaries were, without knowing and often without showing it, the bourgeoisie, attacking a changed but still essentially 'feudal' aristocracy. It is largely from the English Civil War that the concept of a seventeenth-century 'bourgeois revolution' originated. Many familiar facts appear to uphold it: the comparatively backward north and west were mainly Royalist, the south and east, the clothing towns, and the men with a controlling voice in London, the other cities, and the ports were more likely to be Parliamentarian. Puritanism, the religion of the hard-working, the thrifty, and the self-made, was as firmly associated with Parliament as Catholicism was opposed to it. But the closer these identifications are examined the less convincing they appear. The geographical alignment relates at least as much to military control as to political sympathies. Corporations and merchant communities were deeply divided among themselves. In the most prominent social group, the landed gentry, there are too many ways in which the facts can be selected to fit the theory. It is more difficult still to show the assorted enemies of Mazarin's government, or the narrow urban oligarchies who supported de Witt and the dominance of Holland, as representative of an emerging capitalist class. What has to be recognized is that the quest for demonstrable Marxist explanations has provided some of the most powerful analysis of the rebellions and of the societies in which they occurred. Other general theories of revolution have not proved more convincing, and not hitherto as long-lasting. Some have started from the idea of an 'equilibrium' in communities that broke down through the failure of rulers to adapt to new social and economic conditions; obedience to government and acceptance of inferiority in a hierarchy then broke down too. There have been adaptations and elaborations of the theory dating back to Tocqueville's work on the French Revolution that men rebel not when deprivation is greatest but when hopes are raised and frustrated. However crude its original form appeared, it does take account of human behaviour as well as of collective patterns. The immensely complex evidence now available can easily lead to the despondent conclusion that no interpretation covering large expanses of place and time has much validity.

The difficulties in finding the common characteristics of rebels can lead back to the old concentration on governments. The 'Court', the central élite of monarch, office-holders, and resident aristocrats, was everywhere recognizably the same, while the 'Country' had endless variety. The extravagance of kings and magnates on ceremony, offices, perquisites, and wars appeared to cause the burdens of taxation. The absolutist state could be attacked by almost any section of society excluded from a share in the spoils. Against the king and his officers the lord might well be the ally of the peasant. It is possible from this point of view to show how the character of the revolutions differed according to the particular sins of the regime, from Spain where monarchy was at its worst to the Netherlands where the Orange dynasty threatened only a mild reversion to the evils that had already been overthrown. The connection is clearly not a simple one; and it is difficult to reconcile it with the claim that the 1640s and 1650s were a unique moment of change. The evils and the resistance to them had existed all through the century; and though, in the west at least, the widespread victories of the monarchies made further violence less feasible, the conflict of interests changed only very slowly. Perhaps no explanation of the major revolts can be satisfactory if it is excessively rational. The closer men come to collective violence, the further their reasoned aspirations fall into the background.

POPULAR REVOLT

The first essential in a revolt of any kind was that a number of people should band together. Governments were – as most of them still are – alarmed about any gathering of their subjects. Anything from the meeting of a parliament to a parish festival could be an occasion for collective discontent. The line between revelry and rioting was dangerously thin; rural disturbances could notoriously begin at fairs or religious processions, and occasionally they merged into more widespread violence. The urban crowd was a greater danger. The emotions and actions of the masses in Lisbon, Barcelona, Naples, Paris, or London were more important at critical moments than anything the political leaders could do. Crowds great or small, urban or rural, were unpredictable. It was possible to appeal to their loyalty or their realistic hopes; but often they were moved by irrational fear. Rumours of bandits, armies, papists, witches or werewolves could lead some to bar their doors and others to band together in arms. The presence of armed but undisciplined soldiers, common in every country during or after a war, could touch off a riot that rumour could magnify into incipient revolution. The usual response of governments was brutal and indiscriminate punishment.

THE FRENCH *EMEUTES*

French historians have made in recent years an intensive study of the rural and urban revolts of the seventeenth century. It was to France too that the Russian historian Porchnev turned for an investigation of the same question. It has consequently become a matter of controversy going far beyond the events themselves. Small rebellions were not necessarily more significant in France than elsewhere; but they are probably the best-recorded. There were few if any years, in the first half of the century at least, when there was not a popular rising somewhere in the French country-side. In towns, major violence was liable to occur at almost any time. 1623, 1629, 1633, and 1642 were years of insurrection in Lyons, 1634 and 1639 in Rouen. Bordeaux had two of its worst riots in 1635 and 1675. Most of these risings of the *menu peuple* were apparently unconnected with those of the great men. They were widespread in years of crop failure, plague, urban unemployment, and foreign war. But the worst of the disasters did not usually lead immediately to the most forceful rebellions. It was in the mid-twenties that the risings of the *croquants*, which had happened sporadically ever since the Wars of Religion, became almost a nationwide phenomenon. Royal officials, tax-collectors, army commanders demanding freequarter, lawyers and judges might all be attacked as manifestations of oppressive authority. The alignments were unpredictable. *Parlements*, and local office-holders hostile to the intendants, sometimes made use of the rebels. Small landholders were often ready to identify themselves with the cause of the peasants, and were alleged to be arming their rebellious tenants. The clergy too could be either victims or allies. Relations between rural rebels and townsmen varied. The appearance in a market-town or outside city walls of a gathering of peasants armed with scythes and pikes, sometimes with muskets or fowling-pieces too, might touch off a sympathetic assembly of townsmen; or the urban militia might prove reliable defenders of property. The great fear of the government was unity of the many groups opposed to Parisian authority. The fear of property-owners great and small was that any rising was liable to turn into an indiscriminate attack on buildings and crops. The house of the *élu* – the local tax-collector – might be attacked first, and the rebel landowner see to it that his hated neighbour's vines were torn up. But once destruction had started, the distinction between those who crushed the peasant with taxes and those who demanded rents, tithes, or labour dues could cease to matter. The simple element of poor versus rich was always somewhere in the background. For the central government the most serious development was when local rebellion became identified with the separatist ambitions and loyalties of provinces. It was then that conspiracies of the great nobles against the Crown found a basis in popular support. It happened in Languedoc in 1632, when the provincial governor, the Duke of Montmorency, put himself at the head of the long-simmering resistance to the extension of royal administration into the region. Languedoc was then closer than any other French province to functioning as an independent state. With the backing of its elected Assembly of Estates and of some of its bishops he was able to raise an army that could fight a pitched battle against the royal force sent against it. He was defeated and beheaded.

From 1635, when the war with Spain brought enemy armies into France, and almost doubled the burden of taxation, waves of rural disorder appeared each spring, often dying away of their own accord when the harvest had to be gathered. The central government did not panic at the wild rumours of plunder and massacre. A policy of dividing the rebels, making concessions to townsmen to encourage them in resisting the peasantry, and using troops occasionally but decisively had some success. These were not aimless riots: many of them involved meetings where political and practical aims were decided. In 1636 a great revolt in the country round Angoulême was ended when an assembly of delegates from the towns and villages agreed to stop all rebellious activities in return for concessions on taxation and promises to hear petitions of grievances. In 1637 a rising of the *croquants* in Périgord was organized as a regular military operation under its elected leader, a local *gentilhomme* who was accused of betraying the cause after his forces were defeated. Then, in the summer of 1639, there came the fiercest and most concentrated of the rural revolts – that of the *nu-pieds* in Normandy. Years of plague and bad harvests had brought poverty to towns as well as the countryside. A long succession of new taxes for the war had been proclaimed, of which the most hated was the order tightening up the *gabelle*. Towns such as Rouen, exempt from the *taille*, had their trade ruinously taxed. Soldiers were quartered on the province; Spanish prisoners were taken there and left ill-guarded. Rumours of revolt which seem to have filled the province before there existed much real basis for them quickly turned into reality. Sometimes towns were attacked by armies of peasants; sometimes the townsmen rose first. Offices of tax-collectors were burned, and here and there individuals suspected of being obnoxious officials were killed. Avranches became the alleged headquarters of the mythical Jean Va–nus-pieds in whose name printed orders were distributed calling on men to arm themselves 'for the service of the king'. By the winter the grand army of the *nu-pieds* moving through Normandy was said to be 20,000 strong. It had leadership of a sort – townsmen, a few impoverished nobles, perhaps one or two clergy. Local office-holders, angered by the government's creation of new posts, supported the rebels. The situation was serious enough to bring out an army from Paris, which crushed the rebels fairly easily and indulged in indiscriminate killing of any who could be caught.

It was against this background of almost incessant popular unrest, supported by many groups at every level of society, that the chaotic revolutionary upheaval of the Fronde began. It was only because the political conflict so easily touched off risings in Paris and in the country that the state was brought close to anarchy. How much coherent purpose there was behind the mass movements has been bitterly disputed. There was nothing to compare with the emergence as leaders of the parliamentary cause in England of people previously below the level of central politics and stirred by radical ideas. One man who became momentarily the most successful popular leader was the arch-aristocrat and turncoat Condé, another the unprincipled Cardinal de Retz, a third the aged *magistrat* Broussel. Certainly the breakdown of government was the occasion for a succession of revolts against urban and provincial authority on a larger scale than ever before. Landlord and tax-collector were permanent villains, Mazarin the personification of tyranny. But every popular movement became swamped by the cynical and shapeless quarrels among political leaders great and small. The calamity was that the oppressed had as little sense of purpose and as great a devotion to petty faction-fights as the oppressors.

The restoration of order, and Louis XIV's achievements in winning the loyalty of the provincial *noblesse* and strengthening the authority of the state, changed the character of revolts. It did not end them. In Artois and in the Bourbonnais 1662 was another year of revolts against taxation and high prices; from 1664 to 1666 the outbreaks were mainly in the south. They were punished efficiently and quietly. The Dutch War of the 1670s, like that against Spain in the thirties and forties, produced still more new taxes and military burdens. In 1675 the biggest of the provincial rebellions under Louis XIV broke out in Brittany. It was a province where more judicial power remained in the hands of landlords than elsewhere but where many of the minor *noblesse* led a life not much different from that of the peasants. Impositions like the tax on tobacco and the notorious stamp-duty on paper were the occasion for successive revolts throughout the peninsula. Alarm about possible Dutch invasion had led to the recruiting of an armed peasant militia, which could easily become a nucleus for rebel bands. The movement had a good deal of co-ordination, and was even linked, through coastal shipping, with the simultaneous rising in Bordeaux and its countryside. It produced not only protests against taxation and poverty, but demands for the removal of the barriers of privilege and status that separated the peasant from even the poorest *gentilhomme*. At the end of the summer royal troops could be spared to put down the rebels in both Brittany and Bordeaux, and to remain there in winter quarters to punish and plunder as they thought fit. There were no more risings on such a scale. But at the turn of the century there appeared a form of rebellion that seemed to revert to an earlier generation. The *Camisards* of the Cévennes were a Protestant group led by visionary prophets. It became a big enough movement to attract the interest of the Dutch and English. For a time Catholic bands of the same character fought a local guerilla war against them. But governments no longer felt that religious warfare was to be taken too seriously as a threat to their power.

THE IRISH REBELLION

Sixty years before the *Camisards* one remote corner of Europe had produced a rebellion in which religion was uppermost among the familiar ingredients. The Irish rising of 1641 was the outburst of an oppressed nationality against alien rule. It was also the protest of a religion which the majority accepted and the minority forbade. Its leaders were landlords who had lost their estates, local ruling families who had lost their power, priests and friars whose activities were permanently illegal. It was linked with the whole network of Catholic politics in Europe and with court intrigues in England. And it was one of the immediate origins of a prolonged civil war. Yet nothing in it happened at high pressure. Most of the oppressed did not rebel at all; and those who did were cautious and discriminating in their vengeance. The plotting by Catholic lords and gentry was a tangle in which it was hard to say who were the rebels and who the rulers – so much so that while some of its threads led to the pope others were connected to the king. Almost certainly the authorities in Dublin Castle, or some of them, could have stopped it but preferred not to do so. The Irish rebellion that had an undoubted effect existed not in reality but in the skilled imagination of Pym and the English Parliamentarians.

For many of those outside it, Ireland seemed more closely

connected with Europe than with England. In the Irish seminaries of France, Italy, and Spain, and in Irish companies among the armies in Germany and the Netherlands men talked of heroically rescuing their land and its faith. The active conspirators did nothing heroic at all. Rory O'More and Sir Phelim O'Neill were the descendants of traditionally rebellious clans. Another O'Neill, Owen Roe, was a mercenary officer in the Spanish armies who made extravagant promises of men and money from abroad. The talk of a rising was turned into specific plans by the conflict in England. While the Long Parliament was thought likely at any moment to add to its reforming programme the complete destruction of Irish Catholicism, Charles, in his typically indirect and half-informed way, was involved in schemes to re-establish the Irish army that had been disbanded under parliamentary pressure and to seize control of Dublin Castle and the central administration. Cautiously, and with neither of them fully understanding the purpose and prospects of the other, the two conspiracies were in touch.

In the summer of 1641 there emerged the scheme for a rising in Ulster at the same moment as a *coup d'état* in Dublin to overthrow the ruling group in the Castle. Some at least of the plans were revealed to the English Lords Justices, Parsons and Borlase. How far they deliberately allowed the rising to come to a head is impossible to say. Since the Castle was not taken over, and the leaders of the plot fled or were arrested, the provincial insurgents were left without the armed support they had expected. Even so, it was at first largely a military demonstration led by the Catholic gentry who recruited a disciplined army. The true peasant movement grew more slowly as the news and rumours of the rising spread. Then the plundering and burning and killing began. The Dublin government, officially supported by both Charles and the English parliament, was able to send an army that attacked the peasant bands and their homes with enough ferocity to remove any restraint from the rebels. There were a few pitched battles; but the truth behind the stories of huge massacres seems to have been a short period of widespread unco-ordinated violence different in scale but not in kind from the local peasant risings familiar everywhere. From the successive enquiries and depositions and the later manipulation of them there is not much prospect of arriving at any meaningful figures of the dead. One well-established fact suggests both some degree of control and a limitation of the possible number of victims: the Ulster Scots, far more numerous than the English, were largely left alone – on the instructions of the leaders who thought them possible allies against the English parliament. Another is that many of the rebels had originally the simple and attainable object of driving English settlers away from lands and houses they regarded as belonging legally to the Irish, rather than of attacking landlords, or Protestants, as such. Not many of them can have been aware of the political demands drawn up in the name of Sir Phelim O'Neill after the rebellion was more or less over, for the restoration of Catholicism and the return of confiscated lands. A document whose existence was probably more widely known was the alleged royal proclamation giving Irish Catholics permission to seize the property and persons of English – but not Scottish – Protestants. It would be interesting to know how far this notion of a king devoted to Catholic interests was held. There were many at Charles's court who would have been glad to encourage it. In fact, once the Ulster rebellion had begun, the need to restore order and security seemed to English royalists at least as important as scoring points against the Parliament. To everyone with property to lose, popular rebellion was even in this situation a dangerous weapon to handle.

RUSSIA

The local discontents of the French and the politically manipulated rising of the native Irish were events on a scale that could be matched in many western countries. Switzerland had a long series of peasant revolts against the wealth and power of the towns. In most of the Italian states, quite apart from the rebellions against Spanish rule in 1646–7, bandit attacks and sporadic violence by peasants were common. But all these seem trivial manifestations of forces that appeared in their full horror and splendour only in the east. As we have seen on p. 35, Russia and Poland had in the Cossacks something like permanent rebellion on a huge scale. They had also, in the forest zones especially, the little bandit groups, supported by some villagers, feared by others, that could always form a nucleus of wider repudiation of authority. The Russian government had its department of banditry that tried to limit their activities. For the peasant the prospects of improvement within the village community, and the incentives to compromise for the sake of peace and stability, were far less remote from reality than the hope of improvement through political action. The whole of the 'Time of Troubles' (see pp. 425–8) was in part a succession of rural and urban disorders instigated but never fully controlled by the political and military groups. In 1606 they culminated in the mass rebellion that spread northward and eastward from the Ukraine to affect something like half of European Russia. Partly it was an offshoot of the movement exploiting the 'false Dmitri', partly a response to the belief that a new and even more brutal government of the Boyars had taken, or was about to take, power in Moscow. Its leader, Ivan Bolotnikov, 'the Thief', brought to his banner an astonishing assortment of followers. There were serfs and slaves, free peasants, deserters from the armies, Cossacks and townsmen; but also many of the provincial *dvoriane* who were ready to use any weapon against the Boyars and did not take Bolotnikov's propaganda too seriously. His war-cries were the wildest of revolutionary threats: slay the landlords, seize their houses, land, and women; abolish every kind of restriction and taxation. But he claimed also a loyalty to the 'true tsar' who seems to have been vaguely imagined as ruling over a peasant democracy. Behind the despair of the peasant was a half-legendary belief in a lost freedom that would be restored when the usurpers were overthrown. Bolotnikov's host expanded at fantastic speed. It was supported by more organized forces under one of the politically ambitious nobles, Prince Shakhovskoy, who saw it as a possible source of power for himself. But Bolotnikov soon had his own 'court' with more authority, for the moment, than that of the tsar. He was at the gates of Moscow before he suffered his first setback. Once the illusion of victory was broken, a better disciplined royal army began to break up the host and take its revenge. By the end of the year Bolotnikov was defeated and in hiding.

For the next forty years local risings of the peasants continued, even under the 'good Tsar' Michael. Every landlord ran the risk of a village revolt that might end in the burning of his house and destruction of his crops. Then, in the peak period of political revolution in the west, there came the great rising of the Ukraine that turned agrarian revolt into international war. The Zaporozhian Cossacks who owed a nominal allegiance to the Polish

Crown had long been in a state of intermittent warfare against it. Repeatedly the Polish nobility and Crown officials had used the opportunity of a defeated rising to curtail Cossack privileges and exemptions and to confiscate land. 'Registered' Cossacks were taken in large numbers into the Polish forces. In 1637 a new hetman of the independent Cossacks, Pavluk, attempted a mass attack on the Poles and those who accepted their rule. It was a big enough affair to encourage peasants, in the Dnieper region especially, to begin a new wave of manorial revolts; but Pavluk's army, after it had captured a few towns, was destroyed by the Polish cavalry. The Polish government organized a vast campaign of retribution, hanging the men of rebel villages, driving out peasant families, handing over lands to whatever Poles were prepared to buy or lease them. The autonomous status of the Zaporozhie was repudiated and even the loyal Cossack regiments were put under Polish officers. It was the hope of Vladislav IV that eventually he would be able to use the Cossacks as an instrument of his own military power. But in 1648 there appeared the leader who turned their resistance into a united war against the state.

Bogdan Khmelnitsky was among the most successful of all upperclass leaders of popular revolt. He was a small landowner, son of a registered Cossack, and an officer in Polish service who had fought for the French in the Netherlands. It seems to have been largely personal grievances that made him put himself at the head of a few thousand Cossacks and attack the new Polish fortifications. His victories produced a sudden surge of support and the most widespread of all the agrarian risings. He got military help from the Tartars of the Crimea and created out of the Cossack host a modern disciplined army. But the explosion of peasant fury was soon beyond his control. The whole of the Ukraine was filled with crudely armed men, burning, killing, destroying, and vaguely aware that all this was an act of liberation. Despair alone had never sustained rebellions for long; and in this one there was also a religious element that provided a streak of hope. The Catholic Church and its Jesuit missions had worked long and persistently to drive Orthodox Christianity out of the Polish Ukraine. The Cossacks had sometimes been militant supporters of the Orthodox priesthood and had set up a new Metropolitan of Kiev under their protection. The rebel cause could now be held up as that of the accepted religion; and for the few there was the prospect of a share-out of the lands of the Catholic Church. In 1649, the year of the final imposition of serfdom in Russia, Khmelnitsky was able to approach the feeble Polish government almost as a victor making peace with the vanquished. Polish troops were to be withdrawn, Jews and Jesuits expelled, Cossack autonomy restored and the numbers of registered Cossacks increased. Grievances of the peasantry were no longer of much interest to him.

For two years Khmelnitsky ruled the Ukraine in regal splendour – with the help of approved Polish officials. But his military power was slowly being eroded as he expounded his schemes for becoming the hereditary monarch of a vast new state. In 1651 he began to negotiate with the tsar who, after long hesitation, agreed to the incorporation of the Cossacks into the Russian state. The status and possessions of Cossack leaders were to be guaranteed; but politically there was room for a good deal of doubt about how much Cossack autonomy would survive. War with Poland was the main preoccupation. Khmelnitsky remained in power in the Ukraine during the years when in England the leader of a different kind of military rebellion was Lord Protector. Each was succeeded by a less effective son who relinquished his post – though Yuri Khmelnitsky, unlike Richard Cromwell, became a priest.

The Ukrainian revolt produced neither strong government nor relief for the peasants, but the 'years of ruin' in which armies of Poles, Russians, and eventually Turks completed the devastation. It was not the only Russian rising during the 'crisis' decades of the west. In 1648 Moscow had one of its most savage outbreaks of mass violence, in which the rebels occupied the Kremlin before the foreign mercenaries of the palace guard drove them out. In the 1650s the tighter imposition of serfdom made banditry more tempting than ever; and rebels now had the support of the Old Believers. A village priest giving to enemies of the tsar and the patriarch assurance of divine approval was an excellent recruiting agent. Then, in 1667, there appeared the rebel leader who more than any of the others played the part of the messianic saviour rather than the politician or soldier. Stenka Razin, real though he was, belonged to the line of Robin Hood and Jean Va-nus-pieds. Within a few months of his appearance at the head of some Don Cossacks, his symbol of the horsetail was known everywhere from the Ukraine to Persia and was spreading northward into Muscovy. The throngs who joined him included serfs and refugee peasants, soldiers from all the armies, priests, the urban poor, landlords impoverished by taxation or war. Razin became a liberator who could work miracles, fly through the air, rise from the dead. Sometimes he was himself acclaimed as the true tsar who had come to recover his throne from the usurpers; sometimes he insisted that his only aim when the traitors had been defeated was to live among the peasants as a brother, serving God, the Virgin, and the Tsar. Sometimes he was proclaiming an almost anarchic Cossack freedom and equality, sometimes a powerful state that would rescue the poor from the landlords and rule through elected assemblies. But always in Razin's message the idea of social revolution was uppermost. It was partly this, partly a sheer rivalry for power, that produced a split between his followers and the established Cossacks. Whatever Razin's aim, his method was destruction – of houses and crops and cattle, of landlords and tax-collectors, of the whole apparatus of oppression. In 1670 he captured Tsaritsyn (Stalingrad, Volgagrad) and led his throng northwards with the cry 'To Moscow against the Landlords'. Peasants rushed to join him; townsmen overthrew their rulers and welcomed – at first – the 'liberators'; monasteries saw him as the saviour of the Old Believers. But it took only a few victories of government forces to make the legend collapse. Razin himself was handed over to the 'enemy' and publicly executed in Red Square with spectacular tortures. The campaign of vengeance that followed was probably as devastating in its destruction of property and order as the rebellion itself. It did not produce any significant reduction in the number of local risings in town and country: their pattern was still the same when Pugachev, the greatest of all the Russian rebels, began his peasant war a century later.

CENTRAL EUROPE

The Empire and the lands of the Habsburgs were only a little further removed than Russia and Poland from a condition in which rebellion was a constant threat to the rule of law. The Bohemian revolt of 1618 that merged quickly into more widespread war, and was so successfully and brutally suppressed, might have had very different consequences if its popular and nationalist elements had been less entangled in noble politics. Often during the wars there are glimpses of a truly independent resistance to the depredations of the armies. In 1626 the peasants of Upper Austria, where Maximilian of Bavaria had brutally attacked Protestantism and left his soldiers to make the most of the process of enforcing his edicts, found a leader – Stefan Fadinger – who for a few months had a rebel army big enough to defeat the Imperial forces. There were popular risings against the occupying armies in Silesia and Moravia. In 1633 the peasants of Bavaria succeeded in compelling Maximilian to take his troops away from the areas of worst starvation. But the greatest danger to the emperor's prospects of achieving stable government in the areas under his sovereignty came from Hungary. After the Peace of Westphalia 'Royal' Hungary looked like becoming a new Bohemia, more dangerous because of the heathen intervention which any disturbance there was liable to bring.

As the 'bulwark of Christianity' against the Turk, the Hungarian nobility from time to time asserted a claim to greater protection by the emperor than his western subjects. One form they would now like it to take was help in imposing on their peasants the serfdom that profitable cultivation of their lands seemed to require. But the ambiguity of imperial policy towards Hungary was demonstrated after the victory over the Turks at St Gotthard in 1664 when, far from driving the enemy out of the rich territory of the Danube plain for the benefit of Christian land-owners, the Emperor Leopold made the Treaty of Vasvár that gave to the sultan roughly what he had before. To the Hungarian nobility treatment like this left no good reason for loyalty to the Habsburgs. A conspiracy of nobles in the next few years was so mismanaged and so lacking in any national support that both the French and the Turks decided it was not worth backing. In 1671 the 'three counts' who led it were executed; many of their followers who escaped death went as galley-slaves to Italy; an Austrian army was quartered in the country; new taxes were imposed; the last remnants of Protestantism were persecuted. It was all reminiscent of what had happened after the White Mountain fifty years before. Gradually a wider and deeper movement of revolt developed, helped by the great outbreak of plague in 1678 and the poor harvests of the next year. Exiles who had fled from Austrian vengeance formed on the northern frontiers the partisan army of the *kurucok*, organised first by the Transylvanian

Calvinist noble Teleki and then by the young Lutheran grandson of one of the executed counts, Imre Thököli. In him the Hungarians had what Bohemia had so conspicuously lacked – a successful popular leader. Peasants, landlords, and townsmen joined an army that began to take on some characteristics of a Cossack-like community. Ignoring frontiers, it moved into Slovakia, Silesia, and Moravia. Thököli and the Transylvanian princess he married claimed a half royal status, producing their own coinage, receiving the envoys of Louis XIV and the sultan, establishing a military regime that destroyed the authority of imperial officials. Royal Hungary and many of the regions beyond it came largely under his control. But against the *kurucok* there appeared a similar rival organization, the *labanc* in support of the monarchy. Between the two fighting was inconclusive. In 1681 Leopold made to the Hungarian Estates far-reaching promises of 'liberties' (see p. 373). It amounted to a surrender, as a political necessity to the 'national' rebellion. A year later Thököli reached agreement with the Turks for a joint attack on imperial forces in Hungary. The 'popular' rebellion was submerged by foreign invasion.

In Bohemia the succession of plague and famine led to peasant movements that for a moment seemed near to being a general revolt against serfdom. Peasants in the north began to act in unison and with some political awareness. They sent deputations to Leopold to complain of the increased burdens. Alarmed landowners hastened to use their influence at the imperial court to get a decree prohibiting such actions and strengthening the authority of landlords still further. In the spring of 1680, risings of serfs reached a scale large enough to call for a military campaign against them. The familiar bands of crudely armed peasants merged into an 'army' big enough for artillery to be used against it. Within a few weeks the gatherings had ended. While order was being restored with the help of indiscriminate hanging and beheading, Leopold issued a new decree ostensibly fixing the maximum obligation of serfs but in fact giving them no worth-while protection against their lords.

A good many other specimens of rebellion could be added to these. No-one could claim that any popular insurrection suceeded in changing for long the distribution of wealth or power. Few of them consistently advocated any such ideas. The mixture of material and emotional incentives that determined the behaviour of the masses had a great deal in common with the motives of politicians. Groups and strata in the countryside and the streets came together and split apart with as little consistency as palace cliques or alliances of nations. The policies of rebel leaders were twisted by their ambitions and jealousies as much as were those of ministers. But in the protests there appeared, sometimes hazily, sometimes stated with inspiring clarity, the belief that the organized community need not always be run in the interests of the rich and the privileged. It was better to resist in vain than to acquiesce.

NOTES AND REFERENCES

1   J. H. Elliott in *Past and Present*, no. 42 (1969).

2   On the aristocratic element in the opposition, see the articles by B. S. Manning in *Past and Present*, no. 9 (1956) and V. F. Snow in *Journal of Modern History* (1960).

11

WAR

Just as the history of government is seen through the eyes of the rulers, the history of wars has, at least until recent decades, been written largely from the viewpoint of the men of power who brought them about and the commanders who organized them. Their effects on the participants, the civil populations, and the whole economic and political life of the countries involved in fighting and preparing for wars have been less conspicuous. The tedious diplomatic arguments before hostilities and the even more tedious treaties after them that have been made to seem similarly important. Hardly anyone would now doubt that though one of the greatest changes in seventeenth-century Europe was in the character of warfare, it mattered less because of victories or defeats than because of its connections with the life of the community. Wars came, more and more, to be fought only by states; and states became, more and more, institutions for fighting wars. The developments are not easy to define: there were no inventions comparable to gunpowder or aeroplanes, no decisive events like Hiroshima. Innovations in weapons such as the flint-lock, the paper cartridge, and the rifle were adopted slowly and erratically. Soldiers were recruited and trained in the old ways long after new ones had become familiar. Attempts to build bigger and better ships were generally unsuccessful. It is safe to say that far more resources were spent on wars; but much of the information we need is very hard to quantify. Where statistics are available the historian can be deceived by figures that were meant to deceive someone else. (Unending controversy about the effects of the Thirty Years War shows how some of the problems of evidence extended to civilian affairs too.) It is difficult also to see the many wars in their true proportions. As with other topics, we still devote too much attention to western Europe. The warfare that had the largest effects was not that about scraps of territory in the Rhineland but about control of the Danube countries, the Balkans, the Mediterranean and of course the huge areas outside Europe whose fate wes decided by comparatively small forces. We shall not entirely escape the distortions here.

ARMIES

Of the many changes in warfare during the century, by far the greatest was in the size, and hence the cost, of armies. In 1600 war was within the means of individuals. A large landowner could raise and maintain an army that was virtually his own. It was nearly always said to be for the service of the monarch; but everyone knew that it might be used against him. The French Wars of Religion and the Revolt of the Netherlands had shown that wealthy subjects could control forces well able to challenge the Crown. In the Thirty Years War, armies largely independent of political rule ranged from the mighty force of Wallenstein to the little democratic bands of Landsknechter that wandered in the most depressed areas. On the death of Bernard of Saxe-Weimar Richelieu concluded a treaty with his army, not with his state. Kings who recruited large forces kept them for a single summer's campaign rather than for a prolonged war, and were certainly not expected to maintain them in peacetime. Even when an army was firmly loyal to a state, its management was not necessarily under close state control. Commanders like Spinola provided men and supplies largely on their own initiative. The armies most closely controlled by rulers were perhaps those of the petty German princes who went into the trade themselves and hired out their forces as profitably as they could. But by 1700 almost every state that could claim true independence had, more or less permanently, armed forces far too large and too expensively equipped to be matched by any private enterprise. Their recruitment and management formed a major part of the work of governments, their supplies a means of wealth for industrialists and financiers; and in one way or another the sections of society that held political power continued to regard military command as a natural part of their functions. How much of the available resources of the world was wasted on armies active or inactive is beyond calculation.

SOLDIERS

The quality of any armed force depended on the men who served in it – not only how many but their efficiency, the likelihood of their staying there and obeying orders, and how much it cost to keep them. In 1600 major battles could still be fought between armies of 20,000 or so. The decisive change in the west came when Louis XIV, from the Dutch War onwards, kept almost continuously a force of between 200,000 and 300,000, recruited mainly in the north and east of France. No other country could equal it – except perhaps the Turks who sent 200,000 men into Hungary and kept a large eastern army as well. Even the Russian national forces, after all Peter's efforts, were no bigger than those of Louis. Larger armies could be worse ones. It was a frequent complaint throughout the century that only the 'meanest sort of people' served in the infantry, and there were many arguments about how the quality of soldiers could be improved while finding enough of them and making them serve continuously.

In the vestiges of feudal theory that could occasionally be renewed, most men were under some sort of obligation to serve and most landowners were bound to raise and command forces. To some extent the notion of universal military service had been revived to produce such forces as the French *ban* and *arrière-ban* and the English militia; but these were primarily for local defence. Free tenants who had been persuaded by tradition or threats to serve under the command of their lords could not easily be made to leave their own area, let alone go abroad on a long campaign. National armies had to consist of men who were driven to join them, either by more or less legal conscription or by the lack of any better livelihood. In the east the need for soldiers gave the state a direct interest in extending serfdom. In the west a mixture of forcible conscription, pay, and occasionally appeals to patriotic duty produced the national element in armies. Feudal obligation was replaced by what could be dignified as the sovereignty of the monarch but consisted in practice of the miscellaneous devices of his administrators. It was in the poorest communities that armies could most easily be gathered: Spain and Sweden owed some of their military strength to this. But national armies were not enough. In the major states of Europe the fully trained soldier was likely to be a mercenary who might or might not have some loyalty to the monarch he was serving. The supply of soldiers was a great international business. The professional fighting-man served where his prospects were best, sometimes for a middleman who hired out troops in bulk, sometimes by applying to a commander with a good reputation as an employer. Switzerland was throughout the century regarded as the source of the highest-quality soldiers; but Scotland was not far behind. Even in the Spanish Succession war, English and Dutch armies consisted more of German and some other foreign troops than of their own nationals. Small German states found it profitable to recruit men and provide them for service abroad in return for subsidies: the line between hiring out soldiers and making an alliance was not always clear. Since commanders of mercenary forces often had themselves a vested interest in the preservation of their men, and desertion was usually easy, it was not a particularly dangerous occupation. Nor was service in a foreign army in any way disreputable: a few years of such experience, even in the ranks, attracted many sons of wealthy families. But the ordinary soldier depended on his pay. To the homeless, war was better than vagabondage. Religious persecution added to the numbers who found military service a tolerable refuge; and the victims of devastation could survive by joining the armies that had caused it. Wars, in fact, helped to create the conditions in which people were willing to take part in them.

OFFICERS

Feudal theory had made military and social rank inseparable. In 1600, though the merits of professional commanders and soldiers had been recognized occasionally for at least two centuries, it was still assumed everywhere that normally armies were commanded by great noblemen and that within them large units were commanded by the owners of large estates and holders of high civil titles. In English terms the colonel of a regiment was likely to come from a leading county family, the captain of a troop of horse or company of infantry from the manorial gentry. These or their equivalents were the two basic grades of officer, originally derived from the ability of the landlord to call out his tenants. At the beginning of the English Civil War, parliamentary no less than royalist armies were commanded by peers. In Poland many land-owners were still obliged by the deeds of their estates to raise soldiers and to fight in war. In France it was accepted that members of the nobility were entitled to hold commissions in the army if they wished, and that no-one else could. Even so, they often had to pay for them. In most countries military offices were increasingly acquired, like civil ones, by purchase or patronage. They conferred their own prestige, and they could sometimes be a profitable investment. It was commonly said that officers made fortunes, by collecting pay for non-existent soldiers, by holding multiple commissions, by profiteering in the sale of arms and supplies, by using their power over the civilian population to extort money for themselves, and in the end by selling their commission at an enhanced price. It is impossible to know how common these practices were: French officers were apt to complain that they had been ruined by the expense of their army careers. If many holders of military titles stayed at home or at the royal court, many others died in battle. It is one of the most surprising survivals from earlier custom that the highest officer of all, the king, could appear on the battlefield himself. Not only such warriors as Gustav Adolf and John Sobieski but the unwar-like Charles I thought it a natural part of their functions. The portraits of kings in armour on horseback may well have done more to maintain loyalty than those showing extravagant splendour.

Governments were not eager to overthrow the existing systems of army command. The successes of the New Model Army in England, when it was, briefly, possible for low-born soldiers to rise to officer level, were a dubious precedent: armies that seized political control were to be avoided at all costs. But there was no escaping the fact that when warfare grew in scale it became increasingly a matter for the full-time specialist. The most obvious compromise was to persuade the old-style officers to learn new methods. Military academies and military textbooks, unenterprising though they often were, did something to spread a knowledge of what was needed. As armies became more heavily dependent on central governments for finance and the organization of supplies it was easier to infiltrate the direct authority of the state without upsetting aristocratic control too much. When Louis XIV's ministers introduced the ranks of major, lieutenant-colonel and brigadier, which were supposed to be awarded by the Crown for merit and to provide opportunities to rise in the hierarchy without purchase or influence, the example was followed in many other countries. Indeed one of the striking characteristics of European armies, at least in the west, was that they became so much alike. Officers easily recognized and respected the ranks of their enemies as well as of their allies. The authoritarian rule that could still occasionally be resisted by civilians was exercised by much the same governing élites in their capacity as army officers, with death as the penalty for any indiscipline. The barrier between officers and others became virtually uncrossable. Armies collectively were an institution that imposed unquestioning obedience to the commands of men closely connected with those who ran government and justice. The officers who paraded at every opportunity their uniforms and medals, and taught the proud traditions of their regiments, were contributing all the time to the stability of the social and political hierarchy.

WEAPONS AND BATTLES

Most of the soldiers in the big armies were, throughout the period, infantry. Naturally only foot-soldiers could build and man the defences of a town, or besiege them. The foot-soldiers also occupied territory and held its population in obedience. How far they also played the decisive part in winning big battles was more arguable. Part of the difficulty was that cavalry was still assumed to be superior in status: the idea that 'the scum of the commons' could now fight on horseback was deeply resented. The feeling that the most impressive and prestigious part of the army ought also to be the most victorious was hard to avoid, and undeniably the cavalry charge did sometimes produce a sudden victory. The cavalry soldier was paid more – a reasonable enough discrimination when he was expected to provide and maintain his own horse. He sometimes claimed to be entitled to a larger share of booty that was being divided. It was less easy to preserve the social distinction when the state or army was responsible for providing horses. The decline of the cavalryman's prestige did not make the horse itself less indispensable in the organization of warfare. In 1600 cavalry normally used the 'great horse', ponderous and slow but capable of carrying the heaviest armour. This was now commoner than the much smaller 'northern horse'. During the century Arab horses became increasingly fashionable for racing and hunting, though they were often thought unsuitable for fighting. The notorious successes of Turkish and Polish cavalry might have thrown some doubt on that; but light horses ridden by men without metal armour were another weakening of the social difference. Not until the wars of Louis XIV was it accepted that horses bred for speed rather than weight were a vital part of armies. The distinction between the types of horse used for different purposes was by no means rigid: at a pinch the same animal could be employed for transport, fighting, and ploughing. Soldiers habitually took them – officially or illicitly – for use or for profit. After a prolonged war the scarcity of horses was a major problem both for agriculture and for the armies themselves. Probably more horses than riders were killed in battle, and a horse could be harder to replace than a soldier.

At the beginning of the century the main weapons of the horseman were two wheel-lock pistols, of such short range that massed pikes were a good defence against them. The fashionable operation was the 'caracole', an intricate manoeuvre which was supposed to enable successive squadrons of horsemen to trot close to the enemy, first from the right and then from the left, and having fired each pistol to leave the way clear for the next attempt. It was seldom very formidable. The caracole originated as an attempt to break a new formation of foot-soldiers introduced by the Spaniards, the 'tercio'. This was based on the two standard infantry weapons, pike and musket. Pikes were eighteen feet long (though their bearers often reduced this by sawing a few feet off). Massed together in a square formation they made a fearsome barrier that could gradually move forward. Muskets were unwieldy objects loaded through the muzzle with powder and ball and fired with a spark burning on the end of a length of 'match.' In the tercio this slow process was achieved by musketeers, about equal in number to the pikemen, marching in front of the pikes and then retreating to reload. To keep up a steady fire eight relays of musketeers were needed. Though less mobile and with a lower rate of fire than the unduly discredited longbow, and so inaccurate that skilled marksmanship did not help much, the musket could penetrate armour, which became increasingly useless. The tercio had the advantage that inexperienced and unreliable men could take part. Anyone big enough could wield a pike; and from the middle of the square it was difficult to run away. But its drawbacks in wasting manpower and slowing down movement had long been argued by military writers. The introduction of more adaptable formations was one of the changes in warfare that had first been conspicuous in the Netherlands revolt where Maurice of Nassau was a commander free from the entrenched habits of monarchies and armies.

Maurice was an intellectual among military leaders, a student both of classical strategists, particularly Vegetius, and of contemporary theorists like Justus Lipsius, an admirer of Roman warfare. He developed ideas of linear rather than square formations, of small units capable of quick tactical manoeuvre, and above all of the need for highly trained soldiers. His battalion of pikemen, fifty wide and only five deep, with the musketeers on either side, could hold its ground well. Its training made it less expendable; and Maurice's armies, which set the fashion for Protestant Europe especially, tended to avoid major battles if they could. His other main improvements were also defensive – the devising of better fortifications with greater fire-powder against the besieger. So long as commanders found it more profitable to establish garrisons and occupy territory than to seek out and destroy enemy armies, the siege was one of the most important military operations; and to the contest between artillery and fortifications much of the new technology of the day was applied. Maurice's friend Simon Stevin designed elaborate defences that kept pace with the casting of heavier siege guns and the more accurate calculation of range. The other royal commander who had most to contribute to the reforms was Gustav Adolf, the aggressor fighting beyond reach of quick retreat to his homeland, who put new power into attack. His sudden decisive assaults were delivered by the pike in linear formation and musketeers firing a single simultaneous salvo. His cavalry was armed with sabres and trained to charge at speed. Light field artillery, able to move during battle, replaced the heavy guns drawn by huge teams of horses that had tended to sink irrevocably into mud; and artillery regiments were formed instead of the loosely organized companies of gunners. Indeed the essence of both Dutch and Swedish reforms was close integration of all the weapons under a co-ordinated command; and this meant that orders must be given through a hierarchy of well-trained officers whose numbers and status were related to the way the armies fought rather than to the way they were recruited and paid.

PAY AND PLUNDER

The new methods of managing armies led only very slowly to changes in the life of ordinary soldiers and in their impact on the rest of the population. The almost universal complaint was that they were unpaid, if not unfed. At the beginning of the century the soldier could expect to receive on joining his regiment a sum large enough to prevent him from immediately deserting. With luck he might get some more when he was discharged. During his service he was probably entitled to pay comparable to that of a labourer, out of which he was supposed to feed and clothe himself; but since more often than not it was far in arrears, armies in fact lived mainly at the expense of the countryside they occupied. At best this was done by organized billeting, either as avowed freequarter or for sums which the householder had a poor prospect of getting. At worst it was done by plunder. Between the comparatively mild complaints in England against billeting of soldiers and the devastation wrought by armies in the Palatinate or East Prussia, every degree of hardship to civilians occurred. It was common for towns to be sacked and the countryside destroyed as a matter of military policy: a commander's principal object was often to find territory which he could exploit for supplies, and to deprive the enemy of it. If he ran his army independently for profit, he had even more incentive to leave it to feed itself; and a defeated army quickly disintegrated into the 'bands of soldiers' that were the worst terror to the civilian.

As states gradually took over the task of supplying their forces, first during campaigns and eventually in peacetime too, they found themselves creating much the biggest economic organizations of the time. Resources were now extracted from the countryside partly by the administrative work of clerks and commissaries employed in what became the early forms of a war-office and a general staff, partly by private civilian suppliers who ran the business with great profit to themselves. More and more of the cost to the community took the form of money payments by the government, and consequently of taxation. The soldier became, however unwillingly, a lifelong servant of the state, which had an interest in preserving his loyalty and efficiency. One manifestation of this was in his dress. The ordinary soldier in 1600 was not provided with uniform, and was distinguishable from a labourer, if at all, by the knapsack that held his possessions and the leather coat that protected him against the weather and even against sword-thrusts. Colonels sometimes found it paid to supply their regiments with distinctive colours of cloth, buying it in bulk and deducting the price they fixed themselves from the pay they promised. But for an army as a whole the 'token' worn perhaps as a scarf or in the hat was the only identification. Mercenaries naturally found this conveniently easy to change. The red coats of the New Model Army, adopted under the Protectorate for all English forces, were one of the first 'national' uniforms. Gradually it seems to have been realized that identical dress varied by badges of rank contributed to a change in the whole outlook of the soldier. With strict parade-ground drill, marching in step, and enthusiastic ceremonial it helped to create the warrior who would remain a faithful automaton even in face of death, and a spirit of emotional identification with the success of the state that spread beyond the ranks of the army to the whole community.

THE FRENCH ARMY

By the end of the century the state and its armed forces could often be seen as a single entity devoted to the contest for power; but the military state could still take many different forms. The development of three of them, France, Brandenburg, and Russia, will show how the characteristics varied. Though Richelieu had made some efforts to restrict the independence of commanders, he had not seriously altered the French army's social character. It was already a standing army in the sense than ten or fifteen thousand men remained in the guards and provincial regiments during peace, many of them officers paid to keep a skeleton of their units in being. The prospect of war in 1666 was the signal for many of the nobility to seek commissions to which they felt entitled, and to recruit companies more or less by force. Nevertheless, the army was already showing the first benefits of the great achievement of turning war into a huge nationalized industry. Michel le Tellier had held since 1643 the office of Secretary of State for War, and during Louis' minority had produced a series of ordinances bringing order into the previously chaotic methods of recruiting, supplying, and disciplining the army. His bourgeois origins and consequent exclusion from military command did not endear him to the high military officers whose position was soon threatened. Some of the traditional offices, like that of colonel-general of the infantry, were abolished; the title of Marshal of France became an empty honour; the military power of provincial governors was gradually eroded. Absentee colonels lost their regiments and their profits. Louis alone was the head of his armed forces, and under him Le Tellier quietly continued his work. Despite the contempt of the old school of commanders, the technicians and administrators came to the forefront. The Marquis de Chamlay as *Maréchal Général des Logis* (a post he had to buy) produced the arrangements for supply and communications, the maps, the calculations, the grand strategies that made victories on the eastern frontier predictable rather than merely possible. From 1662 Le Tellier was less conspicuous, though not in fact less active, than his son the Marquis de Louvois, Secretary of State. Louvois was the great advocate at court of the army's claims, and associated the call for glory with the new militarism. It was Louvois too, moving among the armies in the provinces and the war zones, who became the notorious enemy of corruption and incompetence. Every aspect of the army was investigated ruthlessly by his intendants. The *passe-volant* who paraded in place of non-existent soldiers on the pay roll, the absentee colonel, the idle commissary went in fear of his personal attention. But Louvois was as alert to positive innovations as he was to removing inefficiency. Production of the efficient army was a continuous process. In the 1660s Martinet earned the unlikely reward of making his name a part of the English language by his relentless drilling and marching and firing. In the seventies the main innovations in armament began. The ring bayonet, fitted to a flintlock musket – often with a rifled barrel – which seems to have been common first in the emperor's armies, gradually became standard equipment in France. The sabre, long familiar in the east, at last became a normal weapon for the French cavalry, whose charges were a feature of the great battles in the Spanish Succession War. Grenadiers and dragoons became an essential part of the foot regiments. Artillery which previously had been a haphazard private enterprise largely independent of the army command, was reorganized into regiments. Industrial development made iron and brass cannons far more reliable than before. Control of the engineers, the men who applied the new techniques of fortification, became involved in the quarrel between the Louvois and Colbert factions, until in 1667 Louvois' expert Vauban was appointed commissary-general in charge of the whole task. The outcome of the wearisome but vital sieges on the eastern frontier depended largely on the technical struggle between the builder of the defences and the master-gunners and mining engineers who attacked them. In practice the siege and eventual capture seem often to have followed an easily predictable pattern and even timetable – to the benefit of everyone involved.

Almost every improvement depended for its application on adequate new supplies. One lesson of the 1660s had been the need for reliable methods of sending arms and provisions to the frontiers in far greater quantities; and again it was Le Tellier and Louvois who established an adaptable system of reserve stores and planned mobility. Behind it were industries and factories, some owned by the state directly and others by privileged entrepreneurs, into which huge funds were poured. The need for competent officers was met by offering a military education to people whose origins would not previously have made them acceptable as commanders. The cadet colleges set up in the 1680s were not altogether welcome to those of the *noblesse* who had spent large sums on buying commissions. As with civilian office, it became possible to attain high rank in the army through hard work and the favour of superiors, and – theoretically after three generations – to attain thereby the status of nobility.

Lists of reforms can easily give a false impression of their extent. In the Spanish Succession War the French army, despite all the expansion and improvements since 1660, still suffered from the inefficiency of officers whose commissions depended on rank and wealth and from soldiers recruited from the very poor or bought from abroad. It was nothing unusual if half the army deserted at the end of a campaign. The main army units still 'belonged' to their aristocratic commanders, for whom war, like hunting, might be more a part of the good life than a full-time profession. At regimental level the state could not produce the great social change that would give it full control over its forces. At the top it was often felt to control them too much. The sole authority even for day-to-day decisions was Louis himself, and he seldom had enough information to take them well. An obedient general found more favour than a victorious one. This was partly Louis' fault; but it was also a characteristic of national war. Fighting was no longer an affair of the individual but the main object of a vast state machine. In it the brilliant independent commander could be a dangerous misfit.

THE BRANDENBURG ARMY

The rise of the military state in the seventeenth century is usually associated above all with Brandenburg. The danger in stressing this obvious example is that too much can be read from later Prussian militarism: other German states, Bavaria especially, were at this stage developing their forces in comparable ways. But the Great Elector was certainly outstanding in creating almost from nothing an army that was the avowed focus of all state activity (see p. 365). In 1640 he had four or five thousand men, many of them deserters from other German states, or from companies that had turned almost into independent nomadic tribes. By the time of Westphalia the most irresponsible colonels and their regiments had been eliminated, and a useable force of perhaps eight thousand was being paid by the various Estates, whose interest was solely in defending their own territory. After the peace, when they refused to go on paying, the army almost disappeared. The compromise between the Elector and the Estates in 1653 made possible a permanent nucleus of five thousand mercenaries and volunteers. With the Northern War of 1655 there began the process of ruthless conscription that enabled Frederick William in the next thirty years to expand the army to nearly 100,000 in war and 30,000 in peace. To the Junker families military office was an economic and social necessity; but they now performed it as servants of the state, not as entrepreneurs. The Great Elector's commander, Otto von Sparr, and the administrative head of the army, Claus Ernst von Platen, achieved a centralized control much more complete than that of the French. Pay, recruiting and commissioning were gradually taken out of the hands of the colonels, and all officers became part of a unified hierarchy. Even the rank-and-file soldier, however harshly disciplined, was a comparatively privileged person, maintained at the cost of the agrarian serf. To turn military service into a way of life rather than a temporary adventure or disaster there arose the scheme for making disbanded officers and soldiers remain in the care and at the call of the state, in civilian government services or on estates taken out of the electoral domain. How far in fact the Junkers underwent a change of outlook, giving up political privilege to become loyal allies of the Elector and his military state is a matter of doubt. Certainly militarism and centralization developed together; the 'General War Commissariat' was the name not just of an army department but of the principal governing institution of the state.

THE RUSSIAN ARMY

In Russia the provision of fighting men formed an even larger part of the work of government than it did in the west. Service in the army was one aspect of the service to the state on which the whole structure of society depended. Descriptions of the recruitment and organization of the tsar's forces are not usually very lucid or consistent, partly because they changed so much from time to time and from place to place, partly because the government itself rarely had more than a rough idea of what units it could command. Total figures can vary enormously according to which of the huge more or less independent forces are included. The most we can attempt here is to arrive at a general impression of the kind of developments that took place during the century.

Ivan the Terrible's first concern had been to bring under his control the armies of the great Boyars and to establish the *streltsi* ('archers') as a loyal garrison force in Moscow. With a regular wage and living-quarters and a well-defined regimental organisation, these garrison soldiers – now mainly musketeers – were intended to form the most reliable part of a full-time standing army. But most of the campaigning troops were brought together when they were needed, and then abandoned. Under Michael Romanov this part-time force was recruited mainly by selective conscription, with villages each providing a specified number of soldiers according to how many houses they had. Training hardly existed, and central organization was extremely hazy. The great change in the middle decades of the century was the rise of a permanent army on western lines. Professional soldiers from Scotland, Poland, Sweden, and above all Germany became the officers and technicians of new regiments; foreign mercenaries came into the rank and file of what were now called *soldati* (infantry), *reitari* (cavalry), and *draguni*; many were settled in militarized districts where land was allotted to them. With the *streltsi* and some of the 'registered' Cossacks they formed a reasonably well-equipped force. But the fate of the army always depended on internal politics. During the struggles for power in Peter the Great's childhood the old type of force seems to have revived as an instrument of the nobility. By the time he began to rule there was not much left of the 'foreign' army. For his first campaigns troops were brought together haphazardly from the villages. Apart from these there were only two professional regiments and two regiments of *poteshnye* that had developed out of the live toy-soldiers of his boyhood war-games (see p. 436). The defeat at Narva seemed to uphold the familiar complaint that Russian forces were an ignorant rabble.

At first Peter's reforms were concerned only with maintaining a large force in spite of the enormous losses from disease and desertion, and battle. The number of men demanded from the villages was increased and the principle of the 'immortal' soldier firmly established: for every man who disappeared or died a replacement had to be supplied. By the time of the victory at Poltava (1709) the regular forces probably numbered something like 100,000. More important, they were now being trained in centres where 'western' discipline and tactics were taught, and equipped from a military budget that accounted for four-fifths of the tsar's entire revenue. At this point army reform became inseparable from the attempt to reconstruct the Russian nobility as a whole. The series of decrees that began with the measures for registering the *dvoriane* in 1711 and culminated in the 'table of ranks' in 1722 turned the theory that noble status and landholding depended on service into an inescapable reality. Two-thirds at least of the young men in the families of *dvoriane* were to be conscripted for military service, all but the highest ranking families beginning as ordinary soldiers. The rest went to civil offices. Promotion was to be only by merit and commoners who achieved a commission as lieutenant were supposed to acquire hereditary nobility. By the end of the reign the permanent army of something like 200,000 gave Russia, for what it was worth, the status in western eyes of a great power.

WAR AT SEA

Fighting at sea played, in 1600, a part in the affairs of European states entirely different from fighting on land. Some states took little or no part in it – and not only those without a coastline. France in the sixteenth century had nothing that could be called a navy. Spain quickly made good the losses of 1588 and maintained fleets both in the Atlantic and in the Mediterranean. But under Philip III most of the ships were left in harbour, eaten away by the worm and dry-rot that were the curse of all the shipping of the day, until Olivares revived the policy of a strong navy. Then, in the Battle of the Downs in 1639 and off the Brazilian coast a year later, the Dutch destroyed almost the whole battle fleets of Spain and Portugal. Thereafter England and the Netherlands were the only powers with a worldwide naval strength. It is well known that Richelieu founded the French navy. Colbert gets as much credit for exactly the same initiative thirty years later. A good deal of Richelieu's effort it is true produced Mediterranean galleys rather than the Atlantic fleet Colbert demanded; but again the main reason is that two decades of neglect were enough to reduce fighting ships to a state of useless decay.

To look at ships built for war and owned by governments gives little idea of the real resources on which warfare at sea relied. While armies still had in their organization traces of private enterprise, navies depended overwhelmingly on the ships of merchants and even fishermen. Throughout the first half of the century the armed merchantman, hired or seized by the state, was the commonest fighting ship, and the regular troop-carrier. Any ship on an ocean voyage would necessarily be armed, and its chances of being involved in fighting before it returned were usually high. Even in peace, the rule of law and the sanctity of private property could not be relied on at sea. Attacks on the Spanish treasure fleet were only the most spectacular part of a process that made the distinction between war, piracy, and legitimate commerce extremely hazy. The 'letters of marque' from their governments gave the captains of ships almost a free hand to get involved in hostilities. Sometimes local clashes were encouraged by governments as acts of provocation. For maritime nations formally at war, the destruction of each other's commerce was as always a major activity, which could be indulged in without the risk of total disaster involved in big naval battles.

PRIVATEERS

Fighting ships often belonged more to a port than to a state. The French king's fleet did not assert its power as readily as did the privateers of Marseilles, Toulon, St Malo, and above all Dunkirk. For every small island privateering was a major industry. Encounters with the ships of Jersey, Malta, Corsica, and the West Indies were part of the normal hazards of trading. A large share of the slave-trade was run by heavily armed privateers. Most notorious of all, the 'Barbary Corsairs' from Algiers, Tunis, and Tripoli, attacked the shipping of every European maritime state, claiming to be subjects of the sultan or not as the occasion required. Major wars enormously expanded the privateering business without changing its character. The Spanish Succession War saw the century's greatest activities of this kind. The defeat of the French fleet at La Hogue in 1692 put an end to its hope of achieving complete domination of the seas. But it was reasonable to argue that France as the most self-sufficient nation and one with good land communications would suffer less in a destructive commercial war than her enemies England and Holland. The navy became therefore hardly distinguishable in its functions from the ships of the great syndicates that made privateering a profit-making business on a sound financial basis. The ships, cargoes, and ransoms that were seized in this way became the subject of elaborate legal and administrative procedures in the Prize Courts, which ensured that the state got its share of the reward. It was this state-sponsored piracy that made the heroic reputation of Jean Bart, the fisherman from whose home port of Dunkirk a hundred ships were reported to be involved in the warfare. While Bart's Drake-like fame took him eventually into the ranks of the *noblesse*, a good many sons of ancient nobility who had expected to command ships in battle were glad to turn to privateering instead.

SHIPS

The character of naval warfare naturally depended largely on the design and effectiveness of ships. Throughout the century there were two contrasting means of propulsion – sail and oars. No-one doubted that in ocean waters sail was essential. The Atlantic fleets of Spain, France, England, and the Netherlands consisted of sail-powered ships, most of them now built entirely for war. But in the Mediterranean the galley still had its merits. It did not need to be as strongly built as a sailing-ship and its demands on timber were less exacting. The oarsmen cost virtually nothing, since most them were prisoners or criminals who had to be maintained somewhere, and if it was destroyed it was better to lose them than skilled seamen. How brutally they were treated varied; on the whole they must have suffered one of the worst lives on earth. Though the galley was still in use even under Louis XIV, the advantages of the 'great ship' were well established. Its purpose was to carry artillery which was fired broadside, sometimes at enemy ships, sometimes at ports. The heavy cannon had to be mounted near the waterline, or their recoil could be disastrous – and this seems in any case to have been the factor that limited the size of naval guns. The main defence was to hold the ship together with massive pillars and stays. It took in fact an enormous amount of shot to sink a large ship: usually the worst that gunfire could do was to break the masts – and it was so inaccurate that this was a matter of luck. In favourable conditions a few old hulks used as fireships could be far more damaging. But once a ship had been put out of action it could do little but await destruction or capture. A lost battle at sea was likely to be more expensive than one on land.

An outstandingly large warship was naturally a great thing to have for prestige. The *Couronne* in Louis XIII's fleet and the *Sovereign of the Seas* in Charles I's were both well over 1,000 tons – though statements like this would be more significant if the method of reckoning the naval 'ton' had not varied. The largest normal ships of the line were said to be 800 or 900 tons, carrying perhaps a hundred guns of which twenty might be the largest cannon. The smallest – the English 'fourth-rate' ships – were not less than half that size. By the end of the century it was sometimes argued that the light swift frigate,[1] low in the water, was a better weapon than the great ship – whose size, an eminent ship-wright assured Pepys and Evelyn, was only for the vanity and comfort of Gentleman Commanders.[2] It was always hoped that much larger vessels could be built; but there was no method of joining the heaviest timbers end to end with adequate strength. Size was limited by the extent of the beam that could be constructed on the traditional principles and by the belief that the ship intended to fire broadsides could not be much longer than three times its width. The fate of the *Vasa* – another royal showpiece – was the result of attempts by the Swedes to build big ships four or five times as long as their beam. In 1628 this pride of Gustav Adolf's fleet sailed into Stockholm harbour for her first trial, rolled over, and went to the bottom. The natural curvature of timbers was another important factor: Protestant winds were believed to have favoured the English not only by dispersing the Armada but by producing the 'gnarled oaks' ready to be cut into just the shapes the shipyards needed. The techniques and theories which Peter the Great picked up from Dutch and English shipbuilders, and which were expounded in works like Renaud's *Architecture Navale* did not differ much from those used a century earlier. But they had become a matter of bitter argument between the practising experts and the scientists. The Royal Society had many discussions on shipbuilding; and in Paris a conference of mathematicians and naval designers in 1681 tried to settle some of the disputes.

Every naval power had, in one way or another, its worries about the supply of materials for building and repairing ships. In England there had already been alarm about timber shortage under Elizabeth. Royal woodland had been sold and exhausted rapidly under the early Stuarts, and the Commonwealth period became notorious for its squandering of timber resources. But only the Baltic countries could now build fleets entirely with their own materials. England, France, and Holland all used firs from

Riga for mainmasts. The danger of being cut off from naval supplies was an important factor in diplomacy. By the end of the century American firs were proving a bigger and better substitute for Scandinavian ones. Whatever the sources and the means of obtaining them, navies were by the accepted standards of state expenditure extremely costly. It was a great blow to the States General to find that in mid-century the fleets it could put to sea were smaller and less well-equipped than those of England. The Dutch had many advantages. Amsterdam supplied not only merchant ships but naval ones too to almost every European country. Dutch contractors controlled much of the supply of hemp and tar from the Baltic. Nowhere else was so high a proportion of the population able to serve as crews of warships. But the division of responsibility among the separate admiralties, which in turn relied on the contributions of individual towns, meant that the money and labour actually diverted to naval building was not enough. It was normal in most countries to make the navy a charge partly on the profits of the trade it protected; English Ship Money, the Danish sound dues, and the tolls imposed on merchants by Gustav Adolf were all examples of this. But in the Netherlands decentralization proved a serious obstacle to financing as well as organizing a national fleet. 'Everywhere', Tromp complained in 1653, 'fine new ships remain ashore only partly finished.[3] By the time of the Spanish Succession War the Dutch navy was only a minor reinforcement for the English.

SEA POWER

How important did naval warfare in European waters prove to be? The famous battles do not seem in themselves to have produced any vital changes. Perhaps the most significant episode was the absence of a battle: neither the French nor the English fleet was ready to prevent William of Orange from landing in England. The consequences of this were greater than anything that happened as a result of the Anglo-Dutch wars. England could, with luck, inflict defeats on the Dutch fleet; the Dutch, when the luck went their way, could still horrify the English by sailing into the Medway and the Thames. But each of the wars ended without decisive loss to either side. Blockade and bombardment were less exciting than naval battles, but often more effective in achieving a limited purpose. De Witt within two years – 1657–58 – ended French interference with Dutch trade by a mere threat to blockade the coast, punished the Portuguese for their intervention in Brazil by a blockade of Lisbon, and preserved Dutch interest in the freedom of Baltic trade by rescuing both Danzig and Copenhagen from the Swedes. Naval power was in fact generally more important in the Baltic than in the open seas: Sweden's successes in war depended entirely on the ability to convey troops and supplies safely and to cripple her enemies by blockade. Mediterranean naval war was an activity highly important to western states when their merchant shipping was threatened; but for long periods the little republic of Venice was left to fight largely on its own what the powers occasionally regarded as the Turkish menace to Christendom. When a fleet of eighty Turkish galleys attacked Crete in 1645, the Venetians showed that the government of even a small state could, by putting all its power and resources into the effort, maintain quite a formidable fleet. For nearly twenty-five years they kept up a war that prevented any full Turkish control of the eastern Mediterranean, in the course of which the English, Dutch, and French who benefited from this took over what was left of Venetian trade. It was one of the many unheeded demonstrations of the real cost of war.

THE MILITARY REVOLUTION

The changes in warfare between 1560 and 1660 have been called, not surprisingly, 'the military revolution'. They were, according to the originator of the phrase, not just a matter of new tactics and strategy or of the growth of armies but a revolution that 'stands like a great divide separating medieval society from the modern world.'[4] Once again the use of the term 'revolution' risks the kind of arguments that attach great importance to the meaning of a word. It has also raised the inevitable claim that it all started earlier than the idea even of a century-long 'revolution' requires, and that pre-revolutionary characteristics remained long afterwards. But controversy on these lines has not been as heated as many aspects of the debates about the 'general crisis'. Developments in war were, it seems to be agreed, bigger and faster than at most other times. It is less easy to see in perspective the connections between new ways of making war and the life of societies that were, at least intermittently, at peace.

Governments were already well aware at the beginning of the century that the cost of a major war was far greater than any peacetime expenditure. It was greater still by the time of the Thirty Years War, when Spain spent something like nine-tenths of state revenues on the wars in the Netherlands, Germany, and northern Italy; Gustav Adolf used every possible expedient to divert the country's wealth to war; and in much of France the *taille* doubled or trebled in ten years. A generation later it was impossible for most governments to get anywhere near to meeting the costs of war out of their immediate resources. They had to borrow; and if possible they had to find subsidies from richer allies. The cost of armies, navies, and weapons was a main reason for the development of international banking and lending systems. The Dutch above all other nations became the financiers of other people's wars, both through the state itself and through Amsterdam merchants. The French supplied outright subsidies rather than loans. How far war was responsible for developments in commerce and industry is less easy to define. Certainly huge amounts of materials and manpower went to the supplying of the armed forces. Bigger wars required increased economic resources; increased economic resources made possible bigger wars. The profits of war were made at every level, from the local blacksmith whose trade flourished through the presence of a garrison or leaguer to the great international dealers in timber, lead, saltpetre and many more commodities needed by the forces. But whether a military revolution was a crucial stimulus to the development of capitalism is not a helpful question. War was part of the way of life of states and communities: we cannot isolate its ultimate effects on their economy.

It is difficult also to say whether the innovations in warfare altered people's attitudes to it. War has always produced two opposite responses. Victory is an occasion for rejoicing and the qualities of the soldier are upheld as virtuous; killing and devastation are condemned, brutality denounced as wicked. It is naturally in the interests of rulers to establish the assumption that all evil comes from the enemy; but this depends on each side being united and identifiable. Religious hatreds were a great help in achieving emotional loyalty to what might otherwise have been an objectionable government or a meaningless territorial unit. But even in the first half of the century religion was often more relevant at the level of the regiment, where preachers or priests had a captive audience, than at that of governments. France's Protestant allies and Catholic enemies are the most obvious example of politics overriding religious loyalties. Cromwell's belief in a divinely ordained Protestant alliance was established after he had with some hesitation, rejected an alliance with Spain in favour of one with France. One of the dangers he recognized was that the Emperor might join with the Danes and even the Dutch to defeat Sweden. If religion anywhere determined whether a government went to war, and against whom, it was not so much among the large states as among the small ones. In Germany especially rulers could feel their survival threatened by religious opponents and could go to the help of their fellow-believers at least partly in a crusading spirit. After 1660, despite such episodes as the reign of James II in England, there was little likelihood that the religious allegiance of states and peoples would be changed by conquest. Coalitions of Catholic and Protestant against France were repeatedly made and broken; and in the north Sweden achieved the distinction of being attacked by Catholic, Orthodox, Lutheran, and Calvinist enemies together. In the propaganda encouraging support for wars God had to appear more as the upholder of virtue than as requiring the destruction of the wrong kind of Christianity. There was more room for the other religious explanation of war – that it was a divine punishment possibly inflicted on both sides. It was easier too for distinctions to be drawn between just and unjust wars.

The notion of the just war – and hence of the unjust one – had been argued ever since the days of Athens. Theorists – religious, legal, and philosophical – in nearly every century asked in what circumstances it was right to take part in war and what kinds of warfare were permissible. The most widely known seventeenth-century authority on the subject, Grotius, came close to arguing that everything was justifiable in war. Wars, he thought, were no longer fought for religious ends: hence every kind of attack, including the killing of civilians and the destruction of their homes, had to be accepted. But his purpose was to show the horror of warfare that was growing in his time. (*De jure belli ac pacis* was published in the midst of the Thirty Years War.) The evils should be mitigated first by international laws establishing, among other things, that wars for revenge, for the conquest of territory or for national glory were unjust, and second by an accepted morality that would diminish the atrocities that laws could not rule out. It was the kind of compromise that did more to assuage guilt than to offer any real improvement. If military developments did anything to make wars less disastrous it was mainly because soldiers were under tighter discipline; but the devastation of the Palatinate in 1688 and 1674 and of Bavaria in 1704 suggested that restraint could be abandoned at any moment. The most that could be claimed as mitigation of warfare was that commanders of armies accepted the conventions that limited the barbarity of armies towards each other. Their professional duties did not, on the whole, demand the total destruction of the enemy. When the human and material cost of a war became too high, statesmen would usually arrive at a compromise peace. It seldom lasted long. Nothing in the 'military revolution' made governments either more ready or more reluctant to go to war. So long as the military structure within a state was a major part of the political establishment, there had to be potential conflict. Standing armies required standing enemies. Religion no longer provided them automatically; nor do the origins of most later seventeenth-century wars give much support to the idea that economic rivalries replaced it. Wars were justified by supposed dangers to the state itself; and these could be assumed to come from whatever power seemed to threaten the precarious stability – territorial commercial, or just diplomatic – that was for the moment accepted. Enemies destroyed the peace; friends redressed its injustices. The whole social and political system implied the existence of wars; and to seek too hard for the reasons that touched off any particular one can be unprofitable.

NOTES AND REFERENCES

1   Use of the term 'frigate' varied; but this meaning seems to have been generally accepted by 1700.

2   *The Diary of John Evelyn* (ed. E. S. de Beer), vol. 5, p. 10

3   Quoted in P. Geyl, *The Netherlands in the Seventeenth Century.* (1963), vol. 2, p. 33.

4   Michael Roberts, 'The Military Revolution' in *Essays in Swedish History* (1967), p. 195.

12

FRANCE, 1598–1660

This was the century of France. By the end of it, French language, culture, manners and dress had permeated the richer levels of the whole European community. French wars and diplomacy dominated western political affairs, and influenced eastern ones too. The French treasury seemed to have inexhaustible supplies of money with which the king and his ministers could buy the dependence of other states and fight wars largely of their own choosing. They spent it too on the splendour of the court and the patronage, direct or indirect, of literature and art. The glory may not have been apparent to the peasant starving in a year of famine, or the beggar in the streets of Paris, or the soldier plundering the ruins of a frontier town. The legend that grew in the great days of Versailles makes it easy to forget both how little there was to show for the victories and how unstable the French state had been before the effective rule of Louis XIV began. The political history of France in the seventeenth century is sharply divided by the chaotic years of the Fronde. Before it royal and ministerial governments struggled continually and with no decisive success to prevent the breakdown of the state. Far from being an example of steady progress towards the absolutist ideal, the France of Richelieu and Mazarin showed how narrow the division was between order and anarchy. It is this long period of uncertainty that we shall examine first.

HENRI IV

The year 1598 can now be seen as the beginning of a century in which a stable French monarchy overcame one by one all the threats to its power and established the authority that was unshaken until the Revolution. At the time no dramatic change was evident. The Edict of Nantes was an elaborate compromise with the Huguenots, and the Peace of Vervins ended the fighting with Spain. But there was no guarantee that either would last longer than the assorted pacifications of the previous century. Two years later French armies were at war once more – against Savoy; by 1610 the Huguenots were again thinking in terms of military action. It was not even certain how far Henri's abjuration of the Huguenot religion in 1593 meant that he was now firmly Catholic: negotiations on the subject with the papacy were inconclusive. Everything depended on whether the king could build quickly enough a government that would change France from an insecure state only half administered from the centre into one where servants of the Crown were the normal rulers and powerful subjects found loyalty expedient.

Nothing in the rest of Europe could compare with the Edict promulgated by Henri while he was at Nantes at the head of his army. Perhaps one in ten of the population were now Huguenots. They were strong in the *Midi* and in numerous small enclaves throughout the south and east. In La Rochelle, Montauban, Tours and many other towns their communities were powerful enough to hold something approaching the independence of German Free Cities. But only continuing support among the noble families made them politically dangerous to their renegade monarch. The Edict, with its associated 'secret' articles and *brevets*, gave not only the right to undisturbed religious services in specified places but state subsidies for fifty military garrisons and for their clergy. The ban on extending their religion any further seemed a fair return. The elaborate provisions of the '*chambres mi-parties*', in which Huguenots were guaranteed a large share in legal proceedings affecting them, helped to maintain their support among lawyers who profited from them. Part of the Edict was registered by the Paris *parlement*; but essentially it came from the king and could be revoked or modified at any time. They could not expect more: whatever dreams of a Protestant France existed, they had no prospect of replacing the royal government.

The religious division was not the only one in which France had an uneasy tinge of the conditions familiar in the Empire, Spain, and the Netherlands. French provinces in their relations with the central government stood somewhere between the status of a German principality and that of an English county. Some – Languedoc, Provence, the Dauphiné, Burgundy, and the newly assimilated Brittany – had their own provincial Estates that voted and administered taxation. Others were subdivided into *élections* in which the collection of taxes was in the hands of royal officials. To complicate matters, Normandy had both – but its Estates for most of Henri's reign successfully reduced the amount they were asked to vote. One of Henri's greatest but least advertised achievements was that bit by bit, partly through political persuasion and partly through ignoring the protests, he overrode provincial powers and whittled down the liberties of the towns. It was by fairly high-handed as well as efficient methods that the government managed to become financially strong. Inevitably there was resistance. Popular local revolts against tax-collectors were easily suppressed. A measure of the government's success was that the most serious aristocratic resistance of the reign, when in 1602 Biron, Governor of Burgundy, and the Huguenot Duc de Bouillon were involved in a conspiracy sponsored by Charles Emmanuel of Savoy, failed to get any general support. Biron was executed after a scrupulously legal trial before the Paris *parlement*.

The penetration of the central administration into the whole life of the country was accomplished in a great variety of ways, ranging from the king's carefully planned journeys through the provinces to the work of royal supporters inserted into town governments in regulating industry through the guilds. It did not add up to any master plan for creating absolute monarchy. But Henri had a forceful group of ministers – the Chancellor Pomponne de Bellièvre and his successor Silléry, Villeroy, the former Catholic Leaguer whose allegiance had been bought at a high price, and the *surintendant des finances* Maximilien de Béthune, Marquis de Rosny, who acquired his final title of Duc de Sully in 1606. Sully was in general the enemy of conciliar government, and tends to get – as no doubt he would have wished – credit for the work of his rivals. The immediate question was, as for so many governments, debt. It was not a matter of repaying all that was owing but of reducing the total enough to give the confidence that made it possible to borrow more. Henri had taken over the debts of the government he had overthrown as well as his own. He owed large amounts to the English, the Swiss, and to Christian of Anhalt (whose successors were still claiming it after the Napoleonic Wars – with the interest), as well as to French towns and individual lenders. The temporary ending of the major wars made possible some reduction in the cost of armies; corruption and extravagance at court were said to have been reduced. But Sully's great boast was that he had created, in face of opposition from all those who were taking more than their share of the revenue, a system of accounting at every level. By 1608 he claimed to have paid off in ten years nearly half the debts, redeemed the mortgages on Crown property, and accumulated a large reserve in the treasury. This did not exist just on paper, but in huge boxes and sacks in the Bastille – still a normal way of holding government funds. One achievement needing great tact was to buy out many of the Parisian *rentiers*, who sometimes complained that interest was in arrears without stressing that they had not paid for their bonds but took them as a free gift.

How government revenue could be increased is always a political as much as a financial question. Sources that had been alienated to great men could be bought back when money was available. Lower-grade profiteers like local tax-farmers could be made to take smaller and more regulated amounts, and to buy their offices in competition. But the most expedient devices were to reduce or reapportion the *taille* and other direct taxes from which the central government received too small a share and to increase more efficiently administered direct taxes. The *gabelle*, the unpopular salt-tax, was raised to the point where it provoked riots. The sale of offices was not a major part of Crown income until Henri's last few years: it was more important in breaking the dependence of office-holders on the nobility and building up their vested interest in the monarchy. True, the highest office of all was sold in 1600. Having secured a papal annulment of his first marriage, Henri was now able to negotiate with the Grand Duke of Tuscany, to whom he owed three and a half million *livres*, for the appointment as the new French queen of Marie de Medici, in return for a dowry that amounted to nearly half the debt. Only remotely related to Catherine de Medici, she had no personal importance; but she fulfilled her main task of giving Henri what the last three kings had lacked – legitimate male heirs. It was the best possible guarantee of the permanence of the régime; and that in turn enabled Sully to carry out the reforms of the national economy for which he is best known. Spending money on roads, land-drainage, and agricultural improvements became a regular way of advertising enlightened government, though none of Sully's good works cost as much as even a reformed court. Nor did they cost as much as the scheme that was for Henri the first object of financial improvement. He had long worked to build up a block of French allies among the German states. When the ruler of the small but strategically important Rhineland duchies of Jülich and Cleves died without heirs in 1609, and the emperor asserting his right of succession 'sequestered' the duchies, France was ready to exercise its military power. Assassination saved Henri from the dismal anti-Habsburg enterprise which might have diminished considerably the legend of the enlightened and benevolent king. Molten lead, boiling oil, and the four horses that tore Ravaillac asunder could not extract from him any evidence of political motive or employers. The stories of great plots to overthrow the monarchy and start a new civil war did not last long. But Louis XIII was nine years old: the question was whether the new royal government could survive without a king.

MARIE DE MEDICI

For those in Parisian politics the immediate need in 1610 was to attach themselves to the regency. There was no opposing faction able to offer better prospects for the ambitious – yet. Henri had left no firm direction for the trusteeship of his kingdom on his death. But the queen had been brought into more prominence by a belated coronation; and as Henri had intended to lead his troops personally to the capture of Jülich and Cleves he had provided for her to hold power in his absence. All who believed in the stability of the state needed now to support her regency. The method by which she was proclaimed was a significant assertion of legality: the gouty President of the Paris *parlement*, which was already in session in its various chambers for legal business, was summoned from his bed to hold a *lit de justice*, where princes, peers, cardinals, and all the great officers of the Crown should inaugurate the new reign in an ancient court superior to all the upstart councils created by this or that monarch.

The greatest resistance to Marie's power would certainly come from these men – *les grands* – whose ambitions Henri IV had thwarted. They included Henri of Condé, second cousin of Louis XIII but his nearest adult relative and a possible claimant to the throne if Marie's marriage could be invalidated; Condé's uncles, Soissons and the Prince of Conti; Henri Duc de Longueville; and Henri IV's illegitimate son the Duc de Vendôme. All these were 'Princes of the Blood', claiming as of right a share in the power of the monarchy. Hardly less powerful were the non-royal holders of formerly independent principalities such as the Duc de Nevers and the Duc de Bouillon. These leaders of the great families, who now hurried to Paris with their huge retinues, were from their mere existence and outlook a potential threat of renewed civil war. But the new generation of *grands* saw more hope in dominating the monarchy than in overthrowing it. They still had little less than absolute control over their territories and virtual subjects; the competition for power at the king's court was now thrown open again. Henri IV had by no means completely separated the running of central government from court service or noble birth. The king's council still in theory included men who were there by birthright or by the holding of ceremonial office. Like the Paris *parlement* it could be regarded as the descendant of the ancient 'Curia Regis'. But it had long been a highly adaptable and sometimes almost unidentifiable body, divided and subdivided in ways that could produce, amid endless disputes, specialized committees of administrators. From Henri's inner circle of ministers, by now usually called the *Conseil d'Affaires* or some such name, the principal survivors in 1610 were Sillery, Sully, Villeroy (in charge of foreign affairs), and Jeannin (the president and virtual minister of justice). They had neither bought nor inherited their offices, though there is a hint of how quickly such a group could solidify itself in the fact that Sillery's son married Villeroy's daughter and acquired a place on the council. On Henri's death the foundation of their power and unity had gone. They agreed with Marie in throwing open meetings of the council to anyone at court who chose to attend, so that no-one could claim to be excluded. Sully, the only one to oppose the policies of the regent from the beginning, was turned out of office in 1611 (with a pension of 24,000 *livres*); the others remained. But against this power of the *barbons*, the grey-beards of the old regime, there were aligned the noble families and the clerical circles whose influence had already been strong in Henri's court. Neither would have things all their own way.

Marie soon had working a 'court' government centred not on the French magnates but on the *confidante* she had brought with her from Italy, her half-sister Leonora Dori. Leonora was a witch – or so the *parlement* later decided. At all events she exercised remarkable power over the regent and the court, into which a throng of Italians penetrated. The two thousand French men and women who made up its competitive hierarchy could not be expected to welcome them. Marie bestowed on them most generous pensions out of the funds accumulated by Sully's careful management. Leonora's husband, Concini, made himself the greatest figure in court and political affairs, and became, by gift or purchase, Marquis d'Ancre, Marshal of France, Governor or Lieutenant-General of several provinces. He won enough power to be hated, but never became a ruling minister of the type of Richelieu or Buckingham. The great men of Henri IV's court did not come off too badly in this; but however much they were given, it appeared that but for the upstart Italians they might have had more. Some hard bargains were driven before pensions were renewed: the regent's aims seemed to be to buy their loyalty as cheaply as possible, and to leave scope for acquiring by similar means the support of lesser nobles and office-holders.

THE REGENCY, SPAIN AND THE CHURCH

The immediate political question for a new regime was the expedition to Jülich and Cleves which Henri IV had been about to lead. Fighting had begun when Dutch troops had tried to occupy the Duchies and had been driven out by Spinola's Spanish army acting on behalf of the emperor. Though the affair was not expected to begin a major war it would certainly intensify the alignment of European diplomacy into what would seem to be Catholic and Protestant teams, with France committed to the Protestants. Marie and Concini felt themselves to be on the Catholic side: the Protestant war was hastily called off. The succession dispute was temporarily settled in 1614, when Cleves went to one of the main claimants, the Elector of Brandenburg, and Jülich to the other, Wolfgang William of Neuburg, who had hastily become a Catholic.

France's withdrawal was not entirely a matter of foreign policy. The supporters of Henri's schemes, apart from the Protestants who had naturally rejoiced to see him still a friend of their cause, were the *bons français*, the believers in strong central monarchy and a sovereign state. In turning to Spain and Catholicism, Marie was identifying herself with the *Catholiques zélés*, with the Jesuits, and to some extent with all who preferred a weak state to a strong. Spanish diplomacy did not at this time miss its opportunities. The success of the Spanish Ambassador and of the Papal Nuncio was decisively proclaimed in the double betrothal of the eleven-year-old king to Philip III's daughter, misleadingly known as Ann of Austria, and of Philip's heir to the king's sister Elizabeth.

NOBLE REBELLION

In 1613 the great men rose in revolt. They were not really rebelling against anything: they were asserting themselves. Marie's court, and fights with each other for precedence, did not provide an adequate outlet for their importance. When they had displayed their power, they expected to be paid, and to return to the court. A feeling of frustration among a few princes and dukes could have drastic effects on France. While they were in Paris, central government – however corrupt and incompetent – worked. When at the end of 1612 they returned in anger to their 'own' territories there was a partial disintegration of the kingdom. The lesser *notables* hurried to line up behind their leaders; denunciation of the regency became the accepted orthodoxy. A manifesto appeared complaining of how ill-used everyone was. The clergy were being deprived of their power, the nobility 'impoverished and ruined'; most of all, Condé and his friends purported to sorrow for the ordinary people whose burdens provided the rewards of the rich. Nothing much happened. The princes took possession of a few towns; their armies marched about the western provinces. Marie put herself at the head of an army, but with no intention of fighting. She met the rebels, negotiated, and agreed to distribute money and governorships among them. She also agreed to summon the Estates-General.

THE ESTATES-GENERAL

There was already a hint of antiquarian solemnity in calling together, after twenty years, a body which no-one supposed had now a serious function in the working of French government. The conflicts and bargaining that took place were largely between the three Estates themselves. The one demand debated at some length was the article '*de la sûreté des rois*' asserting that the king held his crown from God alone, and that no power on earth, spiritual or temporal, had a right over the kingdom to deprive him of it. It was a declaration, supported by the great majority of the Third Estate, against ultramontane Catholicism in its political form; but it produced a conflict with the clergy which neither the Third Estate nor the Crown eventually felt it expedient to push to a conclusion. In the tedious arguments about this article, a more practical one demanding regular meetings of the Estates-General was largely forgotten. Discussion of taxation also turned into an internal dispute, between the nobility and the office-holders who formed a majority of the Third Estate. This was beyond doubt a fundamental social conflict, however much administrative technicalities obscured it. The Second Estate, claiming that commoners were acquiring in perpetuity offices that should be the preserve of the nobility, demanded that the *paulette* should be abolished. The *Tiers* suggested that the loss of revenue could aptly be made up by cutting the pensions paid largely to the nobility. The council agreed, though the changes did not last long. The dispute between the Estates meant that the council neither worried about the demand for a reduction of the *taille* by a quarter nor sought any support for a better-administered system of collection.

THE END OF THE REGENCY

The Estates-General did nothing to upset the palace clique that monopolized power; but habitual leaders of conspiracies among the *grands* were increasingly keen to get rid of Concini's circle. They had a new incentive when Louis XIII, proclaimed of age in 1614, was about to celebrate his marriage to the Infanta: no-one was so good as the Spaniards at keeping their friends and dependants in power. Henri, Prince of Condé, was one of the men with no cause to support and a large private army that could only be kept in being by occasionally allowing it to fight and plunder somewhere. Another Henri, the Duke of Bouillon, whose frontier lands enabled him to pose, when it suited his purpose, as an independent subject of the emperor, was Condé's principal ally in trying with only slight success to get Huguenot support for a widespread rebellion. In the chaos of intrigues that followed their feeble rising of 1616, the loyalty of great men was bought by sharing out several millions of livres and the control of provinces. Condé found himself first on the royal council and then in the Bastille. But if Concini could outwit rebellious princes, he was not secure against palace revolutions. The king himself was now inevitably a centre of rivalry to the hangers-on of the regent.

Louis, a bad-tempered, sickly sixteen-year-old, divided his interest, in normal royal fashion, between the exercise of power through patronage and the management of horses, dogs, and falcons. The master of the royal falcons was Charles d'Albret, later Duke of Luynes, whose outlook seems to have been limited entirely to the life of the court and its opportunities. He had no interest in extending or in opposing the 'Catholic' and 'Spanish' policy of the government – merely in killing off the previous favourites. The 'great men' of the provinces were not likely to object to this, and the law of the land was not an obstacle but one possible instrument. So in 1617, with Louis' approval, Concini was stabbed, Leonora tried and publicly burned alive, Marie virtually banished from Paris. Luynes became the effective head of government. With Marie, as her private chaplain, went one of the men to whom Concini had given high office, Armand Jean du Plessis, later Cardinal and Duke of Richelieu. He contrived to support her without losing his contacts with the king. In 1619 he was largely responsible for bringing about a reconciliation between Marie and her son instead of a civil war.

THE HUGUENOTS

With the royal government at so low a point, there were bound to be Huguenot leaders attracted by the opportunity of joining the contest for power. A million supporters, including some of the highest nobility, concentrated in a few strongly defended areas but existing everywhere else as a zealous minority, were something most European leaders of resistance could scarcely dream of. Henri IV's scheme had envisaged that they should have their share of high office in the state – a prospect that now seemed to have gone. The greater their seclusion, the more attractive their cause was bound to appear to all opponents of the government. When Europe seemed to be dividing into religious alliances, the more militant wing of the Huguenots asserted itself. The strength of Catholicism at court, the growing activity of the Jesuits, and the continued existence of private armies of Catholic nobility were undeniable threats to the settlement. Sully's son-in-law Henri de Rohan became a typical noble leader, prepared like all the others to be bought off with a court pension but returning to opposition when it suited him. But Huguenot organization was not an affair of the nobility. The 'circles' they established in 1610 on the German model each had its assembly that revealed in military as well as civil activity something of a popular character. Within the Huguenot movement there was the same division as outside it between those who wanted to accept the authority of the state and those who were ready for any opportunity to create disorder and see what they could get out of it. The Crown's methods of asserting state power did not do much to encourage the pacific element.

In 1620 Louis proclaimed the restoration of Catholicism in Béarn, Henri IV's little territory north of the Pyrenees which claimed to be still independent. It was the occasion for a splendid demonstration of court unity. Louis set forth with a retinue of princes and dukes, among them the Queen Mother and Condé, both back in favour. An indignant Huguenot general assembly prepared for war and for two years there were conflicts round some of their fortresses. The Treaty of Montpellier in 1622 deprived the Huguenots of a good many of their opportunities for militancy: they lost most of their military strongholds, and their general assemblies were forbidden. Those of the right status received suitable pensions and offices. The 'war' had also brought more immediate benefits for Louis: Luynes died of the fever he caught, and Condé departed for Italy. In an atmosphere of comparative harmony at court, Richelieu came back into the Council and by 1624 was its effective leader.

RICHELIEU AND THE STATE

Nearly all great ministers of the century reached the top by winning the competition in intrigue, self-assertion, and favouritism that occupied the royal courts. Richelieu's rise was normal enough. His family of second-rank nobility in the Poitou area had already served at court and in the law. Armand entered the church to keep the Bishopric of Luçon in the family. It was a fortunate decision. By the time he entered the royal council he was a cardinal, which gave him precedence over the other members – though he did not use his clerical status to dominate the king as his confessor. Theology, like war, was not something to believe or disbelieve but a part of the life of the French upper classes. It was an episcopal group in the Estate of the Clergy in 1614 that sponsored him for the minor post at court that led to his brief experience of political power under Concini. But he was slow to jump onto the wagon of Louis XIII. When he returned, it was as the favourite of the Catholics against the survivors of the *barbon* group whom Louis had recalled. He was already known as a friend of the aristocratic Capucin François de Tremblay – Father Joseph. Both were in touch with the militant Catholic circle of the Duke of Nevers, and with Bérulle and the Oratory. The man who was to make destruction of Habsburg power the purpose of the French state came to prominence as the great hope of the pro-Spanish *dévots*.

It is tempting to suppose, on the strength of the *Testament politique*, that Richelieu's ministry was the fulfilment of a clear-cut plan to create the strong state and the absolute monarchy. That was clearly the impression the *Testament* was meant to convey. But there is doubt not only about when it was written – perhaps as late as 1638 – but about how much if any was Richelieu's own composition. The 'plan', it claims, was set out in a promise to the king that he would 'use all my industry and all the authority it has pleased you to give me to ruin the Huguenot party, to humble the pride of the great men, to bring your subjects to their duty and to raise your name abroad to the place that is its due'.[1] It is not a very constructive policy. The first three aims concern the removal of immediate internal dangers rather than the reform of the system; the fourth is as vague as any peroration on foreign policy could be. It may indeed be showing unintentionally that

Richelieu's one permanent objective, other than keeping himself in office, was to preserve and extend the authority of the government by whatever means seemed feasible. A more specific programme was in fact drawn up in 1626 and presented to the Assembly of Notables, a body court and government officials intended to be of more practical use than an Estates-General. Richelieu and other ministers – Marillac speaking on finance, Schonberg on military needs – called upon these governing men, great and small, to help in the reform of commerce and of taxation, to get rid of the ruinous cost of civil disorder, and to make the country strong on sea and land. The fact that the object of all this was war on Spain was scarcely noticed.

Richelieu was well aware that the success of his schemes depended on finance. The government in 1626 was spending over half as much again as in 1607 – though there were big year-to-year variations. Almost all the increase was in the cost of the army and of pensions. The extra revenue came from loans and above all from the sales of offices. Richelieu held out hopes that taxes would be reduced and the *paulette* abolished. Freed from some of its burdens, the French economy would catch up with the Dutch and the state would become solvent. Nothing of the kind happened. In the 1630s expenditure was more than doubled. Sales of offices certainly declined, and by 1643 had almost stopped – but more through the fall in demand than through deliberate policy. Payment of office-holders, now greatly exceeding the revenue from sales, fell into arrears. The *taille* in 1643 was two and a half times what it had been under Henri IV. The sale and mortgaging of Crown lands continued. The difficulty in all schemes for improving state finances by taxes, loans, or sales was that so many men of power benefited from the injustice and inefficiency of the system. Innovations had to be pushed as far as proved feasible and withdrawn when they failed to bring in revenue or risked too much resistance. The troubles of the treasury were not entirely the fault of either taxpayers or the government. Prices had begun to fall; harvests were bad; there was a general shortage of bullion. Industrial and commercial activity declined, partly because there was little investment in them by owners of land or profiteers from office. Richelieu was heavily influenced by writers like Montchrétien who saw foreign commerce as more of a drain on bullion than a source of wealth. In 1635 he confessed to the new *surintendant des finances*, the improbably named Claude Bullion, that he was ignorant of financial matters and would leave it all to the expert. In face of all the obstacles the revenue did increase, erratically. There were even some areas, including the royal household, in which expenditure was reduced. But the achievements were more than outweighed by the cost of war preparations, and especially of the new navy that was one of Richelieu's cherished projects. Accordingly debt rose again.

The financial problem was as much administrative as economic. As long as collection was erratic, and the orders of the central government could be evaded in the regions, calculated improvements could not get far. The surviving distinction between the *pays d'élections* on which finance ministers could lean heavily and *pays d'états* where local autonomy was not attacked openly, had already been seen by Marillac as a great obstacle. It was a well-established practice for central departments to send into the provinces *commissaires* of one kind or another to put their orders into effect more actively than local officials liked. No firm decision led to the establishment of a permanent body of such agents under the name occasionally used before of *intendants*. But from 1635 onwards they were sent into every part of the country, originally to investigate the collection of the *taille* – with, it could be claimed, the intention of reducing it. In the *pays d'élections* one *intendant* was sent to each of the revenue-raising units known as *généralités*; in the *pays d'états* it was necessary at first to accept that the province must be the unit – an unhappy recognition of the difference. Their functions grew; their appointments were continued; and where there were serious disputes with a provincial governor it was he rather than the *intendant* who was likely to be removed. But Richelieu was not prepared to provoke a major conflict with the old authorities. The official line was that those who did their job would benefit from the strengthening of the Crown. Like Strafford and Olivares he resisted disruptive forces within the state – especially any that might threaten his own position – by whatever means seemed feasible at the time.

All the centralizing governments sought the help of religion: only in France and England was it now liable to provide instead the great foundation of opposition. It was not only the Huguenots whom Richelieu had to fear. His ideal was a higher clergy in his own image – men with property and ability who could teach their inferior churchmen to conform. Already the state exercised a more effective control over the revenues of the Church and over its assemblies than in other Catholic countries. But both the movement for Gallican liberties and the growing hostility of the *dévots* and of the Jesuits as the state became again the open enemy of Spain were an embarrassment that led to strict censorship. Ultramontane and extreme Gallican writings were suppressed more severely than Protestant ones. The belief that the Huguenots would eventually be brought within the ordinary working of the state was not abandoned, and proved to be more than half true. Full-scale war against them, for which the *dévots* worked hard, was no way to achieve such an end. The policy of the *bons francais* was to make closer involvement in the state more attractive to them.

HUGUENOT REBELLION

Like all internal opposition groups, the Huguenots were dangerous when they attracted foreign support. Their control of military and commercial outlets to the Atlantic was inevitably of interest to the English; and in 1627 they became part of one of Buckingham's twisted political manoeuvres. The mismanaged expedition of English ships to the Île de Ré off La Rochelle gave the opportunity for a showpiece of siege warfare. To the *dévots* it was a Catholic crusade, making Spain an ally against England. To the government La Rochelle was more than just the head-quarters of the Protestants. It was also a privileged municipal community with the same mixture of interests as independent cities everywhere. State-sponsored monopolistic trading companies, for whose benefit new ports were being developed, seemed likely to divert commercial profit from La Rochelle in particular, and also from the merchants generally to the court. There was therefore something of a three-cornered commercial struggle between the French government, the town, and the English. When Buckingham's force appeared the leading Rochelais merchants preferred the security offered by the French government, while many of the lesser inhabitants welcomed their allies in the worldwide Protestant cause. Rohan in Languedoc tried to build up a great Huguenot force to join in the struggle, but found less support than he had hoped. Neither Buckingham's expedition nor its successor under Denbigh proved very determined; but the threat of an English base on French soil supported by the Huguenots was grave enough for Richelieu to turn all his resources against it. The year-long siege of La Rochelle was made possible by a great feat of military engineering – the barrier built across the harbour. An equally remarkable achievement was that when the starving city eventually surrendered the soldiers were prevented from destroying it. The *dévots* naturally claimed the fall of La Rochelle as a victory for their cause, and bitterly denounced the Peace of Alais in 1629 as a shameful compromise with rebels. But by removing the political and military rights of the Huguenots without attacking their religious ones Richelieu turned them into a reliable part of the French community. Once they had lost their attraction for the enemies of the regime, their religion ceased to imply political resistance.

NOBLE CONSPIRACIES

'As a party' the Huguenots had, so Richelieu justly claimed, been ruined. His second subsequently professed aim, 'to humble the pride of the great men', had to be undertaken cautiously. He did not regard the *noblesse* as enemies of the state: they were its most vital part. The danger came only from those who, if they were excluded from a share of central power, could revert to territorial independence. Their whole life was a defiance of sovereign law. The huge escorts of horsemen that blocked the streets of Paris behind Condé or Guise and threatened civil war if they met at a cross-roads were a frequent reminder that the days of the religious wars were not very far away. Men like Vendôme in Brittany, Guise in Provence, or Montmorency in Languedoc could almost ignore the central government in the day-by-day exercise of their hereditary power. Lesser noble families borrowed the customs with which the great displayed their superiority to central law. The duel was an assertion of status with remote memories of the feud and of chivalry. Richelieu's edicts against it were a recognition of the fact that to kill an individual according to the strict rules of aristocratic etiquette was as much a repudiation of the state as was armed rebellion. The notion that fighting was an occupation superior to all others, and the natural role of the nobility, appeared in their houses, their pseudo-military retinues, their hunts. The lower down the scale, the feebler the substitutes had to be. It was an attitude attacked in a popular work of the period, Turquet de Mayerne's *De la Monarchie Aristodémocratique* (1611), which denounced the devotion of the nobility to the art of war as an 'iniquitous and destructive disease'. They ought, he said, to occupy themselves productively in commerce or the professions.

Richelieu's technique was to avoid a showdown and always to assess realistically his own strength. He dealt with the major plots against his regime by selective revenge. He would hold an execution as high up the scale as was safe. The arch-plotter by birth and temperament, Louis' younger brother Gaston of Orleans, remained beyond his reach, appeased when necessary with governorships and wealth. The 'Chalais' conspiracy of 1626 was a tangle of court plots around Gaston, the queen, and the most dangerous of the court ladies, the Duchesse de Chevreuse, widow of Luynes. It was meant to involve the assassination of Richelieu, perhaps of the king himself. The Marquis de Chalais, not the chief offender, was a person Gaston could safely denounce and Richelieu safely punish; and as his friends had foolishly locked up the skilled executioner, he suffered a more than normally painful death. The 'great storm' of court opposition which Richelieu met and survived between 1629 and 1632 was a far more professional political job. It was a palace conspiracy; but it was also a struggle between two coherent policies. The party of the *dévots* was still the strongest influence on Marie; behind it, as always, was the power of the Church and of Spain. Things were harder for them now that an adult king exercised the authority of monarchy. His personal support, if expressed with even a moderate amount of energy, could outweigh all the intrigues of the court ladies and their allies. It was by no means clear on whose side it would be exercised. Marie had new allies whose challenge to Richelieu was less irresponsible. Marillac, from his place at the centre of court politics, saw what appeared to be a consistent tendency to identify France with the anti-Habsburg cause. His objection to this was not the simple one of the committed Spanish party, but the harm he believed it was doing to the cause of strong government and sound finance. Richelieu's foreign policy was already expensive; in 1629 he had sent armies into Italy which were soon devastated by the plague. There was

obvious likelihood of greater wars before long. Foreign commitments were preventing the suppression of internal disorder. With
his brother Louis, a military officer who had also won promotion
with remarkable ease, and Bassompierre, the Marshal and
diplomat, Marillac joined Marie and her palace clique in urging
the king to dismiss Richelieu. On 10 November 1630, the 'Day
of Dupes', Louis, faced with Marie's passionate fury, accepted the
seizure of power by Marillac's party, and left Paris for his
hunting-lodge of Versailles. Richelieu followed, and proved
himself superior both in political manoeuvre and in theatrical
professions of devotion to the king. Louis, defying his mother and
the triumphant palace *dévots*, restored the Cardinal to power.
Marie survived in exile, Michel de Marillac and Bassompierre in
prison. Only the lesser Marillac perished. The success was not lost
on Louis: thereafter Richelieu managed to hold the king in a
complex bond of loyalty, fear, and self-interest. But it was a task
to which he had to devote an energy and a vigilance as great as
those he put into manipulating the diplomacy of all Europe.

The two remaining great conspiracies of Richelieu's day
showed how hazy was the line between noble rebellion and
foreign war. To men on the level of Princes of the Blood, such
places as France, Languedoc, Spain, Lorraine were alike territorial
units, differing in size and in the practical relationship they could
have with individual magnates, but able to command equal
emotional or legal attachment. In their efforts to prevent the
French state from depriving them of the freedom this situation
implied, the great men would naturally use whatever other territorial units might be helpful. Gaston now spent his time partly
in the Spanish Netherlands, where money from Madrid was
usually available to pay an army that might be used in support
of the Spanish cause in France, partly in Lorraine where he
married the ruling duke's sister, one of the queen-mother's large
circle of politically active women. Resentment in Languedoc at
the extension of the government's taxation machinery in defiance
of the province's rights as a *pays d'états* was an opportunity for
its governor Henri de Montmorency to raise, in 1632, a fairly
formidable army to which Gaston was willing to add his own.
The provincial estates and the towns declared their loyalty to the
king and joined in what they regarded as a demonstration against
the central government. When the rebel forces were beaten, the
Toulouse *parlement* was willing enough to be used as the legal

instrument for sentencing Montmorency to death. It was thought safer to carry out the sentence in private.

France, as Marillac's supporters had feared, became more deeply involved year by year in anti-Habsburg conflict. After 1635 Gaston, abandoning a brief reconciliation, was eager to rouse and exploit complaints against military failures. The central government, he argued, was defying the rights of towns and provinces in impoverishing them through costly and useless war. He found new allies. The Comte de Soissons, a Prince of the Blood and, like Montmorency, a feudal magnate in the old tradition, was the centre of one plot that ended in a minor battle, with Imperial troops aiding the conspirators. Soissons was conveniently killed in action. The Marquis de Cinq-Mars was a court favourite in the Buckingham style, pushed forward partly by Richelieu himself but firmly appropriated by the opposition. In 1641 by what amounted to a formal treaty with the enemy power it was agreed that Spain would supply money and troops while the French conspirators organized a scheme to kill the cardinal and take over power in Paris. Naturally the Spaniards would be repaid in territorial concessions and their French friends in offices and titles. The documents setting out the scheme came smoothly into Richelieu's hands through his network of espionage. Cinq-Mars was executed; Gaston once again went free.

RICHELIEU AND SPAIN

It is easy to build up a picture of Richelieu as the master-mind behind all the wars of his time, planning from the beginning the defeat of the great Habsburg enemy, manipulating from his position of power and wealth every move on the 'Protestant' side and finally, at the pre-arranged moment, throwing his own invincible forces into the conflict. Such a version fits in well with the view that the Thirty Years War was a single fight to the death between the powers of the future and those of the past in Europe – and to some extent with Richelieu's own retrospective claims. Certainly Spain was from his early years of power an enemy: internal politics alone would have made it so. But it was only in 1629, after five years of intrigue and uncertainty at home and abroad, that he wrote to Louis of his 'perpetual design to stop the progress of Spain' and of the necessity to make gateways into all the neighbouring states and 'guarantee them against the oppression of the Spaniards'. Open war, he explained, must be avoided 'as far as possible'. The enemy was Spain, not the Habsburgs, still less an alliance of all 'Catholic' powers; and the method was encroachment on the frontiers – Metz, Strassburg, Navarre, and wherever opportunity for progress arose.[2]

The Valtelline had already provided one specimen of the intricate connections between local conflict and large-scale alignments. It formed part of two military routes. For the Habsburgs it was part of 'the Spanish Road', the overland route from Spain to the Netherlands; for the French it was the most reliable military road to Venice, the one ally among the Italian states. (There were roads through Savoy; but Savoy was liable to switch unpredictably from the French to the Habsburg side.) The valley, running eastward from Lake Como to Tirano and thence northward towards the Rhine, involved difficult mountain passes for both countries. Its mainly Catholic population was ruled by the Swiss canton of the Grey Leagues, the *Grisons*. In 1618 a local Catholic revolt was fiercely put down, and Catholic leaders began a campaign for outside support. The sudden importance of the Palatinate and the approaching end of the Dutch truce (see pp. 386, 473) made the military routes an urgent matter. In 1620, after a spectacular massacre of Protestants, Spanish troops occupied the valley. But as in the larger episodes of the Thirty Years War, Spanish and French governments drew back from war with each other. The Valtelline, it was agreed, would be occupied by papal troops. Richlieu's first escapade in foreign affairs was to confirm, in 1624, a scheme to invade the valley with the help of Venice and Savoy. Then, in face of opposition at home, he repudiated the actions of the army commanders and by the vaguely worded Treaty of Moncon in 1626 allowed the Spaniards sole use of the route. The French ambassador in Madrid, it was claimed, had ruined a better diplomatic scheme by signing the treaty without authority.

It was one thing to have a general conviction that Spain was an enemy to be thwarted, another to resolve at any given moment the balance of advantages between toughness and concessions. In 1628 the French Duc de Nevers produced a claim to the Duchies of Mantua and Montferrat in the Lombardy plain which gave another opportunity for a limited campaign. In the spring Richelieu led an expedition to the fortress of Casale, but had to call it off without any decisive success in face of the continued dangers at home. The problem was that while a successful foreign expedition, backed by a dominant party at court and occupying the great men happily in the fighting, was a political asset, failures played into the hands of the pro-Spanish circle round Marie. When a second expedition was prepared for the following spring, Richelieu purported to leave to Louis the choice between war – at the cost, as he warned, of abandoning economy and reform at home – and peace at the cost of abandoning power in Italy. Louis was for the moment reconciled to Gaston, and the two set out in full splendour for the battlefields. French forces occupied a large part of the lands of their former ally Savoy, including the fortress of Pinerolo. Sieges and the feeding of troops brought the familiar miseries to the places overrun. Mantua was devastated by Imperial forces. Then the fighting was almost stopped by the plague that shattered all the armies and sent the king and the great men home in panic. Such was the warfare that could be treated by the *noblesse* as an extended hunting-trip.

Richelieu's success on the 'Day of Dupes' gave him a wider range of freedom in which to display his diplomatic strength. It did not mean that he would become the captain, on or off the field, of a Protestant team united in sportsmanlike solidarity. There was still a gap between the anti-Spanish contest and the anti-Catholic one that was being fought out in Germany. Nor was there any praiseworthy skill in his evasion of its implications. The diplomacy that produced treaties with both Sweden and Bavaria (see p. 347) made little sense except as a means of postponing irrevocable commitments. However many allies Father Joseph could twist to his purpose, the triumphs of Swedish armies were capable of reducing it all to a slightly comic process of mutual deceit. When Swedish troops appeared on the Rhine and in southern Germany, it was so manifestly embarrassing to Richelieu that cynics asked who paid the unidentified Croats responsible for Gustav's death at Lützen. The contraction of Swedish power was only one of the developments in Germany that led to the armed intervention of France. Richelieu remained as subtle as ever in his determination to keep open every possible line of action but to avoid or at least postpone full military commitment. He offered troops to the Dutch, who throughout the more spectacular German fighting had, since 1621, been resisting the Spanish armies at great cost. He made new treaties with Savoy; he opened negotiations with the best surviving freelance commander, Bernard of Saxe-Weimar. At any point he was ready, if it became the most expedient course, to send French troops into the war. But it was the defeat of the Protestant alliance at Nordlingen in 1634 that made the decision inescapable. 'It is certain', he told Louis, 'that if the Protestant party is ruined, the power of the House of Austria will turn against France'.[3] Saxony and all the other German states would, unless they soon saw some source of help, each act in its own interests in a way that would leave nothing of the alliance. The alternatives were no longer peace or war, but an immediate war in Germany that might, with the help of the Protestant allies, be won quickly or a war alone against Spain and Austria that France could certainly not afford. The memorandum, like all Richelieu's expositions of political problems, was carefully directed against the arguments of his opponents. The idea that it would be a short victorious campaign was not borne out by the strategic plans.

There were for the French two wars. There was the German struggle, which in 1635 Richelieu complained the princes too readily abandoned in making terms with the emperor at Prague (see pp. 352–4); and there was the war against Spain. If the great danger was really a Habsburg conspiracy to dominate Europe, the princes had as much reason as France to defeat Spanish forces, in the Netherlands especially. Not many of them saw it that way. Though Richelieu refrained from any fanciful theories about the 'natural frontiers' of the kingdom, many of his preparations had consisted of strengthening his positions on the German border, a process which the neighbouring states did not view with enthusiasm. But it was from the Spanish Netherlands that the greatest danger came. In 1636 an army under the Bavarian general Johann von Werth and the 'Cardinal-Infant' Ferdinand moved into Picardy. Northern France, if not the capital itself, was threatened with the same fate as so much of Germany. The invasion at least helped to achieve what Richelieu had long attempted: the French armies and the *noblesse* at every level were united in alarm. Condé and Turenne were able to build up forces as powerful as any of the armies that had appeared in the earlier stages of the German wars. Rohan, the Huguenot general, was welcomed back from his exile to join them. One German commander remained who was prepared to sell his services to France. Bernard of Saxe-Weimar, who had turned down Richelieu's earlier offers, had now agreed to provide an army of 18,000 men. In 1638 he fought a successful campaign in the southern Rhineland and captured, after a long siege, the fortress of Breisach. There was a violent quarrel about whether Bernard or the French should hold it: his ambition now was to annex the whole of Alsace. When the dispute was ended by Bernard's death, the French were able to hold his army together in their pay and continue the German war.

Very slowly the French armies, pressing forward on the whole frontier but never committing themselves too far inside enemy territory, proved superior to the Spaniards and their allies. The capture of Arras threatened the whole Spanish defensive system in the Netherlands. The Dutch fleet by destroying a Spanish squadron off Dover in 1639 cut their sea-route from Spain. The Catalan revolt made possible the capture of Perpignan, securing the French frontier in the Pyrenees. In 1634 Condé shattered the main Spanish forces at the fortress of Rocroi in the Ardennes. The victory had an effect on the political situation even greater than its military consequences. Spain, with 8,000 of her best troops killed, was now regarded as a defeated power. Bavaria became again the faithful ally of France; Saxony let in the Swedes and pretended to have been on the anti-Imperial side all the time. France would clearly be in a position to have the decisive voice in a German settlement (see pp. 357–60). But neither Richelieu nor Louis XIII lived to see the triumph.

MAZARIN

The great test of the policies and systems of government created by any minister or monarch was how far they survived when their originator had gone. It was a grim misfortune for the upholders of centralized administrative power in France that Richelieu's death in December 1642 should be followed by that of Louis in the spring. Again there was an infant king; again the regency fell to a woman, and a Habsburg woman at that. Louis XIII's will naming Anne of Austria as regent had made things no better by directing that she should act on the advice of a council in which Gaston of Orleans, as Lieutenant-Governor of France, was the most distinguished figure. Richelieu too had long ago designated his successor, the inscrutable Father Joseph. But Joseph died in 1639 and was replaced as unofficial heir by a man far less easily acceptable to Richelieu's admirers. Jules Mazarin, formerly Giulio Mazarini, had first been prominent at the French court as Papal Nuncio. Within a few years after 1639 he became a Frenchman, a cardinal, and the lover of the queen. (Whether he ever secretly married her is a question for endless argument on unsure evidence.) The one good fortune was that the change-over did not come until the moment of Spain's military defeats, when devotion to Madrid looked a far less attractive policy for the queen's circle than it had in the past. Mazarin's management of court intrigue immediately justified Richelieu's confidence in his diplomatic skill. By a process of intricate deception, the cardinal and the queen outwitted the leaders of the rival court factions and won the support of the men of the *robe* by putting on a show of legality. The Paris *parlement* was made to look like a supreme constitutional authority in granting the regency unconditionally to Anne alone. It did not prevent the survival of the *cabale des importants*, a group whose principal members were the survivors, or the sons and widows, of the principal conspirators against Richelieu.

By the time of the Westphalia treaties France appeared to be the one stable and victorious state in Europe. The settlement was not quite dictated by the French; but no-one else had a bargaining power comparable with theirs. To that extent at least Richelieu had won, posthumously, the contest on which he had so cautiously entered. Inside France, the price was still being paid. In the struggle between efficient central government and the decentralised authority of provincial magnates the centre had achieved a good deal; but it had done so at the cost of building up widespread resentment. Instead of the sectional rebellions and palace opposition with which Richelieu had learned to cope, Mazarin faced in 1648 a revolt against the whole central government that involved the *robe*, in its institution of the Paris *parlement*, the urban masses, and eventually all those in the provincial communities who were willing or compelled to participate in a new disorder of the magnates.

THE FRONDE

It is easy to treat the whole affair of the Fronde as a farcical interlude in the rise of absolute monarchy. That is what it became in the end. Though many of the demands put forward strikingly resembled those of the English Parliamentarians, the Fronde was not a repetition of the English Civil War. No leading ministers, let alone kings, were executed; no battles on the scale of Naseby or commanders of the stature of Cromwell appeared. For much of the time French armies continued to fight the Spaniards. The very name, from the slings used by Paris children to throw stones at the carriages of the rich, suggested that it was not to be taken too seriously. But there was nothing superficial about programmes that would have made France a country governed by a constitution protecting the citizens' liberties and restricting ministerial and bureaucratic power. The successive popular insurrections were at least as widely supported as any in England; officials more readily abandoned their posts; the legal system, which in England continued with only local and partial interruptions throughout the war, provided in France the basis of a new government. What France lacked most conspicuously was the nationwide alliance of propertied society that in England had destroyed the 'personal rule' of Charles I. The Paris *parlement* was supported by a much narrower section of professional and merchant interests. Its shifting alliances with the mass movements and the noble factions were not held together by any common beliefs: Huguenotism had lost almost all trace of the ideals of puritanism. Only the resistance to taxation gave a common purpose. The ruinous cost of the war and of ministerial incompetence and dishonesty made men who normally shared in the spoils of the office-holding system rebel against the faction in power. In only one way had the French opposition an advantage. It was never easy in England to show how fighting against Charles I was compatible with loyalty to him. But Anne of Austria and Mazarin were foreigners, abusing the authority they derived from the boy-king: everyone could be on the side of the monarchy, saving it from the villainy of others.

Mazarin had learnt in 1643 what French rebellions were like. The *cabale des importants* failed in a plot to murder him. Its leader, the Duc de Beaufort, was arrested; the others retreated into the country and continued their more or less public conspiracies among the provincial nobility, with the brothers Condé and Conti, Gaston of Orleans, and Gondi (the future Cardinal de Retz) on the fringes. There was no need to worry: the war against Spain was going well, and most of the rebellious nobles were willing to accept service in the army. But in 1648 things were different. There were no more victories, but no peace with Spain. It was more necessary than ever to extract still larger amounts from the country: tax-farmers and *intendants* alike were ordered to collect more, and the sale of new offices depressed the value of the old. Every Parisian property-owner was hit by a succession of manoeuvres to raise money, which benefited a few who owned the best official positions. The revival of a penal tax on building outside the walls and the manipulation of the *rentes* were more obnoxious devices than Ship Money and the English forced loans had ever been. In January 1648 a new group of money-raising decrees was presented to the *parlement* at a *lit de justice*. The regent ordered that they should be duly registered. It was not a leader of popular opposition but the king's Advocate-General, Omer Talon, who in formally presenting the decrees challenged the constitutional right of the government to use such a procedure. In the wrangle between the *parlement* and the monarchy that followed, high principles did not triumph on either side. But at least the *parlement* was prepared to show solidarity with the three lesser sovereign courts in Paris, whose members, together with those of provincial *parlements*, would only have their offices renewed at a greatly increased cost. The threat to the security of office-holding led to the meeting, in defiance of the regent, of delegates from the four courts. In July this assembly in the *Chambre de St Louis* seemed to be heading for a peaceful constitutional revolution. It proposed reforms that would demolish much of the system of centralized power established under Richelieu, eliminate the worst of the financial rackets, and turn the *parlement* into something approaching a legislative body with control over taxation. There were concessions by the government, some of them transparently unreal. Meanwhile the foreign war continued as usual. In August Mazarin chose the occasion of an official celebration of Condé's long-awaited victory at Lens to stage a sadly blundering attack on the opposition leaders. The one prominent figure actually arrested was old Pierre Broussel, a radical whose incorruptible disrespect for the government had won the amused affection of Parisians. No-one could have been less the leader of mass insurrection; but it was his name that touched off the *émeute*. There was more of the demagogue in Paul Gondi, the unscrupulously ambitious Italian cleric, who having failed to sell his services to the regent as the man who could put down the rebellion, bought his way into the confidence of the townsmen and appeared on the barricades to convey God's blessing to the rioters. If, he seems to have calculated, he could be the means of linking the mass rising with an adequate alliance of nobles he could well become Mazarin's successor. The support of the parish clergy proved to be one of his means of turning diverse elements of resistance into the 'party' of the Fronde. But he was no hero of revolution. 'We were all', he wrote later, 'playing a comedy.'

The *frondeurs* faced the same problem that had bedevilled peace negotiations between king and parliament in England: Anne and Mazarin, like Charles I, would be able, once they had an army at their command, to repudiate any agreements made under duress. The Declaration of St Germain in October 1648 granted practically everything the *Chambre de St Louis* had thought of. The peace treaty signed at Münster at the same moment, though it did not affect the war with Spain, would soon make it rather easier to bring up an army against the Parisian forces that were now on the side of the rebels. While Mazarin kept in the background the royal court solemnly returned to Paris. Matthieu Molé, the President of the *parlement*, made patient efforts to make the settlement a reality. Then, in January, with an army under Condé ready to blockade the city, Anne revoked the concessions, ordered the *parlement* out of the capital, and returned with the king to St Germain. It was a moment when a revolution on the English pattern could well have swung into radical denunciation of the monarchy and its whole corrupt establishment. But in Paris every protest remained within the cage of faith in a sovereign. There was little support in the *parlement* for talk of a representative assembly. The most scurrilous of the *Mazarinades*, the leaflets in verse and prose that had been appearing incessantly, never attacked the system of royal government as a whole. Even when the idea of ministerial responsibility to a court or assembly emerged, it had to be hazily reconciled with royal absolutism. There was more interest in the performance of the group of princely nobles – Conti, Longueville, Beaufort, and others – who proclaimed themselves allies of the rebels and made desultory attacks on Condé's small besieging army. One manoeuvre showed how far apart the princes and the *parlement* were. To Conti it seemed an obvious move to seek the aid of Spain: Molé and his patriotic friends were horrified.

The revolt of the great nobles of the Sword replaced the Parisian rebellion of the Robe by nationwide disorder. Some of it was in the form of sporadic urban and agrarian popular risings against the sheer misery that had continued to grow. Mainly it was a return to the days of the Wars of Religion, but with alliances that were far less solid. The 'Treaty of Rueil' in March 1649 renewed the court's concessions to the demands of the *parlement* and ended the siege. Whatever was left of constitutional theories disappeared in the chaos. The *parlement* was left as one of many warring factions, sometimes under Gondi's guidance, still allied with rebellious nobles but aware that its own privileges depended in the long run on the survival of a centralized state. The divisions within it naturally grew wider as its positive programme ceased to be relevant. The intrigues of the nobles, and of the women who played an outstanding and utterly unscrupulous part in them, were in themselves as insignificant as the most petty episodes of international diplomacy; but they had the same effect of killing, maiming, and starving large numbers of people. Glimpses of the events of the next four years are enough to suggest how the natural rulers of the people were now behaving.

In January 1650 Condé, Conti, and Longueville were reunited – in the prison to which Mazarin with the help of Gondi had been able to send them. There were celebrations in Paris and opposition to Mazarin almost disappeared. Some of Gondi's *frondeurs* accepted places in the government. But armies were being collected by many provincial nobles. Despite all the efforts of the court and the ministers to build up loyalty and continue the war against Spain, the anarchy of private armies spread through the country.

In February 1651 Mazarin was in precipitate flight across the frontier and Anne virtually a prisoner in her palace. His fall had come mainly through an alliance between Gondi and Gaston of Orleans, who persuaded the *parlement* to demand the release of the imprisoned princes and the dismissal of the minister. Condé and his allies after a triumphal entry into the capital called together an assembly of the *parlement* and the nobility where there was talk of an Estates-General, and even preparations for summoning it. The *parlement* disliked the idea. As Mazarin himself predicted, the unity between the two Frondes could not last long. During the summer Anne had some success in winning the support of the *parlement*.[4]

In January 1652 Mazarin felt it safe to join Anne at Poitiers and had a small army of German mercenaries at his command. Condé with his regiments of dependants was in the south. He had now become an ally of the invading Spanish forces and a leader of those nobles who proclaimed themselves in revolt against the regent. It was whispered that he would soon be crowned king. In Paris Gondi had abandoned a brief alliance with Condé and was using all his powers of public and private persuasion on the side of Anne, who had persuaded the pope to grant his burning ambition of holding the title of Cardinal. Nearly all the men of the *parlement* now agreed that Condé was the traitor.

In July 1652 Condé's army captured Paris. Scattered warfare had gone on throughout the year – good fun for the nobles, disaster for the peasants. Support for the royal side had generally increased, though only because no-one else could offer a prospect of peace. Condé was saved from defeat in Paris only by the ludicrous affair of Mademoiselle de Montpensier ordering the guns of the Bastille to fire on the army of the regent's hired commander, Turenne. With at least the passive acquiescence of Condé, a mob attacked the Hôtel de Ville, murdered many of the leaders of the sovereign courts and the municipal government and began another day of plunder and destruction. Condé had established a Paris government of his own: at its head was the man whose arrest had begun the first rising in 1648, Broussel. But the support for any form of resistance had almost disappeared. The judges and lawyers of the *parlement*, the tough *frondeurs*, the noble supporters of Condé alike began to disappear from the city. Only in Bordeaux did the '*Ormée*', in which municipal leaders had joined with artisans and apprentices to form a broadly-based popular movement, hold out against the royal army. Some of its members even spoke of alliance with the English Republic. In October Condé himself left to return to his command of the Spanish army. As soon as he had gone the king and the regent entered their capital. There were the most loyal demonstrations of joy. Mazarin returned in February 1653, with no less enthusiasm from the citizens, to be received at the court of Louis XIV.

Of the movement towards constitutional monarchy nothing

remained. A succession of decrees revoking all the concessions, forbidding the *parlement* to interfere in finance or in the 'general affairs of state' and imposing massive new taxation was dutifully welcomed. Gondi, consoled with his title of Cardinal de Retz, was imprisoned. Duretête, leader of the *Ormée*, was broken on the wheel. In many parts of the country parish registers showed that the number of children born and surviving to be baptized had fallen in the years of the Fronde to half the normal number or less. Nearly all the main elements that form the political history of the century had been made to appear ineffective and irresolute – ministerial government, legal and representative institutions, popular and aristocratic revolt. A decade later the absolutist state of Louis XIV had been established unshakeably. We shall leave its triumphs and failures to make the end of the story, and look first at the other states of Europe.

NOTES AND REFERENCES

1   *Testament politique*, ed. L. André (1947), p. 95. The arguments on its authenticity are summarized in G. R. R. Treasure, *Cardinal Richelieu and the Development of Absolutism* (London, 1972), p. 246.

2   D. L. M. Avenel, *Lettres du Cardinal de Richelieu* (Paris, 1853–77), vol. 3, pp. 179–90.

3   Quoted in G. Pagès *La Guerre de Trente Ans* (Paris, 1949), p. 181.

4   See p. 495 for the proclamation of Louis XIV's majority.

13

THE THIRTY YEARS WAR

The Thirty Years War has become firmly established as a single topic in the history of the century, unified in a way other periods of complex fighting were not. It is not obvious that this is justified. The phrase was used occasionally soon after 1648, in England and in Germany.[1] But few contemporaries saw it as a distinct historical event. To the Netherlands the German conflicts were part of the Eighty Years War that began with their own revolt. To the French and Spaniards their wars with each other were more important than German affairs and were not interrupted for another decade. When the thirty years are divided into 'periods' of Bohemian, Danish, Swedish, and French prominence, the impression of coherence becomes less convincing still. Nevertheless, for the inhabitants of large areas of central Europe this was a generation of warfare more continuous and more devastating than they had heard of before. Armies became more significant than states. Their presence – actual or feared – dominated the life of town and country more than the landlord or the emperor ever had. They moved, in summer at least, incessantly; they lived on what they could seize; they spread disease, poverty, chaos. Those who initiated and tried to control their movements had an immense variety of motives, most of which were in one way or another connected with the power of the Habsburg monarchy or the Catholic Church. It was the Peace of Westphalia in 1648, which appeared to settle many of the boundaries between Habsburg and non-Habsburg, Catholic and Protestant, that led to the idea that a unified period of warfare had ended. But there had been too much confusion of purpose for any settlement to be a permanent solution to it all. At every level there were motives of faith, loyalty, and tradition as well as of greed, anger, and self-aggrandisement. If religion was sometimes a prime influence, it was often to the foot-soldier a war-cry and to the statesman a factor that influenced, but not too strongly, the choice of allies.

In this chapter we shall look at the Thirty Years War mainly as part of the wretched history of the peoples of central Europe. It was also part of the twisting tangle of diplomatic and military hostilities that affected in greater or less degree almost every government. The affairs of the Palatinate were a vital issue in English politics; Poland was as much the victim of Swedish ambitions as was Germany; even Russia had an interest as a temporary ally of the Swedes. The greatest influence from outside was certainly that of Richelieu. For him the enemy was Habsburg power: all possible forces must be aligned against it, and if Protestant states did most of the fighting, so much the better. How far the warfare was begun and maintained by the French for their own benefit is still disputable. The emperor argued, not often convincingly, that his cause was that of Catholic rulers and the Catholic faith everywhere. Protestant governments could, when it suited them, agree that a struggle against the emperor was part of their devout resistance to the all-pervading evil of popery.

CATHOLIC AND PROTESTANT ALLIANCES

By 1600 Catholics in the Empire, or at least in southern Germany and Austria, had seen the Counter-Reformation win back much of what they had lost. Jesuit education was succeeding in driving out Lutheran doctrines; Protestant landowners were returning to Catholicism and Protestant townsmen abandoning their authority or even their homes. In Styria the Archduke Ferdinand almost destroyed Lutheranism as an active force; in Vienna Rudolf II himself ordered the closing of Protestant schools and churches. During the wars against the Turks that ended in 1606 he used the presence of imperial armies in Hungary and Transylvania as an opportunity to attack Protestantism there. There was seldom much resistance; but in some places, particularly the small German states that had a well-established degree of toleration, religious divisions persisted. In 1606 the Imperial Free City of Donauwörth, in Silesia, was the scene of a clash between townsmen and clergy typical of many others. It mattered only because Maximilian of Bavaria persuaded the emperor to allow him to use it for a demonstration of imperial and electoral authority. Maximilian was the most ambitious of the German princes and the least impossible rival to the Habsburgs as emperor. The intervention of his armies, in a town outside his own territory, became the occasion for an outburst of Protestant anger which led to bitter accusations and demands at the Diet of Regensburg in 1608. A group of Protestant princes walked out and established the 'Protestant Union', a body designed to appeal to the religious loyalties of German and European rulers. Maximilian, whose predecessors had organized various unimpressive alliances of Catholic states, was now able to set up a more effective 'Catholic League' with a sound financial system and a unified army. It seemed for a moment that a great religious war was about to begin; but most German states, suspicious of the aims of anyone who tried too hard to align them in larger units, remained uncommitted.

The Union had as its figurehead the prince who was to become an especially unfortunate victim of other people's ambitions. The Elector Palatine Frederick V, grandson of William the Silent and married in 1613 to James I's daughter Elizabeth, ruled the widely separated territories of the Rhine Palatinate and the Upper Palatinate. He was an unassuming youth with no evident zeal for leading anything, least of all a rebellion. But he was managed by an able and unscrupulous politician, Christian of Anhalt, in whose care he had been educated on rigid Calvinist lines. As one of the three Protestant Electors he was bound to be an important figure at a moment when the succession to the throne of the Empire was in doubt. Rudolf II, unmarried and approaching old age, had been trying for many years to prevent the succession of his brother Matthias, who with the support of most of the leading members of the Habsburg family contrived to take over the running of the Hungarian kingdom and to ·a great extent of Austria and Bohemia. The quarrel seemed an opportunity for Estates and Electors of every kind to assert their influence. Matthias's Chancellor, Melchior Khlesl, hoped to use the League as an institution for gathering support in the German states; if Lutherans could be persuaded to identify their cause with the League rather than the

Calvinist-dominated Union he would not make Catholicism a barrier. Anhalt, on Frederick's behalf, was not prepared to support the rival ambitions of Albrecht, the younger brother of Rudolf and Matthias; but he had hopes that the Habsburg family quarrels would leave the Union as the greatest power in Germany. Only Rudolf's sudden death in 1612 enabled Matthias to become emperor without a disputed election.

BOHEMIA

In all the rivalries about the imperial crown it was vitally important to the Habsburgs that they held the Crown of Bohemia and hence its electoral vote. Its various territories straddled the vague border between Slav and Teuton. In the north the Duchies of Silesia and of Upper and Lower Lusatia were German, and claimed that their only connection with Bohemia was that their duke was its king. Bohemia itself, and the Margravate of Moravia in the east, were mainly Slavonic but with strong German minorities. The German language was spreading, helped by the Lutheran Church. German landowners were steadily acquiring Bohemian lands. The lesser native nobility who were being deprived of power and estates were a possible source of united opposition to the monarchy; but few of the magnates showed any interest in national unification. The Diet, which had once been a thriving political institution, was now mainly a tax-voting machine. Moravia was said to be governed by fifteen families who naturally foresaw little benefit from any independent government in Prague. The lands of the Bohemian Crown were a large source of Habsburg revenue. For it was, comparatively, a rich kingdom. The peasants were fairly prosperous, paying rents and dues in money. Towns had been thriving in the sixteenth century, though Dutch merchants were now beginning to oust local ones. Rudolf II, to escape the intrigues of Vienna, had made Prague his capital and it became a major centre of European diplomacy and culture.

It was this alien and divided monarchy with its ponderous court maintained at the expense of the native nobility who were largely excluded from it, that brought the Bohemian landowners to the condition in which armed revolt was conceivable. For a time the Protestant Churches, which still claimed the allegiance of nine-tenths of the population, benefited from the court rivalry. Matthias thought it expedient to reach agreement with the political leaders of the various Protestant groups; Rudolf to outbid him produced in 1609 the 'Letter of Majesty' purporting to impose equality and freedom of choice between the Catholic Church and the compromise 'Czech Confession' which had been agreed between the Lutherans and the Bohemian Brethren, a sect whose antecedents went back to the Hussite wars of the fifteenth century. The assumption was that there would be separate communities each with its own political institutions: an elaborate system of arbitration gave the Protestants elected 'defenders' who could appeal to the Crown. Behind the political compromise, Protestant enthusiasts tried to build up a more united and educated clergy able to resist the Jesuits. But the family quarrels of the Habsburgs could not be relied on as a basis for religious toleration. Matthias, once his succession was secure, saw no reason to keep the goodwill of Protestants: Khlesl, still his chief minister, began to erode the guarantees by censorship, restriction of meetings, and so on. The militant Catholic party at the imperial court hoped to do better than this. Its moving spirit, the Spanish ambassador Don Balthasar de Zúñiga, had returned to Madrid and was persuading Philip III to take an interest in central Europe. Matthias, old and childless, was likely to be succeeded soon by his cousin Ferdinand of Styria, an ideal product of Jesuit education obsessed with the need to save his soul by extirpating heresy from his dominions. In Prague, now that the court had gone back to Vienna, the central government was run by the Chancellor Lobkovitz and a council of regents carefully chosen for their Catholic loyalty. These rich and energetic office-holders, among whom Jaroslav Martinitz and Vilém Slavata were the most prominent, were ready for an uncompromising attack on the Protestant community. The largest landowners, many of them recent converts to Catholicism, could well benefit from any victory over the mainly Protestant lesser nobles and knights.

The development of an opposition party was not helped by the alarm of Protestant landowners at any sign of popular insurrection. But it had a military leader in Count Matthias Thurn, a mildly Calvinist German noble who had become commander of the army of the Bohemian Estates. Thurn, almost alone, opposed the vote of the Bohemian Diet in 1617 when, accepting the pleas of the dying Matthias and the threats of Lobkovitz, it elected as 'king designate' the Archduke Ferdinand of Styria who had the support of Spain and the Jesuits. When Lobkovitz began a general attack on concessions to Protestantism, whittling down the provisions in the Letter of Majesty about building new churches, Thurn was able to get enough support for an organized show of resistance. He was now in touch with Protestant forces in Germany and beyond it. Austria, Transylvania, and the Palatinate were possible sources of help. The notion of a coming conflict between the forces of good and evil was already growing among European Protestants, who tended to underestimate the reluctance of governments to be involved in a distant war, especially one started by rebels.

THE BOHEMIAN REVOLT

In March 1618 the Protestant 'Defenders' summoned, as the Letter of Majesty entitled them to do, an assembly of the Estates which petitioned the emperor against the anti-Protestant activities of the regents, in particular the transference of Crown lands to the Catholic Church. A suspiciously prompt royal reply rejected the petition and banned further meetings. It produced in Prague one of those surges of popular anger that can be turned in almost any direction. Thurn became for a moment the acclaimed leader of Protestant nationalism, Martinitz and Slavata the embodiments of alien tyranny. When the assembly met again and was ordered to disperse, its numbers had grown and the streets filled. In the early morning of 23 May a procession of delegates took a new petition to the Hradčany Palace, surrounded by demonstrators, many of them armed. In the Council Chamber they were met by four of the deputies of the royal government. The argument that followed turned into a summary trial, in which those of the crowd who had got into the room agreed that Martinitz and Slavata were guilty of treason. Thurn himself, remembering that the Hussite revolt in 1418 had begun with a 'defenestration', took the lead in dragging the two to the window; and the crowd outside had their historic moment of joy when the representatives of the king and emperor were tipped over the window-ledge into the moat, followed at a suitable distance by their secretary. Reports differed about whether their lives were saved by a miracle or by a dung-heap. In any case the defenestration provided a story to be circulated with delight or horror all over Europe. It did not prove to be the beginning of an immediate national revolt. Thurn commanded a few thousand troops, with the backing of some of the nobles and knights, a few royal officials, and most of the elected delegates of the towns. Nothing had yet been done to organize similar movements in the Duchies or in Moravia. There was little effort to build up popular support in town or country. Thurn did not even put himself at the head of a new state. Power was held by thirty-six 'directors' who tried to create a conscript army. But neither they nor the Estates had the resources to keep large numbers of troops supplied and paid. Eventually, by seizing the royal treasury, confiscating lands of Church and Crown, and raising loans from landowners and townsmen they had a workable system of finance. To match the wealth of the Habsburgs they would have to gain the active support of German and European Protestants. Emissaries were sent to plead with all the Protestant states of the Empire. At this stage only the Palatinate, where Frederick and Christian were already planning to acquire the Bohemian crown, was eager to be deeply involved. Everywhere else there was careful calculation of the odds and the profits. No-one could be sure whether this was the beginning of the great confrontation or just another local episode.

It was through the Palatinate that some European help emerged. In England Frederick's agents campaigned vigorously against Gondomar and the 'Spanish' faction at court; in Denmark and Sweden they were encouraged to hope for help someday, though preferably from someone else first. One positive offer of help came from Charles Emmanuel, Duke of Savoy, whom Christian had dishonestly suggested might be a good candidate for the Bohemian throne himself. He was employing, under Ernst von Mansfeld, the best mercenary army in Europe. It was, for the moment, idle; and the duke offered to make it available not directly to the Bohemians but to the Elector Palatine. In Hungary Gabriel Bethlen saw the revolt as an opportunity to renew his attacks on the emperor. Cautiously the other lands of the Bohemian Crown accepted the rebel government in Prague. In the summer of 1619 they joined in a federal constitution and the Estates formally offered the crown to Frederick. It was a calamitous decision. Whatever his standing in Europe he was neither a military leader nor the possible head of a national revolt. The

Palatinate bordered on the great military road by which Spain
maintained its armies in the Netherlands, and there the truce was
due to expire in 1621. It was already clear that the hopes of the
Bohemian revolt would depend heavily on how strongly Spain
was prepared to intervene against it.

On the Habsburg as well as on the Bohemian side there had
been long hesitations and conflicts of interest. The first attacks on
Thurn's forces came from comparatively small imperial armies
which made progress largely because Moravia did not resist them.
From Madrid, where there were disputes about whether to send
troops to the emperor or to Algiers, only a grudging supply of
money was granted. During 1619 the incentives for Spain to
intervene decisively grew. In March the Emperor Matthias died.
Ferdinand was duly elected as his successor, but only after John
George of Saxony had extracted promises that his territory would
be protected by Spanish troops. By May Thurn had so much
enlarged his army that it was able to threaten Vienna itself. In
August Bethlen began a campaign in Hungary that drove imperial
forces out of much of the country. But success proved disastrous:
Catholic rulers were now alarmed enough to risk involvement in
war, if they had some assurance that Spain would come to their
rescue. The crucial moment came not in any dramatic call to arms
but in a secret deal between Maximilian of Bavaria and the
Spanish ambassador in Vienna, Count Oñate, who like his
predecessor Zúñiga, was among the militants in the governing
circle at Madrid. Oñate, apparently without any authority, promised a force of cavalry and infantry from the Spanish Netherlands.
He also got the agreement of Ferdinand that Maximilian should
have the Upper Palatinate and eventually the title of Elector
Palatine. The Catholic League was brought together again and at
the end of 1619 recruited a new army of its own effectively
controlled by Maximilian. Its commander, the Flemish general
Tilly, whom a Jesuit upbringing had impressed as deeply as
Ferdinand's own, imposed on his soldiers an almost monastic
discipline: the story of a 'Catholic Crusade' he thrust on them
may have made them a little less reluctant to fight than were their
enemies. The Protestant Union did agree to raise an army, but
only for defence against the League. While Spain was becoming
committed to intervention, James I in England moved away from
the Palatine cause. Louis XIII, anxious to avoid any Protestant
successes on his borders, sent his own emissaries into Germany

and prevented a confrontation between the armies of the League and the Union at Ulm. The truce there meant that Tilly's army, now thirty thousand strong, could move into Austria and crush a threatened revolt by the Protestant Estates. Then, in September 1620 he marched into Bohemia. Despite tensions between Ferdinand's commanders and those of the League, the Catholics were more united than their enemies. On 8 November, when the main armies met on the White Mountain, a low chalk hill west of Prague, there was little sign of a Protestant alliance. Bethlen's troops were plundering twenty miles away; Mansfeld was holding back most of his forces and arguing about a new contract. Contingents had appeared from the Netherlands, England, Scotland, and Saxe-Weimar: on the whole they managed to remain in reserve. The battle lasted little more than an hour. Frederick was dining happily in the palace when the first fugitives from his shattered army reached the city.

The challenge of Czech nobility, gentry of Silesia and Upper Austria, scheming politicians and rioting townsmen had not added up to a serious danger to Habsburg power. Nowhere had a clear alternative to imperial rule emerged. When the strongest of the Protestant Electors, John George of Saxony, invaded Lusatia he did so on behalf of the emperor, claiming a few concessions to the Lutherans in return: Germany was much as it had been. Only the firm presence of Spanish forces in Frederick's former Rhineland territories was new. But for Bohemia as a nation with a culture and tolerance of its own the price of defeat was destruction. It was not a sudden planned vengeance. At first only twenty-seven leading Protestants had their lands confiscated and distributed to imperial officials and Catholic nobles. The process developed over a period of seven years into a scramble for free or cheap lands in which most of the great estates were transferred to adventurers from many parts of Europe, with great profit to the Crown as well. The new Governor in Prague, Liechtenstein, a convert to Catholicism who envisaged Bohemia as a showpiece of the Counter-Reformation, sentenced rebel leaders to death. The Papal Legate, Carafa, organized the final establishment of Jesuit education. Protestant clergy lost their livings or experienced a sudden conversion. At every level of society, security could only be won by acceptance of Catholicism. Continued plunder by armies led to ever-deepening poverty. The greater the misery, the more easily miracles and festivals did their work. Belief in witchcraft grew too, and was persecuted as savagely as heresy. A Protestantism as old and deep-rooted as any in Europe was completely overthrown.

THE RISE OF THE ARMIES

The next ten years can provide specimens of most of the factors that provoked seventeenth-century wars. One, usually concealed behind a political façade but now blatantly displayed, was that the professional commanders of armed forces like to use them, to increase them, and to take control of policy. Princes and statesmen shared their influence on events in and around Germany with Mansfeld, Tilly, and above all with Wallenstein, one of the greatest organizers of the war industry in history. Albert de Valdstein was by birth a Bohemian and a Lutheran, from a family of impoverished nobility. After changing his name and religion, he built up an immense fortune by marrying a rich and dying widow, by sharing in the company that produced a new Bohemian currency, and especially by buying up confiscated Protestant lands. Soon he was able to make loans to the emperor on almost the scale of the Fugger a century earlier. He was never primarily a strategist: he entered the emperor's military service by contracting to supply 20,000 armed men, farming out the recruiting with great profit to himself. Food and equipment of every kind were supplied by Wallenstein's own organization, with his officers as middlemen. Soldiers got their pay or not as the situation required: if they could live entirely by plunder, so much the better, but in emergency Wallenstein's Bohemian wealth could give support. Desertions became fewer than in other armies, and were provided for in his calculated recruiting programmes. The terms he made with Ferdinand gave him stage by stage completely independent control over the use of his forces. But Wallenstein having become a political power identified himself completely with the cause of the Empire. More than Ferdinand himself, he worked for a reunited imperial and Catholic power, dominating the German princes and the lesser states of Europe. The emperor began to reward him with lands and titles in Germany, the Catholic princes waited for the moment when they could demand his dismissal.

Many German princes were themselves behaving more as military commanders than as rulers. But for them it was the holding and expanding of territory that mattered. From the emperor himself down to the pettiest count, everyone with control of some sort over a piece of land was faced with the fear of annexation and devastation, and with the possibility through careful choice of alliance or neutrality, that he might in the end benefit from the wars. For the great men like Maximilian, continuing war increased the opportunity to build alliances they could dominate. Since the division of Germany into Catholic and Protestant groups was roughly matched by the division of Europe, the prospect of intervention by the great powers lay behind every policy. For Frederick it was the only hope. Anhalt made his own peace with the Emperor soon after the Bohemian collapse; the Upper Palatinate and most of the Rhine Palatinate were in enemy hands; nearly all the German Protestant rulers and their Estates had in one way or another repudiated the Palatine cause. The Protestant Union was formally dissolved. James I, though still publicly demanding the restoration of his son-in-law to his Palatinate lands, saw himself more as a European peacemaker than a Protestant leader. When the war between Spain and the Netherlands was resumed in 1621, Spinola, probably the most competent and best-equipped general in Europe, was ready both to complete the conquest of the Palatinate and to use it as a base for his attack on the Dutch. It was not a time for them to get involved in fighting deep in Germany. Yet it was partly the hope of eventual Dutch support that encouraged the rash enterprise of a Protestant ruler who had so far remained aloof – King Christian IV of Denmark.

DENMARK

Christian was an unusual monarch. While most rulers were struggling to find new devices for raising funds, his steady income from taxes and from the Sound Dues enabled him to lend money to his landed subjects in return for loyal support. He could, in a modest way, start a war whenever he chose. The most likely enemy appeared to be Sweden, the one rival for control of the Sound. But Christian was also Duke of Holstein, and hence had an interest in German affairs not shared by his Danish subjects. His German territories might, he hoped, be extended by acquiring one of the great bishoprics on behalf of his son. The troubles of Germany offered still better prospects: to conquer lands on the German coast and control the entrance to the Elbe and the Weser would give further control over Baltic commerce. Conversely either a sweeping Habsburg victory in the north or a successful intervention by Sweden would threaten his whole position. The plight of the Protestant states offered him the chance to become a hero of the anti-Catholic cause – in other words a link between the German and the European conflicts. Christian really believed in the Protestant cause. Not only the Netherlands but England and even his old enemy Sweden had, he was convinced, a duty to follow his new leadership. No such alliance materialized. England eventually sent a few conscript soldiers to join the cosmopolitan army of Mansfeld; Dutch bankers raised a small subsidy; Gustav Adolf, with no desire to help Danish ambitions in the Baltic, refused to have anything to do with such schemes. Only the little states of the Lower Saxon Circle, faced with the threat of Tilly's army, agreed to make Christian their president and to let him recruit freely in their territory. With no more encouragement than this, Christian sent in his army. His only reward was to bring into northern Germany and into Denmark itself the full horror of the marching soldiers. The little states were looted repeatedly: the pitiful efforts of George William of Brandenburg to keep forces out of his territory by agreeing with almost anyone only added to the complexities of the fighting there. It was in the summer of 1625, when Christian had hopes of a victorious campaign that would leave northern Germany under his control, that Wallenstein's army was ready for the emperor's service. He was willing to bring it into the north, and thought the Duchy of Mecklenburg might be an appropriate reward. (One result of this was that Mecklenburg escaped most of the fighting.) The Danes and their allies among the princes soon had to face Wallenstein as well as Tilly. Even so, Christian was able to patch up an agreement by which Mansfeld would be under his command and England and Holland would contribute money for a great southward campaign in 1626. It did not work. Despite the inevitable disputes with Wallenstein, Tilly defeated Christian at Lutter in Brunswick. But the victory did not benefit the emperor much. His threats to inflict decisive punishment on the Danes and destroy the Protestant states of the north so alarmed Maximilian and the Catholic princes of the League that they tried in vain to arrange a compromise peace. This was now Ferdinand's great difficulty: Catholic rulers were no less threatened than Protestant ones by any extension of Habsburg power. A prospect of unlimited triumph for the emperor brought to the surface the neutrality movements and the particularism of the states great and small. Wallenstein at least was well aware of the danger in making too many enemies; and it was largely his pressure that led in 1629 to the reasonably generous Peace of Lübeck which removed the Danes from the war without grievous punishment. Wallenstein's realism was shown in his treatment of the city of Magdeburg. While it resisted, his besieging army would show it no mercy; when it was prepared to submit to the emperor its religious privileges must be maintained and even the demand for huge amounts of money relaxed. Mecklenburg was a different matter: Wallenstein took the whole territory for himself and set up his court there as duke.

THE BISHOPRICS

The ending of the Danish episode speeded up the land-grabbing in Germany. The most tempting morsels had, ever since the Reformation, been the former Catholic bishoprics. Some in Protestant areas had been completely 'secularized' and were now principalities heritable like any other; some kept their theoretically clerical chapters of canons but were controlled by a lay 'administrator' who took the profits. They were often a welcome solution to the problem of providing for the younger sons of great families. While English gentlemen found parochial livings for their dependants, the emperor acquired for his son the bishoprics of Strassburg and Passau, and the electoral families of Brandenburg and Saxony had half a dozen bishoprics between them. Episcopal possessions could be expanded no less than others: the Bishop of Speier got Ferdinand's authority to recover whatever lands he could claim had once belonged to his diocese. Out of the scramble for bishoprics, the successive confiscations, and the general insecurity of territorial possession, there developed among the ministers of both Ferdinand and Maximilian the scheme for giving legal and religious blessing to Catholic acquisitions which emerged in 1629 as the 'Edict of Restitution'. All Church property that had been alienated since 1552 was to be restored to the rightful successors of its former owners – episcopal lands to Catholic bishops, monastic ones to re-established religious houses. Protestant 'administrators' were declared to have no legal rights at all. Only the Lutheran religion was recognized as benefiting by the old principle of '*cuius regio eius religio*'; and Protestants of any kind who now found themselves back under a Catholic ruler could change their faith or get out. It would mean the destruction of many Protestant princes, the imposition of Catholicism on Protestant towns like Augsburg and Dortmund, the re-establishment of many hundreds of monastic foundations. The fact that it was an Imperial Edict, issued without reference to the diet or the princes, was in itself a defiance of the accepted division of power. Ferdinand had acted quickly enough to ensure that he rather than Maximilian and the other Catholic princes got the greatest benefit. It would have been hard to devise a better combination of the war-provoking motives of property, power, and belief.

The Edict was in itself an indication of how possession of land was merged with political power, and religious with secular control. There was room for endless arguments on such questions as its application to the Imperial Free City of Augsburg which was also the Protestant centre of a Catholic bishopric. The Imperial 'Commission' that purported to hear the legal arguments was in practice part of the process of ordering armies to carry out the transfers. When the Augsburg citizens had heard what Wallenstein's army could do to places that resisted the execution of the Edict, they surrendered without a blow. Eight thousand Protestants were later said to have fled from the city. On the whole the spoils were distributed with due regard to the realities of power. Maximilian, who after supporting the idea of the Edict had drawn back when the emperor seemed strong enough to get more for himself, was pacified with the sees of Verden and Minden for the Wittelsbach family. Magdeburg, Halberstadt, and Bremen had already gone to the Habsburg Archduke Leopold. Believers in the triumph of the Catholic faith could claim it as a great victory over the forces of evil. In fact the scramble for lands brought out more bitterly than before the conflict between the emperor and the Catholic princes, while for Protestant princes withdrawal of the Edict became a major aim.

EMPERORS, PRINCES AND FOREIGN POWERS

It was typical of the German situation that in the midst of the forcible seizures of territory and with the armies still the most effective power in a country suffering disastrous impoverishment, the emperor in 1630 resolved to invite the electors, Catholic and Protestant alike, to assemble at Regensburg and give formal recognition to his son as successor to the throne. They were also expected to approve of imperial support for Spain against the Dutch. This, Ferdinand hoped, would be the moment when Germany would re-unite against its outside enemies – which meant, as the Electors soon saw – the enemies of the Habsburgs. The Electors of Saxony and Brandenburg refused to take any part in the meeting. The others were determined to use the opportunity to diminish the emperors's military power. Their principal demand was that Wallenstein should be dismissed. For Ferdinand to fling away his great source of armed strength seemed incredible folly. But the emperor like the Electors was suspicious of the growing power of the commander who seemed to be running a foreign policy of his own. The Spanish party at Ferdinand's court, hoping to get Wallenstein's forces put under its own nominee, and hence at the disposal of Spain, was also in favour of his dismissal. At the moment when Germany was invaded by Swedish armies the man most able to resist them was persuaded to 'resign'.

The Regensburg meeting marked a further stage in the development of the wars in Germany into the centre of a single European struggle. But the great powers were still cautious in their commitments. While Ferdinand's Jesuit confessors had growing hopes of a new Catholic Empire in which both German and Spanish Habsburgs would be loyal instruments of the Church, the great aim of the Spaniards was to get German troops to fight against the Dutch. Saving Catholic Germany from Protestant aggression was no concern of theirs: they had already shown a cynical readiness to negotiate with Frederick for the restoration of the Palatine to his family under Spanish protection. Richelieu, feeling that home affairs now left him a little freer to manoeuvre against Spain, had been working to strengthen the German princes, and keep Ferdinand's Empire divided. The Capucin secret diplomats Father Hyacinth and Father Alexander had long been involved in intricate chicanery on his behalf; and at Regensburg Father Joseph himself turned up to take charge of it. Franco-Spanish rivalry was now involved in the affair of Mantua (see p. 322). Under Spanish pressure, and despite the hostility of the princes, Ferdinand had asserted his authority over the disputed Duchy and sent imperial troops against the invading French. They won some surprising military successes, which did a good deal to weaken France's position in Germany.

There is no reason to suppose that any of the participants in these chaotic rivalries had deeply subtle plans, let alone consistent principles. Richelieu, though always glad to see Habsburg power diminished, preferred confusion in Germany to firm alignments. He encouraged the electors to demand Wallenstein's dismissal, and suggested to Wallenstein that it might be a way of proving how indispensable he was. Catholic and Protestant princes alike were possible allies of the French. In particular it was important to let Maximilian of Bavaria especially see the benefits of relying on French support rather than making terms with Ferdinand. (Maximilian for his part felt so strong, with Wallenstein out of the way, that he could accept French help without making any binding commitments.) But Richelieu intended to leave open as long as possible the option of keeping up peaceful relations with the emperor. Father Joseph actually signed an agreement by which France would withdraw all help from the princes in return for a favourable settlement of the Mantuan war. Richelieu, unwilling to be bound by any firm commitment, repudiated it. His intervention at Regensburg had been far from a triumphant success. One satisfaction that remained was that Ferdinand had been even less successful. Another was that in July 1630 Gustav Adolf's well-prepared and well-advertised invasion force had landed at Peenemunde.

Though Richelieu had long been encouraging, cautiously, the schemes for Swedish intervention, it was a complication that made it harder than ever to build up an alliance of German states within a French system. Gustav was no-one's mercenary soldier. It was not until January 1631 that he reached agreement with Richelieu in the Treaty of Barwälde. In return for a subsidy not big enough to be vital to Sweden's plans, Gustav agreed to tolerate Catholicism, to make no separate peace, and to keep out of Bavarian territory if Bavaria remained strictly neutral towards Sweden. Since Gustav was pledged to restore the Elector Palatine to his lands, the prospects of this part of the treaty being effective were not good. In May Maximilian, alarmed not so much by the Swedes as by Spain's apparent threats to the Palatinate, made with France the agreement at Fontainebleau by which each side promised to uphold the other's possessions and give no assistance to their enemies. The difficulty of reconciling the two treaties looked formidable. It was some satisfaction that in April the Peace of Cherasco ended the Mantuan war in favour of the French claimant; but it also released imperial and Spanish troops for other purposes. At least it indicated that the emperor felt himself in a weaker position than he had at Regensburg.

THE SWEDISH INVASION

Gustav's landing was a spectacular achievement. Within a fortnight the Pomeranian capital of Stettin was occupied and the Dukes of Pomerania and Mecklenburg quickly became his first German allies. After that, progress slowed down. Gustav was not the ideal saviour of German Protestantism, since he was obviously hoping to acquire for himself Baltic territories that were in Protestant hands. His successes were especially unwelcome to John George of Saxony, who had his own schemes for outbidding Maximilian as leader of the anti-imperial cause. A meeting at Leipzig in the spring of 1631, attended by nearly all the Protestant states and cities, was able to proclaim that they were now an alliance for the defence of the imperial constitution. Neither the emperor nor any foreign power could expect their support except on their own terms. The threat of a genuinely independent Protestant force was not very convincing. John George, for the moment, was rich enough to pay for a substantial army, and Wallenstein's second-in-command, von Arnim, found no more difficulty in transferring to the service of Saxony than he had formerly in invading his native Brandenburg. But Brandenburg was the first large state to show how easily any Protestant alliance could be broken: Gustav Adolf, after a well-timed invasion of

Pomerania, was able to persuade his brother-in-law the Elector George William to promise Sweden a benevolent neutrality.

In May 1631 the rulers and their political servants were still deeply involved in the refinements of professional diplomacy. Swedish troops had occupied much of Pomerania and lived at the expense of its people; then they had moved on to take and plunder Frankfurt-on-the-Oder. But ever since the autumn of 1630 the great Protestant city of Magdeburg, which had rebelled against its 'restitution' to Catholic control, had held an essential place in Gustav's programme. Both in strategy and in propaganda, its possession was immensely valuable. He promised repeatedly to come to its rescue; and he needed to do so in a spectacular way that would establish his role as Protestant saviour. Tilly's subordinate Pappenheim was besieging it with an ill-supplied force. It could, Gustav believed, hold out until the Swedish army, depleted by the need to hold down the territory it had occupied, could be reinforced. There were long negotiations to try to get John George of Saxony to help in its relief. Tilly decided that a final assault on the city was the chance for a great blow to Swedish prestige. Its success was not quite what he had hoped.

When the city's resistance ended, soldiers suddenly released from inactivity into a source of wealth and drink robbed and killed indiscriminately; and somehow there began the fires that merged into the total destruction of the city, of the supplies the Catholic commanders had hoped for, and of most of the inhabitants and soldiers alike. Whether Magdeburg experienced the phenomenon of a 'fire-storm' that three centuries later produced the greater horrors of Hamburg and Dresden is impossible to say; but probably the holocaust was exceptionally great only because it was a very windy day. At all events, it became in Germany and in Protestant Europe the basis of a story of Catholic atrocity that provided a new incentive for war. Tilly made amends in his own way: he attended a mass to mark the restoration of the city to the true faith, and urged the surviving soldiers that they ought to marry the women they had seized for themselves. But Magdeburg had not changed his main problem – to find supplies for his army. Maximilian, still hoping to lead an alliance of princes and discouraged by Richelieu from an encounter with Gustav, did not want the Catholic army to attack John George. But for Tilly the needs of the army were an end in themselves: at the end of August 1631 he invaded Saxony. A fortnight later John George signed a military alliance with Gustav, and at Breitenfeld, north of Leipzig, enough of Tilly's army was destroyed for the Swedes to be sure of living successfully for some time off the Catholic states.

SWEDEN AND GERMANY

In the next year, as Gustav continued to lead his armies through south Germany, his ambitions expanded. Instead of the hastily improvised extraction of wealth from the countryside to support the alien army, he began to consider, with Oxenstiern, reorganizing the 'Circles' to provide a new government for conquered territory. Even Richelieu took seriously the awful possibility of a Swedish Empire extending to the Rhine. In Bohemia, though John George's activities often looked more like the familiar plundering than liberation, there was briefly a hope that Protestantism might be restored. For among the countless secret soundings that went on between all the parties in the conflicts Gustav was in touch with Wallenstein. If revenge for his dismissal was a motive, Wallenstein could hardly do better than get troops and money from the Swedes to reconquer for Protestantism his native Bohemia. Gustav evidently decided the risks were not worth while. Ferdinand, now that the Pope, Spain, and Poland were all for their different reasons refusing to give him substantial help, might soon be completely at the mercy of the Swedish army. Only by making what seems, from uncertain accounts of it, to have been a humiliating bargain with Wallenstein, who acquired practically the status of an independent sovereign ally, could the emperor acquire a new army. Catholic Germany had shown no sign of uniting against the Swedish invader. On the contrary, there was, in the winter of 1631–32, a reasonable chance that one of Richelieu's many alternative schemes might be brought off – an agreement for the Catholic League to remain neutral while Gustav fought the emperor on Protestant territory. The negotiation failed, less perhaps through any reluctance of Gustav to limit his freedom of action against Catholics than because he needed to let his army live off the produce of Catholic lands. The distinctions between ally and enemy had come to matter less than the contest between all armies for what food was left, and the efforts of rulers to send the soldiers elsewhere. Maximilian tried to hold an awkward balance between preserving his Bavarian lands from destruction by the armies and preventing a Swedish victory that might deprive him of them altogether. In the end he decided to fight as best he could.

There was no more progress towards a united Protestant cause in Germany than there was towards a Catholic one. John George of Saxony had not got far with the discouraging task of becoming leader of an alliance of the princes and at the same time furthering his own territorial interests. One unexpected prospect of help for Sweden and Protestantism came from Transylvania. Gabriel Bethlen, who had been a Calvinist magnate before he acquired his more or less independent throne, was not an enemy the emperor could afford to treat lightly. Not only was Transylvania itself a thriving state with an efficient army; when Bethlen had proclaimed his support for the Bohemian rebels in 1619 he had brought in Turkish troops, a menace to the Habsburg lands as great as any European power. He had also married a sister of Gustav Adolf. Twice Ferdinand had bought him off with promises of large additions to his territory, and twice he had renewed hostilities. After Bethlen's death in 1629, a new Transylvanian prince, George Rákóczy, had established himself. The Swedish advance led him to hope that he could make an alliance with Gustav Adolf and share in a glorious victory over the emperor. Gustav decided Transylvanian help was too remote to be worth the terms Rákóczy demanded. But at least his envoys had better treatment than the ludicrous delegation of Crimean Tartars who turned up in Stockholm with an offer of 30,000 men. They were sent off to Germany to see the King of Sweden if they could find him – which they never did.

The emperor's fears that Swedish forces might, in 1632, overrun the Catholic states of Germany and even reach Vienna itself were exaggerated. Only far more reliable help, with supplies if not with men, from inside Germany would have enabled Gustav Adolf to win a campaign in the south. For much of the summer his main army faced Wallenstein's outside Nüremberg and both avoided a major battle. Soldiers were now suffering as much as civilians, from hunger, from flies and rats, and inevitably from plague or other unidentified diseases. Some died; some deserted. At the end of the campaigning season the Swedish army turned back towards the north, where the Elector of Saxony was an unreliable ally. Wallenstein had occupied a large part of Saxon territory and was about to give up warfare for the winter when, in mid-November, the Swedes attacked his headquarters at Lützen. He had withdrawn from the battle and decided to leave Saxony when he heard, incredulously, the news that Gustav Adolf had been killed on the field. It was more important for the emperor than any victory. The hero-myth had gone from the Swedish cause: no-one else could become a figurehead for the enemies of the Habsburgs.

It was ironic that of the two men whose personal successes had most influence on the fighting the king should die on the battlefield and the professional soldier be the victim of politically motivated assassination. There is no great mystery about Wallenstein's conduct in the years after Gustav's death. Since his first agreement with Ferdinand he had remained in part a manager of the business of war, selling his services where he thought best, in part a politician with the same standards of conduct as the rest of them. He had therefore been in frequent touch with many leading figures on whatever at any given moment was the 'other side'. Wallenstein's 'treason' in being prepared to reach agreements with the French, with Protestant Electors, with his fellow-soldiers Bernard of Saxe-Weimar and Arnim, or with the Swedes differed from the normal honourable proceedings of diplomacy only because he was still on the borderline between subject and monarch. Perhaps if he had added a touch of Cromwellian passion to his wealth and ability he might have become a Lord Protector of the Empire. But an essential part of the business was to hold the loyalty of his mercenary soldiers and subordinate commanders; and his prospects were now too uncertain for all of these to follow him unquestioningly against the emperor. Nor had he won popular support in Bohemia: none of his astrologers had revealed to him that Prague might have been worth a Protestant sermon. In 1634 Ferdinand agreed to his dismissal and, it appears, to a secret order that he should be captured or killed. So for his disloyalty to the German emperor he was murdered by the conspiracies of men with such names as Butler, Gordon, Leslie, and Devereux, officers in the imperial armies.

THE PEACE OF PRAGUE

The forces that remained in Germany were gradually abandoning such coherence as they had had in the days of the great commanders. Mansfeld in 1626 had lost the support of his army in Silesia and died obscurely in the mountains of Bosnia. Tilly had been fatally wounded in a minor encounter with the Swedes. An alliance of the smaller Protestant states concluded at Heilbronn in 1633 did little more than thwart the schemes of Saxony for making peace. Clearly the French would before long have to decide whether to forsake German politics or intervene directly. It was the extension of French control over German Protestant politics that encouraged a new Catholic commander to bring help to the emperor. Philip IV's brother Ferdinand, the 'Cardinal-Infant', governor of the Spanish Netherlands, was not a man to allow his high sacred office to prevent him from becoming a highly skilled soldier. He was delighted to have the opportunity of taking an army into Germany to practise his theories of war. In September 1634 his force, with the remains of Wallenstein's army, fought the Swedes and the German Protestants organized by Bernard of Saxe-Weimar at Nordlingen. It was a victory for the emperor's cause formidable enough to end the resistance of most of the princes, and to bring nearly all southern Germany under the control of imperial commanders. In the spring of 1635 the Elector of Saxony completed his long negotiations and signed with the emperor the Peace of Prague. John George was to have the reward of Lusatia and the bishopric of Magdeburg. The whole principle of the Edict of Restitution was to be quietly abandoned and lands to revert to those who had held them in 1627 – but only for a period of forty years, during which, by some conveniently unspecified process, the disputes would be settled. Lutheran worship was to be tolerated in some imperial cities. In return John George was to assist the imperial government against such princes as refused to join the settlement. Few of those that mattered did refuse. Bavaria and Brandenburg, the Rhineland bishoprics and the Duchies of Mecklenburg were equally ready to accept. Only Bernard of Saxe-Weimar, still in command of an army but not of any territory, decided that his future lay in a Wallenstein-like existence as a mercenary sovereign with dreams of becoming the saviour of Germany. It was by no means the end of the fighting or the plundering. But the German war as such had petered out. The eighteen years of destruction had settled that Maximilian of Bavaria should rule the Palatinate, that Bohemian Protestants should continue to be persecuted, and that a number of bishoprics should be shared out equitably among the younger sons of the emperor and the princes. The emperor, to whose new army Catholic and Protestant states were expected to contribute, had reason to be moderately pleased. But when he died in 1637 he had few illusions about the struggle with France that faced his son.

DEVASTATION

To incalculable numbers of men, women, and children the warfare in Germany meant the loss of homes, crops, and livestock; their possessions were stolen, their families broken up; they were in constant danger from plague and famine. Many towns suffered in greater or less degree the fate of Magdeburg; many villages were abandoned. None of this can be denied; but attempts to be more specific about the extent, causes, and consequences of the damage have led to incessant controversy. The 'all-destructive fury' of the war has been denounced as a 'myth', and it has been argued that those thirty years in Germany were not essentially different from earlier and later decades there and elsewhere. Historians have no doubt been guilty of a variety of blunders. One is to accept, or imply, that accounts of the worst horrors were typical of the whole period or area. Another is to rely on descriptive writers who had a natural tendency to report the most spectacular events, or even had an ulterior motive for doing so. Samuel Pufendorf, the Great Elector's official historian, has been accused of using the miseries of the war in Brandenburg to contrast the glorious achievements of his master. The most quoted of all the accounts, Grimmelshausen's *Simplicius Simplicissimus*, was a novel written in 1669. But he was drawing both on his own recollections and on the mass of news-sheets and pamphlets that had appeared everywhere, many of them illustrated with vivid engravings. Reports of the devastation spread everywhere, and fear spread with them. Some estimates of the loss of population – a half or even two-thirds – have indeed been produced by extending too crudely the figures or impressions from the worst-hit places. Not all those who disappeared from a village or district had necessarily died, though to say that they had merely 'migrated' does not make it unimportant in human or economic terms. A modern calculation suggests an average of a third in towns and two-fifths in the country. In some areas evidence for a loss of something like half in the total population is strong and consistent. They include Mecklenburg and Pomerania in the north, Würtemberg and the Rhine Palatinate in the west. In similar places such as Oldenburg and Hanover the losses were comparatively small. Much of lower Saxony suffered badly at the beginning of the war but before it ended had shown how rapid recovery could be. Bavaria did not suffer its worst losses until the 1630s. The destruction of Magdeburg was almost complete; but a few towns such as Hamburg had an almost uninterrupted rise in population and commercial activity. In the towns and cities that escaped devastation the main demand of governments and armies was for money. Some municipal rulers were able to buy off a besieging army; some had to accept a garrison and pay towards its maintenance. It all led to borrowing; and in the tangle of debts that the war produced some people were impoverished and others enriched. As always, many forms of commerce and industry benefited from the requirements of warfare. Buying and selling continued; and the monetary system on which they depended never broke down completely. But the possibility of sudden ruin was seldom far away.

Even more difficult than piecing together the facts about Germany in these years is to decide how far the war itself was responsible for immediate and for lasting changes. Most of western and central Europe experienced some form of depression during the second and third decades of the century. Epidemics, crop-failure, riot and the brutality of the powerful were ordinary parts of life. In many German states and cities food-prices had risen, coinage had been debased, commerce had declined before 1618. But it would have been hard to persuade a peasant who saw soldiers destroy his means of living that this was merely part of a phase of economic contraction. Here and there the actual fighting – battles, sieges, and planned devastation – was the greatest calamity. More commonly disaster came from the very existence of the armies. The separate field armies were often larger, but not immensely larger, than had been seen before. Gustav Adolf had at most 170,000 men under his direct command, Wallenstein 100,000. To maintain them far greater numbers were enlisted at one time or another. Many, even in the German armies, came from abroad: Switzerland, the Netherlands, Croatia, Poland, Hungary, and Scotland were sources of mercenary troops; though to the town or village that had to feed them it did not matter whether they came from a hundred or a thousand miles away. Recruiting was partly an administrative operation, partly a private enterprise. The regiments had their attractions: they offered, even if they did not always provide for long, food, clothing, pay, and the benefits of authorized or unauthorized plunder. But increasingly as the needs of the commanders grew, the arrival of recruiting officers was a new moment of terror. It was the poor, including the victims of the wars themselves, who filled the infantry companies. Cavalry tended to be either professional soldiers or men rich enough to provide their horse and equipment: most of them took servants with them to the war.

Servants were a small part of the great trains of followers often more numerous than the armies themselves. Women and children, artisans, carriers, salesmen, beggars, families whose homes and livelihood had been lost attached themselves to the armies and like the soldiers lived off the countryside through which they passed. Here amid the flies, rats and dirt a variety of diseases flourished and spread into the rest of the community. (Whether bubonic plague was increased by armies or had its independent fluctuations is another matter of argument.) The suffering was not always accepted without protest. Below the war of army against army there developed here and there the revolts of civilian against soldier, oppressed subject against authority. Upper Austria in 1626 and Bavaria in 1633 were regions that saw what was described as a new peasants' war. The peasant was not always the loser: if he failed to preserve his stores and animals from the soldiers he could sometimes steal them back. Trading in horses and in hoarded food could be very profitable. In chaotic conditions some might escape altogether the tax-gatherers and the rent-collectors who completed the ruin of others. The most lasting upheavals came when the land was abandoned altogether. Along the main marching-routes especially, small villages were deserted not only until the soldiers had gone away but sometimes permanently. Descriptions of columns of peasants in Bavaria leaving their villages and moving into the mountains do not say how many returned or on what terms. It was possible for a landlord or prosperous tenant to take over abandoned lands, increasing the size of holdings and the number of landless labourers. Some owners of small estates were reduced to almost the same condition of poverty as their former tenants and disappeared from their territory. Land prices collapsed and speculators, often from far away, moved in. 'Social mobility' – a phrase that would have seemed bitterly ironic at the time, was sharply stimulated.

THE PEACE OF WESTPHALIA

Wars can continue only as long as governments pay for them and subjects can be led to accept them. Peace was eventually made in Germany when first the states of the Empire and then the European powers found it impossible, or at least inexpedient, to let it go on. The Peace of Prague seemed to mean the end of resistance to the emperor inside Germany. After it Richelieu had at last to fight his battles with French resources. In May 1635 he issued a solemn declaration of war against Spain. The fighting in Germany became a minor part of the European conflict – a conflict almost as incoherent as the German ones. Round the western frontiers of the Empire, from northern Italy to the Netherlands, a struggle for territory was fought at great expense for little reward. The French, though they continued to seize what lands they could on their eastern border, were glad to leave German warfare to their Swedish allies and to Bernard of Saxe-Weimar. Gradually the Swedish generals Lennart Torstensson and Johan Banér recovered control of the north from the Saxon and imperial armies. Swedish forces went through Bohemia with the intention of joining George Rákóczy, whom the sultan had allowed to undertake a sporadic campaign against the emperor in Hungary. In the south Bernard won a series of victories over the Bavarian and imperial troops. One by one the new Emperor's allies deserted him. Brandenburg and Saxony made separate truces with the Swedes. Bavaria in unavailing efforts to keep the armies away made and broke agreements with almost everyone. More and more the armies remained in being only because there was no means of getting rid of them safely. It was notorious that soldiers disbanded and with no other livelihood were a threat to what was left of the country even worse than that of organized forces. Everywhere a popular demand for peace became the main theme of the pamphlets and news-sheets that had once been concerned with upholding a cause. Lutheran churches were generally the first to denounce the evils of the warfare. A succession of plays performed at princely courts had the same message. As years went by with no decisive change in the internal power-struggles, the princes slowly accepted that making peace of some sort was the only policy they could safely follow. The emperor too wanted a peace settlement and would make it if he could by negotiating with all the European powers without much reference to the electors or the lesser rulers. In 1645, when news of what was happening to Charles I in England gave every monarch cause for concern, Ferdinand III conceded that all German rulers should have a share in the peace-making.

Both the French and the Spanish governments had their own incentives to get out of the German wars. Each of them had over the years paid more in subsidizing the fighting than their financial systems could afford; and each had lost the regime that had involved them in it. In France after the succession of rebellions and the deaths of Richelieu and Louis XIII, Anne of Austria and Mazarin were unsure of the strength of their regime and anxious to concentrate all their resources on the war against Spain. It would be a great help if they could establish the neutrality of the emperor. In Spain the rebellions of the 1640s were even more dangerous and the state's finances even more overstretched. In 1643 the defeat at Rocroi left the Spanish Netherlands open to invasion from both France and Holland. Olivares, who had long been insisting that commitments in Germany must be cut down was overthrown. It was then accepted that he was right: peace must be made with everyone except the French. For more than five years a multiplicity of negotiations went on. Munster, where Spain and the Catholic German states first met, and Osnabrück which was the base for the Swedes and the Protestant states became centres of what began to look like a large peacemaking industry. Nearly two hundred rulers, most of them of course from small German states, were represented by several thousands of diplomats and their entourages. It gave almost endless scope for arguments about procedure and protocol that postponed the need to decide anything of substance.

Great treaty-making Congresses are easily overrated as turning-points of history. The various agreements that made up the Peace of Westphalia in 1648 did not put an end to the one major conflict still being fought in the west – between France and Spain; nor did they much affect the strength or interests of the northern and eastern states whose intermittent wars were soon resumed.

Sweden achieved part of Gustav's original aim in Germany – West Pomerania and some smaller territory on the Baltic, and the bishoprics of Bremen and Verden on the North Sea. France established absolute sovereignty over the long-disputed frontier towns of Metz, Toul, and Verdun, and a position in Alsace militarily strong, but so unpopular and legalistically so complicated as to ensure future wrangles. Breisach and Pinerolo were two other desirable fortresses returned to the French. As a settlement of the internal affairs of Germany and the Habsburg Empire, Westphalia was important, though the conflicts it officially ended had exhausted themselves years before. The essential point, nowhere put in black and white, was that though the German states were still, in varying degrees, linked by the institutions and traditions of the Empire, the strongest of them could become completely sovereign units. The clause that came nearest to recording this was the one giving the German states control over their relations with each other and with foreign powers – provided that they did not form alliances against the Empire. There was room still for renewed conflict between state and imperial power. In general the crimes and the acquisitions of territory since 1618 were obliterated; but in the vital question of the tenure of ecclesiastical lands, though there was no longer any question of reviving the Edict of Restitution, it was possible to bargain about the 'normal year' to which conditions should return. At the Peace of Prague 1627 had been more or less agreed; now it was 1624. Calvinist rulers were to have most of the rights granted in 1555 to Lutherans. There was even some protection for subjects who found themselves under a new sovereign of a different faith. But for any who persisted in rejecting the beliefs prescribed under the territorial settlement, the one concession was that they could flee from their homes and even take their goods with them. For the Bohemian Protestants there was no relief at all. Ambitions of the Churches to extend their dominion no longer interfered much with dynastic and diplomatic aims. The problem of the Palatinate was typical: Maximilian used all his bargaining power to keep the gains that had always cost him the hope of Protestant support, and Frederick's son Charles Louis had no friends among the European powers. The balance was eventually expressed by giving Charles Louis only the shattered Rhine Palatinate, though a new electoral seat was created for him. Maximilian kept the Upper Palatinate and its electorate. Brandenburg, in exchange for the lost Baltic lands, acquired Magdeburg and the Bishoprics of Halberstadt, Minden, and Kamin. Its title to East Pomerania was confirmed – though without the vital port of Stettin.

Details of the German agreements are on the whole trivial and tedious, though to the inhabitants of a town whose future depended on some unscrupulous bargain it may have seemed that diplomacy could be as cruel as war. The settlement registered, even if it did little to determine, two great changes. The boundary between Catholic and Protestant ceased to be, within Germany, a major source of conflict – in practice though not in imagination; and the Habsburg Empire had a different character. Both changes were shown in the country where the war had started. Bohemia had lost all prospect of an independent national existence. The Protestant churches had been crushed; most of the old landowners had been dispossessed by outsiders, mainly army commanders claiming their reward, who had acquired the confiscated lands. German became the language of the aristocracy and the administrators. The effective government was in Vienna, where the emperor as King of Bohemia made it a model of centralization. He was still in theory Holy Roman Emperor, chosen by the Electors and sharing power with the Diet. In fact the hereditary Empire of the Habsburgs was now the significant unit. Vienna had become the capital not of a German Empire but of a miscellany of peoples held together by their subjection to the House of Austria. However destructive the war had been, it had not destroyed the Habsburgs.

REFERENCE

1   See F. L. Carsten in *History*, vol. 43 (1958) and Geoffrey Parker, *The Thirty Years War* (London, 1984), p. 237, n. 1.

14

GERMANY AND THE
HABSBURG EMPIRE, 1648–1713

BAVARIA, SAXONY, AND BRANDENBURG

The history of Germany after 1648 tends to be treated as chapter one of the 'rise of Prussia'. Probably we should hear less of the Great Elector if he had not been the forerunner of Frederick the Great and Bismarck; but it cannot be denied that Brandenburg was made into a successful state out of material that would have been unpromising even without the various ill-effects of the war. At this stage Brandenburg and its associated territories seemed less likely to achieve prosperity for its people and power for its rulers than either Bavaria or Saxony. Maximilian of Bavaria had already, by the time of his death in 1651, encouraged cautious rehabilitation, re-settling land that had gone out of cultivation, disbanding the army rapidly, importing horses and cattle to make good some of the wartime losses. His son Ferdinand Maria seemed to have good prospects of establishing an absolutism as secure as any in Europe. The Wittelsbach dynasty were the only serious rivals to the Habsburgs, and became eventually the longest-lasting of all ruling houses – from the twelfth century to the twentieth. They had remained firmly attached to the Catholic cause, and could reasonably claim to have done more than the Habsburgs to turn back the advance of Protestantism without having allowed the numerous clergy to gain much political power. Bavaria, on the other hand, had not much opportunity of economic progress. Cut off from the sea, and with no long-distance river transport, its only commerce was by land; and though Munich was a junction of alpine routes it had not become a major city. Nor was there a body of powerful magnates to whom the Wittelsbachs could turn in the formation of an impressive court, or whose quarrels they could exploit. Landed estates were seldom large; peasants were not, by German standards, unduly oppressed – and indeed were able after 1648 to benefit from a shortage of labour; the armies that had flourished during the war did not become a permanent source of support for the government or for landed families. Ferdinand Maria handled his political problems well. Evading pressure to permit regular meetings of the Estates, he developed the small self-perpetuating committee of 'deputies' that took over the function of granting taxes and petitioning for redress of grievances. A conciliar system of government was soon working efficiently enough, with the usual assortment of specialized councils and local commissaries. Revenue rose, and an active Chancellor, Caspar von Schmid, showed some enthusiasm for reviving the textile and mining industries and encouraging agricultural improvements. But there was no attempt to organise the state for war until the arrival in 1679 of an Elector with dynastic and military ambitions. Maximilian Emmanuel was soon able to claim credit for rescuing the emperor from the Turks at the siege of Vienna; but he then reverted to the alliance with France that proved disastrous in the Spanish Succession War. Bavaria suffered the unexpected punishment of being occupied by Austrian armies. But it was not annexed: the momentary possibility that would have made the Austrian Empire into more of a German state than an eastern one would not have been welcome to the allies at Utrecht.

Saxony had little in common with Bavaria except its remoteness from the sea and its German language. It was, or had been, the richest of the Protestant states in the Empire. Silver and tin had made it the most commercially successful region in eastern Germany. Leipzig and Dresden were thriving cities, exercising enough power in the Estates to compel the landed nobility to make some contribution towards the revenue. The Electors of the Wettin dynasty had managed to get a large share of the profits of the mines into their own hands. Even so, they were glad of any financial assistance they could conveniently arrange from other German states. There was one likely source of support: Saxony's third city, Wittenberg, was the headquarters of Lutheranism. Despite unscrupulous manoeuvres in the days of the Schmalkaldic League, the Electors were seen by Lutherans everywhere as their protectors against the recovery of Catholicism. Any such prospects disappeared in the Thirty Years War, when the opportunist Elector John George I used his armies, eventually, on the imperial side. Though Gustav Adolf had regarded him as the most likely ally in Germany, he proved reluctant to take part in any general Protestant alliance. Even when Saxon forces were fighting in alliance with Sweden, the Elector seemed more concerned to move the war out of his own region than to defeat the emperor. In the end duplicity appeared to pay. In the settlement of 1648 Saxony was allowed to keep the territories of Upper and Lower Lusatia its forces had occupied. Its recovery from the effects of the war was at first quicker than in most areas of fighting. John George seemed to have succeeded in getting rid of the Estates and substituting committees vaguely claiming to be representative, which voted taxes that increased smoothly. But in his last years, far from working to improve the security and unity of Saxony, he was preparing to divide it among his relations. Though no-one doubted that a state could be treated in this way, John George II, on his accession as Elector in 1656, was determined to avoid any division of his inheritance. Largely for that purpose he accepted the pressure of townsmen and landowners to recall the Diet. Amid formidable constitutional entanglements, representative bodies of one sort or another continued until the end of the century to hold a real share in central authority. Taxes were voted for limited periods, and continued to rise without provoking more than manageable resistance. Out of the funds allocated for the forces it was possible to pay for a standing army, with which John George III became another ambitious participant in the war against the Turks. It was a moderately successful demonstration of Saxon military power. The one grievous piece of electoral aggrandisement came in 1697, when Frederick Augustus I became involved in the costly competition for the crown of Poland (see p. 422). He won the prize, but only at the cost of a conversion to Catholicism that angered a nobility already hostile to the demands for still more taxation and involved in disputes with the towns about the extension of excise duties. The century ended with the Estates and the Elector still quarrelling over the rights to levy taxes – in terms that early Stuart parliaments would have understood. It is not easy to see why Saxony escaped the development of military despotism that in Brandenburg was laying the foundations of the future Prussian state.

Saxon Electors were usually better off than those of Brandenburg, but they too spent money on armies; Saxony was about as much involved in wars as Brandenburg. Both governments were constantly harassed by disputes about finance;, and both found excise duties, on alcohol especially, an essential source of funds. In establishing a rich capital city and a spectacular court Saxony had all the advantages. There was certainly a difference in social structure: the Saxon aristocracy was prosperous without relying on state-supported privileges and without being dependent on a magnate élite. Urban communities were strong and assertive; the peasantry was largely free. On the whole it was not a basis for military despotism, even if there had been Electors or ministers who wanted one. Saxon governments seldom sought a fundamental change in their functions. Their bureaucracy did not greatly expand; their armies did not seem likely to gain much by political activity. The Estates never won all they demanded, but efforts to get rid of them were thwarted both by financial necessity and by pressure from the nobility. Stability, in the long run, outweighed dangerous initiative.

THE GREAT ELECTOR

Brandenburg-Prussia was the most accidental of all the large units in Germany. In the early seventeenth century dynastic schemes had worked out well: John Sigismund inherited the Duchy of Prussia as a 'fief' of the Polish Crown, divided from the Electorate by West Pomerania, which was a part of Poland itself, and by East Pomerania which was seized by the Swedes before a Brandenburg claim to inherit it could be enforced. In the west the affair of the Duchies of Jülich and Cleves (see p. 306) was eventually settled by a division that gave Brandenburg an excellent base for provocation and bargaining. At the wrangles in 1648, Brandenburg as a French client did undeservedly well. Schwarzenberg, the brilliant minister of the Elector George William, had used the misfortunes of the war to establish a War Council, predominantly of commoners, as a professional ruling institution. He may well have had ambitions to be one of the great military-political figures of the war. When Frederick William succeeded at the age of twenty in 1640, he was regarded as the enemy of

Schwarzenberg and the bright hope of the landowners, restoring the old Privy Council and negotiating cautiously with the separate Estates in each of his dominions (see pp. 251–2). It involved dissolving Schwarzenberg's army and starting afresh with a force he could hope would be loyal to the Elector alone.

The Great Elector's army of the 1640s was one of the lesser forces in Germany (see pp. 290–1) and his political tergiversations were rapid even by the standards of those years. It was the resumption of war in the north from 1655 to 1660 that enabled Frederick William to establish his military state. The use he made of his army was on the same lines as before: after triumphantly entering Warsaw as the ally and military equal of Charles X of Sweden, he accepted the efforts of Ferdinand III's diplomat Franz von Lisola – a man with almost French standards of conspiratorial skill – to get him to switch to the Polish side. There was no point in taking his soldiers deeper into the east for the benefit of the Swedes. They were not a mercenary force to be discarded when no longer useful but a part of the machinery of the state. The General War Commissariat was a body in which civil government was merged with the administration of the army. Its officers were outside the hierarchies and patronages of the separate dominions, and independent of the Estates. They established themselves so successfully that the Commissariat was able to survive the peace and become the ideal instrument of the Elector's rule. The war had been financed at first as German wars had been in the 1640s – by taking money from those who had it with only perfunctory regard to the theoretical tax on property voted by the diets. To expand the army and the central administration in peacetime would involve a permanent source of revenue. The method that seemed most likely to produce it was an excise of roughly the type on which the Netherlands government appeared to flourish.

The long struggle with the Estates that centred round the question of taxation produced what amounted to a tacit agreement between the government and the landed nobility. The state would demand no sacrifices from them. It would uphold the extension of their power over the peasants and leave them almost sovereign rights over their lands. In return they would support the army and the civil authority without demanding political control. The men who now dominated the Estates of both Brandenburg and Prussia were the lesser nobility – the *Jung-Herrn* or Junkers – who had in many places begun to exploit their lands with great success through new agricultural techniques and investment of capital. Unfree labour and tax-exemption seemed to them necessary to their prosperity and to recovery from the wartime devastation that had completed the ruin of many of the towns.

The process in Brandenburg was absurdly tedious: collective privileges of the Diet still meant more to many representatives of towns and to the nobility than immediate economic benefit. The first effort in 1653 to introduce an excise failed completely. Through the years of war and after the peace in 1660 the government continued to put on all the pressure it could to get a permanent source of revenue. It had to do so by making use of the split between townsmen and nobility that arose originally from the fact that total taxation was supposed to be divided in a fixed proportion between the towns and the tenants of the tax-free nobles. A powerful group of the townsmen saw an excise as the only way of shifting some of the burden off themselves. The outcome of the quarrels was a gradual and complicated extension of the excise system, partly by royal decree. The towns soon had cause to regret the support they had given to it: every device that would have lightened their payments was stopped, and the split in the Estates had enabled the Elector almost to eliminate them as a political force. Town and country quickly became separated by a rigid system of customs barriers, and industries had every incentive to move outside the urban boundaries. The state's economic programme largely disregarded old-style urban power.

The nobility correspondingly benefited from the industries attracted to their territory. Fortunes were alleged to be made from the tax-free inns on their estates. Lucrative offices in the government were still their preserve. But above all the landowners, who had regarded the Elector's wars as no concern of theirs unless their own territory was affected, began to accept military service as a matter of social prestige. A unified landed class was coming to feel that its interests were permanently identified with those of the state. The Elector's well-known economic innovations – the trading companies, the artificially stimulated industries, the land improvements – were in part intended to put Brandenburg on the level of the great powers. To extend serfdom and to welcome refugees from persecution were equally desirable parts of a way of statesmanship that drew no distinction between the well-being of the government and that of the landed class. It is easy to exaggerate the achievement, to stress the 'progress' or the

'Colbertism' in economic life and in 'unification' and forget the hostile and impoverished towns, the tolls and monopolies, the dismal rural poverty. If Frederick William rejoiced that his Prussian territories were now freed from their antiquated status as a 'fief' of Poland, he thought in similar terms himself when he repeatedly amended his elaborate wills to bequeath bits of his supposedly unified state as sovereign principalities for his younger sons. It was only his less celebrated successor Frederick who began to play the part of the Versailles-style monarch.

THE HABSBURG MONARCHY

The Peace of Westphalia had for the time being removed two threats to European stability – that western Europe would be dominated by the Habsburgs and alternatively that their Empire would be dismembered by predatory states inside and outside it. One great anomaly remained undiminished: German states still constituted an Empire with an elected monarch, while the lands claimed by the Habsburgs as their inheritance were a part of eastern Europe rather than of Germany. For the rest of the century Habsburg lands were as much as ever the scene of successive wars. They were, as became urgently apparent, the main defence of Christendom against Turkish invasion by land – though this was more often an opportunity for their European enemies than a stimulus to assistance from their friends. With their three crowns, of Austria, Hungary, and Bohemia, and their multiplicity of peoples, creeds, and languages, they formed a unit manifestly unsuitable for the development of a centralised absolutist state. But the next general settlement, Utrecht, left them with by far the greatest territorial gains of any of the combatants and with a government as secure and efficient as any in Europe. It was also no doubt the beginning of the decline of the Habsburgs; but a decline that went on for the next two hundred years was quite an achievement.

Leopold I was never regarded as one of the epoch-making monarchs. His reign, from 1657 to 1705, is inescapably the 'age' of his cousin and brother-in-law Louis XIV. The wealth and assertiveness of France, the 'Gallomania' of the time, and the French culture that upheld it left little opportunity for Austrian influence in the west. The imperial court at the Hofburg, on a restricted site in a Vienna that was not then regarded as one of the great cities of Europe, was a very inferior imitation of Versailles. Leopold was not among the most industrious crowned bureaucrats. He hunted, like the rest of them; but he also composed and performed music, collected pictures, and read widely. The thousands of letters he wrote in Italian, German, and Latin show that, though he had no great political initiative, he was never out of touch. Above all he was a fanatical Catholic, convinced of his mission to destroy Protestantism. He was of course poorer than Louis XIV. While French bribes were a constant, if sometimes exaggerated, influence on the politics of the Empire, Leopold's money seldom got further afield than the Electors and their officials. He could not prevent the sinister activities in Vienna of foreign diplomats who cultivated their own parties at his court. Louis XIV aimed simultaneously at having a group of client states within the Empire, encouraging dissention in Hungary especially, and yet keeping the alliance of the emperor himself. It was evident that France had a growing body of enemies in Vienna.

Leopold succeeded without difficulty to the nominally elective crowns of Royal Hungary and of Bohemia. The Empire was a different matter. Though the possibility of a non-Habsburg emperor was remote, it was just conceivable enough for the Electors, under French influence, to extract unusually onerous conditions, as well as bribes, for accepting Leopold. He was not to support Spain in the still unfinished war against France, and in a variety of ways he was to uphold local rulers against their Estates. He also had to accept the existence of the French-sponsored 'League of the Rhine'. It lasted only ten years; it included, even when the Elector of Brandenburg eventually joined it, a minority of princes; and it became more and more openly an instrument of French penetration. But it was also, in a small way an attempt to create, within a political system shaped by conflict between the states, a German organization that would keep internal order. The Elector of Mainz, Philip von Schönborn, gave it a permanent headquarters in Frankfurt, and an army that might someday compare with those of the great powers. To Leopold it was merely one more alliance between the princes and his foreign enemies, and one more reason for turning away from Germany and towards the east. The 'German Party' in Vienna was no match for either the French or the Spanish.

To some extent the Holy Roman Empire could function independently. From 1633 the Imperial Diet at Regensburg was
deemed to be in permanent session. Its long and trivial deliberations made it a laughing-stock in Europe. Nevertheless its support
was worth keeping. It continued to vote money to the emperor
who claimed, as Elector of Bohemia, to be a member of the first
of its three houses. (In 1692 Leopold on his own authority created
the Electorate of Hanover to make a ninth seat.) The Diet had no
means of enforcing its decisions on the princes who formed the
second house, or on the Free Cities who formed the third. Yet
despite its inefficiency and its devotion to the particularist interests
of its members, it provided men and money for imperial wars in
increasing amounts. In 1681 it was laid down that an army of
60,000 should be raised. For the Spanish Succession War the
number was raised to 120,000. In theory contributions were
shared out among the ten 'Circles' that were supposed to join
states and cities to form administrative units of the Empire. In
practice it was from the western circles, and that of Bavaria, that
imperial forces came.

The states that gave support to the Empire naturally expected
to maintain their share in the chaotic mixture of governing institutions in Vienna that confronted Leopold on his accession. The
innermost policy-making body, the *Geheimer Rat* or secret
council, consisted of half a dozen ministers or courtiers, rarely
German in origin. Its leader was the *Oberhofmeister*, a title significantly meaning master of the court, not of the government.
There was a treasury, the *Hofkammer*, which sought to intervene
in everything; and there was the war council, the *Hofkriegsrat*
which sometimes extended its interest from military to diplomatic
matters. The complexities arose from the existence of overlapping
and rival bodies. The 'Court' or 'Austrian' Chancery, the *Hofkanz-
lei* and the 'Imperial' Chancery (*Reichskanzlei*) had much the
same administrative powers, and neither readily accepted territorial limitations. The *Reichshofrat*, with a name that seemed to
attach it to both the Austrian court and the German Empire,
claimed to deal with disputed powers, but had its own rival, the
Reichskammergericht. The aim of building up Habsburg-controlled
institutions at the expense of German ones was achieved partly
by splitting up the less amenable bodies into committees and
inserting non-German officers when the chance arose. Much
depended on a few active ministers. Wenzel Lobkowicz, a Czech

prince who presided over the war council, also became the *Ober-hofmeister* in the *Geheimer Rat*. In 1674, when his by then too openly pro-French policies led to his dismissal, he was succeeded by an Italian marquis. Below the highest level, central adminis-tration was run by an assortment of office-holders drawn from the lesser nobility and occasionally the merchant communities of every part of the Habsburg dominions. Increasingly, and at every level, clergy were involved in government: to Leopold church and state alike ruled his peoples.

Behind all the complexities of administration and diplomacy lay the one consistent purpose of Leopold's regime. The Catholic Church must be restored not only to a monopoly of religious belief but to a position from which it would uphold the monarchy and the existing social structure without question. It was to be the completion of a process that had developed all through the century. The attack on Protestantism in Austria had begun even before the Thirty Years War. Threats that lands could be confis-cated, and promises that the return of Catholicism did not mean that the Church would reclaim all its lost estates, had brought many Austrian landowners, and hence their parish churches, back to the religion some of them had abandoned only recently. In Bohemia the restoration of Catholicism had been part of the outright destruction of Czech society (see p. 340). Even in Hungary and Transylvania, where Calvinism had won promises of toleration, there had been some progress in establishing Cath-olic landlords. Under Leopold no compromises and no under-ground Protestantism would be allowed. His was a campaign to inculcate absolute faith and obedience. Parish priests, of whom there were not enough, bishops, and the Papacy itself were seldom as zealous as the emperor wished. It was the Jesuits and sometimes Franciscan and Dominican orders, who undertook the main tasks of organizing the great conversion campaigns. Submission to the Papacy was not emphasized too much: the central feature was the cult of the Virgin Mary, whose pictures and statues proliferated everywhere. The one theological doctrine that became the test of orthodoxy was that of the Immaculate Conception (see pp. 132–3). Though cardinals and professors continued to argue about a notion that could not easily be supported by scripture, Bohemian, Hungarian, and Slovak peas-ants responded enthusiastically to it. Protestantism had nothing comparable to offer. In other matters the Jesuits, as always, were realists. While the mass was conducted in Latin and government business often in German, Jesuit preachers knew the value of local languages. They were even ready, sometimes, to defend villagers against indiscriminate punishments. By a mixture of propaganda and ruthlessness, Leopold's ambitions were achieved: unlike anywhere else in Europe, regions that had been Protestant in 1660 were reclaimed permanently for Catholicism.

HUNGARY, THE TURKS AND THE WEST

The frontier between the Habsburg Empire and that of the sultan was now formed by the narrow remnant of the Hungarian kingdom which the Habsburgs had acquired through the marriage of Ferdinand I. To the south it was more or less united with the kingdom of Croatia, which gave it a few miles of Adriatic coast; to the north was the principality of Transylvania, ruled – when the Turks relaxed their hold – by Hungarian magnates chosen in theory by its Diet. In 1660 George Rákóczy II was struggling to keep his throne. The imminent threat of further conquest by the Turks and the remote prospect of regaining the rich lands of the old Hungarian kingdom dominated the lives of the landed families. This was above all others a land of great aristocrats. Thirty or forty families, including an inner circle of ten, owned the land, formed in effect the representative assemblies, controlled the law and the economy. The Esterházys, who in 1687 were given the title of Prince of the Empire, were recognized as the top magnates, though like many of the others they had risen only in the last hundred years. The Zrinyi in Croatia, the solidly loyal Pálffys, and the Nádasdys who rebelled in 1671 had estates almost as big. It was through the great families that the triumph of the Catholic Church was achieved. In 1600 many of the magnates were still Protestant. The collapse of Protestantism in Bohemia and the firm alignment of the Empire may have helped the great majority of them to be converted; and with all the zeal of the convert they worked for the establishment of a powerful Catholic Church. Monastic orders were patronized; churches, schools, and colleges were built; ancient shrines appeared mysteriously where none had been before. The cult of St Stephen upheld glorious memories of Hungary's medieval traditions.

The campaign was not simple. However readily the magnates accepted Catholicism, it could not expect an easy victory in the towns and villages. Transylvania under Gabriel Bethlen had been an outpost of Calvinism. Heinrich Bisterfeld, a puritan scholar and a friend of Hartlib, became the leader of a radical Protestant movement encouraged by the anti-Habsburg rulers. In the 1640s the familiar schisms had appeared between a left wing, in touch with English Independents, and the more cautious episcopal puritanism that George Rákóczy was prepared to uphold. Puritan pamphlets and preaching spread into the market-towns and villages of Hungary; Hungarian students travelled to the universities of the west, and brought back news of revolutions. Rákóczy, with some hesitations about dealing with regicides, sent envoys to Cromwell to discuss the idea of a Protestant Union. But an alliance between western radicalism and Hungarian aristocracy was too improbable to concern the Vienna government much.

The other great contribution of the Hungarian magnates to the Empire was the day-to-day defence against Turkish incursions. Many of the richest estates were within easy reach of Turkish raiding parties or of more serious invasions; and the castles of their owners were fortresses with garrisons of retainers. A whole 'frontier culture' had developed, in which the luxury of the great house and its court was combined with the life of the warrior chief. It was always uncertain how far the emperor and his council would support these defenders of his realm. The fate of Transylvania did not encourage the Hungarians. In 1661 George Rákóczy was killed in a desperate battle against a formidable Turkish invasion that he had fought with little help for three years. Only then did Leopold send an army, under his successful General Raimondo Montecuccoli. It was too late to save Transylvania from complete Turkish control. In the spring of 1663 the huge forces of Ahmed Kiuprili began to move rapidly towards Vienna. Imperial envoys were sent round the capitals of Europe to plead for help. For a moment the almost inconceivable happened: Louis XIV, Philip IV, the Pope, the Great Elector, and a variety of other German rulers – including those in the League of the Rhine – united in sending men or money or both in the cause of Christianity. Louis XIV, though he gave up the idea of leading the enterprise, sent 6,000 of his best soldiers. In 1664 their victory at St Gotthard, fifty miles from Vienna, ended the immediate danger. Crusading enthusiasm disappeared when the emperor hastened to make the

Peace of Vasvar. By this Transylvania, under Turkish suzerainty, was demilitarized and the Turks kept the vital fortresses on which imperial defences had previously relied. Hungary was to remain divided between Austrian and Turkish rulers.

Leopold and his council, which it was noticed seldom included Hungarians, were now felt in Hungary as in the west to have betrayed the cause of Christian (and aristocratic) security. They had, it was suspected abandoned the war partly because they preferred a divided Hungary to a free and united one, partly because the succession question in Spain was becoming more important to them than the interests of their subjects in the east. The rebellion that was initiated by a small group of landowners was half-hearted and inefficient (see p. 275). But it provided the opportunity to treat the Hungarians almost as the Czechs had been treated after 1620. An army of occupation was permanently quartered on the country; estates were confiscated and sold or given to Austrian and other foreign owners. Local privileges were suppressed. Three outstanding magnates, Nádasdny, Zrinyi, and Frangepan, were executed. It brought to the surface the hostility, in every social group, to 'Germans', as the Austrians were generally called. A ruling council, the *gubernium*, consisted half of Hungarians and half of the other nationalities of the Empire. It was a generally passive instrument of the real ruler, Johann Ampringen. He was not the most effective of dictators. Years of sporadic resistance and economic depression produced, in 1679, renewed revolt, with an aristocratic leader who drew in support from all but the most loyal of Catholic families. Imre Thököli was the young protestant son of a family with close Catholic connections. The army he raised in the north-east of Hungary with unofficial help from France and Poland threatened to start a real civil war, until in 1681 Leopold called a meeting of the Hungarian Estates and announced a new constitution that restored the powers of the landowners. There was even some relaxation of the laws against Protestantism. Some of Thököli's Catholic supporters were happy to return to the Habsburg side; but nothing that renewed the old authority of magnate families was likely to appeal to townsmen or peasants. The *kurucok* army – a name originally meaning 'crusaders' – grew; and in what to many of its original sponsors seemed an astonishing betrayal, Thököli negotiated with the Pasha of Buda to plan a joint attack on Hungary by the rebels and the Turks. It was not an alliance that could last for long. But it provided an illustration far removed from western diplomacy of the unlimited propensity of military and political leaders to make agreements completely contrary to their proclaimed ideals. Thököli could claim that his ultimate purpose was a Hungary freed alike from Turks and Habsburgs; and briefly in 1682 he was accepted by both as ruler of a large part of the kingdom. The Turks were preparing their great attack on Europe; and the emperor had made a satisfactory realignment in the west.

Until 1672 the 'French' faction at Leopold's court had been dominant. Lobkowicz as its leader could convincingly claim that peace with the strongest western power was essential for success in the east. There was also the distant question of the Spanish Crown. But when the French occupied Lorraine, which was at least in name part of Leopold's German Empire, the arguments of his leading diplomat, François Lisola, that he should construct an anti-French alliance were irresistible. For the next six years most of Leopold's resources were devoted to the defeat of France. The Protestant Electors, as well as the Dutch, became his allies. Their envoys to Vienna, along with those of Spain, tried hard to establish hostility to France as a permanent imperial policy. But when the Peace of Nymegen removed the immediate dangers, it was again the Turks who seemed a more potent enemy. In 1683 they launched their new attack. Leopold tried until the last moment to buy them off. When the huge invading armies were on their march his role as the defender of Christendom was thrust upon him. For three horrifying months Vienna was besieged. This time there was no Christian alliance. The French tried in vain to extract conditions for doing nothing. Of all the foreign powers only John Sobiesky and the Polish Diet thought the danger to their own country great enough to justify sending an army, paid for almost wholly by the Empire. Within Germany negotiations with Brandenburg broke down on the question of price. Bavaria was already committed to provide help against the Turks in return for subsidies. The Elector of Saxony, with a large unemployed army, was glad to lead it himself to be fed and billeted in Austria. Only when the worst danger was over did Innocent III announce his 'Holy League' for the salvation of Christian Europe. The only power he was able to bring into formal alliance with the Empire was Vēnice. But the Church's propaganda was not addressed solely to governments. Its own financial resources were poured into the crusade. From all over Europe money and volunteers were contributed. In 1686 Russia joined the League. Only France, England, and the Netherlands firmly resisted the appeals. The League could soon claim that it had ended once and for all the threat of the infidel in central Europe. Leopold's response to the liberation of Hungary from Ottoman power was to re-establish his own authority. In 1687, when the allied armies had recaptured Buda and again heavily defeated the Turks at Nagyharsány, near Mohacs, the Hungarian Estates were made to declare that the throne was now hereditary (Sobiesky was suspected of having an eye on it) and that the medieval notion of a right of resistance to kings who did not observe the liberties of the nobility was repudiated.

LEOPOLD AND THE SPANISH SUCCESSION

It might have been supposed that the victories over the sultan's most powerful assault on Europe would have made Leopold the monarch of a triumphant Empire. While Louis XIV was spending vast sums of his subjects' money on capturing a few patches of Rhineland territory, Leopold by the end of the century recovered Hungary, Transylvania, and a large part of Serbia. It was not easy: in 1690 the Turks recaptured Belgrade, and imperial forces in the Danube region were in a more or less permanent state of war. Frederick Augustus of Saxony and then Prince Eugen of Savoy were commanders who took charge of the campaigns without much regard to orders from Vienna. By getting more and more deeply entangled in the claims to the Spanish inheritance, Leopold again made the western diplomatic game rather than the great east European Empire the principal use for his resources and energy.

In 1684 Leopold's Spanish schemes were changed by the birth of his second son, significantly named Charles. Since he would not, presumably, inherit the Empire, it seemed possible that the monarchs who would reject any idea of reuniting Spain with the possessions of the Austrian Habsburgs could be manoeuvred into accepting the lesser family link. To Charles, it was proclaimed in Vienna, were transferred the rights claimed under the will of Philip IV by Leopold's daughter Maria Antonia, wife of the

Elector of Bavaria. This the Spaniards especially regarded as cheating: Maria Antonia in 1692 produced a son to whom her alleged inheritance ought to go. The efforts to establish in Madrid an 'Austrian' party to uphold Leopold's interests were badly bungled; and there was little prospect of reaching any agreement with Louis XIV – who, like Leopold, was Philip III's grandson. Protestant powers saw little to choose between the pretensions of Leopold and Louis XIV's dreams of putting a Bourbon candidate on the Spanish throne. But in the end it was Louis whose greed proved the more realistic. One partition treaty giving most Spanish possessions to the Bavarian, Joseph Ferdinand, with some Italian territory for the Dauphin was ruined when Joseph Ferdinand died. A second was making progress when Charles II, still implacably alive, made a new will leaving it all to Louis' younger grandson Philip. It might seem to be a piece of harmless comedy revealing the childish behaviour that was disguised in pompous diplomatic exchanges; but from this there arose the war that brought the most prolonged and destructive international fighting of the time.

Of all the participants in the Spanish Succession entanglements Leopold alone was interrupted in his machinations by repeated rebellions on the part of some of the subjects whose lives could be changed by a marriage, a testament, or a treaty in some far-off capital. It was not of course any awareness of the struggles to choose a king of Spain that made another Hungarian magnate organize, in 1703, the biggest rebellion so far. Ferenc (Francis) Rákóczi, grandson of the George Rákóczi who had lost Transylvania to the Turks, had inherited estates in Hungary which the family had continued to build up until they were possibly even bigger than those of the Esterházys. Leadership of the *kurucok* army had come to him not through any Cromwellian qualities but because he was the stepson of Thököli. The alliance of his fellow Catholic magnates with whom he embarked on a new challenge to the Habsburgs in Leopold's dying years was as unreliable as those of earlier generations. Once the rebellion had brought in independent peasant forces and Transylvanian Calvinists it was unacceptable to those with everything to lose if the security of law and inheritance broke down. When a new emperor, Joseph I, succeeded Leopold in 1705 the rebellion had ceased to alarm the Viennese court. A few constitutional promises were enough to ensure that when Joseph died in 1711 his brother

Charles VI was crowned amid the loyal plaudits of the magnates as King of Hungary.

ITALY AND THE NEW EMPIRE

Ever since the retreat of the Turks after the siege, the emperors and their entourage in Vienna had preferred to treat the east as a secondary concern. Inevitably the dynasty was at the centre of the continuing Spanish Succession turmoils and of the wars against France. Agreements about Spain itself seemed fated to break down through one mishap or another in the lives of European royalty. The Austrian contribution to the chaos came when Joseph I failed to produce a son, or even a daughter, and the Archduke Charles consequently inherited the Empire at a time when he was claiming to be Charles III of Spain. In 1705 he had taken advantage of Catalonia's hostility to government from Madrid by landing, with the help of English and Dutch warships, at Barcelona and proclaiming it as his capital. He had also been welcomed in the Spanish Netherlands. But the one territory that the allies had been prepared for him to keep was the Duchy of Milan. Italy was an easier and more profitable region for the almost bankrupt Austrian government to occupy in his name. In spite of the economic decline it would be a profitable source of taxation and a place where armies could live off the country. The invasion of northern Italy was begun in 1701 under the leadership of the best general the Empire had employed since Wallenstein. Prince Eugen of Savoy, son of Mazarin's niece, had been trained as a priest, applied unsuccessfully to Louis XIV to be enlisted in the French army, and in 1683 offered his services to Leopold instead – a common enough attitude to the Church and to nationality. His organization of the campaign against French forces in Italy was a startling success; but it was part of the swiftly moving career that took him to the Turkish frontier, to Vienna as President of the War Council, and to all the major battles on the French frontiers. Without him the army in Italy moved slowly southward: in 1707 it captured Naples, and by the time of the Utrecht negotiations it had occupied the whole of southern Italy. Charles VI insisted that Italy was his by right rather than by conquest. The regions under imperial control were probably better treated than they had been by Spanish governors, though such trivialities were not of much concern to diplomats in the intricate negotiations that produced the Utrecht settlement (see pp. 525–7). The Austrian technique in these was generally to refuse subtle bargaining and insist that what they had they held; and at the separate Treaty of Rastatt that settled their claims an Empire was established larger and more diverse than the western allies had contemplated. With miscellaneous legalistic reservations, the southern Netherlands, the Milanese, all Italy south of the Papal States, and Sardinia (which was later exchanged for Sicily) became the hereditary lands of the Austrian Habsburgs. But there had been no revival of the Holy Roman Empire. The Austria that on the map looked so extensive was now, in Germany, one of two states that were to confront each other for the next century. In 1700 the Elector Frederick of Brandenburg had sold his support to Leopold in return for the apparently harmless recognition of the title of King of Prussia. Northern Germany, Protestant, military, and increasingly prosperous, had gone for ever outside the Habsburg sphere.

15

SPAIN

The Spain of which Philip III became king in 1598 had been united under a single monarch since 1580, and remained so until 1640. But Portugal, joined to Castile in much the way that Aragon had been a century earlier, kept its separate institutions and economy; in Aragon rebellion aiming at separation had been finally defeated in 1572. The Netherlands war now left little hope of recovering the richest provinces there. The treasury was empty, the armed forces outmoded, the government corrupt, incompetent, and insecure. Between a peasantry kept down to subsistence level and the great consumers of riches there was hardly any commercial or industrial class making use of the opportunities for profit and investment that the colonial empire provided. The only consistently prosperous institution was the Church. Yet Philip III's empire was incomparably the most populous in the world, comprising virtually the entire continent of South America and a multitude of settlements in Asia and Africa. The paradoxes were scarcely noticed. It seemed that a long reign of strife could be followed by one of stability and – for those at the top – of luxury.

PHILIP III AND LERMA

The stern old bureaucrat-king whose personal decisions had dominated Spanish government was replaced by a young sovereign with comparatively little capacity or inclination for work.

Philip III's interest turned in time from the luxury of the court to priests and miracle-working relics. At either stage the way was open for the rule of a minister; and it was on the conduct of ministers that the country's political fate now depended. The first of them, Francisco de Sandoval y Rohas, Duke of Lerma, was one of the aristocratic politicians whose success did not involve much beyond amassing power and wealth for himself and his dependants. His position at court was one that in other countries was familiar but not so blatantly recognized: he was the *privado* or *valido*, the favourite of the king. In one form or another enormous grants from Crown property found their way to him to his family. It naturally meant that he encouraged the central institutions that were within his patronage at the expense of provincial ones. The King's Council of State was still an active administrative body composed mainly of the old aristocracy with a few newly risen office-holders; but more and more of its work was delegated to smaller groups: the inevitable rivalries among them grew (see p. 244). The most startling change was that for long periods neither Lerma nor the king took part in the daily work of government. Philip and his court travelled through the provinces and demanded hospitality from the high nobility. Valladolid became the main residence of the monarch while the government institutions remained in Madrid. So too did the Castilian Cortes, which survived as one means of raising money by taxation. There were, as almost everywhere, two categories of increasing expenditure; one was the central government together with the court; the other was the armed forces, including those subsidized but not employed by Spain. Much of the cost of the court was in fact not spent on collective splendour but on the place-holders and bribe-takers who devoted it to their own estates and households. Lerma's personal fortune was reckoned at twice the annual revenue of the Crown. After Philip II's successive repudiations of Crown debts, no-one could suppose that gold and silver imports – which in any case had only produced a quarter of the revenue – were an inexhaustible source of funds. Taxes, particularly the *alcabala*, the 10 per cent sales tax, were absorbed by tax-farming and corruption. The *millones*, the levies on wine, meat, and oil that had been introduced at the time of the Armada, were administered more effectively, though there were still ways in which the nobility evaded payment. The Spanish Crown joined in the now familiar process of living by selling things – its own lands, offices, and privileges. Occassional promises of more equal burdens on the provinces and genuine taxation of the rich were not fulfilled.

The most startling decision of Lerma's ministry was to expel from Spain the people who were the most economically assiduous part of the community. The Moriscoes had, after attempting repeated insurrections in the middle decades of the sixteenth century, been deliberately dispersed by Philip II over the southern half of Spain. They had been accused of secretly adhering to the Moslem faith, avoiding taxation – largely by not drinking – helping the Barbary pirates, and being too prosperous. They were not allowed to own land, though some still held it on long leases and by good technique and labour made it profitable to both landlord and lessee. They were excluded from office and were unwelcome in commercial activities. However remote their connection with the Turks, they were an ideal target for racial and national hatred. In 1609 there began the series of decrees that expelled them first from Valencia, where they formed an organized community amounting to perhaps a third of the population, and then from their more scattered centres. Most of the quarter million who left probably died in North Africa from poverty and persecution. It was a spectacular blunder; and though its eventual contribution to economic failures may have been exaggerated the loss of labour and rents in Valencia was an immediate disaster.

The expulsion of the Moriscoes brought to perfection the one great source of Spanish unity – the relentless grip of the Church on every activity, individual or communal. The Inquisition now had few serious doctrinal errors to punish: it spent much of its time on blasphemy, rural witchcraft and such illicit contacts with foreign culture as the import of books. It became not so much a religious body as a political police, imposing in its own courts a totalitarianism as efficient as any Europe had known. The clergy, poor though many were, formed a privileged Estate extracting even more of the country's resources than the court. With the occupants of an enormous number of monasteries and nunneries added to the parish priests, they were the only occupational group that was thriving and expanding. (The Castilian Cortes was told in 1626 that there were 9,000 monastic institutions for men.) Education and charity were their monopolies; popular anti-clericalism hardly existed until the later part of the century. There was much to be said for the life that religious orders could offer the individual compared with his prospects outside, but little for their effect on the economy of the country. They may even have been an appreciable factor in the decline of population.

THE REFORMS OF OLIVARES

The one mitigation of the evils of royal courts was that a brilliant politician could usually make his way to the top if he tried. Incompetent favourites tended eventually to be overthrown by competent ones. While Philip III, desperately ill, was calling for the corpses of saints to diminish his prospects of eternal damnation, a palace conspiracy replaced Lerma in 1618 by his son the Duke of Uceda. The immediate difference was imperceptible; but in Uceda's gang was Gaspar de Guzman, Count of Olivares and Duke of Sanlúcar, the ambitious son of one of Philip II's former viceroys. When the king died in 1621, his sixteen-year-old son Philip IV was firmly under the control of the clever and hardworking statesman who was the real successor of Philip II. The 'Count-Duke' combined with his lust for power a manicdepressive instability of temperament; but he supervised the new monarch constantly, accompanying him throughout his days of work and ceremony and his nights of varied entertainment. The Lerma family and its hangers-on were disgraced, imprisoned, or exiled. Olivares at once became the hope of the *arbitristas* (see p. 224). In contrast to the inertia that had been the normal way of life in every part of the government, he was known to have a 'zeal for reformation' and a determination to revitalize the monarchy to which he was intensely loyal. Whether the revitalizing was to be more for the benefit of the Spanish people or of Spain's imperial glory was not certain.

Cautiously, Olivares began to erode the worst privileges that made the idleness and pride of Spaniards proverbial. The Church was made to pay a bigger share of taxation; its acquisition of land was restricted. The Inquisition felt that its political power was being undermined, and became a dangerous enemy of Olivares. He made no secret of his intention to curtail drastically court extravagance, the multiplication of offices, the whole corrupt and parasitic idleness of the aristocracy. The one celebrated success in his sumptuary laws was in banning the ruff, the ludicrously expensive status-symbol of its day. (An acceptable substitute was produced from cardboard, said to last for a year without washing.) To take away the uniform of a social group does much to destroy its exclusiveness, and the action was at least a symbol that the great days of the grandees were ending. But of the numerous other reforms produced with the help of the long-established *Junta de Reformacion*, most were soon evaded. A miscellany of royal decrees reduced the numbers of office-holders, restricted their retinues, investigated their more flagrant forms of enrichment, and sent a good many back to their estates. There could not of course be an open attack on the privileges of nobility as such. Perhaps a fifth of the population was included in the well-demarcated ranks that ranged from their Excellencies the Grandees of the court to the provincial hidalgos, and the sale of honours was constantly increasing their number. Yet gradually, and without diminishing the demand for titles, Olivares was able to evade the aristocracy's exemption from taxation. The Cortes of Castile successfully opposed his schemes for a national and a complete reform of the fiscal system that would have replaced the *millones* by new direct taxes. Some of his measures hit the few native merchants so hard that they were blamed for the final collapse of the commercial activities he claimed to be encouraging. Long-term projects, ranging from the improvement of communications to restricting the teaching of Latin in order to limit the number of unproductive careers, had little serious effect. His economic achievement was not to increase the total wealth but to allow more of it to be wasted by the state and less by the individual.

If the country could not be saved from poverty, it might at least be better governed. Olivares' political ideas, set out in his memorandum to the king in 1624, amounted to a practical instead of a bogus centralisation. Though the 'liberties' of other provinces would have to be curtailed and uniform laws imposed, the programme was not to be merely 'Castilianization'. The whole country must share the benefits of strong government as well as the obligations. Offices should be open more freely to non-Castilians. Intermarriage between families from different provinces should be encouraged. Philip should become more effectively the King of all Spain and of its possessions, with a residence in each part of the peninsula; and in his absence viceroys should be his personal servants unconnected with the region they governed. An essential part of the reform would be the 'Union of Arms': all the king's dominions, including even the Indies, were to contribute to a reserve army, part of which would be immediately available for whatever region was attacked. The most effective reform was the further reduction in the powers of the old councils, efficient instruments of administration under Philip II, but now increasingly in the hands of nobles and hidalgos who bought their places. The Council of State itself lost most of its real powers to the *Junta de Ejecucion*, drawn from the highest court nobility, and for every new administrative task a special Junta was set up, directly responsible to Olivares. These reforms too had only limited success. Few of the men at the top took kindly to the imposition of virtuous ways; Olivares' own group of dependants, though less vicious than Lerma's, became as ridden with patronage and favouritism; the Cortes of Aragon, Catalonia, and Valencia were roused to the defence of their privileges. But as usual the final obstacle to good government was foreign war.

SPAIN IN EUROPE

The 'Spain' seen by foreign peoples and rulers was not the 'Spain' seen by a Castilian courtier or an Andalusian peasant. Internal poverty was in part the price of external success, and there was no apparent decline in the amount Spanish governments could spend on foreign enterprises. The servants of the Spanish Crown outside the peninsula worked in a very different tradition from that of the Madrid court: their reward was the power they built in the country or province allotted to them, and it was this service that attracted most of the gifted politicians. Sometimes European politics still seemed to be managed by the viceroys and ambassadors of Spain. Gondomar in England, Zúñiga and Oñate, successive ambassadors to the emperor in Prague, Bedmar, ambassador in Venice, and Feria, Governor of Milan, were men at the summit of international politics. Spinola was respected even by his enemies as the greatest expert on war. They had no need to consider very deeply what cause they were serving. In Philip III's view it was more that of the dynasty than of the nation – the scoring of points for the Habsburg side against its enemies. Those who wished could easily equate this with furthering the triumph of the Catholic faith. Neither Philip nor Lerma wanted to assert

Spanish power at the cost of further involvement in European war. They were ready enough to abandon the struggle in the Netherlands as soon as it could be done without excessive humiliation. But they lacked both the ability and the effort that would have been needed to maintain a pacific policy within a diplomatic system whose purpose was to win allies for war. Spaniards abroad were preparing for a new age of military glory.

For the time being their schemes had to be developed slowly in face of strong resistance and suspicion. Though the Stuart regime appeared to have ended the Elizabethan tradition of Protestant war, Gondomar never quite succeeded in establishing the secure dominance of a 'Spanish Party' in James I's government. At the French court Spain could encourage and organize opposition to Henri IV; but French pressure during the negotiations for the Netherlands truce made its terms more favourable to the Dutch. Discussions about a marriage alliance between France and Spain were broken off, and only the death of Henri IV in 1610 averted a war. The regency that followed was much more amenable to Spanish influence: in 1612 the double marriage between the children of the two royal houses was agreed (see p. 309). The defensive alliance that accompanied the marriage agreement provided for mutual help against rebels as well as foreign enemies. It was naturally in Prague, for the time being the effective capital of the Empire, that Spanish power was most firmly established. Zúñiga was deeply involved in the formation of the Catholic League. In his view it was to be no mere alliance of German states but the core of a great European system to which the pope, the emperor, and the Spanish king would contribute in their different ways. His successor Oñate took the decisive step of offering Spanish support to Ferdinand of Styria as a candidate for the imperial throne (see p. 336). On Ferdinand's accession, Oñate became his principal adviser, and in alliance with the emperor's Jesuit confessor filled him with the notion of triumphant war for the Church and the Habsburgs. Philip III was not so sure of its benefits.

THE SOUTHERN NETHERLANDS

In 1621 the new king and the new minister found themselves committed to a more aggressive policy without having planned it, but equally without any desire to resume what seemed the discredited inactivity of Philip III. The Bohemian revolt had added to the difficulty of renewing the Netherlands truce that expired at the moment of Philip's death. The Orange party in the north was eager to take part in the Protestant war; the Portuguese had long been pressing for revenge on the Dutch for their unscrupulous commercial expansion and piracy during the truce; the large armies maintained in the southern Netherlands had, not surprisingly, cost almost as much in peace as in war. Spinola was convinced that success in a new war would depend even more than before on the transport of men and money from northern Italy. The route that began in the Valtelline included the fifty miles of the Rhine controlled by the Elector Palatine; and it was a stroke of luck that Frederick involved himself in war with the emperor. Spain could now invade the Palatinate and contribute to the imperial cause without sending troops outside her immediate sphere of interest. Their success would still depend heavily on the resources of the southern Netherlands. There the Archduke Albert and his wife Isabella, sister of Philip III, were nominally independent sovereigns of the Netherlands. When Albert died in 1621, Isabella remained as regent, but was expected to be no more than a viceroy of the Spanish king. By Spain's low standards, the Netherlands were well governed. Because of the obvious dangers in provoking a new rebellion the burden of taxation was not outrageous, and the administration became what Pirenne was to call a 'modified absolutism'. The principal offices were held by Spaniards and important matters were referred to a committee in Madrid which usually failed to settle them; but on minor questions a good deal of autonomy was allowed. Under Albert the Spaniards held the support of the rural gentry and nobility, good Catholics and enemies of the suspect townsmen, contented with rising rents and reliable markets. Olivares was as anxious to reduce the powers of the Netherlands Council and of Isabella as he was those of the provinces of the peninsula itself. Between 1629 and 1632 hostility to Spain became widespread: losses caused by the renewed war, and the beginnings of tighter Spanish control, led to attempts at rebellion by groups of nobles with some popular support. They were prevented from growing into a national rising largely by the initiative of Isabella, who ignored instructions from Madrid and summoned a States-

General, where arguments and petitions gave time for the revolt to fade away.

SPAIN AGAINST FRANCE

At this stage Spanish forces were at least holding their own. Funds had been provided, largely by the minting of twenty million ducats in *vellón* – which now meant pure copper – for a great increase in the armies and the navy. Spinola's capture of Breda in 1625, after nearly a year's siege, and the defeat of a Dutch fleet off Gibraltar in 1626 suggested that Spain was far from collapse. Amid a tangle of diplomatic bickerings with the emperor and Maximilian of Bavaria, Spanish forces remained in occupation of a large part of the Palatinate, and English support for the Protestant cause there ended with a ludicrous attempt to attack Cadiz. Yet there remained a world of difference between the real Spain, staving off a financial and administrative collapse, and the Spain envisaged by Richelieu as a menace to the rest of Europe. Olivares had even better reason than Richelieu to avoid a major war; but neither could back out of the local territorial conflicts. The more dependent the Madrid government became on the money and troops it could raise outside the peninsula, the greater the need to prevent French encroachment on the fortresses and the lines of communication. The episodes of the Valtelline in 1621 and Mantua in 1628 developed without any firm plan either for limiting or for extending them (see pp. 321–2). Spinola from the Netherlands and Córdoba, the Governor of Milan, were left to their own devices in a dreary and unsuccessful campaign that could easily be used as evidence of continued Spanish aggressive designs. By the time the Treaty of Cherasco in 1631 registered the Spanish defeat, both sides were acting on the assumption that a major war was the inevitable next stage. More money had to be found for the forces in Italy; the Empire had to be supported in its worst years of danger from Protestant attack; the struggle in the Netherlands had to go on. It meant making the non-Castilian provinces contribute more than ever before to the cost of wars that seemed to bring them only misery.

In 1634 a new saviour of the Spanish Netherlands was found – Philip IV's brother Ferdinand, the Cardinal-Infant whose influence Olivares was glad to remove from Madrid. It was his army, on its way north, that won the victory at Nordlingen which made possible the restoration of Habsburg control in southern Germany (see p. 353). But the success had disastrous consequences. It confirmed Richelieu's decision that he would soon have to intervene openly in the war; and that the forces of Spain were a greater threat than those of the emperor (see pp. 323–4). He did not plan to attack Spain itself, which might induce the Catalans at least to contribute more readily to the cost of the war, and would be a bad risk with no-one to share it. He preferred to attack the whole strategic line from Italy to the Netherlands. In the first years of the war Spain on balance did well. Rohan in 1635 drove Spanish forces out of the Valtelline, but only at the cost of so alienating the Grey Leagues that eventually they defeated the army of occupation and agreed to give Spain access to the valley in return for guarantees of religious liberty. In the north the Cardinal-Infant, with German reinforcements, occupied territory as far west as the Somme, and made Paris itself expect a siege. But gradually the slightly greater efficiency of Richelieu's France in the organization of war had its effect. The vital fortresses of Breda, on the Netherlands dividing-line, and Breisach, on the upper Rhine, were lost, and the fleet was all but destroyed by Tromp. By 1639 both the land and the sea-routes to the Netherlands were cut. Once Spanish support seemed to be useless, the emperor abandoned dynastic solidarity and concentrated on saving his own power in Germany, leaving Olivares to think bitterly of the Spanish funds that had paid imperial soldiers. The project for an invasion of France from Catalonia, which Olivares hoped would arouse some enthusiasm for the war, led only to the loss of the Spanish frontier fortress of Salses, and the siege that followed increased rather than diminished Catalan hostility to Madrid. 'God', wrote Olivares to the king, 'wants us to make peace; for he is depriving us of all the means of war.'[1]

It was in this condition that the government in Madrid faced those consequences of defeat which Olivares had long feared. The greater the burden imposed on the outlying dependencies of Castile, the nearer the moment came when they would attempt to go the way of the northern Netherlands. The message instilled at every possible point by Richelieu's collaborators was becoming undeniable: Madrid squeezed the provinces dry for a war that was no concern of theirs, failed to defend them against external enemies, held them in poverty while the life of luxury at the court continued. The question was whether and where the inescapable movements of rebellion would turn into revolutions capable of breaking up the Spanish monarchy entirely. Olivares would not let this happen without a heroic struggle.

REVOLT IN CATALONIA

The story of the revolts reveals as much about the behaviour of governments as of subjects. Philip IV might well have been left as King of Castile – a succession that would have been hardly worth fighting for. But only the full collaboration of the French could have brought the rebels such a success; and though statesmen readily fomented discontent against each other as a normal part of the competition, when it came to actual support and exploitation of popular rebellion, they were fumbling and cautious. At the end of it all, Portugal was the only major possession lost.

The rising in Catalonia contained almost all the familiar ingredients of rebellions. Partly it was an agrarian revolt touched off by the latest additions to the oppression of the peasants; partly it arose from the resistance of men of property who wanted not separation from Spain but a larger share in the power and profits of office. There was an element of national sentiment and one of religious fervour; and in the end the resistance was both used and destroyed by the foreign enemy. Under Philip II Catalonia had been a place where bandits who had cut themselves off from organized society formed something like a permanent rebellion. In parts of the countryside their power was notoriously greater than that of the government. The wars and depressions in the first decades of the century kept them in being. A good many of the rural nobility, for whom the feud was still a normal part of life, were involved in bandit activity, though by now more and more of them were drifting into the towns, as were their tenants. Commerce was increasingly linked with France, and gave Richelieu's agents opportunities they did not overlook. Indeed, the fear of French heresies was a reason for the Inquisition being more active there than in the rest of the country. When French troops crossed the Pyrenees in 1638 the Catalans did not give the support

Richelieu had hoped for; but they showed no enthusiasm for raising an army or building fortifications in their own defence. Olivares decided that the opportunity should be taken to crush the recalcitrant province as well as the invaders. Soldiers, both Castilians and alien mercenaries, were quartered in Catalonia and left there unpaid to live off the country through the winter. There was no surer way to incite rebellion.

The revolt that exploded in the spring of 1640 was both rural and urban. Catalan villages had grown accustomed through the years of brigandage to join in self-defence. When the town of Santa Coloma de Farners refused to billet soldiers and appealed for help against the expedition sent to punish it, church bells called together peasants in the surrounding villages, and within days armed revolt had spread through the province. Such united action was only possible with the help of the clergy. Catalan priests were the most heavily taxed section of the population, and high offices in the Church were as much a preserve of hated Castilian outsiders as those in the state. Castilian as well as French troops were blamed for the destruction of churches and images, and reforms derived from the Council of Trent were regarded as Castilian innovations. Royalist commanders accused the clergy of 'rousing the people and . . . inducing the ignorant to believe that rebellion will win them the kingdom of heaven'.[2] The towns sometimes tried to protect themselves from the plundering peasants; but many, including the city of Barcelona, opened their gates to let the insurgents join with the urban mob of poor and homeless. The climax of the revolt in Barcelona came when the Segadors, the labourers who flocked to the city in the summer to be hired for the harvest, joined in the fighting. Many of the surviving royal officials and judges fled for their lives, and the viceroy, Santa Coloma, was murdered. In other towns the municipal oligarchies were the first victims of the rioters. More and more the social and political purposes of the rebellion were lost amid the plundering, and the rumours of nameless disasters, unknown enemies, miracles and witchcraft. Among it all, since it was a year of drought, incongruous processions of prayer for rain continued to win great support.

Catalonia never produced a real rebel leader – not even a mythical one. At the height of the revolt there appeared letters threatening destruction to towns that resisted the rebels, some of them signed by the 'Captain-General of the Christian Army', who in

Madrid was reported to be a galley-slave released from prison. But he failed to emerge as an identifiable hero. The fate of the rebellion depended a great deal on the attitude of those political leaders who had built up their own resistance to Madrid. There had been a prolonged quarrel between the Viceroy and the *Diputació*, the small executive committee which was chosen by lot from the rural, urban, and clerical oligarchies and controlled most of the local patronage. Its president, Pau Claris, was a cleric connected with some of the leading families in the country and in Barcelona. Without being a separatist, still less a believer in social revolution, he saw himself as the defender of Catalan liberties against the misgovernment of Castilian officials. His chief supporter in the *Diputació*, the aristocratic representative Francesco de Tamarit, was arrested in March 1640 for his resistance to the billeting measures, and was released from prison by the insurgent mob in Barcelona. The *Diputació* was in a dilemma familiar to moderate revolutionaries: it was appalled by the threat to propertied society, but at the same time ready to use the situation to win from Madrid concessions for Catalan liberties.

In the capital advocates of stern repression were for a time resisted by those who saw a need to pacify Catalonia with concessions in the interest of unity against France. Olivares at first supported the new viceroy, the Duke of Cardona, in trying to conciliate Claris and his supporters. But it was doubtful whether Catalonia could now do anything to resist French invasion. Many of the nobility, seeing no move coming from Madrid to save them from revolution, abandoned their estates and left for other parts of Spain. Nevertheless, Olivares delayed the decision to send a punitive expedition until it was known that Claris had begun serious negotiations with the French. For a moment an independent Catalan Republic claimed to exist under French protection; but it then had to accept Richelieu's demand that Louis XIII should be recognized as its sovereign. Allegiance to the new state now meant not the opportunities that the Catalan nobles had hoped for, nor a relaxation of burdens on the lesser men, but a foreign domination in place of a Castilian one. It put an end to the hope that the whole of Aragon might join in the revolt. Catalan resistance lasted, in theory, until the citizen army of Barcelona was at last defeated in 1652. But the ten years were a period not of successful revolution but of military occupation and intermittent warfare, of economic ruin, and, at the end, of plague and famine. Eventually the surviving rebels received a royal pardon and a vague promise that the traditional privileges of Catalonia would be respected.

REVOLT IN PORTUGAL

One revolt against Spain was apparently successful – but successful only because the movement of protest was absorbed by a national war of liberation. Portugal, with its own language and traditions, a separate colonial Empire, a large and prosperous merchant class, was the most recent acquisition of the Spanish Crown. The union of 1580 with Spain and hence with its empire, contrived by many of the nobility, had brought some commercial benefits; but they were more than offset by the wars. The Dutch and English were happy to attack Portuguese shipping and colonies when opportunity arose; the Spaniards demanded Portuguese men and money without, it was felt, doing enough to retrieve the American territories lost to the Dutch. Cadiz was driving Lisbon out of the Atlantic trade; and in the general economic decline Castilians kept for themselves an increasing share of what remained. Both Lerma and Olivares incurred the resentment of Portuguese aristocrats by finding profitable offices for Castilians. The king's cousin Margaret of Savoy was sent to Lisbon in 1634 with a body of Castilian counsellors whose task was to build up enough power to make Portugal pay a regular contribution to Spanish war expenses. Two years later there came the real onslaught of Castilianization. In the years of minor revolts and party rivalries that followed, French agents were hard at work. A more unexpected source of support for resistance was the Archbishop of Lisbon and the leading Portuguese Jesuits. The Catholic institutions of Portugal, including the Inquisition, remained indepedent and, excluded from the temptations of the Madrid court, took a stern view of Spanish sins. The parish clergy were as willing to support popular revolt as their superiors now were to join in a palace conspiracy. But the union of the two might well have been impossible without the emotional loyalty in both town and country to the old ruling house of Braganza.

For two generations there had existed one of the superstitions, deeply rooted in primitive religion, about the return of a suppos-

edly dead leader who would redeem his people from their sufferings. This was King Sebastian, who had died in 1578. Several
claimants to his identity had already achieved momentary success.
The real Braganza heir, Duke John, was now bullied by his wife
Luisa de Guzman, despite her Spanish birth, into accepting the
role of a national leader. She also found an able political organiser,
Professor Ribeiro. In the hope of thwarting two revolutions at
once, Olivares ordered the Duke of Braganza and many of the
Portuguese nobility to command the expedition against Catalonia
in November 1640. The planned revolt could only succeed if it
began at once. On 1 December, while a French fleet was off the
coast, a group of court nobles cut to pieces the chief Spanish
representative, Vascollenos, and proclaimed the reign of John of
Braganza as King John IV. Simultaneously there was a mass rising
in Lisbon, and the Spanish fortifications throughout the kingdom
were seized. There were in fact few Spanish troops left in
Portugal, and none that could be spared to go there. Opposition
to the new régime had to consist of bribery, counter-plots, and
propaganda. One device was to make sweeping offers to the
Christian-Jewish community for their support: the Grand Inquisi-
tor himself was induced to promise that their persecution would
cease. It all made little difference. Portugal had one outstanding
asset that made it possible to sustain a struggle against Spain – the
Brazilian sugar fleet. Though the war went on until 1668, the
Spaniards were fighting against a nation with a sounder economy
than their own, and a strong material incentive to defend its
independence.

THE FALL OF OLIVARES

Every European statesman who faced revolt of one sort or
another in the provinces or dependencies of his country had also
to keep a close eye on the response at the centre. Aristocratic plots
against the régime of Olivares had always been one of his minor
burdens. He was well aware, from the beginning of the Catalan
rising, and especially after the failure of his first attempts to
suppress it, of the new threats to his authority in Castile itself.
The movement that he discovered in 1641 combined both palace
conspiracy and provincial separatism. The Duke of Medina

Sidonia, brother of the new Queen Luisa of Portugal, was at the centre of a group of Andalusian grandees who planned a revolt that could lead to the overthrow of Olivares or to an independent Andalusian kingdom, or even to both. This time the plan was betrayed to the Count-Duke and broken before it could take effect. But every failure in the wars and every increase in the economic chaos they were producing added to the chances that the king would before long make a scapegoat of his minister – and hence to the number of courtiers who thought it expedient to be on good terms with his enemies. Like Richelieu, Olivares had maintained his position by never allowing the king to escape from his day-to-day influence and by keeping careful track of the manoeuvres against him at the palace. It was always a difficulty that from time to time the king chose to leave his capital. Olivares did his best to dissuade Philip from undertaking a journey to the armies in Catalonia. Though it was more of a ceremonial excursion than a serious attempt to intervene in the organization of the campaign, it was bound to reveal how dangerous the situation was and to leave Madrid at the mercy of the enemies of Olivares. In the spring of 1642 the king insisted on going; Olivares decided that the lesser evil was to go with him. The queen, the Count de Castrillo who was left in charge of the administration, and all the opposition group made the most of their opportunity. When Philip returned in the winter he was faced with an organized and apparently universal demand for the dismissal of his minister. The best Philip could do was to save him from Strafford's fate and send him to die in exile. Richelieu had just died – in power.

REVOLT IN ITALY

While Mazarin was establishing his position as Richelieu's successor, no-one in Spain made any open attempt to take over the position left by Olivares. The king made it known that he intended in future to rule as Philip II had done, with a large Council of State restored to its old supremacy. To some extent he does appear to have devoted himself to administrative tasks, though his political views came increasingly under the influence of the church, and in particular of the mystical abbess Sor Maria de Agreda. Luis de Haro, a nephew of Olivares, was able to emerge from the former opposition group to become an effective minister who, with none of the ostentation of Olivares, made himself almost as powerful in both home and foreign affairs. It was his realistic assessment of the military situation that led to the agreement with the Netherlands in the Westphalia negotiations recognizing, after eighty years of war, that there was no longer hope of crushing their 'revolt' (see p. 473). The fact was made a little clearer by the outbreak of rebellion in yet another part of the European Empire.

In the two provinces of southern Italy Spanish government was at its worst, and local political ambition at its feeblest. The administration of both Sicily and Naples had been, even under Philip II, a conflict between attempts at efficient central control and a great variety of local forces. The Inquisition had often proved a better instrument for maintaining loyalty to the Crown than were the viceroys and their officials. There was a vast difference between the two territories. Sicily was still regarded as one of the richest parts of the Spanish Empire: it exported grain to Spain and to northern Italy, and one of its specific grievances in the 1630s was the attempt to buy the crops at cheap monopolistic rates for the armies. It had a tradition of representative institutions that made possible the startling claim that the only parliaments in Europe that kept their powers were in London and Palermo. But the secular powers that really resisted royal government were those of the great landowners and the towns. The Sicilian nobility were at the stage where the quest for office, with all its opportunities for extortion and corruption, was slowly changing the habits of territorial independence and baronial warfare. The towns, with their governments more or less dominated by the guilds, clung to their control over justice and taxation and their rivalries with each other. Anything begun in Palermo was inevitably opposed in Messina. Viceroys survived – usually not for long – by exploiting disunity and buying support with titles and offices.

The harvest of 1646 was a disastrous failure; and in the following spring there were not only the expected sporadic riots in the countryside but a succession of full-scale urban risings. The pattern was fairly uniform: houses of officials held responsible for the taxes or the hoarding of grain were attacked first; then for two or three days there was indiscriminate plundering and fighting. But behind the hunger-riot there was a good deal of well-informed political motive. In Palermo a goldbeater, Giuseppi Alessio, became the spokesman of demands for the restoration of Sicilian privileges, the abolition of new taxes, and the removal of the viceroy, the Marquis of Los Velos. After three days of anarchy in Palermo, the viceroy fled for his life and announced almost unlimited concessions. But although the revolt had a political programme, no-one could produce the means of putting it into effect. There was irreconcilable conflict between the pro-French party in Palermo (carefully fostered but not much helped from Paris) and those rebels who shouted their loyalty to a king of Spain remote enough to be something of a legend himself. The real Philip produced a tougher viceroy who restored order.

The Kingdom of Naples was a poorer region with none of the remnants of Aragonese liberties. Power was shared between the viceroys and the small councils of the nobility, the *sediles*, among whom titles and offices were lavishly distributed. The heavy taxation benefited the Genoese tax-farmers and the Spanish armies, but not the Neapolitans. Peasant revolts, brutally suppressed, were a common enough feature of rural life, and the city had a large population of the homeless and starving. It was the revolt of 1647 in Naples that produced the most spectacular of the messianic demagogues in the west. Thomaso Aniello ('Masaniello') was a fisherman with a genius for popular oratory. He first appeared as a mob leader when a normal market scuffle, involving a petty Castilian official, had turned into a riot against the latest piece of war taxation – a levy on fruit which was the only food the poor could get in summer. Within a few days the crowds were spreading palms beneath his feet. At his behest they attacked the palace, the prisons, the tax-collectors, everything that was part of the machinery or display of Spanish government. The pitiful efforts of the viceroy, the Duke of Arcos, to hold off the rioters with promises and at the same time organize a plot to murder Masaniello turned the agitator into a paranoiac dictator whose alleged enemies were executed in the streets. But the hysteria of the crowd produced conduct as irrational as Masaniello's own. When, in response to a more subtle move on the viceroy's part, he was invited to negotiate as an equal with the Spanish authorities, there was a sudden movement against him. He was shot and beheaded by a gang of obscure origin; his corpse was dragged through jeering and celebrating crowds; and next day he was venerated as a martyr. Four hundred priests and a hundred thousand spectators were said to have attended his funeral, where the body miraculously pieced itself together to give them a saintly benediction.

The Masaniello episode in the city was only the beginning of a revolt that spread through the whole of southern Italy. Too many of the Neapolitan landowners had a stake of some sort in the Spanish regime for anything like a national resistance to be possible. By the autumn a war of peasants against the landlords had merged with the eternal local feuds and rivalries. The man now regarded by the rebels as their leader, Prince Massa, was an eccentric nobleman half in league with the viceroy but also seeking power for himself as the restorer of order. When a Spanish fleet appeared in the bay, leading some of the revolutionaries to believe that the king across the water had at last come to their rescue, Massa negotiated with the commander, Don Juan; but the viceroy demanded that the city should be bombarded. The gunfire and the Spanish troops who landed gave the revolt a new realism and purpose. It was Massa who now became the traitor to be killed, and Naples was proclaimed a republic. Realism also meant that help from a powerful state must be found; the source of it could only be France. In November one faction of the rebels called on Henry Duke of Guise, who had a remote claim to a Neapolitan throne, to come from Rome (where he was arranging his divorce) and lead a war against the remaining Spanish garrisons. The spectacle of a member of the House of Guise heading a rebel republic did not appeal to Mazarin. Any serious attempt to exploit the revolt as a weapon against Spain would have to be organized by the French government. Fear of proletarian revolutionaries made him, as he later admitted, miss 'the finest opportunity' for a triumph in Italy. The fleet he eventually sent to Naples proved almost as hostile to the rebels as the Spanish one. Guise escaped arrest by Mazarin only to be caught by the Spaniards instead. Six months after it began, the revolt disintegrated into aimless recriminations.

THE SPANISH FAILURES

The crisis of the 1640s and the defeats in the European wars put an end to the lingering belief that Spain was a mighty power in Europe and the world. Whether it was suffering an impoverishment unequalled anywhere else is still arguable. As so often in the seventeenth century, the great difficulty is that few general statements can be applied to the whole of a country. But it can hardly be doubted than in Castile at least both countryside and towns now had a lower standard of living for all but the highest levels of society than the rest of western Europe. Despite the efforts of Olivares to distribute the burdens of the state more evenly, it was Castile that bore the main cost of the court and the wars; and Castile had been throughout the century suffering more than most of the peninsula from a diminishing population, a lower output of food and exportable raw materials, and a reduction in almost every form of commercial activity. The power of wool-producers in the sixteenth century had helped to make Spain dependent on imported grain; but wool had enabled many peasants to earn a little money. Now it was in smaller demand. The less profitable agriculture became, the greater the temptation for both landlord and peasant to abandon it entirely. Often their debts left them with no alternative. The lord might then try to get a living at court, the tenant in a town. But the towns were if anything in a worse plight than the country. As the colonies became more self-sufficient, their demand for goods exported from Spain shrank. The crushing and unpredictable taxation imposed on native merchants increased the tendency for trade to be run by foreigners. Though the extent to which Spain had lived on imports of silver can be exaggerated, the steady fall in the yield as mines became less profitable to work added to the government's difficulties and hence to the tax-payer's burden. The Atlantic trade of Seville collapsed in the 1640s; and the disaster was completed by the plague of 1649 in which half its people were said to have died or fled. Such epidemics were often blamed for a decay that had more lasting causes.

The floundering attempts of the ministers and bureaucrats to solve difficulties that were partly of their own making produced one of the most startling symptoms of economic disease: more than any other country, Spain, and Castile especially, experienced a succession of violent inflations and deflations. Ever since 1617, when the Cortes of Castile released the king from a promise to use only silver coinage, *vellón* was repeatedly minted to pay government debts. A period of rising prices in the 1620s was brought to a sudden end by Olivares when he stopped payment of the government's debts to Italian bankers, tried in vain to fix prices by decree, and then, in 1628, halved the value of all existing copper coins. (The government's profits from this were lost in the Mantuan war and the subsidies to imperial forces.) By the 1640s, Castilian coins were being repeatedly restamped to raise or lower their value, bringing momentary relief to the Crown and disaster to almost everyone involved in commerce or finance. Since silver seemed a safer form of wealth than copper, its disappearance was completed by hoarding. In 1660, when the war with France was over, there was another effort to stop the inflation by introducing a completely new copper coinage with greater intrinsic value; but within a few years the price of silver and of commodities generally was higher than ever. Eventually, in 1680, the desperate measure of 1628 was repeated: the value of the new coins was halved. This time the collapse of the economy in Castile seemed complete. After an outburst of rioting and robbery, the choice for most people lay between leaving Castile altogether and living on what they could produce or acquire by barter.

Bad as it was, the economic failure was not unrelieved. For the lucky or enterprising few there were ways of prospering. Fortunes could be made as well as lost by smuggling and hoarding foreign coin, silver, and scarce commodities. Lucrative offices could still be bought. The Church offered riches on earth for its higher clergy as well as holy poverty for the majority of priests. But it was only the holders of large landed estates who, by avoiding economic enterprise and living on the misery of their peasants, could achieve secure luxury. Such property became concentrated in the hands of fewer and fewer families as the hidalgos increasingly shared in the general decline. The costs of war and rebellion naturally varied. Though taxation was grievous everywhere, it was Castile that suffered most from the follies of the central government it housed. One of them had been the Portuguese war. In a wide frontier area towns and villages were garrisoned against the Portuguese raids; billeting of soldiers, losses of crops, animals, and houses to the forces of both sides shattered the already wretched economy. Taxation and recruiting extended further still. The peace of 1668 was therefore an opportunity for recovery. In Catalonia too the effects of the rebellion were being overcome and the peace with France brought relief. With their own coinage and a smaller proportion of unproductive population to maintain, the non-Castilian provinces had preserved more links with the economy of the rest of Europe and could now expand their trade.

Barcelona, abandoning the old Mediterranean commerce, began to export more textiles to northern Europe as well as America. The benefits of new commercial enterprise were limited by its tendency to fall under foreign control. Native merchants, and a new generation of *arbitristas* complained of the concessions made to the Portuguese and later the Dutch and English. But any economic stimulus was better than none; and foreign immigration was in the long run as beneficial to Spain as it was to Russia. Astonishingly, even Protestants were not excluded: provided they kept their religion to themselves, foreigners were not subject to religious persecution. To the French, land in Spain was cheap, and opportunities for skilled artisans attractive. While European statesmen were interested in Spain only as the kingdom without an heir, there was in many parts of it by the end of the century a slow return of economic stability.

When Philip IV died in 1665, there was not much left of the legend of Spanish power. At the Peace of the Pyrenees in 1659, Artois and the outlying defences of the Spanish Netherlands had been surrendered to France. So had the Catalan province of Roussillon, and a large part of Cerdagne. The marriage of the Infanta Maria Theresa to Louis XIV instead of to an Austrian prince, though it was in the well-established tradition of Franco-Spanish royal matches, looked like a futher recognition that the Habsburg axis was broken. Ironically, Spain remained at the centre of Europe's diplomacy, but as the victim to be dismembered rather than the feared leader. The question was how far the centralized monarchy would disintegrate of its own accord before the succession question brought the great powers to fight over its fate. As the diplomats were soon to be reminded, it was still accepted in Spain that the will of a deceased king could determine in some detail the management of his possessions. Philip IV showed an unusual amount of perception and initiative in the schemes he laid down for the long minority of the four-year-old Charles II. Philip's illegitimate son, whose name of Don Juan was his chief qualification for the role of saviour of the country, was excluded from the power he had assiduously prepared for. The regent, contrary to custom, was to be the queen, Philip's second wife Maria Anna. Effectively, the authority of the Crown would be exercised by a Junta of Regency. Though it included two leading figures from the old government, the Counts of Castrillo and Peñaranda, its other members came from outside Castile. There seemed a possibility that it would constitute a deliberately inactive central power representing the interests of the provinces.

One obstacle to any happy solution on federal lines was that a queen-regent, however ineffective herself, was bound to be exploited by the power-seekers of the court. Maria soon came under the control of her Austrian Jesuit confessor, Father Nithard, who was able to reduce the Junta to the level of a powerless advisory body. Against him Don Juan mounted in 1669 a short-lived but spectacular rebellion. The support he had built up in Aragon enabled him to stage a triumphant march on Madrid where he was received as a popular hero. Nithard hastily departed for Rome, and if – as was already thought imminent – Charles II had died, Don Juan could well have become the new king. He was not the man to lead an armed rebellion; and when the king made the first of his many unexpected recoveries the queen was able to end the episode by making Don Juan Viceroy of Aragon. In Nithard's place she adopted as favourite an upstart courtier from Andalusia, Fernando de Valenzuela, who in his turn became a hero of the Madrid populace. If Don Juan had been something of a False Dmitri, Fernando behaved like one of the less reputable Roman Emperors, entertaining the plebeians of the city with circuses and the court with lavish and amorous banquets. The grandees were scandalized: he was not even of noble birth. When Charles attained his official majority – the age of fourteen – Don Juan had the support of a solid party of courtiers for a second descent on the capital, this time at the head of an army. For two years he held power – the years in which Franche-Comté and a few more Netherlands fortresses were finally lost to the French. When he died in 1679, the enthusiasm of the court and the capital had turned into ridicule. The Council of State was left to preside, with no perceptible policy or leadership, over the worst years of monetary chaos.

Charles II himself has always been known only as the moribund half-wit whose lack of an heir produced the 'Spanish Succession Question'. Obviously this offspring of a series of marriages between cousins, which made him the descendant of Charles V by six or seven tangled lines, was not a paragon of health or intellect. But the fact that he reigned for thirty-five years in spite of the incessant torment inflicted on him by his doctors suggests that he was tougher than those in Spain and abroad who were preparing for the moment of his death liked to believe. It may well have been a beneficial change when the doctors were largely replaced by exorcists. His deep suspicion of everyone around him, which was reported as a sign of madness, seems in the circumstances entirely reasonable. As the succession loomed larger in European politics, palace rivalries in Madrid took on the character of a struggle between French and Austrian parties. In 1689 Charles's second marriage, to the Emperor's sister-in-law Maria Anna of Neuburg, brought a strong 'Austrian' contingent to the court, led by the new queen's confessor Father Gabriel. For the moment Charles had found in the Count of Oropesa a minister who was showing some ability and determination in trying to sort out the economic calamities and establish a workable system of government finance. In 1691 the pressure of courtiers whose interests he threatened to override was enough to remove him. Nevertheless it was Oropesa's favoured candidate for the throne, the Bavarian Joseph Ferdinand (see p. 376), whom Charles decided to name as his heir. The French and Austrians, though they were fighting against each other a desperate battle of court conspiracy, agreed that this was another proof of royal insanity. In fact it was the best hope of avoiding surrender to one or other of the great powers whose rivalries now seemed likely to end in the invasion and break-up of the Spanish possessions. Everything Charles could do in his last wretched years to preserve his Empire he carried out, however slowly, in face of mercilesss diplomatic and palace intrigue. When the Bavarian candidate died, nearly all the favoured advisers of the king agreed with the French that Philip of Anjou was now the most desirable successor. Despite all the efforts of the queen and her clerical allies, Charles kept firmly to his decision to make a new will leaving all his territories to Anjou. If the French refused, the Austrian Archduke was to succeed instead. The only important condition was that the new king was not to become the sovereign of any other power as well. In November 1700, a month after the signing of the will, the news was proclaimed that the last of the Spanish Habsburgs really was dead.

NOTES AND REFERENCES

1   Quoted in J. H. Elliott, *Imperial Spain 1469–1716* (London, 1963), p. 388.

2   Quoted in J. H. Elliott, *The Revolt of the Catalans* (Cambridge, 1963), p. 487.

16

SCANDINAVIA AND POLAND

The lands that surrounded the Baltic Sea brought together some of the most thickly tangled threads of seventeenth-century history. It was through the Baltic that eastern Europe had its main economic links with the west. The exchange of surplus grain from the great estates of Poland for southern manufactures and produce had made Baltic ports the most desirable of territorial prizes and gave to the Dutch and the English a special interest in Baltic politics. As forest products began to rise in importance at the expense of grain, and Russian markets became more accessible, the tsars were increasingly concerned too. The Empire had nearly four hundred miles of Baltic shore; and the Habsburgs soon found to their cost that Scandinavian politics were anything but remote from theirs. Poland as a Catholic power brought the religious alignment into Baltic affairs, and even linked them with the Danube and the ebb and flow of Turkish pressure.

In 1600 frontiers and political predominance in the whole region were a matter of dispute principally between the three kingdoms with which we shall be concerned in this chapter, Denmark, Sweden, and Poland. This was in itself something fairly new. A century earlier the Hanseatic League, and even the Teutonic Knights whom the Poles had defeated, were still in their different ways at least as great as the kings. The Danish Oldenburg dynasty reigned over the whole Scandinavian peninsula, the Polish Jagiello kings over Lithuania, much of the Ukraine, and – less directly – Prussia. The estates of the great nobles, spreading through all these territories, had often been more effective units than the kingdoms. But the conflict of dynasties was now more decisive than the interests or passions of any of their subjects. When the Swedish Vasas, helped by the merchants of Lübeck, were finally able in 1523 to break the 1396 Union of Kalmar with Denmark, there remained two kingdoms eager to expand, and divided from each other by fears and ambitions beside which the new bond of Lutheranism counted for very little. Sweden had strong incentives to acquire the rich provinces on her own side of the Sound still held by the Danes, to gain a more secure outlet to the Atlantic, and to win control of Baltic commerce. Danish kings still hoped to regain their hegemony over all Scandinavia. For both an immediate aim was to annex the lands round the Gulf of Finland, and especially Livonia, a largely German region which contained the rich port of Riga.

In the Baltic as much as anywhere else, economic and military purposes were complicated by the personal ambitions of monarchs, who at the beginning of the century had only shaky connections with the countries over which they reigned. In 1587 the elective throne of Poland had been won by Sigismund (Zygmunt) III, who was also recognized by the dominant faction in Sweden as heir to his father John III. The chaotic affairs of his Swedish kingdom were of more concern to him than Poland, where he felt that his job could prove temporary. As it turned out he was thrown out of Sweden and survived for forty-five years in Poland. The Lutheran Swedish nobility had been alarmed to find that he was a Jesuit-inspired crusader for the Counter-Reformation, with eccentric ideas about re-union of the churches. After appearing originally as an anti-imperial candidate, he married a Habsburg princess. The conspiracies against him led by the uncle who became Charles (Karl) IX made him conclude that even Poland was better than that. He left Sweden and in 1599 was deposed by the Riksdag; but his hope was to return as a conqueror with a Polish army. That would have meant a victory for Catholicism that would have been a frightening blow for European Protestant states.

As King of Poland Sigismund was also involved in the endless territorial disputes with Russia, and he came within reach of overthrowing the disorganized Russian state and seizing the tsar's throne for himself, or for one of the Polish-sponsored defenders. The prospect of a vast Polish Empire that would absorb Russia, Finland, and then Sweden was not quite as ludicrous as it later appeared. The Swedes took it seriously enough to intervene in

Russia themselves. Swedish and Polish armies successively got as far as Moscow. The Swedes, heavily defeated by a Polish army that included Cossacks and Tartars, were further exhausted by wars in the north intended to subdue the Lapps and secure the White Sea for commerce; and in 1611 Christian IV of Denmark took the opportunity to attack. The 'War of Kalmar' enabled the Danes to capture the fortress of Älvsborg on Sweden's tiny outlet to the North Sea and demand an enormous ransom for it. Every country in the region had the same ingredients of war – insecure monarchs and frontiers, magnates on the verge of rebellion, peasant populations ready to supply soldiers. Sweden's hero-king Gustav Adolf began his reign at war with Poland, Russia and Denmark and having few resources. Fortunately wars could be ended as quickly and irrationally as they began.

THE DANISH MONARCHY

Of all these rivals for expansion in the Baltic area, the one that by any material tests looked most likely to achieve it was Denmark. She had a comparatively large population, productive soil, and easy access to the European mainland without a long southern frontier to defend. The Sound Dues were a source of revenue large enough to be envied by most states, and provided valuable bargaining power. If Norway was an almost colonial area too poor to be beneficial, at least there was no need to fear its hostility. By the standards of the time Christian IV was a prosperous monarch able, for instance, to offer subsidies to James I. He also had private resources in his large German estates, and had long been eager to acquire full sovereignty over Schleswig and Holstein, duchies which in the sixteenth century were partitioned between the King of Denmark and his brothers. German was still the language of government and of the court. Though Christian, like Sigismund, regarded war on Sweden as the reconquest of his own kingdom and the means to complete control of the Baltic, expansion in northern Germany was for him a great personal ambition. He was one of the monarchs who tried to be a strong, centralizing reformer, but never quite escaped the position and outlook of a landed magnate.

The Danish Crown was elective. The Oldenburgs retained it only by granting at each election a 'capitulation' confirming a system of government in which the monarch shared his power with the nobility and its council the Raad. The Assembly of Estates had become completely ineffective, with the peasant estate no longer meeting at all. Of the other three the clergy were helpless dependants of the nobles, and the burgesses tended to represent family cliques in towns that had retained their medieval constitutions but not their privileges. Political power was in the hands of the nobility alone, and indeed was hardly distinguishable from land ownership. With an expansion of the great estates many peasants had become labourers not far removed from serfdom, and the Crown was in the same position as other great landowners in being able to tax the peasants on its own estates and no others. Christian and his group of court supporters were involved throughout his reign in a half-hearted and largely unsuccessful conflict with a nobility that resisted every measure of reform. Eventually he did, in spite of the opposition, set up trading companies, build roads and harbours, strengthen municipal governments. Both Christiana (Oslo) and Copenhagen were largely his creation. But for the first decade of the century the Raad in resisting royal policy could complain that Christian's wars of reconquest would not bring much benefit to them: Sweden now looked so poor that it would be a drain on the funds of any invader. A useful bargaining point for Christian was that he could, as Duke of Holstein, undertake a war without the approval of his Danish kingdom.

SWEDEN, THE GREAT POWER

It was reasonable in the west to think of Sweden as a minor contestant in the power-game and commercially on the outer fringe of profitable activities. The fact that such a kingdom could for the rest of the century play so large a part in the military, diplomatic and economic affairs of Europe has always been one of the historical problems of the period, though there is plenty of evidence that a nation's external successes were not related in any simple way to conditions at home. By any European standards, Sweden was a poor country. There were a few wheat-growing areas, which the conquests increased; barley was the major crop, produced by a peasantry many of whom had little connection with markets or active landlords. Most of the land was forest. In the north a semi-migrant population could be deemed to belong to whatever state succeeded for the time being in collecting taxes from it. Elsewhere the Swedish Crown seemed to be even less competent than most in the task of diverting a steady share of what resources there were into its own hands. The great asset was minerals. The Crown, in its eagerness to get quick funds for itself, allowed the celebrated Falun copper-mine to be worked in ways that diminished the long-term benefits. The Swedish currency had been in frequent trouble. A great deal of internal trade in the sixteenth century was by barter, and many taxes were collected in kind. In 1625 Gustav Adolf decreed that marks should be minted only in copper worth their face value. Thus the amount available for export would fall, and since Sweden had virtually a monopoly, the price on the Dutch market (which had been sinking disastrously) would rise while the Crown would still draw profits from the increasing output. The silver for which it was exchanged abroad would be kept for the government's foreign expenses, including repayment of loans raised in Holland to pay the ransom for Älvsborg. The most visible effect of this was that Swedes found themselves, when they had anything to pay for, pushing around carts loaded with ludicrous coins nine inches in diameter, as well as suffering all the usual effects of inflation. In the end Gustav began the process, familiar in the west, of keeping the Crown solvent by selling its lands. It was soon clear that the Swedish nobility – again like many of their western counterparts – were the real beneficiaries.

The system of government seemed no better fitted than the economy for a century of foreign wars and alliances. The effective powers of the Crown still depended on the state of its perpetual conflict with the ancient nobility. Charles IX had begun his reign by executing four of the leading members of the Råd who had supported Sigismund too long. He had also made some attempt to restrict noble influence by creating a secretariat from men without landed property. This was not the line suggested to the young Gustav Adolf by Axel Oxenstiern (see pp. 242–3). Stable monarchy, the new Chancellor believed, would depend on a nobility actually serving the state. The Ordinance which the king and minister persuaded both Råd and Riksdag to accept in 1617 was the first stage in their plan for a monarchy run by the landowners and upheld by every section of the community. The old aristocracy and new office-holding families were to join with lesser landowners in a 'first estate' that would fill the posts needed by an expanded central government. In 1626 their gradations and precedence were firmly laid down: nobility, a status hitherto acquired or asserted as a recognition of military obligations, was made to depend wholly on royal patent. There was a rapid expansion of numbers; and generous grants of royal land to the newcomers did not endear them to the old noble families. Symbolically the centre of life for the nobles was to be not the court but the newly built 'Riddarhus', which was primarily the meeting-place of the First Estate. Equally symbolically the building was not completed until 1660.

The 'Form of Government' of 1634,[1] framed by Oxenstiern after Gustav's death, purported to complete the king's work. By a system of administrative 'colleges' the departments of state were organized under the Råd whose members became 'working statesmen' in Stockholm rather than provincial magnates. Oxenstiern may have gone beyond Gustav's intentions in relegating the Riksdag, whose powers the 1617 Charter had in theory upheld, to a minor role. The aristocratic politicians used the opportunity of the regency to impose permanent restrictions on the monarch. They had not much success. The royal prerogative remained the ultimate authority and both Råd and Riksdag were more important in winning acceptance for decisions that in making them. If the Riksdag had none of the theories of the English Parliamentarians, Gustav had none of those of the Stuart monarchs. His way was to avoid prescribed forms of government where it suited him, and deal directly with those able to expedite or resist his projects. This was part of the answer to the problem of Sweden's victories. A king who was one of the military entrepreneurs as well as one of the unhampered sovereigns could create an army as formidable as any of its rivals without needing the population and materials of a large state. Once it was involved in the wars, it had the chance to 'live of its own'. Moreover Swedish power is measured by Baltic and north German rather than by western standards. Had they been enemies rather than clients of the French, or faced greater risks of invasion, their triumphs could hardly have lasted so long.

THE MID-CENTURY CONFLICTS: SWEDEN

The Baltic countries did not experience in the 1640s internal conflicts that can readily support theories of a mid-century crisis. Certainly the rising of the Cossacks in 1648 came nearer to destroying an entire state through mass rebellion than anything the west could imagine (see p. 414); but it did not arise directly from conflicts in ordinary Polish society or politics. Sweden in 1650 was in danger of a peasant revolt – but one that was directed against landlords, not against the Crown. Eventually monarchies were strengthened throughout the region; though it was not until 1680 that the Swedish Crown made decisive progress in escaping the control of the landed aristocracy. In Poland it did not escape at all. Only Denmark provided, in 1660, a specimen of peaceful surrender by the nobility to royal absolutism. It did not mean that the Baltic is irrelevant to theories of crisis and revolution.

At the death of Gustav Adolf the new Queen Christina was six years old. Even more than in France a long minority would be a dangerous time for the Crown and its ministers. When peace was made by Sweden's German allies in 1635 there was nothing to show for Gustav Adolf's much-vaunted campaigns. Oxenstiern resisted the pressure to abandon military exploits altogether. With a closely united ministry, formed from his relations and dependants, he had an unexpected success when in 1643 he ordered a sudden attack on Denmark. In little more than a year the restored army was able to impose a peace by which the Danes surrendered their complete control of the Sound Dues by handing over the North Sea province of Halland to Sweden, as well as the bishoprics of Bremen and Verden, the islands of Gotland and Osel, and two Norwegian provinces. A profitable victory was the ideal way to set the reformed constitutional machinery working and the armies fighting, on a more modest scale, in Germany. It did not prevent the nobility from exploiting the financial difficulties that a slow war entailed. The Crown had throughout the century sold or given away land and revenues from its estates, mainly to the old or new nobility. The process was now speeded up, increasing the division between those who benefited from the activities of the state and those who suffered. At first the Crown's finances were improved by exchanging lands for lump sums in money, and the support it bought enabled it to impose heavy indirect taxation. When Christina took a hand in government herself, and handed out huge indiscriminate rewards to the returning commanders, the situation got worse. In ten years the number of counts and barons was multiplied by six. The revenue of the Crown fell by 40 per cent.[2]

409

In 1650, after the harvest had proved to be the worst for half a century, the peasants seemed on the verge of a major revolt. The Estates of townsmen and clergy joined them in denouncing the nobility and attacking alienation of lands, abuses in office-holding, and private jurisdiction. The peasants were afraid – not merely of poverty but of serfdom, or something near to it. Nobles, to whom the Crown alienated the right of taxing freeholders, were easily able to confiscate their land for arrears, reducing them to the status of landlords' peasants and thereby depriving them of most of their legal rights. The view was aired that only nobles were direct subjects of the Crown. Against this threat to the constitutional settlement and to the Riksdag (see p. 250), ideas familiar in the English parliaments of the 1620s were put forward in combined resolutions of the three non-noble estates. Far more than in England the reformers saw the nobility as the enemy. The Råd, though it had become a narrow oligarchy of office-holding families, was supported by the upper Estate; while the lower Estates claimed to uphold the power and independence of the monarch.

Queen Christina was not prepared seriously to support peasants against nobles: though she regarded the social order like everything else as open to intellectual questioning, the culture to which she was devoted was that of a rich leisured class and an extravagant court. The queen who gathered round herself many of the leading scholars of Europe, and claimed to debate on equal terms with Grotius and Descartes, showed no great interest in wider aspects of government. She gave some harmless promises of sympathy for peasant grievances, and welcomed the discomfiture of the nobility as a chance to insist on the recognition of her cousin Charles as her hereditary successor – since she had long since decided not to marry. She was ready enough to see the non-noble Estates resist any extension of noble power, but also to help the nobility in avoiding any really dangerous attack on the system. A few more privileges for the clergy, a few offices for leaders of the urban oligarchies, and death for the leaders of a faction that got as far as trying to involve the heir in treasonable conspiracies – actions like these proved enough to make sure that the rebellious atmosphere cooled. The popular demand for a *reduktion* – resumption by the Crown of the estates it had alienated to the nobility – was firmly put aside. So was the pressure for an extension of office-holding outside the ranks of the nobility.

POLAND UNDER SIGISMUND III

The Polish monarchy was now the least effective in Europe. Sigismund, like the previous foreign kings, had bargained for his election by making what amounted to a contract of employment, the *Pacta Conventa*, with the Seym (see p. 255) and hence in effect with the nobility. In theory taxation, declaring war, raising troops, and a share in appointing state officers and judges were in the hands of the nobility. Even a right of resistance to kings who broke the agreement was, rather uncertainly, included. This did not mean that the Polish central assembly had won all the powers and more that the English parliament was soon to seek. Under Sigismund the magnates continued to extend their control; but it was in the local assemblies, the Dietines, that the constitutional part of it was exercised. Their tyranny as landlords and their influence as patrons probably mattered more. Much of the Crown's authority came from its position as the largest landowner. There was nothing like the royal courts of western Europe that were also centres of administration. Those aristocrats who held central offices, virtually for life, came commonly from the German-influenced western areas. In the east and in Lithuania magnates were becoming as independent as princes of the Habsburg Empire. The bureaucracy in Warsaw was small and feeble. The revenue of the royal treasury has been put at one-twentieth of that of French kings at the time. It was not kept down by any great impoverishment of the country, as distinct from its peasantry. Polish agriculture was producing a large surplus of grain over local consumption. Until the middle of the century the grain trade through Danzig thrived, by exploiting the labour of peasants who were being driven into tighter serfdom. Cracow and Lwow flourished too, and Warsaw was becoming something of an industrial city. But there was no assertive Polish bourgeoisie: German and Jewish communities ran the commerce and often the administration of towns, in western areas especially. Poland was seen as a place of refuge from the harsher wars and persecutions of most of Europe. Every religion had its adherents there. Sigismund's aim of strengthening the Catholic Church as a national institution, with rich monastic lands and a politically powerful episcopate, was continuing the work of his predecessors. It was not entirely welcome to the provincial nobility, who regarded patronage of the Church as part of their inheritance. Many joined in the complaint that 'our ancestors . . . were born nobles rather than Catholics. . . . Poland is a political kingdom, not a clerical one.'[3] Though only Catholics now had full political rights, Protestants, Jews, and Muslims could worship freely. The Polish Brethren, with doctrines like those of the most extreme puritan sects in England, were one of the many unitarian groups that survived local suppression. The fears among all Sigismund's non-Catholic subjects that religious unity was being imposed as part of a policy of creating a unified state led to active resistance. In 1606 the Palatine of Cracow, Nicholas Zebrydovski, started one of the few rebellions against the monarchy. Though a Catholic himself, he joined with Protestant nobles to resist the pro-Habsburg court party that Sigismund, with Jesuit support, was building. The rebels were defeated but not punished. Their assertions of the right of nobles to almost unlimited power on their estates were only half-heartedly rejected.

It was remarkable that a monarchy so unstable, in a state surrounded by enemies on the long and indefensible land frontiers that are usually held to account for its subsequent partition, was able to fight simultaneously wars against two or three of its neighbours with apparently as good a chance of victory as anyone else. They were possible only because the nobles thought it in their own interests to put their resources into warfare. Poland was a popular source of mercenary soldiers. Foreign rulers and generals who recruited them needed the goodwill of the nobles from whose estates they came, or of the king. The line between supplying troops for a war and fighting in it was not a rigid one. Sigismund's campaigns in Russia began when the False Dmitri acquired a Polish army and with it the backing of many Polish nobles opposed to the Crown (see pp. 426–7). A practical reason for the king's assertion of his own claims to the Tsardom was that it might at least bring him some territory on his eastern borders. When his expedition collapsed in 1612 the army retreated in disorder and recompensed itself by plundering Polish estates and coercing the Seym into voting its arrears of pay. Five years later the Russian career of Sigismund's son Vladislav was ended partly by the mutiny of his mercenaries against the prospect of a winter with little food or pay.

The wars of Polish kings that were intended to serve their own ambitions or the Habsburg cause in the west were a different matter. The Seym successfully resisted an attempt by Sigismund to join as an ally of the emperor in war against Gabriel Bethlen of Transylvania who in 1619 thought the Bohemian war would give him the chance of conquests in Hungary. Ferdinand had to buy his Polish soldiers for himself. It was hardly to be expected that the emperor would then respond to Polish requests for help against the infidel: he was happy to see Turks and Poles destroy each other. But the great Turkish victory at Cecora in 1620 aroused the fears of the magnates and some national enthusiasm for revenge. In 1621 the Poles defeated a large Turkish army to recapture the fortress of Khocim (Chocim), and the sultan had to abandon his hopes of conquests on the Danube. The two sovereigns agreed to discourage their subjects from further fighting: neither could promise that they would obey. The victory made Polish claims to be the great defender of Christendom look more plausible. It came in time to avert the danger of a Russian attack, and released some resources for use against Sweden. The opposition of even loyal nobles to the Swedish wars had to be appeased by lavish grants of lands and offices in such territories as were conquered. Few of them remained in Polish hands for long. The Truce of Altmark in 1629 was generally welcomed as the beginning of a period of peace. But the outlook remained the same: military leaders kept their influence, and Sigismund would happily make agreements with the Danes, the Russians, or anyone else who would help to uphold his regime.

POLAND IN THE MID-CENTURY CONFLICTS

For Poland there was without doubt a crisis in the middle of the century; but 'the deluge' was not originated by any political or social tensions there. In 1632 Sigismund's son Vladislav IV was elected to the throne easily enough. He too would have preferred the Swedish Crown to the Polish, and was not averse to the idea of becoming tsar. His prospects of either were even worse than his father's; nor did he make much progress towards establishing a stronger monarchy in Poland. The landowners, as suspicious as ever of royal diplomatic schemes, forbade him to claim Estonia or Livonia from Sweden as hereditary possessions. The Treaty of Viasna that ended another Polish invasion of Russia in 1634, and the Treaty of Stuhmsdorf a year later promising peace for twenty-six years, brought only minor material gains. An alternative path of glory might be found by becoming a mediator in the Thirty Years War. At one time or another Polish diplomats approached almost every ruler, from Charles I to Wallenstein, and were snubbed so effectively that in the end they were not even present at the Westphalia negotiations. Vladislav's final hope of triumph, a war against the Turks, was again opposed by the Seym. Paradoxically, the reign of a king who sometimes seemed to regard Poland as merely a base and recruiting-ground for his armies was one of comparative peace. Yet Vladislav was not merely a warrior: he had plans for a unified and enlightened kingdom. Protestant and Orthodox Churches were to have better protection, with reunion as a distant goal. He made some attempts to introduce western culture to the capital – a theatre, a Rubens painting, Italian opera. Galileo and Grotius were favoured with his correspondence. Such things were no more attractive to the Seym than dynastic wars. They not only objected to paying money, but obstructed all efforts to raise it by customs dues. Poland remained too much a federation of the half-independent estates of magnates and gentry to be ruled effectively by its kings. It now became more of a battle-ground even than Germany in the worst of the Thirty Years War. But if elected monarchs could not rule it, neither could conquering ones. The conditions that let invaders in did something to ensure that they drove each other out.

Sigismund III's second son John Casimir, formerly a Jesuit and a Cardinal, took over from his brother both the throne and the Queen, Marie Louise de Nevers. It was at the moment of his election, in 1648, that Poland became involved in the most catastrophic of all the mid-century revolts (see pp. 272–4). There were many allies in Poland whose help the Cossack leader Khmelnitsky could seek against the Warsaw government – the peasants who saw him as a saviour from serfdom, the Orthodox Church to whom he offered domination over Catholicism, the Lutheran nobility. The quarrels of the magnates about relations with the Cossacks were the occasion for the first completely unscrupulous use of the *liberum veto* to dissolve the Seym. But the constitutional procedure was simply the reflection of the political situation. The outlines of a Polish state survived less through any strength of its own than because its enemies failed for the time being to agree on partition. Before long it became the centre of the first general 'northern war'.

THE NORTHERN WAR, 1655–60

When Charles X of Sweden attacked Poland in 1655, a year after his accession, he seems to have had no other motive than un-defined hopes of aggrandisement or at least of escaping his inter-nal problems and employing his armies. It was not difficult for him to capture Warsaw, drive John Casimir into exile, and win hasty assurances of loyalty from Polish gentry and Polish generals. The success did not last long. Charles's commitment in Poland offered to both Russia and Denmark the chance to redeem some of their Baltic territories. He could find only one active ally – the Elector of Brandenburg, who for the first time had to be reckoned as one of the powers in the Baltic contest. As Duke of Prussia he held the rather absurd status of a vassal of whatever Polish king there happened to be, and was ready to fight for complete sovereignty over his territories. A Poland invaded by the armies of Sweden, Russia, the Tartars, and the Cossacks and with central government shattered might well have seemed beyond survival. Land was going out of cultivation, serfdom on the demesnes of the nobility increasing, industry disappearing. But faintly, out of the total misery of the occupation, a Polish nationalism, Catholic and predominantly western in outlook, began to emerge. There was a brief attempt, initiated partly by the queen, to reform the constitution and set up hereditary monarchy. Townsmen plundered by the armies, and peasants disillusioned by Charles's indifference to serfdom, began to harass the Swedes in guerilla fighting. For John Casimir an elective throne, however feeble, was something to bargain with: he was ready at one time or another to promise it to almost anyone. By offering to support the tsar's own candidate he won a truce with Russia in 1656. A year later the prospect of a Habsburg succession brought an Austrian army to rescue him from the Swedes. Nevertheless it was the French influence of the queen's circle that dominated court policy; and a French candidate seemed the most likely successor to the child-less John Casimir. Nobles, gentry, and army officers saw their 'liberties' threatened by any foreign candidate for the throne who might think it expedient to bring in resources to strengthen the central government.

It was easier for armies to devastate and occupy large areas of land than for governments to destroy each other completely. The tendency for diplomats to hand back what generals seized was shown repeatedly in the northern wars. When Swedish troops withdrew from Poland in 1657 Charles X was already involved in war with Denmark. It was in this campaign that the nobility of Zealand, who thought themselves and their estates safe from the dangers of the war they had demanded, and rejoiced that the hard winter had cut off the invading Swedes from their bases, were punished by the dramatic spectacle of Charles's armies marching over the frozen sea of the Great Belt to occupy the island and besiege Copenhagen itself. Instead of hoping to rule the Baltic, Denmark was soon faced with appalling losses. By the Treaty of Roskilde she handed over her remaining possessions on the Swedish side of the Sound, together with the Norwegian province and port of Trondheim and the Baltic island of Bornholm. Within a few months Charles invaded Denmark again – an act for which it is again difficult to find any better reason than his personal craving to have another war somewhere. His apparent intention of destroying Denmark completely was not likely to be tolerated by the diplomats of western Europe, and he was soon faced by a formidable alliance of Dutch, Austrian, and Polish forces. Since at this moment he died, to the general relief, the powers were able to conclude in 1660 the treaties of Oliva and Copenhagen which confirmed Denmark's surrender of the Swedish provinces (but not of Bornholm and Trondheim). The Elector of Brandenburg, who changed sides at the right moment, won his sovereignty over East Prussia.

CROWN AND NOBILITY IN SWEDEN, 1654–97

In 1654 Christina had dramatically announced her decision to abdicate. Her conversion to Catholicism made her by law ineligible for the throne, and the cultured life of Europe attracted her more than the problems of Swedish finance. Oxenstiern died soon afterwards, and though his office-holding dynasty had seemed as well established as the Vasas themselves, the son who succeeded him could not aspire to the same dominant position. Charles X owed nothing to the goodwill of the old nobility: he was even prepared to attempt again the formidable task of recovering some of the Crown lands so rashly handed out to them. The *reduktion* of 1655, in which a quarter of each new estate was handed back to the Crown in return for security of tenure for the rest, was not so severe a blow as to alienate the nobility from a government that still protected their status. But it touched off a conflict between the great aristocracy, who were the principal sufferers, and the lesser and newer nobles. Many of the latter, as office-holders, had an interest in Crown prosperity: gradually, the division between a bureaucratic and a territorial nobility was becoming deeper and firmer.

It took another twenty-five years of intermittent war, and the rule of an increasingly corrupt Council of Regency after Charles X's death in 1660, to bring about the decisive attack on the great ruling families and their cliques. During Charles XI's minority, opposition in the Estates grew. When the king came of age in 1672 he quickly broke away from the inner group of high nobles led by Magnus de la Gardie. The alliance with England and the Netherlands, made in 1668, was abandoned and Sweden became Louis XIV's ally in his Dutch war (see pp. 420, 507–10). In 1675 Charles left Stockholm to lead his armies in the field. Inspired by his new minister Johan Gyllenstiern he saw bright prospects for monarchical absolutism with popular support. Both king and minister determined to put an end to court extravagance, to the power of the great families, and eventually to the expense of fighting Louis XIV's wars. In the Riksdag of 1680 the former regents and the great landowners were bitterly attacked by the 'service-nobility' and by the free peasants. They demanded further 'reductions' of noble estates and the return of money supposed to have been squandered or filched under the regency. The old nobility having consented to a *reduktion*, in the hope of winning Crown support for their privileges, found the security of their property and offices completely destroyed. Their power was not replaced by a constitutional one. Without much political manœuvring on his own part, Charles got an assurance from the Estates that he was not obliged to consult them at all (see p. 251). Throughout his reign more specific extensions of royal power were recorded as occasion arose, until in 1693 he and his heirs were declared 'absolute, sovereign kings, responsible for their actions to no man on earth'. But Swedish despotism rested less on political developments than on financial security. By the end of Charles XI's reign the Crown could, in peacetime, 'live of its own' without calling on the Estates for supply, and could raise properly secured loans when it needed them. Much of the land recovered from the old nobility was occupied by the servants of the Crown. The peasants who worked it paid rent directly to the Crown which used it to pay the office-holders – the system of *indelningswerk*. In one way or another the peasants still bore a heavy burden for the state. But compared with most of their counterparts in other countries they were fortunate: their complaints were heard and their status protected by a Crown that valued their support.

CROWN AND NOBILITY IN DENMARK, 1648–99

The Danish nobility had lost none of its political power through the disasters of the German wars. Frederick III signed at his accession a 'capitulation' virtually handing over to the magnates in the Raad all the powers of the Crown. Denmark, like Sweden, went through a period of alienation of Crown land to the nobility. It was supposed to increase revenue but in fact benefited almost entirely the purchasers. A decade of corrupt and inefficient government and defeat in war produced by 1660 the complete collapse of government finances. The cession to Sweden of the provinces on the further side of the Sound, which meant that dues could now only be collected with the consent of Denmark's main enemy, was a final blow to the system of aristocratic rule. A meeting of the Estates in 1660 achieved something like a bloodless revolution. The Copenhagen townsmen, in alliance with the clergy and with one of the rival groups at the court, repudiated the policies of the Raad. An excise, with no full exemption for nobles' estates, was introduced; the powers of provincial governors were restricted; Frederick, in defiance of the nobility, solemnly accepted Denmark from representatives of its people as a hereditary kingdom. In 1665 a new and absolutist constitution was proclaimed, asserting the theory that royal power was derived from this contract with the Estates as the equivalent of the whole body of subjects. Most subjects were not even allowed to know in detail what the constitution said.

The Danish peasantry, most of whom were already in a state of dependence not far from serfdom, gained nothing from the constitutional changes. Though the nobility could not escape taxation entirely, it remained a privileged class, active in administration and justice, and economically thriving. While the Swedish Crown was recovering its lands, in Denmark Frederick's reforming minister Sehested handed over most of the remaining Crown possessions to pay off debts accumulated in the wars. But it was not the old-established aristocrats who benefited most. A new nobility of civil and military office-holders, many of them German by origin, slowly supplanted the old families. Lacking resources of its own, the Crown now depended on a well-administered general land-tax, levied on the king's sole authority. The Rigsraad disappeared entirely. Under Christian V a centralized administration was developed, with civil divisions replacing the old fiefs as the local units, and a Privy Council closely controlled by the king. The real creator of the system was Peter Schumacher, later Count Griffenfeld (see p. 243), the merchant's son who at Christian's accession in 1670 became his all-powerful chancellor. Besides his reform of government, he did his best to be a Danish Colbert, but without the resources for a successful commercial power. Beginning as an advocate of peace and neutrality, he was soon committed to the anti-French alliance, and to the attempt to exploit the military misfortunes of Sweden.

One region which escaped the worst effects of Baltic wars was Norway. It was not a possession the Danes could afford to lose. The timber trade through its many little ports was more significant to the free peasants than to big commercial concerns; but there were iron, copper, and silver mines. Gustav Adolf did not regard it as territory worth conquering, or even bargaining for. To the Danish nobility estates and offices in Norway offered opportunities for exploitation well away from the control of the central government. Though there was a Norwegian Diet, administration was almost entirely kept by the Danes in their own hands. It was in the war of 1657 that they came nearest to losing Norway altogether, when the Swedes briefly occupied Trondheim as well as a good deal of territory in the south. Since the Dutch disliked the presence of what was now beyond doubt the stronger Baltic power on the route to the White Sea, most of the Norwegians in 1660 found that they were back under Danish rule and in theory 'consenting' to the new hereditary monarchy. In fact they had some reason to welcome it. The reformed administration, even though it still treated Norway more or less as a backward area, destroyed the power of the Danish nobility over its estates there. A rigid alien government and taxation system was probably for most of the peasants a lesser evil than total subjection to landlords.

THE BALTIC POWERS, 1660–1700

Charles XI of Sweden was much less consistent and resolute in trying to reduce the amount of resources devoted to war than in achieving monarchical absolutism. To say that the need for French subsidies compelled him, in 1674–75, to make war on Brandenburg and Denmark is no explanation: the war cost more than the French ever paid. After Brandenburg had defeated the Swedes at Fehrbellin in 1675, German forces occupied the Swedish lands in Pomerania. When Denmark joined in the war there was for a time a risk that the provinces of southern Sweden annexed by Charles X would be lost again. In 1679 it was made clear that Baltic wars were now a subsidiary part of the European contest: peace was made almost entirely by the French, who permitted only small territorial changes. There was for the Baltic states one possible way out of this role of pawns to be sacrificed or preserved by the western powers. If Denmark and Sweden made a firm alliance, the French and Dutch would have to fight without them. Behind the Treaty of Lund in 1679 which publicly settled the frontiers were secret articles that did envisage some such long-term agreement. Both in fact still based their military and diplomatic activities on the assumption that war between them would be renewed. The Swedes were anxious to control Holstein–Gottorp (a Baltic equivalent of the little duchies on the French frontiers), which would be a base for attacking Denmark from the south. In 1681, at the cost of abandoning attempts to drive the Dutch out of Baltic trade, Charles made at The Hague an alliance with the United Provinces which inevitably led Louis XIV to make Denmark his Scandinavian assistant instead of Sweden. A long and insecure semi-peace in the Baltic was maintained only because none of the major powers felt it worth while to extend their wars there.

To the Poles, Baltic affairs after the Peace of Oliva were as always only one of many dangers and ambitions. The 1660s were a period of territorial as well as economic disaster. The war against Russia, resumed in 1658, continued despite the pacification on other frontiers. Nine years later, by the armistice at Andrusovo, Kiev, all the Ukraine east of the Dnieper, and large areas in the Smolensk region were handed over to Russia. The Polish–Lithuanian state lost something like a fifth of its land – an area larger than England and Wales. Not much of it was inhabited by Poles. In 1665, with Russian armies occupying much of the country, another internal revolt had begun. A successful general, Jerzy Lubomirski, who had been convicted of treasonable dealings with the emperor, formed an armed confederation that attacked royal forces, ostensibly to prevent the very mild reforms put forward by the court party. The only indication of any remaining strength in the Polish Crown was that when, in 1668, John Casimir happily abdicated, at least five foreign countries were involved in the electoral intrigues. The younger Condé was one subject who thought that a throne, even of Poland, would be worth having. For once most of the nobility agreed that a native candidate was less likely to involve them in any further calamitous wars. Michael Wisnowiecki was chosen as a king only vaguely committed to the Habsburg cause.

The settlement with Russia did nothing to preserve Poland from the other eastern invaders. In 1672 a new Cossack attack provided the opportunity for the intervention by the Turks that was a prelude to their last big advance in Europe. In the decade of war that followed, Poland was dominated by the army. The grain trade collapsed; so, in many areas, did the whole internal economy. Small estates became even smaller as their owners grew hopelessly indebted; urban markets disappeared; great aristocrats ruled their estates with even less regard than before to the central government. For a few there were opportunities to acquire land cheaply; for others service in the army at any level became an attractive means of escape from misery. It was in these conditions that Jan Sobieski, son of one of the richest Ruthenian magnates, built his career as diplomat and soldier. His status as a national hero and Christian idealist was established by an almost treasonable defiance of the monarchy. King Michael had signed, in 1672, the humiliating Peace of Buczacz which handed over to Turkish suzerainty Podolia and most of the Ukraine as well as promising a large annual tribute. Sobieski ignored the treaty, made appeals to national loyalty, and while the Seym was objecting to the surrender but doing nothing to recreate the army, raised new forces at his own cost. By a stroke of political luck he not only won a brilliant victory over the outraged Turks but did so at Khocim, remembered as the scene of the heroic siege of 1621, and on the day after the death of the king. At the head of a triumphant army he marched on Warsaw and was elected to the throne with little resistance. Even so, his accession in 1674 as John III was not unanimously welcomed. He was attached to the 'French' party in opposition to the 'Austrians'; and his actions as king mingled the familiar diplomatic chicanery with his crusading ambitions.

Sobieski (who is one of the few monarchs to be referred to commonly by his surname) did not earn his successes by any major reforms of Polish government. The armies were trebled in size and the Cossack and Tartar regiments more firmly incorporated in them. But central administration, and central taxation, were as erratic as before. The armies could be paid only with foreign subsidies. Secret treaties with the French and the Swedes in 1675 held out hopes of an alliance against Brandenburg that would lead to the recovery of some lost territory; but the price of a large French subsidy was an agreement with the sultan that left under his control most of what King Michael had given away. In 1678, when that scheme had been abandoned, the Holy League against the infidel again became Sobieski's dominant idea. Gradually he abandoned his ties with Louis XIV in favour of the alliance with the emperor that made possible his dramatic exploit as saviour of Vienna in 1683 (see p. 374). The achievement that momentarily made Poland look like a European power again did not in fact bring much benefit to the country or its king. Wars against Turkey dragged on until Sobieski's death, shaped more and more not by devotion to Christianity but by his zeal to conquer Moldavia as a sovereign principality for his son. It would be an excellent base from which to work for the establishment of a hereditary Sobieski dynasty in Poland.

The hope did not materialize. At the election in 1697, the year after Sobieski's death, the successful candidate, in spite of French opposition, was Frederick Augustus, the Lutheran Elector of Saxony (see p. 373). He had been supported by one of the most energetic enemies of the Swedes, John Reinhold Patkul, leader of the resistance by the Livonian nobility to the alleged oppression by the Swedish government. Like Henri IV of France a century earlier, Augustus decided that a crown was worth a mass, and as soon as he was established in his joint capitals of Warsaw and Cracow, began the soundings for an anti-Swedish alliance. It was a great help that in 1699 he was able to join in the Treaty of Karlowitz between the emperor and the sultan and regain some of the lost Ukrainian territory. It was in 1697 too that Charles XII inherited the Swedish throne and succeeded, at the age of fifteen, in disposing of the regents appointed by his father and taking power himself. His boyhood had been devoted entirely to his training as a military sovereign. A great new conflict in the north was obviously at hand.[4]

NOTES AND REFERENCES

1   Printed in *Sweden as a Great Power*, ed. M. Roberts (London, 1968), pp. 18–28.

2   M. Roberts, 'Queen Christina and the General Crisis' in *Past and Present*, no. 22 (1962), p. 39.

3   Quoted in N. Davies, *God's Playground: a History of Poland* (Oxford, 1981), vol. i, p. 342.

4   The Northern War is described in the next volume in this series, M. S. Anderson, *Europe in the Eighteenth Century* (3rd edn, London, 1987).

17

RUSSIA AND THE OTTOMAN EMPIRE

Western textbooks have still not completely escaped from the habit of treating the history of Russia before Peter the Great as a minor appendix to the more significant affairs of Jülich-Cleves or Pinerolo. As for the Turks, though they are well known as a 'menace' to Europe proper, their internal regime and society tend to be seen as an Asiatic phenomenon unrelated to the development of civilized countries. Yet whatever the boundaries of the continents are taken to be, tsar and sultan between them claimed something like half Europe as their territories. Eastern empires were experiencing on a larger scale than the west the same conflicts in the establishment of a unified and centralized state. The power of landowners, administrators, and armies, the impact of Churches, and the threat of famine were fundamental in the life of communities; the ancestry of Byzantium and hence of Rome was a hazy background. Russia by the end of the century was beyond doubt a monarchy in the western style, and a part of the European international entanglement. The Ottoman Empire was in a period of retreat; but there was no reason to doubt that it would recover as it had before. The rulers of both countries had achieved more successfully than any of their western counterparts the universal aim of applying their resources to military power. There are many difficulties in the way of making the comparisons as enlightening as they ought to be. Barriers of language and accessibility still make the work of Russian historians slow to penetrate to the west; and in both Empires the seventeenth century left a limited range of surviving sources. Too many questions will have to go unasked.

RUSSIA IN THE TIME OF TROUBLES

'The Time of Troubles' is a term applied aptly enough to the whole generation between the death of Ivan IV in 1584 and the reign of Michael Romanov. In 1598 it had seemed that the outlook for the monarchy might be improving. Boris Godunov, who as regent had the credit of freeing the Russian Church from its nominal dependence on the Patriarch of Constantinople, had the backing of the Church and of a strong group of boyar leaders in claiming the throne. But he chose to be 'elected' by a *Zemski Sobor* that was at least a symbol of wider support (see p. 254). To prove that despite this unheard-of procedure he was a real tsar, Boris asserted his power with executions, tortures, and allegedly sorcery. None of these disposed of his worst enemy, the famine that hit central Russia in 1601 (see p. 99). The collapse of many landed estates as peasants fled towards the frontiers reduced any tolerance of the regime. Crown officials were blamed for inaction and corruption; revenues fell; conspiracies among noble families exploited, on a Russian scale, the forces that in their smaller way such rebels as the magnates of the French religious wars had used. It was easy to find claimants to the throne. The story which began to circulate that Dmitry, the murdered son of Ivan IV, had survived or miraculously risen from the dead, was nothing unusual in the mythology surrounding tsardom. Nor was there any difficulty for the boyars excluded from the court in finding allies among men of their own kind whose estates happened to be under the Polish instead of the Russian Crown. Surrounded by his Russian and Polish sponsors and backed by the forces they could raise as easily as could monarchs, the 'False Dmitry' enjoyed a triumphal entry into Moscow and a brief reign in which he retained some of the popularity of the rebel hero. Who he really was remains a matter of speculation. The Poles proclaimed that he had become a Catholic, and there were hopes among the Jesuits of a movement for the reunion of the two Churches. For the moment no-one seemed to expect any policy or promises from him: merely to be the enemy of the existing regime was enough to win the support of many great families, of peasants, of smaller landholders, and of the Moscow townsmen. But the pseudo-tsar was no mere Perkin Warbeck: he showed signs of an almost progressive outlook, complaining of boyar ignorance and isolation, rejecting both the brutality and the ceremonial of palace custom. It was not a situation that could last for long. Like later occupants of the Kremlin, 'Dmitry' became more and more afraid of treason among his supporters. His Polish allies were not in a position to defend him with adequate force, and rivals of those boyars he favoured could easily denounce him as an instrument of the foreigners. In 1606 a new mass rising in Moscow was organized – ostensibly to defend the tsar from the Poles – and 'Dmitry' was murdered. The head of one of the greatest boyar families, Vasily Shuisky, was proclaimed as the true tsar who would restore the traditional forms of Russian paternal rule.

Shuisky appears to have made some effort to play the part of an upholder of law rather than a wholly irresponsible boyar-sponsored despot. Whatever constitutional ideas could be read into his promises did not matter much. Nor did it really improve his security when he arranged that the Church should prove the fraudulence of the False Dmitry by bringing the remains of the Real Dmitry to Moscow and showing them working miracles. Shuisky's fumbling efforts to win the support of the Church included what later proved an important move: he repudiated the appointment as Patriarch of Filaret, the head of the boyar family of Romanov. Outside Moscow none of these palace manoeuvres seemed to matter much; for it was at this moment that the rising of the Cossacks (see p. 271) threatened to destroy the entire apparatus of the state. Shuisky, once the rebels had been turned back from Moscow, put all the armed force he could raise at the disposal of his supporters in the provinces to punish their enemies.

No consecutive account of the events between 1606 and 1610 can make much sense. There was in 1607 a second Polish-sponsored False Dmitry, and a blockade of Moscow which led Shuisky to make an agreement with Sigismund of Poland. It did not last long; and the tsar was soon seeking support of the Swedes instead. At the rebel capital at Tushino Russian opponents of Shuisky gathered whatever forces they could get, including Poles acting independently of their king. The more ingenious or widely connected nobles, as well as ambitious lesser men, contrived to play off one source of authority against another and demand rewards from both. Marina, the Polish wife of the first False Dmitry, turned up at Tushino with the claim that the new one must obviously be her husband too. In 1610, when Sigismund had established a headquarters at Smolensk, the Tushino leaders rallied round his son Vladislav as tsar. Shuisky was overthrown by a military defeat and by another Moscow urban rising; and slowly power seemed to be passing into Polish hands everywhere except in the Swedish-dominated areas of the north.

There was still a strong 'Cossack' element in the peasant population that aimed not to take over the state but to dissolve it or simply escape from it. But there were also many among the rebels of various allegiances who retained their hope of a stable propertied society in which they would share. The increase of Polish and Swedish power produced, in towns and among the *dvoriane*, an element of national resistance. The Church, though rightly regarded as one of the most merciless landowners, was an influence on the side of order. In 1611, with the Poles occupying the Kremlin, the Swedish army in Novgorod, and hordes under Cossack inspiration imposing a military rule of terror on much of the countryside, there developed a movement in favour of some kind of collective national stability. It came chiefly from what can reasonably be described as the middle classes – the propertied townsmen and the provincial *dvoriane*. Some of Sigismund's supporters had already attempted to get the Poles to commit themselves to a document that would guarantee a stable form of administration and in particular give a better legal and social status to landowners below the boyar level – a move which the boyars had then tried to frustrate. One of the military leaders responsible for Shuisky's fall, Prokopy Liapunov, went some way towards becoming a national leader of the *dvoriane*, with a strongly conservative religious element in his appeal and a vague promise to get rid of foreigners. His movement became such a tangle of incompatible aims and alliances that it easily fell to pieces when he was murdered by disillusioned Cossack supporters.

It seems a ludicrous notion that a country as large as European Russia could be in danger of being partitioned between its Polish and Swedish enemies. But that, as civilian administration and the stable society of landlord and peasant crumbled, was now a real possibility. Only an independent military force was likely to preserve the existing state. In 1612 a new army did emerge, recruited partly by an urban leader, Kuzma Minin – a butcher, in the literal sense, from Nizhny-Novgorod. Its commander was a boyar, Prince Dmitry Pozharsky, who had kept well away from the murders and executions of Moscow. Their range of support was meant to extend from the peasants to the great landowners; Cossacks, and the palace nobility, were as much the enemy as were foreigners. The appeal to all seekers of order and peace was strengthened by calling a Zemsky Sobor, to meet at Yaroslavl. The 'assembly of the land', however uncertain its power, was a means of reconstituting out of the local communities a Russian state separated from the foreign invaders and their discredited princely allies. It had surprising success in collecting men and money for an attack on Moscow and the Poles. The leaders of the assembly were by no means high-minded patriots rejecting the sordid world of alliances and compromises. Pozharsky was quite prepared to reach an agreement with the Swedes, or to become a candidate for the throne himself. Eventually he became the ally of the Cossacks in forming an army under Prince Trubetskoy which decisively beat the Poles. The army was soon the one effective political power; at its headquarters a new Zemsky Sobor assembled in 1613. Besides the Cossacks and soldiers all sections of the landholders down to the free peasantry had a voice, as well as the towns and the church. It was this body that proclaimed as tsar Filaret's sixteen-year-old son Michael, the first of the Romanov dynasty. Though the Romanovs were not much different from any other great family, there was just enough of the *politique* and the nationalist in the regime of Minin and Pozharsky to establish a feeling that the boyars and the foreigners had been more decisively beaten than before and that the disbanding of armies could begin. No-one took very seriously the talk of written constitutions or guarantees against unacceptable royal power.

THE RUSSIAN SERVICE-STATE

The re-establishment of a comparatively secure monarchy was bound up with the creation of the Russian 'service-state'. There was nothing new in the insistence that every Russian owed an almost unlimited duty of service to the tsar. Ivan IV's *Oprichnina* had been an extravagant version of the principle that a subject's status depended on the way in which he served. It was still the theory that social and economic status was a subsidiary matter, and was itself derived from the individual's relationship to the state. Much of the effort of Michael Romanov's government was put into constructing an administrative system in which obligations to the state were not evaded. A surprising amount of bureaucratic work was achieved. An elaborate census, completed in 1628, though obviously it could not really list and classify the entire population, did something to make legal resistance to the flight of peasants easier. The Treasury, pressing for an increase in revenue, produced a survey of the armed forces it maintained and their cost. It revealed that in spite of the state's devotion to military service the available *dvorianin* force only amounted to 40,000 men. Trivial grievances of provincial officials found their way to Moscow in enormous quantity; and slowly the gulf between the theory of the centralized state and the actual life of peasant communities began to narrow. But the crucial part of the service concept was at the top: the highest ranks in the boyar nobility, the armed forces, and the central bureaucracy should be united in dependence on the tsar. High military and civil officers could achieve the rank or at least the social level of boyars; more of the landed nobility became active servants of the state. As landed estates became less secure, the holding of prestigious office was welcome. The *Duma*, originally a council confined to the narrow circle of top boyar families, became a larger body, membership of which was a mark of belonging to the highest service élite. By the time of Peter the Great's re-ordering of ranks the boyars as such had disappeared in an increasingly tangled system of status.

The erosion of exclusive boyar privilege did not destroy the *mestnichestvo*, the institution, or legalised custom, of the boyars by which a strict order of prestige depended on the holding of offices. It established the assumption that though an office itself was not hereditary the status it conferred was – and extended to the whole family of the holder. Once the status was achieved it was an intolerable derogation to have anyone inferior in the rating appointed to a higher office than one's own; so that to introduce new men to the bureaucracy and to create or abolish posts within it were matters of immense complexity. Throughout Michael's reign the '*mestnichestvo* feuds' hindered the development of a competent central administration. Nevertheless, departmental organization did expand, more through the empire-building efforts of those already in high office than by a rational plan. The *prikazy* – departments of central government – multiplied. Their size, function, and survival depended mainly on personal rivalries that surrounded them. The armed forces came in theory under the same system: there were *prikazy* for the cavalry, the artillery, even the Cossacks. Locally the *voevoda*, originally military commanders, organized every aspect of government in the districts they controlled, and were generally undermining the power of older institutions less dependent on the Crown. Two or three hundred of them shared out all but the most sparsely populated areas. Some were almost completely independent rulers, others intermediaries between central and local authority. The almost unanimous view expressed in complaints from the provinces was that they were more corrupt and oppressive than any former authority. But as outsiders they were inevitably open to such accusations. In theory they held office for only a few years and had no opportunity of profitably controlling taxation. To the peasant the Moscow-appointed official was merely one more creator of poverty to add to the landlord, the moneylender, and the priest.

Conditions in Moscow as Michael's government gradually became established did not make efficient administration easy. For his first six years the tsar, like many weak sultans, was dominated by his mother. This was 'Martha the Nun', whose connection with the Church was more the result of the Troubles than of religious zeal. Round her a palace group of relations and dependants collected. Her husband Filaret, who had been captured by the Poles, was released under the truce of 1619 and took up his office as Patriarch. He claimed to be an equal ruler with the tsar, and became effectively the head of the state. He was one of the clerical statesmen of the time who made no pretence of defending ecclesiastical in preference to civil power. His Church was to be a tightly organized body with a hierarchy of its own equal, at the top, to that of the state; but ultimately it would accept the sovereignty of the tsar and his ministers. What mattered to Filaret was that he could add to his power in the state direct control over the huge domains of the Church. Having sent Martha back to her nunnery and carried out the normal purge of her dependants, he established a carefully restricted princely circle of his own in the highest court offices. Only in the Holy Synod, which claimed a status almost equal to that of the Duma, could the high clergy assert independent influence.

By the time of Michael's death in 1645 the Russian government was more stable than at any time since 1598. The wars against Sweden and Poland had been settled at the cost of abandoning the Smolensk lands and the Baltic region. Resistance to the Turks had been left largely to the Cossacks. When they captured the fortress of Azov at the mouth of the Don and offered to cede it to the tsar, Michael, with the approval of a Zemski Sobor, refused. It did not mean that Russia was becoming a peaceful constitutional monarchy. Alexis I, who inherited his father's throne as a youthful tsar surrounded by the familiar palace gangs, was faced in his first years with risings in Moscow and Novgorod, and then with the great Ukrainian revolt (see pp. 271–4). In the midst of it, in 1649, the Moscow government undertook the production of a comprehensive legal code, the *Ulozhenie*, which was supposed to incorporate the pleas for reform that had been brought before it. It was an attempt to assert in a solemn documentary form the total power of the state over the Russian people, and to give to those who administered it a practical new instrument. There had been such Codes before; but the latest was a century old and had little relevance left. In nearly a thousand articles, the *Ulozhenie* brought together a mixture of legal practices and principles, assembled hastily from a great variety of sources. Some of them were familiar parts of Russian tradition, some originated in the requests of the Zemsky Sobor. But the essential articles were those that froze the existing social structure and completed the legal imposition of serfdom.[1] Nothing could be done that would deprive the state of a taxpayer; the Church could no longer expand its estates; townsmen could not leave their towns, nor outsiders compete in town trade; no-one outside the ranks of the *dvoriane* could come into them; no-one could use slavery as an escape from obligations. Existing landholdings were generally confirmed, and the hereditary rights of the boyar families were strengthened. In spite of its size and complexity, the Code did not really define the legal relationship between lord and peasant closely. There were rules about circumstances in which the lord could move his peasants from the land – designed not to protect the peasant but to prevent tax-evasion. What legal rights remained to the serf, in such matters as ownership of his household goods, depended on incomplete rules rather than any comprehensive principles. Where there were doubts, it was clear that the landlord and the knout would normally settle them.

With the defeat of the Ukrainian rebellion and the imposition of the Code, the state seemed to be on the verge of an unprecedented efficiency. It was achieved not by brutal treatment of its subjects – except of course that the vast majority of them who lived at the lowest levels of society – but under the reputedly gentle and

431

cultured Alexis. A problem that grew was that of the Orthodox Church, which had not abandoned its hopes of regularly intervening in political affairs. The Patriarch Nikon, elected in 1652, rose to power by capturing the devotion of his sovereign. His proclaimed purpose was to restore the Church to its ancient purity of observance and efficiency of organisation (see pp. 147–8); but his first ambition was to re-establish the dominant role in the state of which he alleged the 'satanic law' of 1649 was meant to deprive it. Before long he had achieved the same status as Filaret – the equal in majesty of the tsar. But that was not enough. His Church had to recover the unity of the Orthodox faith and become superior to the states within it. The great reforms that made some sense of Russian religion created an opposition not only among the clergy and their congregations but among courtiers who were always ready to line up against a royal favourite. By 1658 the great quarrel between Alexis and Nikon had begun. In one sense it demonstrated the strength of the royal government, since it was conducted with no alarming violence and no outside intervention. The reforms had their attractions for the tsar. A united Orthodox Church under the leadership of Moscow would be a great asset in extending Russian power and influence southward. But the settlement by which Nikon was dismissed and his reforms retained was a victory for the state won at the cost of establishing a minority faith round which opposition could collect (see pp. 148–9). In the resistance of the Old Believers and the use made of them by rebels of every kind, the Russian government for the first time experienced the inconvenience for the state of religious minorities. It was not backward in taking revenge.

PETER THE GREAT

Alexis married twice. His first wife, from the great Miloslavsky family, produced a daughter Sophia and the two defective sons who became the tsars Fedor III and Ivan V. The second wife of Alexis, Natalia Naryshkin, was a very different character. The daughter of a provincial noble, she was related, through the foreign service of another of her family, to the Scottish Hamiltons and had been educated in a household corrupted – as all good Russians saw it – by western culture. Her son Peter was born in 1672. There was nothing that an older generation of Muscovites would have thought unusual in the events that followed the death of Fedor ten years later. The Miloslavsky and the Naryshkin families were naturally the centre of a palace feud, involving accusations of witchcraft, poisoning, and treason. The Naryshkins had Peter 'elected' tsar at a mass meeting in Red Square. But by superior bribes and promises the Miloslavsky had won over the rank and file of the *streltsi*, the large part-time army of Moscow guards. They now invaded the Kremlin, mudering all the Naryshkins they could find. With the help of a city mob they attacked the houses of boyars, rich merchants, and – in the name of the Old Belief – clergy. Peter, who had watched the proceedings, was allowed to remain 'joint tsar' with Ivan; Sophia was to be regent. For five years the rival parties continued to use torture, public flogging, and execution as their normal weapons. Sophia and Peter, on different occasions, fled for their lives to the Trinity Sergius monastery. Eventually she was defeated and spent the rest of her days under guard in a nunnery; many of the *streltsi* ended theirs on the block. By 1689 Peter's family were in fairly secure control, though the tsar himself was in no hurry to devote himself to politics.

Peter's reign was a translation into Russian terms of the absolute monarchy of the west. In the imagination of the peasants he kept some of the mystery of tsardom. To those who knew him he was the 'sovereign emperor', and the man in disguise at the dockyards or at the riotous parodies of court and church ceremonial. To the Old Believers he was either a simple usurper or another manifestation of Antichrist. Peter's elaborate week-long orgies of blasphemy and promiscuity with the Most Drunken Synod were no more incompatible with efficient monarchy than was the ceremonial life of Versailles. Western kings went hunting three times a week and had their enemies killed in moderate numbers, usually with the help of the law. Peter occasionally wielded the axe himself, and executions were counted in hundreds. Russian tortures were not more blood-curdling than those applied, for instance, to Henri IV's assassin, Ravaillac – they were merely more numerous. High office was used for personal gain: Alexander Menshikov, who despite his illiteracy and obscure origins acquired leading posts in state and army under Peter, became the owner of 90,000 serfs; but western ministers seldom died in poverty. The difference was not so much in the conduct of absolute monarchs as in the range of Peter's activities and in his defiance of tradition.

The Great Embassy to the west in 1697 was certainly unique. Though its immediate purpose was to seek help in defeating the Turks rather than to prepare for the westernizing of Russia, Peter's acquaintance with the isolated German community in Moscow had made him see how remote in culture and economy Russia had become, even by the standards of a nation that was not itself in the forefront of western civilization. As the half-incognito Peter Mihailov, he contrived to give western court society something of a lesson in not taking itself too seriously. He met the Elector of Brandenburg, the Emperor Leopold, the King of Poland, and William III. He took a short gunnery course in Berlin, worked in Dutch shipyards, studied architectural and engineering drawing. There was time too for the happier activities that disillusioned Bishop Burnet, who had thought him a 'holy man', and made John Evelyn send for Wren to estimate the cost of repairs after the royal party had borrowed his house. When Peter returned it was to deal with a new revolt of the *streltsi*. As soon as he arrived in Moscow he organized the punishment of the already defeated rebels, with a bloodbath of tortures and executions, in which Peter gave practical assistance. It was not entirely incongruous that he combined this with appearing in western dress and encouraging others to do the same. Whether or not it is true that he brandished shears to cut off the beards of courtiers, the story is plausible. Beards, held by the Old Believers to be necessary for salvation, were a cherished symbol of patriarchal authority. God, as everyone knew, had a beard and man was made in his image. Attempts to make the Russians enjoy themselves in the image of Peter, with tobacco and sex to help, were rightly seen as an attack on the crushing of thought and enterprise in which the Church had a leading part. More seriously, Peter initiated an expansion of lay printing and publishing. Textbooks on geometry, engineering, and geography, translations of western literature, and even a newspaper appeared – all in a simplified Slavonic alphabet.

Peter's reforms of Russian government did not spring from any sudden inspiration to 'westernize' a 'backward' country. They fluctuated in immediate aim and method; but the consistent purpose was to win military victories. In them his ruthless energy impinged on the old conflict between central and local, territorial and bureaucratic powers. The greatest need was of course money. One of the first features of western economy to be introduced was repeated debasement of the currency followed by a rise in prices.

With no merchant and banking community able to lend large sums, the Crown lived on the direct income from lands, and on taxes, a large part of which got lost in the central administrative machine. In 1699 a new central institution, the *Ratusha* run by the merchants of Moscow, was put in charge of the taxation of all the towns. Indirect taxes on almost every purchase and a poll-tax on every individual, though it was claimed that they trebled the revenue, were a new cause of flight and revolt. The assessment of these was closely supervised from the centre. But Peter's policy in the first decade of the new century was to run down the old Moscow administration and rely on the eight provinces into which the whole country was now divided, each responsible for its own unit of the army. Only when the new capital at St Petersburg was usable – at first, like other reforms, it was in con-stant danger of sinking into a swamp – did a more effective central government appear. The Senate, originally a small body picked by Peter to exercise some of the tsar's authority in his frequent ab-sences at the wars, took advantage of the decline of the old depart-ments. With the help of its vague judicial powers, it became something like a ruling council. But it had to fight for its authority against the *oberfiscal*, who by rooting out corruption was supposed to augment the revenue. In fact, he became the head of a secret service that acquired power by denunciation. 'We all steal,' said Yaguzhinsky, procurator-general and the tsar's chief link with the Senate, 'some on a bigger scale than others'.[2]

Beside the Senate there began to flourish the new-style depart-ments, the Kollegii, modelled on the theories of Leibnitz and on Swedish practice and to some extent staffed by Swedes and Ger-mans. The notion of territorial division had gone: the 'colleges' exercised their departmental function over the whole country. Commerce, industry, and mining had their 'colleges'; one dealt with taxation, another with state expenditure. They were sup-posed to combine the virtues of committee decisions with pro-fessional expertise. But they were also one more addition to the complexities of the competition for central power. The presidents of the 'colleges' became bureaucrats engaged in contests for supremacy which, despite the great personal authority of the Procurator-General and Peter's occasional violent interventions tended to make government as heavy and almost as inefficient as before.

The effect of the 'Petrine reforms' has ever since been an inexhaustible subject for historical dispute. In the west they have often been imagined far too vividly as a moment when Russia was suddenly translated from barbaric isolation to second-class membership of the community of civilized states. To contemporaries what mattered was the burden of service that the tsar's government could impose; and in this Peter was merely a little more relentless and thorough than most. Much of the 'westernizing' was certainly a façade that collapsed. Though there was some increase in textile and metal production, and even some improvement in agriculture, too few of the people were far enough above a bare subsistence level for enterprises maintained by monopoly and urban serfdom to develop into a thriving native capitalism. Cities did become safer and, for the fortunate, freer places to live in. The worst religious taboos were less easily enforced; begging, brigandage, and the oppression of women diminished. The apparently preposterous 'Table of Ranks' of 1727 marked a real success in replacing the intricacies of status and privilege by distinctions that the state could exploit more effectively. Hereditary nobility became the automatic reward for service as officers in the forces or in comparable grades of the bureaucracy. It was a further step in the subordination of the landed nobility to the state, and to its increasingly urgent function of defeating its enemies abroad.

RUSSIA AND TURKEY AT WAR

Peter as a child had liked to play at soldiers. His first regiments were his boy-companions; then young men of the court volunteered to serve in them; real horses, artillery, specially built fortresses were provided for him to play with. For his make-believe wars German officers and technicians were recruited to teach methods of fighting unknown to the old Russian armies. His commander-in-chief, Patrick Gordon, was a Catholic Scot. The two 'regiments of boy-soldiers' became a part of the Russian forces. It was hard to say where the game ended and reality began. (Western kings and western generals thought themselves different from Peter.) Of the thirty-five years of the reign, Russia was at peace for about two. The wars were not unproductive frontier clashes or dynastic quarrels of the kind that kept western soldiers occupied: they involved great territorial hopes and fears on fronts a thousand miles apart. The three great enemies – Poland, Sweden, and Turkey – were still capable of inflicting almost unlimited destruction; and the Turks, in spite of their retreat after 1688, still seemed to Russia the greatest menace.

The last great manoeuvres of Peter's make-believe armies led, in 1695 and 1696, to attacks on the Turkish fortress of Azov, with Peter as a bombardier and then as a captain in his newly built fleet. The capture of the strongpoint that Russia had previously refused as a gift from the Cossacks was in itself no great triumph for Peter, and a minor addition to the disasters that were threatening the Turks; but it was a demonstration of the success of the technical advances in both land and naval armaments for which Peter had begun to employ western engineers. Except as an oratorical convention, the Christian crusade against the infidel was not at this stage more imporant to Peter than it was to his allies in the 'Holy League'. But the prospect of a great drive against the Turks became much more attractive to Peter after the capture of Azov: it was an enterprise in which he could win and exploit the close support of the western powers. The great Embassy was intended to make Russia for the first time a leading partner in European warfare. Unluckily it came at the moment when the western powers, involved in the profundities of the Spanish Succession, were anxious to take their gains from the successes in the east and establish peace. The Treaty of Karlowitz (see p. 445) was from the Russian point of view a misfortune, which destroyed the prospect of consolidating their power on the Black Sea. The splendid new fleet could not be used without risking a war on too wide a front.

In 1700, with vague hopes of support from the Poles and the Danes, Peter switched his military activity to the north. The 'window on the west' was even less of a deep-laid policy than the 'crusade': the object was victory for its own sake wherever it could be won – though Peter was well aware of the possibilities that Baltic conquests could involve. His defeat at Narva, by a far smaller Swedish force than the 40,000 soldiers the vast Russian recruiting system could still supply did not for a moment suggest to him that the resources of the state might be better used for other ends. He began immediately on the schemes that were to produce an army to fight the Swedes on equal terms. Numbers were still the principal aim. But modernization of arms and equipment, with the help of a renewed supply of western technicians, was an essential part of the plan. It was just as important to built up a diplomatic 'presence' in the courts of Europe. While the sultan remained a remote and alien potentate, whose envoys to Europe were unthinkable as members of the ambassadorial 'club', Peter's lavishly spending embassies and well-informed political intrigues were becoming an accepted part of the scene. In 1709 the Battle of Poltava, which destroyed the army Charles XII had taken into the Ukraine, established Russia unshakeably as an ally or enemy that no-one could ignore. With Russian forces securely in possession of a Baltic coastline, Peter could at last become the mighty liberator of Christians from the Turk. Ten thousand Moldavian soldiers and twenty thousand Serbs were, their secret envoys were said to have promised, ready to rise in support of their champion. 'Peter, Emperor of the Russo-Greeks', as his portrait, circulated in the Turkish possessions, was inscribed, could dominate the Black Sea and the eastern Mediterranean, with limitless lines of expansion open to him. It was a dream that he managed to reconcile with anxious diplomatic negotiations in Constantinople designed to prevent the Turks from assisting their embarrassing guest Charles XII. The anxieties soon proved more realistic. In 1711, on the banks of the Pruth, Peter's modern army found itself at the mercy of the horde, 200,000 strong, that the decadent Empire of the sultan could still assemble. Only negotiation on the spot saved him from the final irony of being taken prisoner by the forces of the east.

THE TROUBLES OF THE TURKS

If the Russian conflicts can appear to western eyes as one caricature of the affairs of powers that thought themselves politically more advanced, the Ottoman Empire provided another – but by an artist with an even more extravagant imagination. To the Turks Europe was still a region for military expansion, a source of slaves, and a place that supplied a growing variety of manufactures with no effort on the part of the consumer. It also provided some useful military technicians and tradesmen. But nothing in the cultural, political, or economic life of the Christian unbelievers seemed likely to affect very much what was clearly the centre of universal civilization. It could not be denied that the power of the

Ottoman Empire on its western fringes has been badly shaken in the second half of the sixteenth century. But the naval defeat at Lepanto had not put an end to Turkish activity in the Mediterranean. Egypt, the vital north African possession that was a source of grain, remained secure. Though the allegiance of the Danube lands depended on the fluctuating military and diplomatic position, the treaty of Zitva-Torok in 1606 was important mainly because it was a document in western form, signed outside Constantinople, which involved recognizing the infidel Habsburg emperor as in some sense an equal of the sultan. On the whole none of these matters seemed as significant as the long and at first unsuccessful wars against the Persians. It was not yet apparent that the successes of the Habsburgs were leading the Turkish occupiers of the Danube lands to return gradually to Anatolia and add to the pressure on its resources.

Constantinople was not in danger of disasters comparable with the occupation of Moscow by foreigners. Nevertheless, the first two decades of the century were a period of chaos. Mehemet III had a normal enough career, serving in the provinces before his accession in 1595 and killing nineteen of his brothers. But when he died in 1603 there was some danger that the Osman dynasty, like the Tudors, might run out of heirs. For Mehemet had left only two sons, both children. The elder, Ahmed, was accepted as the new sultan; the younger, Mustafa, was regarded as such a helpless idiot that he could safely be allowed to live, strictly secluded in the palace. On Ahmed's death in 1617, Mustafa was the only feasible candidate for the throne. His support came mainly from the *ulema*, who saw some prospect of bestowing on an imbecile prince the role of a saintly sovereign. The rival civil and military élites round the palace fought a tangled struggle for power that involved some popular revolts in Constantinople and the other towns. Royal wives were prominent in it, especially the always-influential figure of the *valida*, the mother of the sultan. Mustafa was soon deposed, but briefly re-appeared after the murder of his successor, Ahmed's son Osman. The second deposition of Mustafa brought to the throne a much more formidable figure, Ahmed's next son, Murad. There was even, in the midst of the instability, a pretender on the European frontier. Jachia ben Mehemet claimed to be a son of Mehemet III, hidden away to escape the strangling and educated in the Greek Church. Throughout the Thirty Years War he wandered round the courts of Catholic Europe with schemes for the liberation of the Balkan Christians and a great crusade against the Turks. It was a diplomatic weapon to keep in reserve.

The Turkish troubles had lasting effects. A comparatively minor one was that the 'law of fratricide' was abandoned. The brothers of the sultan not only survived but regularly succeeded him in preference to his sons. The theory that loyalty to the sultan could be upheld by excluding native Muslims from his entourage had failed. Moreover, as wars were less successful, the supply of men from the *devshirme* was inadequate. Armies were bigger and costlier; revenue was not rising enough to pay them or maintain the roads and the frontier defence systems. The distinction between a Domain of Islam devoted to the life prescribed by the Prophet and a Domain of War from which came the unbelievers whose offspring maintained the state and the economy was breaking down. But the sultan/caliph remained; and on his behaviour everything else still depended.

Murad IV was a succesful sultan. When he came of age, after taking the throne as a minor in 1623, he beheaded, strangled, or drowned everyone who caused him even trivial irritation, and did so with enough speed and confidence to prevent conspiracies against him. More important for his success, he was able to reconquer most of the territories lost to the Persians in the war of 1602 –18 and to distribute lands that won him supporters and revenue. Fiefs that had ceased to supply funds were confiscated. The Janissaries and Sipahis were denounced for their rebellious conduct and purged of their political leaders. Not only viziers but a Grand Mufti and a Greek Patriarch lost their heads on suspicion of disloyalty. He was also a puritan in the colloquial sense of the word: smoking was prohibited on pain of death, idleness treated as evidence of criminal intent.

Ibrahim I was an unsuccessful sultan. Though he executed the Grand Vizir and planned a general massacre of Christians, he was regarded as weak, effeminate, and interested more in ostentatious luxury than government as the function of the palace. He also had the bad luck to be in power at the time of the alarming success of the Venetians in the Balkans and the Mediterranean that enabled them to blockade the Dardanelles. Cossack invasions in the north were producing repeated losses of territory; governors and armies in the frontier provinces were mutinous. So in 1648 the Turks too held their revolution – a palace conspiracy that led to the murder of Ibrahim and the accession of his seven-year-old son Mohammed IV.

THE TURKISH REVIVAL

The decline of central authority in the worst periods of both Russian and Turkish misrule was helped by the fact that neither system now enabled a strong ministerial government to supply the deficiencies of hereditary monarchs and warring nobilities. The tsars had never had an official like the Grand Vizir who had sometimes, in the sixteenth century, been a man with the immense industry and skill needed for central government on such a scale. The Grand Vizir had been head of the 'slave' system of government. But his power had declined, through venality, the strength of the military cliques, and the dominance of the harem. Nevertheless, it was still possible for a strong Vizir to emerge from the palace intrigues. It happened briefly in 1652, when Tarkhan, the sultan's Russian mother, secured the appointment of Tarhondju Ahmed – a highly efficient administrator who unfortunately quarrelled with the corrupt Grand Mufti and was beheaded after only a year in office. It was Tarkhan too who in 1656 won the office for Mohammed Kiuprili.[3] Seventy-years-old, unworried by the prospects of dismissal or death and – though hardly literate – immensely experienced in both central and provincial office, Kiuprili made his own terms for accepting the post. In a manoeuvre with the sultan and his mother reminiscent of Richelieu, Kiuprili won what amounted to guarantees of absolute power. In his remaining five years of life he carried out a merciless purge of the governing establishment in the capital and the provinces. For any office-holder guilty of corruption or disloyalty the doubt was not whether he would keep his place or lose it but whether he would be strangled or beheaded. The nearest to the position of a Gaston of Orleans too powerful to be a victim was the Chief Eunuch, who escaped with exile. Every execution meant an estate that could be used for the benefit of the central Treasury. Whether the totals quoted for the number of victims, which range from 30,000 to 60,000, are exaggerated or not, Kiuprili certainly brought about a startling change in the sultan's effective power. There were rebellions, organised by frightened office-holders, but with an element of popular resistance to the more efficient taxation. They were crushed because the armies were loyal; and the loyalty was maintained by victories. In the Mediterranean the Venetian advanced bases were recaptured: in Hungary and Transylvania there was the beginning of the new expansion that threatened the Habsburgs. Armies, Kiuprili impressed on the sultan, must be kept on the move; and he added that the same applied to the sultan himself. Kiuprili's vision was in fact a return to the old days of the military empire. Stability, rich estates, and corrupt palace politics had been the causes of disaster – all of them characteristics of the western monarchies. It was the mobile, aggressive power, based on a well-regulated financial system, that avoided rebellion and rewarded its loyal subjects.

Kiuprili's reign of terror is one side of Turkish government. The other, less conspicuous, is the beginning in the same period of the slow extension of western influence and western administrative methods. Most of the empire's commerce was in the hands of Greeks, whose activity already extended into government. Dutch, French and English trading companies were inclined to support anyone who would give them a competent administration to deal with. Keeping well clear of the political struggles, the Greeks were able not only to preserve their lives but to build up a system of patronage and hereditary office-holding of their own. The post of Interpreter became the centre of a circle of Greek bureaucrats. In the western provinces a few of the Greeks were able, in spite of their origin, to become powerful landed aristocrats. The rules that shaped both government and society were becoming unrealistic.

Hereditary power was not one of the forms of decadence that alarmed old Kiuprili: he was succeeded in office by his son Ahmed Kiuprili. The second of what became almost a dynasty of Grand Vizirs could hardly have been more unlike his father. Ahmed represented the old cultural traditions of the empire rather than the military. Poets, historians, and astrologers were as conspicuous in his entourage as executioners in that of his father. He was also a professional politician who defeated the palace intrigues so successfully that he kept his office until his death in 1676. His concern for central administration did not mean that he, any more than his equals in the west, absented himself from military campaigns. He kept the armies in Europe under his direct command. Neither the Hungarian campaigns that ended in 1664 nor the invasion of Poland in the 1670s produced any lasting success, though Kiuprili had no difficulty in posing as a victorious hero for the benefit of the sultan and the people of Constantinople. In the Mediterranean success was more decisive: the surrender of Crete by the Venetians re-established the security of the Empire's homeland from western attack. Kiuprili was naturally well aware of the repercussions his activities were having on the wars among Christian monarchs. Most of them now had their regular diplomatic representatives in Constantinople. But in making western alliances and exploiting other people's conflicts the Turks were still backward. They did not join in the custom of sub-sidising supporters to exercise political pressure in foreign courts. It was not even possible to exploit the competition for Mediter-ranean commerce except as a source of minor economic ad-vantage. Privileges in Constantinople went to the representatives of whichever power seemed for the moment to be strongest. The French victories over the Dutch in the 1670s won them the sultan's permission to trade in the Red Sea – which may well have been in the end more valuable than any European frontier gains. But the Turks did not in return see any increased prospect of a second front against their European enemies. On the contrary, the growth of French trade to the east led to talk in Paris of an attack on Egypt and development of the Suez route.

TURKISH ATTACKS IN EUROPE

Ahmed Kiuprili was a statesman able to recognize the limits to his reasonable ambitions. To expand the area of warfare too much was to risk defeats that could not be concealed. His successor Kara Mustafa, son-in-law both of the elder Kiuprili and of the sultan, set no bounds at all to his schemes to extend Ottoman power and his own. He had already made an immense fortune before he ac-quired the highest office: a household of 2,000 slaves and 1,500 con-cubines was enough to make life at Versailles look frugal. 'Red Apple', the project for an attack on Vienna, was not his invention. The memory of 1529 was still strong in Turkish military tradition, and hopes had risen again during the campaigns of the sixties in Hungary. The Turks had accepted western diplomatic customs to the extent of regarding the Treaty of Vasvar (see p. 373), made with the emperor in 1664 and timed to remain in force for eighteen years, as at least a strong deterrent to outright attack on Austria. Consequently 1682 had become a date to which advocates of the western invasion looked forward. Mustafa virtually committed himself to a great new advance somewhere when he made with Russia the humiliating Treaty of Radzin (1681) by which Turkey practically withdrew from the Ukraine. The cautious support given to Thököli did not mean that the Hungarian rebel ruler was to play any major part in Turkish plans; but it provided one useful occasion for war. Envoys sent by Leopold to negotiate a renewal of the Treaty of Vasvar mysteriously died. (The Turks saw it as Allah's condemnation of the Christian emperor; the Austrians could think of other possible reasons.) In the spring of 1683 the march that was to subordinate Christendom to the rule of the sultan began. By July Vienna was summoned to surrender and to accept the true faith of Islam (see p. 374).

It is easy to find reasons on the Turkish side for the failure of the last of all the invasions of Europe from the east. Though Louis XIV gave a firm promise of neutrality, the sultan's only allies were the Crimean Tartars, who were afterwards blamed for failing to hold the relieving army on the Danube. Turkish artillery was not up to the standard against which western defences were now designed to survive. Discipline was not good enough to maintain the long siege while the surrounding countryside was there to be plundered. Fortresses that threatened the Turkish supply-lines were not captured. Nevertheless, it is perfectly conceivable that, at any rate if help had not been forthcoming from John Sobieski, Vienna might have fallen. As it turned out, the victory of the allied force in September began an unprecedented disaster for Turkish power. The army, apart from the Janissary corps, disintegrated. Mustafa was strangled; but his death did not prevent the development of a movement against the sultan himself. When the Holy League of European powers opened in 1684 its uncoordinated but widely successful attacks on all the western frontiers of his Empire, Mohammed IV still showed no great interest in its defence. The Grand Mufti and many of the army commanders joined in the palace revolution of 1687 that finally overthrew him. His brother Suleiman II, who had been kept a virtual prisoner to prevent conspiracies to put him on the throne, was coerced into accepting the succession of which he was very reasonably afraid.

A year later Belgrade fell to the armies under Maximilian of

Bavaria. The Venetians, steadily destroying what was left of Turkish Mediterranean power, had occupied most of Greece. A final attack on Constantinople itself seemed possible. But if Islam was in a grievous condition of internal conflict, Christendom was even worse. It was clearly in Louis XIV's interest to keep Turkish forces in the field against the Habsburgs. The French ambassador in Constantinople was able, with plausible assurances that the sultan's principal enemies in Europe were in a desperate plight, to prevent a peace treaty with the emperor. Under the third Kiuprili Grand Vizir new armies were conscripted and much of the lost territory retaken. The basic military situation was unchanged: whenever a first-rate western force was available it could now defeat any that the Turks could put into the field. European technology in firearms and in defences was better than Turkish; European capacity to devote resources to war hardly less. While in the west the machinery of government could operate tolerably well with no outstanding leadership, accidents of personality still determined the strength or weakness of the sultans. In 1697, when the emperor was for the moment free to send his best forces against the Turks, the victory of Eugene of Savoy at Zenta left the sultan no escape from a peace settlement that would involve a heavy loss of territory. The Treaty of Karlowitz in 1699 secured the whole of Hungary for the emperor and the Dalmatian coast for Venice. Otherwise most of the sultan's losses in the Balkans were restored.

NOTES AND REFERENCES

1 Extracts from the Code are translated in *Readings in Russian History*, ed. T. Riha (London, 1964), pp. 173–9.

2 Quoted in V. O. Klyuchevsky, *Peter the Great* (London, 1958 trans.), p. 244.

3 Köprülü, Koeprili, and Kuprili are among the other versions. The transliterations used here aim to be familiar rather than scholarly.

18

BRITAIN AND THE NETHERLANDS

Nearly everywhere kings and their immediate dependants were as firmly in control of central governments in 1700 as in 1600. But in two of the great states of the west, the power of hereditary monarchs had been resisted with some success. By an oddly appropriate combination of design and accident, William of Orange, who had brought the Netherlands[1] closer than ever before to dynastic rule, arrived in 1689 on the throne from which English political leaders had, for the second time in half a century, in effect deposed their king. Throughout their internal conflicts, the affairs of the two countries had been interwoven by rivalries, alliances, and similarities of theory and practice. Each had been bitterly divided between centralizing and decentralizing forces, between rival economic interests, between versions of Protestant Christianity that served to rouse emotion and belligerence. Each had a single great city so rich that governments could not easily resist its political demands. After repeated commercial and military struggles against each other, they now seemed firmly united in the exhausting wars against France. They were agreed in offering a limited toleration in religion and in political ideas, combined with intense suspicion of their Catholic minorities. They were agreed too in accepting as a permanent part of their governing machinery a central representative body. A large share of power was held, in Holland and England more than in the countries joined to them, by men whose wealth came from the accumulation and use of capital rather than simply from land. If the two stories are set side by side they may throw some light on each other.

The accession of James I in 1603 and the truce in the Netherlands six years later each produced a political agglomeration in which one state was dominant over the others. But to most Englishmen their Irish colonial territory and their monarch's separate realm of Scotland were far less important than were the lesser Netherlands provinces to the inhabitants of Holland. In both countries it became clear how different was the central power of the court and the dynasty from that of the economic capital. Charles I and the House of Orange both drew their support more from the outlying regions than from the centre of wealth. In England this was less obvious because the long-established monarchy had collected round itself a large number of allies and beneficiaries – office-holders, monopolists, higher clergy, and all whose aspirations, traditions, or connections drew them towards the court. The Netherlands, much to its economic benefit, had no court, and no established royalty. But the members of the Orange family soon came to represent no less than the Stuarts the hereditary principle, the power of the rural nobility, and foreign policies based on dynastic ambitions. One of their attempts to gain prestige was the marriage of Maurice's nephew William to Charles I's daughter Mary. That, ironically, was in 1641, the moment when royal power in England was about to collapse.

POLITICAL AND ECONOMIC POWER IN ENGLAND, 1603–21

James I came to the stable, broadly supported English monarchy from a land where heads of great clans could still fight for control of the Crown. The murder of his father and the execution of his mother were only two of the more spectacular episodes in the stormy career that had taught him a lot about the dangers and the skills of monarchy. As soon as he arrived in England courtiers and ministers indicated respectfully that they would not tolerate a preponderance of barbarous Scots in the English court or council. Not all Elizabeth's kingdom was a model of advanced civilization. Ireland, at the moment of Elizabeth's death, had just been brought back under military control; but despite Tudor efforts to impose an English system of landownership and government on the Irish chiefs, only the Pale of Dublin with its English gentry and official class was reliably administered on the queen's behalf. Out-

side it the process of turning Ireland into an area of new colonization was still far from complete. In England itself local loyalties
and, faintly, the possibility of local rebellion survived. The Council in the North and the Council in the Marches of Wales were
designed to impose royal justice on troubled regions, but could do
so only with the unreliable help of local magnates.

Nevertheless, by the standards of the time James inherited the
most centralized and well-governed of states. There were no significant internal customs barriers; the privileges of towns were
limited to administrative matters; in the counties the ruling community of the JPs, the Sheriff, and the lieutenancy formed a stable
link between local interests and central authority. Justices in Assize, who took the authority of central courts into every part of the
country, kept the Crown well-informed of defects in the system.
The king's Privy Council was a governing body whose powers,
through proclamations, commissions, and influence on the
'prerogative' courts of justice, seemed to be growing continually.
Aristocracy and gentry formed a coherent society: their traditional tendency to fight the monarch or each other seemed to have
diminished. They had not, despite centuries of intermittent conflict, evolved local institutions likely to challenge the national
ones. Regional representative assemblies were unheard of. Certainly the efforts of the English representative assembly to extend
its political influence were a familiar problem. Elizabeth's parliaments, in their dealings with the Crown, had learnt to combine fulsome assurances of loyalty with toughness on specific points. But
the range within which financial pressure and bargaining about
spheres of authority could operate seemed fairly well defined.
There was no reason to think their relations with James would be
much different.

Behind his verbiage about Divine Right, the new king accepted,
as had Elizabeth, that the most decisive way of making or declaring law was by parliamentary statute. It was not an indispensable
one: most of the actions of the central government were carried
out through proclamations and the other recognized devices of
the Crown. James – again like Elizabeth – found little difficulty
so far as law-making was concerned in doing without parliaments
for many years in succession. Peers and MPs did not deny that the
king was entitled to call and dissolve parliament when he saw fit,
or that in emergency he could exercise virtually unlimited powers
of government. The notion of collective resistance to a monarch,

to which the United Provinces owed their very existence, had scarcely arisen in England. If parliament opposed evil ministers of the Crown, this was in principle the same thing as resistance to rebels – the upholding of the state against those who would harm it for their own ends. Nowhere else did the possibility of civil war seem so remote.

The first four decades of the century have produced some high-powered disputes among scholars – disputes that can involve fundamental implications about the purposes and methods of history. The events of the 1640s and 1650s were so shattering that there was, and still is, an almost inescapable tendency to see some earlier period as 'leading up to' the Civil War. How far back this goes can vary. Clarendon (born in 1609) saw the accession of Charles I in 1625 as 'the entrance into these dark ways' though he added sardonically that others more sharp-sighted 'discerned this rebellion contriving from if not before the death of Queen Elizabeth'.[2] Later writers have seen tension increasing more or less continuously, with or without a definable starting-point. It is only in recent years that a widely upheld argument has stressed that until a late stage opposition to the policies of the Crown was sporadic, and limited to a few topics and a few people. It depends in the first place on what questions are being asked: a study of the origins of the Civil War will have a different way of selecting what is important from, say, a study of the impact of James's financial problems on his foreign policy. The complaint is that the quest for 'origins' leads to an inflation of the signs of conflict. Speeches by two or three MPs on a specific issue can be quoted as the opinions of 'parliament'; approval of royal sovereignty can be written off as conventional or self-protecting. If all the emphasis is put on opposition, religious or political, we are left with a distorted impression of what was being opposed, and still more so of the large areas where existing assumptions were unquestioned. James and Charles can be pictured as incompetent monarchs confronting angry subjects at a time when to most European rulers the Stuarts seemed to be having an easy life. But revision of the older views has its own dangers. The case against the king's ministers was expressed not just by an inner circle of politicians but in massive amounts of writing, preaching, petitioning, and demonstration. Amid all its diversity a constant theme was that from James's reign onwards a harmonious constitution was being progressively overthrown by the 'malignant party' of the royal court. Charles's anger in 1629 at the 'unsufferable disturbance and scandal' that had 'daily grown' and been tolerated until then by his father and himself was perhaps normal rhetoric for the occasion.[3] But it was not unfounded. Conflict and conformity both existed; and materials for the eventual explosion had accumulated for a whole generation. They did not make it inevitable.

The most obvious distortion has been to exaggerate the activities of parliament. In the thirty-seven years from the death of Elizabeth to the crisis of 1640 the periods when parliament sat totalled three and a half years. After the widely separated sessions of 1604 to 1611, the brief Addled Parliament of 1614 was the only one until 1621. In 1629 the eleven years of non-parliamentary royal government began. Peers and MPs were surprisingly slow to claim outright the most essential privilege of parliament – the right to meet. They asserted, at tedious length and with eventual success, their personal freedom from arrest, their right to settle disputes about elections, their freedom of speech – first on limited topics that did not encroach on royal prerogative and then, in 1621, on anything they chose. But they accepted that their survival depended in theory on the will of the monarch, and in practice on his uncertain need for taxation. Since taxes were still supposed to be granted only on special occasions, a parliament could be regarded as an unusual event. In 1610 the Commons spent many months debating a possible solution to the financial problems which might have greatly reduced the necessity for summoning parliaments. The 'Great Contract' would have abolished wardship, purveyance, and other 'feudal revenues', and in return guaranteed a permanent income from taxes that was supposed to enable the Crown to live comfortably. When it came to details, it was evident how many people were linked to the Crown by the profits involved in these matters. The Commons demanded more concessions by the court; ministers became alarmed at the widening split between royal and parliamentary views of the Crown's needs. The idea of the contract was abandoned.

The failure to establish an agreed financial system marked the end of the least troubled period of James's reign, in which government had been largely controlled by Robert Cecil, Earl of Salisbury. As son of Elizabeth's successful minister, and already in 1603 an experienced politician himself, he provided one direct link with the old regime. He kept his power, and collected offices for himself, in careful alliance with the dominant aristocratic faction of the time – the Howards. There is no firm evidence for the extravagant theory that he invented the gunpowder plot to build up anti-popish panic, or for the opposite picture of him as a defender of government integrity. None of his devices for increasing Crown revenues prevented large amounts of what was collected staying in private hands, including his own. The one safe claim that can be made for him is that after his death extravagance, incompetence, and corruption got much worse. Yet even at its most lavish, James's government was not hopelessly insolvent. The loss of revenue through selling Crown lands, and through the failure of many remaining assets to keep up with inflation, was partly offset by the increase of customs duties as new impositions were added and trade, erratically, grew. Since the Commons, as was customary, had voted 'tunnage and poundage' to the king for life, this was a source that lay on the frontier between the monarch's own revenue and parliamentary assistance. James's attempts to extend the levies angered both the Commons and the merchants. (Sir John Eliot claimed that the Dutch got more revenue by encouraging trade through a low rate of duty.) Indeed nearly all the Crown's expedients for solving its financial difficulties took forms that made the majority of gentry and merchants represented in the Commons more hostile to those groups of royal dependents and beneficiaries from which most of them were excluded. The feudal right of the king to the 'warship' of heirs who were minors was a frequent disaster to landed families, the benefit of which was shared by the treasury and those to whom the Court of Wards handed on its profitable tasks. 'Purveyance', the compulsory purchase of supplies for the court at low prices, gave obvious opportunities for profit. 'Monopolies' was a term that covered a great variety of economic privileges, some with an element of genuine state regulation and support, some amounting simply to an unearned rake-off. Granting a monopoly was not always clearly distinguishable either from farming out tax-collection or from the sale of an office: the harmfulness of all these depended partly on how much revenue the Crown lost to private profit, partly on the corruption and faction-fighting involved.

It was not easily seen that in Robert Cecil's time the government and many of its subjects had a great advantage over their predecessors: they were living in a period of good harvests, expanding industry, and comparatively stable prices. Wool was bringing greater profits to the sheep-farmer and the clothier;

landowners were finding new sources of income in minerals; exports and shipping flourished. The difficulties of the exchequer came not from any decline of national resources but from failure to get enough of them for itself. State intervention in industry and commerce was doing nothing to ensure that the successes would continue. The English economy was not doing as well as that of the Netherlands, where Amsterdam merchants had an élite of their own in many ways more powerful than the government. In 1614 the notorious scheme of the London alderman William Cockayne showed the difference clearly. For many years the Dutch carrying-trade and local industry had profited from importing unfinished English cloth which was dyed and re-exported. English exports were handled mainly by the most powerful of state-sponsored companies, the Merchant Adventurers; and it was in opposition to them that Cockayne persuaded the government to prohibit the export of any but finished cloth. He claimed confidently that he could pay the Crown £300,000 a year and make even more for his own company. The monopolists controlling alum and dye-stuffs would benefit too. The scheme was a disaster. The Dutch were adaptable enough to retaliate by banning all imports of English cloth and supplying the market themselves; English merchants could neither get all their cloth finished at home nor provide the shipping to take it to the Baltic ports where it had been most in demand. But a single blunder could not reasonably be blamed for the general economic decline that followed. For a time the export of new and lighter textiles to the Mediterranean continued to flourish. In 1618 commerce generally seemed to have recovered and the harvest was good. Then, from 1620, there began the great depression, the causes of which were argued passionately on lines that have been familiar ever since. World, or at least European, conditions certainly contributed to it: the currencies and trading practices of other countries changed, much to England's disadvantage. It had long been supposed that England was short of money, particularly of silver coins. The merchant economists Gerard Malynes and Edward Misselden suggested government controls that would prevent the export of currency. Thomas Mun was the first to make widely known the idea of a balance of trade that was unfavourable when goods that came into the country were of greater value than those that left it. Luxury imports and the activities of aliens in England were two of the worst evils. (Some modern historians think that monetary problems were decisive in themselves and imports one of many origins of them.) There were other very different ways of approaching the question. The wrath of God might be appeased by ending the peace with Spain – which incidentally would give opportunities for profitable attacks on shipping and markets.

From the beginning of his reign James had proclaimed himself as the bringer of peace: the end of the war with Spain was to be a step towards the universal peace that God had chosen James to inaugurate. Few of his subjects were convinced. The most widespread complaint against the royal court was that a 'Spanish Faction' there was attracted to the Habsburg style of absolute monarchy and, secretly, to the Catholic Church. When one of the most skilful Spanish politicians, Count Gondomar, arrived as ambassador in 1613 and established himself in the innermost circle of James' associates, he was assumed to be at the centre of a conspiracy to make England an ally, or client, of Spain. The worst suspicions were confirmed when it became known that terms were being discussed for a marriage between Prince Charles and the Infanta. England would make many concessions, including a relaxation of anti-Catholic laws; but in return there was talk of a dowry in the region of £600,000 – enough to solve the immediate financial problems. The danger of England being involved in costly foreign wars would recede. It was a prospect attractive enough to win approval from most of the holders of high government office. They included Francis Bacon, Attorney-General and afterwards Lord Chancellor, Lionel Cranfield, and Bishop John Williams, as well as the more obviously pro-Spanish courtiers such as Cottington and Digby. To those whose opinions derived from Elizabethan Puritanism, finance was unimportant and peace impossible when the great struggle between the forces of Christ and Rome was imminent. They included George Abbot, Archbishop of Canterbury, and the Earl of Pembroke whose family was now the centre of a powerful web of patronage. They too had a policy for England that was linked to a marriage alliance, between James's daughter Elizabeth and the Elector Palatine. They were married, with lavish festivities, in 1613, and James thereafter was inescapably involved with the Protestant side in German politics. When Frederick's disastrous reign as King of Bohemia led to the invasion of the Palatinate by Spanish forces, James's attempt to be both a friend of Spain and a Protestant champion seemed wrecked. With the economic depression at its worst and the Spanish

marriage in the balance, he was under a heavy obligation to find
an army to rescue German Protestantism.

PARLIAMENT IN THE 1620s

In this unhappy situation James agreed to make a new attempt at
governing with the support of a parliament. The peers and MPs
who assembled in May 1621 were willing enough to co-operate
with the king, and even – for the moment – with his new favourite
George Villiers, Marquis and future Duke of Buckingham. They
voted subsidies worth £140,000 for a war in Germany that was expected to cost more like a million pounds. Most of them envisaged
a war for the Protestant Cause in alliance with the Netherlands
while James and the 'Spanish' party in the council still hoped
somehow to fight the imperial forces only. MPs were happier to
accept James's other request – that they should suggest remedies
for the depression. It was a great opportunity to resume the
familiar attacks on monopolies, corruption, and waste. It also
enabled them to carry out some of their ancient function of bringing to the government the grievances of the localities. But it was
soon evident that the equally ancient question of parliament's
rights would not be dispelled by a few royal concessions. In
debates, petitions, and the multiplicity of committees and conferences they encroached, pretty timidly, on areas of government
that the king claimed as royal prerogative. Since not one of their
many bills for economic reforms was ever completed, they were
not in a strong position to demand more parliamentary powers.
But one method of attacking the misdeeds of the king's servants
proved important. This was the revival of impeachment – putting
ministers and others on trial with the Commons as accusers and
the Lords as judges.

Introducing 'the law' as an element in the sharing of political
power or in theories of 'sovereignty' had not on the whole been
a success. Sir Edward Coke's efforts to exalt the Common Law
into the ultimate constitutional authority tended to give power
to a small group of successful lawyers. After his dismissal in 1616
the Crown was able, though never with certainty, to keep the
judges on its side. No-one denied that parliament was itself a court
of law; and its power to put ministers and others on trial offered

a means of attacking specific actions without appearing to question the working of the state or the security of its regime. A man shown to be a lawbreaker could not be regarded as rightfully representative of the Crown. The line between crime and policy was sometimes blurred. The use of this procedure against Bacon, the greatest intellectual figure of his day, and Cranfield, the only minister to have had some recent success in handling government finance, was hardly an auspicious beginning. But from it developed, slowly, the possibility that Buckingham himself might be impeached. He was in many ways the personification of what opponents of the court believed was wrong. Having exploited James's homosexual propensities to make himself the king's inseparable counsellor, he became the unrivalled head of the patronage system. But he did not uphold a 'court' policy against a parliamentary one. For whatever reason, it was on his initiative that the Commons at the end of 1621 agreed to petition the king to make war on Spain and find a Protestant bride for Charles. Possibly he foresaw the royal anger at this that put an end to the parliament. In 1623 he escorted Prince Charles to Madrid, and came back without the promised bride, amid public rejoicing. Then he adopted parliament's demand for war on Spain as his own. It did not win him much of a following in the Commons: his support of the French monarchy against the Huguenots was almost as bad as the Spanish alliance. When that in turn was reversed and France became the enemy he had to carry the blame for the failure of the 1628 expedition to assist the Huguenots in La Rochelle. There was, it seemed, no policy and no individual he would not take under his protection and control if it furthered his own power. The most eloquent exponent of parliamentary rights, Sir John Eliot, owed his original rise to Buckingham. But Eliot, like many other clients of the duke, recognized after Charles I's accession in 1625 that the continued dominance of Buckingham was a barrier to that 'right understanding' between king and parliament that he believed to be a permanent basis for stability. When Buckingham was assassinated in 1628 the campaign to impeach him was on the brink of success.

Buckingham was a poor substitute for a great minister: all his expedients made the running of the government more chaotic and support for the monarchy itself less confident. But opposition to him did not lead to any firm parliamentary policies. In 1624 there was a spate of completed legislation that carried out some of the specific demands such as the reform – up to a point – of industrial monopolies. In 1625 the prospect of serious war in Germany made evident the inconsistency of those who had pressed for it. The Commons offered to grant 'tunnage and poundage' – the regular customs duties – to the new monarch not for life but for one year. There was no intention of providing to a mistrusted regime anything like the funds needed for an effective military force. When customs duties were collected without parliamentary authority and more money raised by forced loans, it could be argued that it was all done to make possible what parliament itself demanded. The attacks on 'illegal' taxation were seldom as high-minded as they seemed. In denouncing above all the tax-farmers who profited at the expense of both Crown and merchants, parliamentary spokesmen were not only finding a way to avoid disloyalty: behind every financial dispute lay the conflicting interests in the city with which more and more of the nation's wealth was becoming involved. It was easier for the Crown to do without parliament than to do without the support of an adequate part of London's financial community.

Parliamentary debates, even then, were long, repetitive, and seldom completely frank. But they were followed avidly, through letters, manuscript journals, and personal reports, in the country generally. It was good publicity for parliament when in 1628 it achieved the not very convincing success of the Petition of Right. The typically antiquarian title was given to a document – the ancestor of many longer ones – that denounced, in a style recalling Magna Carta, unparliamentary taxation and arbitrary imprisonment. Its other two clauses, directed against martial law and the billeting of soldiers, concealed behind these immediate grievances of southern England, the anxiety that the king would use his control of the armed forces as an indirect political threat. Charles responded with his first open demonstration of weakness and evasiveness. After successive attempts to delay and qualify his acceptance, he eventually assented to the Petition in the form the Commons demanded. In theory it was a statement of unchanged law. In practice there was a growing demand for a shift in the distribution of power. Under the energetic leadership of Sir John Eliot, the Commons were now prepared, despite their devotion to royal sovereignty as a symbol of order, to challenge ministerial rule much more decisively. In each of the great issues – taxation, religion, foreign policy, and the privileges that upheld the status of parliament – MPs were demanding a degree of control that was manifestly new. The line between supporters and opponents of the parliamentary demands was rapidly hardening. Sir Thomas Wentworth, until now a prominent opposition spokesman, entered the king's service. In the second session of the parliament, in 1629, Charles despaired of conciliation and was about to announce the dissolution. There then occurred the dramatic episode in which the Speaker was held in his chair while another – though not very novel – set of resolutions was read. That done, members obeyed the royal command to go home. Their demonstrations had not done much to secure the permanence of parliament.

THE PERSONAL RULE OF CHARLES I

It is no longer possible to imagine the eleven-year 'personal' rule of Charles as an interlude of unprecedented tyranny. Seen from outside, England merely seemed to be following belatedly the general trend for central representative bodies to fade away and monarchical government to extend its activities. For seven or eight years both financial disaster and dangerous opposition were avoided. The county aristocracy and gentry seemed to be running justice, administration, and even taxation with only a manageable amount of discontent. The Lord Treasurer, Richard Weston, Earl of Portland, who had been under threat of impeachment when parliament was dissolved, proved a competent manager. His miscellany of devices suggested that the Crown could indeed live in peacetime without parliamentary subsidies. At least the yield was enough – when the new depression of 1629–31 gave way to a period of comparative prosperity – to persuade many London merchants to co-operate with the Crown. Royal government proved in many ways to be moderately beneficial. The personal rule was certainly not a 'welfare state'; but Charles in his quest for order and stability wanted to remove sources of discontent as well as preventing any dangerous expression of it. The royal court was to be reformed, though not so much as to make it unattractive; gentry and nobility were to spend more time running their counties instead of enjoying the corruptions of London. The Book of Orders in 1630 directed JPs to enforce a mass of economic regulations and punitive measures, under the supervision of the Justices in Assize who were themselves closely watched by the Privy Council. Bodies like the Commission for Depopulation were supposed to protect the ordinary citizen from the unscrupulous exploiter, but also to make money by selling exemptions. One of Charles's personal schemes was the 'perfect' or 'exact' militia, his vision of a nation armed against invasion and internal disorder. Out of the existing ill-managed and ill-equipped amateur forces in each county he hoped to build a body of men, some properly trained and all capable of action in emergency. The Lords Lieutenant, aristocrats often attached to the court and the council, would exercise real control over their local deputies. It never matched Charles's hopes; and its consequences were unpredictable. Awareness of armed force on English soil was possibly a more important prelude to civil war than many of the political disputes. So too were the innovations in religious practice, the most evident proof that the Stuarts were breaking down an old-established way of life. To Charles they were an essential part of his programme. The Church was to instil the habit of obedience to authority and respect for hierarchy that was symbolized by the altar rail, the fixed liturgy, the avoidance of dispute and 'curious search'. It meant that every surviving puritan congregation was part of a ready-made network of opposition ideas. Against the apparent author of the changes a resistance could be concentrated that claimed full divine support.

William Laud, Archbishop of Canterbury in 1633, leader of the Treasury Commission and of the Foreign Affairs Committee of the Council in 1635, seemed a living demonstration of the link between religious and political innovations. But he was never a dominant royal minister. The other unswerving upholder of the personal rule, Thomas Wentworth, was for most of the eleven years based far from London, as President of the Council in the North and from 1632 Lord Deputy of Ireland. He was, in the eyes of political opponents, the arch-renegade who had found favour at court and made a fortune out of his offices, though he can now be seen as exemplifying the insistence that opposition in parliament did not mean opposition to the king. Between them Laud and Wentworth established the doctrine and practice of 'thorough', and exchanged their half-humorous complaints about its opposite 'the Lady Mora' – delay, incompetence, and timidity. It was Wentworth who described most eloquently how the state and the social order, the administrative institutions, the Church, and the law were all parts of that 'arch of order and government' whose keystone was the monarchy. Many of its other builders – Francis Windebank, William Juxon, John Finch, and Francis Cottington among them – tended to dispute the size and details of the 'arch'; and the queen was a constant source of irresponsible advice. Even so, the court and council in the 1630s were nearer in quality to those of Elizabeth than to the deplorable servants of James I.

The dissolution of parliament in 1629 was a blow to an opposition that had achieved at least an intermittent coherence when they had met so often at Westminster. But as the government continued to offend the interests and ideas of large sections of the parliamentary classes, new centres of opposition appeared. Besides the puritan congregations, the colonizing ventures that combined religious zeal with commercial enterprise were a centre of leadership. Family connection was more important still. The original generation of parliamentary leaders had been depleted. Sir John Eliot died in prison in 1632, Sir Edward Coke in quiescent retirement in 1634. They were succeeded by a new inner group of peers, ex-MPs, and lawyers, many of whom were connected with one or more of the puritan trading ventures, the Massachusetts Bay, Saybrooke, and Providence Island companies. John Pym, the formerly inconspicuous Somerset gentleman patronized by the Earl of Bedford, was one. John Hampden, rich, respectable, and far from fiery, was another. Laud and Wentworth had good reason to complain that men who in their view should have upheld the regime could not be trusted. Great aristocrats like the Earl of Pembroke and Montgomery, courtiers like Sir Henry Vane, bishops like John Williams showed little gratitude for the offices they held. Aristocratic faction, political management, and religious idealism made a shapeless but alarming barrier to the advance of 'thorough'.

In 1637 there came the opportunity to create a nationwide movement of defiance. Many of the financial expedients by which the Crown had maintained its solvency – the forced loans, the compulsory knighthoods or fines in default, the extension of antiquated feudal revenues – had aroused complaints and occasional legal cases. When 'ship-money' was extended from the ports, which were accustomed to finding ships for defence or paying money instead, to inland areas where it amounted to widespread new taxation, there came the deliberately contrived *cause célèbre*, in which Hampden was an ideal figurehead. No-one could have been less of a fanatic or a natural rebel. When the legal argument produced a division of opinion among the judges there began a widespread campaign of respectable disobedience. There was popular disobedience too. Prynne, Burton, and Bastwick, sentenced in Star Chamber for their opposition to Laud, became the martyr-heroes of mass demonstrations. Economic depression stimulated the demands for a new parliament.

Predictably, it was the need to pay for a war that eventually made a parliament inescapable. But the war itself was another act of resistance by Charles's own subjects, in Scotland. Since the days of Knox the Scottish Church had been closer to continental Calvinism than was the English, and its quarrels between the strict and the less strict had been complicated by the imposition of a half-hearted episcopacy, as well as by the traditional clan and regional loyalties. Opposition to Laudian religion in Scotland was a more popular movement than in England. In 1638 most of the landowners, clergy, lawyers, leading townsmen, and eventually many ordinary men signed the Covenant, the long document upholding the existing religion. It marked a startling unity of the whole people in all but the Catholic areas. When Scottish forces invaded the north of England in the 'Bishops Wars' of 1639 and 1640 they demonstrated not only the disunity of Charles's kingdoms but the incapacity of his English armies. To the English opposition the Scots proved in the next decade highly embarassing allies – plundering barbarians in popular opinion, treacherous in the eyes of statesmen and soldiers. To Charles the failure of the first war was a disaster, from which he hoped that Wentworth, summoned from his rule in Ireland and encouraged with the Earldom of Strafford, could somehow rescue him.

THE ENGLISH CIVIL WAR

The 'Short Parliament' in the spring of 1640 showed Strafford how wrong he was in expecting to manage an English assembly as he had the Irish. Putting aside the government's demand for an immediate vote of money, the Commons made the whole history of the personal rule a matter for debate. Pym established himself as a master of parliamentary tactics. After three weeks Charles angrily dissolved the parliament, which was beginning to demand peace with the Scots. No-one expected another period of personal rule. For the new parliament that met in November a long and high-powered election campaign was organized – something new in English politics. A spate of supposedly spontaneous petitions from the freeholders of many counties demonstrated the solidarity of opposition among the gentry, combining local with national complaints, religious liberties with the interests of landowners. In the next twelve months there was a peaceful revolution in government. By legislation which a large majority of the Commons actively supported and the Lords accepted, the institutions of prerogative rule were demolished one by one. When the plan to impeach Strafford failed for lack of any 'crimes' plausible enough to convince the hesitant peers, he was executed by the process of an Act of Attainder. Fewer than one-eighth of the MPs voted in his favour. High Commission, Star Chamber, and the other prerogative courts were abolished; so were unparliamentary taxation and the political power of the bishops. At least as important as the legislation was the rapid increase in parliament's participation in the actual work of government. Having at last secured control over its own dissolution and reassembly, it began, by the work of committees whose number multiplied incessantly, to insert itself into the running of finance, of the armies, and of countless minor administrative affairs. When the royal government in the capital broke down completely, there was already a sketchy substitute for it.

It was a godsend to Pym that in the autumn of 1641 rebellion broke out in Ireland (see p. 268). Stories of Catholic atrocities in the land Strafford was supposed to have pacified seemed to confirm the great legend of the popish menace. The Armada, the Gunpowder Plot, the wars on the continent had all been used to demonstrate that a vast conspiracy existed to overthrow Protestantism and its adherents. Strafford was alleged, on shaky verbal evidence, to have hinted at using an Irish Catholic army in England. The armies that fought the Scots were said to have been dominated by Catholic officers. Could Charles and his suspect councillors be trusted to fight the Irish rebellion? It was this suspicion that gave Pym the opportunity for a further extension of parliamentary demands. The 'additional instruction' to the envoys to the king, now in Scotland, threatened that unless he would employ such counsellors and ministers as were approved by parliament, they would take control of the army themselves. It would destroy the king's power to govern as he chose; and for the first time it made control of the armies a matter of open dispute.

The strongest objection to seeing the growth of parliamentary opposition since the 1620s as a sufficient explanation of the Civil War is that almost every political demand had now been conceded. The king had no support that would enable him to restore his authority by armed force, and hardly anyone in parliament or the country thought war against the monarch an immediate possibility. Yet in the next few months there came into being a royalist party and a royalist army ready to fight against the parliament that was now ruling the country. It was created not by devoted supporters of King Charles, but by those who felt that on balance he was now less of a threat to their society and their religion than the parliamentary leaders. The new and moderate royalists were, roughly speaking, the men who had condemned Strafford in May but who refused in November to support the Grand Remonstrance. This was the long rambling document in which Pym's party set out their view of the history of Stuart government and their demand for a parliamentary monarchy. Pym had contrived to put on the shelf one great source, or perhaps symptom, of division among his followers – the demand of the more militant puritans for the 'root and branch' abolition of episcopacy. But it proved impossible to find a compromise on the future structure and teaching of the Church that would be generally accepted by old-style Anglicans. There was no guarantee that the unspecified 'grave, pious, learned, and judicious divines' who were to settle religion would not be far more puritan than the Remonstrance implied. A division was hardening between those who were ready to risk the overthrow of Church and state in their existing form and those who believed that they had gained enough and could hold it without going further. When the Remonstrance was passed by eleven votes, the fears of its opponents were confirmed by a seemingly unpremeditated proposal – that it should be published. Pym's hope that a call for mass support would 'bind the people's hearts to us' produced a spate of horrified protests. To 'remonstrate downwards' was clearly felt to be the beginning of social revolution. There were already signs of it in London. Every rumour and every provocation could touch off a demonstration by apprentices and other 'tumultuous people'; and citizens once firmly on the side of order were increasingly liable to become tumultuous themselves. The immediate protests were against bishops, papists, and those army officers who seemed to threaten the city. But it was an indefinable enemy, or a mass emotion, that turned protest into insurrection. At the end of December the Lords and Commons were helpless in face of the crudely armed crowds that filled the streets of London and Westminster every day. Only the imprisonment of the twelve bishops who had been, on poor evidence, identified as the worst enemies of the Londoners relieved the panic. Pym, for once, seemed to have miscalculated. No-one in either House could openly support policies that were seen to condone popular rebellion. He was lucky that Charles perpetrated, in January 1642, the fiasco of his personal appearance in the House of Commons to arrest five opposition leaders who were not there. Nothing could have demonstrated more dramatically the king's ill-intentions and incompetence. In the next six months a torrent of proposals, counter-proposals, and petitions did little to enable either side to believe in the good intentions of the other. The Militia Ordinance, by which parliament took control of Charles's much-favoured county forces, was a decisive step in establishing the hideous possibility of a civil war; but it arose, as did the collecting of weapons in towns and great houses, as a supposed contribution to maintaining order. As usual, preparation for war made peace less likely: to gather men and money it was necessary to denounce someone else as evil and dangerous. Professions of loyalty to the king and of revulsion from fighting were not always convincing: there were lords who liked to put themselves at the head of the tenantry, preachers who liked to call for action in defence of the faith. There were too the multifarious conflicts in counties, towns, villages, even families between the powerful and the less powerful, the successful and the resentful. To explain how the conflicts were aligned, and which side dominated any particular locality, seems to become more difficult with every increase in knowledge. The crude divisions between a more royalist north-west and a more parliamentarian south-east, or between urban and rural, are made up of a vast complexity of local, personal, and accidental pressures. The rigid division between two sides was a military phenomenon, which inevitably became an emotional one. Religious, economic, social, and philosophical divisions continued to exist as much within each side as between the two.

There was no passionate drive towards war: even after the fighting began, demands for a settlement were almost as strong as the alignment of hostility. There were always peace proposals. There were always movements, open or clandestine, towards neutralism.

At every level people changed their allegiance, casually or thoughtfully. Charles's declaration of war, in August 1642, was symbolic in ways he did not intend: the solemn call to arms from the sovereign took place in an insignificant town remote from the capital. Few spectators had assembled; and the royal standard, it was said, blew away. But the rallying power of monarchy was still deep-rooted. With the support of most of his great aristocracy, the king was able to come close to victory. Parliament won in the end by gradually acquiring better resources of men, money, and materials. At first its military effort was financed almost entirely from London and a few nearby counties. Then, in his last great feat of political management before his death in 1643, Pym produced the series of financial measures that enabled all the areas under parliament's control to be exploited mercilessly for war. Taxes on land and goods were collected on a scale that made all the impositions of the past thirty years insignificant. Huge forced loans were demanded. An excise, the most hated of all forms of taxation, was imposed for the first time. All the estates of royalists were liable to be 'sequestered' for the use of parliament. Committees of Parliament, with their executive body the Committee of Both Kingdoms which brought the Scots their share of power, took complete charge of the work of government. Committees in every county brought together in the vastly increased work of local administration the parliamentarian gentry and others below their level. The victory was made certain in 1645 with the creation of the New Model Army to replace the fumbling decentralized forces of rival generals and county authorities. From the beginning two kinds of warfare had gone on side by side – the rapid movements of the main armies, with their occasional mostly indecisive battles, and the war of garrisons and leaguers on which control of territory depended. Royalist power was largely destroyed at Naseby in 1645, both because parliament now had the better soldiers and because it had more territorial resources. A year later Charles sought refuge, ironically, with those of his subjects who had been the first to fight against him, the Scots.

REVOLUTION IN ENGLAND

In 1647, when the Scots had handed over the king as a prisoner to parliament, he had not lost hope of recovering his authority. His great source of comfort was the divisions among the victors. Once the fighting ended, hostility became more open between the peacemakers, now misleadingly referred to as 'Presbyterians', and the 'Independents', a word applied in its loose political sense to those supporters of the army who demanded a settlement that would give a good deal of power to men below the level of the county gentry. The Independents were not, as a whole, democrats or egalitarians. They were the spokesmen of an assortment of lesser property-owners – principally of those to whom the war had brought unaccustomed power. Ireton and Cromwell, as leaders of the army officers, assumed that, since government was concerned primarily with property, only those with a 'permanent fixed interest' in the nation, however small, should have a voice. They now encountered new and frightening doctrines. The army, idle, angry about its arrears, steeped in puritan preaching, created a representative system of its own; and in the Council of Officers and Soldiers Rainsborough and Wildman argued passionately the democratic ideas that Lilburne, Overton, and Walwyn were expounding in a torrent of popular pamphlets (see pp. 226–8).

It was not the extreme left that vehemently demanded the execution of the king, though few of them opposed it. His trial was brought about by the army leaders and the small group of active 'Independents' in the Commons. In 1648 some of his new supporters – English 'Presbyterians' and Scottish adherents of the secret 'Engagement' to bring an army to his aid – made possible the scattered battles known as the Second Civil War. It demonstrated again that whatever Charles might say or sign, once he was back in his capital and the army disbanded nothing could prevent him from restoring a great deal of the old form of government, recompensing the plundered royalists at the expense of the victors, and punishing the leaders of the rebellion. In December, with a nominal show of force at Westminster, the army removed from parliament those members who refused to renounce further negotiation. On 30 January 1649 Charles showed more strength of character at his death than at any time in his life, and helped to establish the legend of the martyr-king. The Leveller movement, easily defeated by the renewed imprisonment of its leaders, perished less gloriously, though its ideas achieved in the end a greater renown.

Killing the king by judicial process was, in the eyes of the western world, an outrage comparable only to the crucifixion –

though the analogy could not be pressed too far. It would presumably be followed by other spectacular disasters, or by the dawn of a new age of freedom. In fact, as was soon evident, no-one knew what to do next. For ten years successive English governments tried in vain to find what seemed easier for the Dutch – a stable form of republican state and moderately tolerant religion. The 'Rump' of the Long Parliament (or rather, since the House of Lords was abolished along with the monarchy, of its House of Commons) survived until 1653, a core of twenty or thirty active politicians with perhaps another hundred who turned up at one time or another. Its executive 'Council of State' was dominated by army officers; and in the army Oliver Cromwell was now an unrivalled leader. When his campaigns against the remains of royalism in Scotland and Ireland were over, Oliver became the óne decisive force in English government. The most potent of all great ministers had risen from the ranks of lesser landowners by challenging everything on which ministerial absolutism was based. Like so many successful statesmen, he combined ruthless self-aggrandisement with political idealism. He dragged his decisions slowly out of a tangle of doubts and quests for support; but he had the gift of convincing himself and others that they were right – which often was enough to make them work. He had the energy of puritanism without its pigheadedness, and the rare quality among despots of wanting others to share his power – if only they would agree with him. The period of his political dominance was a ceaseless search for the institutions that would make 'healing and settling' possible. As he tentatively admitted, there was much to be said for a government with 'somewhat of monarchical in it'. Having won the fight for the power of parliament, he now found. himself dismissing one parliament after another more brutally than James or Charles had ever done. In April 1653 the Rump surrendered tamely to his soldiers and his angry denunciations. The 'Parliament of Saints', nominated to some extent by the Puritan congregations, but largely in effect by the army officers, produced impressive proposals for reforms, but no machinery for carrying them out or defending its power. In December 1653 the 'Instrument of Government', the only written constitution England had known, made Oliver a half-monarch, changing the title at his insistence from 'King' to 'Lord Protector'. Meetings of parliament (to be elected every three years on a franchise that brought in more of the lesser gentry, but hardly anyone below that level) were to last at least five months. Lunar months, Oliver decided – when he could not wait another few days to drive out a body that had insisted on debating the constitution itself. In 1656–7 the second Protectorate Parliament was no less critical, and a new constitution moved closer still to the old order, with a nameless 'other house' and an installation for the Protector that was a coronation with everything but the crown. At his death in 1658 'healing and settling' were not much nearer. Part of the blame for the failure of the Protectorate certainly rested on the constitutions. The semi-official propagandist Marchamont Needham praised them because the legislative and executive powers were separate – a notion that has been a curse of written constitutions ever since. The Council of State was the permanent centre of authority that attracted the power-seekers; and the occasional parliaments, despite the exclusion or expulsion of undesirables, were inevitably centres of opposition. There was no plan for a return to purely civilian rule, and nothing to re-establish an accepted system of government in the counties. The 'Major Generals', appointed by the Protector in 1655 as virtual military governors of the eleven regions into which they divided the country, aimed to impose a more rigid state control than Laud and Strafford had dreamed of. They were seen as an intolerable threat to the landed community and provoked resistance more dangerous than any they were supposed to quell. The Lord Protector did little to gain the mass support a revolution would need. More surprisingly, he failed to gain the backing of a broadly acceptable religious system. There was to be a state Church, with clergy paid and supervised by central authorities in a framework of Presbyterian *classes*. Almost any doctrines untainted by popery were to be tolerated. But the zeal of Puritanism in opposition was lost when Puritanism had won. Sects and independent churches thrived and quarrelled, but did not help to preserve the regime on which their liberty depended.

It might have been assumed that the regicide state would be ostracised for ever by the monarchies of Europe, and by Catholic ones most severely of all. It was not so. One of the most astonishing episodes in seventeenth-century history, upholding apparently the most cynical views on war and diplomacy, was the rivalry in 1655 between Spain and France for an alliance with England. Oliver and the Council had, in the end, little hesitation in rejecting the Spaniards and joining in France's war against them. He was able, with typically modified truthfulness, to expound the vision of the Protestant Alliance and the economic benefits of peace with the Dutch and war against Spain in the West Indies. He was less explicit about the cost of the army and navy. England was now a major military and naval power, whose allies as well as enemies were keeping a close eye on the possibility that the Protectorate might be overthrown. There were good grounds for resisting any diminution of the army and the fleet; and Oliver was never able to shake off the influence of the military magnates. He had no solution to the greatest problem of all – the royalists, or ex-royalists. As long as a large section of propertied society was excluded from power and subjected to fierce penalties and restraints, normal political stability was unattainable. The claim that all royalist families had lost most of their possessions and that Oliver's leading supporters had grown rich on plundered estates was greatly exaggerated; but it was believed. So was the hope that all injustices would be remedied by the restoration of the king. Charles II, as he could claim to have been since 1649, was not much impressed by the minor royalist plots: he was content to wait for the moment when he could come back with the acclaim of a dis-illusioned majority. Only a strong and tolerably stable regime could prevent his support from growing; and after 1658 the Protectorate was neither.

Any attempt to follow the chaotic events of the eighteen months after Oliver's death in 1658 needs more space than it is worth here. The story is aptly symbolized in the slow, inexorable march from Scotland to London of General Monck, a professional soldier who, while keeping all possibilities open, certainly meant at some unpredictable time to 'restore' the king. An opposing force under Cromwell's former associate John Lambert melted away without a battle. The quarrels between the various military and civilian groups that hoped to dominate central politics were becoming ludicrous. The decisive power favouring restoration was that of the City of London, on whose financial support any successful government was bound to depend. Every opinion had its adherents in London; but the government of the city since 1641 had been firmly on the right wing of the parliamentarian side – which meant now that it was royalist. At Westminster the parlia-ment of Richard Cromwell, as ineffectual as the second Protector himself, had been replaced by the restored Rump, to which, under the aegis of Monck, the survivors of the members driven away in 1648 now returned. In March 1660 they made way for the newly elected 'Convention' parliament that invited King Charles to his throne.

POLITICAL POWER IN THE NETHERLANDS

Stuart England had inherited the stability of a century of Tudor administration, with frontiers and internal boundaries seemingly immutable. The United Provinces of the Netherlands were still uncertain of survival as a unit after their thirty years of war against Spain. The outward form of government could hardly have been more different from England's. The alliance of provinces against Spanish rule had never produced agreement on the kind of state that was to be established when the military Union of Utrecht was succeeded by a permanent peacetime system; and in 1609 it was assumed, rightly, that the twelve-year truce would be as short as it said. Both William the Silent and his son Maurice had come close to establishing a monarchy, and had drawn back in face of widespread opposition. There had been an attempt to set up an ecclesiastical Synod with political powers. Mistrust within and between the various provinces led to a requirement of unanimity not only in the Estates-General but for many purposes in provincial assemblies too: it has been reckoned that a decision could depend on the assent of 1,200 individuals.[4] The Council of State, itself composed of provincial representatives, was pushed into comparative insignificance. To foreign governments willing to incur the displeasure of Spain by establishing relations with the new state there were many diplomatic problems. Their Noble High Mightinesses the States General were not an easily acceptable substitute for a king. It seemed natural to regard Maurice as an effective head of state. But it was Johan van Oldenbarnevelt who, from his position as leader of the Holland delegation, established himself as a virtual chief minister. He and his immediate circle of dependants initiated policy, conducted internal and external negotiations, and formed increasingly a governing political party. His office of Grand Pensionary and Advocate of Holland did not exist in the other provinces, and easily came to be regarded by his supporters as making him the civil head of the Union.

The hostility between Oldenbarnevelt and Maurice, Count of Nassau and from 1618 Prince of Orange, gradually aligned the many different strands of dispute during the twelve-year truce. It was Oldenbarnevelt himself who had urged the Estates of Utrecht, Overyssel, and Gelderland to elect Maurice to the office of Stadtholder, primarily but not entirely a military position, which he already occupied in Holland and Zeeland. (His cousin William Louis was Stadtholder of Friesland and Groningen.) Though the immediate aim was to avoid further danger of monarchy, it was also a move towards a real federation. By the time of the truce the prospect of unity seemed to the Regents of Holland to depend on their own hegemony over the rest of the provinces. So long as each state ran its own army and fleet, raised its own taxes, and pursued its own interests in foreign affairs and war, the one whose economic strength was overwhelmingly the greatest could not easily be resisted. National forces were almost entirely mercenaries. Maurice had good reason to oppose the growth of the power of Holland. It meant in effect rule by a narrow and closed group of rich Amsterdam families, interested primarily in destroying the economy of Antwerp and monopolizing European and overseas commerce. As administrative offices grew in number, they became the virtual property of the Regents – and it was doubtful whether this was much better in its effects than the system of venality in royal courts. Amsterdam was by no means united in support of the rulers of Holland. The majority of its burgomasters and merchants resented the power of the East India Company, a preserve of the Advocate and his circle who resisted the rise of the new West India Company (see p. 84). Whatever the constitutional theory, the little group of active politicians seemed to be depriving the city of its power. No part of the United Provinces, except possibly Friesland, could be said to have a widely representative political system. But as the Regents of Holland gradually lost their direct connection with commerce and became pure financiers and exploiters of office, the Netherlands developed some of the worse characteristics of aristocratic government. On paper it all seemed to add up to a state as bad as Poland. In practice it achieved a prosperity and a culture unrivalled in Europe.

The constitutional debates in parliament that have appeared to be the centrepiece of conflicts in England had no parallel in the Netherlands. Meetings of the States General consisted of an unspecified number of delegates from each province who saw the assembly as a small *ad hoc* conference rather than a solemn institution. Revenue was not a major topic: the provinces provided the agreed amounts by collecting them each in their own way, and the central expenditure was usually much less than the provincial. It took so long for the Estates to arrive at any decision that they could not become much of a political force. It was in religious disputes that England and the Netherlands had recognizably comparable stories. Quarrels about the details of Protestant worship were highly effective in both countries as a means of turning a complex assortment of rivalries into a clash between two impassioned causes. But the political implications of the struggles between strict Calvinism and the more relaxed Protestantism of the Arminians were very different (see pp. 87–8). They were not mere clerical debates. It was felt to be annoying but not astonishing that James I in 1611 formally conveyed to Oldenbarnevelt and the States-General detailed arguments on predestination and denunciations of the heretical doctrines being taught at Leiden. The offending professor, Vorstius, was dismissed. Oldenbarnevelt and the majority of the Regents of Holland saw in the Church's claims to enforce its dictates a threat both from within Holland and from the Union as a whole to their own political power. Dutch Arminianism was therefore unlike the later English movement that borrowed its name in that it represented, as its 'Remonstrance' showed, a generally tolerant and Erastian attitude. In 1614 the Holland Estates carried Oldenbarnevelt's resolution condemning the imposition of extremist doctrines. They could not enforce their policy in towns whose burgomasters disliked it. Those in Amsterdam who had wanted to continue the war with Spain that brought them great commercial benefits backed the Counter-Remonstrants, in spite of a brilliant lecture from Grotius on the virtues of secular state government. As the quarrel spread from clergy to congregations there was a good deal of popular resistance to whichever side was in power: at The Hague Counter-Remonstrants were driven to worship outside the town; in Amsterdam it was the Remonstrants who had to hold their services in warehouses.

The real threat of civil war came when Maurice of Nassau, not normally a religious zealot of any kind, decided to use the dispute for a showdown with Oldenbarnevelt. As the accepted leader in war, Maurice had disappointed the opponents of the truce with Spain by agreeing to Oldenbarnevelt's negotiation. Since then he had on various political issues moved nearer to the Calvinist side. While Oldenbarnevelt was trying to maintain good relations with the French government, Maurice became involved in intrigues with the Huguenot nobility. Instead of France he saw a possible ally in England – a prospect unwelcome to some of his supporters in Amsterdam. Though Maurice stood for the supremacy of the Union in war and diplomacy, there was never a simple division between central and local power. The Remonstrant party worked to establish the authority both of the Estates of Holland and of those town magistracies that supported them. In 1617 the Estates after long debate carried the 'sharp resolution', asserting their supremacy in religion, authorizing the recruitment of local mercenary forces – the *waardgelders* – and demanding oaths of obedience from the national armies. Maurice and William Louis as Stadtholders, and Reinier Pauw the leading Burgomaster of Amsterdam, were ready to act as decisively as they could against this threat to the very existence of the Union. If either side had found solid support it might well have resorted to armed attack; but every assembly and every town and province was divided. Though in most places the Counter-Remonstrant cause was the popular one, it had little connection with ideas of resistance. The only consistent theme in the flood of propaganda was that the Remonstrant party was secretly in league with Spain and Rome – a notion the Catholics themselves did hardly anything to justify. In face of the hostility of the majority in every provincial government except Holland and Utrecht, the Remonstrants gradually abandoned what had never been a whole-hearted struggle. Maurice was able one by one to turn out the Remonstrant magistracies in towns outside Holland and disband the *waardgelders*. When he had eliminated serious opposition elsewhere he staged what amounted to an invasion of Holland with a national army, purging the town magistracies and so creating a Counter-Remonstrant majority in the Estates. In May 1619 a specially created court sentenced Oldenbarnevelt to death and Grotius to the life imprisonment from which he soon escaped to exile (see p. 214).

Maurice's success against Oldenbarnevelt and Holland, and the demonstration of unity at the Synod of Dort, did not noticeably strengthen the authority of the Union. It showed the lack of any central political or judicial institutions through which his personal supremacy could work. His brother Frederick Henry, who in 1625 succeeded him in the five Stadtholderates and the office of Captain-General, had – for what it was worth – the advantage of appearing as the next war leader. The end of the truce in 1621 brought a new and exhausting war with Spain. Though there was no serious hope of reconquering the south, Frederick Henry's victories at 's Hertogenbosch in 1629 and Maastricht in 1632, and the capture of Breda in 1637, gave him popular glory. On the other hand he was blamed for the troubles of the navy, largely through his reluctance to appoint professional admirals. The tendency to give such offices to men of noble family was part of his one consistent aim – to turn the Netherlands into a monarchy under the House of Orange. His court, in various newly built palaces, gave to the nobility a fresh unity and ambition. It was corrupt, French in speech and culture, isolated from provincial politics. Gradually court influence was inserted into the government of the smaller provinces and poorer towns by securing the appointment of its nominees to local offices and hence to the Estates. But Frederick Henry had no coherent plan for creating a central government: his concern was with the European status of a future Orange dynasty. The one institution he developed was the '*Secreet Besogne*', a foreign-affairs committee of the Estates-General, now effectively dependent on the Stadtholder. Through it he was able to establish his policy of alliance first with France and then, in 1641, with the tottering Stuart monarchy. The first could be justified as part of the struggle against the Habsburgs; but the support of English royalism looked like an attempt to buy dynastic status in defiance both of Calvinist principles and of commercial interests. When it became clear that Frederick Henry was trying to bring the Netherlands gradually to the point of intervention against the parliament, the Estates of Holland gave instructions to their representatives at The Hague that amounted to repudiation of the authority of the *Secreet Besogne*. Worse still, Frederick Henry just before his death in 1647 was found to be involved in a Spanish proposal to hand over the southern Netherlands to France in exchange for Catalonia, giving Antwerp to the Stadtholder as a reward for his assent. (The return of Antwerp to the Union was the last thing Amsterdam merchants would welcome.) The prospect of final peace with Spain found the provinces as disunited as had the truce negotiations forty years earlier. Before the peace treaty was signed at Münster a good deal of Spanish gold was alleged to have been distributed. It meant abandoning the alliance with France, and the hope of new conquests in the south. But the success of William the Silent's rebellion was at last, after eighty years, accepted by the King of Spain.

THE NETHERLANDS REPUBLIC

The House of Orange seemed to epitomize the misfortunes of European royalty, or pseudo-royalty. William II, in his three years as Captain-General and Stadtholder of the five provinces, provided a refuge for his exiled relations Elizabeth of Bohemia and the younger Charles Stuart. Unmoved by their fate, he brought the disputes between the Orange and Holland parties to a new crisis. While he contemplated the benefits to the dynasty of rescuing the English monarchy in alliance with France, Holland was ready to negotiate with the parliament. He opposed, without effect, the cuts in the cost of the army demanded by Holland, which then refused to pay its share. When he formally 'visited' the towns of Holland, appealing for support over the heads of the provincial Estates, the gates of Amsterdam were closed against him. Only after his cousin the Stadtholder of Friesland had brought an army to the city did the burgomasters agree to a compromise. Then, in 1650, William died. The birth of his son a few days later inflicted on the House of Orange the longest possible minority, and meant that the Netherlands like England were to have a royal family waiting in the wings. In 1651 the Estates of Holland, 'their noble great mightinesses' as they called themselves, invited the other provinces (whose Estates had the lowlier status of 'noble mightinesses') to join in a sort of constituent assembly. It produced a great many words, but agreed only on dividing up control of the armed forces to prevent a revival of the office of Captain-General. It looked an inexpedient move at a time when popular demand for a war against England was growing; but it was part of the schemes to replace pro-Orange sentiment by the supremacy of Holland. Amid the quarrels of William III's guardians, the Regents of Holland were able to impose the 'System of True Liberty'. This pompously unconvincing slogan denoted the federated anti-royal and anti-clerical government through which, from 1653, the new Grand Pensionary, John de Witt, ruled the Netherlands more securely than Cromwell ever ruled England. His precautions against Orange revival included a secret pledge by the Estates of Holland never to accept a member of the Orange dynasty as Stadtholder or agree to his appointment as Captain-General. By an elaborate piece of deception the States General were made to accept this Act of Seclusion. It was one among many demonstrations of how complete the domination of Holland's ruling families had become.

'True Liberty' meant the liberty of local élites in the towns and provinces to run their own affairs under the supremacy of the Hollanders. For many municipal and provincial councillors, office was now a full-time occupation and a matter for competition, patronage, and venality. More rigidly than ever, the governing families cut themselves off from outsiders, even from leading merchants. Prosperous though these remained, commerce expanded less in the period of unchallenged rule by the oligarchy of Holland than under the Orange family. Amsterdam was as pre-eminent as before in banking and bullion exchange; but the carrying trade suffered from the decline in Baltic grain exports and possibly from English competition. Unemployment and high food prices in the towns helped to produce an active popular opposition which not only the Orange party but also the Calvinist Church tried to use. Calvinist clergy and elders were drawn largely from the lesser merchant or even artisan level in towns, and tenant farmers in the country: the Regents did not intend to allow them a share of political power. A policy of tolerating sectarian religion, and allowing the large numbers of Catholics who remained almost everywhere to go unmolested was on the whole in the interests of the Regents. Dutch Puritanism had little of the radical idealism in political and social matters that was part of the life of English sects. But tolerance, easier for the Dutch than for most countries, had become a well-established ideal that could not easily be overthrown. It was not a contribution to peace: if decline of anti-popery made peace with Spain possible, it also removed an obstacle to war against Protestant nations.

ENGLAND AND THE NETHERLANDS AT WAR

The war between the United Provinces and England from 1652 to 1654 was not sought by de Witt, or by Cromwell. The two new governments had almost everything in common. Both were Protestant and Republican; both had emerged from long and exhausting warfare; both were threatened by former ruling dynasties and upheld by merchants who had the whole world to exploit and the retreating commercial empires of Spain and Portugal to overthrow. Cromwell, on his idealist tack, repeatedly sought alliance and even union with Holland as the other great Protestant power. In 1651 a commercial clique in London and in the Rump parliament, seeking protection against a more successful competitor, pushed through the House the Navigation Act. It was designed primarily to exclude the Dutch from their carrying trade with English colonies; but it also represented a general strengthening of the commercial motive in British politics that proved more lasting than the republican constitutions. The Dutch demand for a war of reprisal brought popular resentment on to the side of those merchants most affected by the English economic aggression. As Blake's fleet was now a match for Tromp's, there was no prospect of a decisive Dutch victory. In the peace treaty Cromwell was able to appease his commercial supporters by insisting that the Dutch should concede almost every substantial demand made by the English merchants. In 1660, when every action of the Interregnum ought, politically, to have been anathema, the Navigation Act was renewed and made more workable. But England's role in Dutch politics was reversed. Downing, Cromwell's ambassador to The Hague, returned under Charles to become a leading advocate of the Orange cause. Fighting between the two powers was renewed overseas in 1664, with little regard to diplomatic manoeuvres. In 1665 it became official. It was a merchants' war; and the Peace of Breda in 1667, without settling much of the quarrel, marked the stage at which they more or less agreed to cultivate their own patches of trade. It also marked, for both England and Holland, the beginning of a new era of diplomats' wars – an era in which the constantly shifting alliances were determined by personal persuasion and corruption. The expansive power of France was the one constant factor: for the Dutch and the English, as for most other states, it was arguable whether they would do better by alliance with or against the French.

De Witt, in spite of Colbert's tariffs and in spite of actual French annexations on the frontier of the Spanish Netherlands, on the whole preferred alliance with France. It was essential, as the moment when William of Orange would be of age approached, to build up the strongest possible support for the republic. In 1668, with many misgivings, de Witt accepted the Triple Alliance with Sweden and England. The Dutch did not mind much that Sweden, against whom they had briefly intervened in the Baltic wars, was soon back to her normal alliance with France: all the Netherlands needed was moderate hostility between Sweden and Denmark (see pp. 420–1). The real disaster, of which de Witt was only dimly aware, was that Louis XIV now determined that the Netherlands should be the victim of his quest for land and glory. The full terms of the Treaty of Dover between England and France in 1670 remained unknown. Its mere existence was alarming enough. The Triple Alliance had enraged Louis against the Dutch at a time when Colbert was also happy to make a commercial agreement with England against them. So there emerged the vague fear of a plan for England and France to take their pick of Dutch territories, and to impose an Orange monarchy on what was left. There was little prospect that any other European power would promise aid to the Netherlands.

THE HOUSE OF ORANGE RESTORED

The war with England and France in 1672 (see pp. 508–10) made certain what already seemed likely, that de Witt's republic would not long survive the coming-of-age of William of Orange. De Witt had tried to prepare for it by a fierce attack on the Orange politicians, by putting William's education under the supervision of the Estates of Holland, and by the 'Eternal Edict' of 1667 which abolished the office of Stadtholder of Holland altogether. Though provincial Estates eventually accepted the theory that William might be a Captain-General without other office, it would, even in peace, be impossible to ignore his political influence. Inescapably he was drawn into the affairs of the inland provinces, and everywhere the Orange movement revived to unify all the hostility to the oligarchy. Faced with war and invasion, the Netherlands rallied to William with at least as much enthusiasm as, twelve years before, England had shown for Charles. Provincial nobility, urban oppositions, and rioting crowds backed by the preachers demanded William's appointment to all the offices of his ancestors. De Witt despite his resignation was the victim of a savage mob murder. But the crowds did not get, and apart from a little pamphlet literature did not demand, a popular government. The monopoly of the old urban oligarchies was broken to the extent of letting in some Orange supporters hitherto outside the charmed circle. Otherwise the Stadtholder – to whom royal titles were still refused – found the distribution of power and the disunity much as before.

The very fact of his lack of a crown may well have strengthened William's determination to demonstrate his full membership of the dynastic war-and-peace-making club. Since the triumphs of his great-grandfather, the dynasty had always been most successful as leaders in war. Now, at the moment of his arrival in power, he was presented with the opportunity to appear as another saviour of his country from the foreign and popish enemy. More than Louis himself – perhaps more than any other ruler – William was devoted to war. The peace with France in 1678 was made by the States General against his wishes. His marriage to Mary Stuart a year earlier had naturally increased suspicion that his dynastic ambitions were unlimited and unrelated to the interests of Amsterdam especially. Yet gradually in the ten years before the crucial moment of 1688 he built up his pseudo-royal power. More and more offices came under his control; more and more allies were bought or won in the states of the Union. The journey to England, when it came, involved no fears of resistance at home.

THE STUARTS RESTORED

The English Restoration had been a vastly greater change – almost, it seemed, a complete return to Stuart absolutism. The king's reign was dated from 1649 and the legislation of the Interregnum annulled; but judicial proceedings, on which innumerable property transactions depended, were in general confirmed – as indeed they had been through all the changes of regime. For the parliament of 1661 the old system of elections was resumed. Even at the beginning it was not entirely a 'Cavalier Parliament', and at the many by-elections in its seventeen-year course former Parliamentarians came quietly back. By a variety of expedients a great many royalist estates confiscated or sold since 1642 found their way to the former owners or their heirs. Generalizations about the ultimate effect of the land settlement are still uncertain; but it is clear that, though some royalist families suffered, very few of the 'upstarts' were able to keep their status. Perhaps the most surprising phenomenon was the disappearance of Presbyterianism. Charles had promised toleration, and a synod to settle official doctrine. But at the Savoy Conference in 1661 between bishops and Presbyterian leaders the Puritans won no concessions. Parliament and the Convocations of the Church established an Anglicanism that avoided everything firmly Calvinist, but fell short of Laudianism. Ejected ministers came back and unsurpers were put out in their turn, though a good many former Presbyterians found their way into livings. In Presbyterian London, solid resistance by those who controlled the supply of funds would have been very hard to resist; but after some argument the aldermen dutifully went to St Paul's to welcome their bishop. The 'Clarendon Code' meant that 'dissenters' escaped the' worst forms of persecution at the cost of exclusion from politics and from the chance to propagate their ideas. Though Quakers and the other sects continued to resist the state and to suffer for doing so, it was a sad end to the mighty victories of the saints. But it was also a sign that, despite all the appearances to the contrary in the conflict that lay ahead, religion was not quite as closely or as universally linked with political loyalties and hostilities as it had been.

The old symbols of royal 'tyranny' had gone for good. There were no prerogative courts or 'feudal' exactions; traffic in offices no longer dominated the working of government, and in the seventies tax-farming was quietly ended; MPs were no longer imprisoned for their speeches; the new Habeas Corpus Act of 1679 protected the ordinary citizen too from 'arbitrary' imprisonment, leaving him to the mercies of the lawyers. Parliament's survival seemed secure: no-one worried much that the Triennial Act of 1664, unlike that of 1641 which it repealed, contained no precautions against defiance by the Crown. The worst failure was to establish any effective parliamentary control over the choice and policy of the king's ministers. Opposition to Clarendon in 1667 and to the Earl of Danby in 1679 had to take the old form of impeachment. There was a great difference between the two cases. Clarendon had managed without any firm support in parliament; his fall came when the disappointments of the Dutch war were added to a multiplicity of minor grievances, and his unpopularity at court made him the obvious scapegoat. Danby had seen the need for a parliamentary following – though he built it up more by bribery and patronage than by policy. He too was a victim of hostility at court. But he was blamed for two things – the alleged concealment of the imaginary Popish Plot that threw the nation into hysterical panic in 1678, and the secret negotiations with France. The latter he had certainly supported, however reluctantly. To save him, Charles dissolved the parliament that had lasted since 1661. The election, with the 'Plot' still raging, was a startling failure for government management. Danby was lucky to get away with five years in the Tower.

Very slowly, the question of Catholicism had once more come to be all-important. It was made inescapable by accidents of personality and genealogy. Like Elizabeth, though for different reasons, Charles failed to produce a legitimate son. His brother James, unless his Catholicism could be made a legal ground for excluding him, was the undoubted heir; and when James made a second marriage in 1673 it was likely that a son would be born to continue the Catholic line. Meanwhile the next in succession was Mary, James's Protestant daughter by his first wife Anne Hyde. Danby had arranged her marriage in 1677 to William of Orange. Advocates of a Protestant monarchy were now faced with a Dutch connection that not everyone saw as preferable to the Stuart links with France. The course of the conflict was set partly by Charles's views on religious policy. Protestantism, or so he had cause to believe, contained a latent threat to monarchy. Repeatedly he attempted without success to win enough support for such measures as the Declaration of Indulgence that would have removed the disabilities of both Catholics and Protestant non-conformists. In return for Louis XIV's promises of support he added the secret clauses to the Treaty of Dover in 1670 promising in due course to declare himself a Catholic. He recognized that it would be difficult to convince a large enough proportion of the aristocratic and gentry families that Catholicism was the best form of religion for defending the Restoration monarchy which upheld their power – difficult, but not impossible.

The prospect was made much more hopeful by the Crown becoming once again less dependent on parliament for its revenue. The greatest weapon of the old parliamentary cause seemed to have been allowed to rust. The customs, and the hated excise, had been settled on Charles for life, together with other revenues such as the 'hearth tax' invented in 1662. (None of these fell directly on land.) At first the revenue they produced was less than the rather arbitrary estimate made in 1660, and the Crown depended heavily on loans from the city and on more closely controlled and non-recurrent parliamentary grants. The rapidly rising cost of gifts and bribes, under various names, helped to produce the shortage of money that culminated in the disastrous 'Stop of the Exchequer' in 1672. But then the Crown's position improved. Indirect taxes, taken out of the hands of tax-farmers, increased automatically with the expansion of trade, until – just at the time when parliamentary control of finance would have been decisive – the Crown could almost 'live of its own' again. The notorious subsidies from France, though they rescued Charles in some difficult moments, were too small a proportion of the total to have a major effect on the outcome of a long conflict.

Charles was right in thinking that a substantial part of landed and political society would accept Catholicism – not in the sense of being ready converts themselves, but to the extent that, if faced with a choice between resistance to the Crown and loyalty to a Catholic king who would bring about equality of status between Catholic and Protestant subjects, they would not risk another rebellion. Men had to choose between the fear of popery and absolutism and the fear of civil war, with the threat to property which this would involve. The 'Exclusion Crisis' produced three parliaments between 1679 and 1681. They were not only concerned with fears for the future but, like the parliaments of the 1620s, with current grievances which only a constitutional change would remedy. Charles, despite the Triennial Act, resolved to rule without parliaments. Louis promised his support. It was in these years that the old 'Court' and 'Country' groupings became recognizable as the two 'parties' of the next century, under the nicknames that compared them to the Whiggamores of Scotland and the Tories of Ireland. (There was no greater insult than association with popular rebels, and Celtic rebels at that.) To exclude James from the throne by legislation would greatly alter the division of power between parliament and the monarchy. Shaftesbury's Exclusionist party, the immediate ancestor of the Whigs, had an unmistakable if pale resemblance to the party of Pym. It included a group of political leaders, peers among them, in whom William of Orange began to take an interest; gentry outside rather than inside the established ruling circle in the counties; many merchants and their associates; and many dissenters who contrived to evade the restrictions enough to take some part in political life. It was associated too with movements well below the level of parliamentary politics – a fact its enemies were quick to exploit. Anglicans who, whether from a connection with royal government or simply from a belief in non-resistance, supported the Crown convinced themselves that James (who still lacked a son) would not seriously interrupt the power of the Protestant ruling classes. By using royal authority to revoke the charters of many boroughs and eventually of London itself, the Tory ministers were able to remove the main electoral strongholds of the opposition. There was no serious doubt that Charles had won.

JAMES II AND THE 'GLORIOUS REVOLUTION'

The peaceful accession of James II in 1685 was an astonishing success for those who sought a strong monarchy at almost any price. At the decisive moment, many who had believed in the Popish Plot, who had voted for exclusion, and who had regarded themselves as unshakable supporters of parliament and Protestantism, preferred acquiescence to rebellion. When a new parliament met, it seemed to have been tamed at last as Strafford had long before believed it could be – by efficient manipulation of franchises and elections. Two members out of five held some sort of Crown office; four out of five were new. It voted a generous revenue, which James was able to supplement by the willing assistance of Louis XIV. When Charles II's most energetic bastard, the Duke of Monmouth, made his theatrical attempt to claim the throne, the extent of acquiescence was demonstrated still more clearly. It became not a revolution but a local popular rebellion reminiscent more of Tudor risings than of the Civil War. Yeomen, clothiers, and miners in the south-west were no substitute for the support of peers and gentry which Monmouth sought in vain. John Wildman, veteran of the democratic movement of 1647, failed to get any substantial following for the Duke in London.

One effect of the rebellion on James was to increase his determination to have a loyal army, commanded as far as possible by Catholics. Another was his decision to punish the rebels with a ruthless demonstration of the authority of law. The 'Bloody Assizes' of Judge Jeffreys were by any standard a brutal affair, which the Whig politicians who had kept well away from the rebellion afterwards exploited as propaganda. James, like Charles I, had a great capacity for making blunders. Step by step it lost him the support of those who at first were eager to seize any opportunity of reaching a compromise with the Crown that would leave them a share of power. Anglican Tories were not likely to be reassured by the insistence that concessions were being sought for all dissenters, Protestant and Catholic alike. If anything was worse than outright popery, it was tolerance that would enable Puritans to resume their attack on the monopoly of office held by established families. But it was significant that some of the Quakers and other non-conformists were willing to take the king at his word and accept the liberty and the ending of their legal disabilities that he offered. It was no longer universally agreed that religious doctrines were inseparable from political. It seemed to most people strange, if not sinister, that William Penn, the Quaker coloniser, should be a confidant of James. A generation earlier it would have been ininconceivable. The *Letter to a Dissenter* from one of the most skilful of practical politicians, the Marquis of Halifax, did a great deal to convince the most cautious non-conformists that any favours offered from Rome would prove to be traps for the unwary.

James's pose as the benevolent devotee of tolerance was not made more convincing when he established an army, under Catholic officers, on Hounslow Heath just outside London. If fears were diminished by the reports that the English soldiers were more likely to mutiny than to terrorise the citizens, the army that was being created in Ireland seemed to prove that there was a real threat of popery being imposed by force. Less obviously, James was time after time going a little further in the direction of prerogative rule than those who in general were ready to support him would accept. His 'High Commission' for the exercise of the Crown's ecclesiastical powers, not being a court of law, was not strictly illegal under the terms of the Act of 1641 – but it was made to look like a defiance of the opposition to such bodies. His use of the 'dispensing power' to insert his nominees into Universities was seen, with good reason, as an effort to undermine the future strength of Anglicanism. The judges, when those less amenable had been removed from office, were used as the most authoritative upholders of the doctrine that the king could dispense individuals from the operation of the law. More and more the actions of the king grew horribly reminiscent of Charles I; but no second Pym appeared. There was no second Strafford either. Robert Spencer, second Earl of Sunderland, was like Wentworth in being a former opponent of the Crown who became its chief minister; but he had no heroic devotion to the principle of monarchical rule. He despaired of the Catholic policy sooner and more decisively than did James, and at the last moment departed for Holland and tried to persuade the future king that he had long been working in favour of the revolution. The theory that he deliberately led James into more extravagant policies in order to destroy him has no convincing proof. But he certainly did nothing to prevent the follies that in 1687–88 drove believers in stable monarchy to the conclusion that James must go.

James had not allowed parliament to meet since November 1685; but sooner or later he would need to call another. Success in this, as in everything else, would ultimately depend on the acquiescence of a sufficient number of the politically active landed proprietors. Charles had got away with an attack on borough charters that enabled him to increase the influence of the government. James attacked them a second time with the intention of replacing respected county families by unheard-of landless dissenters, in accordance with his policy of merging concessions to Catholics with those to Protestant non-conformists. The scheme was such a failure that the proposed new parliament had, for the moment, to be abandoned. Faced with this first sign of mass opposition, James demanded a new demonstration of his control over the church, which he believed, more and more justifiably, was ceasing to preach the doctrine of unquestioning obedience and even giving positive encouragement to resistance. The first Declaration of Indulgence in 1687, suspending all religious discrimination, was an extension of his questionable use of royal authority, but not a deliberate defiance. There was a soothing promise that the declaration would be submitted to a future parliament. When it was reissued in the spring of 1688 with the instruction that it was to be read in every cathedral and church, James seemed to be openly challenging the Anglican clergy to resist. Nine-tenths of them did so. Sancroft, the Archbishop of Canterbury, and six of the bishops, drew up the petition against it. Between the presentation of the petition and the trial of the seven prelates, deliberately designed by the government to give maximum publicity to the expected confirmation of royal authority, James's son was born and the prospect of a Protestant succession ended. On 30 June the bishops were acquitted after a trial in which their fate had been linked with the question of the king's power to dispense with the law. The people of London saw it as a great victory. Sancroft, far from becoming a rebel hero, resumed his efforts to persuade James to compromise with his Church. On the day of the acquittal another group of seven – some of the most prominent English peers – sent off their invitation to William of Orange.

William had controlled his ambitions with unexpected skill. A single prematurely overt move might have identified opposition to James with support of a foreign invader. Soundings among the English aristocrats had been carried out cautiously; careful assessments were made of the possible extent of James's support. One obvious risk was that James's patron Louis XIV might come to his rescue. Another – which Louis himself, fortunately for William, thought would benefit the French more – was that there might be a civil war. If that happened, William insisted, he would refuse to come. As part of his elaborate preparations, he had copies of his soothing Declaration ready for immediate distribution all over England.

The States General had to be handled tactfully too: use of the national fleet and army depended on their consent. So had the Burgomasters of Amsterdam, whose opposition to the scheme would have produced an intolerable political division for William to leave behind. As it turned out there was enough public enthusiasm to suppress the doubts of some of the commercial interests. James, still in the best Stuart tradition, tried, when it was far too late, to reverse his entire policy. It was imposible now to alter the unformulated but clear decision of the 'political nation'. Loyalty to the monarch was still the creed of the ruling section of society. But the loyalty must be transferred, with as little fuss as possible, to a different monarch. There were to be no cries of 'King in Parliament', no armies to develop dangerous democratic ideas, no elaborate paper constitution. The problem of what, in constitutional theory, had happened could be solved with no very painful stretching of the truth. The throne was 'vacant': William and Mary, with the unconditional invitation and assent of the nation, subsequently ratified in parliament, occupied it. God, the Church proclaimed, had upheld divine right by sending a deliverer. There was no need to dwell on such awkward details as the fact that James had fled (at the second attempt) only after William had landed and made him a virtual prisoner.

ENGLISH GOVERNMENT AFTER 1688

When the embarrassing episode of James's departure was over, it was not difficult to contrive the performances which would avoid admitting that a monarch had been overthrown or that another had been appointed after bargaining with his prospective subjects. The 'Convention' – not yet, for want of a royal summons, a parliament – produced the 'Declaration of Rights' which was read out immediately before William and Mary accepted the ceremonial offer of the Crown. By the end of 1689 the Declaration had been turned into a Bill which could receive the royal assent in the normal way. It was not the kind of document to be recited on patriotic occasions, or to settle legal disputes, but a mixture of specific and hazy assertions. Catholics were barred from the throne. The king's power to suspend laws, and the dispensing power 'as exercised of late' were to be abolished. (A later clause adds that a statute must not be subject to royal dispensation unless it said it was.) Money was not to be levied, nor an army raised in peacetime, without parliamentary consent. There was to be freedom of parliamentary speech and elections; there were to be no 'cruel and unusual punishments'; parliaments were to be 'frequent'. It all sounded enlightened, without laying down anything that was likely to prove a serious obstacle to a ministerial government acceptable to normal gentry and aristocrats. There was no hint of parliamentary control of the king's ministers. Foreign policy and religion were quietly left to the Crown. Certainly monarchs now had to promise that they would maintain 'the Protestant Reformed Religion established by law'; but that was in the Coronation Oath and seemed to leave room for the law to change. There was no attempt to define what parliament was, or to protect it from the loss of initiative that representative assemblies everywhere risked. The Crown, and aristocratic patrons, could continue unimpeded to manage parliamentary elections and to persuade members to go on supporting those to whom they owed their seats. In general the narrowed borough franchises imposed under Charles and James were kept: almost a third of MPs represented boroughs with fewer than a hundred voters. The cost of controlling a seat was rising, and it was more and more necessary to reach the agreements that avoided contested elections and eliminated the voters from any share in choosing those who 'represented' them. There were some later clarifications of the rules. The Triennial Act of 1694 stated that there must be every three years at least not only a meeting of parliament but a new election. The Act of Settlement of 1701, besides arranging the succession in favour of the descendants of the Electress Sophia of Hanover, included provisions supposed to protect the independence of the judges and – absurdly – to prevent discussion of major matters of state outside the Privy Council. Much more significant than the constitution-making was the lifetime grant to William of £700,000 a year. It was enough in time of peace for the cost of a fairly modest court and the payment of existing office-holders, but not for foreign wars or expanded armies and navies. When parliament voted additional taxes, it did so for short periods. Money bills had to be driven through the Commons by careful bargaining and manipulation: it was always possible that they would be amended or rejected in ordinary political conflicts. The twentieth-century routine of ministers revealing to the House once a year the secret of what taxes it was about to vote would have seemed an astonishing triumph of absolutism.

The settlement of 1689 left plenty of scope for the creation of a powerful ministerial government and a docile parliament. But the gentry who dominated the House of Commons and the peers who were still the normal leaders of politics and administration were not going to relax their concern with matters of state. Conflicts at Westminster were part of their way of life. Every parliament was the scene of incessant disputes and manoeuvres; every ministry depended for survival on winning the contests. How far they can be seen in terms of two-party politics is still a matter of controversy. Rivalry for seats and offices was now predominantly between Whig and Tory. It did not mean either that ministries were formed exclusively from one party or that Lords and Commons were divided into two unchanging sides. Least of all did it mean that Tories were the party of strong monarchical government and Whigs that of radical non-conformity, parliamentary independence, and hostility to the court. In the first six or seven years of his reign William had to be taught by Sunderland that a change,

almost a reversal, was taking place in the character of the two parties. 'Whenever the government has leaned to the Whigs, it has
been strong; when the other has prevailed it had been despised.'⁵
The Whigs moved away from their dangerously democratic allies
in town and country to become the defenders of the constitution
eager to build within it a strong and efficient executive machinery.
The Tories increasingly drew their support from the less politically active county families. They liked to appear as defenders of
the church against the insidious spread of dissent, and of an
economy soundly based on landed property against the risky and
unscrupulous financial dealings of the Whig bankers and war
profiteers in the city. As before, at every level, in every district and
every occupation local and personal rivalries could be aligned,
often irrationally, by party loyalty. But the alignment was growing weaker rather than stronger. The 'independent country
gentlemen' were a group in the Commons larger than any other
– sometimes as many as two hundred. Their decisions, on both
great questions and small, could be influenced not only by the
pressure of party and government organizers but by arguments in
the House and by the views of their electors. This too was a situation inconceivable in twentieth-century democracy.

THE WARS WITH FRANCE

One question on which parliamentary opinion could be decisive
and on which it emerged from a great variety of pressures was that
of war or peace – a matter still in theory left entirely to the Crown.
In 1689 there was no doubt that in welcoming William, England
was committing herself to war with France. The Netherlands
declared war in 1689 at the moment when William made his formal acceptance of the Crown; and his odd dual status was
demonstrated when, as King of England, he made a treaty with the
States General for the joint use of his two navies against French
forces. The early stages of the war seemed to threaten the overthrow of William's rule. With Louis at last giving James his full
support, a simultaneous invasion from France and Ireland looked
possible. William's victory in the battle of the Boyne brought the
Irish back under the unrelenting rule of Protestant Englishmen;
but it was not until 1692 that the allied fleet was able to avenge

the defeat it had suffered off Beachy Head. Land warfare was a fruitless use of men and money. Once the invasion scare was over, complaints in the Commons against the war grew. It was hinted that William was proving himself a foreign king employing in his continental wars the armies that were meant for the defence of England. His occasional use of the royal veto did not help his popularity. Only because enough MPs were involved in the forces or in the supply of war materials was the risk averted that the Commons might refuse outright to vote further supplies.

The war cost at least three times as much as Charles II's war against the Dutch, seven times as much as the regular revenue voted to William. It was paid for partly by a land tax, which in 1692 rose to four shillings in every pound of rental, partly by the excise. Regular government borrowing was essential to the financing of the war, and indeed to the whole economy of the country. The creation of the Bank of England in 1694 was only the most conspicuous single event in a long process of establishing a financial system in which bullion became a far less important form of wealth and government debts produced stability rather than weakness. The more the government borrowed, the larger the number of subjects who had a heavy vested interest in its survival. The costlier wars became, the greater the incentive to invest in the concerns that supplied their material. Nevertheless, financial exhaustion, in England as in the other states involved, was one major cause of the temporary peace settlement at Ryswick in 1697 (see p. 518).

William, in the two years before his death in 1702, had to fight against a strong anti-war feeling among the gentry in the Commons. The successive schemes, open or secret, for the partition of the Spanish possessions were not an obvious reason for England to prepare for the renewed war against France which was the centre of William's whole policy. When the 'Junto' of Whig ministers was found to have agreed in the absence of a parliament to the second partition treaty (see p. 376) – though William had negotiated it without consulting them – the newly elected Commons set in motion the clumsy impeachment procedure. Whig peers were in a strong enough majority to defeat it. The question of war or peace became the main difference between the two parties. Those eager to resume the fight with France were saved by pressure from outside parliament. Daniel Defoe took over the leadership of a campaign of public propaganda and petitioning, smearing the Tory advocates of peace as hirelings of the French and stressing the threats implied in Louis XIV's recognition of James III as King of England. In the Netherlands too William did not find it easy to keep up enthusiasm for war. Before Ryswick, while London had on the whole supported the continuance of the fighting, Amsterdam had been the centre of the peace movement. News of Charles II's will in 1700 was received there with general relief on the assumption that the powers would accept it. William relied on his close ally Heinsius, the Grand Pensionary, to bring the city round to support of war, while he himself took on the harder task of defeating the peacemakers in England. 'I hope to conduct myself', he wrote, 'with such circumspection as will carry them along gradually without their noticing it.'[6]

William before his death had appointed John Churchill as commander of the forces of both nations. Under Anne – who in her first year as queen created him Duke of Marlborough and made his duchess the most powerful figure at court – he and the treasurer Godolphin had little difficulty in keeping support for the campaigns. They had the advantage not only of a well-managed and generally enthusiastic parliament, but of an administrative system which had slowly, since the days of Charles II, become a complex but tolerably efficient professional service. Though offices were still regarded as rewards, the old venal hierarchies had gradually been replaced by a system of departments completely detached from the court, with the Treasury as the recognized superior body. The number of court places had fallen; that of departmental jobs rose continually. The process of government by committee, which parliament in the Civil War had improvised from within itself, was now developing rapidly outside it – though many of the Boards remained under close parliamentary scrutiny. While Anne continued to attend, without much influence, formal meetings of the Privy Council and of smaller groups of ministers, the growth of a recognized Cabinet was beginning. It remained unsure of parliamentary support.

In the first years of the war the ministry was predominantly Tory. The most extreme of its members, Nottingham, resigned in 1704 when his efforts to take a tougher line against dissenters were unsuccessful. Robert Harley and Henry St John, Tories less dogmatic and more devoted to political manoeuvre, came into the government. But the general trend was for Tory supporters of the war to work in alliance with the moderate Whigs. After the election of 1705, when the Whigs increased their strength in the Commons, the ministry became a coalition within which the Whigs were able gradually to establish themselves in complete power. By 1708 Marlborough and Godolphin were the only Tories left. Harley and St John worked both at court, where they exploited Anne's reliance on her confidante Mrs Masham, and in the country to bring about a decisive rejection of the Whigs and of Marlborough. In the distance there lay the prospect of another succession problem. But the Tories did not make the blunder of appearing to be Jacobites. Their great rallying-cry was the one raised by Henry Sacheverell in his much-publicized sermon at St Paul's in 1709 – 'the Church in danger'. To the Whigs his authoritarian line appeared as a denial not only of even the most limited toleration, but of the whole principle of the 1688 settlement. Their attempt to impeach Sacheverell played into the hands of the Tories, who made him a hero of the reactionary country gentry and clergy, and of an emotional London mob. A more rational motive for opposing the ministry was that the war, and the taxation it involved, now seemed to be prolonged quite unnecessarily. In 1710 Harley became the leader of a new government, and had no trouble in getting a reliable Commons majority in his favour at the election that followed. The ruthless political intrigues of the next year destroyed Marlborough. He was charged on very thin evidence with dishonest financial dealings; but his real offence was that he had been reluctant to complete the long negotiations for peace. So were many of his fellow peers: it was only when they faced the threat that new titles would be created to produce a majority in the Lords that they agreed to the Utrecht terms. The contrast between England's status in the world of diplomacy and the squalid political scene at home could hardly have been greater.

THE NETHERLANDS AFTER 1688

While William III (who, conveniently, was the third William to be Stadtholder of Holland as well as the third to be King of England) was concerned mainly with his English kingdom and his European wars, he had little cause to worry about the affairs of the Netherlands. Before 1688 he had faced constant opposition from the Amsterdam Regents, who claimed that his government was run for the benefit of a court nobility and of the Orange dynasty. But as King of England he was in an unchallengeable position. There was no question about the need to resist the French in the Spanish Netherlands as well as to protect the territory of the Union itself, and the danger would have been immeasureably greater without the English alliance. Fortunately for the republicans, the chances of a permanent union of the English throne and the Dutch Stadtholderate receded. William remained childless, and announced that his heir in the Netherlands was the Stadtholder of Friesland, John William Friso, who was fifteen when William died in 1702. The only possible rival was the new King of Prussia. It was therefore easy for the republicans in Holland and William's other provinces to seize control. The movements in many towns by which the Orange party was swiftly removed from its offices were victorious demonstrations rather than acts of rebellion – though in Nymegean the ex-Burgomaster who attempted a counter-coup was executed. The rival parties continued to fight a bitter political struggle throughout the Spanish Succession War. No new Stadtholder was elected; and the misfortunes of the Orange supporters were completed when John William died leaving another minor as heir.

In many ways the effective successor of William III was the Duke of Marlborough. In 1702 the States General agreed to his appointment as 'Lieutenant-Captain-General' of the Netherlands forces; but every effort was made to restrict his authority by attaching to him the 'Deputies' whose approval had to be given to all plans for the use of the army. These were the men whom Marlborough blamed for frustrating his bold strategic concepts by their belief in old-fashioned garrison warfare. After the Blenheim campaign he was in a strong position to argue that with better Dutch support the war might have been won outright. The States General became more ready to accept Marlborough's direction of the war, and concentrated on winning from the English government the 'barrier' agreements that promised a strong defensive line extending into the southern Netherlands.

It was not only military considerations that they had in mind. If Austria was to replace Spain as ruler of the southern provinces, at least the Dutch could prevent a revival of the commercial rivalry of Antwerp or any of the other towns. Moreover they could extract from England a share in the commercial benefits that were expected to accrue from the victory over France and the break-up of the Spanish European Empire. On the face of it the Netherlands economy survived the war well. Despite the enormous burden of taxation and the general depression of the years around 1710, there was no major financial crisis and no spectacular industrial or commercial collapse. In 1715 Dutch shipping was as prosperous as ever. But it gradually became apparent that the relative position of Britain and the Netherlands, both economic and diplomatic, had changed. While Britain's commercial and industrial activity expanded, and the cost of the great colonial and European wars seemed to be absorbed without greatly hindering the rising investment in all kinds of economic development, the Dutch lost their pre-eminence in the carrying trade. They were not in a position to replace it by new industrial activity. Yet helped by their neutrality in most of the wars of the next seventy years they remained the masters of international finance. Nor was there any evidence that the people of the Netherlands were worse off than the British for lack of glory.

NOTES AND REFERENCES

1   The term 'Netherlands' is used here for the United Provinces of the north, as distinct from the Spanish Netherlands.

2   History of the Rebellion (ed. Macray) Book I, para 4.

3   The King's Declaration, March 1629.

4   R. Mousnier, *Histoire générale des civilisations*, vol. 4 (Paris, 1956), p. 168.

5   Quoted in J. H. Plumb, *The Growth of Political Stability in England, 1675–1723* (London, 1967), p. 135.

6   Quoted in P. Geyl, *The Netherlands in the Seventeenth Century* (London, 1964), part 2, p. 275.

19

LOUIS XIV'S FRANCE AND THE EUROPEAN WARS

THE KING

The reign of Louis XIV has generally been regarded as the epitome of royal absolutism in the seventeenth century. It is a story, like so many others, of mitigated disaster. To give its tragic elements the firm structure approved by the dramatists of his time, Louis would have needed to destroy himself amid the ruin of his state. Instead he lived to see slow deterioration and indecisive defeat. It was never apparent to him that the cost of the state, its monarchy, and its wars impoverished the country, still less that in the long run a state identified with too narrow a privileged élite would collapse. But he could hardly fail to see that the glory he so assiduously manufactured lost its magic. At the beginning of the reign the eulogies were unanimous. Ten years before its end Fènelon wrote:

Even the people . . . who have so much loved you, and have placed such trust in you, begin to lose their love, their trust, and even their respect. They no longer rejoice in your victories and conquests: they are full of bitterness and despair. They believe you have no pity for their sorrows, that you are devoted only to your power and your glory.[1]

Louis had grown up as a king who was both an object of adulation and, from time to time, a refugee. His memories were of hazardous journeys into and out of a half-rebellious capital and through a kingdom where his mother, to whom he was devoted, was clearly not treated by her important subjects as a ruling sovereign. Amid the treachery and intrigue he received the approved education in the classics and the arts, with a large dose of carefully selected history. Mazarin took a personal interest in the political training of, as he saw it, his own successor. Louis' first great experience of public life was significant. In September 1651, the day after his thirteenth birthday, there was held in the Paris *parlement* the *lit de justice* at which his majority was proclaimed. Paris was still the centre of chaotic warfare and unconcealed treason. But now the streets that could at any moment be the scene of mob violence were lined with the most orderly and loyal of crowds. Through them passed the vast procession of the king's cavalry, the heralds, the court nobility, the great clergy, the provincial governors, the warring princes of the blood. Only Condé humbly excused himself on the grounds of the danger he would be in. The English diarist Evelyn, watching the ceremony with his friend Hobbes, was deeply impressed by the appearance and manner of the king his people 'idolized'. When it was all over the desultory civil war was resumed. In June 1654 there was a very different ceremony – the coronation at Rheims. Few of the great men of the kingdom bothered to attend. It was no longer of any benefit to Mazarin or the court that attention should be drawn to a king who was already making some effort to assert his powers. But in August 1660 he had again a central part to play. The celebration of his marriage to the Infanta was to mark the peace with Spain which formed the climax of Mazarin's achievement. It was also a sign of the restored harmony between Paris and the government that had at last achieved peace. The ceremony had been planned in lavish detail: one part of it was the homage to the king by representatives of every section of his rich and respectable Parisian subjects, another the great procession through streets decorated with the utmost baroque extravagance. This time Condé, undeterred by the fact that he had been fighting for the enemy, took his place with the other princes.

These were the beginnings of the splendours that for the next twenty years were to be not a relaxation from the business of the state but a vital part of it. In 1662 the birth of the Dauphin was celebrated with the '*caroussel*', a gorgeous mixture of procession, ballet, and charade to which the royalty and nobility of all Europe were invited. Louis appeared as an improbably jewelled Roman emperor, Orleans and Condé as Persian and Turkish generals,

Guise as a commander of Red Indians. Royal dignity was certainly not equated with stuffiness. Splendour became a permanent and brilliantly organized form of public service. Though the monarch was the centre of it all, it was carefully designed to demonstrate the superiority of the state to other institutions. The courtier and the holder of central office were expected to show extreme courtesy to their superiors as well as to the king but also to show a formal and consistent contempt for those outside the circle of government. At the beginning of the reign public devotion to the king and his entourage had to be adapted to a mobile court. Louis progressed from place to place, though seldom far from Paris, taking with him a mass of servants and equipment that included much of the apparatus of government. His entertainment varied according to the place and season: usually a lavish amount of scenery, fireworks, or fountains had to be added to the first essential, costume. Many royal occasions contained an element that has since become inseparable from state ceremonial: the armed forces had to accept elaborate displays as part of their function. The line between the inclusion of the army in festivities and a visit by the king to a frontier campaign was not always clear. War could for the moment be made to appear picturesque rather than squalid.

Outdoor spectacles and cardboard castles were not an entirely satisfactory representation of the triumph of France. From the beginning of the reign Louis was much concerned with fine architecture. All the royal palaces were repaired, extended, ornamented. Paris got public buildings and monumental archways. An enormous park was constructed round the hunting-lodge of Versailles, where in 1664 was held the nine-day festival proclaimed as the '*Plaisirs de l'Ile Enchantée*'. In 1671 the decision was taken to make this the site of the chateau that was to provide splendour as a truly national institution. It was more than a decade before the full court was permanently established there; and building was still going on until a few years before the king's death. Tens of thousands of workers had been employed on it, a good many of whom died from the fevers they caught there. When it was occupied, seven or eight thousand of the king's dependants lived amid discomfort and dirt that must have been worse than even the grim conditions moderately prosperous Parisians accepted. One of Louis' remarkable qualities was the physical toughness that kept him alive while most of those around him, from royal children to workers on the fever-striken canals, were dying at an earlier than average age. The king did not escape disease. Smallpox, gonorrhea, intestinal worms, and the anal fistula that led in 1686 to the excitement of the royal operation, were some of the incidents from which he was restored to health. At frequent intervals, when the smell of the palace became intolerable even to seventeenth-century noses, the court went on its travels while the gorgeous rooms were cleaned up. As a symbol of the French absolutist state it could hardly have been improved on.

The attractions of Versailles seemed, to those who were within reach of court society, irresistible. Apart from the pleasures of food and drink and promiscuity, the great competition for the highest favours offered the prizes of wealth, title, and office. Success depended on a mixture of patient skill in forming alliances with the unpredictable luck that could produce triumph or disaster in a moment. The most secure were those who had built up family connections, of which the Le Telliers and the Colberts were the most conspicuous. But Arnauld de Pomponne, raised through the alliance of Louvois and Colbert to be foreign minister, was thrown out by them and restored after Louvois' death. Colbert's son, the Marquis de Seignelay, lost his place on the Council of State when Louvois was trying to diminish the Colbert faction. It was even more risky to use the patronage of the king's current mistress. Ultimately the price of competing for position at court was likely to be the gradual impoverishment of the family as neglected estates were burdened with the debts incurred in keeping up an impressive retinue of followers and a conspicuously lavish way of life. Versailles was never a means of persuading the magnates to accept exclusion from power: at most it made them compete more ruthlessly to keep it. To the Parisians, and still more to most provincials, it meant that the monarchy had become more remote. Louis' boast that French subjects had free and equal access to the king became increasingly absurd. The early Louis, playing the part of the young Apollo with great success – despite his lack of height – had been seen as the long-awaited saviour of his people. Then, as the glory grew more costly, it was not so easy to persuade the populace that they somehow shared it. The image of Louis, however carefully it was presented, changed with his mistresses. Louise de la Vallière, the 'little violet', detached from the normal palace intrigues, was a link with the lesser nobility and the *robe*. Her replacement by the gorgeous and ill-tempered Mme de Montespan (whose husband successfully publicized his misfortune) seems to symbolize all the capriciousness and the contempt for outsiders of the Versailles circle. Intrigues to remove Mme de Montespan became a major court preoccupation. When at last Louis permanently shifted his affections, it was to the daughter of a minor noble who by a normal piece of good fortune in exploiting connections had become governess to Mme de Montespan's bastards. Mme de Maintenon, secret wife of the king from about 1683, acquired an almost unchallengeable influence. Though the original splendour of Versailles was to a great extent under her management, she seems to have become the principal instrument through which Louis was captured by the *dévots*. Even in the first years of Versailles, religious observances had been strictly enforced. Now compulsory gaiety turned gradually into compulsory respectability and holiness. Whether or not the story is true that the Duke of Orleans had the complete works of Rabelais between the covers of his book of devotions, there must have been many who found the change difficult.

KING AND MINISTERS

Splendour was one part of what Louis regarded as the proper function of a king; but it was not the main one. The *métier du roi* to which he justly claimed to devote himself was that of managing the state. It was the death of Mazarin in March 1661 that marked the real beginning of his reign. Both the cardinal and the young king had intended that from that moment there should be no more ministerial despotism: Louis would do the whole work of sovereignty. He was one of the rare and enviable men who appear to pack into a day activities that for most people would fill two or three. In spite of the ritual, and the mistresses, and the hunting, his rigorous timetable was so arranged that, according to Colbert, he spent six or eight hours a day at his desk. From it, within a few years, he reconstructed the central machinery of the state. In England Charles II's accession after a revolution that had appeared completely victorious marked only a return to the regime accepted in 1641. Ten months later Louis' assumption of power after the pseudo-revolution of the Fronde was a decisive moment in the shifting of power in the state. The king's council at the centre had become a body where high birth and the possession of great hereditary office ensured political power. All but three of its members Louis peremptorily expelled. The new *conseil d'état* (see p. 245), or *conseil d'en haut*, consisted first of three survivors from the government of Mazarin who were unconnected with the great families and free from any suspicion of conspiracy. Hugues de Lionne had been involved in diplomacy from his earliest youth through being the nephew of one of Richelieu's secretaries of state. Under Mazarin he was already virtually a foreign minister. Michel Le Tellier, lawyer and former intendant, had been secretary for war for nearly twenty years. Nicholas Fouquet, *surintendant des finances*, had also come from a *robe* family, and held among his minor offices that of *procureur-général* to the *parlement* of Paris. But unlike the others he had not limited his ambition to administrative power. He had become, by the obvious means open to him, immensely rich. In Paris he was a lavish patron of the arts and the centre of a large circle of dependants. He built for himself one of the most ostentatious of all private chateaux in France, and made the mistake of entertaining the king in a week of wildly expensive festivity. Louis decided that this was a man of too much eminence to belong to his innermost circle. Fouquet was tried for treason and eventually imprisoned for life. With him many of the *financiers* were punished too, with fines large enough to remove the wealth they had acquired at the state's expense. The office of *surintendant* was abolished. In the next fifty years only seventeen men became members of the council to which the great men had once assumed they had a right to belong. Fouquet's fall was, at least in part, contrived by the man who replaced him, Jean-Baptiste Colbert. The bourgeois origin of the great minister, which he made ludicrous efforts to hide, merely demonstrated that, as in most political systems, the energetic, ruthless, and fortunate could get to the top. His father was an unsuccessful member of a fairly prominent merchant family. His cousin was a brother-in-law of Michel Le Tellier, through whom Colbert came to the notice of Mazarin. As Mazarin's 'intendant for personal affairs' he began to build up the elaborate connections at court that led eventually to the 'Colbert dynasty' and its grip on appointments. Jean-Baptiste soon saw himself as Fouquet's successor at the head of financial administration. His other offices he collected one by one, partly through his technique of taking over the functions first and claiming the titular appointment next. By 1669 he had formally acquired control of every department except those of war and foreign affairs.

CENTRAL AND LOCAL POWERS

Of the other holders of high office in the period of peace and internal reform down to 1672, only Le Tellier's son Louvois, already assured of the succession to his father's post, could compare in status with the three great men over whose deliberations the king presided two or three times a week. The rest – the *conseillers d'état*, the *maîtres de requêtes*, and the thirty provincial intendants – formed a small and close-knit administration, outside which the mass of office-holders exercised little power. One estimate is that in the whole work of central government not more than a thousand men were employed. Against the possible dissentients a slow process of attrition was begun. The 'great men', from Condé and Séguier downwards, found their most important administrative functions gently removed. The 'sovereign courts' were told that all decisions taken in the Council must be accepted, and had their title reduced to *cours supérieures*. The local office-holders, who had been regarded as initiators of revolt during the Fronde, were rendered harmless, sometimes by buying back their offices, sometimes by drastically diminishing their powers. Far more thoroughly than Richelieu, Louis and his ministers were able to replace the authority of the *officier* by that of men wholly dependent on the continuing goodwill of the central power. Colbert selected for special attack the *trésoriers de France* – the finance officials who, with their clerks, did more to defraud than increase the revenue. Even provincial governors were limited to three years' tenure of office – renewable on good behaviour – and prevented from residing permanently in their provinces. Provincial nobility had still to be handled with care. Visitations, of which the *Grands jours d'Auvergne* in 1665 was the most drastic, revealed that local tyrannies upheld by private armies were still common. They were not eliminated; but sometimes titles could be found invalid, high-sounding rewards for good behaviour agreed on, loyal families raised above the unreliable ones. It was all a matter for skilled manoeuvre; and money shared between the state and its servants was still a means of moderating the rigour of most official policies.

There was a steady campaign against the surviving 'liberties' of provinces and towns. The Fronde had not shown that the Estates of Brittany and Languedoc were capable of offering any deeply entrenched resistance to the Crown, and the other *pays d'états* had been even less dangerous. Even so, there were the remains of a process by which they had struck a bargain about their own taxation and linked it with the presentation of 'grievances'. Without stirring up any issues of principle, the government now contrived to reduce these to a complete formality. Municipal liberties were treated in the same way. Town governments could often be persuaded, by the mixture of threats and corruption that was the key to success in all these matters, that exemptions from free-quarter, or privileges in taxation, or free election of municipal officials should be voluntarily renounced while any local customs of a purely decorative kind could rely on the blessing of the Crown. Paris was a different problem. However much the *parlement* and the municipal governments were reduced to obedience, the capital was still the centre, to which there came the growing numbers of starving poor from the countryside, disbanded soldiers, hopeful fortune-seekers. Retainers of the great men were still a major source of disorder. It was here that the state really needed to show its strength. Nicolas la Reynie, carefully chosen for the new post of *'lieutenant-général pour la police'*, imposed on Paris a regime that authorities in every other European city could envy. One side of it was the cavalry that paraded the streets, the spies who watched every threat of the formation of gangs, the censorship that put an end to the presses that had produced the *mazarinades*. The other was the improvement of the town itself: six thousand street lanterns, the rudiments of a drainage system, the feeding of the beggars even in the grim conditions of the *hôpital général* all helped to make a dangerous *émeute* less likely. Elsewhere resistance to the government was put down fiercely. Peasants who demonstrated in their villages were liable to be sent to the galleys. The city of Bordeaux was punished for resisting new taxes on commerce in 1675 by having eighteen regiments billeted there, and the entire *parlement* of Rennes was banished from its town. Though Paris remained peaceful, the king and his ministers seem to have been constantly afraid of what might happen there.

STATE FINANCE

The gradual erosion of sources of independent power – even of those that had grown up as part of the centralized administration in the previous reign – was one side of the new absolutism. The other was the building of a state more efficient, and above all economically sounder. This was the task to which Colbert devoted a personal energy that made even the king's life look leisurely by comparison. The process of government by paper that had occupied the cardinals for a large part of their time, and in which Louis himself was closely involved, was almost the whole of Colbert's life. His attitude to the job was that of every twentieth-century civil service. The raw material of the work of governing is information – detailed, precise, and capable of being distilled into manageable brevity. The danger that between the original reporting and the drawing of conclusions the picture can become grievously distorted was as readily pushed aside then as now. The essence of his method appeared in the financial reports he presented to the king. The three 'registers' – the receipts, the expenses, and the 'journal' – were used to produce a monthly summary and a final yearly balance-sheet. Each October the financial commitments for the year ahead were laid down in something very like a modern British budget. It was Colbert's boast that every item of finance came before the king six times from the first order to the *état au vrai* that showed the final reckoning. A bad activity properly accounted for, he asserted, was better than a good one with no accounts.[2] Le Pelletier, the *contrôleur-général*, soon found that the money in the treasury did not in fact tally with the elaborate balances. But the reports Colbert accumulated on the state of the country's industries, trade, communications, justice, and public order were no doubt capable of giving under his skilled scrutiny a clearer picture than had existed before. The second stage, the evolving of a line of action, or of a number of alternatives, lay largely in the minister's own hands; and though every important decision was officially taken by the king from the reports presented to him, Colbert seems to have been a master of the art of 'overwhelming the king with paper'.[3]

When all allowances have been made for falsification, the record of Colbert's reform of national finances is impressive. No-one could have come to power with better justification for blaming economic difficulties on his predecessor and on circumstances beyond his control. The famine of 1660–61 came at a time when the yield of taxation was already declining. Mazarin, it was claimed, had committed the whole expected revenue for the next two and a half years to the financiers from whom he had borrowed. But one great cause of the state's comparative poverty was that more than in other countries its revenues were absorbed by the tax-farmers and the office-holders at every level. More was lost too in the tangle of exemptions and irrational assessments. If the evil was worse than ever, it was also a moment at which it could be attacked without dangerous resistance. As early as 1661 there was established under Séguier and Omer Talon the fiscal *Chambre de Justice* which began to investigate malpractices of farmers and officials. By backing negotiation with menaces and inflicting exemplary sentences on those least able to offer opposition, the court eventually recovered more than a year's normal revenue. Once there was some money in hand it was possible to begin the buying back of offices and of the *rentes* so that the total of such charges was halved. The reforms of the royal forests deprived many people of a regular income they had derived from defrauding the king of his revenues; and gradually all the royal lands were subject to the process of minute investigation that brought profits back to the Crown.

Colbert's efforts to improve the return from taxation without any revolutionary change in the system relied on the same methods of minute investigation into individual peculation. The tax-farmers who had taken fantastic amounts for themselves were faced with the alternative of making a reasonable bargain or losing their position. The use of troops to collect taxes was gradually abandoned in most areas. Tax exemptions illegally sold or conferred by local nobles were eliminated. The privileged position of the *pays d'états* was eroded. Unless the official statistics are more consistently misleading than seems likely, the worst victims among the peasantry had their burdens reduced, and at the same time revenue rose. It was claimed that the net total doubled in the ten years after 1661. Much of the Crown debt was either paid off or repudiated as fraudulent, and it was even possible to buy back a few of the alienated lands. But such reforms never lasted long enough to have any decisive social effect. Their failure was part of the price of glory.

WAR AND DIPLOMACY: THE 'WAR OF DEVOLUTIONS'

The history of Louis' reign is inescapably punctuated by wars on which convenient names are bestowed and by treaties called after the irrelevant places where they were signed. But the distinction between war and peace was not a rigid one. To the nobility, high and low, the army was a more important part of the ways of life open to them as the range of other functions narrowed. At the few times when Louis was not providing military activity they could seek it elsewhere. (In 1685 Turenne and a succession of military men about the court asked the king's permission to go and fight in Poland.) To the administrators the army was a sphere of control like any other, to be made the subject of competition among themselves, purged of the more outrageous forms of corruption, transformed from a mainly private enterprise into a mainly state one. It all meant that a military campaign was an inescapable part of the routine of court and political life. Royal diplomacy proceeded on this assumption. (See pp. 287–90).

The Peace of the Pyrenees had marked at least a major pause in the conflict with Spain. It had not removed the habit of regarding the Spaniards as the 'other side' to be outmanoeuvred at every opportunity. The king's Spanish marriage was the occasion for establishing a convenient source of future conflicts when France's renunciation of the right of succession to the always dying Charles was linked, not too clearly, with an unpayable dowry. In the first few months of Louis' effective power, demonstrative anti-Spanish diplomacy became a major preoccupation. There was the celebrated 'incident' in London when the French ambassador refused to continue an unofficial arrangement by which he and the Spanish ambassador had avoided a public scramble for precedence. Two processions, reinforced for the occasion, met, and the Spaniard won. It was vital that France should extract from Spain, with the maximum publicity, an admission that precedence was due to the French. The Ambassador to Rome, by getting involved in quarrels about the extension of the area of his embassy's privileges, was involved in another infantile brawl. French troops avenged the insult by occupying Avignon and threatening to march on Rome itself. The pope made an abject surrender. It was in this atmosphere that Louis involved himself in the preposterous legalistic tangle of the 'devolutions'.

The French attitude to the chaotic dependent and independent territories on the eastern frontier was much less cautious now than it had been in Richelieu's day. It was assumed that France ought to acquire whatever lands she could, just as she needed to acquire bullion and markets. The simplest method was the one used with Dunkirk. In 1662 Louis bought it from Charles II of England as any peasant proprietor might buy a field from his neighbour. Vauban, as chief engineer in Turenne's army, used it as his first showpiece of design in fortifications. The Duchy of Lorraine, where France already had some complicated rights of passage, was nearly acquired by paying its Duke Charles and making his whole family 'Princes of the Blood' of France in return for a promise that Louis would be his successor. There were loud objections; a small French army was sent to keep the duke to his bargain; for many years there was argument about whether a valid agreement existed or not. With the same merging of the concepts of sovereignty and property, a list of territories was presented to the Spaniards as a bill for the first instalment of the Infanta's dowry. Franche-Comté, Luxemburg, Hainault, and Cambrai would do to begin with. It was not, of course, expected that they would be handed over; and at this point there was devised, apparently by one of Turenne's secretaries, the claim that in some of the desirable areas property descended to the children, even females, of a first wife in preference to those of a second. Louis therefore, in his anxiety to prevent injustice, required that lands – not restricted to those where such a custom did apply – should be handed over to his wife Maria Theresa as heiress to her father. On this argument the will ma 'e by Philip IV, who died in 1665, was invalid. By it he exclude . Maria and her descendants from all inheritance (see pp. 375–6). The 'devolutions' theory was more in the realm of war propaganda than of practical diplomacy. It could hardly be expected to satisfy believers in divine right or dynastic solidarity; but it sounded sensible to lawyers and bureaucrats. While the reasons for a quarrel with Spain were being worked out, Turenne and Louvois were building up the forces they intended for the occupation of Spanish towns in Flanders. In 1666 the entire court was invited to see the reorganized armies, and to accept the fact that they were there to be used.

In the summer the parades turned into genuine war. With no great difficulty town after town was besieged and occupied. If nothing but military success had mattered, the whole Spanish Netherlands could have been annexed. But there was also the diplomatic score to be reckoned. Ever since the Peace of the Pyrenees, Louis and Lionne had continued the policy of the two cardinals in collecting as many allies as possible without worrying too much about conflicting obligations. Portugal, Sweden, and Denmark all got their share of French money. The Swiss cantons, for once, united in a grand embassy to establish their alliance with France and collect the rewards. The agreement made in 1662 with the United Provinces proved momentarily embarrassing. It was an advantage to get the Dutch to accept the prospect of the Spanish Netherlands being conquered by France rather than the notion that was being canvassed of some sort of independent federation or 'cantonment'. But Louis was committed to support the Dutch at the moment when they were involved in war with another desirable French ally, England. The solution was not difficult: in 1666 France, fulfilling her treaties, declared war on England and attacked the very small Caribbean island of St Christopher. It was made clear to Charles how grateful he should be to Louis that no more serious harm was done.

The Empire was another problem and opportunity. It had become normal French practice to make, and where necessary pay for, alliances with whatever German states were amenable, vaguely directed against the emperor. Hence the support of Brandenburg and Bavaria, and the separate treaties with Rhineland states that kept alive the general idea of a 'League of the Rhine'. How much more in accordance with French grandeur it would be to arrange with the emperor himself a future division of the possessions of the Spanish monarchy. In January 1668 the agreement was signed in Vienna in which lands ranging from Spain and the West Indies to the towns of St Omer and Douai were dealt out and exchanged like cards from a pack. France's eventual collection, on the death of Charles II of Spain, was to include the Netherlands, Naples and Sicily, North Africa and the eastern Philippines. Spain, Milan, the West Indies, and Sardinia were to go to the emperor. Lionne and Louis were delighted with their ambassador's triumph, which unfortunately could not be made public. The one practical effect of the agreement with the emperor was that within a few days Condé marched his small army into Franche-Comté. It was a most unconventional time of year for an invasion; but with no risk of serious resistance the troops and inhabitants could be relied on to accept it passively.

The shape of the conflicts emerged not from any master plan but from a succession of minor frustrations and successes in which the military leaders were constantly at odds with the diplomats. To Turenne, Condé, and Louvois the easy victories in Flanders were an obvious opportunity to crush the United Provinces. To Lionne it seemed certain that any further military advance would wreck the system of alliances. Almost at the same moment as Louis' partition treaty with the emperor, England and Holland had made the alliance which French diplomacy at once sought to break by the secret approaches to Charles II (see p. 480). Sweden by joining it had become the first renegade from Louis' party. Since the fighting had no particular objectives in the first place, there was no loss of face in making the 'magnanimous' peace of Aix-la-Chapelle in May 1668 at which Franche-Comté, with its defences destroyed, was returned to Spain and only an illogical assortment of fortifiable towns in the Spanish Netherlands retained. The diplomats, with their eyes on the Spanish succession, only gradually accepted that the next move should be a war against Holland. But the party of the army that was working for it gained in the four years of inactivity the decisive support of Colbert. France was losing the commercial struggle with the Dutch: it must become a military one.

THE DUTCH WAR

We have seen something of Colbert's efforts to apply the power of the state to industrial and commercial expansion (see pp. 87–90). As they developed, he became, more than the military or diplomatic policy-makers, obsessed with the need to defeat the Netherlands. It was humiliating that French goods should be carried in Dutch ships; that France should still find it necessary to import both luxuries and war materials from Dutch merchants; that Dutch overseas companies should treat their French imitators with unworried disdain. In a trade war with the Netherlands, all the natural advantages ought to have been on the French side: France was larger, able to supply almost all the raw materials she needed, ruled by an ideal monarchy instead of a heretical, unstable, and decentralized bourgeois oligarchy. To defeat the Dutch at their own game seemed not just economically advantageous but morally necessary. England was as much affected by the tariff war as Holland; but the two were, in Colbert's eyes as in those of Louis and Lionne, by no means the same. Though Colbert may not have known all about the prospects held out by the Treaty of Dover in 1670, by which Charles II agreed to join in an attack on the Netherlands and to become – some day – an avowed Catholic, England was clearly less dangerous as a centre from which the material rewards of Protestantism and revolution could be shown to the French. Nor could she claim any superiority so offensive to the notion of a proper hierarchy of nations as the 16,000 ships that Colbert's information showed, wrongly, the petty state of Holland to possess. With England there were long and unsuccessful negotiations for a tariff agreement. The Dutch did not wish to negotiate: they retaliated, with measures that amounted to a complete ban on French imports. 'It is impossible', Colbert announced in 1670, 'that his Majesty should tolerate any longer the insolence and arrogance of that nation.' The alternatives he offered to Louis for his decision were to abolish the United Provinces altogether, taking over for the benefit of his French subjects the most profitable parts of the trade and industry of his new Dutch ones, or to leave them their sovereignty on condition that they handed over their colonies and trade. It was a choice the king was unlikely to have to make.

In April 1672 Louis set forth in person on his most glorious excursion so far. Every preparation had been made: the alliances had been reconstructed, and England – most necessary to the success of an attack on the greatest naval power – had declared war already. The army of 120,000 was probably the biggest western Europe had seen. The king, so the Parisians were officially informed, was about to punish the Dutch for the ill satisfaction he had received from their States-General. There were more sieges, more surrenders. In June there was the great occasion of the crossing of the Rhine, which opened the road to

Amsterdam. Condé would have risked everything to take the city without which the survival of the Netherlands state was inconceivable. Louvois and Turenne wanted further sieges; Louis wanted the ceremonial restoration of Catholicism in the Cathedral of Utrecht. So the Dutch army survived; the dykes were opened; the fleet still had secure bases from which it was beating the English. A month after the first invasion the party of de Witt, in favour of a compromise peace, had offered to Louis all the territory he had occupied and more, together with a large payment in cash. Louis suggested more territory, more money, more commercial concessions. But above all the Dutch must agree to an annual mission to Paris to present to him a formal token of their submission. The Dutch envoys went home. Louis returned to France to receive the triumphant welcome of a hero whose conquests were not yet quite complete.

The conduct of the Dutch war was not simply a series of follies in which vanity overcame military and diplomatic good sense. But it was nevertheless the point at which unbounded French ambitions for territory and for glory made European countries that had previously been within the orbit of Louis' alliance-building see the defeat of France as a common necessity. The once glorious invading armies spent the next year burning villages, living off a countryside that gradually fell into desolation, here and there falling back into French territory. In 1674 the English, despite all Charles's secret commitments, made peace. William of Orange built his coalition, with Spain and the Empire fighting as the principal allies of the Protestant power. The lesser states began to follow the example of Brandenburg in being prepared to desert and rejoin the French as expediency required. A frontier war and a display of military glory for the French court turned within a couple of years into a struggle for the survival of French prestige and long-term hopes. It was a war of many different aspects. In the Mediterranean the French fleet won a succession of improbable victories. In Franche-Comté there was another conquering military parade, with the festivities seldom interrupted by any resistance. In the north there were long and hard-fought sieges. In Alsace and deep into the German Rhineland the war became a succession of marches and battles in which the object was to obstruct the enemy's movements by destroying the country off which he tried to live. Even among the French commanders there were a few who protested against the brutality. Imperceptibly, the dreary negotiations that continued for most of the last two years of war became more realistic as every state involved suffered heavier costs. In 1678 the separate treaties known as the Peace of Nymegen[4] distributed the frontier towns in a manner that reduced a little the intermingling of fortifications without humiliating either side. But the French had to abandon the fiercest of the tariffs against Holland. Their only serious gain was the territory of Franche-Comté which the Spaniards had written off long before. Their loss was the end of Colbert's economic expansion.

WAR AND THE NATION

The costs of the wars in 1667–68 had been borne without much difficulty: the Treasury had ceased for a couple of years to show a credit balance, but the activities of the state had not been restricted nor the burden of taxes increased. From 1672 the change in government finance was unmistakable. Month by month the precisely summarized accounts showed a growing deficit: by 1676 the normal revenue was meeting only two-thirds of the expenses. Solvency had once more to depend on the *affaires extraordinaires*. Offices that had been bought back by the Crown were sold again; new rights of inspection and monopoly were created to be sold; exemptions from the *taille* could be bought for a lump sum; royal lands were put on the market, new direct taxes imposed and the rate of old ones raised. State borrowing in the form of *rentes* at the equivalent of 7 per cent interest, loans from bankers at even higher rates – every device short of debasement of the currency had to be used. This was merely the inescapable condition of a state of war, and far better controlled than usual. France, with the help of the financiers, proved that the cost of a big war could be met. But it could only be done by reducing the state's support of the economy. The overseas companies, carefully fostered as a part of the effort against Dutch supremacy, failed when the government's support was withdrawn. The royal manufactures, sustained by subsides and state purchases, became as indebted as the Treasury itself.

To judge the immediate effect of the wars on the French economy is still, in spite of the intensive studies of economic historians, difficult. Against the complaints of growing debts and falling profits must be set the evidence that France in the 1680s was, even by Dutch standards, a land of booming commerce and high standards for all but the poorest. St Malo rose from comparative obscurity to be one of the great ports of Europe; Marseilles and Toulon had a huge trade with eastern markets. Some of the expenses of the wars found their way from the armament-makers, the suppliers of the armies, and the financiers into capital investment. On the other hand the peasant and his landlord had often good reason to feel that the good days were over and the familiar succession of disasters beginning again. From 1677 there were several years of poor harvests. Coming after the neglect and depredations of the war they led to frightening local shortages of food. Epidemics became more frequent; so did the local rebellions that the armies, in the intervals of campaigning, were ready to repress.

RELIGION IN THE SERVICE OF THE STATE

Maintaining order and obedience by the brutal crushing of opposition was hard to reconcile with the ideal of a harmonious state which king and ministers still professed to uphold. If the army and the taxation that paid for it were destroying that ideal, it was more necessary than ever that it should be supported by the Church. The pompously named 'Peace of the Church' in 1669 whereby the terminological concessions on behalf of the nuns of Port Royal had put an end to what was regarded as a dangerous controversy did not remove Jansenism from the social and political scene (see p. 143–5). It had for many of the intellectuals and the ladies of fashion the attraction of a minority circle that conferred a sense of moral superiority without the stigma of heresy or disloyalty. But its success among the clergy had made it a nationwide movement too. It was a pair of southern Jansenist bishops who brought the controversy back into political prominence by protesting against what began as a comparatively minor manifestation of royal supremacy and administrative tidiness – the extension in 1673 of the *régale*. Appointments to offices in the Church were a matter of agreement between the Papacy and the Crown, largely settled by the Concordat of Bologna in 1516. It seemed reasonable to claim that the arrangement should be extended to territories to which it had not originally applied or which had bought exemptions. The issue affected not only noble and clerical society, but Crown revenues: by the *régale spirituelle* benefices in a vacant diocese were filled by the king; and by the *régale temporelle* he had the right to the episcopal revenues. It was bad luck that three years after the decree the amenable Pope Clement X was succeeded by Innocent XI, supposedly a pro-French candidate but as it turned out a *pape de combat* who was not prepared to take any snubs from Louis. The *régale* turned into a burning issue of ecclesiastical and national politics reviving all the ancient emotions about Gallican Liberties. The Jansenists became almost accidentally the defenders of clerical interests against the Crown. Louis had no difficulty in finding other clergy to support him in a struggle against the pope; and there were many ready to follow the lead of Bossuet in devising formulae that would satisfy both sides. An Assembly of the Clergy, convened under a certain amount of royal manipulation, produced in 1682 the 'Four Gallican Articles'. Apart from the first, which simply reaffirmed the king's sole authority in temporal matters, their precise meaning was comprehensible only to the ecclesiastical mind. The second favoured, with some circumlocution, the supremacy of General Councils; the fourth, more obscure still, indicated that the pope was not infallible. The crucial article was the third, which upheld Gallican liberties without defining them. The Assembly then expressed its unlimited obedience to and admiration for the pope. The pope denounced the Assembly so forcibly that a French breach with Rome began to seem possible at the moment when England was awaiting the accession of a Catholic king. As neither pope nor king would accept bishops appointed by the other, the number of vacant sees was rapidly increasing. Louis, and Madame de Maintenon, had the task of reconciling their religious duty with political necessity. It was in these circumstances that the rights of the Huguenots became a question of renewed political significance.

In 1609 Philip III of Spain had expelled the Moriscoes, an action commonly believed to have added substantially to his economic difficulties. In 1685 Louis XIV signed the Edict of Fontainebleau which put an end to the rights of co-existence which the Huguenots had enjoyed – decreasingly – for nearly a century. Louis has been bitterly denounced for his bigotry and stupidity. The insatiable territorial ambitions, the indiscriminate hanging of

possibly rebellious peasants, the savage devastation of enemy
territory have often been excused as the normal behaviour of the
time, by writers who nevertheless found the revocation unpardonable. In the light of history it was certainly ill-advised: the
economic consequences – even though they have sometimes been
exaggerated – obviously outweighed any advantages in national
and international politics. But Louis' decision arose from an
accumulation of immediate incentives with much the same
mixture of petty self-assertion and administrative tidiness as most
of his others. The principal difference was that the existence of
the Huguenot problem was itself so astonishing.

At the beginning of the reign there were probably well over
a million Huguenots, with six or seven hundred churches, still
– in spite of Richelieu's erosion of their privileges – more secure
and less penalized legally or socially than almost any religious
minority in Europe. As their total inactivity in the Fronde had
shown, Huguenotism was no longer the weapon of a section of
the nobility and had no political cohesion of its own. Huguenots
survived as village communities loyal to their traditional faith, or
as individual townsmen, or as families often of noble or prosperous mercantile status. Louis in 1661 believed – as had Henri
IV – that they would come to 'consider from time to time
whether there was any good reason to deprive themselves of the
advantages that they could have in common with the rest of my
subjects'.[5] They were therefore to receive no royal benefits, but
no persecution. There were obvious reasons for refraining from
any open attack on them: the 'Protestant' foreign policy which
had in the past always been an obstacle to any religious activity
that would arouse the wrath of France's allies was not destroyed
by the peace with Spain. Colbert could provide a list of Huguenot
bankers, merchants, arms manufacturers whose loss would be
calamitous, quite apart from the large numbers of prosperous
artisans. It was however possible to hold out greater incentives
to conversion. Once the *'converti'* became a familiar figure, it
would be clear how readily he acquired state favours. Sometimes
he was exempted from taxation that his 'old Catholic' neighbours
continued to pay.

The drive to convert the Huguenots originated however less
from the state than from private enterprise. Paul Pélisson, himself
a convert, became in 1676 the controller of the *caisse de conversions*:
Huguenots who renounced their faith were 'compensated' from

the revenues of vacant abbeys for pecuniary losses that were not always too closely scrutinized. The complementary process, to which many of the *dévots*, the judges, and the clergy applied themselves zealously, was the stringent enforcement of every penalty and disability that a careful scrutiny of the wording of the Edict of Nantes could extract from it, and the banning of every activity not specifically and unambiguously authorised. Visitations of the Huguenot areas arranged by the Assembly of Clergy were able to demonstrate that the Huguenots had gradually extended their teaching and worship beyond what had originally been permitted. By steady pressure normal life for the Huguenot communities could then be made impossible. The saving of Huguenot souls did not contribute to unanimity among Catholics: while Jansenists were energetically instructing those ex-Huguenots for whom six livres a head – the minimum payment from the *caisse* – was felt to have been only the means towards divine grace, Jesuits resented Pélisson's success and claimed that his converts were becoming a heretical sect within the Church, with Huguenot pastors still dominating it. All the political influence of the Jesuits was used to get a dramatic royal move that would destroy French Protestantism and identify the majesty of the king with that of the Church. In 1685 an assortment of circumstances gave them their way. One of them, paradoxically, was the success since 1681 of greatly increased state persecution. In Poitou the 'dragonnades' organized by the intendant René de Marillac, in which soldiers were encouraged to treat Huguenots with unlimited brutality, aroused such protests that Louis intervened to stop them. Elsewhere they were successfully imitated. They had produced tens of thousands of conversions; but they were bad for discipline and for the unity of the state. The European situation too, with James on the English throne, the Turks in retreat, and the Truce of Ratisbon registering a new set of territorial gains for France, seemed to have set a scene for Louis to appear as the leader of triumphant Catholicism. Revoking the Edict would make it difficult for anyone to question the king's staunchness as an ally of the Church. Besides, it would now be cheaper to throw the remaining Huguenots out than to pay the cost of further conversions.

The devout and the loyal in France celebrated the 1685 revocation enthusiastically. European Catholics – even the pope – offered rather tepid approbation. To Protestant statesmen the misfortune of their co-religionaries was a godsend. Louis had proclaimed himself the brutal persecutor of Protestantism, and had done so in a way that brought material as well as moral strength to his enemies. Something like a quarter of a million refugees took their skill and their capital to the states that were aligning themselves more firmly against the French. In England the demonstration of what Catholic rule might mean to Protestants could hardly fail to damage the prospects of James II. The effects inside France were not merely to remove a small section of the population that was on balance an economic asset. Huguenotism itself was turned from a declining and passive form of dissent into a militant faith of permanent resistance. In the Cévennes and here and there throughout the old Huguenot regions, secret Protestant congregations and occasional open revolt were met with an unpredictable mixture of ferocity and disregard. But gradually the sacred duty of extirpating heresy ceased to enthuse even the devout. By 1715 it no longer seemed to matter very much whether Huguenots survived or not.

FRANCE AND EUROPE IN THE 1680s

The peace treaties and truces marked changes in the activity of armies but not, for any length of time, in the habit of hand-to-mouth acquisitions on the frontier and vast schemes for European hegemony, to mature at the happy moment when Charles of Spain would die. The years from 1679 to 1688 were a period of 'peace'. In it Louis scored quiet victories over the emperor by buying the Poles away from him, backing the Hungarian rebels, encouraging the advance of the Turks. 'Peace' also meant that the armies of 200,000 well-equipped men which Louvois kept constantly available were used less in major warfare than as the threat that made it possible to get away with a succession of piecemeal pseudo-legal annexations. The idea of the '*réunions*' was on much the same level as that of the devolutions; but it depended not on juggling with the laws of private property but on research into the fantastic tangle of dependencies and fiefs that had arisen during centuries of warfare and robbery in Alsace and Franche-Comté. The Treaties of Münster and Nymegen had – in some cases no doubt intentionally – failed to specify precisely all the 'dependencies' of territories that changed hands. Colbert de Croissy, who as one of his brother's dynasty of ministers was now Secretary for Foreign Affairs, carried through the *parlements* and municipal Councils the supposedly judicial decisions that 'reunited' to French territories villages and fiefs that had been assumed to belong to Spain or to one or other of the states of the Empire. Louvois was ready with occupying forces. Sometimes the only effect was that the nobles who held the lands involved were expected to do homage to Louis. But two acquisitions were of strategic importance and hence scored immediate points against the other side. Casale, the Milanese fortress, was only included in the process by elaborate bribery and diplomatic trickery. Strassburg was one of the few towns that in the Thirty Years War had got its neutrality respected. Now, after an army thirty thousand strong had surrounded it, its reunion with France was celebrated by the entry of Louis in person.

French diplomacy was soon faced with a new opportunity that needed careful management. The emperor was temporarily unable to fight in the west because of the advance of the Turks; and in 1683 the folly of the Spaniards in declaring war was an occasion for Louvois to move his armies forward in the Netherlands. But there were still some limits to the public cynicism of western sovereigns and aristocrats. It would be inexpedient for the prospective master of Christendom to take advantage too openly, for his immediate gains, of the coalition formed by the emperor to defend its eastern frontiers. It was better to assure the Turks privately that France, despite the pope's threats of hell, would as usual do nothing against them, and make a settlement with Leopold that would not appear too outrageous. Some day Louis might still be able to emerge as a valiant champion of the cross against the crescent. The Truce of Ratisbon, or Regensburg, in 1684 – which was supposed to last for twenty years – accepted most of the *réunions* and the French seizure of Strassburg and Luxemburg. As it turned out, this was the height of French power. Helped by the Protestant indignation at the Revocation of the Edict of Nantes, the movement in Europe for an anti-French coalition began to grow. At home, some of the old 'Colbert Party' now hoped that territorial claims might really be ended and the cost of 'the enterprises of M. Louvois armies' diminished. But the militants were firmly convinced that further triumphs were to come.

The only result of the truce was that for a short time French power was asserted against the smaller states outside the Empire: Venice, Genoa, Algiers, and the Papacy continued in their different ways to serve as victims for the advertisement of French authority. When the marriage of the emperor's daughter Maria Antonia to the Elector of Bavaria raised the hideous complexities of the Spanish Succession affair again, a large French army appeared on the Pyrenees as a warning. A quarrel about the choice of a new Archbishop of Cologne was added to the dispute with the Papacy. In September 1688 the armies were brought into action again. The Habsburgs, Louis proclaimed, had spurned the generosity shown at Ratisbon; they had created, in the 'League of Augsburg', an aggressive coalition against France; they had thwarted his just policies in Cologne and his claims to lands in the Palatinate. The emperor was required to accept the French proposals within three months, and to convert the truce into a formal treaty. Meanwhile a few more frontier towns would have to be temporarily occupied. Three days later the massive attack along the whole eastern frontier began. In the winter, under Louvois' direction, there was carried out the destruction of the Rhine Palatinate and its population which became the most notorious atrocity of its kind in the century. The party of war had taken decisive charge of French policy at the moment when William of Orange was at last in a position to bring an even greater force against it.

WAR, DEPRESSION, AND RECOVERY IN THE 1690s

The alliance against France was probably the strongest any power had yet faced. Louis failed to prevent in 1688 a success for William of Orange that made his own schemes for acquiring territory either by inheritance or by conquest look clumsy and futile. Under William England and the Netherlands together became allies of the already formidable league of the emperor, Sweden, Spain, Savoy, and several German states. The war was fiercer and more costly in lives and material than any of the frontier struggles. For the first time the Anglo-Dutch navies effectively cut off French commerce. Colonial governors, commanders, and traders seized the chance to step up their hostilities. The French armies won victory after victory on the frontiers with little to show for it. Then, as every government found itself unable to keep up the supply of men and materials, the pace slackened and talk of peace became more serious. Yet the treaties made in 1696 and 1697 were due less to exhaustion than to firm reports from Spain that at last the helpless invalid king was on the point of death. Since William III was on the whole in favour of ending the fighting and Louis was prepared to pay a good territorial price, Leopold was the main obstacle. His position was greatly weakened in 1696 when Savoy was bought out of the war by the secret Treaty of Turin. France abandoned Casale and Pinerolo and restored the occupied territories of Duke Victor Amadeus, who was happy to bring his army over to the French side. At Ryswick in 1697 the French sacrificed most of their gains since Nymegen. The fortresses of Trier, Phillipsburg, Breisach, and Freiburg were handed back. Only Strassburg remained as an addition to French defences. Almost all Lorraine was restored to its duke. The French forces that had invaded Catalonia were withdrawn; Luxemburg, Charleroi, Ath, Mons, and Courtrai became Spanish Netherlands strongpoints again. Louis at last accepted that William III was a king and not a rebel against James II.

Once again Charles II did not die. Once again the carefully calculated improvements in French national finance and the commercial and industrial progress had been sacrificed in vain to the demands of war. Le Pelletier, who had been quietly reducing the government's debt, took the astonishing step during the war of resigning his post rather than resort to the financial evil for which he held Louvois' lust for power responsible. But the war had not been a complete financial disaster. So long as harvests remained good, the yield of the *taille* was increased. The *gabelle*, the *aides*, and the Crown's other resources had risen for a year or two and then fallen back. When the war was at its height it was costing almost double the revenue from taxes and from the various *dons gratuits* of the clergy and of those other nominally exempt classes who could be pressed to pay. Consequently the familiar 'extraordinary' devices were used again. Pontchartrain, *contrôleur-général* from 1689 to 1699, manipulated the currency, anticipated future revenue by the sale of exemptions, collected royal and noble plate to be melted down, pushed the venality of honours further than ever by supplying to intendants blank patents of nobility that could be sold to the highest bidder. Up to a point, the cry of the nation's honour and glory had its effect. Estates and municipal councils did vote higher sums than before – though less willingly as the demands were repeated. Most remarkable of all was the scheme, first publicly advocated by Vauban, for a capitation tax that would override all exemptions except that of the clergy. In 1695 it was introduced as an addition to older levies. Despite a crude grading by social class rather than wealth, men who had never paid anything to the state before, unless for their own profit, did for two or three years contribute to the cost of the war. If victory depended on resources and the means of diverting them, Louis would not be easy to defeat.

France had not only the capacity to pay for wars – however grim the impoverishment for most of the people. She was also able to make quicker recovery than the central, let alone the eastern, nations from a whole succession of calamities. In 1694 it was shown once again that small changes in barometric pressure could determine how much the lives of the great majority of the population were affected by the follies of statesmen. From 1691 to 1693 there was a succession of bad harvests. Probably the natural failure was no worse than the normal fluctuations. What mattered was that the fall in supply coincided with the greatest demand of the armies, the loss of manpower, the insecurity aroused by fears of invasion, and the maximum burden of taxation. All these contributed to the spiral of famine: rising prices were an incentive to hoarding which led to further rises; impoverishment of employers produced shortage of work, which increased the starvation of the labourer. The extent of the depression of course varied very much even within quite small areas; but the reports and statistics that were produced in increasing quantity and complexity give, when all allowance has been made for motives that might tempt their compilers to exaggerate, a consistent picture of decline. The yield of taxes never returned to the amounts reached in Colbert's day; the numbers of beggars rose, the value of land fell. It is easy to imagine that the entire economy of the country was collapsing. Yet eighteenth-century France could hardly be regarded as one of the poor or materially backward states of Europe. The peasants, on the whole, did not go desperately short of food for long, but did not achieve for themselves any general increase in prosperity. They provided a surplus which the state and the landlords and the merchants absorbed in rapidly changing ways.

The peace of 1697 happened to follow a few years of improved harvests. Taxation fell; industrial activity revived; exports rose at unprecedented speed. The efforts in overseas trade of the Colbert period and the steady growth of ports and shipping could now show their real value. For the first time French goods became a main part of European exports to America, both north and south – making possession of the Spanish Empire more tempting than ever. Amsterdam and Cadiz were no longer needed as *entrepôts*. The harvest of 1698 was not good – but the increased price seems to have been accepted with no great suffering. (One suggestion from the demographic studies is that the deaths of so many old and unproductive people four years before had made life easier for the survivors.) The burdens imposed by the state were to some extent diminished without any weakening of the central authority. The intendants and their *subdélégués* were now a permanent feature of life in every part of the country. The naval war was an occasion for establishing them for the first time in Brittany. Only the privileges of towns and of the nobility restricted the scope of the intendants' powers. But once the war was over there were even ways in which the state could appear as a beneficent paternal authority. The horror of the *milice* – selective conscription at the expense of the parish – ended. The *lieutenant de police*, an office extended from Paris to towns everywhere, was of course an instrument for enforcing conformity and obedience; but he could also offer some protection against the worst oppressions of the petty officials and taxgatherers. An enlightened despotism – even the glimmerings of a state concerned with the well-being of its people – seemed on the point of emerging from the gloom whenever war ceased to be the one essential purpose.

FRANCE AND THE SPANISH SUCCESSION

The end of the war in 1697 had brought France little benefit either in territory or in prestige. To give up so many of the frontier fortresses when they were firmly held by French armies was a remarkable assertion of diplomatic over military attitudes. Vauban, and Madame de Maintenon, were enraged. But the 'diplomatic' party could claim that by leaving open the possibility of agreement with almost any of their former enemies except the emperor they were playing for the prize of a share in the imminent carving-up of Spanish territories, either without war at all or with a war in which it would be France's turn to have a large coalition on her side. The diplomats could well have proved right. In the two Partition Treaties French demands were not those of an insatiable aggressor: they were intended to win the support that the emperor by his more blatant hopes of expansion was losing. France would be content with Naples and Sicily, plus – in the second version – Lorraine or perhaps Savoy. When the Spanish king made his second will leaving all his possessions to Louis' second grandson Philip of Anjou, there was some doubt about whether so dazzling an offer should be accepted. Colbert de Torcy, the latest French foreign minister, recognized that there was in any case a risk of war against the emperor, who had refused to agree to the Partition Treaty. If France stuck to the treaties, there was hope that England and the United Provinces would be her allies; if she accepted the will instead almost any alignment of the powers would be possible. The optimists believed that the Dutch and English would be at least as hostile to a Habsburg seizure of Spain as to a Bourbon one, and that the Spaniards themselves would be on the side of France. To reject the will meant a risk that the old nightmare of France being surrounded by a solid Habsburg barrier would come true; to accept it gave hope of a commercial as well as military alliance that would solve the economic troubles of the nation. It was not simply dynastic ambition that led Louis to accept the inheritance. The question was hotly debated in the Council and the court. The weight of opinion clearly favoured the will; even heredity of this kind was felt to uphold divine right.

It took a year and a half from the death of Charles II to the outbreak of war between France and a new 'Grand Alliance', in the spring of 1702. Once the possibility of war was obvious, the pressure to begin it appeared irrestible. An ambiguous pronouncement on the French attitude to the succession left a way open for breaking the agreement that Philip V of Spain should not also become King of France. French troops occupied the Netherlands frontier fortresses – in the name of the Spanish king. A French company acquired from Spain the immensely valuable '*asiento*' for the supply of negro slaves to the Spanish colonies, formerly held by the Dutch. When the former James II died a few days after the formation of the alliance of The Hague, Louis, in spite of his promises at Ryswick, greeted the pretender as James III. To each major pressure-group – the military, the commercial, and the Catholic – Louis had conceded a measure that played into the hands of those in Holland and England who were avidly seeking popular reasons for war.

The French appeared to have a reasonable prospect of defeating the new coalition. Their agreements with Spain, Bavaria, and – for the time being – Savoy gave them excellent bases for moving forward against the Empire. They spent money lavishly on the armies and on buying support. There seemed every hope that the emperor, interested mainly in the Spanish throne, could be divided from the English and Dutch who sought to beat the French and get what spoils they could. France's defensive fortifications in the east were strong and almost continuous. In the first year of fighting on the eastern frontier and in Italy the advantage, such as it was, went their way. But this proved to be a war in which long sieges, cautious occupation of territory, and evasive marches took second place. On both sides improvements in weapons (see pp. 283–5) gave to armies larger than ever before the power of rapid destruction. Marlborough, appointed in 1702 captain-general of the Anglo-Dutch forces, and the emperor's general, Eugene of Savoy, both believed in swift movement and ruthless, decisive battles. Both held at this stage enough political influence at home to keep full control of the fighting, while Villeroi, Vendôme, Villars, and the other French commanders suffered constant interference and supervision from Versailles.

The first serious misfortunes for France were diplomatic: in 1703 Savoy went over to the emperor's side, and Portugal in the Methuen Treaties became a military ally and economic dependant of England. Part of the price was that all the members of the coalition recognized the claim of Archduke Charles to the Spanish throne (see p. 375). Against this France could set the chance of a great victory over the emperor. French and Bavarian armies joined in an advance towards Vienna. At the same time a new rising in Hungary under Francis, grandson of George Rákóczy (see p. 376), had produced with French help a large force able to threaten the city from the east. In August 1704 Marlborough, Eugene, and Louis of Baden shattered the French armies at Blenheim, with heavy losses to themselves. Germany was brought almost completely under allied control. In the same month the English and Dutch navies captured Gibraltar. With the allies in command of the Mediterranean, 'Charles III' was soon able to land in Catalonia and win popular support as an enemy of Castile.

Not all the allied efforts were as forceful as the Blenheim campaign: there was pressure, notably from the Dutch, to move carefully and even to have some regard for the cost in lives. In 1706 Villeroi, with a new but inferior French army, was ordered to take the offensive in the Netherlands and suffered at Ramillies a defeat on almost the scale of Blenheim. From northern Italy too the French were driven out. There remained one unexpected source of hope: Charles XII of Sweden was winning decisive victories in Saxony. If France could buy him as an ally the Empire would again be in danger. But neither side could make the Swedes involve themselves in western quarrels: Russia was more important to them. In 1708 another effort by Vendôme's army to recover the Spanish Netherlands ended with his defeat at Oudenarde. Lille, one of the key points in Vauban's line of defences, was occupied. With the enemy on French soil, Louis began to consider terms for a settlement. There was now a well-defined peace-party, with the Duc de Beauvillier as its spokesman in the Council. Its great source of strength was the misery of France, and the poverty of the Crown.

DEFEAT AND DEPRESSION

The war had soon increased government expenses to three times the ordinary revenue. Many devices, old and new, were used to supplement it. The issue of receipts for loans developed into the printing of paper money, which circulated at far below its face value. There were repeated efforts to make profits for the government by devaluing the *livre*, the ordinary circulating currency, in terms of the *Louis d'or* and the *écu*. In 1709 a general recoinage was announced, so that loans would be repaid in coins worth three-quarters of their former value. A capitation tax on those exempt from normal taxation was tried again. Revolts in the Cévennes in 1704, which diverted large forces from the war, were an indication of the dangers if things got worse. As before, it was when bad weather was added to the burden of war that the worst suffering came. There was a grim winter in 1709: the cold that was killing off the armies of Charles XII in Russia extended far enough to freeze the Rhône. Both grain and vines were destroyed almost everywhere. In face of the English blockade, such corn as could be imported had to be used to keep the armies alive while the poor died. The intendants reported with growing panic the gathering of armies of rebels, against which they had not the means to act.

A great difference from earlier wartime crises was that now the court and the government and literate society were full of critics of the war and its management. Madame de Maintenon was convinced that the frosts were an indication of God's disapproval of the war. Chamillart, the latest finance minister, announced as early as 1707 that France could not afford to go on fighting. His successor Desmarets was soon of the same opinion. In broader terms their views were upheld by successful writers. Pierre de Boisguillebert, *lieutenant de police* at Rouen, had written before the war his *Détail de France* expounding the follies of the economic system and demanding a real tax on the rich. The *taille*, he said, was 'the ruin of goods, of bodies, and of souls'. His sustained campaign on these lines was now backed by Vauban, old and respected, who just before his death in 1707 published an attack on the crushing of the *menu peuple* by taxation. Fénelon and Saint-Simon were blaming not merely administrative defects but royal absolutism itself. Round the Dauphin and his son the Duc de Bourgogne there gathered shifting groups of nobles interested in the movements for reform and their probable effects on the distribution of power. The Dauphin died in 1711, the Duc de Bourgogne and his elder son in 1712. If, as seemed likely in the epidemics that were sweeping the court, the Duc de Bourgogne's younger son and the Duc de Berry also died, Philip V of Spain would be the sole survivor of the Bourbon line. There was talk of legitimizing some of the royal bastards, and hasty realignments among the court factions.

There were of course important Frenchmen who neither suffered from nor opposed the war. The lower the credit of the state sank, the greater the opportunity of profit for the financiers. The bigger the scale on which wars were fought, the bigger profits there were in supplying the material for them. Samuel Bernard, the greatest of the financiers, was involved in the hoarding of grain, in manipulating the exchanges, in shipping and munitions and the *asiento*. His bankruptcy in 1709, from which the government had to rescue him, was a mere incident in the accumulation of his millions; though it was also part of a general financial upheaval that brought some of his kind onto the side of peace. From time to time, the most unscrupulous of the profiteers were made to repay some of their gains. But on a less spectacular scale there were opportunities at every level for taking a share of the money that was flowing into and out of the Treasury. The sale of office and of patents of nobility remained a source of benefit for both government and subject to which there seemed no limit. Those who had capital to lend continued to regard the *rentes* as a safe investment. In the last years of the war, government borrowing increased at an unprecedented rate. There was no longer any question of paying for the war out of revenue in a foreseeable time. While the state itself was accumulating a vast debt, its subjects were divided sharply into those who suffered and those who gained.

THE UTRECHT SETTLEMENT

In investigating the possibilities of peace, the French hoped that the enemy alliance would as usual be divided by the prospect of territorial gains. At first this seemed unlikely. Marlborough's victories produced powerful groups in England and in the Netherlands determined to achieve a total defeat of France. By demanding that Louis should abandon Philip completely, and even fight against him, and by talking of the occupation of French territory, the allies momentarily evoked in France an indignant enthusiasm for the war, even among the former peace-makers. The fall of the English Whig ministry in 1710, followed by the dismissal of Marlborough, changed the situation completely. In 1711 there came the last of the changes in the tangle of the Spanish Succession: the Emperor Joseph I died of smallpox and was succeeded by his brother Charles, the allies' claimant to the Spanish throne. In keeping the succession away from the French, England and the Netherlands suddenly found themselves faced with a revival of the vast Habsburg Empire of Charles V. The objections to Philip V immediately became far less serious. Ignoring their commitments to their allies, the English ministers

Harley and St John began negotiations with the French and ordered the new military commander, Ormonde, to avoid further fighting. The Dutch and Austrians were not even to be informed. French armies were naturally able to win some victories that improved their position appreciably.

The new emperor at first refused to have any part in the negotiations with the French, which were initiated by what he reasonably denounced as English treachery. The Dutch abandoned their militancy and decided to get what they could out of the conference. Portugal, Savoy, and Prussia also joined in the meetings at Utrecht. In the negotiations and the separate treaties that emerged from them it made little difference which nations had been allies and which enemies. The proclaimed intention was 'to establish the peace and tranquillity of Christendom by a just balance of power (*équilibre de puissance*), which is the best and most solid basis of mutual friendship . . .' In practice it meant that the Spanish possessions would be shared out and other adjustments of territory made in accordance with a more or less recognized order of precedence among the powers and with regard to both strategic and economic interests. The agreement between France and Britain was signed first, in April 1713; the other powers continued to bargain within its general assumptions. It was only in March 1714 that the emperor made peace with France at Rastatt. Portugal, getting little gratitude from Britain for her help, did not submit to Spanish demands until 1715.

From the terms of the settlement it might be supposed that the emperor was the one triumphant victor. The Spanish Netherlands, Milan, Naples, and Sardinia were handed over to him, and French conquests on the right bank of the Rhine restored. (Sardinia was then exchanged for Sicily which had been the main reward given to Savoy.) The diplomats, seeking an arrangement that would not provoke immediate further wars, had produced a far bigger change than any military conquests.

Britain collected some colonial territories from France – Newfoundland, Hudson Bay, Acadia (the eastern part of modern New Brunswick), and St Christopher (St Kitts) – and Gibraltar and Minorca from Spain. The French accepted the Hanoverian succession in Britain, at the expense of the Jacobites. There was an elaborate commercial treaty between Britain and France; and Spain conceded to Britain for thirty years a monopoly in the shipping of 4,800 negro slaves a year to America.

For Louis XIV the outcome was far better than had seemed likely in the black days of 1709–10. He kept Alsace, Franche-Comté, and a frontier with the new Austrian Netherlands much the same as in 1679. His ally the Elector of Bavaria got his former territories back. Philip V, having confirmed his renunciation of any claims to the French succession, not only retained Spain – including Catalonia which tried hard to escape – but the South American possessions too.

The Dutch, who now ranked fairly low in the diplomatic hierarchy, eventually gained most of the barrier fortifications they wanted, and were enabled to thwart any commercial rivalry from Antwerp by closing the Scheldt. The King of Prussia, with his new title formally recognized, acquired Guelderland, the outlying bit of the former Spanish Netherlands adjoining his Rhineland possessions.

Utrecht, like any settlement of its kind, contributed at least as much to future conflicts as to the 'tranquillity of Christendom'. The Empire was if anything an even more irrational agglomeration than before; France still held isolated scraps of territory amid the Duchy of Lorraine; the boundaries of the Netherlands had no other justification than the military one. The monarchs and ministers had devoted themselves to making their states into mechanisms of enormous power and complexity, concerned with nearly every aspect of the lives of their subjects. Yet when they came to settle the vital question of what lands and people they ruled, they behaved like children or like brigands. What the diplomats spoke of pompously as a 'system' and an 'equilibrium' meant in practice that territories and their inhabitants were disposed of by their sovereigns in whatever way the bargaining permitted. It sprang not from villainy or stupidity but from the fact that political authority was held by men who had acquired, at first or second hand, the outlook of a landed nobility, and treated sovereignty as the equivalent of ownership. They assumed equally that war, which for many of them was a major interest in life, should be one of the prime purposes of the state. There were of course other considerations as well. Religious allegiances, which had been crucial in earlier peace settlements, no longer caused much difficulty. Instead the commercial treaties that were coupled with the territorial ones gave the settlement some connection with the material interests of subjects. It was true also that acquisitions of territory, especially colonial, could bring economic benefits. But on the whole if Utrecht ushered in a new era it was not one in which 'enlightenment' had much place in international affairs.

NOTES AND REFERENCES

1 Fénelon, *Ecrits et lettres politiques*, ed. C. Urbain (Paris, 1920). There have been doubts about the authorship of the letter.

2 Quoted in E. Lavisse, *Histoire de France* (Paris, 1905), vol. 7, part 2, p. 185.

3 P. Goubert, *Louis XIV et vingt million français* (Paris, 1966), p. 89.

4 Many different spellings remain in use for the town whose modern Dutch name is Nijmegen. The treaty between France and the Empire was not signed until February 1679, that with Denmark in September 1679.

5 Quoted in P. Gaxotte, *La France de Louis XIV* (Paris, 1946), p. 241.

CHRONOLOGICAL LIST OF POLITICAL EVENTS

1598 The Edict of Nantes establishes the rights of the Huguenots. Philip III of Spain succeeds Philip II. Peace of Vervins between Spain and France.
Boris Godunov succeeds Fedor I as tsar.

1599 Swedish Riksdag deposes Sigismund III.

1600 Henri IV of France invades Savoy.

1601 The Earl of Essex executed for rebellion.

1602 Attack on Geneva by Charles Emmanuel of Savoy repelled.

1603 James VI of Scotland succeeds Elizabeth on English throne.

1604 Peace between England and Spain.
Charles IX recognized as King of Sweden.

1605 Death of Boris Godunov and murder of his son Fedor. The first 'False Dmitry' crowned as tsar.

1606 The 'False Dmitry' murdered: Vasily Shuisky proclaimed tsar. Treaty of Zitva-Torok between the Empire and Turkey.

1608 The Protestant Union formed in Germany. The Emperor Rudolf II cedes Austria, Hungary, and Moravia to his brother Matthias.
Second 'False Dmitry' in Russia.

1609 Twelve-year truce in the Netherlands.
Catholic League formed in Germany. Rudolf II grants the 'Letter of Majesty' promising religious liberty in Bohemia. Sigismund III of Poland invades Russia.

1610 Henri IV of France murdered: Louis XIII succeeds him, with Marie de Medici as regent.
Vasily Shuisky overthrown: Vladislav proclaimed tsar.

1611 War between Sweden and Denmark. Gustav Adolf succeeds Charles IX of Sweden.

1612 Matthias succeeds Rudolf II as emperor.
Polish invaders defeated in Russia.

1613   Michael Romanov elected as tsar by a *zemsky sobor*.
       Gabriel Bethlen becomes Prince of Transylvania.
       Peace of Knaeroed between Sweden and Denmark.
1614   Meeting of the Estates–General in France.
1615   Rebellion of princes in France.
1616   Richelieu's brief term as Secretary of State.
1617   Treaty of Stolbova between Russia and Sweden.
1618   Revolt of Bohemia; the 'Defenestration of Prague'.
1619   Ferdinand of Styria succeeds Matthias as Emperor; Bohemians
       elect Frederick, Elector Palatine, as their king in place of
       Ferdinand.
       Oldenbarnevelt executed.
1620   Agreement at Ulm between Protestant Union and Catholic
       League.
       Frederick of Bohemia defeated at Battle of the White Mountain.
       Turks defeat Poles at Cecora.
1621   Philip IV succeeds Philip III of Spain; Olivares chief minister.
       War between Spain and the Netherlands renewed.
       Religious war in France.
       Sweden invades Livonia.
1622   Peace of Montpellier between Huguenots and French Crown.
       Tilly wins victories in Germany.
1623   Urban VIII succeeds Gregory XV as pope.
       Maximilian of Bavaria made Elector Palatine.
       Murad IV succeeds Osman II as sultan.
1624   French invade the Valtelline
       Richelieu becomes chief minister.
1625   Charles I of England succeeds James I.
       England at war with Spain.
       Frederick Henry succeeds Maurice of Nassau as Stadtholder in
       the Netherlands.
       Huguenot revolt in France.
       Danes enter the war in Germany.
1626   Christian IV of Denmark defeated at Lutter.
1627   Huguenot revolt: siege of La Rochelle.
1628   The Petition of Right in England; Buckingham assassinated.
       The Mantuan War.
1629   Huguenot wars ended by Peace of Alais.
       Edict of Restitution and Treaty of Lübeck in Germany.
       Truce of Altmark between Sweden and Poland.
1630   'Day of Dupes' in France.
       Swedes invade Pomerania; Wallenstein dismissed.
       Victor Amadeus succeeds Charles Emmanuel as Duke of Savoy.
1631   Treaty of Barwälde between France and Sweden.
       Mantuan War ended by Treaty of Cherasco.
       Sack of Magdeburg.
1632   Rebellion of Gaston of Orleans defeated.
       Gustav Adolf killed at Lützen; Christina Queen of Sweden.
       Vladislav IV succeeds Sigismund III of Poland.

1633 League of Heilbronn in Germany.
      Laud becomes Archbishop of Canterbury.
1634 Wallenstein murdered; Swedes defeated at Nördlingen.
      Treaty of Polianov between Poland and Russia.
1635 Peace of Prague between emperor and Protestant states.
      France declares war on Spain.
1637 Ferdinand III succeeds Ferdinand II as emperor.
      Charles Emmanuel II succeeds Victor Amadeus as Duke of
      Savoy.
1638 'Ship Money' trial in England; National Covenant in Scotland.
1639 First Bishops' War in Scotland.
      French invade Alsace.
      Tromp defeats Spanish fleet in the Downs.
1640 Short Parliament and opening of Long Parliament in England;
      Second Bishops' War in Scotland.
      Revolts in Catalonia and Portugal.
      Frederick William succeeds George William as Elector of
      Brandenburg.
1641 Execution of Strafford in England; the Irish Rebellion; the
      Grand Remonstrance.
1642 Civil War in England; John Pym parliamentary leader.
      Conspiracy of Cinq-Mars in France; death of Richelieu; Mazarin
      chief minister.
      Imperial army defeated by Swedes at Breitenfeld.
1643 Louis XIV succeeds Louis XIII; Anne of Austria Regent.
      Fall of Olivares; Spain defeated by France at Rocroi.
      Solemn League and Covenant; Westminster Assembly; death of
      Pym.
1644 Parliamentary victory at Marston Moor.
      Innocent X succeeds Urban VIII as pope.
      Sweden makes war on Denmark.
1645 Execution of Laud; Self-Denying Ordinance; formation of New
      Model Army; parliamentary victory at Naseby.
      Treaty of Brömsebro: Sweden gains territory from Denmark.
      Beginning of peace negotiations in Germany.
1646 Charles I surrenders to the Scots.
1647 Charles I handed over to the English parliament; the Putney
      Debates.
      William II succeeds Frederick Henry as Stadtholder.
      Rebellion in Naples.
1648 The Peace of Westphalia.
      Beginning of the *Fronde* of the *parlement*.
      Second Civil War in England; Pride's Purge.
      Frederick III succeeds Christian IV of Denmark; John Casimir
      King of Poland.
1649 Charles I executed; monarchy and House of Lords abolished;
      sack of Drogheda and Wexford.
      Legal Code establishing serfdom in Russia; revolt in the
      Ukraine.

1650   Cromwell defeats the Scots at Dunbar.
      Condé imprisoned.
      Death of William II: republican government in the Netherlands.
1651   Charles II crowned in Scotland, defeated by Cromwell at
      Worcester; the Navigation Act.
      Mazarin leaves France; Condé enters Paris, becomes ally of
      Spain
1652   War between England and the Netherlands.
1653   Barebone's parliament; Cromwell becomes Lord Protector.
      De Witt becomes Grand Pensionary of Holland.
      End of the Fronde; Mazarin back in Paris.
1654   Coronation of Louis XIV.
      Peace of Westminster ends Anglo-Dutch war.
      War between Russia and Poland.
      Queen Christina abdicates: Charles X King of Sweden.
1655   Swedes declare war on Poland.
1656   Mohammed Kiuprili becomes grand vizir.
      Alliance of England and France against Spain.
1657   'Humble Petition and Advice' creates new upper house in
      Cromwellian parliament.
1658   Death of Oliver Cromwell; Richard Cromwell Protector.
      Leopold I succeeds Ferdinand III as emperor.
      Peace of Roskilde between Sweden and Denmark followed by
      renewed war.
1659   Peace of the Pyrenees between France and Spain.
      Richard Cromwell abdicates; Long Parliament restored.
1660   Charles II restored to English throne.
      Charles XI of Sweden succeeds Charles X; Peace of Oliva ends
      Northern War.
1661   Death of Mazarin; effective rule of Louis XIV begins.
      Ahmed Kiuprili becomes grand vizir.
      Cavalier parliament meets; first measures of the 'Clarendon
      Code'.
1662   England sells Dunkirk to France; Colbert becomes finance
      minister.
1663   Turks declare war on Austria.
1664   Turks defeated at St Gotthard: peace agreed.
1665   Charles II of Spain succeeds Philip IV.
      Second Anglo-Dutch War.
1666   Schism in the Russian Church begins.
1667   War of Devolution between France and Spain.
      Peace of Breda between England and Netherlands.
      Peace of Andrusovo between Russia and Poland.
1668   Triple Alliance of England, Sweden, and Netherlands.
      Treaty of Aix-la-Chapelle ends War of Devolution.
      John Casimir of Poland abdicates.
1669   Michael Wisniowiecki elected King of Poland.
      Venice surrenders Crete to the Turks.

1670   Treaty of Dover between Louis XIV and Charles II of England.
Stenka Razin's revolt in Russia.
Christian V succeeds Frederick III of Denmark; Griffenfeld chief minister.

1671   John Sobieski elected King of Poland.

1672   De Witt murdered; William III becomes Stadtholder.
England and France at war with the Netherlands.
War between Turkey and Poland.

1673   Test Act in England excluding Catholics from office.

1674   Peace between England and the Netherlands; Spain and the Empire join in war against France.

1675   Swedes attack Brandenburg; defeated at Fehrbellin.

1676   Fedor III succeeds Alexis as tsar.
Innocent XI becomes pope.
Kara Mustafa succeeds Ahmed as grand vizir; peace between Turkey and Poland.

1677   War between Turkey and Russia.

1678   Treaties of Nymegen between France and the Netherlands, France and Spain.
Popish plot in England.
Thököli becomes national leader in Hungary.

1679   Cavalier parliament dissolved; first 'Exclusion Parliament' meets.
Further treaties at Nymegen; Treaty of St Germain between Brandenburg and Sweden.

1680   '*Chambres de Réunion*' on French frontier.

1681   Peace of Radzin between Russia and Turkey.

1682   The Gallican Articles.
Turks make war on Austria and Poland.
Ivan V and Peter I joint tsars; Sophia as regent.

1683   Vienna besieged by the Turks.
French invade Spanish Netherlands.

1684   Twenty-year Truce of Ratisbon between France and the Empire.
'Holy League' against the Turks.

1685   James II succeeds Charles II of England; Monmouth's rebellion
Revocation of the Edict of Nantes.

1686   League of Augsburg against France.
Buda recaptured from the Turks.

1687   Turks defeated at Mohacs; Mohammed IV deposed and succeeded by Suleiman III; Venetians bombard Athens.

1688   War of the League of Augsburg begins; devastation of the Palatinate.
William of Orange lands at Torbay; James II flees.
Frederick III succeeds the Great Elector of Brandenburg.

1689   Convention Parliament declares William III and Mary joint sovereigns; the Bill of Rights.

1690   James II defeated at the Battle of the Boyne; Anglo-Dutch fleet defeated by the French off Beachy Head.
Turks recapture Belgrade.

1691 Innocent XII succeeds Alexander VIII as pope.
      Turks defeated by imperial armies at Salem Kemen; Mustafa
      Kiuprili killed.
1692 Massacre of Glencoe.
      Anglo-Dutch fleet defeats the French off La Hogue.
1693 French victory over William III at Neerwinden.
1694 Augustus the Strong becomes Elector of Saxony.
1695 Mustafa II succeeds Ahmed II as sultan.
1696 Peter the Great captures Azoff.
1697 Treaty of Ryswick between France and the allies.
      Peter the Great's visit to western Europe.
      Charles XII succeeds Charles XI of Sweden.
      Augustus II succeeds John Sobieski of Poland.
      Eugene of Savoy defeats the Turks at Zenta.
1698 First partition treaty to settle Spanish Succession.
      Revolt of the *streltsi* in Moscow.
1699 Peace of Karlowitz between Turkey and Venice, Poland,
      Austria.
      Peter the Great's reforms of Russian government.
1700 Second treaty for partition of Spanish possessions; death of
      Charles II.
      Northern War begins; Charles XII defeats Russians at Narva.
      Peace of Traventhal between Sweden and Denmark.
1701 Fighting between French and Spaniards in Italy; alliance of
      England, Netherlands, and Empire against France.
      Frederick III of Brandenburg crowned King of Prussia.
1702 Anne succeeds William III in England; Heinsuis and the States-
      General take control in the Netherlands.
      War of the Spanish Succession begins.
1703 Portugal and Savoy join the alliance against France.
      Foundation of St Petersburg.
1704 The French defeated at Blenheim.
      Stanislas Lesczynski elected King of Poland.
1705 Josef I succeeds Leopold as emperor.
1706 The French defeated at Ramillies; Marlborough's troops occupy
      the Spanish Netherlands; French driven out of Piedmont.
1707 Union of England and Scotland.
1708 The French defeated at Oudenarde.
1709 Russian victory over the Swedes at Pultava; Charles XII takes
      refuge in Turkey.
      Peace negotiations with France; Marlborough and Eugene take
      Tournai, defeat French at Malplaquet.
1710 Tory ministry in England; peace negotiations break down;
      indecisive fighting in Spain and Netherlands.
1711 'Charles III of Spain' succeeds Josef I as emperor.
      Peace between Russia and Turkey.
1712 Negotiations at Utrecht; deaths of Louis XIV's son and
      grandson; Philip V renounces claim to French throne.

1713 Peace of Utrecht: France makes treaties with Britain, Prussia, Netherlands, Savoy, Portugal; England makes treaty with Spain.
1714 Treaty between Spain and Netherlands; Peace of Rastatt between France and the emperor.
      George I succeeds Anne in England.
1715 Death of Louis XIV.
      Jacobite rising in Scotland.
1718 Death of Charles XII of Sweden.
1721 Peace of Nystad between Sweden and Russia ends Northern War.
1725 Death of Peter the Great.

BIBLIOGRAPHY

GENERAL

The aim in selecting this small proportion of the secondary works now available has been to choose first works written in or translated into English and then those in French, with a few from other western languages. (The omission of those in Russian is due only to ignorance.) Books, among them a good many collections of new or reprinted essays, have generally been preferred to articles in periodicals; but there are enough specimens of the latter to give an idea of their proliferation.

The *New Cambridge Modern History* is the most useful source of fuller information on nearly all the topics dealt with here. The three seventeenth-century volumes are vol. IV, *The Decline of Spain and the Thirty Years War 1609–1648/59* (ed. J. P. Cooper, 1970); vol. V, *The Ascendancy of France, 1648–88* (ed. F. L. Carsten, 1961); vol. VI, *The Rise of Great Britain and Russia, 1688–1725* (ed. J. S. Bromley, 1970). Some of the chapters are in themselves important historical works, and a few are listed in the appropriate sections below. The *Atlas* (1970) and the *Companion Volume* (ed. Peter Burke, 1979) are also well planned. In the *Fontana History of Europe* the volume by John Stoye, *Europe Unfolding, 1648–1688* (London, 1969) is probably the best of its size. William Doyle, *The Old European Order, 1660–1800* (Oxford, 1985) has an arrangement by topics that makes every part of it illuminating for the seventeenth century. G. N. Clark, *The Seventeenth Century* (Oxford, 1931) is a collection of lucid short essays. Pierre Chaunu, *La Civilisation de l'europe classique* (Paris,

1966) is a very French blend of the oratorical and the quantitative.

All bibliographies for this period encounter the contrast between the vast output of works on the obvious major countries and the lack, or at least obscurity, of those on other states and regions. For these the short histories covering many centuries may be the only accessible source. They include T. K. Derry, *A Short History of Norway* (London, 1957); E. Bonjour, H. S. Offler, and G. E. Potter, *A Short History of Switzerland* (Oxford, 1952); R. W. Seton-Watson, *A History of the Roumanians* (London, 1963); H. C. Darby and others, *A Short History of Yugoslavia* (Cambridge, 1966) – which treats each of its constituent states separately; H. V. Livermore, *A History of Portugal* (Cambridge, 1947).

For quick reference W. L. Langer, *An Encyclopaedia of World History* (London, 1975) gives dates, summaries of events, and genealogies, from 'man's animal ancestors' to space-travel.

CHAPTER 2: PEOPLES AND STATES

The term 'Europe' and its changing meaning are examined in Denys Hay, *Europe, the Emergence of an Idea* (Edinburgh, 1957) and in an article by H. D. Schmidt, 'The establishment of "Europe" as a political expression' in *Historical Journal*, vol. 9 (1966). Two books on historical geography differing in scope are Clifford T. Smith, *An Historical Geography of Western Europe before 1800* (revised edition, London, 1978) and N. J. G. Pounds, *An Historical Geography of Europe, 1500–1804* (Cambridge, 1979).

On race W. Z. Ripley, *The Races of Europe* (London, 1900) is a sound old-style account; Julian Huxley and A. C. Haddon, *We Europeans* (London, 1935) is an entertaining short survey. On Jewish history one of the many books by Cecil Roth is *The Jewish People* (London, 1936). S. W. Baron, *A Social and Religious History of the Jews* (New York, 1980) deals with western Europe in volumes 14 and 15 and with Poland in volume 16. Brian Pullan, *The Jews of Europe and the Inquisition of Venice, 1550–1670* (Oxford, 1983) has general as well as local material, J. P. Clébert, *The Gypsies* (English transl., London, 1963) is attractive.

Historical demography is now a major subject in its own right. A good introduction to it is Carlo Cipolla, *The Economic History of World Population* (London, 1962). M. W. Flinn, *The European*

Demographic System, 1500–1800 (Brighton, 1981) is a reliable authority. Several of the general works listed on pp. 536 and 539 have substantial chapters on population; the most helpful are K. F. Helleiner, 'The Population of Europe' in *The Cambridge Economic History of Europe*, vol. 4; F. Braudel in his *Civilisation and Capitalism*, vol. 1; and Roger Mols, 'Population in Europe, 1500–1700' in *The Fontana Economic History of Europe*, vol. 2. The much larger work by Roger Mols, *Introduction à la démographie historique des villes d'Europe* (3 vols, Paris, 1954–56) surveys in detail methods and conclusions from the fourteenth to the eighteenth century. There are articles relevant to the period in D. V. Glass and D. E. C. Eversley (eds) *Population in History* (London, 1965) and many others in the periodicals *Population Studies* and (in French) *Population*. Among studies of particular countries short indications of the massive researches on France include J. Dupâquier, *La population francaise aux XVIIe et XVIIIe siècles* (Paris, 1979); J. Meuvret, 'Les crises de subsistances et la démographie de la France de l'ancien régime' in *Population*, vol. 1 (1946) and M. Reinhard, 'La population française au XVIIe siècle' in *Population*, vol. 13 (1958). Examples from other periodicals are Aksel Lassen, 'The population of Denmark 1660–1960' in *Scandinavian Historical Review*, vols 13 and 14 (1965 and 1966) and Irena Gieystorova, 'Research into the demographic history of Poland' in *Acta Poloniae Historica* (Warsaw, 1968). Intensive study of English population is explained in the large book by E. A. Wrigley and R. S. Schofield, *The Population History of England* (London, 1981). J. D. Chambers, *Population, Economy, and Society in pre-industrial England* (London, 1972) is more manageable. Disease and epidemics are an aspect of scientific as much as of demographic history. L. F. Hirst, *The Conquest of Plague* (Oxford, 1953) and W. H. MacNeill, *Plagues and Peoples* (Oxford, 1976), extend to other periods and continents. Dates and places of outbreaks and full accounts of the diseases are in Jean-Noel Biraben, *Les hommes et la peste en France et les pays européens et mediterranéens* (Paris, 1975). M. W. Flinn, 'Plague in Europe and the Mediterranean Countries' in *Journal of European Economic History*, vol. 8 (1979) is lucid. An example of regional studies is B. Bennassar, *Recherches sur les grandes épidémies dans le nord de l'espagne* (Paris, 1969). The obscure subject of restriction on population is investigated in Hélène Bergues (ed.), *La prévention des naissances dans la famille* (Paris, 1960).

General works on the empires and states are in the bibliographies to Chapters 12 to 18.

CHAPTER 3: THE ECONOMY

The vast output of works on economic history, ranging in area from the world to a village and in approach from the uncritically descriptive to the abstrusely mathematical make this the most difficult of the bibliographies to select. Two comprehensive surveys of moderate length, each by a single author, are Jan de Vries, *The Economy of Europe in an Age of Crisis* (Cambridge, 1976) and Hermann Kellenbenz, *The Rise of the European Economy: an economic history of continental Europe from the fifteenth to the eighteenth century* (London, 1976). Kellenbenz is solidly informative, with many examples from central Europe; de Vries is more concerned with the development of a capitalist economy. The three splendid volumes by Fernand Braudel, translated into English with the combined title *Civilisation and Capitalism in the 15th to 18th Century* are *The Structures of Everyday Life* (London, 1981), The *Wheels of Commerce* (London, 1982), and *The Perspective of the World* (London, 1984). They bring together material from every continent and include sidelights often ignored by earlier historians. Many general economic histories are of course collaborative. *The Cambridge Economic History of Europe*, vols 4 and 5, both edited by E. E. Rich and C. H. Wilson (Cambridge, 1967 and 1977), has chapters that differ in approach and level of detail. An easily obtained shorter survey is *The Fontana Economic History of Europe*, vol. 2, *The Sixteenth and Seventeenth Centuries* edited by Carlo M. Cipolla (London, 1974), which draws eminent contributors from several countries. Cipolla is also the editor of *The Economic Decline of Empires* (London, 1970), where essays on Spain, Italy, the Ottoman Empire, and the Netherlands in the early modern period can be compared with those on China, Arabia, and Byzantium. P. Léon (ed.), *Histoire économique et sociale du monde*, vol. 2, *1580–1740* (Paris, 1977) is one of several multi-volume French works on the subject. C. Wilson and G. Parker (eds), *An Introduction to the sources of European Economic History*, vol. 1 (London, 1977) has well-summarized statistical information.

New evidence and theories about climatic change appear

constantly. E. Le Roy Ladurie, 'History and climate' in Peter Burke (ed.), *Economy and Society in Early Modern Europe* (London, 1972) – a collection of essays translated from *Annales* – is a critical account of methods and ideas. H. H. Lamb, *Climate, History, and the Modern World* (London, 1982); M .L. Parry, *Climatic Change, Agriculture, and Settlement* (Folkstone, 1978); and T. M. L. Wigley, M. J. Ingram and G. Farmer (eds), *Climate and History* (Cambridge, 1981) are all involved in the arguments. The pursuit of one unconfirmed theory about the seventeenth-century deterioration is shown briefly by John A. Eddy in 'The Maunder Minimum: sunspots and climate in the reign of Louis XIV' in Geoffrey Parker and Lesley Smith (eds), *The General Crisis of the Seventeenth Century* (London, 1978). E. Le Roy Ladurie, *Times of Feast, Times of Famine* (New York, 1971) treats the problem of fluctuation in a more human way.

There are surprisingly few general books on European agriculture in the period. A standard authority is B. H. Schlicher von Bath, *The Agrarian History of Western Europe* (English transl., London, 1963). His chapter in the *Cambridge Economic History*, vol. 5 (see p. 539 above) is more recent and extends to eastern Europe. Of the older writings N. S. B. Gras, *A History of Agriculture in Europe and America* (2nd edn, New York, 1940) is still relevant. No work on Europe as a whole is as comprehensive as *The Agrarian History of England and Wales*, edited by Joan Thirsk, vol. 4 (Cambridge, 1967) and vol. 5, parts 1 and 2 (Cambridge, 1984 and 1985). On France the *Histoire économique et sociale de la France* – general editors F. Braudel and E. Labrousse – vol. 1(ii) edited by E. Le Roy Ladurie and Michel Morineau, *Paysannerie et croissance* (Paris, 1977) has the modern French approach. Examples on other countries are R. E. F. Smith, *Peasant Farming in Muscovy* (Cambridge, 1977) and Wilhelm Abel, *Geschichte des deutschen Landwirtschaft* (Stuttgart, 1962). A more general book by Wilhelm Abel is translated into English as *Agricultural Fluctuations in Europe* (London, 1980).

Industrial developments in their practical aspects are described in *A History of Technology*, ed. C. J. Singer and others, vol. 3 (Oxford, 1957). E. Lipson, *The Economic History of England*, 6th edn, vol. 2 (London, 1956) contains a reliable survey of each of the main industries. B. E. Supple, *Commercial Crisis and Change in England, 1640–1642* (Cambridge, 1959) includes a clear explanation of old and new draperies. Three works by J. U. Nef,

Industry and Government in France and England, 1540–1640 (London, 1957), *The Rise of the British Coal Industry* (2 vols, London, 1932) and his essays in *The Conquest of the Material World* (London, 1964) can be compared with the criticisms of them in Sybil M. Jack, *Trade and Industry in Tudor and Stuart England* (London, 1977). Some of the best sources for industrial history generally are such local studies as G. D. Ramsay, *The Wiltshire Woolen Industry in the sixteenth and seventeenth centuries* (Oxford, 1943) and W. H. Court, *The Rise of Midland Industries, 1600–1838* (Oxford, 1938). There is abundant material on industry in many of the French regional studies such as P. Goubert, *Beauvais et les Beauvaisis* (Paris, 1960). Henri Sée, *L'évolution commerciale et industrielle de la France sous l'ancien régime* (Paris, 1938) is still useful. In the *Histoire économique et sociale de la France* mentioned above, vol. 1(i), edited by Pierre Chaunu and Richard Gasern, is entitled *L'état et la ville.*

Urban history is another rapidly developing subject. Philip Abrams and E. A. Wrigley (eds), *Towns in Societies* (Cambridge, 1978) shows many of its themes over a wide period. Jan de Vries, *European Urbanisation, 1600–1800* (London, 1984) is a study involving some formidable mathematics. P. Lavedan, *Histoire de l'urbanisme: renaissance et temps modernes* (Paris, 1941) has more about the physical form and construction of towns. Venice is the subject of constant study, to which F. C. Lane, *Venice, a Maritime Republic* (Baltimore, 1973) is a good introduction. Of the various works on Venice by Brian Pullan, *Service to the Venetian State* (Florence, 1965) is a short consideration of links between the economy and the ruling élite, which is also the main theme of Peter Burke, *Venice and Amsterdam* (London, 1974). Violet Barbour, *Capitalism in Amsterdam in the Seventeenth Century* (Ann Arbor, 1963) is a straight survey of its whole economy. The two cities are the basis of wider comparisons in the second section of Braudel, *The Perspective of the World* (see above, p. 539). London commerce and institutions are examined in Robert Ashton, *The City and the Court 1603–1643* (Cambridge, 1979), and the expansion of the city in N. G. Brett-James, *The Growth of Stuart London* (London, 1935).

Accounts of overseas trade concentrate on the great companies and the intervention of governments. C. R. Boxer, The *Dutch Seaborne Empire, 1600–1800* (London, 1965) and *The Portuguese Seaborne Empire, 1415–1825* (London, 1969); J. H. Parry, *The*

Spanish Seaborne Empire (London, 1966); and G. D. Ramsay, *English Overseas Trade During the Centuries of Emergence* (London, 1957) are well established. R. Davis, *English Overseas Trade, 1500–1700* (London, 1973) contrasts European with colonial trade. N. Steensgaard, *Carracks, Caravans, and Companies: the Structural Crisis of European Trade in the Early Seventeenth Century* (English transl., Lund, 1973), is a solid analysis.

E. Hecksher, *Mercantilism* (revised transl., 2 vols, London, 1935) remains a standard but much-criticized work. Some later views are in D. C. Coleman (ed.), *Revisions in Mercantilism* (London, 1969). On prices a decisive statement by F. P. Braudel and Frank Spooner forms chapter 7 of the *Cambridge Economic History of Europe*, vol. 4. The well-known essay by E. H. Phelps Brown and Sheila V. Hopkins, 'Seven centuries of the prices of consumables compared with builders' wage-rates' is reprinted in E. M. Carus-Wilson (ed.), *Essays in Economic History*, vol. 2 (London, 1962). Large statistical compilations include W. H. Beveridge and others, *Prices and Wages in England from the Twelfth to the Nineteenth Century* (London, 1939) and N. W. Posthumus, *Enquiry into the History of Prices in Holland* (2 vols, Leiden, 1946 and 1965). Some of the controversial essays on prices are in Peter Burke, *Economy and Society* (see above, p. 540). An essay on economic cycles by W. W. Rostow, 'Kondratief, Schumpeter, and Kuznets: trends and periods revisited' in *Journal of Economic History*, vol. 35 (1975) shows how the theories were derived from nineteenth-century fluctuations.

CHAPTER 4: SOCIETY

Social history is now an essential part of every general survey. A short separate treatment is S. J. Watts, *A Social History of Western Europe, 1450–1720* (London, 1984). Henry Kamen, *European Society, 1500–1700* (London, 1984) and earlier *The Iron Century* (London, 1971) are comprehensive. V. G. Kiernan, *State and Society in Europe, 1550–1650* (Oxford, 1980) studies social changes and their political manifestations in each country separately. The chapter by Sir George Clark, 'The Social Foundations of States' in the *New Cambridge Modern History*, vol. 5 (Cambridge, 1961) looks at France, Britain, and the Netherlands. No country has been as productive in social history as France. R. Mousnier, *The Institutions of France under the Absolute Monarchy*, vol. 1: 'Society and the State' (English transl., Chicago, 1979) is a massive analysis of the French 'society of orders'. R. Mandrou, *Classes et luttes de classes en France au début du XVIIe siècle* (Florence, 1965) and P. Sagnac, *La formation de la société française moderne*, vol. 1 (Paris, 1945) are less exacting. An article by Robert Brenner, 'Agrarian Class Structure and Economic Development in Pre-industrial Europe' in *Past and Present* 70 (1976) giving a marxist explanation of the role of land-tenure in various countries led to a 'symposium' in *Past and Present* 78 (1978) and to the book T. H. Aston and C. H. E. Philpin (eds), *The Brenner Debate* (Cambridge, 1985).

Studies of peasant society especially have been strongly influenced by the great French regional and local works. P. Goubert, *Beauvais et les Beauvaisis de 1600 à 1730* (2 vols, Paris, 1960) and E. Le Roy Ladurie, *Les paysans de Languedoc* (2 vols, Paris, 1966) are two of the best-known studies that preceded Goubert's *The French Peasantry in the Seventeenth Century* (English transl., Cambridge, 1986). On farm labourers in England there is a chapter by Alan Everitt in the *Cambridge Agrarian History*, vol. 4, listed above. The new serfdom is a main theme in J. Blum, *Lord and Peasant in Russia* (Princeton, 1961). The *Journal of Peasant Studies* has some relevant articles.

Works on the history of the family have proliferated since it became in the mid-1970s a recognized historical topic. J. Goody, *The Development of the Family and Marriage in Europe* (Cambridge, 1983) shows its scope, though mainly from earlier periods. Michael Anderson, *Approaches to History of the Western Family, 1500–1914* (London, 1980) surveys the varied methods and conclusions, some of which can be seen more fully in the essays collected in J. Goody, Joan Thirsk, and E. P. Thompson (eds), *Family and Inheritance: Rural Society in Western Europe, 1200–1800* (Cambridge, 1976). A pioneering study was P. Ariès, *Centuries of Childhood: a Social History of Family Life* (English transl., London, 1962). R. Mousnier, *La famille, l'enfant et l'education en France et en Grande-Bretagne du XVIe en XVIIIe siècles* (Paris, 1975) is a lecture-course.

M. L. Bush, *The European Nobility*: vol. 1, *Noble Privilege* (Manchester, 1983) is far-reaching in time and place; most other studies of the aristocracy are based on a single country or region.

Articles by J. H. Habakkuk on 'English Landed Families, 1600–1800' in *Transactions of the Royal Historical Society*, vols 29–31 (1979–81) deal with a larger section of society than the much-debated book by Lawrence Stone, *The Crisis of the Aristocracy, 1558–1641* (Oxford, 1965). Recent work on French aristocrats is surveyed in an article by Alex Grant, 'The Nobility in Early Modern France' in *European Studies Review*, vol. 12 (1982). D. Bitton, *French Nobility in Crisis, 1560–1640* (Stanford, 1969) is less academic than J.–P. Labatut, *Les ducs et pairs de France au XVIIe siècle: étude sociale* (Paris, 1972). R. O. Crummey, *Aristocrats and Servitors: the Boyar Élite in Russia, 1613–89* (Princeton, 1983) adds some comparisons with the Ottoman nobility. On other countries there are J. C. Davis, *The Decline of the Venetian Nobility* (Baltimore, 1962); E. L. Petersen, 'La crise de la noblesse danoise, 1580–1660' in *Annales*, vol. 23 (1968); D. J. Roorda, 'Ruling Classes in Holland in the Seventeenth Century' in E. H. Kossman and P. Bromley (eds), *Britain and the Netherlands*, no. 2 (London, 1962).

Crime as a social phenomenon is the subject of the varied essays in V. A. C. Gatrell, Bruce Lenman and Geoffrey Parker (eds), *The Crime and the Law: the social history of Crime in Western Europe since 1500* (London, 1980). M. R. Weisser, *Crime and Punishment in Early Modern Europe* (London, 1979) is concerned with the victim and the prosecution as well as with the criminal. Michel Foucault, *Madness and Civilisation* (English transl., 1967) studies the whole 'excluded' population in early modern France.

CHAPTER 5: RELIGION AND THE CHURCHES

The abundant works on religion vary in quality more than most: those written by the clergy or other devotees of the faith they concern can be impeccable but they need to be approached with care. There seems usually to be less on the established religion of a country, and less comparative study, than on dissenting churches. An article by P. Chaunu, 'Le XVIIe siècle religieux: réflexions préalables' in *Annales*, vol. 22 (1967) suggested that religion needs to be studied from outside the churches and that a new attitude to its history was beginning to appear. But there is still no survey of the whole century with the same breadth of approach as parts

one and two of P. Hazard, *The European Mind, 1680–1715*
(English transl., London, 1953). Kaspar von Greyerz (ed.), *Religion and Society in Early Modern Europe* (London, 1984) has some
enterprising but difficult chapters. J. Bossy, *Christianity in the
West, 1400–1700* (Oxford, 1985) is a short investigation of what
was actually believed. His article on 'The Counter-Reformation
and the People of Catholic Europe' in *Past and Present*, no. 47
(1970) examines the decline of popular collective religion. On this
as well as on the previous century three works that were at the
centre of a celebrated controversy in the 1930s are still relevant:
Max Weber, *The Protestant Ethic and the Spirit of Capitalism*
(English transl., New York, 1930); R. H. Tawney, *Religion and
the Rise of Capitalism* (London, 1926); and E. Troeltsch, *The Social
Teaching of the Christian Churches* (English transl., New York,
1931).

For factual detail there are several multi-volume authorities such
as L. von Pastor, *The History of the Popes*, vols 25 to 32, transl.
and edited by E. Graf (London, 1938–40); E. Fliche and V. Martin
(eds), *Histoire de l'église depuis les origines jusqu'à nos jours*, vols 18
and 19 (Paris, 1955–60); P. Fargues, *Histoire du christianisme*, vol.
5 (Paris, 1939); and E. G. Léonard, *Histoire générale du protestantisme*, vol. 2 (Paris, 1961). K. S. Latourette, *A History of the Expansion of Christianity*, vol. 3 (London, 1939) deals dispassionately with
missionary activities. On a smaller scale there are the volumes in
the *Pelican History of the Church*, vol. 3; Owen Chadwick, *The
Reformation* (London, 1964) and vol. 4, G. R. Cragg, *The Church
in the Age of Reason, 1648–1789* (London, 1960). Cragg touches
on east as well as the west. Differing opinions of the Jesuits are
in J. Brodrick S. J., *The Economic Morals of the Jesuits* (Oxford,
1934) and F. A. Ridley, *The Jesuits: a study in Counter-revolution*
(London, 1938). H. Boehmer, *The Jesuits*, (Philadelphia, 1928) is
still helpful. A controversial interpretation of a belief at the
opposite extreme – Frances Yates, *The Rosicrucian Enlightenment*
(London, 1972) – raises wider religious questions.

The French Church in all its aspects is dealt with in René
Taveneaux, *Le catholicisme dans la France classique, 1610–1715*
(2 vols., Paris, 1980). There are few surveys of Huguenotism later
than E. Léonard, *Le protestantisme française* (Paris, 1955); but three
of the essays in Menna Prestwich (ed.), *International Calvinism,
1541–1715* (Oxford, 1985) are on France. J. Orcibal, *Louis XIV
et les protestants* (Paris, 1951) includes popular attitudes as well as

political motives. English Puritanism is an inexhaustible topic. Of the many writings by Christopher Hill, *Puritanism and Revolution* (London, 1958), The *World Turned Upside Down* (London, 1972), and *Religion and Politics in Seventeenth Century England* (Brighton, 1986) contain his major essays. W. Haller, *The Rise of Puritanism* (New York, 1938) and *Liberty and Reformation in the Puritan Revolution* (New York, 1955) extend from Elizabeth I to the Civil War. The Laudian Church is examined in Nicholas Tyacke, *Anti-Calvinists: the Rise of English Arminianism* (Oxford, 1987) and the re-establishment of Anglicanism in R. S. Bosher, *The Making of the Restoration Settlement* (London, 1951). Works on Jansenism abound. René Taveneaux, *Jansénisme et politique* (Paris, 1965) illustrates some effects on the country. Two wide-ranging studies of the religious ideas in Jansenist and other writings are R. A. Knox, *Enthusiasm* (Oxford, 1950) and L. Goldmann, *The Hidden God* (English transl., London, 1964). A. Sedgwick, *Jansenism in Seventeenth-Century France: voices from the wilderness* (Charlottesville, 1977) includes the European background.

On Spain parts 3 and 4 of R. Garcia-Villoslada, *Historia de la Iglesia en Espagna* (Madrid, 1980) are authoritative. Henry Kamen, *The Spanish Inquisition* (London, 1965) is extended by his *Inquisition and Society in Spain* (London, 1984). Among accounts of the Russian Orthodox Church P. N. Miliukov, *Outlines of Russian Culture: vol. 1 Religion and the Church* (English transl., Philadelphia, 1942) stresses the spiritual and W. K. Medlin, *Moscow and East Rome* (Geneva, 1952) the political aspects. R. O. Crummey, *The Old Believers and the World of Antichrist, 1694–1855* (London, 1970) has more on this period than its dates suggest. There is an essay on the Swedish Church by Michael Roberts in his *Sweden's Age of Greatness* (London, 1973). In *The Cambridge History of Islam* (Cambridge, 1970), the opening chapters offer a short explanation of the Muslim faith.

R. H. Popkin, *The History of Scepticism from Erasmus to Descartes* (Assen, 1960) looks at the whole topic of doubt and knowledge. Among the many works on Bayle are P. Dibon (ed.), *Pierre Bayle* (2 vols, Paris, 1963–64) and W. Rex, *Essays on Pierre Bayle and the Religious Controversy* (The Hague, 1965). H. Margival, *Richard Simon et la critique biblique au XVIIᵉ siècle* (Paris, 1900) is still valuable.

Witchcraft is now as prominent in historical scholarship as are any Christian subjects. N. Cohn, *Europe's Inner Demons* (London, 1975) analyses the seventeenth-century panics in the light of medieval beliefs. Keith Thomas, *Religion and the Decline of Magic* (London, 1971) uses mainly British evidence for the wider supernatural setting. Christine Larner, *Enemies of God: the Witch-hunt in Scotland* (London, 1981) has European as well as Scottish material. H. C. E. Midelfort, *Witch-hunting in South-West Germany, 1564–1684* (Oxford, 1972) compares Catholic and Protestant areas.

CHAPTER 6: SCIENCE

Plenty of works comprehensible to the non-scientist deal with the movement in general. Robin Briggs, The *Scientific Revolution of the Seventeenth Century* (London, 1969) is a short summary. A. Koyré, *From the Closed World to the Infinite Universe* (English transl., Baltimore, 1957) is by the leading French specialist. E. J. Dijksterhuis, *The Mechanisation of the World Picture* (English transl., Oxford, 1961) sees the process as extending from the Greeks to Newton. It is arranged for easy reference. Herbert Butterfield, *The Origins of Modern Science* (London, 1949) remains an attractive introduction. A. R. Hall, *The Scientific Revolution, 1500–1800* (London, 1954) is rather more technical than his *From Galileo to Newton* (London, 1962) and its companion volume by Marie Boas, *The Scientific Renaissance 1450–1630* (London, 1963). A. C. Crombie, *Augustine to Galileo* (2nd edn, 2 vols, London, 1959) stresses continuity rather than revolution.

For the links between scientific and social changes, see the controversy between Christopher Hill, Hugh Kearney, T. K. Rabb and others in C. Webster (ed.), *The Intellectual Revolution of the Seventeenth Century* (London, 1974) or the original articles in *Past and Present*, nos 27–32 (1964–65). R. K. Merton, *Science, Technology, and Society in Seventeenth-Century England* (New York, 1938, reprinted 1970) is a firm defence of the causal connections. G. N. Clark, *Science and Social Welfare in the Age of Newton* (Oxford, 1937) attacked some specific Marxist claims. Other comments are in A. G. R. Smith, *Science and Society in the Sixteenth and Seventeenth Centuries* (New York, 1972) and P. Matthias (ed.), *Science and Society, 1600–1900* (Cambridge, 1972).

Studies of individual scientists include Frances Yates, *Giordano Bruno and the Hermetic Tradition* (London, 1977); Paolo Rossi, *Francis Bacon – from Magic to Science* (English transl., London, 1968); M. Boas, *Robert Boyle and Seventeenth-century Chemistry* (London, 1958); G. Whitteridge, *William Harvey and the Circulation of the Blood* (London, 1971); M. 'Espinasse, *Robert Hooke* (London, 1956); R. Lenoble, *Mersenne, ou la naissance du mécanisme* (Paris, 1943); Max Caspar, *Johannes Kepler* (English transl., London, 1959). Giorgio de Santillana, *The Crime of Galileo* (Chicago, 1955) is mainly on the conflict with the Church; S. Drake, *Discoveries and Opinions of Galileo* (New York, 1957) is a short selection of his writing; A. Koyré. *Etudes galiléennes* (new edn, Paris, 1963) and E. McMullin, (ed.), *Galileo, Man of Science* (New York, 1967) are detailed commentaries.

On Newton only partial understanding is open to non-mathematicians. The books by Frank Manuel, *A Portrait of Isaac Newton* (London, 1968) and *The Religion of Isaac Newton* (London, 1974) are general commentaries on his scientific and unscientific thought; S. Brodetsky, *Sir Isaac Newton* (London, 1927) is one of many biographical studies. I. B. Cohen, *An Introduction to Newton's Principia* (London, 1971) is an encouragement to look at the *Principia* itself, available in a revised English translation by Florian Cajori (London, 1934). Descartes is the subject of a vast amount of philosophical, religious, and scientific writing, to which Anthony Kenny, *Descartes* (New York, 1968) is a short introduction. J. F. Scott, *The Scientific Work of René Descartes* (London, 1952) is helpfully selective.

Scientific societies are another subject of debate. M. Purver, *The Royal Society, Concept and Creation* (London, 1967) has to be compared with Christopher Hill, 'London Science and Medicine' in his *Intellectual Origins of the English Revolution* (Oxford, 1965) and with the articles in Webster, *Intellectual Revolution* (see above). *Royal Society Notes and Records* especially vols V (1947), XV (1960), and XXIII (1968) has other contributions. H. Hartley (ed.) *The Royal Society, its Origins and Founders* (London, 1960) is a collection of lectures. French societies are investigated in Harcourt Brown, *Scientific Organisations of Seventeenth-century France* (Baltimore, 1934) and R. Hahn, *The Anatomy of a Scientific Institution – the Paris Academy, 1666–1803* (London, 1971). A wider survey is M. Ornstein, *The Rôle of Scientific Societies in the Seventeenth Century* (Chicago, 1928). The 'Ancients and Moderns' debate is described in R. F. Jones, *Ancients and Moderns – a Study of the Rise of the Scientific Movement in Seventeenth-century England* (2nd edn, St. Louis, 1961). A. G. Debus, *Science and Education in the Seventeenth Century* (London, 1970) has facsimiles of the dispute between John Webster and Seth Ward.

A few miscellaneous works on aspects of the scientific movement can be added. T. S. Kuhn, *The Copernican Revolution* (Cambridge, Mass., 1957); H. C. King, *The History of the Telescope* (London, 1955); D. C. Allen, The *Star-crossed Renaissance* (Durham, North Caroliona, 1941); A. O. Lovejoy, *The Great Chain of Being* (Cambridge, Mass.; 1966); A. Koestler, *The Sleepwalkers* (London, 1959) – a non-academic commentary centred on Kepler; J. F. Scott, *The History of Mathematics* (London, 1958); R. S. Porter, The *Making of Geology* (Cambridge, 1977).

CHAPTER 7: EDUCATION AND THE ARTS

Most cultural aspects of the period are discussed very briefly in F. B. Artz, *From the Renaissance to Romanticism* (Chicago, 1962). Preserved Smith, *The Origins of Modern Culture, 1543–1667* and *The Enlightenment, 1687–1776* (New York, 1934) made an attempt, often condemned for old-fashioned liberal and materialist ideas, to correlate developments in politics, science, religion, education and the arts. Peter Burke, *Popular Culture in Early Modern Europe* (London, 1978) reveals a world almost ignored by writers on the culture of the educated élite.

W. Boyd, *The History of Western Education* (11th edn, revised, London, 1975) is still a standard authority. S. d'Irsay, *Histoire des universités* (2 vols, Paris, 1935) has a limited amount on this period. M. H. Curtis, *Oxford and Cambridge in Transition, 1558–1642* (Oxford, 1959) relates the topic to religion and to society. R. Chartier, M-M Compère, and D. Julia, *L'éducation en France du XVIe au XVIIIe siècle* (Paris, 1976) examines both universities and schools. R. L. Kagan, 'Universities in Castile, 1500–1700' is an article from *Past and Present* 49 (1970) reprinted in L. Stone (ed.), *The University in Society*, vol. 2 (Princeton, 1975). F. Paulsen, *The German Universities* (English transl., London, 1906) is one of the few books on central European education in English. An account of reform proposals is J. E.

Sadler, *Comenius and the Concept of Universal Education* (London, 1966).

The role of the printed word and picture is analysed widely in Elizabeth L. Eisenstein, *The Printing Revolution in Early Modern Europe* (Cambridge, 1983). H.-J. Martin, *Livre, pouvoirs, et société à Paris au XVIIe siècle* (2 vols, Paris, 1969) also has a great breadth of modern outlook, and extends well beyond Paris. C. Cipolla, *Literacy and Development in the West* (London, 1969) faces the difficult problem of uncertain evidence.

National histories of literature are abundant but seldom inspiring. They include J. G. Robertson, *A History* of German Literature (5th edn, Edinburgh, 1966); E. H. Wilkins, *A History of Italian Literature* (London, 1954); J. Fitzmaurice Kelly, *A New History of Spanish Literature* (London, 1926). Those confined to the early modern period range in size from A. Adam, *Histoire de la littérature française au XVIIe siècle* (5 vols, Paris, 1956) to Boris Ford (ed.), *The Pelican History of English Literature*, vol. 3: *From Donne to Marvell* (London, 1956). Examples of varied approaches to the history of drama are L. C. Knights, *Drama and Society in the Age of Jonson* (London, 1937); M. Turnell, *The Classical Moment* (London, 1946) – on Molière, Corneille, and Racine; H. Kindermann, *Theatergeschichte Europas* (Salzburg, 1959); and H. A. Rennert, *The Spanish Stage in the time of Lope de Vega* (New York, 1909). In *XVIIe siècle*, no. 39 (1958) there is a group of articles on 'La vie théâtrale au XVIIe siècle'.

There is a wide choice of commentaries on the visual arts, most of the modern ones lavishly illustrated. One that goes beyond the routine accounts of leading artists and architects is V.-L. Tapié, *The Age of Grandeur* (English transl., London, 1960). Among books on the main countries are R. Wittkower, *Art and Architecture in Italy, 1600–1700* (London, 1958); F. Haskell, *Patrons and Painters – Relations between Italian Art and Society in the Age of the Baroque* (London, 1963); A. Blunt, *Art and Architecture in France, 1500–1700* (London, 1953); J. Rosenberg, S. Silve, and E. H. ter Kuile, *Dutch Art and Architecture, 1600–1800* (London, 1966); E. Hempel, *Baroque Art and Architecture in Central Europe* (London, 1965); George Hamilton, *Art and Architecture in Russia* (3rd edn, London, 1983); M. D. Whinney and O. Millar, *English Art, 1625–1914* (Oxford, 1957); and J. N. Summerson, *Architecture in Britain, 1530–1830* (London, 1953).

The *New Cambridge Modern History* distributes its cultural chapters among the volumes covering the century: J. Lough on 'Drama and Society' is in vol. 4 (1970), R. Wittkower on 'Art and Architecture' in vol. 5 (1961), and W. H. Barber on 'Cultural Change in Western Europe' in vol. 6 (1970). The *Pelican History of Music*, vol. 2, *Renaissance and Baroque* edited by Alec Robertson (London, 1963) sees the musician in his social background.

CHAPTER 8: POLITICAL IDEAS

Commentaries on political theorists are not always more comprehensible than the works themselves; but they are often more readily available and sometimes shorter. A compromise can be found in edited extracts. Andrew Lossky (ed.), *The Seventeenth Century*, (New York, 1967); volume 7 of the series *Sources in Western Civilisation* has passages from Grotius, Bossuet and many others; another collection is R. H. Popkin (ed.), *The Philosophy of the Sixteenth and Seventeenth Centuries*. (New York, 1966). G. E. Aylmer (ed.), *The Levellers in the English Revolution* (London, 1975) has extracts and introduction.

There are a few general surveys. G. H. Sabine, *A History of Political Theory* (London, 1937) has six chapters on the seventeenth century, five of them limited to English writers. F. M. Watkins, *The Political Tradition of the West* (Cambridge, Mass., 1948) is helpful. More valuable for this period is Quentin Skinner, *The Foundations of Modern Political Thought*, vol 2, *The Age of Reformation* (Oxford, 1978) which takes ideas rather than authors as its basis. The *New Cambridge Modern History*, vol. 4 (Cambridge, 1970) has a chapter by R. Mousnier on the exponents and critics of absolutism and vol. 5 (Cambridge, 1961) has a general essay on political thought by Stephan Salkweit, who concentrates less heavily on England than most commentators. On separate countries there are W. J. Stankiewicz, *Politics and Religion in Seventeenth-century France* (Berkley, 1960); N. O. Keohane, *Philosophy and the State in France from the Renaissance to the Enlightenment* (New York, 1980); J.-A. Maravall, *La philosophie politique espagnole au XVIIᵉ siècle* (Paris, 1955); S. K. Utechin, *Russian Political Thought* (London, 1963); E. H. Kossmann, 'The Development of Dutch Political Theory in the Seventeenth Century' in J. S. Bromley and E. H. Kossmann (eds), *Britain and the Netherlands*, vol. 1 (London,

1960). The well-established study by J. W. Allen, *English Political Thought, 1603–1660* only got as far as volume 1, 1603–1644 (London, 1938). Perez Zagorin, *A History of Political Thought in the Puritan Revolution* (New York, 1966) is a shorter introduction.

On exponents of royal right there are W. J. S. Simpson, *Bossuet* (London, 1937) and for Filmer G. Schochet, *Patriarchalism in Political Thought* (London, 1975). J. H. Franklin, *Jean Bodin and the Rise of Absolutist Theory* (Cambridge, 1973) extends to the seventeenth century; F. D. Wormuth, *The Royal Prerogative, 1603–1649* (London, 1939) is a short investigation of the theories behind the Stuart monarchy. W. S. M. Knight, *The Life and Works of Hugo Grotius* (London, 1925) is less ambitious than O. von Gierke, *Natural Law and the Theory of Society* (2 vols, English transl., Cambridge, 1934). E. Thuau, *Raison d'état et pensée politique à l'époque de Richelieu* (Paris, 1966) relates theory firmly to practice.

Radical ideas in mid-century England are an unfailingly attractive subject. An almost random selection of modern commentaries is: W. K. Jordan, *Men of Substance – a study in the thought of . . . Henry Parker and Henry Robinson* (Chicago, 1942); J. Frank, *The Levellers* (Cambridge, Mass., 1955); A. L. Morton, *The World of the Ranters* (London, 1970); H. N. Brailsford, *The Levellers and the English Revolution* (London, 1961); T. W. Hayes, *Winstanley the Digger* (Cambridge, Mass., 1979). The whole of the radical thought in the period is scrutinized in the many essays by Christopher Hill in *Puritanism and Revolution* (London, 1958), *The World Turned Upside Down: Radical Ideas during the English Revolution* (London, 1972); *Change and Continuity in Seventeenth-century England* (London, 1974); and his *Collected Essays*, vols 1, 2 and 3 (Brighton, 1985–86). The thinking of a very different opposition movement – the *arbitristas* in Spain – is analysed in J. H. Elliott, 'Self-perception and Decline in early Seventeenth-Century Spain' in *Past and Present*, no. 74 (1977). A full account is Jean Vilar, *Literatura y economia: la figura del arbitrista en siglo de oro* (Madrid, 1973). (Other works on resistance to governments are in the bibliography to Chapter 9.)

Books in English on Spinoza include Stuart Hampshire, *Spinoza* (new edn, New York, 1961); H. F. Hallett, *Benedict de Spinoza* (London, 1957) and R. L. Saw, *The Vindication of Metaphysics: a Study in the Philosophy of Spinoza* (London, 1951).

The literature on both Hobbes and Locke is enormous. One

work that considers them both in comparison with the Levellers and Harrington is C. B. Macpherson, *The Political Theory of Possessive Individualism* (Oxford, 1962) Among modern studies of Hobbes are D. D. Raphael, *Hobbes* (1977); L. Strauss, *The Political Philosophy of Thomas Hobbes* (Oxford, 1936); M. M. Goldsmith, *Hobbes' Science of Politics* (London, 1966); and H. Warrender, *The Political Philosophy of Thomas Hobbes* (Oxford, 1957). Some of the controversies he has aroused are set out in K. C. Brown (ed.), *Hobbes Studies* (Oxford, 1965). Another collection of differing opinions is J. W. Yolton (ed.), *John Locke, Problems and Perspectives* (Cambridge, 1969). M. Cranston, *John Locke – a Biography* (New York, 1957), J. Dunn, *The Political Thought of John Locke* (Cambridge, 1969) and J. H. Franklin, *John Locke and the Theory of Sovereignty* (London, 1978) are all helpful on his political writing. M. Seliger, *The Liberal Politics of John Locke* (London, 1968) has some European comparisons.

CHAPTER 9: GOVERNMENT

Old-style 'constitutional histories' in which the rules laid down for the working of government were expounded with little regard to the societies in which they arose, or to the practical tasks of administration, have largely disappeared. One work that, for each of twelve countries separately, puts government decisively in its social context is V. G. Kiernan, *State and Society in Europe, 1550–1650* (Oxford, 1980). Perry Anderson, *Lineages of the Absolutist State* (London, 1974) is divided equally between western and eastern Europe in studying government founded on the social supremacy of the landed aristocracy. Charles Tilly (ed.), *The Formation of National States in Western Europe* (Princeton, 1975) has chapters on such topics as finance, policing, and the power of the military. *The Age of Absolution* (London, 1954) is a comparative sketch. Absolutism in general is the subject of some of the essays in Ragnild Hatton (ed.), *Louis XIV and Absolutism* (London, 1976). A much-discussed but not very accessible article by R. Mousnier and F. Hartung, 'Quelques problèmes concernant la monarchie absolue' is in the *Reports (Relazione) of the Tenth International Congress of Historical Sciences*, vol. 4 (Florence, 1955). The controversies it aroused are summed up by J. Vicens Vives in the *Reports of the Eleventh Congress*, vol. 4 (Stockholm, 1960) under the title 'Estructura administrativa estatal en los siglos XVI y XVII'. J. P. Cooper, 'Differences between English and Continental Governments in the Early Seventeenth Century' in J. S. Bromley and E. H. Kossmann (ed), *Britain and the Netherlands*, vol. 1 (London, 1960) questions easy assumptions about the contrast.

The magical aura of kingship is discussed in Marc Bloch, *The Royal Touch* (English transl., London, 1973); and some still more fanciful concepts of monarchy are the subject of M. Cherniavsky, *Tsar and People – Studies in Russian Myths* (London, 1961). Royal courts are portrayed in H. R. Trevor-Roper, *Princes and Artists: Patronage and Ideology at Four Habsburg Courts* (London, 1976) and A. G. Dickens, *The Courts of Europe: Politics, Patronage and Royalty, 1400–1800* (London, 1977).

French and English systems of government have been analysed in a prolific variety of works. An essay by Menna Prestwich, 'The Making of Absolute Monarchy' in J. M. Wallace Hadrill and J. McManners (eds), *France: Government and Society* (London, 1957) is an introductory survey of the period from Catherine de Medici to Louis XIV. At the other extreme in size are two books by R. Mousnier, La *venalité des offices sous Henri IV et Louis XIII* (Rouen, 1945) and *The Institutions of France under the Absolute Monarchy, 1598–1789* (English transl., 2 vols, Chicago, 1979–80). On England G. E. Aylmer, *The King's Servants: the Civil Service of Charles I, 1625–1642* (London, 1961) and *The State's Servants: the Civil Service of the English Republic, 1649–1660* (London, 1973) study in powerful detail both the institutions and the office-holders. The former includes a short chapter on comparisons with Europe. Also by G. E. Aylmer is the chapter on 'Bureaucracy' in the *Cambridge Modern History*, companion volume (Cambridge, 1979). An earlier and shorter work dealing with western Europe generally is K. W. Swart, *The Sale of Offices in the Seventeenth Century* (The Hague, 1949). Pierre Goubert, *L'ancien régime*, vol. 2, *Les pouvoirs* (Paris, 1972) adds brief illustrative documents to its chapters on many aspects of government. Most of the works on great ministers are individual biographical studies (listed here in the bibliographies to later chapters); but one comparative monograph is J. H. Elliott, *Richelieu and Olivares* (Cambridge, 1984). H. F. Schwarz, *The Imperial Privy Council in the Seventeenth Century* (Cambridge, Mass., 1943) is one of the few essays in English on Habsburg government.

Representative assemblies have probably had more than their reasonable share of attention from historians. An attractive introduction is A. R. Myers, *Parliaments and Estates in Europe* (London, 1975). Almost every English parliament, at least until the Restoration, has a full study: Wallace Notestein, *The Parliament of 1604–1610* (London, 1971) and D. Witcombe, *Charles II and the Cavalier House of Commons, 1663–1674* (Manchester, 1966) are differing examples. Conrad Russell, *Parliaments and English Politics, 1621–1629* (Oxford, 1979) introduced many new ideas on the relation of the 1620s to the Civil War. J. Russell Major, *Representative Institutions in Early Modern France* (New Haven, 1980) claims that popular participation in government was greater than is generally thought. J. M. Hayden, *France and the Estates General of 1614* (Cambridge, 1974) has both background and details of the last national assembly. F. L. Carsten, *Princes and Parliaments in Germany* (Oxford, 1959) deals with Bavaria, Saxony and other German States from the fifteenth to the eighteenth century. His earlier book, *The Origins of Prussia* (Oxford, 1954) has a full account of the Brandenburg Estates. Many results of detailed scholarship on almost every country can be found in the multilingual *Études de la commission internationale pour l'histoire des assemblées des états* published at irregular intervals since 1937.

CHAPTER 10: REBELLION

Many of the controversial articles on 'revolution' and 'crisis' are reprinted in two collections – Trevor Aston (ed.), *Crisis in Europe, 1560–1660* (London, 1965) and Geoffrey Parker and Lesley M. Smith (eds), *The General Crisis of the Seventeenth Century* (London, 1978). The essays in Robert Forster and Jack P. Greene (eds), *Preconditions of Revolution in Early Modern Europe* (London, 1970) are less specialized than the title suggests. These and many other contributions are discussed by H. G. Koenigsberger in 'The Crisis of he Seventeenth Century: a Farewell?', chapter 7 of his *Politicians and Virtuosi* (London, 1986). The meaning of 'rebellion' and the other terms are examined by Penry Williams in M. R. D Foot (ed.); *War and Society: Essays in Memory of John Western* (London, 1973). Perez Zagorin, *Rebels and Rulers, 1560–1660* (2 vols, Cambridge, 1982) devotes the first volume to the concept of revolution, with specimens of rural and urban risings, and the second to the major civil wars. Other studies of popular revolt are R. Mousnier, *Peasant Uprisings in France, Russia, and China* (London, 1971) – a translation of his *Fureurs Paysannes* (Paris, 1967) – and P. Slack (ed.), *Rebellion, Protest and the Social Order in Early Modern England* (Cambridge, 1984). E. J. Hobsbawm, *Primitive Rebels* (Manchester, 1959) shows some parallels with the nineteenth century.

As on other aspects of the century, France seems to be more intensively studied even than England. P. J. Coveney, *France in Crisis, 1620–1675* (London, 1977) has general chapters by the editor and by H. Méthivier followed by extracts from the controversy between Mousnier and the Russian historian Boris Porchnev. The French translation of Porchnev's book, *Les soulèvements populaires en France de 1623 à 1648* (Paris, 1963) appeared fifteen years after the original. Mousnier's attack on its Marxist approach first appeared in his article 'Recherches sur les soulèvements populaires' in the *Revue de l'histoire moderne* et contemporaine, vol. 4 (1958). There is a discussion of it by M. O. Gately and others in *Past and Present*, no. 51 (1971). Examples of the regional studies are R. Pillorget, *Les mouvements insurrectionels en Provence, 1596–1715* (Paris, 1975): Madeleine Foisil, *La révolte des nu-pieds et les révoltes normandes de 1639* (Paris, 1970); Y.-M. Bercé, *Histoire des croquants: études des soulèvements populaires dans la sud-ouest de la France* (2 vols, Geneva, 1974); and J. Jacquart, *La crise rurale en Ile-de-France, 1550–1670* (Paris, 1974).

The role of rebellion by 'the middle and poorer sort of people' in the English Civil War is stressed by Brian Manning in *The English People and the English Revolution* (London, 1976). David Underdown, *Revel, Riot and Rebellion – popular politics and culture in England, 1603–1660* (Oxford, 1985) considers differences of culture between regions in relation to revolt. Irish conflicts are examined in the third volume of T. W. Moody, F. X. Martin and F. J. Byrne (eds), *A New History of Ireland* (Oxford, 1976) and in T. L. Coonan, *The Irish Catholic Confederacy and the Puritan Revolution* (Dublin, 1954). Aidan Clarke, *The Old English in Ireland, 1625–1642* (London, 1966) includes a full account of the origins of the 1641 rising. (For the Levellers see the bibliography to Chapter 7.)

On the rebellions in Russia G. Vernadsky, *Bohdan, Hetman of Ukraine* (New Haven, 1941); Cecil Field, *The Great Cossack*

(London, 1947) and P. Avrich, *Russian Rebels, 1600–1800* (London, 1972) are among the few books in English.

Works on the larger-scale revolts are mentioned in the bibliographies to Chapters 11 to 16; but it is worth including here one of the originators of the whole idea of the general crisis – R. B. Merriman, *Six Contemporaneous Revolutions* (Oxford, 1938).

CHAPTER 11: WAR

A short survey by Michael Howard, *War in European History* (Oxford, 1976) extends from the Goths to the nuclear age and is relevant to the whole period. R. A. Preston, S. F. Wise and H. O. Werner, *Men in Arms: a History of Warfare and its Interrelationships with Western Society* (London, 1956) is weightier, as is A. Corvisier, *Armies and societies in Europe, 1494–1789* (English transl., London, 1979). J. U. Nef, *War and Human Progress* (London, 1950) and G. N. Clark, *War and Society in the Seventeenth Century* (Cambridge, 1957) are examples of how old-style military history can be superseded by studies of war in its social context. This outlook is stressed in the introduction to the *Fontana History of European War and Society*, edited by Geoffrey Best, in which the volume by J. R. Hale, *War and Society in Renaissance Europe, 1450–1620* (London, 1985) is to be followed by M. S. Anderson's on the next period. On a different general theme, Michael Walzer, *Just and Unjust Wars: a Moral Argument with Historical Illustrations* (London, 1978) examines the thoughts of soldiers as well as of philosophers. David Maland, *Europe at War, 1600–1650* (London, 1980) is an account of each major conflict.

A much-debated essay on methods of warfare is Michael Roberts, 'The Military Revolution, 1560–1660' reprinted in his *Essays in Swedish History* (London, 1967); but see also the reply by Geoffrey Parker, 'The Military Revolution: a Myth?' reprinted in his *Spain and the Netherlands* (London, 1979). In the *New Cambridge Modern History*, vol. 4 (Cambridge, 1970) has a chapter by J. W. Wijn on military forces 1610–1648 and vol. 6 (Cambridge, 1970) a multiple one on war on land by David G. Chandler, 'Soldiers and Civilians' by J. W. Stoye, and navies by J. S. Bromley and A. N. Ryan. Another chapter by P. G. M. Dickson deals with the crucial topic of war finance. On mercenaries the article by V. G. Kiernan, 'Foreign Mercenaries and Absolute Monarchy' is reprinted in Trevor Aston (ed.), *Crisis in Europe* (London, 1965). A factual account of one type of weapon is H. J. Jackson, *European Hand Firearms of the Sixteenth, Seventeenth and Eighteenth Centuries* (London, 1923). J. Childs, *Armies and Warfare in Europe, 1648–1789* (Manchester, 1982) is comprehensive without being overloaded with technical detail. A scientific account of artillery and its significance is A. R. Hall, *Ballistics in the Seventeenth Century* (Cambridge, 1952). Hall is also the author of the chapter on 'military technology' in C. Singer, E. J. Holmyard, etc. (eds), *A History of Technology*, vol. 3 (London, 1957). Geoffrey Parker, *The Army of Flanders and the Spanish Road, 1567–1659* (Cambridge, 1972) throws light on armies and governments much wider than its specific subject.

On France E. G. Léonard, *L'armée et ses problèmes au XVIIIe siècle* (Paris, 1958) has an opening chapter on the seventeenth century. G. Zeller, *L'organisation défensive des frontières du nord et de l'est au XVIIe siècle* (Paris, 1928) shows something of the disputes on military policy. Colin Jones, 'The Welfare of the French Foot Soldier' in *History*, vol. 65 (1980) has a subject predictably neglected in most military histories. J. H. L. Keep, *Soldiers of the Tsar: the Army and Society in Russia, 1462–1874* (Oxford, 1985) is a fully researched study of military influence.

The Civil War naturally dominates military studies on England. Austin Woolrych, *Battles of the English Civil War* (London, 1961) is less limited than it sounds; P. Young and R. Holmes, *The English Civil War* (London, 1974) is a detailed military account; but C. H. Firth, *Cromwell's Army* (Oxford, 1902) remains unsurpassed. On later years J. Childs, *The Army of Charles II* (London, 1976) and H. C. Tomlinson, *Guns and Government* (London, 1979) are informative. *The Journal of the Society for Army Historical Research* has many detailed articles.

War at sea is as much a part of the history of navigation and exploration as it is of conflict. J. P. Cooper compresses the essential aspects into a dozen pages of the *New Cambridge Modern History*, vol. 4, chapter 7. (Cambridge, 1970). C. M. Cipolla, *Guns and Sails in the Early Phase of European Expansion, 1400–1700* (London, 1965) discusses the whole topic. John Francis Guilmartin, Jr, *Gunpowder and Galleys* (Cambridge, 1974), though mainly on the sixteenth century, clarifies many technical questions. E. G. R. Taylor, *The Haven-finding Art: a History of Navi-*

gation from Odysseus to Captain Cook (London, 1956) is an attractive background work. Examples of more specialized studies are R. Memain, *La marine de guerre sous Louis XIV* (Paris, 1937); P. W. Bamford, *Fighting Ships and Prisons: the Mediterranean Galleys of France in the Age of Louis XIV* (Minneapolis, 1973); J. R. Powell, *The Navy in the English Civil War* (Hamden, Conn., 1962); J. P. W. Ehrman, *The Navy in the Wars of William III* (Cambridge, 1953.) *The Mariner's Mirror* is a scholarly periodical with many relevant articles.

CHAPTER 12: FRANCE, 1598–1660

There are short accounts of the whole century by Robin Briggs, *Early Modern France, 1560–1715* (Oxford, 1977) and – with more narrative but less on recent scholarship – G. R. R. Treasure, *Seventeenth-Century France* (London, 1966). J. H. Shennan, *Government and Society in France, 1461–1661* (London, 1969) is a collection of short documentary extracts with introduction. In the *Nouvelle Clio* series R, Mandrou, *La France aux XVIIe et XVIIIe siècles* (Paris, 1967) considers, among other topics, culture and divine right. John Lough, *An Introduction to Seventeenth-Century France* (London, 1954) has undemanding chapters with apt quotations.

On the early years, Mark Greengrass, *France in the Age of Henri IV: the Struggle for Stability* (London, 1984) is short but scholarly. D. Buisseret, *Sully and the Growth of Central Government in France, 1598–1610* (London, 1968) is condensed from the massive collection of material Sully left. R. Mousnier, *The Assassination of Henri IV* (English transl, London, 1973) adds a consideration of the whole question of tyrannicide. Finance has now been investigated in extensive detail. R. Bonney, *The King's Debts: Finance and Politics in France, 1589–1661* (Oxford, 1981) and Julian Dent, *Crisis in Finance: Crown Financiers and Society in Seventeenth-Century France* (Newton Abbot, 1973) are comprehensible to the inexpert.

For the period of Louis XIII and the two regencies Victor-L. Tapié, *France in the Age of Louis XIII and Richelieu* (English transl., London, 1974) is a comprehensive modern guide. Richard Bonney, *Political Change in France under Richelieu and Mazarin,*

1624–1661 (Oxford, 1978) is mainly on the *intendants* in relation to central and local government; Orest A. Ranum, *Richelieu and the Councillors of Louis XIII* (Oxford, 1963) is 'a study of the secretaries of state and superintendants of finance, 1635–1642'. R. F. Kierstead (ed.), *State and Society in Seventeenth-Century France* (New York, 1975) has sections on the provinces, resistance, and élites. A. D. Lublinskaya, *French Absolutism – the Crucial Phase, 1620–1629* (English transl., Cambridge, 1968), written originally to introduce Russian readers to the western controversies, has incisive criticisms of some English and French authors. It can be compared with David Parker, *The Making of French Absolutism* (London, 1983). There are plenty of lives of Richelieu. The big old *Histoire du Cardinal de Richelieu*, in six volumes, was begun by G. Hanotaux in 1893 and completed by the Duc de la Force in 1947. It is more concerned with wars than government. G. R. R. Treasure, *Cardinal Richelieu and the Development of Absolutism* (London, 1972) is a substantial summary. Mazarin has not acquired as much biographical treatment; but G. Detham, *Mazarin, homme de paix à l'âge baroque* (Paris, 1981) is a comprehensive life. On special aspects there are H. Hauser, *La pensée et l'action économiques du Cardinal de Richelieu* (Paris, 1944) and W. F. Church, *Richelieu and Reason of State* (Princeton, 1972), more closely concerned with the Cardinal himself than the book by Thuau listed on page 552. Aldous Huxley, *Grey Eminence* (London, 1941) is an enjoyable non-academic account of Father Joseph.

On the Fronde, P. Kossmann, *La Fronde* (Leyden, 1954) is still a standard authority – but see also the article by P. Goubert, 'Kossmann et la Fronde' in *Annales*, vol. 13 (1958). P. R. Doolin, *The Fronde* (Cambridge, Mass., 1955) analyses the theories of the various factions. A. L. Moote, *The Revolt of the Judges: the Parliament of Paris and the Fronde* (Princeton, 1971) goes deeply into the social and political origins. D. A. Watt, *Cardinal de Retz: the Ambiguities of a Seventeenth-Century Mind* (Oxford, 1980) and J. H. M. Salmon, *Cardinal de Retz: the Anatomy of a Conspirator* (London, 1970) look at an enigmatic character.

CHAPTER 13: THE THIRTY YEARS WAR

There is an unmistakable contrast between the abundance of

books on France in the first half of the century and the scarcity of those on the Habsburg Empires in languages other than German. Only the Thirty Years War itself has been a popular subject. R. J. W. Evans *The Making of the Habsburg Monarchy, 1550–1700* (Oxford, 1979) is a profound study, concerned less with the wars than with culture and nationality. Evans's earlier work, *Rudolf II and his World: a Study in Intellectual History, 1576–1612* (Oxford, 1973) includes chapters on politics and religion. C.-P. Clasen, 'The Empire before 1618' is a chapter in H. R. Trevor-Roper (ed.), *The Age of Expansion: Europe and the World, 1559–1660* (London, 1968). A more specialized work by Clasen is *The Palatinate in European History, 1559–1660* (Oxford, 1963). V.-L. Tapié, *La politique de la France et le début de la guerre de trente ans* (Paris, 1934) is not confined to the immediate origins. There are articles by P. J. Brightwell in the *European Studies Review* – 'The Spanish origins of the Thirty Years War' in no. 9 (1979) and 'Spain, Bohemia and Europe, 1619–1621' in no. 12 (1982). Simon Adams, 'Spain or the Netherlands: the Dilemmas of Early Stuart Foreign Policy' in Howard Tomlinson (ed.), *Before the English Civil War* (London, 1983) and 'Foreign Policy and the Parliaments of 1621 and 1624' in Kevin Sharpe (ed.), *Faction and Parliament* (Oxford, 1978) are valuable on Europe as well as England. For the political details the old three-volume work by Moriz Ritter, *Deutsche Geschichte in Zeitalter der Gegenreformation und des dreissigjährigen Krieges, 1555–1648* (1889, reprinted Darmstadt, 1974) is still used by modern authors.

Whatever the historical validity of the term 'Thirty Years War,' it has proved useful as a title. Geoffrey Parker, *The Thirty Years War* (London, 1984), with contributions from nine other authors, is a skilful blend of narrative and analysis; H. Langer, *The Thirty Years War* (English transl., Poole, 1980) has detailed accounts of civilian and military life; G. Pagès, *The Thirty Years War* (English transl., London, 1970) is the most broadly European in outlook; C. V. Wedgwood, *The Thirty Years War* (London, 1938) makes full use of the German sources in a fluent narrative; G. V. Polišenský, *The Thirty Years War* (English transl., London, 1971) gives Bohemia the fullest treatment but adds a full discussion of the rest of the war. S. H. Steinberg, *The 'Thirty Years War' and the Conflict for German Hegemony, 1600–1660* (London, 1966) is an outline rejecting the treatment of the war as a single event. T. K. Rabb (ed.), *The Thirty Years War: Problems of Motive, Extent and*

Effect (Boston, Mass., 1964) collects extracts from older and newer writers.

H. Sturmberger, *Aufstand in Böhmen: der Beginn des dreissigjähr-igen Krieges* (Munich, 1959) is a short account of the Bohemian period of the war. Carola Oman, *Elizabeth of Bohemia* (London, 1938) is one of the biographies of the popular heroine. Golo Mann, Wallenstein (English transl., London, 1976) puts into bizarre English the text but not the notes of a long biography published in German in 1971. Michael Roberts, *Gustavus Adolphus: a History of Sweden, 1611–1632* (2 vols, London, 1953–58) is the authoritative account of the Swedish invasion and its origins. His collection of *Essays in Swedish History* (London, 1967) has two chapters on the king's military and political actions. Among studies of less colourful individuals is Dieter Albrecht, *Die auswärtige Politik Maximilians von Bayern, 1618–1635* (Göttingen, 1962).

The never-ending controversies about the devastation caused by the war are examined in articles by T. K. Rabb, 'The Effects of the Thirty Years War on the German Economy' in *Journal of Modern History*, vol. 34 (1962) and by H. Kamen, 'The economic and social Consequences of the Thirty Years War' in *Past and Present*, no. 39 (1968). Günther Franz, *Der dreissigjährige Krieg und das deutsche Volk* (2nd edn, Stuttgart, 1961) has some of the fullest statistical investigation. G. Benecke, 'Death and Destruction in the Thirty Years War' in *European Studies Review*, vol. 2 (1972) examines one small territory. Two firm opponents of the Grimmelshausen picture of disaster are S. H. Steinberg, 'The Thirty Years War: a new interpretation' in *History*, vol. 32 (1947) and Robert Ergang, *The Myth of the All-destructive Fury of the Thirty Years War* (Pocono Pines, Pa., 1956). G. Livet, *La guerre de trente ans* (Paris, 1965) is a well-compressed summary in the *'Que sais-je?'* series.

CHAPTER 14: GERMANY AND THE HABSBURG EMPIRE, 1648–1713

The period is dealt with concisely in Hajo Holbein, *A History of Modern Germany, 1648–1840* (London, 1965). There is an obvious contrast between this and the more far-reaching interpretation in the work on the Habsburg monarchy by R. J. W. Evans mentioned on page 561, which is one of the very few studies to give the non-Austrian parts of the Empire adequate prominence. Prussia under the Great Elector is the subject of Part III of F. L. Carsten, *The Origins of Prussia* (Oxford, 1954) and of his article on the Great Elector in *English Historical Review* 75 (1950). G. Barraclough, *The Origins of Modern Germany* (Oxford, 1946) puts this period in its wider context. Gordon Craig, *The Politics of the Prussian Army, 1640–1955* (Oxford, 1964) has only a little seventeenth-century material. Ferdinand Schevill, *The Great Elector* (Hamden, Conn., 1965) is a straight biography. H. Rosenberg, *Bureaucracy, Aristocracy and Autocracy: the Prussian Experience, 1660–1815* (Cambridge, Mass., 1958) has some striking comments. The standard modern work in German on the monarchy and government is F. Hartung, *Deutsche Verfassungsgeschichte* (Stuttgart, 1964).

'The Austrian Habsburgs' is the title of an especially valuable chapter by J. W. Stoye in the *New Cambridge Modern History*, vol. 6 (1970). J. Berenger, *Finances et absolutisme autrichien dans la seconde motié de la XVIIe siècle* (Paris, 1975) is a well-presented survey that does not concentrate heavily on finance. J. P. Spielman, *Leopold I of Austria* (London, 1977) stresses the emperor's role in Europe. The book on the Imperial Privy Council by H. F. Schwarz mentioned on page 554 is useful for the whole constitutional confusion. J. F. Stoye, *The Siege of Vienna* (London, 1964) has vivid accounts of conditions in the city and in Austria. (It mentions that there were then 2,547 previous publications on the siege.) Nicholas Henderson, *Prince Eugen of Savoy* (London, 1964) is an easily read biography. D. M. Vaughan, *Europe and the Turk* (Liverpool, 1954) gives a short account of the invasions; but the established history of the Turkish wars is O. Redlich, *Weltmacht des Barock: Oesterreich in der Zeit Kaiser Leopolds* (4th edn, Vienna, 1961). Hungarian history appears to have been the subject of thorough neglect by western historians. Laszlo Makkai, *Histoire de Transylvanie* (Paris, 1946) uses his exceptional knowledge of this period, a little of which emerged as an article (in English) 'The Hungarian Puritans and the English Revolution' in *Acta Historica*, vol. 5 (Budapest, 1958). Denis Sinor, *History of Hungary* (London, 1959) has several short chapters on the period, covering both the Austrian and the Turkish-occupied areas.

CHAPTER 15: SPAIN

Spanish history in the early modern period is no longer a comparatively neglected topic: both surveys and controversies in English abound. J. H. Elliott, *Imperial Spain, 1469–1716* (London, 1963) and Henry Kamen, *Spain 1469–1716: a Society of Conflict* (London, 1983) both give more space to the sixteenth than to the seventeenth century, but the earlier part is highly relevant. J. Lynch, *Spain under the Habsburgs*, vol. 2, *Spain and America, 1598–1700* (Oxford, 1969) stresses the importance and success of the South American Empire. R. A. Stradling, *Europe and the Decline of Spain, 1580–1720* (London, 1981) is more concerned with Spain than with Europe. Spanish writers available in translation include A. Dominguez Ortiz, *The Golden Age of Spain, 1516–1659* (English transl., London, 1971) and J. Vicens Vives, *The Economic History of Spain* (Princeton, 1969). Volume 8 of the '*Rialp*' *Historia de España y América* (Madrid, 1986) contains essays by several English historians.

The 'decline of Spain' seems to be a topic of argument as prolific now as it was at the time. Modern discussions often start from the two books by E. J. Hamilton, *American Treasure and the Price Revolution in Spain, 1501–1650* (Cambridge, Mass., 1954) and *War and Prices in Spain 1651–1800* (Cambridge, Mass., 1947). Hamilton's conclusions appear in his article 'The Decline of Spain' in the *Economic History Review*, 1st series, vol. 8 (1938), reprinted in E. M. Carus-Wilson (ed.), *Essays in Economic History*, vol. 1 (London, 1954). Several articles on the subject have appeared in *Past and Present*: J. H. Elliott, 'The Decline of Spain' in no. 20 (1961) is reprinted in T. H. Aston (ed.), *Crisis in Europe 1560–1660* (London, 1965) and in Carlo M. Cipolla (ed.), *The Economic Decline of Empires* (London, 1970), which also contains the chapters by J. Vicens Vives on 'The Decline of Spain in the Seventeenth Century' from his *Economic History of Spain*. Elliott's later article on 'self-perception and decline' is listed on page 552 above. Another *Past and Present* article by Charles Jago. 'The Crisis of the Aristocracy in Seventeenth Century Castile', is in no. 84 (1979); and in no. 81 (1978) Henry Kamen questions the main assumptions.

The first part of the century is examined in detail in I. A. A. Thompson, *War and Government in Habsburg Spain, 1560–1620* (London, 1976), which suggests that the deterioration had begun in the 1580s. James Casey, *The Kingdom of Valencia in the Seventeenth Century* (Cambridge, 1979) is a rare English specimen of the regional studies that are flourishing in Spanish. Casey's article in *Past and Present* 50 (1971) 'The Moriscoes and the Depopulation of Valencia' has detailed estimates of the effects of the expulsion; but the fullest modern work on this is A. Dominguez Ortiz and B. Vincent, *Historia de los Moriscos* (Madrid, 1978). Henry Kamen's books mentioned on page 546 above put the inquisition in its context without claiming to replace the huge work by H. C. Lea, *A History of the Inquisition in Spain* (4 vols, New York, 1906–7).

The rule of Olivares is described in the large-scale biographical study by J. H. Elliott, *The Count-Duke of Olivares: the Statesman in an Age of Decline* (London, 1986). Elliott's earlier major work, *The Revolt of the Catalans* (Cambridge, 1963) investigates the failure of Castilian rule since Philip II as well as the revolt itself. Spain's part in the European conflicts is the subject of several monographs. C. H. Carter, *The Secret Diplomacy of the Habsburgs, 1598–1625* (New York, 1964) and B. Chudoba, *Spain and the Empire* (Chicago, 1952) reveal the methods and extent of Spanish influence on other governments. J. T. Israel, *The Dutch Republic and the Hispanic World, 1606–61* (Oxford, 1982) is a mainly chronological account.

The period of Charles II is analysed in Henry Kamen, *Spain in the Later Seventeenth Century, 1665–1700* (London, 1980). J. Nada, *Carlos the Bewitched* (London, 1962) is a popular biography.

CHAPTER 16: SCANDINAVIA AND POLAND

The supply of modern works in western languages on the region is uneven: Sweden naturally has had more attention for this period than the other countries. There are adequate more or less narrative histories of each country, such as C. I. Andersson, *A History of Sweden* (English transl., London, 1956), which has newer ideas than C. Hallendorf and A. Schück, *A History of Sweden* (Stockholm, 1929); E. Jutikkale, *A History of Finland* (London, 1962); Stewart Oakley, *The Story of Denmark* (London, 1972); and G. E. Slocombe, *A History of Poland* (London, 1942). A short summary of historical problems in the whole area is in the *Nouvelle Clio* series – P. Jeannin, *L'Europe du nord-ouest et du nord aux XVII*e *et XVIIIe siècles* (Paris, 1969). In Göran Rystad (ed.), *Europe and Scandinavia: aspects of the process of integration in the 17th century* (Lund, 1983) there is a chapter by the editor on 'King, Nobility, and Bureaucracy'. The eleventh international congress of historical sciences at Stockholm has amid the usual massive *Reports* in volume 4 articles by Wladyslaw Czaplinski, 'Le problème baltique aux XVIe et XVIIe siècles' and by B. F. Porchnev, 'Les rapports politiques de l'Europe occidentale et de l'Europe orientale à l'époque de la guerre de trente ans'.

On Sweden the outstanding writer in English is still Michael Roberts. For his *Gustavus Adolphus*, see p. 562 above. His short monograph *The Swedish Imperial Experience* (Cambridge, 1979) sets out some of his later thoughts; and his *Essays in Swedish History* (London, 1953) are a varied collection on the whole early modern period. Michael Roberts is also the editor of *Sweden's Age of Greatness* (London, 1973) which has essays by several Swedish historians. Ragnhild Hatton, *Charles XII of Sweden* (London, 1968) is a high-powered biography.

Norman Davies, *God's Playground: a History of Poland*, vol. 1, *The Origins to 1795* (Oxford, 1981) is divided between analysis and narrative, with contemporary comments in prose and verse. J. K. Fedorowicz (ed.), *A Republic of Nobles: Studies in Polish History to 1864* (Cambridge, 1982) has chapters on the 'structure of power', the towns, and the art of war. *The Cambridge History of Poland* edited by W. F. Reddaway and others (Cambridge, 1950) is a source of solid information. O. Laskowski, *John Sobieski, King of Poland* (English transl., Glasgow, 1944) is a standard life.

Two substantial works are on regions that crossed state boundaries – W. E. D. Allen, *The Ukraine, a History* (Cambridge, 1940); and his *History of the Georgian People* (London, 1932). C. E. Hill, *The Danish Sound Dues and the Command of the Baltic* (Durham, N. Carolina, 1926) deals with one of the crucial topics for the whole region.

CHAPTER 17: RUSSIA AND THE OTTOMAN EMPIRE

There are many single-volume histories of Russia in English: two that give reasonable coverage of this period are J. D. Clarkson,

A History of Russia from the Ninth Century (London, 1962) and M. T. Florinsky, *Russia – a History and Interpretation*, vol. 1 (2nd edn, New York, 1953). On a larger scale is G. Vernadsky, *The Tsardom of Moscow, 1547–1682* (2 vols, New Haven, 1969). B. H. Sumner, *A Survey of Russian History* (London, 1944) does its surveying of various topics backwards in time. The classic history by V. O. Klyuchevsky was translated as *A History of Russia* (London, 1913), with vols 3 and 4 covering the seventeenth century; but better versions are now available as *A Course in Russian History: the Seventeenth Century* (English transl., Chicago, 1968), which ends with the Tsar Alexei, and *Peter the Great* (English transl., London, 1958). P. Milioukov, C. Seignobos, and L. Eisenmann, *Histoire de la Russie*, vol. 1 (Paris, 1932) is informative.

Among studies of the ever-changing frontiers at Russia are J. H. Bater and R. A. French (eds), *Studies in Russian Historical Geography* (London, 1983), including a chapter by D. J. B. Shaw, 'The southern frontiers of Muscovy, 1550–1700'; W. H. McNeill, *Europe's Steppe Frontier, 1500–1800* (Chicago, 1964); G. V. Lantzeff, *Siberia in the Seventeenth Century* (Berkeley, 1943).

On the land, the lords, and the peasants there are the books by J. Blum and R. O. Crummey mentioned on page 543 above. J. M. Hittle, *The Service City: State and Townsmen in Russia, 1600–1800* (Cambridge, Mass., 1979) shows the importance of urban élites. R. E. F. Smith, *The Enserfment of the Russian Peasantry* (Cambridge, 1968) is a short collection of documents, with commentaries and also a helpful glossary of Russian terms. Thomas Riha (ed.), *Readings in Russian Civilisation*, vol. 1 (London, 1964) has extracts from both primary and secondary sources, including an essay by Dmitri Obolensky, 'Russia's Byzantine Heritage'.

M. S. Anderson, *Peter the Great* (London, 1978) and the short volume by B. H. Sumner, *Peter the Great and the Ottoman Empire* (Oxford, 1949) add many ideas to the translation of Klyuchevsky listed above; but nothing in English is as detailed as R. Wittram, *Peter I, Czar und Kaiser* (2 vols, Göttingen, 1964). There are some helpful articles in the *Slavonic and East European Review*, including L. R. Lewitter, 'Poland, the Ukraine, and Russia in the Seventeenth Century' in vol. 27 (1948–49) and J. H. L. Keep, 'The Régime of Filaret' in vol. 38 (1960–61).

The Ottoman Empire is, for several obvious reasons, not well covered by western historians, and many of them are happier to study it as an outside influence on Europe than as a state and people. P. Coles, *The Ottoman Impact on Europe* (London, 1968) is an attractive introduction; Dorothy Vaughan, *Europe and the Turk* (Liverpool, 1954) deals with the 'crusade' outlook as well as the more hard-headed military and diplomatic affairs; H. A. R. Gibb and H. Bowen, *Islamic Society and the West* (London, 1950) includes a description of the main institutions. In the *Cambridge History of Islam* (Cambridge, 1970), Part III, chapters 1 and 2, by Halil Inalcik, are genuine national history. In the *New Cambridge Modern History*, vol. IV chapter 20, by V. J. Parry, is on the years 1617–48; and vol. V, chapter 21, by A. N. Kurat, is on the reign of Mehemet IV. H. A. R. Gibb, *Studies on the Civilisation of Islam* (London, 1962) examines Islamic philosophy and society. But for the fullest available details those able to approach the old and ponderous German histories, J. W. Zinkeisen, *Geschichte des Osmanischen Reiches in Europa*, vol. 5 (Hamburg, 1840–63) and N. Jorga, *Geschichte des Osmanlichen Reiches*, vol. 4 (Gotha, 1908) will be rewarded. Among articles in *Studia Islamica* is one in vol. 2 (Paris, 1954) by H. Inalcik on 'Ottoman Methods of Conquest'.

CHAPTER 18: BRITAIN AND THE NETHERLANDS

There is no modern substitute for the large-scale account of British history in the seventeenth century begun by S. R. Gardiner in his *History of England 1603–42* (10 vols, London, 1883–84), *History of the Great Civil War* (2nd edn, 4 vols, London, 1893), and *History of the Commonwealth and Protectorate* (2nd edn, 4 vols, London, 1903). The last of these was continued by C. H. Firth, *The Last Years of the Protectorate* (2 vols, London, 1910), which in turn was finished by Godfrey Davies, *The Restoration of Charles II* (Oxford, 1955). David Ogg, *England in the Reign of Charles II* (2 vols, Oxford, 1934) and *England in the Reigns of James II and William III* (Oxford, 1955) cover a wide range of topics in the later period. Contrasting modern accounts of the whole century are J. P. Kenyon, *Stuart England* (London, 1978) and Christopher Hill, *The Century of Revolution* (Edinburgh, 1961) – the titles are revealing. Ivan Roots, *The Great Rebellion* (London, 1966) is a vivid introduction to the period before the Restoration; Robert Ashton, *The English Civil War – Conservatism and Revol-*

ution, 1603–1649 (London, 1978) incorporates many subjects of modern controversy into a clear narrative; Derek Hirst, *Authority and Conflict, England 1603–58* (London, 1986) and J. R. Jones, *Country and Court, England, 1658–1714* (London, 1978) are volumes 4 and 5 in the *Edward Arnold New History of England.* Many new lines of investigation are shown in volumes of the *Problems in Focus* series – Alan G. R. Smith (ed.), *The Reign of James VI and I* (London, 1973); Conrad Russell (ed.), *The Origins of the English Civil War* (London, 1973); G. E. Aylmer (ed.), *The Interregnum* (London, 1972); J. R. Jones (ed.), *The Restored Monarchy* (London, 1979).

A few of the works on mainly political topics are Conrad Russell, *Parliaments and English Politics, 1621–29* (Oxford, 1979); Anthony Fletcher, *The Outbreak of the English Civil War* (London, 1981); Brian Manning, *The English People and the English Revolution, 1640–1649* (London, 1976); Austin Woolrych, *Commonwealth to Protectorate* (Oxford, 1982); J. H. Plumb, *The Growth of Political Stability in England, 1675–1723* (London, 1967); J. R. Jones, *The Revolution of 1688 in England* (London, 1972).

The productive subject of county society and politics can be represented by Mary Coate, *Cornwall in the Great Civil War and Interregnum* (Oxford, 1940); A. M. Everitt, *The Community of Kent and the Great Rebellion* (Leicester, 1966); J. S. Morrill, *Cheshire, 1630–1660* (Oxford, 1974); David Underdown, *Somerset in the Civil War and Interregnum* (Newton Abbot, 1973).

Biographies abound – though too many are on people who had plenty already. Of the immense number on Cromwell, C. H. Firth, *Oliver Cromwell and the Rule of the Puritans* (Oxford, 1900) and Christopher Hill, *God's Englishman* (London, 1970) make a good contrast; Pauline Gregg, *King Charles I* (London, 1981) is more scholarly than Christopher Hibbert, *Charles I* (London, 1968); H. R. Trevor-Roper, *Archbishop Laud* (London, 1940) and Christopher Hill, *Milton and the English Revolution* (London, 1977) go beyond simple biography, as do Menna Prestwich, *Lionel Cranfield: Politics and Profit under the Early Stuarts* (Oxford, 1966) and R. H. Tawney, *Business and Politics under James I – Lionel Cranfield as Merchant and Minister* (Cambridge, 1958). The second version of C. V. Wedgwood, *Thomas Wentworth, First Earl of Strafford* (London, 1961) has more source-material and is more critical than the first (London, 1938). Some of the best work on post-1660 England is in biographies such as Andrew Browning,

Thomas, Earl of Danby (3 vols, Glasgow, 1951); J. P. Kenyon, *Robert Spencer, Earl of Sunderland* (London, 1958); and K. H. D Haley, *The First Earl of Shaftesbury* (London, 1968). *J. H. Hexter, The Reign of King Pym* (Cambridge, 1941) and B. H. G. Wormald, *Clarendon: Politics, History and Religion, 1640–1660* (Cambridge, 1951) interpret limited periods in the lives of their subjects.

On the Netherlands the indispensable work in English is by Pieter Geyl: *The Revolt of the Netherlands, 1555–1609* (2nd edn, London, 1958), and *The Netherlands in the Seventeenth Century, part one, 1609–1648* (London, 1961 – first published in 1936 as *The Netherlands Divided*), *part two, 1648–1715* (London, 1964). His *Orange and Stuart 1641–72* (London, 1969) is a full examination of relations between the two powers and of the Dutch internal conflicts. There are two short introductions – K. H. D. Haley, *The Dutch in the Seventeenth Century* (London, 1972); and Charles Wilson, *The Dutch Republic and the Civilisation of the Seventeenth Century* (London, 1968). J. H. Huizinga, *Dutch Civilisation in the Seventeenth Century* (English transl., London, 1968) is an important essay. C. R. Boxer, *The Dutch Seaborne Empire, 1600–1800* (London, 1965) and *The Dutch in Brazil, 1624–1654* (Oxford, 1957) have material on internal as well as overseas affairs. The commercial and military conflicts are clarified in C. H. Wilson, *Profit and Power: England and the Dutch Wars* (London, 1957) and Alice Carter, *The Evolution of Dutch Foreign Policy, 1667–1795* (London, 1975). The successive volumes of *Britain and the Netherlands*, papers given to Anglo-Dutch historical conferences, have some important contributions.

CHAPTER 19: LOUIS XIV'S FRANCE AND THE EUROPEAN WARS

John B. Wolf, *Louis XIV* (London, 1968) is a solid narrative of the reign divided neatly into topics. The very short and unadmiring account by David Ogg, *Louis XIV* (Oxford, 1933) is still useful as a rapid introduction. On special aspects of the king's life there are, for instance, G. Mongrédien, *La vie privée de Louis XIV* (Paris, 1938); G. Lacour-Gayet, *L'éducation politique de Louis XIV* (Paris, 1923); J. B. Wolf (ed.), *Louis XIV: a Profile* (London,

1972). W. F. Church (ed.), *The Greatness of Louis XIV* (Boston, Mass., 1959) collects opinions on the king; J. H. M. Salmon in *History Today*, vol. 15 (1965) scrutinizes 'The King and his Conscience'.

Essays on methods of government are collected in J. C. Rule (ed.), *Louis XIV and the Craft of Kingship* (Ohio, 1969), and in Ragnhild Hatton (ed.), *Louis XIV and Absolutism* (London, 1976). On foreign affairs L. André, *Louis XIV et l'Europe* (Paris, 1950) is as lucid a survey as the material permits; C. G. Picavet, *La diplomatie francaise au temps de Louis XIV* (Paris, 1930) has details of the diplomatic system; Ragnhild Hatton (ed.), *Louis XIV and Europe* (London, 1976) has sections both on specific incidents and on general policy; an earlier collection which Dr Hatton edited with J. S. Bromley is *William III and Louis XIV* (Liverpool, 1966). G. R. Symcox, *The Crisis of French Sea Power, 1688–1697* (The Hague, 1974) investigates one factor in the varying balance; and on the final struggle there is H. Kamen, *The War of the Succession in Spain* (London, 1969). *XVIIᵉ Siècle* has published many articles on the political as well as the cultural aspects of the reign: in no. 46 (1960) there are essays on French relations with German and Italian states and with England, together with one by V.-L. Tapié on 'Quelques aspects généraux de la politique étrangère de Louis XIV'. The two books by P. de Nolhac, *La création de Versailles* (Paris, 1925) and *Versailles et la cour de France* (Paris, 1930) are still extremely useful. Roger Mettam, *Power and Faction in Louis XIV's France* (Oxford, 1987) adds to the doubts about 'absolutism'.

Social and economic questions are the main subject of a chapter by J. Meuvert, 'The Condition of France, 1688–1715' in the *New Cambridge Modern History*, vol. 6 (1970) and of P. Goubert, *Louis XIV et vingt million français* (Paris, 1966). On Colbert C. W. Cole, *Colbert and a Century of French Mercantilism* (2 vols, London, 1939) is still the standard work. On conditions and on government, many local and regional studies are as important as general surveys: see F. L. Ford, *Strasbourg in Transition, 1648–1789* (Cambridge, Mass, 1958) and O. A. Ranum, *Paris in the Age of Absolutism* (New York, 1968). H. Fréville, *L'intendance de bretagne, 1669–1790* (Rennes, 1953) and Georges Livet, *L'intendance d'Alsace sous Louis XIV* (Paris, 1956) show the effects as well as the working of administration.

The Huguenots have been examined in works cited on p. 545,

and the effects of the expulsion in W. C. Scoville, *The Persecution of the Huguenots and French Economic Development, 1680–1720* (Berkeley, 1960). Two articles by H. G. Judge, 'Church and State under Louis XIV' in *History*, vol. 45 (1960) and 'The Congregation of the Oratory in France in the Late Seventeenth Century' in the *Journal of Ecclesiastical History*, vol. 12 (1951) have a realistic view of religious complexities.

Among the biographical studies of major figures in court and government are L. André, *Michel le Tellier et Louvois* (Paris, 1943); P. Lazard, *Vauban* (Paris, 1934); M. Langlois, *Madame de Maintenon* (Paris, 1932); G. Guitton, *Le Père de la Chaise: confesseur de Louis XIV* (2 vols, Paris, 1959); and G. Montgrédien, *Le grand Condé* (Paris, 1959).

RULERS AND ROYAL FAMILIES

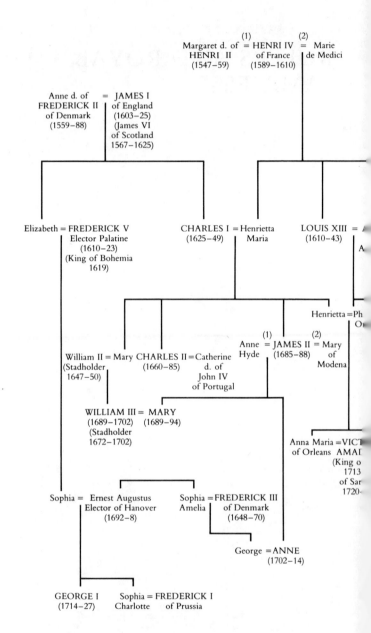

Table 1 The rulers of England, France, Spain, and the Empire

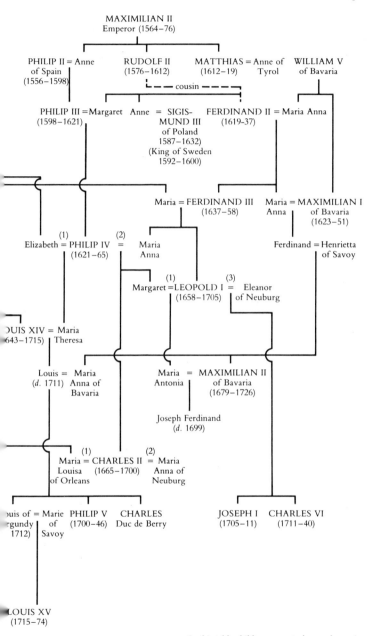

MAXIMILIAN II
Emperor (1564–76)

PHILIP II = Anne
of Spain
(1556–1598)

RUDOLF II
(1576–1612)

MATTHIAS = Anne of
(1612–19)   Tyrol

WILLIAM V
of Bavaria

└ ─ ─ cousin ─ ─ ─ ┘

PHILIP III = Margaret
(1598–1621)

Anne = SIGIS-
MUND III
of Poland
1587–1632)
(King of Sweden
1592–1600)

FERDINAND II = Maria Anna
(1619-37)

Maria = FERDINAND III
(1637–58)

Maria
Anna

= MAXIMILIAN I
of Bavaria
(1623–51)

(1)
Elizabeth = PHILIP IV
(1621–65)

(2)
= Maria
Anna

Ferdinand = Henrietta
of Savoy

(1)
Margaret = LEOPOLD I
(1658–1705)

(3)
= Eleanor
of Neuburg

OUIS XIV = Maria
643–1715) Theresa

Louis = Maria
(d. 1711) Anna of
Bavaria

Maria = MAXIMILIAN II
Antonia   of Bavaria
(1679–1726)

Joseph Ferdinand
(d. 1699)

(1)
Maria = CHARLES II
Louisa   (1665–1700)
of Orleans

(2)
= Maria
Anna of
Neuburg

ouis of = Marie
rgundy   of
1712)   Savoy

PHILIP V
(1700–46)

CHARLES
Duc de Berry

JOSEPH I
(1705–11)

CHARLES VI
(1711–40)

LOUIS XV
(1715–74)

In this table children are not always shown in
the order of their age

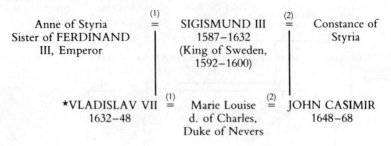

MICHAEL   =   Eleanor Maria
WISNOWIECKI   Sister of Leopold I
1669–73   Emperor

JOHN SOBIESKI = Marie d'Arquien
1674–96

AUGUSTUS II
1697–1704, and 1709–33

STANISLAS LESZCZYNSKI
1704–9

★Also known, by counting only Jagellon kings, as Vladislav IV.

Table 2   The rulers of Poland

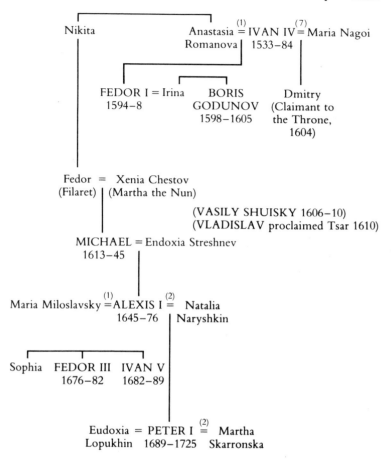

Table 3 The tsars of Russia

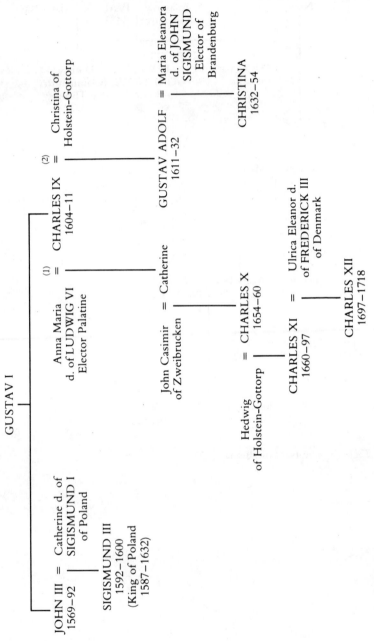

Table 4 The rulers of Sweden

Table 5 Ottoman sultans

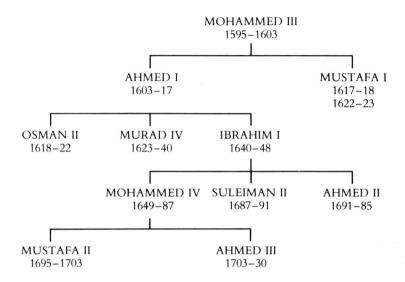

Table 6 Popes, 1592–1721

Clement VIII 1592–1605
Leo XI 1605
Paul V 1605–21
Gregory XV 1621–23
Urban VIII 1623–44
Innocent X 1644–55
Alexander VII 1655–67
Clement IX 1667–69
Clement X 1670–76
Innocent XI 1676–89
Alexander VIII 1689–91
Innocent XII 1691–1700
Clement XI 1700–21

MAPS

Map 1 Europe in the early seventeenth century: frontiers

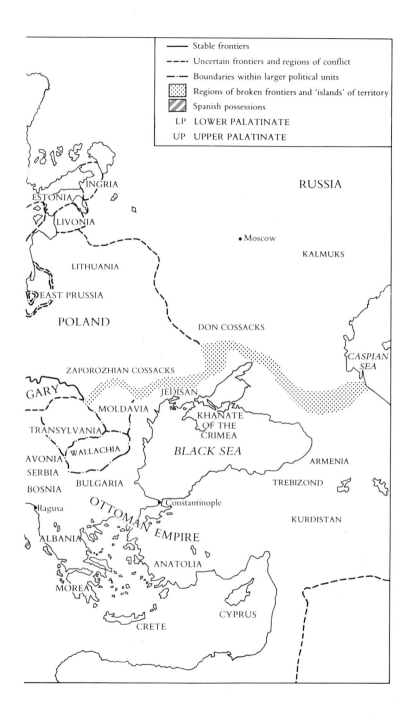

Stable frontiers
------ Uncertain frontiers and regions of conflict
—·— Boundaries within larger political units
▒ Regions of broken frontiers and 'islands' of territory
▨ Spanish possessions
LP LOWER PALATINATE
UP UPPER PALATINATE

INGRIA

RUSSIA

ESTONIA

LIVONIA

• Moscow

KALMUKS

LITHUANIA

EAST PRUSSIA

POLAND

DON COSSACKS

CASPIAN SEA

ZAPOROZHIAN COSSACKS

GARY

JEDISAN

MOLDAVIA

KHANATE OF THE CRIMEA

TRANSYLVANIA

WALLACHIA

BLACK SEA

ARMENIA

AVONIA

SERBIA

TREBIZOND

BOSNIA

BULGARIA

Ragusa

KURDISTAN

OTTOMAN EMPIRE

Constantinople

ALBANIA

ANATOLIA

MOREA

CYPRUS

CRETE

Map 2 Europe in the early seventeenth century: population

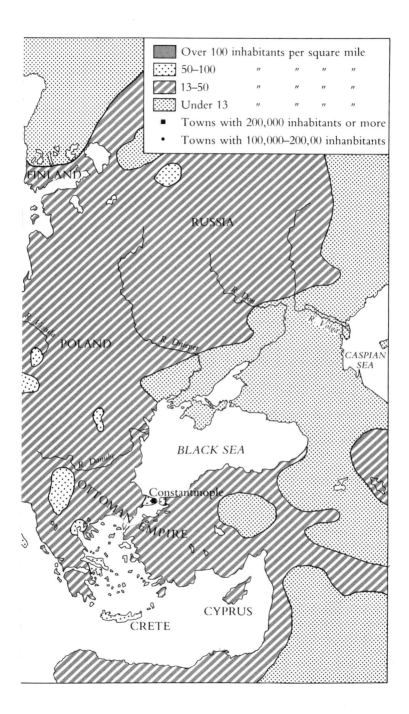

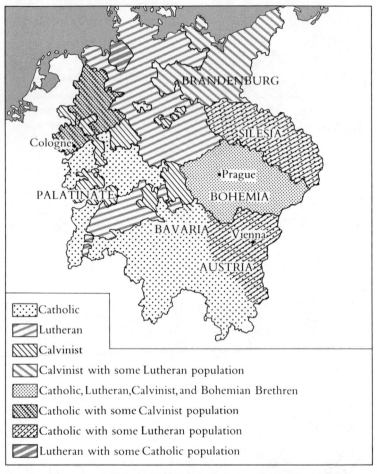

Map 3 Germany: religious divisions before the Thirty Years War

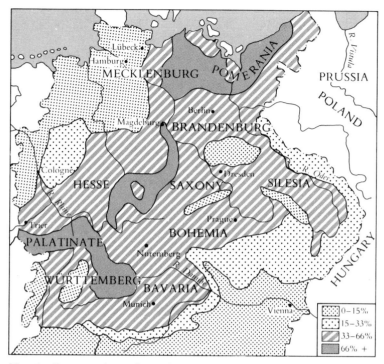

Map 4   Germany: loss of population in the Thirty Years War

Legend:
- Swedish territory from 16th century
- Swedish, 1617–1721
- Swedish, 1629–1721
- Swedish from 1645, 1648
- Swedish from 1658

NORTH SEA

VÄSTERBOTTEN

ÅNGERMANLAND

ÖSTERBOTTEN

GULF OF BOTHNIA

TRONDHJEM
(Swedish
1658–60)

JÄMTLAND

HÄRJEDALEN

KARELIA

Lake
Ladoga

FINLAND

Bergen

DALARNA

ÅLAND

VÄSTMANLAND

Stockholm

GULF OF FINLAND

INGRIA

ESTONIA

Göteborg

Gotland

Osel

LIVONIA

HALLAND

SMÅLAND

Riga

SKAGER RAK

KATTEGAT

KURLAND

Copenhagen

SCANIA

BALTIC SEA

DENMARK

BORNHOLM

Stralsund

Rügen

Danzig

Königsberg

W. POMERANIA
(Swedish
until 1715)

ERMELAND
(Swedish 1629–56)

Bremen (Swedish
until 1715)

Verden

Map 5 Scandinavia, 1600–1721

Legend:
- To Sweden, 1617 ⎱ To Russia, 1721
- To Sweden, 1629 ⎰
- To Poland, 1618; To Russia, 1667
- Under Ottoman control, 1672–99
- Regions of eastward expansion
- Main areas of Razin's rebellion
- To Russia, 1667
- — ·· — Russian political frontiers in mid century
- — · — Other frontiers
- — ··· — Fortified lines

NORWAY

SWEDEN

FINLAND

WHITE SEA

Archangel

GULF OF BOTHNIA

KARELIA
Viborg
L. Onega
L. Ladoga
•Stockholm
St.Petersburg
ESTONIA INGRIA
BALTIC SEA
•Novgorod
Riga
•Pskov
R. Volga
Memel•
KURLAND
•Moscow
•Kazan
Ufa•
Danzig
•Königsberg
R. Dnieper
Smolensk
•Tula
Simbirsk
POLAND
•Warsaw
•Brzesc
•Cracow
R. Dniester
Kiev•
Tretchnikov
R. Don
•Kharkov
R. Dniester
TRANSYLVANIA
MOLDAVIA
PODOLIA
Poltava
R. Prut
ZAPOROZHIAN
COSSACKS
DON
COSSACKS
R. Volga
R. Ural
WALLACHIA
KHANATE
OF THE
CRIMEA
Azov
(Russian
1699–1711)
KALMUKS
R. Danube
BLACK SEA
CASPIAN SEA
•Constantinople
OTTOMAN
EMPIRE

Map 6   Russia and Poland, 1617–1721

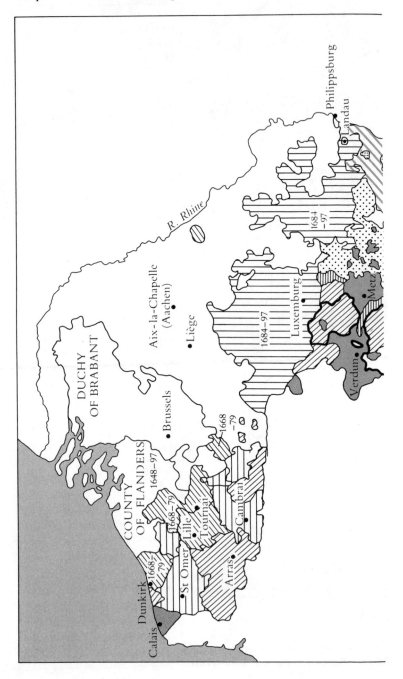

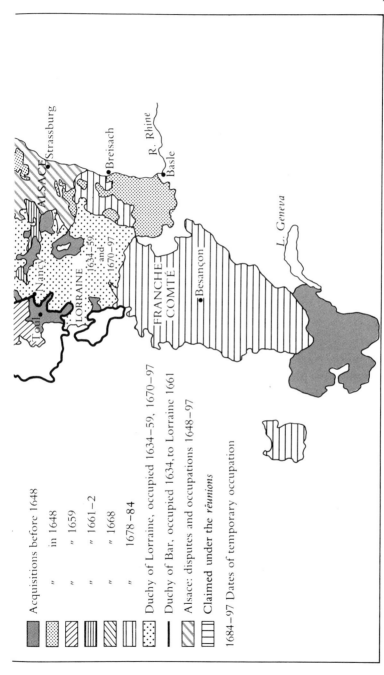

Map 7 France: the eastern frontier in the later seventeenth century (it is impossible to show on this scale all the complexities that arise from fortresses, isolated territories and possessions without full sovereignty)

The map legend reads:

- Acquisitions before 1648
- " in 1648
- " " 1659
- " " 1661–2
- " " 1668
- " 1678–84
- Duchy of Lorraine, occupied 1634–59, 1670–97
- Duchy of Bar, occupied 1634, to Lorraine 1661
- Alsace: disputes and occupations 1648–97
- Claimed under the *réunions*
- 1684–97 Dates of temporary occupation

Map labels: Strassburg, Breisach, R. Rhine, Basle, ALSACE, Toul, Nancy, LORRAINE, 1634–59 and 1670–97, FRANCHE COMTÉ, Besançon, L. Geneva

Map 8 Europe, 1721

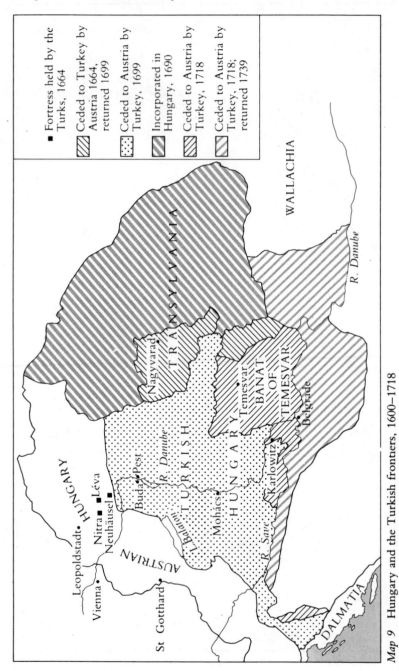

Map 9 Hungary and the Turkish frontiers, 1600–1718

Index